Discovering Christ In Hebrews

Discovering Christ in Hebrews

Donald S. Fortner

Go *publications*

Go Publications
The Cairn, Hill Top, Eggleston, Co. Durham, DL12 0AU, ENGLAND

© Go Publications 2007
First Published 2007

British Library Cataloguing in Publication Data available

ISBN 978-0-9548624-4-2

For information on other Go Publications titles and New Focus magazine:

www.go-publications.co.uk
www.go-newfocus.co.uk

Printed and bound in Great Britain
by Lightning Source UK Ltd

This book is dedicated to:

Doug Hacker

" ... who is my beloved son,
and faithful in the Lord."

Contents

Foreword

Discovering Christ in Hebrews might not appear, at first, to be a particularly difficult task. After all, the Son of God is specifically mentioned in verse two. Furthermore, the Apostle Paul, the believed author, rotates the whole narrative around the person of the Lord Jesus Christ. The excellence of Christ above the angels, his superiority over the priesthood, his uniqueness as a worthy sacrifice to God, are but a few of the accolades applied to the Saviour. Why then the need for 'Discovering Christ in Hebrews'?

Simply this, we can never have enough of the Saviour. Christ is our champion, our pleasure, our joy. We delight in him. We delight to see him lifted up in preaching the gospel, in the study of the Word of God, in the heartfelt praise and prayers of his people and in the midst of a dark world that has lost sight of the only way of salvation. Don Fortner is a preacher and a pastor and it is his constant desire to lift up the Lord Jesus to the view and attention of his hearers and readers. And what better way to do so than to preach, teach and study one's way through Paul's letter to the Hebrews.

The book before you is not a standard commentary. Those looking for a verse by verse breakdown of text and language can refer to other fine material for this. This book is quite different. While not failing to be faithful to the detail of the text, the purpose of the book is to find Jesus Christ in every nook and cranny. Then having discovered the Lord, to declare with the Samaritan woman, 'Come, see a man, which told me all things that ever I did: is not this the Christ?' (John 4:29). Certainly the author covers all thirteen chapters of Hebrews, dwelling longer in some places where Christ is most clearly encountered and allowing the glorious themes of Paul's narrative to speak personally and directly to our heart.

In my experience of Don Fortner's writings I have found that his audience are a broad spread of people. Some use his writings as devotional material, an aid to approach and meditate upon the Lord. Some particularly appreciate the strong free grace emphasis by which Don applies every aspect of salvation to sovereign grace; the eternal love of God for his elect, the substitutionary work of Christ, and the Holy Spirit's quickening power. Yet others draw upon Don's great experience as a pastor writing for today's men and women to guide their own ministry and glean pointers and insights as to how preaching Jesus Christ crucified from everywhere in the Bible ought to be the purpose of every shepherd of men's souls.

Reader, I am confident that you will find the book you now hold in your hand a great blessing and encouragement to you, whether you are a young believer new to the scriptures and seeking to learn more about the Lord Jesus, or a seasoned, old pastor, seeking to meditate upon Christ and fill your own heart and the hearts of your people with the Lord. Christ permeates this work. He is honoured and worshipped, presented and praised on every page. Look here, you cannot miss Jesus.

I do not want to detain you a moment longer than necessary but one final comment, if I may. Today, many books are published and sermons preached on the modern issues affecting Christians. It is said they are popular, sell well and gain a large following because they answer the questions people are asking and give the audience the instructions they need to live in the modern world. No doubt they have their place and perhaps their usefulness. But they are temporary and passing, like a fashion, soon to be replaced by another issue with another new set of questions which publishers and preachers will be happy to answer.

However, Paul writes, 'Jesus Christ the same yesterday, and to day, and for ever' (Hebrews 13:8). We fear the essential and necessary centrality of Jesus Christ to all men of all ages is missing from much of today's Christianity. This is not the place for hectoring, suffice it to say that Don Fortner's ministry in word and print will not scratch itching ears, but it will most certainly bring those who have ears to hear closer to Jesus Christ. That for me is the first and last recommendation for this book.

Peter L Meney

Introduction

Christ is Better
The Psalmist David, speaking prophetically of Christ's great accomplishments as our Saviour, sang, 'His glory is great in thy salvation: honour and majesty hast thou laid upon him. For thou hast made him most blessed for ever' (Psalm 21:5-6). In the book of Hebrews the Holy Spirit tells us of the great glory of our God and Saviour, the Lord Jesus Christ. In the opening words of this magnificent epistle we see that this is the theme of the book.

Truly His Glory is Great in Salvation
We are not told who wrote this epistle, when it was written, or to whom it was written. It was obviously written to men and women of Jewish ancestry who were born of God; but we have no indication where they were located. This lack of information is not accidental. God the Holy Spirit, whose Word this is, intended for every person who picks it up and reads it to read it as God's Word specifically to him.

These Jewish believers, being constantly pressurised by family and friends to go back to their former religion, to go back to Judaism, needed encouragement to remain stedfast, to 'hold fast the confidence and the rejoicing of the hope firm unto the end' (3:6). Like the saints at Galatia, Judaisers were trying to get them to go back to the Mosaic law, back to Jewish ritualism, back to empty, meaningless religious activity, to give up the way of life and faith in Christ. Everywhere, on every side, they were harassed, pressured, and persecuted for the gospel's sake, because they had abandoned the religion of their fathers and trusted Christ alone for righteousness with God.

In a word, they faced the same pressures God's saints face in all places and in all ages. This epistle was written by divine inspiration to God's saints everywhere, inspiring relentless devotion to Christ by showing us his great glory in salvation.

Christ's Work

As we read these 13 chapters describing the greatness of our Saviour's glory in the salvation he accomplished, we should not be at all surprised to see that the focus of the entire epistle is that salvation which the Lord Jesus Christ, the Son of God, has accomplished. We are reminded of four great facts about Christ and his work as our Mediator throughout this epistle.

First, everything that the Lord Jesus Christ did for us as our Substitute and Saviour he did by himself, alone (1:3; 2:14, 18; 7:27; 9:12-14, 25-26; 12:3). There was none to help him. He purged our sins by himself, offered himself, gave himself, and obtained eternal redemption for us by himself. His glory is great in salvation precisely because it is his work alone.

Second, everything that the Lord Jesus Christ did for us, as our Substitute and Saviour, he did just once (7:27; 9:12, 26-28; 10:10). There was no need for anything he did to be done twice. Once was enough. He lived once. He obeyed once. He brought in righteousness once. He died once. He arose once. He obtained eternal redemption once. Once is enough.

Third, everything the Son of God did as the God-man our Saviour, our Substitute, everything he did for the salvation of God's elect, he did for us all alike (2:9; 6:20; 9:12; 10:10, 20; 11:40). He tasted death for us all (2:9). The Son of God died to bring all God's elect to glory. He entered into heaven for us as a forerunner (6:20). He sanctified, by his blood, every sinner for whom he died, and perfected us all forever by his once for all sacrifice for us (10:10, 14). The Lord Jesus has made a way for us all to approach and find acceptance with God (10:20). And all God's elect, every sinner in the universe who believes on the Lord Jesus Christ, shall obtain the same eternal inheritance in Christ (11:40). Abraham, Isaac, and Jacob, Peter, James, and John, Paul, and you, and I shall all be made perfect together.

Fourth, everything that our Saviour did for our salvation, he did perfectly. Nothing needs to be and nothing can be added to it (10:10-14). The Lord Jesus Christ is the perfect God, the perfect Man, the perfect Son, the perfect priest, the perfect Sacrifice, the perfect Altar, the perfect Tabernacle, the perfect Captain of our Salvation, and the perfect Surety.

He has 'perfected for ever them that are sanctified'! And, because everything he did he did perfectly, and because he is the perfect God-man, because all that he did, he did as our Representative, Substitute, and Surety, everything he did is of infinite value and efficacy.

That simply means everything he did has everlasting consequence. It is forever (1:8; 5:6; 6:20; 7:17, 21; 10:12-14; 13:20). His throne is forever. His priesthood is forever. He has perfected and sanctified his people forever. His covenant is an everlasting covenant.

God-man

Nowhere in scripture is our Saviour's eternal deity and glorious humanity more clearly set forth than it is in the first two chapters of Hebrews. Remember, the purpose of this epistle is to show forth the greatness of Christ's glory in the accomplishment of our salvation and to encourage us to remain stedfast in the confidence of our faith in him. What better way could this goal be accomplished than by reminding us at the outset that he who is our Saviour is both God and man in one glorious person? Because he is a man like us in all things, sin alone excepted, he is able to understand all our needs. Because he is God over all, he is able to meet all our needs.

Central Doctrine

The central doctrine of this epistle is Christ's eternal priesthood and his finished, efficacious sacrifice for the redemption and salvation of his people. The book of Hebrews stresses the infinite importance and efficacious power of Christ's sin-atoning blood in obtaining eternal redemption for us, in purging the conscience, and in opening to us the heavenly sanctuary.

Better

The key word in the book of Hebrews is 'better' (1:4; 6:9; 7:7, 19, 22; 8:6; 9:23; 10:34; 11:16, 35, 40; 12:24). One purpose of this book is to show us that Christ is 'better' than all who came before him. He is better than the prophets, better than the angels, better than Moses, better than Joshua, and better than Aaron. He is Surety of a better covenant, established upon better promises, giving a better hope. Christ our Saviour is better than the tabernacle, the altar, and the mercy-seat. He is a better Sacrifice, offering better blood, giving us a better access to and better standing before the holy Lord God. In all things Christ is better than all others. He is infinitely better. He is the best!

Better than the Prophets

Christ is better than the prophets (1:1-4). Each of the prophets gave us a partial revelation of God and his purpose. Reading the prophets and studying their messages, we leave each one thinking (as they intended), 'This is not the final word. There is more to be revealed'. Christ is the perfect, complete, full, and final revelation of God.

The prophets were mere messengers. Christ is the Message. The prophets were mere men. Christ is the Creator, Ruler, Redeemer and Saviour of men. The prophets were sinners in need of atonement. Christ is atonement. By his one sacrifice, 'he purged our sins' and 'sat down on the right hand of the Majesty on high', because his work was finished and accepted.

Better than the Angels

Christ is better than the angels (1:4-2:18). The angels are creatures of God. He is the Son of God (v. 5). The angels were commanded of God to worship the Lord Jesus Christ, his incarnate Son, as God, even in his humiliation as he came into the world (v. 6). God never commanded an angel to sit with him on his throne; but he said to his Son, when he had finished his work of redemption as our Substitute, 'Sit thou on my right hand, until I make thine enemies thy footstool' (vv. 7-13). Christ is one with the Father, in every way his equal. But the angels are 'all ministering spirits, sent forth to minister for them who shall be heirs of salvation' (v. 14).

They minister for those who shall be the heirs of salvation; but Christ is our Saviour (2:6-18). He visited the earth in human flesh, made a little lower than the angels, that he might taste death for all his elect (referred to by the words 'every man' in verse 9). His elect are every man numbered among the many sons he shall bring to glory (v. 10). His elect are those who are sanctified by him, whom he calls brethren (v. 11). His elect are the children the Father gave him to redeem and save (v. 13). His elect, the every man for whom he tasted death, are the seed of Abraham, on whom he took hold to redeem and save (v. 16).

Better than Moses

Christ is better than Moses (3:1-19). Moses, of course, represents the law of God. He was a servant in the house. Christ is Builder and the Master of the house. God's elect, his church and kingdom, are his house (3:6). In this house Moses was a servant for a season. But Moses could not bring the children of Israel into the land of promise because he represented the law, and the law cannot save. It cannot give rest. Moses had to die in the wilderness. Joshua was raised up to take his place and to lead Israel into Canaan, into the land of rest. But Joshua, too, was but a man typical of Christ.

Better than Joshua

Christ is better than Joshua (4:1-16). As Joshua brought Israel into the typical land of promise, the land of blessedness, bounty, and rest, so the Lord Jesus Christ brings God's elect into rest by his omnipotent grace. As Israel's enemies were conquered by the hand of God in Joshua's day, so our enemies were conquered by God our Saviour, our Joshua, the Lord Jesus Christ (Colossians 2:13-15).

Better than the Sabbath

Christ is better than the sabbath (4:9-11). The Old Testament sabbath was, like everything else in Old Testament worship, typical of Christ who is our true Sabbath. The sabbath rest of faith in Christ was typified by God ceasing from his works of creation and resting on the seventh day, and in Israel resting in Canaan. As the Lord God ceased from his works, sinners enter into rest when they cease from their works and trust Christ alone for acceptance with God. Just as surely as Christ our Substitute has entered into his rest in glory, there is a vast multitude of sinners in this world who must also enter into his rest. They must enter in because God ordained it, and because Christ has obtained it for us.

Better than Aaron

Christ is better than Aaron (4:14-7:28). Beginning at the end of chapter 4 and going through chapter 7, the Holy Spirit tells us that the Lord Jesus Christ is our great High Priest, and that he is a Priest better than Aaron, with a better priesthood than Aaron's typical priesthood in Israel.

'Seeing then that we have a great high priest, that is passed into the heavens, Jesus the Son of God, let us hold fast our profession. For we have not an high priest which cannot be touched with the feeling of our infirmities; but was in all points tempted like as we are, yet without sin. Let us therefore come boldly unto the throne of grace, that we may obtain mercy, and find grace to help in time of need' (4:14-16).

All Aaron could do was offer typical sacrifices and make ceremonial cleansings. Christ is a better Priest. His work is neither typical nor ceremonial, but real and sure. He is a Priest who is able to save and save unto the uttermost all who come to God by him. He who is our Priest is the omnipotent Lion of the tribe of Judah (7:11-27). If our Lord, who came not from the tribe of Levi but from the tribe of Judah, was to be our High

Priest, 'there is made of necessity a change also of the law' (7:12). The law regarding these things was disannulled because of its weakness and unprofitableness (7:18; Romans 8:4).

The Lord Jesus Christ could not be our great High Priest before God, except the Levitical law which required the priests to be of the tribe of Levi be set aside and be made of no effect. That legal system under which the Jews lived and worshipped God in the Old Testament was only temporary and typical. Once Christ came and fulfilled it in its entirety, he put and end to the typical, Levitical system altogether (Romans 10:4).

'It is yet far more evident' that our Lord Jesus Christ is a great High Priest infinitely superior to Aaron because those priests were temporary, made priests 'after the law of a carnal commandment', without an oath, for a limited time. Christ was made a Priest forever after the order of Melchisedek and the oath of God in his eternal decree, by the power of an endless life (7:11-27).

A Better Covenant

Christ is the Surety and Mediator of a better covenant (8:1-13). The old covenant was a conditional covenant of law and works. In that covenant the whole weight of responsibility was upon the shoulders of men. The new covenant, of which Christ is the Surety, is an unconditional covenant of pure, free grace. In this covenant nothing depends upon men. In this covenant the whole weight of responsibility was laid upon the shoulders of One who is mighty, our great Surety, the Lord Jesus Christ. This new covenant of grace is that of which Jeremiah spoke (Jeremiah 31:31-34).

'But now hath he obtained a more excellent ministry, by how much also he is the mediator of a better covenant, which was established upon better promises. For if that first covenant had been faultless, then should no place have been sought for the second. For finding fault with them, he saith, Behold, the days come, saith the Lord, when I will make a new covenant with the house of Israel and with the house of Judah: Not according to the covenant that I made with their fathers in the day when I took them by the hand to lead them out of the land of Egypt; because they continued not in my covenant, and I regarded them not, saith the Lord. For this is the covenant that I will make with the house of Israel after those days, saith the Lord; I will put my laws into their mind, and write them in their hearts: and I will be to them a God, and they shall be to me a people: And they shall not teach every man his neighbour, and every man his brother, saying, Know the Lord: for all shall know me, from the least to the greatest. For I will be merciful to their unrighteousness, and their sins and their iniquities will I remember no more' (8:6-12).

A Better Tabernacle

Christ is a better Tabernacle (9:1-28). Everything in the Old Testament tabernacle, and later the temple, was typical of Christ. They were but 'a figure for the time then present ... until the time of reformation'. Christ is the true Tabernacle. He is the true place of worship and blessing.

'Christ being come an high priest of good things to come, by a greater and more perfect tabernacle, not made with hands, that is to say, not of this building; Neither by the blood of goats and calves, but by his own blood he entered in once into the holy place, having obtained eternal redemption for us. For if the blood of bulls and of goats, and the ashes of an heifer sprinkling the unclean, sanctifieth to the purifying of the flesh: How much more shall the blood of Christ, who through the eternal Spirit offered himself without spot to God, purge your conscience from dead works to serve the living God? And for this cause he is the mediator of the new testament, that by means of death, for the redemption of the transgressions that were under the first testament, they which are called might receive the promise of eternal inheritance. For where a testament is, there must also of necessity be the death of the testator' (9:11-16).

A Better Sacrifice

Christ is a better Sacrifice (10:1-39). All the laws, sacrifices, holy days, and religious observances of the Old Testament were only typical rituals. They could never take away sin and give sinners acceptance with God. Christ did and does! Isaac Watts wrote:

Not all the blood of beasts
On Jewish altars slain,
Could give the guilty conscience peace,
Or wash away the stain.

But Christ, the heavenly Lamb,
Takes all our sins away:
A Sacrifice of nobler name
And richer blood than they.

Believing, we rejoice
To see the curse remove:
We bless the Lamb with cheerful voice,
And sing redeeming love!

Christ and his sacrifice, his finished work as our Substitute and Saviour is the whole of our acceptance with God, the whole of our peace from God, and the whole of our assurance before God (10:4-22).

A Better Object of Faith

Christ is the better Object of faith (11:1-40). In chapter 11 the Apostle shows us that Christ is the better Object of faith, better than any that any man may choose, for he is the only Object of faith among God's saints throughout the ages. He alone is the One by whom Abel worshipped God and by whom Enoch walked with God and pleased him. Christ is the Ark of Salvation in whom Noah trusted. He is the One with whom Abraham, Isaac, and Jacob walked. Joseph, Moses, and Joshua, Rahab, Samson, and David, all God's saints of old believed him, lived by him, died in him, and reign with him in heaven today.

Let us, like those countless multitudes of old, trust Christ alone as our Saviour. It is only by believing him that we can know our election by him (11:1-2). It is only by faith in him that we can understand the things of God (11:3). And it is only by believing him that we can please God (11:6).

A Better Motive

Christ is the better motive (12:1-29). The book of Hebrews calls for perseverance in faith, urging us to continue in the grace of God. We have many examples to follow. But our best and only real inspiration and motive is Christ himself.

'Wherefore seeing we also are compassed about with so great a cloud of witnesses, let us lay aside every weight, and the sin which doth so easily beset us, and let us run with patience the race that is set before us, Looking unto Jesus the author and finisher of our faith; who for the joy that was set before him endured the cross, despising the shame, and is set down at the right hand of the throne of God. For consider him that endured such contradiction of sinners against himself, lest ye be wearied and faint in your minds' (12:1-3).

In a word Christ is a better Saviour than any to whom we might look, for he is the only Saviour there is, 'the same yesterday, and today, and for ever' (13:1-25). Those who serve at the altar of freewill, works religion cannot eat at this Altar (v. 10). As he suffered outside the city for us, bearing our reproach, 'Let us go forth therefore unto him without the camp, bearing his reproach' (vv. 12-13). 'By him let us offer the sacrifice of praise to God continually, that is, the fruit of our lips giving thanks to his name' (v. 15). Truly, his glory is great in salvation!

'Now the God of peace, that brought again from the dead our Lord Jesus, that great shepherd of the sheep, through the blood of the everlasting covenant, Make you perfect in every good work to do his will, working in you that which is wellpleasing in his sight, through Jesus Christ; to whom be glory for ever and ever. Amen' (13:20-21).

God, who at sundry times and in divers manners spake in time past unto the fathers by the prophets, Hath in these last days spoken unto us by *his* Son, whom he hath appointed heir of all things, by whom also he made the worlds.

Hebrews 1:1-2

Chapter 1

Read: Hebrews 1:1-2

The Unrivalled Excellence of Christ

If you are ever tempted to imagine that there might be some similarity between the weak, frustrated, helpless Jesus of this idolatrous generation and the exalted Lord of glory, just re-read the opening verses of the book of Hebrews. Here we have the Christ of God revealed to us, the real Christ, our all-glorious Saviour. If the Christ you worship is not this Christ, the Christ you worship is antichrist, a false Christ. In the first two verses, the Holy Spirit shows us the unrivalled excellence of our Lord Jesus Christ in three glorious facts

1. The Word of God

The Lord Jesus Christ is unrivalled in his excellence as the Word of God, the revelation of the invisible God. 'God, who at sundry times and in divers manners spake in times past unto the fathers by the prophets, hath in these last days spoken unto us by his Son' (vv. 1-2).

Though God spoke to men in the Old Testament in the types, shadows, ceremonies and pictures of the law, and by the visions of faithful prophets, all the law and the prophets spoke of and pointed to Christ. And, now, in these last days, God has spoken to us one more time, this time with finality and in one way 'by his Son'.

The Lord Jesus Christ is not one of many revelations. He is the revelation of the invisible God. Christ is not one of many words. He is the Word of God (John 1:1-3; 18). You and I cannot see God, know God, speak to God, be spoken to by God, or come to God except by Christ (John 14:6; Matthew 11:25-27). Christ is the Way. Without him, there is no going to God. Christ is the Truth. Without him, there is no knowing God. Christ is the Life. Without him, there is no living before God. There is no prophet like Christ our Prophet. He is unrivalled in his excellence as the Revelation of the invisible God.

2. The Heir of God

The Lord Jesus Christ is unrivalled in his excellence as the Heir of God, the appointed heir of all things. 'Whom he hath appointed heir of all things' (v. 2; John 3:35). All things belong to Christ, our great Mediator and Substitute. He who is our Saviour holds all things in his hands by rightful and lawful possession. Being heir of all things, he has the absolute right to do exactly what he will with all things. 'None can stay his hand, or say unto him, What doest thou?' (Daniel 4:35). No one is about to slap him on the wrist and say, 'Oh, no, don't do that'. No one in heaven, earth, or hell, is going to call him to account!

Jesus Christ our Lord is the unrivalled Sovereign of the universe (Matthew 28:18; John 17:2). He who is God our Saviour does as he will in the army of heaven and among the inhabitants of the earth. He makes one a vessel of honour and another a vessel of dishonour, one a vessel of mercy and another a vessel of wrath, one to show forth the riches of his grace and another to show forth the severity of his justice, exactly as it pleased him from all eternity (Romans 9:21-23; 11:22).

Christ is the appointed heir of all things personally (Psalm 2:8). He is the appointed heir of all things representatively (Hebrews 6:20). And he who is the heir of all things is the dispenser of all things. 'Behold your God!' Jesus Christ is unrivalled in his excellence as the appointed heir of all things.

3. Creator of All Things

The Lord Jesus Christ is unrivalled in his excellence as the Creator of the Worlds. 'By whom also he made the worlds' (v. 2). There is an obvious reference here to the distinct divinity and personality of our Lord Jesus Christ as God the Son. John tells us that 'All things were made by him; and without him was not anything made that was made' (John 1:3; Colossians 1:14-17).

Everything the triune God does he does through the mediation of Christ. The measurements of the universe were laid down by Christ. The power of the sun and the brilliance of every star is energized by his sovereign, almighty, irresistible will! It was Christ, our Saviour, the great Mediator and Surety of his people, who laid the foundations of the earth! Christ is the Creator of all things! He is not the great Spectator of all things, or great Evolver of all things, but the great Creator of all things!

When the Holy Spirit tells us that the Lord Jesus Christ is the Creator of the worlds, he is not suggesting that there might be more than one inhabited planet. Rather, he is telling us that every realm of existence in the universe was created by the Lord Jesus Christ and is ruled by the Lord Jesus Christ: The Heavenly World, The Habitation of God and the Holy Angels, The Upper World, The Vast Expanse of Space, The Lower World, The Habitation of Man, The World Beneath, The Prison of the Damned.

Christ is Lord of All!

Behold God's vast creation, in all its orderly splendour, beauty, and majesty, and know that Christ is unrivalled in his excellence as our great Creator. Perhaps you think, 'Why is this so important? Why are you so vehemently insistent upon declaring that Christ made all things and rules all things in absolute sovereignty?' Let me show you.

To deny that Christ created all things and rules all things is to deny that he is God. To deny that he is God is to mock him, blaspheme him, and attempt to deny him his glory. To deny that Christ is God, all-glorious and sovereign upon his throne is to deny hope to needy sinners who look to him alone for grace, salvation, and eternal life (John 17:2; Romans 14:9). None but an absolute, sovereign Lord can save. None but an absolute sovereign can be trusted implicitly. None but an absolute sovereign will be worshipped.

A long, long time ago, the prophet Isaiah wrote of the greatness, superiority, and excellence of our Lord Jesus Christ (Isaiah 9:6-7). Then, hundreds of years later, when the angel Gabriel appeared to Mary he announced that, though she was a virgin, having never known a man, she would conceive and bring forth a Son by the power of the Holy Ghost; and that her child would be the Son of God, the Saviour of his people. The angel named him JESUS and said, 'He shall be great, and shall be called the Son of the Highest: and the Lord God shall give unto him the throne of his father David: and he shall reign over the house of Jacob for ever; and of his kingdom there shall be no end' (Luke 1:31-33).

We read in Colossians 1:18-19 that it is the will and purpose of the triune God 'that in all things he (the Lord Jesus Christ, the God-man, our Mediator) might have the pre-eminence. For it pleased the Father that in him should all fulness dwell'. Now, that which God spoke by the prophet, announced by his angel, and proclaimed by his apostles has come to pass.

In Hebrews 1:1-4 the Spirit of God informs us that the Lord Jesus Christ is superior to, greater than, and exalted above all things. In fact, this is really the message of the entire book of Hebrews. A key word in the book is the word 'better'. The primary purpose of this book is to show us that Christ is 'better' than all who came before him, and, by implication, any who claim to come after him. He is better than the prophets, better than the angels, better than Moses, better than Joshua, and better than Aaron. He is Surety of a better covenant, established upon better promises, giving a better hope. Christ our Saviour is better than the tabernacle, the altar, and the mercy-seat. He is a better Sacrifice, offering better blood, giving us a better access to and better standing before the holy Lord God. In all things Christ is better than all others. He is infinitely better. He is the best! He is, in a word, unrivalled. That is clearly the message of the book.

'The Brightness of His Glory'

The Lord Jesus Christ is unrivalled in his excellence as the brightness of the glory of God. 'Who being the brightness of his glory' (v. 3). Christ is the glory of his glory who is Glory! He is God, having the same glorious name, nature, attributes, and being as the Father. Therefore, he rightfully claims worship, homage, and glory from men and angels. He is God, in all the fulness of Godhood; and he is the glory of God, the brightness of the glory of God. That is a statement which simply exceeds the limits of my puny brain!

Christ shows us the nature of God, the purity, brilliance, and splendour of his perfections as God. Yet, there is more. Jesus Christ, the Man who is God, is the glory of the triune God. 'In him dwelleth all the fulness of the godhead bodily' (Colossians 2:9).

'The Express Image of His Person'

The Lord Jesus Christ is unrivalled in his excellence as the express Image of God's person. 'The express image of his person' (v. 3). Clearly, this description of our Saviour implies the equality of the Father and the Son, the sameness of essence within the godhead, and a distinction of persons in the trinity (John 5:17-18). Certainly, that is more than we can begin to comprehend. Yet, there is something here which is commonly overlooked.

The Lord Jesus Christ, our Mediator, is that man who is the image of God in whose image the first man, Adam, was made (Genesis 1:26-27).

The Upholder of the Universe

Christ's unrivalled excellence is also seen in the fact that He upholds all things by the word of his power. Again and again, throughout the Inspired Volume, the Holy Spirit tells us, and emphasizes the fact, that our Lord Jesus Christ governs the universe and all things in it absolutely. He controls what men call 'the balance of nature'. He is the Balancer! He is the One, who as the Lawgiver of the universe, established and controls what scientists call the 'laws of nature'. It is Christ, our God and Saviour, who determines all the affairs of providence. He preserves; and he destroys. He kills; and he makes alive. He enables; and he disenables, not by force of arms, but by the mere word of his power! Jesus Christ, our God and Saviour, rules all things absolutely (Psalm 76:10; 115:3; 135:6; Proverbs 16:1,33;21:1).

No event takes God by surprise. Nothing happens without his direction, from the election of his people to salvation and everlasting glory, to the election of civil magistrates, to the consummation of the universe. Everything in the universe happens, or not, at the will, decree, and order of Christ our God! Even the cursing of Shemei and the kiss of Judas were as much under his rule as the worship of the holy angels around his throne. When the Jews cried, 'crucify him', and Pilate delivered him to their will, when the soldiers nailed him to the tree and the mobs spit in his face, he who was crucified was in absolute control of his crucifiers. I hear him as he hangs upon the cursed tree, covered in his own blood and the excrement of their vile throats, declare, 'Therefore doth my Father love me, because I lay down my life for the sheep ... No man taketh my life from me, I have power to lay it down, and power to take it again!'

Jesus Christ is the Absolute Monarch of the Universe.

Our Saviour is the great King! Nothing more fully shows forth the unrivalled excellence of Christ than his total sovereignty, 'upholding all things by the word of his power'.

Our Redeemer

Our Lord Jesus Christ is unrivalled in his excellence as the Redeemer of his people. 'He has by himself purged our sins'. Glorious word of grace! The Lord Jesus Christ took our sins upon himself, bare our sins in his own body on the tree, was made to be sin for us, suffered all the horror and ignominy of Almighty God's wrath for our sins to the full satisfaction of his infinite justice, and bore them away forever! It is Christ who purged our sins (Hebrews 9:24-26), and he did it by himself (Isaiah 63:1-5). All the sins of all God's elect were washed away at one time in the blood of the Lamb, washed away forever! The Lord Jesus needed no help in doing the work. He did it by himself, without our involvement, without us putting forth our hand, or lifting up our tools (Exodus 20:25, Deuteronomy 27:5). 'He has purged our sins!' This is atonement, blood atonement, a just atonement, definite (limited to our sins) atonement; and effectual atonement. Here is a Priest like no other priest. 'He purged our sins!' Here is a sacrifice like no other sacrifice. All other sacrifices were consumed by the fire of God's altar. Here is the Sacrifice that consumed the fire of God's wrath. Truly, Christ is unrivalled in his excellence as our Redeemer.

Glorious Exaltation

Our Saviour's unrivalled excellence is to be seen in his glorious exaltation. 'When he had by himself purged our sins, sat down on the right hand of the Majesty on high'. Behold the Lamb upon his throne, seated yonder in glory, at the right hand of the Majesty on High! What could be more appropriate? Christ achieved all that he came here to do. He has redeemed his people from their sins. He purged our sins. Now, he sits in glory, the Object of all worship, honour, and praise. This is our God. This is our Saviour. He is seated on the right hand of the Majesty on High. What does that imply? His work is finished. His sacrifice is accepted. 'His rest is glorious!' His people are secure. He is pre-eminent!

His Excellent Name

The Lord Jesus Christ is unrivalled in his excellence by reason of the excellent name he has obtained. 'Being made so much better than the angels, as he hath obtained a more excellent name than they'. Christ is better! Better than all the prophets! Better than all the priests! Better than all the kings! Better than all the sacrifices! Better than all the angels! Christ is better than all. 'He hath obtained a more excellent name than they'. His name is who he his. His name is the name of salvation (Acts 4:12; John 1:12; 20:31). His name prevails in heaven (John 15:16). His name is the name that must be known and acknowledged. We preach that men everywhere may know his name (Acts 9:15). All will one day acknowledge and reverence his name (Philippians 2:9-11). This great, unrivalled, gloriously excellent Christ is the Saviour of all who trust in his name!

Who being the brightness of *his* glory, and the express image of his person, and upholding all things by the word of his power, when he had by himself purged our sins, sat down on the right hand of the Majesty on high;

Hebrews 1:3

Chapter 2

Read: Hebrews 1:3

'Sat Down'

There is a Man in glory! There is a Man risen, exalted, and seated upon the throne of God. Do you realize what that means? Does not the Word of God ask, 'How can he (a man) be clean, that is born of woman?' (Job 25:4) We read in the book of God, 'It is appointed unto men once to die, but after this the judgment' (Hebrews 9:27). Yet, the Holy Spirit here declares that there is a Man in glory, a Man who, 'when he had by himself purged our sins, sat down on the right hand of the Majesty on high!'

No Ordinary Man

This Man is no ordinary man. This Man is himself God. He is the God-man. He became a man that he might redeem men. He lived in this world as the Representative Man, the Representative of God's elect. He lived the full age of a man in perfect obedience to the will and law of God to establish righteousness for men, even the righteousness of God, by magnifying the law and making it honourable. Then, when his hour had fully come, this Man, the God-man, our Lord Jesus Christ, died upon the cursed tree as our Substitute, 'the just for the unjust, that he might bring us to God' (1 Peter 3:18). Now, this Man, who as a man put away sin by the sacrifice of himself, is seated upon the very throne of God in glory, accepted as a man, with God! Hear the good news of that fact. Since there is a Man in glory, accepted of God, there may be another, and another, and another! Because this Man, the God-man is in glory, 'He is able also to save them to the uttermost that come unto God by him' (Hebrews 7:25).

Who is He?

This man, the Lord Jesus Christ, is 'the brightness of God's glory and the express image of his person'. Christ is both God himself and the singular revelation and expression of the glory of God. 'The reference', wrote Henry Mahan, 'is to the sun and its rays. The Father and the Son are the same as the sun and its rays. One is not before the other, and they cannot be divided or separated. He is the perfect revelation and the exact image and character of the Father (Isaiah 9:6; John 1:1-3; 10:30; 14:8-10; Matthew 1:21-23)'.

What has He Done?

Much needs to be said in answer to this question; but allow me to stick with the words of this text, and simply declare that which is the essence of all our Saviour did as the God-man, our Mediator. The Lord Jesus Christ has 'by himself purged our sins!' The Lord Jesus, of himself, by himself alone, and by the sacrifice of himself, made atonement for all the sins of God's elect. He took our sins upon himself, bore them and died under the penalty of them, thereby abolishing them completely and forever (2 Corinthians 5:21; Hebrews 9:26; Colossians 1:19-22; Isaiah 53:4-6).

Where is He Now?

He is yonder in glory, where, two thousand years ago, 'he sat down on the right hand of the majesty on high'. The 'Majesty on high' is God the Father to whom majesty belongs and who is clothed with majesty. His right hand is the place of power, greatness, acceptance, and glory. There sits the Man, Christ Jesus, and all his elect in him. We have been made to sit down with him in heavenly places! (Ephesians 1:3, 20; 2:6; 3:10).

What 'Sat Down' Means

Our Lord Jesus Christ, when he had finished all the work which his Father gave him to do upon the earth as our Substitute, Surety, and Mediator, 'sat down on the right hand of the Majesty on high!' Let me show you something about what that means. Here are seven reasons why the Lord Jesus Christ, the God-man, our Mediator and Substitute, sat down upon the throne of grace, on the right hand of the Majesty on high.

He sat down because his work was finished (John 19:30; Romans 8:33-34; Hebrews 10:10-14). He sat down because God the Father accepted his sacrifice as our sin-atoning Substitute (Isaiah 53:10-11). The Lord God sees of the travail of his soul and is satisfied. The law and justice of God, the righteousness and truth of God, the holiness and purity of God cannot demand more than Christ paid for the sins of his people! Now, God can be and is, both just and the Justifier of all who believe on his dear Son. He is both 'a just God and a Saviour' (Isaiah 45:21; Romans 3:26).

The Lord Jesus Christ sat down in heaven as our great High Priest upon the throne of grace, because he is now, as the God-man our Mediator, the sovereign Monarch of all the universe (John 17:2; Romans 14:9). The Lord Jesus took his place in glory at the right hand of the Majesty on high, because this Man is himself God. The throne of God is his throne (1:8). He was given this place as a man; but it was always his as God; and he took it. He 'sat down' as the God-man, our Saviour! The Lord Jesus Christ sat down upon the right hand of God as the Representative and Forerunner of his people (Hebrews 6:20; 1 John 2:1-3).

Yonder, in Glory Land, upon the very throne of God, is a Man, a Man who is himself God, who incessantly pleads our cause with the Father. Because our Forerunner is there, we soon shall be. The Lord Jesus Christ sat down in heaven, because he has now opened the way for sinners to come to God (Hebrews 10:19-22). The Lord Jesus sat down in heaven as a mighty Victor, a Conqueror whose enemies shall never rise again, whose enemies must and shall be put under his feet (Philippians 2:8-11).

Because Christ sat down in glory, as the mighty Captain of our salvation, our salvation is a matter of certainty. We are now more than conquerors in him (Romans 8:28-39).

'When He had by Himself Purged Our Sins'

The Lord God our Saviour promised that he would remove the iniquity of his people in one day, by one tremendous act of grace (Zechariah 3:9); and he has done it. The Lord Jesus Christ has, by himself, completely purged away and removed forever all the sins of all his people. His blood has not merely covered our sins, but purged them. His blood has not only remitted the iniquities, transgressions, and sins of his people, but removed them. This is forgiveness, pardon, absolution. Sometimes God promises to 'cover' our sins 'Blessed is the man whose transgression is forgiven, whose sin is covered'. Truly, that man is blessed whose sin has been covered by God. Sometimes the Lord speaks of 'blotting out', or 'erasing' our sins. 'I am he that blotteth out thy transgressions for mine own sake, and will not remember thy sins'. The Lord God has blotted out our sins from the ledgers of justice (Isaiah 43:25).

Here, and in Zechariah's prophecy, the Lord describes this great work of redemption and grace as the purging and removal of our sins. How I delight in this! The Lord Jesus Christ has, by his precious blood, purged and graciously removed our sins. Our sins, like a great, high mountain, stood between us and God. We could not climb over it; and God could not cross it. So he said, 'I will remove it!' Sin laid upon us like a heavy, heavy burden on a man's shoulders; and God said, 'I will remove the burden'. He took the burden off our shoulders, put it upon himself, carried it up to Calvary's hill and flung it into his tomb, where he left the dead thing. Christ has finished the transgression, made an end of sin and brought in an everlasting righteousness for his people (Psalm 103:12; Jeremiah 50:20; Numbers 23:21).

What is this Removal of Iniquity?

It is the removal of sin's punishment (Galatians 3:13). That person whom God pardons cannot be punished for sin again. Christ was punished in our stead. 'Payment God cannot twice demand, first at my bleeding Surety's hand, and then again at mine!' (A. M. Toplady).

It is the removal of sin's guilt. To be justified is to be declared, 'Not guilty!' In the court of heaven, we were declared not guilty when Christ died (Romans 4:25). And in the court of conscience, as soon as a sinner trusts Christ, he is declared, 'Not guilty!' (Hebrews 9:14). Miracle of miracles, Almighty God has removed from us the guilt of sin. He sees no sin in us, upon us, or about us!

It is the removal of sin's defilement. Though in ourselves we are yet aware, increasingly aware, of sin's defilement, before God through the blood of Christ, we are pure and holy. Our Saviour says, 'Ye are clean!' (John 13:10).

It is the removal of sin's dominion. 'The position of sin in a natural man is that of a king on his throne, the position of sin in a Christian is that of a bandit hiding in secret places trying to get back its old usurped dominion, but failing in the attempt, for 'sin shall not have dominion over you, for ye are not under the law, but under grace" (C. H. Spurgeon).

It is the removal of sin's being. Soon we shall be delivered from this body of sin (Romans 7:24-25). When we have left this body of sin we shall have left sin!

It is the removal of sin's sorrow. 'God shall wipe away all tears from their eyes' In heaven there shall be 'no more sorrow', not even for sin!

It is the removal of sin's consequences. God has removed from his people all the consequences of sin. And soon, he shall remove the very slime of the serpent's trail from his creation. Sin is the attempt of men and devils to rob God of his glory. But he has foiled his enemies. He will get glory to himself even by the wrath of man (Psalm 76:10), 'The wrath of man worketh not the righteousness of God'. But the righteous God makes even the wrath of man to praise him.

Being made so much better than the angels, as he hath by inheritance obtained a more excellent name than they. For unto which of the angels said he at any time, Thou art my Son, this day have I begotten thee? And again, I will be to him a Father, and he shall be to me a Son? And again, when he bringeth in the firstbegotten into the world, he saith, And let all the angels of God worship him.

Hebrews 1:4-6

Chapter 3

Read: Hebrews 1:4-6

The angels are venerated, and even worshipped by many, as the highest creatures of God. Therefore, the Holy Spirit shows us here the infinite superiority of Christ over those heavenly creatures. In verses 1-3, we are told who Christ is and what he has done. Beginning with verse four, we see numerous displays of Christ's superiority over the angels of God. This is in keeping with the whole theme of the book of Hebrews which was written to show us the excellence, superiority and glory of the Lord Jesus Christ over all creatures, all covenants, all priests and all sacrifices.

Christ Better than Angels

Our Lord Jesus Christ is better than the angels by virtue of his eternal divinity; but he was made better than the angels as a man, as the God-man, by virtue of his success as our Mediator and Surety (vv. 1-3; Philippians 2:9-11). While we thank God for the angels and their work, we must never pray to or worship them (Revelation 22:8,9). Neither angels nor men are to be worshipped, but God alone (Acts 10:25,26; Matthew 23:8-11).

Christ is, in all things, better than, superior to, and more excellent than the angels by an infinite degree. He is the Creator. They are his creatures. He is the King. They are his subjects. He is independent. They are dependent upon him for all things. He is the One worshipped. They are his worshipers. He is the Master. They are his servants. He is the One who sends. They are sent by him. He is the One who blesses. They are blessed by him.

God the Son

God never said to any angel, 'Thou art my Son'. That title is given to the Lord Jesus Christ alone (v. 5). When did the Lord God say to Christ, 'Thou art my Son'? At his baptism (Matthew 3:16-17). At his transfiguration (Matthew 17:5). At his resurrection (Psalm 2:7; Romans 1:4; Hebrews 5:5). Christ is the Son of God by nature. He is God the Son. Angels are the sons of God by creation. God's elect are the sons of God by adoption. Our Lord's office as the Messiah and our Mediator is not the foundation of his sonship. His sonship is the foundation of his office. He was the Son before he was the Prophet, Priest and King (John 1:1,2; 17:1-5).

Angelic Worship

When our Lord Jesus Christ came into the world, the angels of God were called to worship the incarnate God, and they gladly did so. We see the angels worshipping him as God, and serving him as their Master with willing hearts in many places: at his birth, after his temptation in the wilderness, in Gethsemane, at his resurrection, at his ascension, and in heaven (Luke 2:9-14; Mark 1:13; Luke 22:43-44; Luke 24:2-5; Acts 1:10,11; Revelation 5:11-12).

God's Messengers

While it must be acknowledged that we really know very little about the angels of God (because little is revealed), their ministry is very important and should not be ignored. The terrible confusion and utter heresy promoted by many in religious superstition concerning the angels of God needs to be exposed and laid aside. As it is with most spiritual matters, the whole religious world is caught up in superstition, sentimentality, and idolatry about the angels of God. Some venerate, pray to, and worship angels. Many wear idolatrous little 'angel' pins as good luck charms to keep them from evil. Multitudes foolishly imagine that when babies and little children die, they become angels. In light of these facts, the need for clear instruction from the scriptures is obvious.

Before the completion of holy scripture, before the entire canon of this sacred volume was written, God spoke to men in visions and by angels, as well as by prophets and apostles. He confirmed the word spoken in such a miraculous manner by miracles, signs, and wonders. But those days are over. Since that which is perfect has come, now that which was in part has been put aside (1 Corinthians 13:10). We now have the complete Revelation of God in holy scripture. There is no need for, nor can there be, any inspired prophets or apostles with a new word from God. Because we have no new word from God, we do not now live in the age of miracles, signs, and wonders. Those things were needed in the church's infancy to confirm the apostles as the messengers of the Messiah (Hebrews 2:4; 2 Corinthians 12:12). For the same reasons, the Lord no longer sends angels, in visible or audible manifestations, to direct us in his will and ways. We have God's Word for that purpose.

However, that does not mean that the ministry of God's angels has ceased. Far from it. The angels of God are just as active today as ever. The word 'angel' means 'messenger'. An angel is essentially a messenger from God, one created and sent of God. Without question, there is a specific order of heavenly beings called 'angels'. The fallen angels (Revelation 12:4), are commonly referred to as 'devils' or 'demons' (James 2:19). Those fallen angels are messengers of Satan, bent upon the destruction of our souls. Whereas the angels of God are described as, 'ministering spirits, sent forth to minister for them who shall be heirs of salvation' (1:14).

The angels of God are God's messengers of mercy to his elect. They are described in exactly this way in Genesis 32:1-2. Believers have far more friends than we know. As we make our pilgrimage through this world, as we seek to serve our God, as we walk through the midst of our enemies in this world of darkness, if only we could hear, we would hear the rush of angels' wings, 'God's hosts', at our side and round about us. If only we had eyes to see, we would see 'the mountain full of horses and chariots of fire round about' those who dare be faithful to God (2 Kings 6:15-17).

The Angels of the Churches

In Revelation 1:20, and in chapters two and three, the faithful pastors of local churches are called 'angels' because faithful men, gifted and called of God to the work of the ministry are God's messengers to his people. Not all pastors are designated 'angels' but all who are truly God's messengers to the souls of men are to be esteemed as such. Why? Because God has ordained the salvation of his elect by the preaching and hearing of the gospel (Romans 1:16-17; 10:17; 1 Corinthians 1:21-24; James 1:18; 1 Peter 1:23-25).

Proper Esteem

Let no one despise or lightly esteem the ministry of the Word. Rather, we should highly esteem those men who faithfully preach the gospel for their work's sake as the angels of God to our souls (1 Thessalonians 5:12-

13). As the Galatians received Paul as an angel of God to their souls (Galatians 4:14), so all faithful gospel preachers are to be received by those whose souls they serve. This esteem is due them as God's messengers, because God's servants are placed as pastors in his churches to instruct them, admonish them, and lead them in the way of faith and righteousness. Paul's admonition to the saints at Thessalonica to esteem God's servants very highly was enforced by the fact that the unity, peace, and usefulness of every local church greatly depends upon it.

Necessary Work

The ministry of the Word is not an optional addition to, but an essential part of the believer's life. Gospel preachers are essential to both the salvation of chosen, redeemed sinners and the edification of the church (Ephesians 4:11-16). People often say, 'I follow the Lord. I will not follow a man'. Certainly, there is a sense in which this is right. Every man is responsible for his own soul. Each one must search the scriptures, and make certain that the preachers he hears are true to the Word of God. God's servants are not inspired, infallible instructors to be blindly followed, or priests to whom we trust our souls. Yet, if anyone follows Christ, he must hear, heed, obey, and follow those men who are the angels of God to their souls (Hebrews 13:7, 17).

Living Creatures

These faithful men are portrayed as ' beasts' (living creatures) before the throne of God (Revelation 4:6-11). By the gifts and grace of God the Holy Spirit, they are bold as lions, strong as oxen, compassionate as men, and soar to heaven like eagles, seeking a word from God for the souls of men. Like the seraphs described in Isaiah 6, they are humble, conscious of their unworthiness, but swift to do the will and work of God to which they are called. With their eyes always fixed on the blood of the Lamb, they ever set forth the glorious holiness of God. By the unction of God's Spirit, when God speaks by his servants to the hearts of chosen sinners, they expose the sins of men and bring the gospel like live coals from off the altar, and proclaim to all who believe, 'Thine iniquity is taken away, and thy sin is purged!' Gospel preachers, the angels of God to the souls of men, lead sinners in the worship of God, giving glory and honour and thanks to him sat on the throne, and worship him that liveth for ever and ever (Revelation 4:9-10) . Blessed are those people to whom God has sent a faithful man, as an angel of God, to minister to their souls.

And of the angels he saith, Who maketh his angels spirits, and his ministers a flame of fire. But unto the Son he saith, Thy throne, O God, is for ever and ever: a sceptre of righteousness is the sceptre of thy kingdom. Thou hast loved righteousness, and hated iniquity; therefore God, even thy God, hath anointed thee with the oil of gladness above thy fellows. And, Thou, Lord, in the beginning hast laid the foundation of the earth; and the heavens are the works of thine hands: They shall perish; but thou remainest; and they all shall wax old as doth a garment; And as a vesture shalt thou fold them up, and they shall be changed: but thou art the same, and thy years shall not fail. But to which of the angels said he at any time, Sit on my right hand, until I make thine enemies thy footstool? Are they not all ministering spirits, sent forth to minister for them who shall be heirs of salvation?

Hebrews 1:7-14

Chapter 4

Read: Hebrews 1:7-14

Ministering Spirits

God's angels are created spirits, sent forth into all the world to serve him (v. 7). God is the uncreated Spirit. They are his created spirits. They often appeared in the Old Testament and in the gospels in the form of a man; but the angels do not have material, physical bodies. These created spirits are made the 'ministers (servants) of God'. They do his bidding; they attend his presence, and are ready to do as he commands.

They are called 'a flame of fire', because of their power and swiftness, because of their burning love and zeal, and because they are the executioners of God's wrath. The chariot of fire which bore Elijah away was probably angels. Certainly, those chariots of fire surrounding Elisha and his servant were the angels of God (2 Kings 6:17-18).

Enthroned Son

Christ is God's risen, exalted, enthroned Son (v. 8). Our Saviour's excellence, glory, and superiority are set before us in ever-increasing tones in Hebrews 1. If we were reading scales of music, this passage reads like a great cantata rising rapidly to the crescendo. To the Son, Jesus Christ, the Father says, 'Thy throne, O God, is for ever'. Again, we are here told that the man Jesus Christ, our Redeemer and Saviour, is himself God (John 1:1,14; 10:30; Matthew 1:23; Acts 20:28; 2 Corinthians 5:19). His throne is an everlasting throne. The sceptre of his kingdom is the sceptre of righteousness (Psalm 45:6-7).

Obedience Rewarded

Our Saviour's exaltation and enthronement as a man is the reward of his obedience to the Father as our Mediator (v. 9). 'Thou has loved righteousness and hated iniquity'. He showed this in casting Adam from the garden, in the flood, in Sodom, in all his dealing with Israel, and most fully and perfectly in working out a perfect righteousness for us as our Substitute. In the last day, at the bar of God, he will display to all the universe and make every creature see and acknowledge that he loves righteousness and hates iniquity. In that day, every creature shall confess that the sceptre by which he rules is a right sceptre.

The words, 'Thy God', refer to both the triune God (Father, Son, and Holy Spirit), and to God the Father, for the Father is the God of Christ as man (Ephesians 1:3). Because of what Christ has accomplished as the God-man, our Mediator, he has been anointed with the oil of gladness above his fellows (Colossians 1:14-18).

Christ our Saviour

Christ Jesus is the Creator of all things (v. 10). Our Redeemer, our Mediator, our Saviour, the Lord Jesus Christ is the sovereign Creator. These verses (vs. 10-14) are addressed to our Lord Jesus Christ. Throughout this passage great emphasis is laid upon his deity, eternality, wisdom, excellence, and glory as God the Son. Everything in this sin cursed earth is marked for destruction (v. 11). How I wish we could learn this. It is all going to be burned soon (2 Peter 3:7-10). The heavens and the earth in their present form shall pass away (Romans 8:19-22). Soon, our Lord will come again. He will purge all creation with fire. He will remove the curse. He will create a new heaven and a new earth, purified and without sin. But Christ remains as he is, without change, the same yesterday, today, and forever (Isaiah 51:6; Malachi 3:6; Hebrews 13:8).

When our clothes wear out and lose their beauty and usefulness, we fold them up, lay them aside, and replace them with new garments. That is what our Lord is going to do with this world (v. 12). When it has served its purpose, he will fold it up, put it away, and create something better. Yet, he is forever immutable, unchangeable in his nature, in his person, in his offices, and in the virtue of his blood and righteousness. What a consolation this is for our souls! To rest and trust in him is never to die or be ashamed (Job 19:23-27).

Sent Forth to Minister

'To which of the angels said he at any time, Sit on my right hand, until I make thine enemies thy footstool?' (v. 13). God the Father never said anything like this to a mere angel. He never promised dominion to them. He did not prepare a throne for them. This high honour is reserved for Christ, alone.

What, then, are the angels? How do we account for them? What is their purpose? Read verse 14. 'Are they not all ministering spirits, sent forth to minister for them who shall be heirs of salvation?' The angels are servants to the Father, to the Son, and to his people (his elect 'who shall be heirs of salvation'). But how do the angels of God minister to those who shall be the heirs of salvation? They serve God's elect before conversion in prevenient grace, protecting their lives. After conversion, they secretly and constantly continue to watch over and care for believing sinners. At death, the angels of God carry God's Lazaruses up to Glory (Luke 16:19-22). And at the resurrection, they will gather the dust of our flesh into our bodily forms again.

Let us ever thank God for his holy angels; but we do not worship them. We worship Christ, who created, rules, and sends the angels to keep us in our ways and bring us safely into glory, where we shall be the heirs of salvation forever!

There is a special order of heavenly, spirit beings called 'the angels of God', who were specifically created to be 'ministering spirits' to God's elect. These heavenly, ministering spirits were created and sent forth by our heavenly Father to minister to (serve the needs of) those who shall be the heirs of salvation.

God's Elect People

God almighty has an elect people scattered through all the human race, through all parts of the earth, who must and shall be saved. For every chosen, redeemed sinner there is an appointed time of love when he must be called by grace (Ezekiel 16:6-8). It is the work of the heavenly angels to preserve and protect chosen sinners until the time of their calling. They are instruments of God in prevenient grace, whereby the elect are kept, provided for, and secretly directed through all the days of their rebellion, until they are brought at last to the feet of the Saviour.

Heavenly Guardians

The angels' ministry to God's elect is not over once the chosen are called. The superstitions regarding each person having a guardian angel is as foreign to the scriptures as the idea that babies who die in infancy become angels. God's elect do not have a guardian angel. All God's angels are our guardians, given charge from our Heavenly Father to guard his chosen

(Psalm 91:9-11). None of us will ever know, this side of eternity, what wonders the angels of God have done to protect and care for us during the time of our sojourn on this earth. When our pilgrimage here is over, the angels of God carry God's Lazaruses away to glory. The angels of God are highly intelligent spirits, excellent in wisdom and power. They are the secret servants of Emmanuel's kingdom, ministering to all who shall be heirs of God's salvation. Could we see how they watch over us, how they guard us from countless evils, did we but know how safely they keep us in the midst of countless foes, we would like the prophet's servant see the mountains around us full of horses and chariots (2 Kings 6:17).

Angelic Ministry

A single angel destroyed seventy thousand at God's command (2 Samuel 24:15-17), and a hundred and eighty-five thousand Assyrians who came against Israel (2 Kings 19:35). How safe God's elect must be who are protected by the angels of God, kept by the power of God, and are secure in the hands of our omnipotent Saviour! Only in eternity will the heirs of salvation begin to discover what we owe to the perpetual ministry of these ministering spirits. Well may the heirs of salvation rejoice with such heavenly protectors surrounding them and ministering to them with unceasing joy. It was an angel who first announced the purpose of Christ's coming. It was a chorus of angels who first sang the praise of the incarnate God. It was an angel who first announced the resurrection of Christ our Redeemer. It was an angel who sent men to fetch Peter to Cornelius that he might show him the words whereby he must be saved. The angels of God kept us all the days of our rebellion. The angels of God watch over us every hour. The angels of God meet with us in the assembly of the saints. The angels of God always behold our Father's face in heaven. The angels of God will carry us home. There is a far more intimate relationship between the saints of God and the angels of God than any of us yet know (Hebrews 12:22-24).

The Angel of the Covenant

The Lord Jesus Christ, the eternal Son of God, is called 'the Messenger (Angel) of the covenant' (Malachi 3:1). Commonly, in the Old Testament, when we read of 'the Angel of the Lord' appearing to men, as he did to Abraham, Manoah and his wife, etc., the one appearing was the Son of God himself. Those pre-incarnate manifestations of Christ were preludes to the coming of our great Saviour to accomplish the redemption of his people. To say that Christ is 'the Angel of the Lord' does not, in any way, contradict the fact of his eternal Deity. He is both Jehovah and Jehovah's Messenger. In his eternal Deity, our Saviour is God himself, over all and blessed forever. In his mediatoral capacity, as our Surety and Substitute, he is 'the Angel of the Lord'. As the Angel of the Lord, 'the Messenger of the covenant', the Son of God comes to men to reveal and fulfil all the stipulations of the covenant of grace for us (Jeremiah 31:31-34; Hebrews 8:6-13), thereby securing our 'eternal redemption' (Hebrews 9:12). Having fulfilled all the requirements of the covenant as our Substitute, our Saviour now sits upon the throne of universal monarchy, ruling all things according to the purpose of God as our God-man Mediator, to give eternal life to his people (John 17:2; Revelation 10:1-6). He and he alone is able to fulfil the book of God's decrees (Revelation 5:7). He who rules the universe is God in human flesh, our Saviour and Redeemer, 'the Angel of the covenant'. Rejoice!

Therefore we ought to give the more earnest heed to the things which we have heard, lest at any time we should let *them* slip. For if the word spoken by angels was stedfast, and every transgression and disobedience received a just recompence of reward; How shall we escape, if we neglect so great salvation; which at the first began to be spoken by the Lord, and was confirmed unto us by them that heard *him*; God also bearing *them* witness, both with signs and wonders, and with divers miracles, and gifts of the Holy Ghost, according to his own will? For unto the angels hath he not put in subjection the world to come, whereof we speak.

Hebrews 2:1-5

Chapter 5

Read: Hebrews 2:1-5

See how the Holy Spirit calls us to consider in our hearts and minds the excellence, glory, and superiority of Christ and the gospel of God's free and sovereign grace in him. With this word, 'therefore', he tells us to recall, gather up our thoughts and focus our attention upon what he has just told us in chapter one. The word, 'therefore', might be translated 'since'. *Since* God has spoken to us by his holy prophets and his Son; *since* the Lord Jesus Christ is the appointed heir of all things; *since* he who is our Saviour is the Creator of all things; *since* Christ, the God-man, is the brightness of the Father's glory and the express image of his person; *since* he upholds all things by the word of his power; *since* he has by himself purged our sins; *since* he who is our Saviour is the exalted, reigning Monarch of the universe; *since* our great Saviour is so much better than and superior to the angels …

'We ought', the apostle does not say, 'you ought', but 'we ought'! It is as though he said, 'The message I have for you is the message of God to me. I am in the same boat you are. I have the same struggles you have. I face the same dangers you face. I have the same responsibilities you have'.

Gospel preachers are men just like you. Even the apostles and prophets of old were men just like us. All believers are sinners saved by grace alone; sinners in the midst of great conflict; sinners with great trials; sinners in constant need of grace; sinners under the unceasing assault of hell. What is worse, our flesh is in league with hell. Therefore, we must ever watch and pray. We must ever be vigilant. We must constantly press toward the mark, for the prize of the high calling of God in Christ Jesus.

'Therefore we ought to give the more earnest heed' We must, each one, personally and diligently apply to ourselves and faithfully lay to heart, 'the things which we have heard'. It is our duty and responsibility to bow to the Word of God, to bend our wills to God's will, our minds to God's revelation, and our thoughts to God's gospel. We must set our affection upon Christ; we must do so constantly. We must bring our whole man, every thought and imagination, every faculty of our being, into willing captivity and subjection to Christ. It is not enough that we have heard and do hear the gospel, we must apply it to ourselves and set our hearts upon 'the things which we have heard'. The things we have heard are the glorious truths of the gospel set forth in holy scripture.

'Lest at any time we should let them slip'. This is a very unusual expression. It is used nowhere else in the Word of God. It is an expression of real danger, the danger of apostasy, the danger of losing the benefit of the gospel, the danger of eternal ruin. It is impossible to overstate the seriousness of this matter. It is absolutely vital that we persevere in the faith, that we continue in the Word. There are many, who once seemed to have a real interest in the things of God, who have made shipwreck of the faith and of their immortal souls (1 Timothy 1:19). Let us take care that we be not numbered among them (John 8:31; 1 Corinthians 15:1-8; Colossians 1:23; Hebrews 3:14; 4:1; 12:25).

The admonition of Hebrews 2:1 is this. If we would be saved, if we would continue in the faith, if we would avoid making shipwreck of our souls, we must bind the gospel to our hearts and bind our hearts to the gospel (Proverbs 6:20-22).

'How Shall We Escape?'

If those who heard and neglected the law of God, given by Moses through the mediation of mere angels, perished under the wrath of God, how much more surely shall they perish who neglect God's living Word and take lightly the gospel of Christ, which proclaims 'so great salvation'?

The salvation we preach is here called 'so great salvation' with good reason. The Lord Jesus Christ is the great Author of it, 'the author and finisher of our faith'. 'Being made perfect, he became the author of eternal salvation'. Salvation by Christ is great because it reveals the great wisdom of God. Only by the obedience of Christ as our Substitute, only by blood atonement, by which justice is satisfied and righteousness established, is it possible for God to be just and the justifier (Romans 3:24-26). In infinite wisdom, God found a way to be both 'a just God and a Saviour'.

The objects of God's saving mercy and grace in Christ display the greatness of his salvation. It is called 'so great salvation' because it is salvation for great sinners (1 Timothy 1:15).

The Apostle Peter declares the greatness of God's salvation, when he asserts the great cost of it. The price of our redemption is 'the precious blood of Christ' (1 Peter 1:18-20). Let us often meditate upon this fact and remember that, since we have been bought with the price of Christ's own blood, we belong to him exclusively. We are not our own. Let us therefore glorify God in our bodies and in our spirits, which are God's (1 Corinthians 6:20).

The Holy Spirit describes God's salvation as 'so great salvation' because of the great power by which he performs it. The gospel of God's free and sovereign grace, flowing to helpless, needy sinners through the merits of the crucified Son of God, is 'the power (dynamism) of God unto salvation' (Romans 1:16-17).

This gospel was spoken and preached by the Lord Jesus Christ himself. It was confirmed by the apostles who gave us the Epistles of the New Testament. Their authority as God's messengers was established and endorsed by God the Father who gave them great, supernatural gifts and marvellous manifestations of the Holy Spirit. These were credentials or testimonies that they spoke for God and spoke the truth. They spoke in other languages, healed the sick, cast out demons, and even raised the dead (Mark 16:17, 18; Acts 9:40-42). In light of all this, how shall we escape the judgment and wrath of God if we are indifferent to this gospel? The answer is as clear as the noonday sun, we shall not (Matthew 11:20-24; Hebrews 10:38-39; 12:1-4; 1 Corinthians 15:1-3).

Christ's Superiority over the Angels

Angels were highly venerated by the ancient Jews, almost to the point of worship, just as they are by many today. Because so many would put the angels of God in the place of God, making them the objects of adoration, worship and prayer, superstitions abound concerning those heavenly creatures. Therefore, the Holy Spirit gave us these first two chapters of the book of Hebrews to show us Christ's greatness and superiority over the angels. He is the Creator. They are, like us, his creatures.

The angels are, as we read in verse 14 of chapter one, 'ministering spirits, sent forth to minister for them who shall be the heirs of salvation'. It never was God's intention or purpose to put his people in subjection to, or under the rule of angels, or to make them in any way inferior to the angels, neither in this world, nor in the world to come (v. 5).

But one in a certain place testified, saying, What is man, that thou art mindful of him? or the son of man, that thou visitest him? Thou madest him a little lower than the angels; thou crownedst him with glory and honour, and didst set him over the works of thy hands: Thou hast put all things in subjection under his feet. For in that he put all in subjection under him, he left nothing *that is* not put under him. But now we see not yet all things put under him. But we see Jesus, who was made a little lower than the angels for the suffering of death, crowned with glory and honour; that he by the grace of God should taste death for every man.

Hebrews 2: 6-9

Chapter 6

Read: Hebrews 2:6-9

The Question

In verses 6-9, the inspired writer quotes from Psalm 8, raising the question, 'What is man?' What is man that God should be so gracious to him? What is man that the angels of God should serve him? What is man that the world to come should be put in subjection to him?

Whenever we read about, hear about, or think about God's goodness, mercy, love, and grace toward fallen, sinful man, we ought to be utterly astonished. We should ask, 'What is man?' (Job 7:17-18; Psalm 144:3-4).

The Backdrop

Be sure you do not miss the backdrop against which this question is asked. Both the Psalmist (Psalm 8:1-4) and the writer of the book of Hebrews (Hebrews 2:6) raised the question 'What is man? against the backdrop of the glorious greatness of God. We cannot form a right and proper view of anything in God's creation if we fail to see the greatness and glory of God.

The root of all sin, the cause of all unbelief, and the source of all heresy in the world can be found in this one thing: All men by nature have low views of God. Satan could not persuade Eve to sin until he convinced her that God was not as great as she thought he was. We would never doubt his Word if we did not question his greatness. Men would never pervert the gospel, if they did not have very low views of God. Therefore, the first message of every prophet, apostle, and preacher sent of God is,

'Behold your God!' (Isaiah 40:9). Only when we see the greatness of God will we worship him, love him, trust him, and honour him as God.

It is impossible for us to form a proper estimate of ourselves, until we see something of the greatness of God. Neither can we form any proper estimate of God's wondrous works, until we know something of his greatness. It was the realization of God's greatness which caused David to cry, 'What is man, that thou art mindful of him? or the son of man, that thou visitest him?' (Psalm 8)

The Greatness of God

In Psalm 8 the psalmist extols the greatness of God in five distinct ways. First, he extols the excellency of God's name (v. 1). 'O LORD our Lord, how excellent is thy name in all the earth!' Our great God is Jehovah, the God who saves!

Second, David sang about the glorious supremacy and solitariness of God our Saviour. The second line of verse one speaks of the exaltation of Christ, as our covenant Surety and Mediator. 'Thou hast set thy glory (the Lord Jesus) above the heavens'.

Third, the psalm exhibits God's purpose of grace (v. 2). 'Out of the mouth of babes and sucklings hast thou ordained strength because of thine enemies, that thou mightest still the enemy and the avenger'. Read 1 Corinthians 1:26-31, and you cannot miss the meaning of David's words.

Fourth, so great is our God that the whole of his vast creation is set before us as the work of his fingers! 'I consider thy heavens, the work of thy fingers, the moon and the stars, which thou hast ordained' (v. 3). Finger work is work which requires no strength, but great skill, and detail. So great is our God that the vast universe is his finger work!

Then, fifth, in verses 4-9, the psalmist extols the greatness of God by humbly rejoicing in God's universal providence, describing the whole machinery of providence as God's gracious visitations. David knew what the Holy Spirit tells us all believers know, 'that all things work together for good to them that love God, to them who are the called according to his purpose' (Romans 8:28).

The people of God should ever entertain great thoughts of God. Anything that lowers God's character or lessens his greatness is a lie of Satan. Do not tolerate it. Let no doctrine be believed, no sermon be heard, no song be sung, and no thought be received which in any way detracts from the greatness of God. In all things, at all times, 'ascribe ye greatness unto our God' (Deuteronomy 32:3). 'Behold your God', and know that he is great (Isaiah 40:9-31).

Isaiah 40

Read Isaiah 40:10-31 and rejoice in God's greatness. Isaiah did. It is the greatness of God that inspires our confidence in him. He who is God our Saviour is great! Greater than all the works he performs (vv. 12-14). Greater than all the nations he has made (vv. 15-17). Greater than all the gods men have invented (vv. 18-21). Greater than the world he created (v. 22). Greater than the greatest men the world ever produced (vv. 23-24). Greater than the heavens above (vv. 25-26). Greater far than all our troubles (vv. 27-31). Great beyond description, great beyond imagination, great beyond our loftiest praise is the Lord our God!

'What is Man?'

In the light of God's greatness and glory as God, it is an astonishing thing that God should be mindful of man, especially when we see the answer given in the Bible to the question 'What is man?' Man is set before us in the Word of God as the peculiar, distinct object of God's mercy, love, and grace. But what is he?

Anyone who knows and acknowledges the greatness of God, will also freely acknowledge the utter insignificance of man. As soon as David looked up to heaven and spoke to God of his greatness, his heart was humbled, his pride was withered, and he cried, 'What is man, that thou art mindful of him?'

It is impossible for anyone to have both great views of God and great views of man. Those who imagine that man is great think God is insignificant. Those who know that God is great know that man is insignificant.

'What is man, that thou art mindful of him?' Here is greatness and littleness, grandeur and nothingness, excellence and corruption, majesty and meanness, God and man.

'What is man?' The Word of God tells us plainly. 'All flesh is grass, and all the goodliness thereof is as the flower of the field' (Isaiah 40:6). 'Verily, every man at his best state is altogether vanity' (Psalm 39:5). 'Men are a lie' (Psalm 62:9).

'What is man?' Do not ask philosophers what they imagine, educators what they read in books, scientists what they see in microscopes, psychologists what they see in asylums, or sociologists what they learn from tests. Ask God who made us. He declares in his Word that man is fallen, depraved, sinning, sinful, cursed, condemned, helpless, dying flesh. Men are grasshoppers before him. Men are the dust of the earth, nothing more. Man is a lump of clay. Man is a puff of smoke, a mist of vapour, the small dust of the balance, a drop in a bucket. Man is insignificant! All the nations of all men in all the world are less than nothing before the great and infinite God.

Man is nothing. Man has nothing. Man can do nothing. You are nothing; and I am nothing. No matter how many of us nothings you put together, nothing added to nothing is still just nothing. God, teach us to know our nothingness, that we may look to Christ for everything!

For it became him, for whom *are* all things, and by whom *are* all things, in bringing many sons unto glory, to make the captain of their salvation perfect through sufferings. For both he that sanctifieth and they who are sanctified *are* all of one: for which cause he is not ashamed to call them brethren, Saying, I will declare thy name unto my brethren, in the midst of the church will I sing praise unto thee. And again, I will put my trust in him. And again, Behold I and the children which God hath given me.

Hebrews 2:10-13

Chapter 7

Read: Hebrews 2:10-13

The Greatness of Our God

Notice the first word in this verse 'For'. It is important. This is a connecting word. It connects verse 10 with what has been discussed in the previous verses. There the Holy Spirit sets before us the excellence and glory of our Lord Jesus Christ. In verse 9, we have been told that Christ 'was made a little lower than the angels for the suffering of death ... that he by the grace of God should taste death for every man'.

Every Son

I prefer the King James Version to all other translations; but the King James gives a very poor translation of verse 9. The words 'every man' simply should not be in verse 9. A far better reading would be 'every son'. Both the original language and the context will show this. To translate Paul's words as they stand in the King James Version would imply that Christ died to redeem and save all men, which is totally contrary to the Word of God.

To the Jews, the death of Christ on the cross as the sinners' Substitute was a stumbling block and rock of offence. So when the inspired writer mentioned it, he immediately declared the necessity for it in our text. That is the connection. In this 10th verse of Hebrews 2, he is declaring to us the necessity for Christ's suffering and death, in 'bringing many sons to glory'.

Divine Sovereignty

The purpose of God is the salvation of his people. But the declaration of that purpose is meaningless, until we are assured that the God who has purposed our salvation is able to perform it. Therefore, we are first assured that the Lord our God, who is determined to bring us to glory, is that One 'for whom are all things, and by whom are all things'. This is a declaration of God's total, universal sovereignty. This is a description of the Triune God; but it is particularly a description of God the Father, who made his Son perfect through suffering and death, in bringing many sons unto glory.

The Lord our God is glorious in his absolute sovereignty. This is what sets him apart from all his creatures and distinguishes him from all the gods men have invented. He who is God rules everything absolutely. All things are for him, to do his bidding, to accomplish his purpose, to set forth his glory. All things are for him because all things are by him. In their origin, preservation, purpose, and consummate end, all things are by him. This is what the scriptures universally declare (Romans 8:28; 11:36; 2 Corinthians 5:18; Ephesians 1:11). And this will be the subject of God's everlasting praise (Revelation 4:11).

Our Assurance

This declaration of God's greatness as the sovereign ruler of all things is given to assure us of his ability to save. In the matter of salvation, we need One 'for whom are all things and by whom are all things', because no one else can save. Who can create us anew, but the Creator of all things? Who can keep us from falling, but the Preserver of all things? Who can save us from the many perils we face in this world, but the Ruler of all things? If ever we are brought to glory, it must be by that God 'by whom are all things'. If you and I enter into glory it will be by the work of him 'for whom are all things'.

'Bringing Many Sons Unto Glory'

As the Lord God brought Israel out of Egypt, across the Red Sea, through the wilderness, over the Jordan, and into the land of Canaan, so he will bring all his chosen unto glory by his own mighty hand of grace.

The ultimate destination of God's elect is glory, eternal glory. Not one of God's elect will fail to attain it. 'Not a hoof shall be left behind!' Not one true believer in the Lord Jesus Christ will fail to attain perfect, complete salvation at the right hand of the Majesty on high. Wherever God gives grace, he will give glory. As he does not give grace by degrees, so neither will he give glory by degrees. There are no 'sink estates' in the heavenly

Canaan where 'second class saints' live! There are no slums in the New Jerusalem. God is bringing his people into glory, not degrees of glory.

Whoever he was who devised that abominable notion that there are degrees of glory and degrees of heavenly reward to be given to the saints, depending upon their works on earth, knew nothing of the gospel of the free grace of God in Christ. John Blanchard was exactly right when he said, 'Heaven is not a conditional reward, but a consummated relationship'.

Glorious Place

Heaven is a glorious place. The Holy Spirit uses the word 'glory' interchangeably with the word 'heaven'. He makes the two terms synonymous. Heaven is a glorious place. Countless books have been written about it. We sing hymns about it and preach sermons about it; but really we know very little about it. 'As it is written, Eye hath not seen, nor ear heard, neither have entered into the heart of man, the things which God hath prepared for them that love him'. (1 Corinthians 2:9). We will never know the glory of glory until we are in glory.

Glorious Pursuits

In that glorious place everyone follows glorious pursuits. What are the saints doing in heaven? I will not attempt to guess. But this much I know they are serving God and the Lamb. 'And there shall be no more curse: but the throne of God and of the Lamb shall be in it; and his servants shall serve him: And they shall see his face; and his name shall be in their foreheads' (Revelation 22:3-4).

They cast their crowns at his feet, sing his praise, adore his grace, and make known to principalities and powers the manifold wisdom of God in redemption. They gaze upon the face of their beloved Redeemer, God, and Saviour. All the pursuits of heaven are glorious. There will never be anything low, base, or selfish done in glory. There will never be any wearisome toil required. All is glory!

Glorious Pleasures

In that glorious place, with its glorious pursuits, there are glorious pleasures. There we will understand the meaning of David's words: 'Thou wilt show me the path of life: in thy presence is fulness of joy; at thy right hand there are pleasures for evermore' (Psalm 16:11).

In heaven we shall live! Did you ever try to imagine what the pleasures of God must be? What is that which is called 'the joy of the Lord?' What is the infinite satisfaction of the eternal God? What can be the bliss of him who is blessed God? I cannot imagine such things with my puny brain.

Yet, I know that it is this very joy, bliss, peace, and satisfaction into which we shall enter in glory, when our Master says to each of his ransomed ones, 'Well done, thou good and faithful servant: thou hast been faithful over a few things, I will make thee ruler over many things: enter thou into the joy of thy Lord' (Matthew 25:21).

Chrysostom wrote, 'If one man should suffer all the sorrows of all the saints in the world, yet they are not worth one hour's glory in heaven'. Paul said, 'For I reckon that the sufferings of this present time are not worthy to be compared with the glory which shall be revealed in us' (Romans 8:18). Earth has no sorrow that heaven shall not heal. A. W. Pink wrote, 'One breath of Paradise will extinguish all the adverse winds of earth'.

We are going to glory! Heaven is a place of glorious pleasure. As C. S. Lewis put it, 'Joy is the serious business of heaven'. There are no regrets in heaven, no remorseful tears, no second thoughts, no lost causes, no sorrows of any kind. It is written, 'God shall wipe away all tears from their eyes; and there shall be no more death, neither sorrow, nor crying, neither shall there be any more pain: for the former things are passed away' (Revelation 21:4).

Glorious Persons

This glorious place, with its glorious pursuits and glorious pleasures, shall be inhabited by glorious persons. Read again Hebrews 12:22-24: 'But ye are come unto mount Sion, and unto the city of the living God, the heavenly Jerusalem, and to an innumerable company of angels, To the general assembly and church of the firstborn, which are written in heaven, and to God the Judge of all, and to the spirits of just men made perfect, And to Jesus the mediator of the new covenant, and to the blood of sprinkling, that speaketh better things than that of Abel'.

God is there, Father, Son and Holy Spirit. Christ, the Lamb, is there. The holy angels are there. The spirits of just men made perfect are there. There all the saints of God shall be glorious kings and priests unto God, arrayed as kings, holy as God himself is holy, glorious as Christ himself is glorious. Well does the writer of Hebrews use this word when he speaks of heavenly 'glory'. Heaven is Glory!

The Sons He is Bringing

We often talk and sing about heaven and the glory and wonder of that blessed abode prepared for God's elect. We know that in all that he is doing, our God is 'bringing many sons unto glory'. But the wonder of it is utterly beyond us.

All of Grace
In heaven's glory we shall forever adore and praise our great God for the wondrous mystery of his grace, by which we are saved. Everything in the great work of salvation sets forth the splendour of the grace of the Most High God. What do we see in election, predestination, redemption, regeneration, and preservation, but his grace? The whole work of salvation displays God's rich, free, irresistible, almighty, saving grace in Christ. In salvation as well as in creation, all things are of God, all things are by God, and all things are for God. He works all our works in us, and unto him alone all praise must be forever! (Ephesians 2:8-10; Philippians 2:13).

Divine Ability
The greatness of God in his absolute sovereignty assures us of his ability to do all his will and bring all his chosen unto glory at last (Psalm 135:6; Isaiah 14:24; 46:11). We know that God always does all his pleasure because he always, absolutely controls all things. If he did not, we could never be assured of any promise or prophecy made by him. This is our assurance: the great God, our heavenly Father, who has purposed our salvation, is able to fully accomplish what he has planned, because he is that one 'for whom are all things, and by whom are all things!' We are assured that our God, having put his hand to the great work of our salvation, will not withdraw his arm from the work until he has fully accomplished his eternal purpose, to the praise of the glory of his grace. This we confidently declare to every believer, 'He which hath begun a good work in you will perform it until the day of Jesus Christ' (Philippians 1:6).

Difficulties Overcome
Our great God will bring all his sons to glory despite all the difficulties that lie in the way. Every believer shall persevere unto the end because every believer is preserved by God himself. Though ten thousand hells lay between us and glory, though ten thousand satans roared against us, not one of God's elect shall fail to attain unto glory, because the glorious God has undertaken to save us. As Israel was brought from Egypt into Canaan by a constant series of miracles (supernatural, unexplainable works of God), so the believer's path is a path of constant, miraculous grace. Ours is a miraculous life! God Almighty, himself, has undertaken to save us! Can you get hold of that? Our path is not easy, but it is safe. Fight we must, but victory is sure. Temptations we must endure, but our God will uphold us. Trials we must face, but God holds us with the right hand of his righteousness. He feeds us, refreshes us, clothes us, fights for us, protects us, upholds us; and he will bring us unto glory!

The Objects of Grace

Perhaps the greatest wonder of this great purpose and work of God is the many sons he has determined to bring unto glory (1 Corinthians 1:26-29). God has chosen for his sons and daughters those people whom most people on earth would be ashamed to call their children. Those who are passed over by society, the depraved, the debased, the fallen, are the very ones chosen by God, the very ones he is determined to bring unto glory, for 'the praise of the glory of his grace'.

The Captain of Our Salvation

God has purposed that he will bring many sons to glory; but he has determined that he will do so by a chosen Captain, a Captain greater than Joshua, who will fight for his people and bring them safely into the Canaan of glory. Yes, God will bring his sons to glory, but he will do so only by the Captain of our Salvation, Jesus Christ. Sinners cannot come to glory but by this Captain (John 10:9; 14:6). Christ is called the Captain of our Salvation because ...

The captain has all authority and power. The captain of an army is invested with the authority and power of the king himself. The captain's word is the king's word. The king's treasures are the captain's treasures. Even so, the Lord Jesus Christ has all power and authority given to him for the saving of his people (John 17:2).

The captain makes all the arrangements for the army's march. He decides what path the troops will take, where they will camp, and how long they will stay at any place. And he supplies all provisions for them. Even so, our Lord Jesus Christ mapped out our path in divine predestination, supplies us with our needs and directs our steps according to his wise and good providence.

The captain's word is the law by which the whole army is governed. Soldiers are not allowed to do each one what he chooses. The troops do not make up their rules of conduct and principles of warfare as they go along. That is the captain's business. In the Church and Kingdom of God Christ gives the marching orders. They are not optional. His Word is our law. He alone determined what our doctrine and duty is, what our faith and practice must be; and he has given these things to us in his Word.

The captain is more than a commander, he is a leader. The captain leads the way. You will never go in any path of duty, walk through any fiery furnace, go through any deep valley, climb any high hill of difficulty, or endure any temptation, but where you will find the footprint of the crucified One, who is the Captain of your salvation.

The captain encourages his men. When the Lord Jesus appears to us and we hear him say, 'It is I, be not afraid', that is all that is required to calm our hearts and sustain our souls.

It is the captain's delight to reward his followers. As David's spoils were shared equally by all the army, the timid as well as the brave, the weak as well as the strong (1 Samuel 30:24), so the Lord Jesus Christ will bestow upon all the many sons he brings to glory all the glory he has won. We are heirs of God and joint-heirs with Christ (Romans 8:17). That means that all the glory which Christ now possesses as our Mediator shall be ours (John 17:5,22).

The captain is responsible both for the army under his command and for the victory. It is true, we are engaged in a warfare. We must fight continually, resisting sin, contending with the world, the flesh and the devil. But the battle is not ours. It is the Lord's (Exodus 14:13-14; 2 Chronicles 20:15). Christ, the Captain of our Salvation, is the One responsible for our salvation; and 'he shall not fail!'

The Captain Made Perfect

Christ was the Captain of our salvation from eternity. He was our Saviour from everlasting. But in order to save us, in order to bring us to glory, the Lord Jesus Christ had to be perfected as a Saviour. He had to experience something himself if he would be a perfect and complete Saviour. What does that mean?

Christ was not made perfect in his character by suffering. He was always perfect, both as God and as man. But he was made perfect officially, as the Captain of our salvation. To perform the office of a Saviour, to save lost sinners from their just and righteous condemnation, Christ had to possess three things: merit, power and sympathy. The only way he could obtain all three was by those things which he suffered, which consummated in his death as the sinners' Substitute.

Merit, Power and Sympathy

The Saviour of men must have such merit with God that God can, consistently with the perfections of his nature and the requirements of his law, reverse the sentence of condemnation passed upon those for whom Christ suffered and died. He must have such infinite merit that we can through his merit alone obtain all the blessings of grace and glory, without any works of our own, without any merit of our own.

The Captain of our salvation must possess all power, in heaven and in earth, so that he may, by the sheer power of his will make ignorant, depraved, helpless, miserable sinners, wise, and good, and happy. He must have such absolute control of all things that he can make all things work together for the salvation of his people.

Moreover, the Saviour of men must be able to sympathize with his people. He must be able to enter into the feelings of those whom he is to deliver and save. All these things are necessary if the Son of God is to be a perfect Saviour; and all these things were obtained by him through the things that he suffered.

By his incarnation he became a Saviour of infinite merit. The Saviour of men must be a man, because man had sinned and man must suffer. But man, even a perfect man, does not have merit of infinite worth for the saving of other men. Our Saviour must also be God, because none but God has infinite merit to satisfy the claims of divine justice. Christ, the God-man, is both fully man and fully God.

The Lord Jesus Christ obtained the power to save as the reward of his obedience unto death as our Substitute (John 17:2; Hebrews 7:25). This power is the legal, judicial power given to him as our Mediator, the power he earned as the God-man by his obedience unto death as our Substitute.

The Son of God became a sympathizing Saviour by the things he suffered as a man for us (Hebrews 2:18; 4:15). Only one who has suffered can be touched with the suffering of others.

Now, the Captain of our salvation has been made perfect. The Lord Jesus Christ is a perfect Saviour. He has made a perfect expiation of sin. He has brought in a perfect righteousness. His holy heart is filled with a perfect sympathy for his needy people. He is a perfect example for us to follow. He has perfect power, and is able to save perfectly all who come unto God by him!

Forasmuch then as the children are partakers of flesh and blood, he also himself likewise took part of the same; that through death he might destroy him that had the power of death, that is, the devil; And deliver them who through fear of death were all their lifetime subject to bondage.

Hebrews 2:14-15

Chapter 8

Read: Hebrews 2:14-15

Are you Afraid to Die?

Here is a solemn, sobering, serious question. It is a question you might prefer to avoid, but one you cannot avoid. You may suppress it, and postpone dealing with it; but you cannot avoid it. Are you afraid to die?

I have watched a lot of men die, some young and some old, some believers and some infidels, some with no hope, some with a false hope, and some with a good hope. I have seen some die in utter terror and some with great comfort, some in brazen blasphemy and defiance and some with peace and joy. How will it be for you, when you come to death's chilly waters?

I know a good many men and women who do everything they can to avoid visiting a rest home, a hospital, or a funeral parlour. They simply cannot face the fact that they, too, must soon die. Even now, the fear of death terrorizes them. I ask of you, what Jeremiah asked long ago. If sickness and death torment you now, 'then how wilt thou do in the swelling of Jordan?' Are you afraid to die?

A Reasonable Fear

The fear of death is a very natural thing to sinful men. And, the fact is if you are without Christ, you have reason to be afraid. 'It is appointed unto men once to die, and after this the judgment' (Hebrews 9:27). Soon you and I must die. Long ago, a dying man requested that the words below be inscribed upon his tombstone. He wanted all who passed by his grave to be reminded of the brevity of life and the certainty of death. We would be wise to lay them to heart.

Please view my grave as you pass by,
For as you are so once was I,
As I am now soon you must be,
So make your plans to follow me.

Because of your sin and guilt before God, you must die. But death will not end your existence. You will stand before a holy, just, and righteous God in judgment. There you will reap the exact penalty due your sin, the infinite, eternal wrath of God in hell (2 Corinthians 5:10-11; Revelation 20:11-15). This is 'the second death', the everlasting death of your soul in hell. It is a torturous death that never dies!

A Blessed Deliverance

For the believer, however, things are far different. In Hebrews 2:14-15 the Holy Spirit tells us that one great purpose of our Saviour's incarnation was that he might destroy Satan and deliver his elect from the fear of death. The Lord Jesus Christ came into this world for this purpose, that he might 'deliver them who through fear of death were all their lifetime subject to bondage'.

You and I, who are washed in the blood of Christ and living by faith in Him, should have no fear of death. Certainly, we must not expect to have dying grace until our time to die has come. Yet, we ought not to live out our days on this earth clinging to the vanity of mortality and fearing its end. Christ came not only to deliver us from death, but from the very fear of death. He does so by effectually teaching us the gospel, giving us the blessed confidence of faith in himself as our all-sufficient Saviour.

Deliverance from the Fear of Death

There is no deliverance from the fear of death except by looking to Him whose death is the death of death. Our Lord has done many things to deliver us from this fear of death and its bondage. Here are four works of Christ for his people's deliverance:

1. Christ has destroyed the power of death by dying in our place and rising again. Since all of God's elect were partakers of flesh and blood, under the dominion of death, Christ became a man to suffer and die for us.

It was not possible for our Representative to satisfy the claims of divine justice against us unless he lived and died in our nature. By his substitutionary death on the cursed tree and his triumphant resurrection, the Son of God destroyed the power of Satan and the power of the grave over us. We are now more than conquerors in him. Why then should we fear death?

2. The Lord Jesus delivers us from the fear of death by removing our sin. 'The sting of death is sin'. It is sin which causes men torment in death. But in Christ we have no sin. In him we are fully forgiven. By his blood our sins are washed away. If we are born of God, we are in Christ; 'and in him is no sin' (1 John 3:1-5). Be sure you have the forgiveness of sin by faith in Christ, and fear death no more. To die forgiven, 'accepted in the beloved' (Ephesians 1:6), is not really to die at all. It is simply the departure out of this world into the Father's house.

3. The law of God held us in bondage to the sentence of death and condemnation; but 'Christ hath redeemed us from the curse of the law' (Galatians 3:13). 'Christ is the end of the law for righteousness to everyone that believeth' (Romans 10:4). He is the end of the law's power to condemn. In the book of God's holy law there is no legal claim of condemnation upon any believer. Christ satisfied that claim for us. Why then should we fear? If I am in Christ, I am dead to the law (Romans 7:4; 8:1-4).

4. The Lord Jesus Christ delivers us from the fear of death by changing the character of death. For the unbeliever death is a horrible thing. For the unbeliever, anything short of death is mercy. But, for the believer death is a great blessing. The writer John Trapp once said,

> To those that are in Christ death is but the day-break of eternal brightness; not the punishment of sin, but the period of sin. It is but a sturdy porter opening the door of eternity, a rough passage to eternal pleasure.

Why should Israel be afraid to cross the swelling Jordan into the land of promise, with the ark of God before them? The fact is, believers do not die in the sense that others do. Our Lord said, 'Whosoever liveth and believeth on me shall never die'. To the ungodly, death is the penalty of sin; but to the believer it is just a change of location. Death to the wicked is the execution of justice, but to the believer it is a deliverance from sin. To the worldling death is the beginning of sorrows, but to the believer it is admission into glory. To the rebel death is imprisonment, but to the believer it is freedom.

Would you be Free?

Our Saviour has also taken the fear of death away from those who trust him by assuring us that our souls will go to be with him in heaven immediately. His word of promise is, 'Because I live, ye shall live also'. His prayer for us was, 'Father, I will that they also, whom thou hast given me, be with me where I am: that they may behold my glory'. It is written, 'To be absent from the body is to be present with the Lord!' Knowing this, I can no longer fear to die (2 Corinthians 5:1-9).

Our Lord has delivered us from the fear of death by assuring us of the resurrection of our bodies (1 Thessalonians 4:13-18). This body must die, but, blessed be God, we shall arise. This is my satisfying confidence: 'I know that my Redeemer liveth, and that He shall stand at the latter day upon the earth: and though after my skin worms destroy this body, yet in my flesh shall I see God: Whom I shall see for myself and mine eyes shall behold, and not another; though my reins be consumed within me!' (Job 19:25-27). With such a hope, the grave causes me no alarm.

Would you be free from fear of death? Look to Christ in faith as your crucified Substitute, rising from the dead as your Representative, living and reigning in heaven as your Mediator, and coming as your King.

If you would be free from the fear of death, think about death often and meditate on what it is to die in Christ. We know that those who die in the Lord are blessedly safe and happy. Even Balaam saw that and desired to die the death of the righteous. What makes the death of the righteous so blessed?

1. Death will bring us into the presence of many friends. Yes, death takes a wife from her husband, a child from its mother, and a father from his family. But we cheer ourselves with the prospect of a happy reunion in glory.

It is true, above all else, that we will see Christ and be with Him. But it is also promised that we will sit down with Abraham, Isaac, and Jacob. When we die we will leave some behind, but we are going up to 'the general assembly and church of the firstborn, which are written in heaven' (Hebrews 12:23). And we shall know one another then, even better than we do now, even as the disciples knew Moses and Elijah on the mount (Matthew 17:3).

2. When, at last, we come to die in Christ our most earnest and constant prayers will all be answered. How often have we prayed to be free from our trials and temptations? When we close our eyes in death, we will leave this vale of tears behind. For the believer, death is the blessed funeral of all sorrows. Does your soul long to be free from all sin? It will be when this body lies in the grave. Oh, how our hearts long to be more like

Christ! And we shall be perfectly like him in glory when we have put off this body of flesh. We pray for a brighter and clearer vision of Christ in his glory. After we are no longer hindered by the sight of things in this world, our eyes will be opened to see the Son of God as he is. We should never weep for those who have died in the Lord. We might well envy them and be sad for our loss, but do not weep for them.

3. The death of God's saints is accompanied with many comforts. Death can never separate us from the love of Christ. He will go with us through the dark valley. I am sure that the believer never has such full revelations of Christ's love, grace, glory, and greatness as he is given in the hour of death. The Lord will make His people triumphant over the last enemy in that hour. In that hour, all our enemies will be as still as a stone (Exodus 15:16).

The Lord Jesus Christ, our great God and blessed Saviour delivers believing sinners from the fear of death by giving us a foretaste of the glory that will follow it. It is written, 'Eye hath not seen nor ear heard, neither have entered into the heart of man, the things which God hath prepared for them that love Him'. Yet, he has given us his Spirit, which is 'the earnest of our inheritance' (1 Corinthians 2:9; Ephesians 1:14).

We cannot comprehend this glory, but we can think upon it. In Christ heaven is ours, the throne of Christ is ours, the glory of Christ is ours, the crown of life is ours, eternal joy is ours. God is ours. Christ is ours. Heaven is ours. If these things are so, and they most assuredly are, then death is not to be feared, but anticipated!

If you would be free from the fear of death, live every day as though it were your last. Get into the habit of dying to this world. Let us die daily. Hold everything here with a loose hand. Learn to live in this world in the awareness that everything here is perishing. Live not for the perishing things of time, but for the lasting things of eternity. Live here as a traveller through this a strange land. Do not become too fond of it. Soon you will have to let it go. Be prepared at a moment's notice to do so.

I exhort you to walk with God. 'Enoch walked with God: and he was not; because God took him'. Walk with God; and when you die you will walk into glory. Press as much as you can into each day for the glory of Christ and the service of His kingdom. We must soon die. We will be wise to put our affairs in order.

Let us ever be ready for that happy day when the Son of God calls us home. When death comes, let us have nothing to do, but die. I try to think often every day of my last day. I cannot tell you what a blessing it is to do so comfortably. Until we are freed from the fear of death, we will never be free to live.

For verily he took not on *him the nature of* angels; but he took on *him* the seed of Abraham.

Hebrews 2:16

Chapter 9

Read: Hebrews 2:16

The Sovereignty of God's Grace

The sovereignty of God's grace is set before us most clearly in Hebrews 2:16. It is written, 'For verily he took not on him the nature of angels; but he took on him the seed of Abraham'.

When our Lord Jesus Christ came to save fallen creatures, he passed by the fallen angels and laid hold upon the seed of Abraham. He did not take hold of the seed of Adam, but he took hold of the seed of Abraham, God's elect, and delivered them from the bondage of death by the irresistible power of his grace.

We were lost, rushing headlong to destruction, until Christ reached down the hand of his sovereign power and delivered us. Every saved sinner is 'a brand plucked from the burning' (Zechariah 3:2), snatched out of the jaws of hell, snatched out from among perishing men by sovereign mercy and irresistible grace. He passed by the fallen angels, passed by the sons of Adam, and took hold upon the seed of Abraham.

God our Saviour reserves the right of absolute sovereignty in the exercise of his saving grace and in the application of his mercy. As he is sovereign in creation and in providence, our God is absolutely sovereign in the salvation of sinners.

You cannot read through the Bible without being confronted with the fact of divine sovereignty on almost every page. Today we hear much talk about the 'fundamentals of the faith'. Yet, those who boast of being 'uncompromising fundamentalists' seldom ever mention the gospel doctrine of divine sovereignty. When they do mention it, it is only to denounce it and poke fun at those who believe it.

Let men, if they dare, deny it, ridicule it, and rebel against it as they will. God's indisputable sovereignty is a fundamental doctrine of holy scripture, a vital point of Christian theology.

If you doubt the prevalence and importance of this doctrine of God's sovereignty in grace, I challenge you to read the Word of God through one more time. Begin at the book of Genesis and go right through to the book of Revelation. You will find the gospel doctrine of divine sovereignty repeatedly declared, explained, and illustrated throughout the sacred volume. It is set forth, not in a few isolated verses, but upon every page of Inspiration. God has mercy on whom he will have mercy, and whom he will he hardeneth. 'For he saith to Moses, I will have mercy on whom I will have mercy, and I will have compassion on whom I will have compassion. So then it is not of him that willeth, nor of him that runneth, but of God that sheweth mercy' (Romans 9:15-16).

'He Took Not on Him the Nature of Angels'

As it was never the intention of our Lord to save fallen angels, so too, it was never the intention, desire, or purpose of the Son of God to save all men. Thank God! He does save some of Adam's fallen race! 'He delighteth in mercy!' He forgives iniquity, transgression, and sin! But to say that the Lord Jesus Christ wants to save all men, tries to save all men, or provides salvation for all men is both absurd and blasphemous. Notice the wording of Hebrews 2:16. It does not say, 'He took on him the seed of Adam'. It says, 'He took on him the seed of Abraham!'

Blasphemy

Any doctrine which says that Christ wants to save those who perish, tries to save those who perish, and provides salvation for those who perish is nonsense, theological rubbish, and blasphemy. Jesus Christ is God almighty. He is not a whining wimp. What he wants to do he does (Isaiah 46:10). He never tries to do anything. He simply does what he will. His grace, his power, and even his will are irresistible (Psalm 135:6; Daniel 4:34-35). If he wanted to save everybody in the world, where is the force that could stop him from doing so? Any man who worships a god who wants to do what he cannot do, or tries to do what he fails to accomplish is a fool. Such a god, if he existed, would be as useless as a lantern without oil, or a bucket without a bottom. Failure is an embarrassment to man. How much more so it would be to the eternal God.

Useless Redemption

The doctrine of universal redemption, that doctrine which says that Christ wants to save everybody, tries to save everybody, and provides salvation for everybody, tramples the blood of Christ under foot, despises the work of Christ, robs the Son of God of all glory in salvation, and puts him to an open shame. Those who say, 'Jesus loves everybody and died for everybody', proclaim a love and a death which are totally useless for anything more than sentimentalism. They preach a redemption by which no one was redeemed. Universal redemption is no redemption at all. It says that there is no power, merit, or efficacy in the blood of Christ without man's faith to ignite the power. It makes the grace of God nothing but a frustrated desire in God to save. It makes the will of God subject to the will of man, and makes the power of God weaker than the power of man. It robs the Lord Jesus Christ of his soul's satisfaction. It portrays the blood of Christ as a useless waste, shed in vain for many. It makes salvation nothing but a package God offers to man, rather than a work performed by God in man. It makes man his own Saviour. Universal redemption robs Christ of all glory in salvation. If everything is dependent upon man's will, man's power, man's work, man's faith and nothing is really determined by the righteousness, blood, and grace of Christ, why should any man worship and praise Christ?

Redemption was effectually accomplished by Christ on the cross (John 19:30; Hebrews 9:12). And redemption is effectually applied by Christ on the throne (John 17:2). It never was our Lord's intention, desire, or purpose to save all men.

Elect and Non-elect Angels

It was never the intention, desire, or purpose of the Lord Jesus Christ to save the angels who fell. 'For verily he took not on him the nature of angels'. The word 'took' means 'to lay hold of'. Paul's language is very strong. Quite literally, he is saying, 'Christ never took hold of angels to deliver and save them'. Our Lord did not come into this world as an angel. He came as a man. He did not come as a Surety for the angels who fell. He never took hold of them.

There are some elect angels who never fell. The vast majority of the angels are elect. Two-thirds of those mighty creatures were chosen by God. Only one third fell (Revelation 12:4). God would not allow those elect angels to fall. Their preservation was a great act of mercy. Their election by God preserved them. But for those angels that fell, God offered no mercy whatever. They are eternally reprobate, without hope (Jude 6).

This is a hard rock for the Arminian to grind his teeth on. It is sure to give goats sore gums. If it is unfair for God to give mercy to some men, but not all men, would it not be equally unfair for God to give mercy to fallen men if he did not also give mercy to the fallen angels?

Just Suppose

Suppose for a moment that our Lord had taken upon him the nature of angels when he came into the world. Suppose that instead of coming into the world as a man, the Lord of glory had assumed the nature of angels. I think there is something here that will cause us to glorify God for his wisdom, love, and grace toward us in Christ. 'He took not on him the nature of angels; but he took on him the seed of Abraham'.

If Christ had taken on himself the nature of angels, He could not have obeyed the law of God for us or made atonement for our sin (Hebrews 2:9-10). He could not have left us an example to follow (1 Peter 2:21). He could not have been a sympathizing High Priest (Hebrews 2:17-18; 4:14-16). He could never have been one with his church (Hebrews 2:11-12). He could never have delivered us from the fear of death and given us the hope of the resurrection (Hebrews 2:14-15; 1 Corinthians 15:51-58).

How we ought to rejoice in this sovereign determination of our God to pass by the fallen angels and take hold on the seed of Abraham!

How do you Respond to God's Sovereignty?

When the Son of God came into this world, he passed by the fallen angels, he passed by multitudes of fallen men, refusing to lay hold of them, refusing to pray for them, and took hold on the seed of Abraham, God's elect, covenant people, to save them. For them, and them alone, he made intercession. For them, and them alone, he shed his precious blood. For them, and them alone, he obtained eternal redemption. What is your response to this fact so plainly and repeatedly stated in holy scripture? Charles Haddon Spurgeon once said,

> If you in your heart hate the doctrine that God has a right to save or to destroy you, you give me very grave cause to suspect whether you know your own position in the sight of God; for I am quite sure that no humble sinner will doubt God's right to destroy him … I tell you, it is your unhumbled pride that kicks against

> these doctrines; it is your infernal self-conceit, born of hell, that makes you hate this truth. Men have always kicked at it, and they always will. When Christ preached it once, they would have dragged him out to the brow of the hill, and cast him down head long; and I expect always to meet with opposition, if I speak out broadly and plainly; but let me tell you solemnly, if you do not believe God's right over you, I am afraid your heart has never been right before God.

The Call to Surrender

In this day of man centred, man exalting, man pleasing 'will worship', while men everywhere declare God's helplessness, I am determined to lift high the glorious banner of God's absolute sovereignty, calling for proud worms to bow down before God's sovereign throne. I am, in the name of God, calling for lost sinners to lay down your weapons of rebellion and surrender to God our Saviour in his total sovereignty.

Do you ask, 'Where does that leave man?' I answer, it leaves man in the hands of God almighty. Do you ask, 'What about my choice? Have I no choice in this matter?' I answer, you do indeed. You have two choices: Either surrender to Christ's sovereign dominion, or be crushed into hell for your rebellion.

Men rail at God's servants for preaching the sovereignty of his free grace in Christ. They angrily denounce us as Hardshells, Antinomians, and Hyper-Calvinists. I care nothing for their opinions. I am happy to make will worshippers angry. I count it an honour to bear the brunt of their slander and scorn. If a man hates the truth, I shall never be backward about stirring up his wrath. If a man is offended by the character of God, I shall be delighted to offend him (Isaiah 45:5-10, 20-25; 43:1-13). It is the very glory of God to have mercy on whom he will have mercy and to be gracious to whom he will be gracious (Exodus 34:6; Romans 9:15, 18). Those who deny his sovereignty hate the fact that he is God and would rob him of his glory as God. Do not be numbered among them.

An Example of Unbelief

Throughout the Old Testament we are given example after example of God's sovereignty in salvation. One glaring example of God's sovereignty is Pharaoh. God raised him up for no other purpose but to harden his heart and dump him and the entire Egyptian army in the Red Sea so that his sovereign power might be declared throughout the world (Romans 9:17).

Perhaps you think, 'All that was in the Old Testament. God is different now'. Do not be so foolish. The God of the Old Testament is the God of the New Testament, too. He never changes (Malachi 3:6; Hebrews 13:8). His glorious sovereignty is just as clearly exemplified, and even more fully revealed in the New Testament.

When our Lord passed by gathering his disciples, he called Simon and Andrew, but not their father. He chose James and John, but not Zebedee. He healed some, and left others to die. He called some, and passed others by. He saved some who sought him, such as the woman with an issue of blood, and did not save others who sought him, such as the rich young ruler. Christ died for some, but did not die for others (John 10:11, 26). He was gracious to some, but not to others. This is a fact, God does not deal with all people alike.

The New Testament plainly and forcibly teaches the gospel doctrine of God's absolute sovereignty in the exercise of his grace (Matthew 11:20-27; John 12:36-41; Romans 11:5-11, 32-36).

This is something we must see and acknowledge. The God of glory is absolutely sovereign in salvation. He wounds; and he heals. He kills; and he makes alive. It is his sovereign right to either save me or damn me, to either be gracious to me, or to pass me by.

Rebels would be wise to fall down before his sovereign throne, and beg for mercy. Like the Leper, fall down at his feet and say, 'Lord, if thou wilt, thou canst make me clean' (Mark 1:40). Will you perish in your proud rebellion; or will you take your place in the dust and beg for mercy?

> Pass me not, O gentle Saviour,
> Hear my humble cry:
> While on others Thou art calling,
> Do not pass me by!

I tell you without hesitation that this gospel doctrine of divine sovereignty is vital. You will either bow to God's righteous sovereignty, or you will perish in your rebellion.

The Son of God 'Took on Him the Seed of Abraham'

It is the intention, desire, and purpose of Christ to save all the seed of Abraham. 'He took not on him the nature of angels, but he took on him the seed of Abraham'. The Son of God took hold of the seed of Abraham to save them. This expression, 'the seed of Abraham', does not refer to the Jewish race, Abraham's natural seed. It refers to the whole company of God's elect. We are Abraham's spiritual seed (Romans 4:16; 9:6-8; Galatians 3:7, 13-16).

When did Christ Take Hold of Us?

Christ took hold on Abraham's seed as their Surety in the covenant of grace before the world began, and agreed to save them (Genesis 43:9; John 6:39; Ephesians 1:13). He took hold on his elect as our Substitute, legally taking our place under the wrath of God, dying under the penalty of our sins upon the cross (2 Corinthians 5:21; Galatians 3:13).

When our Substitute died, in so far as God's law and justice were concerned, we died in him (Romans 7:4). We were crucified with Christ. In the fulness of time the Good Shepherd comes to each of those sheep for whom he died. He takes hold of them by the hand of his almighty, irresistible, saving grace (Luke 15:4-5).

Blessed be his matchless name forever, our Lord, our God, our Good Shepherd holds us securely in the hand of his almighty grace and will not let us go, until he has brought us safely into the heavenly fold (John 10:28).

What Must Be the Result?

Since Christ took on himself the seed of Abraham, you can be sure of this: All the seed of Abraham shall be saved (Romans 11:25-26; John 10:16). 'He shall save his people' (Matthew 1:21). 'He shall not fail' (Isaiah 42:4). The purpose of God cannot be overturned. The covenant of grace cannot be nullified. The cross of Christ cannot miscarry. The grace of God cannot be frustrated. The seal of the Spirit cannot be broken. The intercession of Christ cannot be ignored. The hold of Christ cannot be broken.

Does man do nothing? Oh, yes, we did much. We did the falling. He did the lifting. We did the running. He did the catching. We did the wandering. He did the fetching. We did the sinning. He did the saving.

Who Are These People?

My friend, you must acknowledge and bow to the absolute sovereignty of God's grace. God can either save you or damn you. 'Be ye reconciled to God'. All who believe rejoice to ascribe the whole of our salvation to the sovereign grace of God in Christ (1 Corinthians 4:7; 15:10). And all who believe on the Lord Jesus Christ are the seed of Abraham! (Philippians 3:3). If you now take hold of Christ by faith, you can be sure of this: He has taken hold of you to save you.

Sovereign Grace Illustrated

The illustrations of God's sovereignty in the exercise of his grace are as numerous as the characters mentioned in the Bible.

Satan led a revolt in heaven against the throne of God. One third of the heavenly angels fell from their holy habitation. As a result of their sin, they were forever doomed to suffer the wrath of God. No mercy was extended to them. No grace was offered to them. No Saviour was sent to deliver them. The fallen angels were forever damned without the least measure of grace.

Then Adam did the same thing. He sinned against the throne of God. He challenged God's right to be God. What happened? God was gracious. God promised the fallen sons of Adam a Saviour, a Redeemer, a Way of mercy (Genesis 3:15). The angels who sinned were passed by, reprobate, without mercy. Yet, when Adam did the same thing, God extended mercy to man. That is divine sovereignty. Why did God pass by the angels that fell? Why did God extend mercy to fallen men? Only one answer can be given, 'He hath mercy on whom he will have mercy, and whom he will he hardeneth' (Romans 9:18).

You can either rebel against this message of divine sovereignty and perish in your rebellion, or bow to the sovereign God and say with Christ, 'Even so, Father, for so it seemed good in thy sight' (Matthew 11:26). Whether you bow to God's throne or rebel against it, the fact remains the same. The God of the Bible is an absolute sovereign. He can save you, or he can damn you. That is his right as God. It is entirely up to him.

Great Grace for Some: no Grace for Others

As God chose some angels who lost their first estate, and passed by others; even so, among the fallen sons of Adam there are some who are chosen of God, to whom he will be gracious, and there are some whom God has passed by, to whom no grace is given.

Adam had two sons, Cain and Abel. God passed by Cain, the older, and saved Abel. Abraham had two sons, Ishmael and Isaac. God passed by Ishmael and saved Isaac. Isaac had two sons, Esau and Jacob. God passed by Esau because he hated Esau, and saved Jacob because he loved Jacob. In the days of Noah, God destroyed the entire human race, except for one man and his family. Why did God save Noah? Because 'Noah found grace in the eyes of the Lord' (Genesis 6:8).

Wherefore in all things it behoved him to be made like unto *his* brethren, that he might be a merciful and faithful high priest in things *pertaining* to God, to make reconciliation for the sins of the people. For in that he himself hath suffered being tempted, he is able to succour them that are tempted.

Hebrews 2:17-18

Chapter 10

Read: Hebrews 2:17-18

Christ our High Priest

The first thing we are taught in Hebrews 2:17 is that the Lord Jesus Christ was appointed by God to be our great High Priest. The word, 'wherefore', does not refer so much to what Paul has said as it does to what he is about to say. He has shown us how that Christ is superior to angels, and that he came into the world, not to redeem fallen angels, but to redeem fallen men. And now he is about to show us how that Christ is superior to Moses, Joshua, and Aaron, as the almighty, effectual Saviour of his people. He begins by telling us that it was necessary for Christ to be made like those people whom he came to save, so that he might be our great High Priest in things pertaining to God.

An Appointed Priest

The Lord Jesus did not assume this office on his own. He was called, appointed and anointed to it by God the Father in the covenant of grace before the world began (Hebrews 5:1, 4-5). Christ was made a Priest by the oath of God himself (Psalm 110:4). Yet, the Son of God voluntarily agreed to become our Priest and to fulfil all that God required to reconcile us unto himself. He said, "Sacrifice and offering thou wouldest not'. The sacrifices of slain beasts offered by sinful men cannot atone for human sin. 'But a body hast thou prepared me', in the everlasting covenant of grace, which I am ready, at the appointed time, to assume and to offer up as a sacrifice to Divine justice for the sins of my people (Hebrews 10:5). 'These eternal decrees and mutual transactions', wrote John Gill, 'are the basis and foundation of Christ's priesthood, and made it sure and certain'.

The Old Testament Prophecies

In the prophetic scriptures of the Old Testament Christ was spoken of as a priest. The promised Messiah of the Old Testament was to be One who would be a Prophet like Moses (Deuteronomy 18:15, 18), a King like David (Zechariah 6:12-13; Psalm 2:6-7), and a Priest like Melchisedek (1 Samuel 2:35; Psalm 110:4). In addition to the plain prophecies that Christ should be a Priest, his priestly work is spoken of in many of the Old Testament scriptures (Isaiah 53:10, 12; Ezekiel 9:3-4; Daniel 10:5-6).

Old Testament Types

The priesthood of Christ was also foreshadowed by the typical priests of that dispensation. There never was but one Priest by whom transactions might be made with God. That Priest is Christ our Lord. All others appointed to the priestly office were called priests, because they represented, pointed to, and foreshadowed him, the true Priest. Only Christ could atone for sin, turn away the wrath of God, and bring men to God in reconciliation.

Christ's Priesthood Typified

In order to be our great High Priest, the Son of God had to be made like unto his brethren. That is the meaning of these words: 'In all things it behoved him to be made like unto his brethren, that he might be a merciful and faithful high priest in things pertaining to God'.

The Necessity

Christ could be our Prophet without becoming a man; and he could be our King without becoming a man; but in order to be our Priest, in order to be a merciful and faithful High Priest, in order to make reconciliation for the sins of his people, the Son of God had to become one of us. Had he not become one of us, he would have had nothing to offer God by which to make atonement for our sins (Hebrews 8:3).

A priest without a sacrifice is like a king without a subject. Had God not prepared his Son a body, he would have had no sacrifice for sin. He must have a body to sacrifice, or his priesthood would be as vain, empty, and meaningless, as the priests of Baal, of Brahma, or of Rome. Being called a priest would be a mockery of him, not a work honouring to him, if he had no sacrifice to offer upon God's altar. Christ our God became a man so that he might be sacrificed to purge our sins.

The Son of God did not have to be our Priest; but if he would be our priest, he had to become a man. The Lord of glory was 'made like unto his brethren'. Those words describe our Saviour's humiliation on our behalf.

They speak not only of his incarnation, but of his life of humiliation, suffering, pain, and sorrow on our behalf. Not only did the Son of God become one of us, he became one with us. We are Christ's brethren by Divine adoption; and everything the Son of God does, he does for the glory of his Father and the good of his brethren.

Made Like Us

Christ was made like unto his brethren in the essence of our human nature by his incarnation (1 Timothy 2:5). Our Lord had a real human body, a real human soul, a real human heart, with real human feelings, emotions, and needs. The only difference between Christ and his people is that he had no sin. His body was not bigger, stronger, or more impressive than any other man's. The experiences of life touched him and moved him, just as they do us. He was and is a real man.

Our Saviour was made like unto us in the temptations he endured as a man (Hebrews 4:15). He was tempted in all points like as we are, only with this one glorious exception, he had no sin. In the main, our temptations arise from within, from our inward unbelief and lusts. Even those temptations which arise from without find a ready and willing companion within. Our Lord's temptations were like Adam's temptation in the Garden. He had no inward inclination to do evil. Yet, his temptations were real.

Our Lord was made like unto us in the things which he suffered, too (Hebrews 5:7-9). What do you suffer? Christ has suffered that. He knows what it is to be hungry, thirsty, tormented with pain, slandered by his enemies, misunderstood by his family, despised by his kin, deserted by his companions, betrayed by his friend, denied by his disciple, put to public shame, scandalized and reproached, and forsaken by his Father.

The Lord of Glory was also made like unto us in the death that he died (1 Peter 3:18). The Son of God, our Lord Jesus Christ, died the death that we should have died, deserved to die and must have died, had he not died in our place, the Just for the unjust, that he might bring us to God.

'A Merciful and Faithful High Priest'

It is this conformity to us that qualifies our Lord to be the kind of Priest we need. He was made a man to be our High Priest. He suffered, being tempted as a man, that he might be 'a merciful and faithful High Priest'.

Christ is moved to compassion and pity by the things that we suffer, being touched with the feeling of our infirmities, because he has also suffered those very things. He is merciful, not only because it is his will as God to be merciful, but also because he has a fellow feeling with those who need mercy.

Our Saviour faithfully shows mercy to us, because the things he suffered, he suffered specifically and distinctly for us. He exercises constant care for all the concerns of his brethren. He lovingly condescends to the wants and sorrows of his suffering, tempted brethren (Isaiah 40:11). Because his compassion does not fail, his faithfulness is great.

Such is the unspeakable love of Christ for us that he willingly endured all that was necessary for him to be our merciful and faithful High Priest. Like Jacob because of his love to Rachel, our Lord was content to submit to any terms, to undergo any sorrow, to meet any conditions, that he might save and enjoy his beloved bride (Ephesians 5:25-26).

The Lord Jesus Christ is our great High Priest, a Priest ordained, appointed, and anointed of God the Father, a Priest worthy of Divine acceptance because he is himself God, and a Priest made like unto his brethren, a Priest who is one of us, God in our flesh!

'To Make Reconciliation for the Sins of the People'

The principal, primary work of Christ as our great High Priest was to make reconciliation, or atonement, for the sins of his people. He is 'merciful and faithful in things pertaining to God, to make reconciliation for the sins of the people'.

The High Priest is one who reconciles God and his sinful people by making an atonement for the sins of the people. This reconciliation, or atonement for sin, is the great work of Christ our great High Priest (1 John 2:1-2). His atonement for sin is the foundation and source of all his other works as our High Priest.

By the sacrifice of himself at Calvary as our Substitute, the Lord Jesus Christ has faithfully executed his office as our High Priest in things pertaining to God and effectually reconciled us to God by the blood of his cross; for by that precious blood he has put away our sins (Hebrews 9:12, 28; Romans 3:24-26). Atonement has been made, reconciliation has been accomplished by the sacrifice of Christ at Calvary. If we are to understand the nature of our Lord's sacrifice and the efficacy of his atonement, certain questions must be answered.

Who was the Sacrificer?

Christ is the Priest. Christ is the Altar. And Christ is the Sacrifice. Christ offered himself to God. He gave himself an offering and a sacrifice of sweet smelling savour (Hebrews 9:14; Ephesians 5:2). It is true, the sword of justice slew our Saviour; but he is the One in whose hand the sword of justice is, for he is God. Our Lord was not made to die by any hand but his own. He gave up the ghost. He laid down his life by his own will.

What was the Sacrifice by which Atonement was Made?
Christ gave himself, body and soul, into the hands of justice, to die as a man for our sins. He laid down his life for us (John 10:17-18; 1 John 3:16). His human nature was the sacrifice. His divine nature was the altar which sanctified the gift and gave it virtue and efficacy to atone for sin.

To Whom was the Sacrifice for Sin Offered?
Our Lord did not offer himself to Satan. Neither does he offer himself to man. He, by the eternal Spirit, offered himself to God as a sacrifice for sin (Hebrews 9:14). Sin is committed against God, therefore the sacrifice must be made to God. It is God whose justice must be satisfied.

For Whom was the Sacrifice Offered?
It was offered for 'the people', Christ's brethren, his elect, 'the seed of Abraham'. Aaron was not a high priest for all men in general, but for all of Israel in particular. And Christ is not a Priest for all men in general, but for the people of God, the Israel of God in particular. Our Lord Jesus Christ offered sacrifice for those for whom he makes intercession (John 17:9, 20). He offered sacrifice for those whose sins are purged, for whom atonement has been made, who are actually reconciled to God by his blood. The sacrifice was offered for those who by faith receive the atonement (Romans 5:11).

What is the Result of Christ's Sin Atoning Sacrifice?
The Son of God is a High Priest of good things to come (Hebrews 9:11). So what good things come to his people as the result of his priesthood and his sacrifice? Much every way ...

The full pardon of sin (Ephesians 1:7)
Eternal redemption (Titus 2:14; Hebrews 9:12)
Complete justification (Romans 3:24)
Perfect sanctification (Hebrews 10:10-14)
Peace and reconciliation with God (Romans 5:10)
Eternal salvation (Hebrews 5:9-10)
All the blessedness of heavenly glory (Romans 8:29-30; John 17:22)

Those who weaken, oppose, or deny the efficacy of Christ's sacrifice and the reconciliation he has made are enemies to the souls of men, enemies to the honour of Christ, and enemies to the glory of God. Either the Son of God accomplished redemption for his people and effectually reconciled them to God, or he is no Saviour. There is absolutely no alternative. Either the Lord Jesus has actually redeemed his people by the sacrifice of himself, or he is a failure; and if he is a failure he is not the Son of God and we are yet in our sins. The doctrine of universal redemption, by whatever name it is called, is utter blasphemy. The Christ of God, whom we rejoice to worship, is an almighty, effectual, sin-atoning High Priest and Saviour. As Augustus Toplady said:

> Complete atonement Thou hast made
> And to the utmost farthing paid
> All that Thy people owed;
> Nor shall God's wrath on me take place
>
> While sheltered in Thy righteousness
> And ransomed with Thy blood!
> Payment God cannot twice demand,
> First at my bleeding Surety's hand,
> And then again at mine!

A Great Gulf

Fallen man, because of sin, has been banished from the presence of God. God will neither speak to man, nor allow man to speak to him. God will neither approach man, nor allow man to approach him. Sin has separated man from God. By reason of sin, there is a great gulf fixed between God and man, which neither God nor man can cross.

The holy Lord God, in and of himself, in his essential Being as God, because he is righteous, just and true, can never span that great gulf and come down to sinful man. Neither can he bring sinful man up to himself. And sinful man, because of his sin, can never span that great gulf and arise to God. Neither can we bring God down to us.

Depraved, helpless and condemned, all men and women by nature are banished from God in this world, and must be banished from God forever in the world to come, unless a holy man can be found who is equal to God himself, and 'able to make reconciliation for the sins of the people'.

A Daysman Needed

Unless there is a daysman found who can stand between the holy Lord God and sinful man, we are all without hope. Unless there is a Mediator found, who can lay his hand upon the holy God and upon guilty sinners to bring God and man together, we all must be forever banished from the presence of God in hell. Unless there is a priest found who can fully satisfy the justice of God by making an effectual atonement for sin, sinful man must forever die.

A Ransom Found

Blessed be God, such a Priest has been found! He is Jesus Christ our Lord, the Son of God. 'Wherefore (because he laid hold on the seed of Abraham to save them) in all things it behoved him to be made like unto his brethren, that he might be a merciful and faithful high priest in things pertaining to God, to make reconciliation for the sins of the people. For in that he himself hath suffered being tempted, he is able to succour them that are tempted'.

The Lord Jesus Christ, the Son of God, became a man so that he might be a merciful and faithful High Priest such as we need, to reconcile us to God and enable us to overcome temptation. Now, the Lord God can be gracious and declares, concerning all his elect, 'Deliver them from going down to the pit: I have found a ransom'. In Christ, the God of glory reveals himself as 'a just God and a Saviour' (Job 33:24).

'Wherefore'

Each of the priests of the Old Testament, in their way, were typical of and represented Christ our great High Priest (v. 18).

Melchisedek

The most eminent type of Christ as our Priest in the Old Testament was 'Melchisedek, king of Salem, and priest of the most high God' (Genesis 14:18). The book of Hebrews tells us three times that Christ is a Priest, not after the order of Aaron, but after the order of Melchisedek (Hebrews 5:10; 6:20; 7:17). This man Melchisedek met Abraham returning from the slaughter of the kings. Abraham was blessed by Melchisedek to whom he gave tithes of all that he possessed, emphasising the superiority of Melchisedek's priesthood. Melchisedek was a remarkable type of Christ.

He was called the King of Salem, the King of Peace. He was called the King of Righteousness. He had neither father nor mother, beginning of days, nor end of life. He was made a priest by the direct ordinance of God himself. His priesthood is perpetual, unchanging and endless. Though we cannot be dogmatic, it seems to me that there is good reason to believe that Melchisedek was more than a type of Christ, as Aaron was. Rather, this man, Melchisedek, was none other than the Lord Jesus Christ himself (Hebrews 7:1-4, 8).

Aaron

Aaron, the high priest of Israel, was also a clear type of Christ, our great High Priest. When Christ came, the Aaronic order was forever abolished. But Aaron served to typify and represent Christ throughout the Mosaic age. Like Aaron, Christ was chosen from among his brethren. He was separated by a holy anointing. The Lord Jesus offered a sacrifice of atonement to God. He entered into the holy place with the blood of atonement. Like Aaron, the Lord Jesus Christ performed his work alone. He is our Spokesman. He carries the incense of his intercession with his blood into the holy place. Christ blesses his people on the basis of the atonement he has made. And, like Aaron, the Lord Jesus Christ represents and performs his work for a specific, chosen people the Israel of God, wearing our names upon his breastplate (1 John 2:1-2).

Levitical Priests

All the common, Levitical priests were also types of Christ. Like Christ, they were ordained from among men and for men, to offer gifts and sacrifices to God on the behalf of the people. Of course, in many ways, the typical priests were clearly inferior to Christ. The type is never perfect. Yet, they were typical of our Saviour. They were many; but Christ is One. They offered many sacrifices; Christ offered one sacrifice. They could never put away sin; Christ did.

In fact, all the sacrifices offered to God from the beginning of the world were typical of and pointed to the one great sacrifice of Christ our High Priest. The sacrifice of Abel was offered up in faith, anticipating the sacrifice of Christ. The sacrifices of Noah, as pictures of Christ, offered by faith in him, were sacrifices of a sweet-smelling savour to God. The sacrifice Abraham made upon the mount, in the stead of Isaac, was a picture of Christ, our substitutionary victim. The passover lamb was a type of Christ our Passover sacrificed for us. The daily sacrifices, offered morning and evening, pointed to Christ, whose one sacrifice for sin, being effectual, is of perpetual merit to God.

Christ is the only priest God will accept and the only sacrifice God will accept. And when he came, he put an end to all the priests and sacrifices that pointed to him. Those priests and sacrifices existed for no other purpose, except to point to and portray Christ.

'In All Things it Behoved Him'

What a sweet word this is! God, the Holy Spirit here declares that Christ, our great High Priest in heaven, is able to succour his tempted people.

A Priest in Heaven

The Lord Jesus Christ ever lives to make effectual intercession for us (Hebrews 7:24-25). Believing sinners come to God by him, by faith in him and by the infinite merit of his blood and righteousness. Because he lives forever, our Saviour's priesthood is unchangeable. Because he lives forever, he is able to save to the uttermost all who come to God by him. Here is a Priest who is able to save and able to help!

Our Lord's presence in heaven is a perpetual and just intercession for the people he represents. His plea before God is his blood; and his plea is effectual. On the basis of his one sacrifice for sin, our great High Priest perpetually asks three things for his people, three things which cannot be denied him: First, the salvation of those sinners for whom his blood was shed at Calvary. Second, the non-imputation of sin to his weak, helpless, sinful people. Third, the everlasting glorification of all his own. Child of God, read the 17th chapter of John's gospel, and rejoice in the on-going, perpetual intercession of your Advocate and great High Priest, the Lord Jesus Christ.

A Help in Time of Need

The Son of God, our great Saviour, the Lord Jesus Christ, is our Help and our Shield. He helps us in time of need by meeting our needs. He promises, in every time of trial and temptation that he will be with us, that he will help us, and that he will deliver us (Isaiah 43:1-7; 1 Corinthians 10:13). He gives us strength to withstand the Tempter's power. He gives us consolation in the midst of trial. He who has sacrificed people and nations for our souls' eternal good, will not fail to deliver us from all evil at the appointed time.

A Blessing Bestowed

Our great High Priest Christ helps us by effectually conferring upon us and communicating to us the blessings of his grace, based upon his sacrifice for sin (Numbers 6:24-26). Aaron pointed to the blood upon the mercy-seat; but Christ points us to his own blood and to himself (the true Passover and true Mercy-Seat), and speaks words of comfort to our hearts, assuring us of his acceptance as our Priest and our acceptance with God in him.

Paul calls Christ our Passover in 1 Corinthians 5:7. He also applies the name 'Mercyseat' to Christ in Romans 3:25, thus showing that Christ was the true mercyseat, the anti-type of the cover of the Ark of the Covenant. Here was where the blood of the sacrifice was sprinkled by the High

Priest on the Day of Atonement (Leviticus 16:15; cf. Hebrews 9:5; 1 John 2:2; 4:10).

A Throne to Supplicate

To call upon the Lord Jesus Christ for help and relief is both the privilege and responsibility of those who are tempted. The word 'succour' implies a call for help. It is help for those who call. Do you need help? Does it seem that Satan has you in his grasp? Are you tempted and tried? Are you weak and helpless? Christ is a great High Priest for men and women like you. He bids you to call upon him in time of need, and promises help to all who do (Hebrews 4:15-16).

'He is Able to Succour Them that are Tempted'

What a sweet word this is! God the Holy Spirit here declares that Christ, our great High Priest in heaven, is able to succour his tempted people. To bring us relief in every distress.

Wherefore, holy brethren, partakers of the heavenly calling, consider the Apostle and High Priest of our profession, Christ Jesus;

Hebrews 3:1

Chapter 11

Read: Hebrews 3:1

The Lord Jesus Christ is a faithful Saviour, worthy of our implicit faith, confidence, and consecration. If you are yet without Christ, you are yet under the wrath of God. You may have many excellent qualities. You may possess much. But you lack the one thing needful. You do not yet believe. You are yet without faith in Christ. Without Christ, you are without life, without forgiveness, without atonement, without righteousness, without God, without hope! It is my prayer that you will now consider Christ for yourself, look him over, observe him fully, discover who he is, and trust him for the glory of God and your soul's everlasting salvation. God help you, now, for Christ's sake, to trust him. But this text is specifically written to those who are here called 'holy brethren'. You and I must always consider Christ, look him over fully, discover who he is, and trust him. In these verses, the Holy Spirit shows us the glory and pre-eminence of Christ over Moses and the law represented by him.

A Description of God's People

Here is a description of God's people 'Holy Brethren' (v. 1). Believers are holy, not because of their birth or because of any merit in them, but because of the sanctification of the Holy Spirit (Ephesians 1:4; 5:27; Colossians 1:21-22).

We are brethren because we have been adopted by one Heavenly Father, into one holy family, indwelt by one Holy Spirit, given one nature, and heirs of one great, holy inheritance with Christ, the firstborn among many brethren (Galatians 4:6-7; 1 John 3:1). We are brethren of 'one Lord, one faith, and one baptism'.

We are also partakers of 'the heavenly calling', because we have been called to life and faith in Christ by the irresistible power and almighty grace of God the Holy Spirit. This call of God is called 'the heavenly calling' with good reason. It is issued from heaven. We are called to Christ, who is in heaven. And it is to heaven that we are called.

The scriptures make it clear that there is both an effectual call and a general call. All men receive a general call (or warning) through nature (Romans 1:18-20), by conscience (Romans 2:14,15), and by providence (Amos 4:6-12); but God's elect, all who have been redeemed by the precious blood of Christ, receive an effectual, irresistible, almighty, saving call (Luke 19:5; Galatians 1:15; 2 Timothy 1:9).

Am I called? And can it be? Has my Saviour chosen me?
Guilty, wretched as I am, has He named my worthless name?
Vilest of the vile am I, dare I raise my hopes so high?
Am I called? I dare not stay, may not, must not disobey.

Here I lay me at Thy feet, clinging to the mercy-seat.
Thine I am, and Thine alone; Lord, with me Thy will be done.
Am I called? What shall I bring as an offering to my King?
Poor, and blind, and naked I, trembling at Thy footstool lie.

Nought but sin I call my own, nor for sin can sin atone.
Am I called an heir of God? Washed, redeemed, by precious blood!
Father, lead me by Thy hand, guide me to that better land.
Where my soul shall be at rest, pillowed on my Saviour's breast.

A Description of Our Saviour

Here is a description of our great Saviour, too. 'Consider', or take a good look at, 'the Apostle and High Priest of our profession, Christ Jesus'. This is he whom we confess as our Lord and Saviour, whom we profess to trust and follow. Let us ever consider him.

He is 'the Apostle of our profession', the Messenger of our faith, the Messenger of the covenant, the One sent of God to preach the gospel of redemption (Isaiah 61:1; Luke 4:18-19) and to secure the salvation of his people by his obedience and death (Romans 5:19; Hebrews 9:26-28).

He is also called 'the High Priest of our profession', because he has entered and resides in the holiest with his own blood atonement. There he intercedes for us with the Father (Hebrews 9:11, 12, 24; 10:19-22).

The Lord Jesus Christ is Jehovah's faithful Servant, 'Who was faithful to him that appointed him, as also Moses was faithful in all his house'. (v. 2). The Jews esteemed Moses most highly, as the servant of God by whom the law was given at Mount Sinai. But Moses was only a man, a sinful man. Christ is God's perfect Servant, completely, perfectly obedient in all things. Moses was typical and representative of Christ. The point Paul is making here is the fact that Christ is far greater and more glorious than Moses.

Moses was faithful to the trust and responsibility put upon him by God. The whole house of Israel was committed to his charge and care. So, too, Christ, as our Mediator and Surety, had all God's elect given to him, entrusted into his hands from eternity (Ephesians 1:12). As our Surety, he became responsible for us to bring us to glory. This he shall do. 'He shall save his people from their sins' (Matthew 1:21). The Good Shepherd will bring all his sheep safely into his fold (John 10:16). 'He shall not fail'. The Lord Jesus Christ shall accomplish all that he was given to do (Isaiah 42:1-4; John 6:37-39).

Consider Christ

This is the one standard by which we should endeavour in all things and at all times to govern our lives for the glory of God. This is the one thing which ought to motivate and inspire, encourage and strengthen us, as we endeavour to walk with God and serve our generation by the will of God. May God the Holy Spirit inscribe these words upon our hearts and make this the rule of our lives 'Consider the Apostle and High Priest of our profession, Christ Jesus'. Consider Christ. Always, in all things, and above all things, consider Christ. Before you make any decision, before you do anything, before you go anywhere, consider Christ.

His Person

Always remember and give consideration to who he is. The Lord Jesus Christ is God, our Saviour. He is our merciful and faithful High Priest. He always bears us upon his heart, making intercession for us in heaven. He does all things for us, rules all things for us, and disposes of all things for us. He never ceases to consider us, his people. Let us, therefore, consider him.

His Sacrifice

Ever consider what the Son of God has done for you. He has saved us by his grace. We are the objects of his electing love and immutable grace. He loved us when we hated him. He came to us when we would not and could not come to him. He wanted us when we did not want him. But, above all, child of God, ever hold this fact in sacred memory and consider it well: The Son of God loved us and gave himself for us. He laid down his life for us, bearing our sin in his body on the tree, that we might live forever with him, without sin!

Our Debt

Consider this, too: We owe him everything! All that we are, all that we have, all that we hope for is because of him. We have, in our baptism, acknowledged that we are his. Let us never fail to remember that fact. Considering Christ, let us unceasingly consecrate ourselves to him, and to him alone.

His Will

What is my Master's will? Nothing is more important to a faithful servant. Ever seek grace to know and do that which is the Saviour's will. Consider Christ, and gladly surrender all things to him, to do his will.

His Glory

What is best for his glory, the interests of his kingdom, the service of the gospel, and the welfare of his people? It is impossible to separate the glory of Christ from the interests of his kingdom, the service of the gospel, and the welfare of his people. If the consideration of these things is the dominant concern of our hearts, we will not greatly err in our behaviour.

'The Heavenly Calling'

There are some people in this world described by the Holy Spirit as 'the called' (Romans 1:6; 8:28). Those who are the called of Jesus Christ are God's elect, those sinners redeemed by the precious blood of Christ, who have been saved by his almighty, irresistible grace. All the rest of the elect shall be called, but those who are saved are 'the called', called from death to life, from unbelief to faith in Christ.

The Means of the Call

All who are privileged to hear the gospel preached are called externally, by the preaching of the gospel. But those who are saved have been called internally, effectually, and irresistibly by God the Holy Spirit. 'The called' are like the Thessalonian saints. Their election, redemption, and calling is made manifest by the fact that the Word of God has come to them, not in word only, 'but also in power, and in the Holy Ghost, and in much assurance' (1 Thessalonians 1:5). There is no effectual call of grace apart from the preaching of the gospel. Yet, the preaching of the gospel will never produce life and faith in Christ without the effectual call of God the Holy Spirit.

The Result of the Call

Salvation comes to chosen redeemed sinners in the experience of grace by the almighty, irresistible, effectual call of God the Holy Spirit. It is this call of which David sang, when he said, 'Blessed is the man whom thou choosest, and causest to approach unto thee' (Psalm 65:4). This is the call the Apostle Paul was talking about when he said, 'God separated me from my mother's womb, called me by his grace, and revealed his Son in me' (Galatians 1:15-16). Paul was talking about this internal, effectual call when he wrote to Timothy, in 2 Timothy 1:9-11, saying, God 'hath saved us, and called us with an holy calling, not according to our works, but according to his own purpose and grace, which was given us in Christ Jesus before the world began, But is now made manifest by the appearing of our Saviour Jesus Christ, who hath abolished death, and hath brought life and immortality to light through the gospel: Whereunto I am appointed a preacher, and an apostle, and a teacher of the Gentiles'.

The Character of the Call

Whenever the Apostle Paul speaks of this call, he seems to be so overwhelmed by it. He seems to be in such awe of it that he cannot find words sufficient to describe it. He calls it …

An holy calling (2 Timothy 1:9).
The high calling of God (Philippians 3:14).
The calling of God (Romans 11:29).
Your calling (1 Corinthians 1:26; Ephesians 4:4).
The heavenly calling (Hebrews 3:1).

Effectual Calling

What is this call of God by which God's elect are saved? What is this heavenly calling of which we have been made partakers by the grace of God? It is described in many ways in doctrinal and theological works: the internal call, the effectual call, the irresistible call, the call of grace. All those terms are good and accurate. But it is best described in the words of holy scripture. This is how God the Holy Spirit describes the call of grace by which chosen, redeemed sinners are brought to life and faith in Christ.

Darkness to Light

This internal, effectual, saving call of grace is a call out of gross darkness into God's marvellous light. 'But ye are a chosen generation, a royal priesthood, an holy nation, a peculiar people; that ye should show forth the praises of him who hath called you out of darkness into his marvellous light' (1 Peter 2:9). As in the creation of the world, God commanded the light to shine out of darkness, so in the new creation of grace God the Holy Spirit shines in our hearts to give the light of the knowledge of the glory of God in the face of Jesus Christ (2 Corinthians 4:6). 'When the apostle Paul was called by grace, a light surrounded him, as an emblem of that internal light which was sprung in him. After that, there fell from his eyes, as it had been scales, as a token of the removal of his former darkness and ignorance' (John Gill).

Engulfed in Gross Darkness

Before God saved us, we were like all other men, engulfed in the gross darkness of our own depraved hearts and spiritual ignorance. God's elect, in their state of nature, before they are converted, are just like all other men, totally ignorant of all things spiritual (John 3:6). Though chosen of God and redeemed by the blood of Christ, we were totally ignorant of God's character, our sin, Christ's person and work, the righteousness of God, the atonement of Christ, the providence of God, the scriptures, the gospel, and the Spirit of grace. We knew absolutely nothing of God, or of faith in his Son, or of eternal life.

Spiritual Understanding

Now, by the effectual call of God the Holy Spirit, the eyes of our understanding have been opened, we are now made to see the light and walk in the light, as the children of the light. God's people are children of light. They no longer grope about in darkness. They have the unction of the Spirit, causing them to know all things. Believers have the mind of Christ, enabling them to understand all things (Proverbs 28:5; 1 Corinthians 2:15-16; 1 John 2:20). Believers understand the truth, believe the truth, and receive the love of the truth. There is no such thing as a believer who despises revealed truth concerning God and his ways, himself and his sin, Christ and his atonement, or grace and salvation.

Being taught of God, born of his Spirit, enlightened by his grace, saved sinners have the ability to distinguish things that differ. They know the difference between grace and works. They know the difference between free grace and free will. We have been called out of darkness into God's marvellous light. We no longer grope about in darkness. 'We walk in the light, as he is in the light'. And walking in the light, we both have fellowship with all who walk in the light and the assurance that we are partakers of God's grace and salvation in Christ (1 John 1:7).

The Word of God describes the call of God by which we are saved as a call out of darkness into God's marvellous light. In Galatians 5:13, the Holy Spirit tells us that the call of grace is a call ...

Unto Liberty

'For, brethren, ye have been called unto liberty; only use not liberty for an occasion to the flesh, but by love serve one another'. We were by nature children of wrath, even as others; but now, in Christ we are freed from all the curse and condemnation of God's holy law. We lived all the days of our lives as home born slaves, under the dominion of sin; but now, in Christ we have become the servants of righteousness. We spent all our days under the power and influence of Satan; but we are now Christ's free men. How I thank God for the blessed liberation of grace! Satan, like a strong man armed, held me in a bondage worse than that of Egypt. Grace has set me free (Deuteronomy 4:31-39; 6:20-23). We who believe have been called unto liberty, even 'the glorious liberty of the sons of God'!

Unto Fellowship

Not only have we been called out of bondage and into liberty, we have been called into the blessed liberty of intimate, sweet fellowship with the Triune God in our all-glorious Saviour, the Lord Jesus Christ! 'God is faithful, by whom ye were called unto the fellowship of his Son Jesus Christ our Lord' (1 Corinthians 1:9).

God calls his people to abandon the world for Christ. Those who are called of God are called to forsake family and friend, like Abram, and follow Christ. We have been, and are continually called by our God, to 'love not the world, neither the things that are in the world'. Being called of God, let us forever abandon and never again seek the riches of the world, the recognition of the world, or the religion of the world Deuteronomy 7:2-6, 25-26; 2 Corinthians 6:14-7:1; Revelation 18:4).

This is no great sacrifice. 'The heavenly calling' of which we are now partakers brings us into far better company than we ever knew before. We now have access to and communion with God the Father, God the Son, and God the Holy Spirit and blessed fellowship with his saints on earth, and even with his saints in heaven (Hebrews 12:22-23). God's house is open to us. The Lord's table is open to us. The very throne of God is open to us. What great privileges! We have been called into fellowship with the eternal God!

God the Holy Spirit calls sinners out of darkness into his marvellous light. He has called us out of bondage unto liberty in Christ. We have been called, by immaculate mercy, into the fellowship of God's dear Son. And God has called us …

To Peace

'But if the unbelieving depart, let him depart. A brother or a sister is not under bondage in such cases: but God hath called us to peace' (1 Corinthians 7:15). The call of God is a call to internal peace, peace of mind and peace of conscience; to which all men are utter strangers by nature. There is no peace to the wicked: but God has called us to peace. He has blessed us with it; with a peace which passes all understanding; with peace in the midst of the tribulations of the world; with a peace which the world can neither give nor take away. Our peace is a peace which arises from the blood and righteousness of Christ, and is part of that kingdom of God which is within us, into which we are brought by our heavenly calling. We have also been called to peace among ourselves, and with all men. 'Let the peace of God rule in your hearts, to the which also ye are called in one body' (Colossians 3:15). We have been called unto peace, and …

Unto Holiness

'God hath not called us unto uncleanness, but unto holiness' (1 Thessalonians 4:7). The call of God is a holy calling. It is a call arising from a holy purpose: the purpose of God! It is a call based upon a holy principle: justice satisfied! It is a call which has brought us into a holy position: justified and sanctified in Christ! It is a call which makes us a holy people: 'an holy nation!', 'a peculiar people!', 'a royal priesthood!'

John Gill wrote, with regard to this call of God's elect, "They are called out of a state of unholiness and sinfulness, into a state of holiness and righteousness; for being created anew in righteousness and true holiness, and created in Christ Jesus to good works, they are called to the exercise of them; to live holily, soberly, righteously, and godly, in this present evil world; 'God hath not called us unto uncleanness, but unto holiness', (1 Thessalonians 4:7) and 'hath called us to glory and virtue' (2 Peter 1:3), to glorious acts of virtue and goodness, becoming the nature of their call, and of him that has called them; 'As he which hath called you is holy' (1 Peter 1:15)."

We have been called unto holiness. Let us ever seek to walk in holiness for the glory of our holy Lord God, and the honour of the gospel, by the power and grace of his Holy Spirit.

Those who are 'the called' are a people who have been called by almighty, irresistible grace out of darkness into light, out of bondage into liberty, out of turmoil into peace, out of enmity into the fellowship of God's dear Son, and out of sin unto holiness. In Galatians 1:6, we are told that God has also called us ...

Into the Grace of Christ

'I marvel that ye are so soon removed from him that called you into the grace of Christ unto another gospel'. We have been called by the grace of Christ. We have been called by the instrumentality of the gospel of the grace of Christ. We have been called into the blessed experience of the grace of Christ. We have been called to be partakers of and to enjoy all the blessings of the grace of Christ.

Salvation is, in its totality, a matter of pure, free, sovereign, unconditional, immutable grace. Let sinners rejoice! The salvation of our souls does not depend upon the works of our hands, the emotions of our hearts, the feelings we have, or the feelings we lack, or even the exercise of our wills. 'Salvation is of the Lord!' He who has called us by his grace has called us ...

Unto His Kingdom and Glory

'That ye would walk worthy of God, who hath called you unto his kingdom and glory' (1 Thessalonians 2:12). Believer, God has called you to a glory which is a kingdom. He has called you into the possession of the kingdom of grace here, a kingdom which can never be taken away from you. And he has called you to inherit a kingdom of glory hereafter. 'The Lord will give grace and glory'. This kingdom and the glory of it are not things we earn, but gifts of God's free grace in Christ. This kingdom and glory to which he has called us is an everlasting kingdom and everlasting glory. We have been called by the grace of God 'To the obtaining of the glory of the Lord Jesus Christ' (2 Thessalonians 2:14), and obtain it we shall (Colossians 3:4).

All who are called are 'called in one hope of their calling' (Ephesians 4:4). All who are called have the same 'promise of eternal inheritance' (Hebrews 9:15; 1 Peter 1:3-4). All who are called are called to and have been given the same glory for their eternal inheritance (John 17:22)

Here is a call which falls from the lips of the Son of God himself. May God the Holy Spirit, by his almighty grace, will to make it irresistibly effectual to all who read these lines. This is indeed 'the heavenly calling'. May God make you a partaker of it, for Christ's sake. 'Come unto me, all ye that labour and are heavy laden, and I will give you rest. Take my yoke upon you, and learn of me; for I am meek and lowly in heart: and ye shall find rest unto your souls. For my yoke is easy, and my burden is light'. Come to Christ, and he will give you rest. Take the yoke of Christ upon you, learn of him, and you shall find rest for your soul. His yoke is easy, and his burden is light.

'Holy Brethren, Partakers of the Heavenly Calling'

Here is a wonderful phrase by which God the Holy Spirit describes every child of God in this world and in the world above. Look at its parts: 'holy', 'brethren', and 'partakers'. With these three words, the Spirit of God tells us three things about all true believers, three things which characterize all who trust the Lord Jesus Christ.

1. All Believers are 'Holy'

All true believers are 'holy'. None are holy by nature. None make themselves holy by something they will, do, or experience. Believers understand this. All who have experienced the grace of God in salvation know, and gladly confess that Christ is 'THE LORD OUR RIGHTEOUSNESS'. Our holiness is a holiness bestowed upon us by grace alone. It is the perfect righteousness of Christ imputed to us in justification and imparted to us in sanctification.

We are made holy by having the righteousness of Christ made ours. That is the work of God alone. God's great work of justification took place outside us, without our aide. Just as Christ was made to be sin for us, though he did no sin, we are made the righteousness of God in him, though we can do nothing righteous (Romans 5:17-19; 2 Corinthians 5:21).

In sanctification, in the new birth, God the Holy Spirit creates a new man within. He makes those who are the recipients of grace to be partakers of the very nature of Christ. He plants within that holy nature which is born of God (2 Peter 1:4; 1 John 3:6-9). This new nature, this new man, that which is begotten of God in us is 'Christ in you, the hope of glory'.

2. All Believers are 'Brethren'

All who are born of God are 'brethren'. Believers, all true believers are brethren. They are all born of God. We all have one Father. We are all partakers of one Spirit. We all share a common hope. We all have one Elder Brother. We are all members of one blessed family, washed in the blood of Christ, and robed in his righteousness.

3. All Believers are Partakers

Being brethren in Christ, we all are partakers together of this heavenly calling of which we have previously spoken. As partakers we believe the same gospel, seek the same things, worship at the same Altar, and are motivated by the same things: the sovereign will and glory of God.

Being brethren, we love one another, forgive one another, encourage one another, and support one another. Being partakers together our common bond is blood, the blood of Christ. Our unifying principle is the glory of God. Our strength is the unity of the Spirit.

Who was faithful to him that appointed him, as also Moses *was faithful* in all his house. For this *man* was counted worthy of more glory than Moses, inasmuch as he who hath builded the house hath more honour than the house. For every house is builded by some *man*; but he that built all things *is* God. And Moses verily *was* faithful in all his house, as a servant, for a testimony of those things which were to be spoken after; But Christ as a son over his own house; whose house are we, if we hold fast the confidence and the rejoicing of the hope firm unto the end.

Hebrews 3:2-6

Chapter 12

Read: Hebrews 3:2-6

Christ Greater than Moses

Because Christ is greater than Moses, he is worthy of greater glory than Moses. Religion magnifies men, things, creeds, works, history, and rituals. The book of God magnifies Christ.

Our Lord Jesus is considered worthy of much greater honour than Moses because Christ is the Builder of his house, the church. Moses is just part of the house, like we are. Christ and Moses are not to be compared, any more than the builder of a house is to be regarded on the same level as the house. Moses (the law) was but a servant. Christ is the Son, the Lord, the Heir (John 9:28,29; 5:45-47). Moses (the law) is of no value unless he is put in his proper place as Christ's servant.

A house does not build itself. Someone conceives the idea, draws the plans, and erects the building. The Planner and Builder of all things is our God. This is a plain declaration of Christ's divinity. The Holy Spirit here states, in the most unmistakable terms possible, that the man Christ Jesus is God. The reference here is to the building of the church and kingdom of God, or the body of believers (Matthew 16:18; 1 Peter 2:5). All God's elect, Abraham, Isaac, Jacob, and even Moses, all the prophets, all the apostles, all believers are built by and upon Christ and receive all their gifts from him (1 Corinthians 3:4-9).

Moses, the Lord's servant, was faithful. He served the Lord with fear, reverence and obedience in all that God called him to do. Yet, his entire life and ministry was a prophecy and type of Christ. All his writings spoke as a testimony to Christ. He wrote of Christ, he spoke of Christ, and he erected the tabernacle, the greatest type and picture of Christ (Luke 24:44,45; 1 Peter 1:9-12).

The Lord Jesus Christ, too, is Jehovah's Servant, but not a servant like Moses. Christ is the Son, the Master and the Heir of all things. 'Whose house are we'. All who trust Christ (whether Jews or Gentiles) are living stones, built up a spiritual house in whom Christ dwells by faith and over whom he reigns (Colossians 2:9,10; 1 Corinthians 1:30), 'If we hold fast the confidence and the rejoicing of the hope firm unto the end'. These words are not to be understood as a condition of grace, salvation, and sonship. They do not indicate that the sons of God might, after all, depart from Christ. Not at all. These words are written to distinguish between genuine believers, born and taught of God, and counterfeit professors. True believers will continue. False professor stones will fall (1 John 2:19; Matthew 10:22; Colossians 1:20-23). All is not gold that glitters; and they are not all Israel who are of Israel.

'Whose House We Are, If ... '

The children of Israel were led out of the darkness and bondage of Egypt by the hand of Moses. The Lord God did many miraculous things before their eyes. Time and again he performed mighty works on their behalf. He defeated their enemies. He fed them with manna. He gave them water out of the rock. By day and by night he led them, comforted them, and protected them. For forty years the Israelites had seen the hand of the Lord in all their affairs. They murmured and complained. But God was merciful and long suffering.

At last the nation stood within sight of Canaan. Many had fallen already in unbelief. But these people had persevered up to the very brink of victory and rest. Yet, at the last, with the promise in sight, we are told that their 'carcasses fell in the wilderness'. At the last, 'They could not enter in because of unbelief' (Hebrews 3:17-19).

In another place, Paul tells us that 'All these things happened unto them for examples: and they are written for our admonition, upon whom the ends of the world are come. Wherefore let him that thinketh he standeth take heed lest he fall' (1 Corinthians 10:11-12).

Perseverance

In other words he says to us, 'Be not high-minded, but fear: for if God spared not the natural branches, take heed, lest he also spare not thee'. Paul is telling us that it is necessary that we persevere in the faith. It is not the person who begins and lives for a long while in faith who is saved and enters into glory. It is the person who begins, and lives, and dies in faith who enters into eternal rest. Not everyone who says to Christ, 'Lord, Lord', is saved; but those who do the will of God, believing on Christ, and enduring in that faith to the end.

The purpose of God the Holy Spirit in this third chapter of Hebrews is to show us the necessity of persevering faith. He is telling us that we must go on, steadfast in the faith. If we do not, if we forsake Christ, like those Jews who fell in the wilderness, we will perish and miss eternal glory.

Eternal Security or False Faith?

I know that all true believers are eternally saved. Not one of God's elect shall ever perish. No true believer will ever cease to believe. No true follower of Christ will ever cease to follow Christ (Ecclesiastes 3:14; John 10:28). Still, all is not gold that glitters; all who profess faith do not have real faith. Therefore, I am compelled to constantly examine myself, and in faithfulness to you I must warn you that there is such a thing as false faith, by which multitudes are deceived.

Many people have a temporary faith which seems, to all outward appearance, real. But in the end they are found among the damned (Matthew 13:18-23). Nothing is more dangerous than a false faith which produces carnal, presumptuous security. True peace is most blessed; but false peace is most deadly.

Let me be very clear. The Word of God emphatically teaches the eternal security of God's elect and the final perseverance of the saints. True believers shall never cease to be true believers. But I do not know, nor can any man know, how near a person may come to the character of a true believer and yet perish.

I take the warnings of holy scripture seriously (Hebrews 6:4-6; 10:26, 29, 38; 2 Peter 2:20-22; John 15:1-7; 2 Peter 3:17; Hebrews 3:12). I know that many who once appeared strong in the faith have, in the end, left the faith (1 Timothy 1:18-20). Therefore, I am compelled to be honest, sincere, and diligent to make my calling and election sure (1 Corinthians 9:27). Let us consider these things seriously.

A Question

Are we truly born of God? Are we true believers? Do we have the faith of God's elect? Or, are we simply deceiving ourselves with carnal security? I would do nothing to shake the true assurance of any child of God. But if you are deceived, if I am deceived, I pray that God will somehow make us to know it and cause us to seek the faith of God's elect. I am quite certain that the man is much more likely to seek God's salvation who knows that he is naked, and poor, and miserable, than the man who says, 'I am rich and increased with goods'.

There is a difference between faith and assurance. I know that many say, 'If you doubt, you're damned'. Others tell us, 'If you don't doubt you're damned'. For my own part, I would rather go to heaven doubting the sincerity and truthfulness of my own heart and my faith in Christ, than go to hell presuming.

The Thing to Examine

The thing to be examined is not 'What have I experienced?' or 'What have I done?' or 'What do I feel?' or 'How do I live?' This issue is 'whether ye are in the faith' (2 Corinthians 13:5). The one issue to be determined is do I, or do I not, trust Christ alone for my acceptance with God? Do I trust Christ's blood alone to atone for my sins, or am I yet trying to atone for my own sins. Do I trust Christ's obedience alone for my righteousness before God, or am I yet trying to establish a righteousness of my own? If Christ is not all in all as the solitary object of our faith, as the solitary object of our trust, we are not yet in the faith.

Wherefore (as the Holy Ghost saith, To day if ye will hear his voice, Harden not your hearts, as in the provocation, in the day of temptation in the wilderness: When your fathers tempted me, proved me, and saw my works forty years. Wherefore I was grieved with that generation, and said, They do alway err in *their* heart; and they have not known my ways. So I sware in my wrath, They shall not enter into my rest.) Take heed, brethren, lest there be in any of you an evil heart of unbelief, in departing from the living God. But exhort one another daily, while it is called To day; lest any of you be hardened through the deceitfulness of sin. For we are made partakers of Christ, if we hold the beginning of our confidence stedfast unto the end; While it is said, To day if ye will hear his voice, harden not your hearts, as in the provocation. For some, when they had heard, did provoke: howbeit not all that came out of Egypt by Moses. But with whom was he grieved forty years? *was it* not with them that had sinned, whose carcases fell in the wilderness? And to whom sware he that they should not enter into his rest, but to them that believed not? So we see that they could not enter in because of unbelief.

Hebrews 3:7-19

Chapter 13

Read: Hebrews 3:7-19

Our Great High Priest

'Wherefore (as the Holy Ghost saith, To day if ye will hear his voice, Harden not your hearts, as in the provocation, in the day of temptation in the wilderness: When your fathers tempted me, proved me, and saw my works forty years. Wherefore I was grieved with that generation, and said, They do alway err in their heart; and they have not known my ways. So I sware in my wrath, They shall not enter into my rest.)'

There are many, very many, who, while professing faith in Christ, yet perish in unbelief. In these verses, the Spirit of God identifies unbelief as the greatest of all evils and gives us a strong warning against it by example (Psalm 95:7-11).

The Israelites professed to be and were called God's people, but they were a rebellious, murmuring, unbelieving people. 'Now all these things happened unto them for ensamples: and they are written for our admonition, upon whom the ends of the world are come' (1 Corinthians 10:11). Four things are here stated about the unbelieving Jews who perished in the wilderness under the wrath of God. Let us lay them to heart and be warned.

Those who perished, perished because they would not hear God's voice as he spoke to them by Moses. God speaks to us by his Son. He declares, 'This is my beloved Son, hear ye him' (Matthew 17:5; Hebrews 1:1-2). God has given us greater light than he gave the Jews. If we perish, as they did, in unbelief, ours will be the greater condemnation.

Those men and women perished because they hardened their hearts. There is a natural hardness of heart with which we are all born; but this text speaks of a wilful, deliberate, voluntary hardness of heart, a hardness of heart that is acquired by the rejection of truth, despising the light of the gospel and the warnings of holy scripture, by a wilful continuance in rebellion and unbelief (Matthew 11:20-24; Proverbs 29:1).

Those who perished in the wilderness perished because they dared to defy God. They tried his patience, despised his long-suffering, and murmured against his providence. Though they had seen his goodness, lived upon his provisions, enjoyed his protection, and witnessed his miracles for forty years, still, they believed him not.

God was grieved with that nation. They wearied him with their sins, displeased him with their unbelief, and provoked him to anger with their complaints. He therefore declared that they could not enter into the land of Canaan, the promised land of rest. So, too, all who harden their hearts against the gospel of God's free and sovereign grace in Christ shall be forever shut out of heaven by their unbelief.

A Warning

The warning in verse 12 is given to all who hear the gospel and profess to believe it, to all who profess to be God's people. We must not follow the example of those who perished in the wilderness and miss Christ, who is our Rest and in whom alone rest is found. Unbelief was the first sin of man and is the mother sin. Unbelief is a wilful denial of the Word of God, a declaration that God himself is a liar, one not fit to be believed (1 John 5:10-13). Unbelief shuts people out of the kingdom of God (Mark 16:16).

An Admonition

Believers should constantly endeavour to encourage one another in the faith, exhort one another to perseverance, instruct one another in the gospel. Perhaps you ask, 'How can we do this?' We encourage, exhort, and teach one another in the house of God, worshipping, praying, and praising God together (Hebrews 10:24, 25). As we study the scriptures, in private and sitting under the ministry of the Word, we learn the things of God and have that with which to assist others in knowing God (1 Peter 2:2; 2 Timothy 3:14 17). In our daily conversation with one another, we ought to talk together about heavenly things and less about foolish, earthly things. When we see signs of indifference and worldliness, we ought to warn one another about the cares of this world and the deceitfulness of riches.

'Partakers of Christ'

The text Hebrews 3:14 does not say, 'We are made partakers with Christ'. That is a precious, comforting truth of scripture. We are joint-heirs with Christ. Because all things are his, all things are ours. But that is not the teaching of our text.

The text does not simply say that 'We are made partakers of the rich benefits of God's grace in Christ'. That, too, is a fact in which we rejoice. All the grace of God in Christ is ours, fully, freely, and perfectly. In Christ, we are partakers of pardoning mercy, adopting love, regenerating grace, sanctification, preservation, and eternal glory. All the blessings of the covenant of grace are ours in Christ.

But the text goes further. It includes all this and much more. Here, Paul tells us that, 'We are made partakers of Christ'. We are made partakers of Christ himself! This is a privilege no tongue can describe. It is beyond the thought of our finite minds. We are one with the Son of God, members of his body, bone of his bone, and flesh of his flesh. Truly, this is a great mystery! (Ephesians 5:30, 32).

Yet, this is the privilege of all true believers. The moment any sinner believes on Christ, that sinner is so vitally and really joined to Christ that he becomes a partaker of Christ. To be partakers of Christ, what can this mean?

Legally

To be a partaker of Christ means that I have a share in his merits. Sinful, though I am, vile, wretched, and unclean, I come to the fountain filled with his blood, I am washed in it, and I am made as white as snow. In that moment I become a partaker of God's eternal Son, the Lord Jesus Christ. Being a partaker of Christ, his merits are my merits.

That which Christ did as my Substitute is actually mine. Did he bear the wrath of God as my Substitute? Then all God's wrath against me is gone. Did he take my sin upon himself? Then my sin is gone. Did he pay the debt I owed to the law and justice of God? Then my debt is paid, nothing more is owed. Yes, it is true!

> Jesus paid it all, all the debt I owed,
> Sin had left a crimson stain:
> He washed it white as snow.

Since my debt has been paid, since in the Person of my Substitute, Jesus Christ, I have paid all that God's law required. God would be unjust to demand more. He cannot require me to pay more than the debt owed.

Payment God cannot twice demand,
First at my bleeding Surety's hand,
And then again at mine.

Being partakers of Christ, his righteousness has become ours. He is 'The Lord our Righteousness'. Not only are we freed from sin by his atoning sacrifice, we are rendered righteous before God by Christ's obedience in life as our responsible Representative. Christ, having obeyed God's law as our Representative and fulfilling all righteousness for us, we have obeyed God's law in him, fulfilling all righteousness. Everything required by God's law has been done by Christ, our Surety.

Being thus partakers of Christ, we are 'accepted in the beloved'. Is Christ accepted of God? Is he fully, perfectly, completely, eternally accepted? Even so, all who are partakers of Christ are accepted in him. God looks upon all his people, all true believers in Christ, and says, 'These are my beloved sons, in whom I am well pleased'.

Experimentally

All true believers have both an eternal union with Christ and an experimental union with him, a legal, covenant union, and a vital, living union of faith. We are partakers of Christ by God's decree; and we are partakers of Christ by faith. We live and feed upon him. His life is our daily bread. It sustains our souls. His blood is the wine that makes our hearts glad. He is our meat and drink (John 6:53-56).

Still there is a deeper spiritual lesson for us. Our union with Christ is so real, so constant, so vital that He is our Life. To be a partaker of Christ is to derive life from him constantly. We live upon Christ, just as the walls of a building stand upon the foundation. We derive life from Christ, just like the branches derive life from the vine. We are partakers of Christ, just as the wife is a partaker of her husband. We are partakers of Christ, just like the members of my body are partakers of my heart and my head.

Eternally

We are so really and truly one with Christ that we are partakers of him in his destiny. When he comes again, his holy ones shall come with him. That he is risen from the dead is the earnest and promise of our resurrection. At the day of his appearing, we shall rise and participate in the fruition of his mediatorial work. We will judge men and angels with Christ. We will join Christ in the destruction of his foes. We will join Christ in the marriage of the Lamb. We will stand with Christ before his Father's throne. We will inherit the glory he has inherited as our Mediator (John 17:22).

Spurgeon said, 'All right and all might, all that can extol or delight, all that forever and ever shall contribute to the glory of Christ, shall be shared by all the faithful, for we are partakers not only with him, but of him of Christ therefore of all the surroundings of glory and honour that shall belong to him'.

By Grace

This is all the work of divine grace. 'We are MADE partakers of Christ' (1 Corinthians 1:30). God himself has made us to be partakers of Christ his Son by the work of his almighty grace. He put us in Christ in election. He put Christ in us in regeneration. He made us partakers of Christ by the gift of faith.

An Exhortation

If we would enter into heaven, if we would obtain eternal life, if we would at last enter into his rest, we must persevere in faith, we must go on trusting Christ to the end (vv. 14-19).

We participate in the blessings and benefits of Christ only by a genuine, persevering faith. True faith never quits. Those who endure to the end shall be saved, no one else (Matthew 10:22). True faith is not a temporary excitement; but a permanent gift of grace (Romans 11:29). We are given many, many examples of false faith in the New Testament (John 2:23-25; 6:26; Acts 8:13, 18-21). Let us be warned. True faith is a genuine, God given, growing confidence in and consecration to the Lord Jesus Christ (Colossians 1:21-23; Hebrews 10:38-39).

In verse 15 the Holy Spirit repeats the warning given in verses 7-8, urging us not to harden our hearts. He makes this repetition because we need it. Not all those Jews who followed Moses out of Egypt perished in the wilderness, but most did. And most who take up a profession of faith in this age, and make a fair show in religious things for a while, soon fall by the wayside and perish.

Though they had many evidences of God's goodness and much light and truth, they did not believe God. Let us take heed that we be not numbered among them. Let us be found clinging to Christ, ever clinging to Christ, lest our carcasses be found at last in this wilderness, lest we miss him at last.

Verse 19 is the summary of the whole matter. Those who perished in the wilderness were not able to enter into the land of rest because of unbelief. They were not willing to believe God, to trust God, to rely on God. Unbelief shut them out (Romans 4:20-25; Hebrews 2:1-3). Let us hear the warning here given, and tenaciously cling to Christ.

Let us therefore fear, lest, a promise being left *us* of entering into his rest, any of you should seem to come short of it. For unto us was the gospel preached, as well as unto them: but the word preached did not profit them, not being mixed with faith in them that heard *it*. For we which have believed do enter into rest, as he said, As I have sworn in my wrath, if they shall enter into my rest: although the works were finished from the foundation of the world. For he spake in a certain place of the seventh *day* on this wise, And God did rest the seventh day from all his works.

Hebrews 4:1-4

Chapter 14

Read: Hebrews 4:1-4

'Let Us Fear'

We ought to fear, lest we also, after hearing the gospel and professing to believe it, fall short of eternal life, like those Jews who perished in the wilderness or those who think they stand yet show no evidence of it (1 Corinthians 10:12; Philippians 2:12). Let us not come up short of the promise of eternal life, like those foolish virgins described by our Lord. Rather, let us ever run with patience the race that is set before us, ever looking to Christ, trusting his blood, seeking his righteousness, seeking to know him (Philippians 3:7-14). May God graciously make our hearts pant for Christ, like David's did, as the hart pants after the water brook (Psalm 27:4; Philippians 3:10).

There is such a divine authority which attends the preaching and hearing of the gospel that the most solemn business on this earth is the business of preaching it, and the business of hearing it (Romans 10:13-21; Proverbs 1:23-33). The word preached must be mixed with faith, received by faith, embraced in the arms of faith, or the word preached is of no profit to our souls.

The gospel now preached to us was preached to the Jews by Moses and Aaron, as it had been by Enoch, Noah, and Abraham. It was preached to them by the types, promises, sacrifices and examples constantly held before them. But it did them no good. It did not save them nor profit them because they did not believe God.

The rest spoken of in verse three is the rest of faith in Christ. It is rest from salvation by works, rest from the yoke and burden of the law, rest from all human effort to gain God's favour. Believers have ease of heart, peace of conscience, and comforting assurance, as we look to Christ alone for salvation. This is rest indeed! God has sworn that those who believe shall not perish (Matthew 11:28-30; Romans 5:1; 8:1, 33-35).

Believers do not keep a seventh day sabbath as they did in the Old Testament, or a first day sabbath as religious legalists would have us do today. We keep a gospel sabbath, the sabbath of rest in Christ. As God ceased from his own works at the end of the first week, so we cease from our own works when we trust Christ. As God rests in his love (Zephaniah 3:17), so we rest, we sweetly acquiesce in our Saviour, resting in his blood and righteousness, goodness and grace, power and providence, promise and person. Christ is our Sabbath.

'Let Us'

Hebrews chapter four is about faith, the blessed rest of faith in Jesus Christ. Yet, it is a chapter filled with exhortations and admonitions, giving us very clear instructions about our responsibilities. Faith in Christ is not a passive, indifferent, or dormant thing. It is a vital, living principle of grace.

When I was in college, my professor of homiletics and pastoral theology used to tell us something every preacher ought to always bear in mind. He repeated it almost every time he talked to us about sermon preparation and preaching. He said, 'Men, where there is no summons there is no sermon.' In other words, every sermon preached ought to call for action, not physical action, but moral, spiritual action. If a sermon does not call for those who hear it to make some kind of response to it, it is not much of a sermon. The same is true of written expositions.

Four times in the sixteen verses of this chapter we are given two words of admonition. Four times the writer admonishes us and himself; to do something. Look at them with me.

1. Something to Fear

Here is something for us to fear. 'Let us therefore fear, lest, a promise being left us of entering into his rest, any of you should seem to come short of it' (v. 1). We ought to fear missing Christ. Christ is the 'one thing needful'. We must have him. If we have him, we have all. If we miss him, we miss all. We must be washed in his blood, robed in his righteousness, born of his Spirit, saved by his grace, united to him by faith.

2. Something to Do

Look at verse 11. Here is something for us to do. 'Let us labour therefore to enter into that rest, lest any man fall after the same example of unbelief'. Let us labour that we may cease from all labour. Faith is ceasing from our works. To trust the Lord Jesus Christ is to quit trying to find acceptance with God by something we do. It is to rely upon him alone for righteousness, finding complete and perfect justification, sanctification, and redemption in him.

3. Something to Hold

Here is something for us to hold. 'Seeing then that we have a great high priest, that is passed into the heavens, Jesus the Son of God, let us hold fast our profession' (v. 14). This we must hold with a death grip, for life and death are the issues, eternal life and eternal death. Whatever we do we must hold Christ.

4. Somewhere to Go

Here is somewhere for us to go. 'Let us therefore come boldly unto the throne of grace, that we may obtain mercy, and find grace to help in time of need' (v. 16). In every time of need come to God your Father, who sits upon the throne of grace; come through the merits of Christ your Saviour, the merits of his blood and righteousness, and get the mercy and grace you need by the power of his Spirit.

The Sabbath we Keep

Every sinner who believes on the Lord Jesus Christ keeps the sabbath by faith, by entering into his rest. 'For we which have believed do enter into rest ... There remaineth therefore a rest to the people of God. For he that is entered into his rest, he also hath ceased from his own works, as God did from his'.

We keep the sabbath of faith, a spiritual sabbath, not a carnal one. We rest in Christ, trusting his finished work, by faith entering into his rest. The believer's life is a perpetual keeping of the sabbath. None of us keeps it perfectly. Our best faith in this world is still unbelief (Mark 9:23-24). But we do keep this blessed sabbath rest sincerely; ever looking to Christ, ever coming to Christ, ever resting in Christ. As the legal sabbath of the Old Testament was a ceremonial picture of both the rest and consecration of true faith, the sabbath we keep is a sabbath of rest and consecration to God by faith in Christ.

Rest

Our all glorious Christ gives rest to every sinner who comes to him in faith. He says, 'Come unto me, all ye that labour and are heavy laden, and I will give you rest'. Horatius Bonar wrote:

> I heard the voice of Jesus say,
> 'Come unto me and rest,
> Lay down, thou weary one, lay down
> Thy head upon my breast'.
> I came to Jesus as I was
> Weary, and worn, and sad:
> I found in Him a resting place,
> And He has made me glad!

The Lord Jesus Christ has given and continually gives us rest. In Christ we have the rest of complete pardon (Isaiah 45:22; Ephesians 1:6), perfect reconciliation (2 Corinthians 5:17; Colossians 1:20-21), absolute security (John 10:27-30; Philippians 1:6; 1 Thessalonians 5:24), and special providence (Romans 8:28).

Consecration

As the ceremonial sabbath portrayed a strict, universal consecration to God, so this blessed sabbath of faith involves the perpetual consecration of ourselves to our God and Saviour, Jesus Christ (Matthew 11:28-30). Taking his yoke, believers find rest. We keep the sabbath of faith when we wilfully, deliberately take the yoke of Christ. If you would keep the sabbath, it involves much, much more than living in religious austerity one day a week. To keep the sabbath is to bow to Christ's dominion as Lord, willingly learning of him what to believe, how to live, what to do, and how to honour God. To keep the sabbath is to bow to his will.

How can a troubled, weary, heavy laden, tempest tossed sinner obtain this blessed sabbath rest? I can tell you, both from experience and from the Word of God, there is only one way you can enter into his rest. You've got to quit working! You have to trust Christ alone for everything!

The Blessed Rest of Faith

Sabbath keeping is not a matter of indifference. It is not one of those areas about which the scriptures give no specific instructions. In fact, the instructions given in the Word of God about sabbath keeping are very specific and clear.

Like circumcision, the passover, and all other aspects of legal, ceremonial worship during the Old Testament, the legal sabbath day was established by our God to be a sign, picture, and type of grace and salvation in Christ. This is not a matter of speculation and guesswork. This is exactly what God says about the matter in Exodus 31:13.

Because sabbath keeping was a legal type of our salvation in Christ during the age of carnal ordinances, like the passover and circumcision, once the Lord Jesus Christ came and fulfilled the type, the carnal ordinance ceased.

Legal Ordinances Forbidden

In the New Testament, we are strictly and directly forbidden to keep any of those carnal ordinances. In fact, we are plainly told that those who attempt to worship God on the grounds of legal ordinances are yet under the curse of the law. They have not yet learned the gospel.

Circumcision is forbidden as an ordinance of divine worship (Galatians 5:2,4). Those who have their babies sprinkled to seal them into the covenant of grace (whether they realize it or not) attempt to retain the carnal ordinance of circumcision. By this act of sprinkling they deny the gospel of salvation by grace alone. They deny the necessity of heart circumcision by the Spirit of God (Romans 2:28-29).

Passover observance is forbidden since Christ our Passover has been sacrificed for us (1 Corinthians 5:7). Those who continue to offer up sacrifices to God, either for atonement or penance, to gain a higher degree of divine favour or to prevent his anger; by their sacrifices, deny that Christ's death at Calvary was an effectual satisfaction for the sins of his people. If something must be added to his blood and his righteousness by us, then his blood and his righteousness are totally useless.

In exactly the same way, those who attempt to sanctify themselves by keeping a carnal sabbath, deny that Jesus Christ is enough to give us perfect acceptance with the thrice holy God. As Paul puts it, they make an outward show of spirituality and wisdom; but it is all will-worship. Such pretences of humility are nothing but the satisfying of the flesh (Colossians 2:23).

Not only that, the whole matter of sabbath keeping is strictly forbidden by the Holy Spirit in Colossians 2:.16-17. Since the Lord Jesus Christ has, by his death at Calvary, blotted out the handwriting of the ordinances that was against us, since he nailed God's broken law to the cross and put away our sins, he alone is our Sabbath. We rest in him (Colossians 2:13-17).

We do not keep a legal, ceremonial sabbath of any kind, because it is specifically forbidden. All carnal sabbath keeping, any form of it, is strictly forbidden on the basis of the fact that in Christ all true believers are totally free from the law (Romans 7:4; 10:4).

The Gospel Sabbath

Yet, the New Testament does speak of a sabbath keeping that remains for the people of God (Hebrews 4:9-11). It is written, 'We which have believed do enter into rest' (v. 3). Believers keep the sabbath by faith, only by faith, finding rest in Christ.

Christ is our Sabbath. He is the One of whom the Old Testament sabbath was a type and picture. Believers keep the sabbath by trusting Christ. As those of the Old Testament ceremonially ceased from their works on the sabbath day, so the believing sinner, as he comes to Christ, ceases from his own works.

Rest Given

The Son of God calls weary, heavy laden sinners to come to him, encouraging us to do so with a great promise. 'Come unto me, all ye that labour and are heavy laden', he says, 'and I will give you rest' (Matthew 11:28).

Fallen man, in his proud self-righteousness, vainly imagines that he can do something to commend himself to God. Therefore, like the Jews of old, he goes about to establish his own righteousness. But he can never atone for past sins, cease from sin in the present, or perform any perfectly good work. Therefore, his conscience is never satisfied. Only when we cease to work and trust Christ alone for all righteousness and redemption do we find rest. This is the blessed rest of faith, a rest which the Son of God alone can give, the rest he promises to give to all who come to him. Come to Christ, and rest. We can never find rest for our souls until we rest in him alone.

And in this *place* again, If they shall enter into my rest. Seeing therefore it remaineth that some must enter therein, and they to whom it was first preached entered not in because of unbelief: Again, he limiteth a certain day, saying in David, To day, after so long a time; as it is said, To day if ye will hear his voice, harden not your hearts. For if Jesus had given them rest, then would he not afterward have spoken of another day. There remaineth therefore a rest to the people of God. For he that is entered into his rest, he also hath ceased from his own works, as God *did* from his.

Hebrews 4:5-10

Chapter 15

Read: Hebrews 4:5-10

'There Remaineth a Rest'

The seventh day rest was a typical day of rest and the land of Canaan was a typical land of rest. The unbelieving Jews did not enter into Canaan but turned around and wandered in the wilderness until they died. They never entered into God's rest.

The multitudes perished in the wilderness, but the Word of God did not and could not fall to the ground. Canaan must be inhabited by Israel. Israel must possess the land of God's promise. Therefore, God raised up Joshua (the type of Christ) to do what Moses (the type of the law) could never do. Joshua led the chosen nation into the land of promised rest.

Do not miss this. The type must be fulfilled! The Lord Jesus Christ, our great Joshua, must and shall bring God's Israel into the blessed rest of eternal salvation, every one of them. The covenant promise must and shall be fulfilled. Some must enter into rest (vv. 5-6). Joseph Swain wrote:

> Sweet as home to pilgrims weary,
> Light to newly-opened eyes,
> Flowing springs in deserts dreary,
> Is the rest the cross supplies;
> All who taste it, all who taste it
> Shall to rest immortal rise.

Today

'Again, he limiteth a certain day, saying in David, To day, after so long a time; as it is said, To day if ye will hear his voice, harden not your hearts' (v. 7). Nearly four hundred years passed between Joshua's day and David's day; but the Word of God was the same (Psalm 95:7-8). And the day in which God speaks to us, 'Today', is our day, the day of grace and salvation.

This seventh verse specifically speaks of this gospel day. God set this day as the day when chosen sinners would enter into this true rest which he promised by faith in Christ. Today, this gospel day, is the day of salvation; now is the accepted time. We have nothing to do with the legal, typical rests (sabbath days) of the Old Testament. We now possess what those days only pictured (Colossians 2:16-17).

Joshua and Jesus

'For if Jesus had given them rest, then would he not afterward have spoken of another day' (v. 8). Joshua's name was changed from Oshea ('Let God save') to Joshua ('God shall save'), when he was sent to spy out the land of Canaan (Numbers 13:16).

The law may bring us into a dry, thorny, desolate wilderness, where we may pray for a Saviour and cry, 'Let God save'. But the gospel brings us into the land of rest and gives us a Saviour, Jesus, who is Jehovah our Righteousness!

Joshua is here called 'Jesus' because his name in the Old Testament means exactly the same thing as Jesus in the New Testament, of whom he was a type. Yet, even the rest he gave in Canaan was only a typical rest and spoke of another, more glorious rest.

The Rest that Remains

'There remaineth therefore a rest to the people of God' (v. 9). The word 'rest' here is 'sabbath' or 'a sabbath keeping'. This rest is Christ our Sabbath, the sabbath rest we find in him. Those sinners chosen of God in eternal election, for whom Christ died, and to whom faith is given, those who believe on the Son of God do enter into a spiritual rest. It will be perfect rest in glory; but it is begun here. Heaven is but a perfection and a continuation of what he begins in our hearts when he brings us to faith (John 6:37-40).

All the sabbaths of the Old Testament, all those sabbaths required by the law of God in the days of carnal, ceremonial worship, were designed to portray this glorious gospel rest and the rest of heaven that shall follow. Ours is a sabbath without end.

The Weekly Sabbath

As the Lord God ceased from his works (Genesis 2:2), so the Jews were required to keep a weekly sabbath day (Saturday), as a typical picture of the believer's rest of faith in Christ (Exodus 31:13). As the Lord God ceased from his works, when he had finished his work of creation, so his people were to cease from their works on the seventh day of every week. When we trust in Christ, we have ceased from our works. The seventh day sabbath portrayed rest in Christ.

The Seventh Year Sabbath

God also required Israel to keep a year long sabbath every seventh year (Exodus 23:10-11). This seventh year sabbath expressed at length the meaning and value of the seventh day weekly sabbath (Leviticus 25:1-7). During this year-long sabbath the ground lay fallow, or rested, from its curse, slavery and toil thus portraying that rest which shall soon come to God's creation and his people (Romans 8:20-21).

The Jubilee Sabbath

The year-long sabbath was kept every seventh year. Then when this series of seventh year sabbaths reached the perfection of seven sevens, totalling forty-nine years, the fiftieth year was also kept as a sabbath; and was heralded by the trumpet of jubilee (Leviticus 25:8-10). Thus a whole additional year was set aside as belonging to the Lord, in which the people rested in and relied entirely upon God.

Emancipation and Restoration

This year of Jubilee is also called 'the year of liberty' (Ezekiel 46:17). During that time all debts were discharged, all mortgages cancelled, all bondmen set free, and all that had been forfeit or lost was restored. What a wonderful picture this is of Christ our Sabbath. We rest in him by faith, and in him alone. There is no place for works. At the 'restitution of all things', all that has been lost to us by sin and death will be restored! (Leviticus 25:1-17; Acts 3:19-21; 1 Corinthians 15:51-52).

The Gospel Sabbath

The Lord Jesus Christ had a work to do in preaching the gospel and in obtaining the salvation and redemption of his people. This work was given him and he finished it. He ceased from these works, never to do them again. He is seated in heaven, having entered his rest (Hebrews 10:5-14), just as we are told God ceased from his works of creation when he had finished them. This is exactly what every believer does when he comes to Christ. We come from a religion of works, and rest in the Lord Jesus. The sabbath into which our Lord Jesus Christ has entered, and into which all God's elect enter when they trust him, is a sabbath without end.

Deliverence to the Captives

This Jubilee is that which Christ has both finished and entered into as our Saviour, and that which is proclaimed in the gospel (Isaiah 61:1-3; Luke 4:16-21). The gospel of Christ proclaims liberty to captive sinners, perfect, complete, absolute, everlasting liberty! In heavenly glory, God's elect shall forever enjoy total liberty from all sin and from all the evil consequences of sin (Revelation 21:3-5; 22:3-6). This is the gospel Jubilee! (Hebrews 4:9-11).

Christ Has Entered His Rest

The word 'rest', which is used over and over and over in Hebrews 3 and 4, means to repose back, to lay down, to be at peace, to cease from work, to be at home. But, the word translated 'rest' in verse nine is an entirely different word. The word here translated 'rest' means sabbatism, or 'a keeping of a sabbath'.

The Holy Spirit here shows us how the Old Testament law regarding the sabbath finds its fulfilment and complete accomplishment in Christ. Hebrews 4 declares that all who believe on the Son of God keep the sabbath by faith in him.

Christ's Rest

Here we are told that the Lord Jesus Christ has entered into his rest, and that his rest is glorious, because he has finished his work (Isaiah 11:10; 2 Corinthians 5:17-21). Our Saviour's rest in heaven is glorious; his rest in heaven is his glory. As God the Father rested on the seventh day, because his work of creation was finished, so God the Son rested and entered into his rest forever, because he has finished his work of making all things new for his people (Romans 8:34; Hebrews 10:10-14).

In Matthew 28:1 we read, 'In the end of the sabbath, as it began to dawn toward the first day of the week, came Mary Magdalene and the other Mary to see the sepulchre.' The verse quite literally reads, 'In the end of the sabbath, as it began to dawn toward the sabbath.' This means that when the Lord Jesus Christ died at Calvary and rose again, the old sabbaths of the law ended and the new sabbath of grace began!

Behold our exalted Saviour! Do you see him seated yonder upon his throne in heaven? There he sits in the undisturbed, undisturbable serenity of his absolute sovereignty. His rest is his glory (John 17:2; Philippians 2:9-11; Isaiah 45:22-25). The fact that our great Redeemer has entered into his rest declares he has finished his work (John 17:4; 19:30). He has, by his obedience in life brought in an everlasting righteousness. And, by his obedience in death, the Son of God has obtained eternal redemption for his people.

Salvation Sure

Because Christ has finished his work, the salvation of his people is certain (Hebrews 9:12). All his redeemed ones must enter into his rest (Hebrews 4:6-7). The works were finished before the foundation of the world in God's purpose (Romans 8:29-30). They were finished in time when the God-man took his seat in heaven as our forerunner (Hebrews 6:20). There is no more work to be done. Christ did it all. Having finished his work, he now sits down in his glory. There he is resting! This is what the sabbath days in the Mosaic economy pictured.

Let us labour therefore to enter into that rest, lest any man fall after the same example of unbelief. For the word of God *is* quick, and powerful, and sharper than any twoedged sword, piercing even to the dividing asunder of soul and spirit, and of the joints and marrow, and *is* a discerner of the thoughts and intents of the heart. Neither is there any creature that is not manifest in his sight: but all things *are* naked and opened unto the eyes of him with whom we have to do. Seeing then that we have a great high priest, that is passed into the heavens, Jesus the Son of God, let us hold fast *our* profession. For we have not an high priest which cannot be touched with the feeling of our infirmities; but was in all points tempted like as *we are, yet* without sin. Let us therefore come boldly unto the throne of grace, that we may obtain mercy, and find grace to help in time of need.

Hebrews 4:11-16

Chapter 16

Read: Hebrews 4:11-16

Labour to Stop Labouring

In the fourth chapter of Hebrews, we are called to rest in Christ, to look to Christ alone for acceptance with God, to trust him alone for wisdom, righteousness, sanctification, and redemption. This is what it is to truly keep the sabbath.

We must labour to stop labouring. There is nothing in all the world more difficult, more contrary to our flesh, than this. Without question, we all, if we enter into Christ's rest, enter into it by degrees. We have a constant struggle with self-righteousness. Therefore, we must strive against that, the most horrid of all sins, that we may rest in Christ.

It matters not whether we say the Word in verse 12 is Christ or the scriptures. What is said here is true of both the written Word and the living Word. Pastor Henry Mahan, in his Bible Class Commentary, explains the passage like this …

> The Word is alive. The word 'quick' is an old English word for alive. This is a living book, the words of our living Redeemer (1 Peter 1:23-25; James 1:18). The Word is the living seed. The Word is powerful. Our Lord and his Word are active and effectual. He spoke for the elect in the council and covenant of grace (Hebrews 7:22). He spoke all things out of nothing in creation (Hebrews 11:3; Genesis 1:6, 9). He spoke and revealed the Father (John 14:10). He spoke and the dead came forth (John 5:24, 25).

The Word is sharp as a two-edged sword. The Word is an edge; it has no blunt side. It is alive all over. You cannot come near the Word of God without its having some effect on you (2 Corinthians 2:14-16). Our Lord comes 'not to send peace but a sword', and that sword begins in our own souls, wounding and killing. However, it kills nothing but that which ought to be killed: our pride, envy, lust and sins.

Christ has Accomplished All we Require

Christ our Lord is the omniscient God: nothing is hidden from him. By his word, he strips us naked and lays us open, exposing the thoughts and intents of the heart. Believers rejoice and find comfort in this, as Peter did (Luke 22:31-34; John 21:17), even in the teeth of our sins and failures. Unbelievers and hypocrites tremble at the thought of our Lord's omniscient discernment.

Our Lord Jesus Christ is a Priest like no other. All the priests of the Mosaic economy were but typical priests. All those who claim to be 'priests' today are mere impostors. The Lord Jesus Christ is the only real Priest there is. All the priests of the Aaronic order died and, therefore, had successors. Christ is our eternal Priest, and has no successor. All other priests were but men of the earth and earthly. Christ is our great High Priest in heaven. Moreover, he who is our great High Priest is a Priest who is touched by that which touches us.

Our Lord Jesus Christ is a compassionate High Priest, one who has been pierced by the very same things that pierce us. He was tempted in all points like we are. Yet, he is a Priest accepted in heaven, because he is a Priest without sin. Still there is more. Christ is a Priest upon a throne, and his throne is a throne of grace. Toplady says:

Awake, sweet gratitude, and sing
The ascended Saviour's love;
Sing how He lives to carry on
His people's cause above.

With cries and tears He offered up
His humble suit below;
But with authority He asks,
Enthroned in glory now.

What reason we have to rest in him! If Jesus Christ is ours, we have all that can be required and all that can be desired to give us peace. Let us ever come to him. Coming to him, we shall find rest for our souls (Matthew 11:28-30). Come reverently, as unto God upon his throne. Come freely, as to a friend. Come gladly to him whose throne is the mercy-seat, the place of grace. Come for the grace you need. Come to Christ our great High Priest who sits upon the throne of grace; to dispense mercy to his people as often as you need it.

Labour to Rest

Self-righteousness is the horrid inclination of our proud flesh. We all want to be saved by something we do. It is a deep natural inclination. Most all religious people talk about grace, and love to sing, 'Amazing grace! How sweet the sound, that saved a wretch like me'. But no sinner will naturally give up his own righteousness and trust Christ alone for salvation.

Strive to Enter

If we would rest in Christ alone and be saved by the grace of God that is in him, 'we must lay aside the sin (self-righteousness) which doth so easily beset us'. We must strive to enter in at the strait gate, because we all want to walk in the broad way. If we would be saved, we must labour to quit working. We must labour to enter into that great, eternal rest of glory with Christ in heaven. 'Let us labour therefore to enter into that rest'.

'There remaineth therefore a rest to the people of God'. There is a great, eternal sabbath to be obtained. In heaven's glory we will enjoy an eternal remembrance of redemption, an endless, perfect consecration to Christ, and everlasting rest. This is the hope set before us.

Some Must Enter

Some have already entered into that rest. 'For he that is entered into his rest, he also hath ceased from his own works, as God did from his'. I have already shown you how this applies to Christ. But the text applies to Christ's people, too. It speaks of the rest into which God's elect enter by faith here, and in heavenly glory hereafter. Many could not enter in because of unbelief. Those who have entered in have ceased from their own works. They have quit trusting in themselves. They have quit trying to do something to win God's favour. There are some who 'must enter therein'. There is a great multitude, chosen in eternity and redeemed at Calvary, who must and shall enter into this rest.

Rest or Death

'Let us labour (strive) therefore to enter into that rest, lest any man fall after the same example of unbelief!' This is what Paul speaks of in Philippians 3:7-14. The penalty for not keeping the sabbath is still death. We will either rest in Christ or die under the wrath of God (John 3:36).

The Power of the Word

It is by the Word of God, specifically by the preaching of the Word, the preaching of the Gospel, that God saves his elect and instructs, directs, and comforts his saints. It is 'the power of God unto salvation' to all who believe (Romans 1:16-17; 10:17; 1 Corinthians 1:21-23; James 1:18; 1 Peter 1:23-25). It is through the ministry of the Word that the Lord God gives consolation and hope to his people and perfects his church (Romans 15:4; Ephesians 4:11-16).

Divinely Ordained Instrumentality

I realize that there are many who object to the fact that this book declares plainly that God saves sinners only by the preaching of the gospel. They tell us that such doctrine limits God's sovereignty. But the teaching of scripture in this, and many other passages, is crystal clear. God has sovereignly ordained the salvation of his elect; and he has sovereignly ordained the means by which he will save them. He chose us 'unto salvation through the sanctification (regenerating grace and effectual call) of the Spirit and belief of the truth' (2 Thessalonians 2:13; Romans 10:10-14). That puts the matter beyond dispute. It is not a matter of opinion, it is not a debatable issue.

If God has purposed something, he has purposed all the means necessary for its accomplishment. Why does the farmer till his ground and sow his seed? He knows he cannot cause seed to germinate and grow. But he also knows that if God gives the increase, it will be through the instrumentality of these means, and that it is only in the use of these means that he can hope to receive the increase.

We know that the means used (gospel preachers) to effect the salvation of God's elect are, in themselves, utterly powerless unless God makes their labours effectual by the power of his Spirit. What encouragement was there for the prophet Ezekiel to prophesy to the dry bones except this: God had determined in connection with his preaching to give them life. What encouragement do we have to preach the gospel of Christ to those who are dead in trespasses and sins except this: God has determined to give efficacy to the Word of His grace.

God has a chosen people in this world; and, as the gospel is the appointed means for effecting the salvation of his chosen, he will send it to those whom he has purposed to save. God had much people in Corinth. Therefore, he sent Paul there to preach the gospel. And by the Word preached, chosen, redeemed sinners were born again and granted faith in Christ.

A Matter of Great Importance

This is a matter of tremendous importance. God saves his people by the Word of the Gospel. Yes, it is the gospel preached, 'By which ye are saved'. (1 Corinthians 15:3; Ephesians 1:13). It is the naked, unadorned Word of God, plainly preached, by which Satan is conquered, dead sinners are brought to life, and our thoughts and imaginations are brought into captivity to Christ. The book of God, and the book of God alone, is our weapon of warfare (2 Corinthians 10:3-5).

Let us never be so foolishly unbelieving that we try to make the Word of God relevant. The fact of its existence makes it relevant! It is utter unbelief, which compels preachers, churches, and religious people to try, by varying methods, to make the gospel effectual. It is God the Holy Spirit alone who makes the gospel effectual. Our responsibility, our only responsibility, our enormous responsibility, is to make the gospel known in the generation in which we live. 'The power of God unto salvation' is not religious programming, religious entertainment, religious activity, or learned methods of evangelism. It is the gospel itself which 'is the power of God unto salvation'. Let us then be found faithful in preaching it, for Christ's sake.

The Design of the Word

Hebrews 4:13 shows us that the Word of God is designed to strip us naked before God. 'Neither is there any creature that is not manifest in his sight'. Christ, our Lord, is the omniscient God. Nothing is hidden from him. By his Word, he strips us naked, and lays us open, exposing the thoughts and intents of the heart. Believers, like Peter even in the teeth of his terrible sin, find great comfort in the fact that, he who is our Lord and Saviour knows all things. Unbelieving religious hypocrites tremble at the thought of Christ's absolute omniscience.

Reverence the Word

Let us ever reverence the Bible as the Word of God. Let us ever come to the holy scriptures for quickening for our own souls. This is our souls' bread. Here we find waters of life for the refreshing of our souls. Here are green pastures in which Christ's sheep may both feed and lay down. It is by taking heed to the Word of God that we cleanse our ways. It is by hiding God's Word in our hearts that we check the evil that is in us by nature.

If we truly reverence the Bible as the Word of God, the Bible alone must determine both our faith and our practice. Let others say what they will about the matter, that man, that church, that denomination has a true, absolutely orthodox creed, whose only creed is the Word of God. Let us reverence the Bible as the Word of God by praying that God will make his Word effectual wherever it is faithfully preached (2 Thessalonians 3:1).

The Word of God is ...

The Word of God is a name for Christ as well as for the scriptures. It is difficult to say whether this text speaks of the written Word (The Bible), or of the Lord Jesus Christ, who is the incarnate Word (John 1:1-3). The fact is, we cannot sever the two. Christ is the Word, of whom all the written Word speaks (Luke 24:27; 44-47). The Word of God is what it is because the Lord Jesus Christ is embodied in it. Hebrews 4:12 tells us seven things about the Word of God. It is ...

1. 'The Word of God'

The Bible is God's final, full, complete, and perfect revelation of himself and his will to man, inspired, inerrant, infallible (2 Timothy 3:16-17; 2 Peter 1:19-21). Since the book of God is complete, we no longer have and no longer need the signs of the apostles. God no longer gives revelation (in the strict sense of the word) to men. The Holy Spirit now gives us illumination by the Word, revealing Christ to us; but he does not give additional revelation.

2. Living

'The Word of God is quick'. This is a living book (1 Peter 1:23-25; James 1:18) and by the living Word comes life. The lively Word is applied by the Holy Spirit, and chosen, redeemed sinners are born again. God's Word has life in itself. It is the living and incorruptible seed. It creates life where it comes, nourishes and strengthens the children of God. Our words pass away. God's Word lives on (Isaiah 40:8).

3. Effectual

'The Word of God is quick, and powerful'. It brings conviction and conversion. It gives comfort to believing hearts and confirms our faith.

The Word of God has power to elevate our hearts and minds to Christ and things above. Christ and his Word are active and effectual. He spoke for the elect in the council and covenant of grace (Hebrews 7:20-22). He spoke all things out of nothing in creation (Hebrews 11:3; Genesis 1:6, 9). He spoke and revealed the Father (John 14:10). He speaks and the dead come forth (John 5:24-25).

4. Cutting

'The Word of God is quick, and powerful, and sharper than any two-edged sword'. The Word is all edge. It wounds, in one way or another, all who touch it. No faithful sermon is ever preached that does not accomplish one end or another (2 Corinthians 2:14-16). It is the sword of the Lord at work. Upon the edge of this sword the conscience of the elect is opened and the sin of the redeemed is put to death. Here self-righteousness is slain and pride falls in the street. The wicked are condemned and the judgment of God is executed.

5. Piercing

'The Word of God is quick, and powerful, and sharper than any two-edged sword, piercing even to the dividing asunder of soul and spirit'. It forces its way into the hardest of hearts. It can find its way to its mark. It penetrates the smallest opening, like the arrow which entered between the joints of the harness (1 Kings 22:34). Although the soul and spirit are invisible and the joints and marrow are covered and hid, so penetrating is the divine Word that it reaches the most hidden and secret things of men and women. It is a discerner of the thoughts and intents of the heart. Christ knows the heart and will make manifest all that is in it by the Word (Luke 16:15).

6. Discriminating

It divides 'asunder soul and spirit'. It separates the precious from the vile, the wheat from the chaff, the sheep from the goats. It divides 'joints and marrow', families and churches, and does so by its own penetrating and discerning qualities.

7. Revealing

'The Word of God is ... a discerner of the thoughts and intents of the heart'. It cleaves a man and exposes the secret corruptions, imaginations, and thoughts of his heart as an axe splits a carcass exposing all within. It shows the sinner how God sees him.

All this we have seen in the preaching of the word of God. Have you not felt it to be so? Does the Word of God pierce your heart? Does it reach your soul? If it does, thank God for it. Does this Sword of the Spirit prick your heart? Does its edge draw out the diseased blood of your heart's lusts? Bless God for it. Would you not thank a surgeon, who used his knife to lance your diseased body, and sever from it a deadly cancer? Though he caused you great pain, you would thank him for his service, and pay him, too. How much more ought we to bless God for his work for, in, and upon our souls by his Word. The puritan, William Gurnall, wrote:

> There is not another sword like this in all the world that can cure with cutting; not another arm could use this sword, to have done thus with it besides the Spirit of God.

O Spirit of God, send your living Word into my heart! Pierce my very soul with that Sword which alone can heal it and give me life!

Christ Our High Priest

'We have a great high priest!' We have no earthly priest, because we need none. Our great High Priest is the Lord Jesus Christ, the Son of God. He is seated in the heavens where he has made every believing sinner a priest unto God in him, a priest to offer up spiritual sacrifices of prayer and praise continually, sacrifices made acceptable to God through the merits of his blood and righteousness.

A Great High Priest

The Lord Jesus Christ, whom we trust, is 'a great High Priest'. Our Redeemer's greatness is spoken of both with respect to his essential person and with respect to his priestly work; herein abides his greatness.

His Solitariness: Christ is our great High Priest because he is our only Priest. His solitariness is his greatness. There is only one Priest and Mediator between God and men; and Christ is that Priest. All men on earth who pretend to be priests are impostors.

His Sacrifice: Christ is our great High priest because his sacrifice alone can atone for sin. He alone has that to offer which God can and will accept for the atonement of our sins. His own life's blood is that by which he has obtained eternal redemption for us.

His Intercession: our great High Priest prays for us distinctly. He said, 'I pray not for the world, but for them which thou hast given me' (1 John 2:1-2; John 17:9-11, 13, 15, 17, 20-26).

Our High Priest

Not only is the Lord Jesus Christ the Great High Priest, he is ours! 'Seeing then that we have a Great High Priest'. What a blessed declaration! This Great High Priest, the Lord Jesus Christ, is mine. 'The Lord is my Shepherd' and the Lord is my Priest! He is our great High Priest by the decree and gift of his Father, by his own, voluntary assumption of our cause, and by our union of faith with him.

A Priest in Heaven

Our great High Priest has 'passed into the heavens' (Hebrews 10:10-14; Romans 8:33-39). That means that his sacrifice has been accepted. Because he has risen from the dead, passed into the heavens and taken his rightful place upon the throne of grace, we are assured that all the sins of his people, which he bore in his body upon the cursed tree, are forever put away and can never be imputed to us. Our High Priest in heaven is our security and our assurance of everlasting, immutable, indestructible acceptance with God.

Divine and Human

He who is our Great High Priest is 'Jesus, the Son of God'. He is 'Jesus' who came here as a man on an errand of mercy, to save his people from their sins (Matthew 1:21). And he is 'the Son of God', God the Son, God manifest in the flesh, who is able to save to the uttermost all who come unto God by him (Hebrews 7:24-28).

A Touched Priest

This God-man, this man who is God, our great High Priest, is 'touched with the feeling of our infirmities'. Because he is a Man who has endured all that men endure, and because his heart is ever toward us, our dear Saviour, that God who rules the world, is touched by everything that touches us. As a loving father is touched by anything that touches his child, so our Saviour is touched by that which touches us. If his people are persecuted, he is persecuted (Acts 9:1-5). If we endure disease, betrayal, bereavement, hunger, thirst, weariness, or any other thing which causes pain, we endure only that which he has endured before us and for us; and it touches him.

A Tempted Priest

He who is our Great High Priest 'was in all points tempted like as we are'. No aspect of our Saviour's mediation is more difficult for us to fathom than his temptation. Yet, no aspect of his sufferings in this world is more comforting to his tempted people in this world. Do the lusts of the flesh seem to overwhelm your soul? Your Saviour knows what you are going through. He has walked that path before you. Do the lusts of the eye seem to constantly pull at your very heart? Your Redeemer knows what you feel. He knows the struggle more keenly than you ever shall. He has been where you are.

Does the pride of life seem to be your constant adversary? The Son of God, who sits upon his throne in human flesh, who intercedes for you in glory, knows what you feel. Not only does he know and feel what you are experiencing, he is able and willing to help you; and he will. He will never leave you, nor forsake you. He will carry you through your earthly woe and bring you at last into your (his) eternal inheritance. But, none of these things would be of any value and benefit to our souls, were it not for this last thing: 'Yet without sin'.

A Holy Priest

He who is our great High Priest is and must be altogether holy. No sinful man can make atonement for another man's sins. Aaron could never make reconciliation for the people. But Christ, our holy High Priest, that One whose very name is 'Holy and Reverend', is a Priest whose Sacrifice and intercession God himself must accept.

Let us take these thoughts with us through the day. Let these blessed assurances of grace arm our souls, as we face the trials and temptations that we must endue. It is upon the basis of Christ's priesthood that we are given this admonition: 'Let us hold fast our profession'.

Perhaps you think, 'But I am weak and sinful, and my temptations are strong. Where can I find the strength to heed this admonition?' The answer is found in verse 16. 'Let us therefore come boldly unto the throne of grace, that we may obtain mercy, and find grace to help in time of need'.

In the book of Hebrews we see the superiority of Christ over the angels, over Moses, over Joshua, over all who came before him. However, the primary feature of our Saviour's excellence, supremacy, and superiority is in his character as our great High Priest.

An Exalted Priest

In chapter one, the Holy Spirit describes him as our great, sin-atoning, almighty, effectual High Priest, who, having put away the sins of his people, is now exalted to the throne of glory. Yonder he sits, a priest upon his throne, our Priestly King, our Kingly Priest!

A Merciful and Faithful Priest

In the second chapter, we are told that our dear Saviour, that God who has redeemed and saved us, is a real man. He came into this world in human flesh that he might become our Saviour, our 'merciful and faithful High Priest'. If he would be our Saviour, if he would be merciful to sinners and yet faithful to his own holy character, the Son of God had to become one of us, bone of our bone, and flesh of our flesh. As such, he had to be made sin, to put away our sins by the sacrifice of himself.

An Inspiring Priest

In Hebrews 4:14-15, the Spirit of God urges us to persevere in the faith, to hold fast our profession, to keep looking to and trusting the Lord Jesus Christ. He does so by showing us the character of Christ as our great High Priest. 'Seeing then that we have a great high priest, that is passed into the heavens, Jesus the Son of God, let us hold fast our profession. For we have not an high priest which cannot be touched with the feeling of our infirmities; but was in all points tempted like as we are, yet without sin'.

Do not miss the argument given in these two verses. We are urged to continue in the faith and in faithfulness to Christ, because he is our great High Priest. If you realize what this means, nothing could be a greater incentive for trusting, honouring, loving, and serving him to the end of our days, faithfully.

'Let us hold fast our profession'. We have, by our words and in believer's baptism, made a public profession of faith in Christ. Like Jephthah of old, we have lifted our hands to God. Let us never go back! We must not allow the religious world to entice us, the material world to seduce us, or anything else to move us away from Christ and his gospel. Let us tenaciously hold to the old paths of solid gospel doctrine (Jeremiah 6:16). Let us cling to Christ alone as our only hope before God, and devote ourselves to him in faithfulness.

This admonition is given in such a way that it suggests both the great value of Christ to our souls ('Unto you therefore which believe, he is precious!') and the danger of dropping him, the danger of letting Christ, his gospel, and his salvation slip through our fingers.

Necessary Perseverance

The perseverance to which we are admonished, without question, is the gift of God's free grace. We persevere because he preserves. It is written, concerning all those to whom God almighty gives eternal life, 'they shall never perish' — and they shall never perish (John 10:27-28; Ecclesiastes 3:14; Philippians 1:6; 1 Thessalonians 5:23-24).

Yet, this perseverance is our responsibility. It is something we must do. It is something all true believers will do. We must hold fast the profession of our faith. We must not be moved away from the hope of the gospel. It will require strength and courage that only God can give. Yet, it is a strength and courage that he gives us by his Spirit, through the use of appointed means, through the ministry of the gospel and the sanctifying influence of his saints in the assembly of public worship.

Let us 'hold fast our profession'. Hold it without wavering, for Christ's sake, for the gospel's sake, for the glory of God, and for the encouragement of other believers. We must do so because it is essential to the everlasting salvation of our souls (Matthew 10:20).

It is the priesthood of Christ that the Holy Spirit here uses as an argument to inspire and enforce our perseverance in holding fast our profession. He is the High Priest of it. He espoused our cause and is ever faithful. He bore witness to the truth of the gospel. He prays for the support of our faith. He pities us and helps us. And he has passed into the heavens, where he appears for us, represents us, owns us, and will own us forever as his brethren.

'The Full Assurance of Hope'

Since we have such a great High Priest in heaven as the Lord Jesus Christ is, one who is touched with the feeling of our infirmities, 'Let us therefore come boldly unto the throne of grace, that we may obtain mercy, and find grace to help in time of need.' Here is a call to prayer that tugs at the hearts of all who need mercy and grace. What a gracious, blessed admonition this is!

I do not pretend to know much about prayer; but I do know what God has taught me and is teaching me. Prayer is one of the most important aspects of every believer's life. Yet, it is one with which we struggle constantly. It is a subject about which there is enormous confusion, even among God's elect. I cannot think of a single text in scripture which gives us more encouragement and reason to pray than Hebrews 4:16.

A Throne

When we approach God on his throne, we rejoice to know that his throne, that throne upon which God our Saviour sits, from which he rules the universe is 'The throne of grace'.

Once it was called 'the mercy seat', but now 'the throne'. In drawing near to God in prayer, we come to God upon the throne. No one approaches

God who does not approach him upon the throne. He who is God almighty is that great and glorious Monarch of the universe who sits upon the throne of total, absolute sovereignty. William Jay has written,

> When God enacts laws, he is on a throne of legislation: when he administers these laws he is on a throne of government: when he tries his creatures by these laws, he is on a throne of judgment, but when he receives petitions, and dispenses favours, he is on a throne of grace'.

The idea of a throne inspires awe, bordering upon terror. It repels rather than invites. Few of us could approach it without trembling. Yet, here is the throne of the King of kings and Lord of lords, the sceptre of total sovereignty, absolute holiness, and immutable justice. Before this great King the greatest earthly monarch that ever wore a crown is but a worm. Before him, all the nations of men are less than nothing and vanity. How dares any sinful man approach him who is infinite majesty? Blessed be his name, we come to him upon his throne, because he sits upon a throne of grace. Therefore, we are allowed, and even commanded, to come to it boldly.

Coming to God

Prayer is coming to God upon his throne. If we would come to God, we must come to him as a King. We must bow before him with reverence, confidence, and submission. Faith, in its essence and in all its exercises, is surrender to the Lord God as our great King.

In prayer we come to this great King as to One who gives as a King. We ask great things from the great King. We ask them with expectation, because he is as magnanimously good as he is great. We ask great things, because he is infinitely rich in grace and in power (Philippians 4:19). He who is our God and King, remember, sits upon a 'throne of grace'. This King sits on his throne on purpose, specifically to dispense grace. It is his design, his object in displaying himself as King, to dispense grace.

Glory Revealed

It is in hearing the prayers of the needy and dispensing grace to them that our God and King is honoured and glorified. It is upon his throne of grace that God our Saviour is revealed in his glory. You will remember that this throne of grace is that which Isaiah saw (Isaiah 6). It was typified in the mercy-seat, which was upon the ark of the covenant in the Old Testament, where atonement was made. This is what John beheld in Revelation 4 and 5, where he saw the Lamb that had been slain.

When he saw the throne of God and of the Lamb, he saw the rainbow encircling the throne, declaring that every act of the throne is according to God's covenant of grace represented in the rainbow. He saw the book of God, the book of God's decrees, full, complete, and sealed. Then, he saw the Lord Jesus Christ, the crucified Lamb of God rise up in the midst of the throne. He saw the God-man take the book and open it. He it is who is the centre of all those decrees. He it is who opens and fulfils them in providence (Revelation 5:9-14).

It is here, in Christ, the crucified Lamb of God, sitting upon the throne, that we behold God's majesty and mercy, his justice and his grace, his truth and his goodness (Exodus 25:17-18, 22; Hebrews 9:1-12; 10:19-22). The Lord God to whom we come and before whom we bow in prayer, even in hearing prayer, acts as a sovereign, but whose sovereignty is the sovereignty of grace. It is to this throne, the throne of the great God, that poor sinners are bidden to come. Oh, what a privilege this is! All who come to the throne of grace have free audience with the King of Grace!

Come Boldly

Let us, therefore, come boldly to God upon the throne, through the merits and mediation of Christ, our great High Priest. Come 'boldly', that is to say, freely, without fear, pouring out our hearts to our heavenly Father. Come with reverence, as before God our King; but come boldly with all the freeness of a child to the most loving father imaginable. Remember, he who is the God of the universe is our heavenly Father. We have every reason to expect him to do us good (Romans 8:32). Come in every time of need for the mercy and grace needed, expecting him to supply the need, for Christ's sake.

For every high priest taken from among men is ordained for men in things *pertaining* to God, that he may offer both gifts and sacrifices for sins: Who can have compassion on the ignorant, and on them that are out of the way; for that he himself also is compassed with infirmity. And by reason hereof he ought, as for the people, so also for himself, to offer for sins. And no man taketh this honour unto himself, but he that is called of God, as *was* Aaron. So also Christ glorified not himself to be made an high priest; but he that said unto him, Thou art my Son, to day have I begotten thee. As he saith also in another *place*, Thou *art* a priest for ever after the order of Melchisedec. Who in the days of his flesh, when he had offered up prayers and supplications with strong crying and tears unto him that was able to save him from death, and was heard in that he feared; Though he were a Son, yet learned he obedience by the things which he suffered; And being made perfect, he became the author of eternal salvation unto all them that obey him; Called of God an high priest after the order of Melchisedec. Of whom we have many things to say, and hard to be uttered, seeing ye are dull of hearing. For when for the time ye ought to be teachers, ye have need that one teach you again which *be* the first principles of the oracles of God; and are become such as have need of milk, and not of strong meat. For every one that useth milk *is* unskilful in the word of righteousness: for he is a babe. But strong meat belongeth to them that are of full age, *even* those who by reason of use have their senses exercised to discern both good and evil.

Hebrews 5:1-14

Chapter 17

Read: Hebrews 5:1-14

The Typical Priesthood of Aaron

In the first four chapters of this epistle, the Holy Spirit has shown us the superiority of our Lord Jesus Christ over the angels, over Moses, and over Joshua, all of whom were highly venerated by the Jews. Perhaps the only thing more highly venerated by them was their sabbath observance. In the fourth chapter, he displayed Christ's superiority over that as well, showing us that Christ is the true Sabbath and that the sabbath rest of faith in him is indescribably better than the observance of legal sabbath days.

In the chapter before us we see the superiority of Christ as our great High Priest over Aaron and all the Levitical priests of the legal dispensation. This seems to have been in the back of his mind all along. I say that because he has mentioned Christ's priesthood twice before (Hebrews 2:17-18; 4:14-15).

Only One Priest

The Holy Spirit's purpose, throughout this epistle, is to show us that the Lord Jesus Christ is the sinner's only access to God. He is the only priest there is between God and man. In fact, he is the only Priest there ever was between God and man. All the priests of the Old Testament were only types and pictures of him. All the pretended priests of all religious orders since the end of the Mosaic age are impostors. The Lord Jesus Christ is the only Priest by whom sinners may draw near to God and God draws near to sinners.

When God gave the law to Moses at Mount Sinai, he instituted an earthly, human priesthood, a priesthood by which sinners could approach him, worship him, and offer gifts and sacrifices to him. The Lord decreed that these priests must be descended from the tribe of Levi and the family of Aaron. Therefore, it is referred to as the Levitical or Aaronic priesthood.

There was one other divinely ordained priesthood mentioned in the Old Testament, that of Melchisedek. You will remember him from Genesis 14. It was this man, Melchisedek, who brought bread and wine to Abraham and blessed him, and to whom Abraham paid tithes. This was done long before any law was given by God concerning the priesthood or tithes.

That fact is important because in Hebrews 5 the Holy Spirit shows us that the Lord Jesus Christ is, like Melchisedek, a priest in every way superior to Aaron. In verses 1-4, he gives us a description of Aaron's priesthood and shows us how it was a type and picture of our Lord's priesthood.

> When Aaron, in the holiest place,
> Atonement made for Israel's race,
> The names of all their tribes expressed,
> He wore conspicuous on his breast.
> So, when our great Melchisedec
> The true atonement came to make,
> Deep in his breast engraved he bore
> Our names, with every penal score.

A Common Man

Every typical high priest under the law was a man. He was a common man, taken out from among them (Exodus 28:1). He was ordained and invested with this great office by that special anointing with oil ordained by God. He was made a priest that he might represent the people of the chosen nation in things pertaining to God.

The high priest presided over Israel in all matters of worship in the name of God, appeared before God in their stead, presented their gifts and sacrifices to God, and blessed them in God's name. God's high priest stood between God and men. The Lord Jesus Christ is our High Priest. We must never attempt to go to God except through Christ. We cannot expect any mercy or favour from God except through Christ.

Israel's high priest was just a man. All the priests of the Old Testament were weak and sinful men. Yet, they were compassionate men who understood and sympathized with the people in their ignorance and in their transgressions of the law. Our Lord Jesus Christ, the Son of God, became a man and knows our frame (Hebrews 4:15; Psalm 103:14).

A Sinful Man

When the high priest brought a sin-offering and made atonement for the people, he first had to offer an atonement for his own sin, and then for the people. The priests were sinners, too. As such, they needed mercy. Israel's high priest even had to make atonement for the holy things (Exodus 28:36-38). Our Lord Jesus Christ is different. He had no sin (Hebrews 7:27).

Divinely Appointed

No man volunteered for the office of high priest, but was called to it (vv. 4-5). The office of high priest was an office of the highest honour. It involved the work of representing the people before God. Only those men who were appointed and ordained of God were allowed to function as priests in Israel. Any who dared, like Uzziah the king, to take the honour to themselves would suffer grave consequences and be brought to public shame.

Even Christ himself did not take this high and holy office unto himself. Neither did he receive it from men. He did not acquire it by family heritage because he was of the tribe of Judah, not Levi. He was not, as a man, of the Levitical, priestly, order. Our Lord Jesus was made a Priest. God the Father made him our High Priest. The Father appointed him to the office, anointed him with the oil of gladness above his fellows and sent him to execute it (John 8:54).

The Superiority of Christ Over Aaron

In these verses the Holy Spirit shows Christ's fitness as our great High Priest by contrasting his priesthood with Aaron's. Aaron and the other high priests in Israel were types and pictures of the Lord Jesus Christ as our great High Priest. Like our Saviour, those priests were men of flesh who understood and had compassion upon their fellow creatures. They were chosen and appointed of God to be high priests. They were intercessors, mediators between God and men. They offered blood sacrifices for sin.

The Contrasts

Yet, in many ways, the priesthood of Christ cannot be typified by men. Those priests of the Old Testament age were many. Christ is the one High

Priest. Their priesthood was only temporary. Our Lord's priesthood is eternal (Hebrews 7:1-3). Those priests offered many sacrifices. Our Saviour offered only one (Hebrews 10:12). Those priests offered the blood of others. The Lord Jesus gave his own life's blood as an offering to God for us (Hebrews 9:12). The sacrifices offered by those priests of the Mosaic age could not put away sin. The one sacrifice of Christ, our Lord, has effectually and completely put away all the sins of all God's elect forever (Hebrews 10:14). The work of the priests of that carnal, ceremonial dispensation was never finished, for thousands of years their fires burned and blood of beasts was spilled. The Son of God, our Saviour, finished the work given to him (John 17:4; 19:30; Hebrews 10:11-14).

The Days of His Flesh

We are told, concerning our great High Priest, that 'in the days of his flesh, when he had offered up prayers and supplications with strong crying and tears unto him that was able to save him from death, and (he) was heard in that he feared'. I have no doubt that there is much, much more in those words than I have yet understood; but that which is obvious is both delightful and comforting to my soul.

'The days of his flesh' refer to our Lord's temporary earthly life. He is still in that body in which he suffered the wrath of God for us and in which he was raised from the dead. There is a Man in glory! And that Man who is our God in human flesh will never put aside our nature.

While our Saviour dwelt upon this earth as our Representative, being numbered and identified with transgressors, he offered prayers and supplications to the Father, with tears. Do you see how truly and fully human he is? He who is our Redeemer, our Saviour, our great High Priest, is fully God and fully man. He lived in this world both in complete faithfulness and by perfect faith. When he knelt in the Garden, anticipating being made sin for us, the weight of our sin crushed his very heart (Luke 22:39-46). However, we must never imagine that our Saviour prayed that he might be kept from dying as our Substitute, or even from being made sin for us. He came into this world for that purpose. His determination to fulfil his covenant engagements for the glory of his Father and the salvation of our souls never wavered.

His prayer described here was a prayer of reverence, consecration, and worship. This Man 'feared' God as no other man ever could, not that he might be kept from dying, but that he might be delivered from death. He was heard because he was perfectly righteous and holy in nature and in conduct. Having fully satisfied the law and justice of God for sin, our Saviour was raised from the dead and declared to be the Son of God. He was thus 'delivered' from death and the grave. We are delivered from death in him. He said, 'He that believeth on me shall never die'.

The Things He Suffered

'Though he were a Son, yet learned he obedience by the things which he suffered'. As a Man, as our Mediator and Substitute, the Lord Jesus Christ learned obedience by that which he suffered.

If the Man Christ Jesus would be our Saviour, he must be 'a man of sorrows and acquainted with grief'. God spared his Son nothing (Romans 8:32). He suffered all that we deserved, both in his life and in his death. Let no one deceive you in this matter. Suffering is not an indication of God's disfavour or disapproval. None of God's children in this world are exempt from suffering (John 16:33). We must all enter into the kingdom of God through much tribulation.

Though he is the Son of God, the Lord Jesus himself could not bring in everlasting righteousness and could not put away the sins of his people, satisfying all the demands of God's holy law and infinite justice, without the things he suffered as our Substitute (Luke 24:44-47).

The Author of Eternal Salvation

Rejoice in this. The sufferings of our Saviour are gloriously effectual! 'Being made perfect, he became the author of eternal salvation unto all them that obey him'. That salvation which Christ accomplished for and gives to his people is an eternal salvation. It is given to those, only those and all those, who obey him, who believe the gospel.

Being perfect in his obedience in life and in death, Christ became the author of a perfect, eternal salvation to all who believe on him. He gives us a perfect righteousness before the law and a perfect justification before the throne (2 Corinthians 5:21). He gives his sheep eternal life, 'and they shall never perish'.

We are assured that our salvation in Christ is an 'eternal salvation', because he is an everlasting Priest with an everlasting priesthood. He is 'an high priest after the order of Melchisedec'.

Obedience Learned

In verse 8 we have another important insight into the work of the Saviour. The Holy Spirit tells us, 'Though he were a Son, yet learned he obedience by the things which he suffered'. Let us learn what God the Holy Spirit teaches us in this text. The lessons here taught are both practical and of immense importance.

Obedience is the Character of the Sons of God

Our Saviour left us an example that we should walk in his steps. He has, by his own example, shown us how we are to live in this world. If we would follow Christ we must yield ourselves to our heavenly Father, in unquestioning universal surrender, to do his will in all things. The extent of our obedience is and must be 'even unto death'.

Obedience to God is a Costly Thing

Obedience to another necessarily involves cost. If I obey another, I subject my will, my thoughts, my possessions, my time, and my energy to the one I obey. It is not possible to be obedient to anyone without cost. But obedience to Christ, as our Lord and God, demands the willing surrender of our lives to him (Luke 14:25-33; 2 Timothy 2:12; 1 Peter 2:19-24; Matthew 5:10-12). God's love for us and our relationship to him as the sons of God do not exempt us from suffering.

Though the Lord Jesus Christ is the Son of his love, he was not spared any suffering and sorrow as a man. He was 'a man of sorrows and acquainted with grief'. The disciple is not above his Master, nor the servant above his Lord. If we are the sons of God, we must through much tribulation enter into the kingdom of heaven (Hebrews 12:5-11).

One old writer, when discussing this matter, said, 'If a sheep stray from the flock, the shepherd sets his dog after it, not to devour it, but to bring it in again; even so our Heavenly Shepherd'. The things we suffer in this world by the will of God are the things by which we learn obedience to the will of God.

We learn not by words, but by experience, not by reading but by tasting, not by instruction, but by correction, not by admonition, but by affliction (Psalm 119:67, 71, 75). It is a sad fact, but a fact nonetheless, that we only learn patience by the trial of our faith. We never learn sympathy until we have walked in the shoes of those who need sympathy. We will never learn forgiveness until we experience forgiveness. We will not learn to help the fallen until we have been helped from a fall. We will never learn what we would or should do in any circumstance, until we are in the midst of the trial ourselves. We will never learn to be weaned from this earth until God graciously weans us from it.

Sonship and Suffering

'Though he were a Son, yet learned he obedience by the things which he suffered'. Suffering is one of the birthmarks which are found upon all who are born of God. Our heavenly Father had one Son, and only one, without sin. He has none without sorrow.

The Father's Rod

Our heavenly Father's discipline is the pledge of our adoption and the badge of our sonship. God chastens none but his own; but he chastens all who are his own. All who are God's look upon his loving rod of discipline as a mark and token of his grace, knowing that 'we are chastened of the Lord that we should not be condemned with the world' (1 Corinthians 11:32).

How we ought to thank God that he does not leave us to ourselves! Painful as it is to feel the rod, let us kiss the hand of our loving Father for laying it upon our stubborn backs. Christian poet and hymnwriter William Cowper wrote:

'Tis my happiness below
Not to live without the cross,
But my Saviour's power to know,
Sanctifying every loss.
Trials must and will befall;
But with humble faith to see,
Love inscribed upon them all.
This is happiness to me.

God in Israel sows the seeds
Of affliction, pain, and toil.
These spring up and choke the weeds
Which would else o'erspread the soil.
Trials make the promise sweet.
Trials give new life to prayer.
Trials bring me to His feet,
Lay me low, and keep me there.

Did I meet no trials here,
No chastisements by the way,
Might I not with reason fear
I should prove a castaway?
Bastards may escape the rod;
Sunk in earthly, vain delight;
But the true born child of God
Must not, would not, if he might'.

Charles Spurgeon once said, 'I bear my willing witness that I owe more to the fire, and the hammer, and the file, than to anything else in my Lord's workshop. I sometimes question whether I have ever learned anything except through the rod. When my school-room is darkened, I see most'.

The Obedience of Suffering

'Though he were a Son, yet learned he obedience by the things which he suffered'. Though our Lord Jesus Christ is the Son of God, he was not exempt from suffering. If he would redeem us from our sins and from the wrath of God, he must suffer all that we deserve as sinners to the full satisfaction of divine justice (Romans 8:32). Though the Lord Jesus Christ is the Son of God, he could not execute a perfect righteousness, to the full extent that the law and justice of God demanded, without a perfect suffering (Luke 24:44-47).

If these things were true of him, how much more so must we expect to experience the same in this world? None of the children of God are exempt. Why does the experience of heartache, sorrow, pain, and trouble surprise us? One of the very last things our Master said to his disciples before he left this world was this: 'In the world ye shall have tribulation' (John 16:33). As our Saviour learned obedience by the things he suffered in this world, so we must learn obedience by the things we suffer. Obedience is learned in no other school.

'Though He Were a Son ... '

The Lord Jesus Christ is uniquely and pre-eminently the Son of God. All who are chosen, redeemed, and born of God, all true believers, are the sons of God by adoption and grace. What a great honour and privilege that is (Galatians 4:6-7; Romans 8:17; 1 John 3:1). But our Lord Jesus Christ is uniquely and pre-eminently the Son of God in that he is the 'only begotten of the Father, full of grace and truth' (John 1:14).

Distinctive Sonship

Christ is the eternally begotten Son of the Father, one with the Father and the Holy Spirit in the Holy Trinity (1 John 5:7). Our Lord Jesus Christ, as a man, is the only begotten Son of God in this sense also: He is the virgin born Son (Isaiah 7:14; Luke 1:26-27; Galatians 4:4-5). Also, our great Saviour is uniquely and pre-eminently the Son of God, the only begotten Son, in his resurrection glory and exaltation as the firstborn among many brethren (Acts 13:27-33; Psalm 2:7; Hebrews 1:5-6; 5:5).

Jehovah's Voluntary Servant

Though he lived in this world as the Son of God, uniquely and pre-eminently the Son of God, our Lord Jesus Christ learned obedience as a man by the things he suffered. Obedience is voluntary subjection to the will of another. If it is not voluntary it is only outward compliance, not obedience (Hebrews 10:5; John 10:16-18). Obedience is owning the authority of another, performing the pleasure of another.

When the Lord Jesus Christ came into the world, he came as Jehovah's servant to do his will as a man. He was made under the law that he might obey, establish, fulfil and satisfy the law as a man. This obedience was essential to his priesthood and to our salvation. While he volunteered to become obedient, he actually entered into the experience of obedience by the things he suffered as a man. He learned obedience by the things he suffered. As Jehovah's voluntary Servant, our Saviour denied himself, pleased not himself (Romans 15:3), and became obedient unto death, even the death of the cross (Philippians 2:5-8). Though he was and is the Son of God, uniquely and pre-eminently the Son of God, our Lord Jesus Christ learned obedience by the things which he suffered.

What were those things which he suffered? They are the very things his people suffer in this world. He suffered poverty (Luke 2:12), endured the temptations of the devil (Matthew 4:3), and the unjustified slander of men (John 10:36). He suffered bereavement, misunderstanding and misrepresentation by both his own disciples and the world. He suffered betrayal by one who claimed to be and should have been his friend, desertion by men who were loved by him, and sorrow like no man ever suffered sorrow. He suffered being abandoned by his Father. The Lord Jesus Christ suffered death, the painful, shameful, ignominious death of the cross, as our Substitute!

Spiritual Immaturity

Men and women who should be instruments of usefulness to others are often spiritually immature. They are like babies and small children, who must be constantly instructed in elementary principles of the faith. This is what we see in Hebrews 5:12-14.

Great Loss

True believers lose much by immaturity. The apostle had many things yet to say about Christ, our great Melchisedec. There were many great treasures to be revealed, many great truths to be taught, many great mysteries to be unfolded; but it was difficult for him to plunge into the great wonders of Christ's work as our Priest before God and the great mysteries of his Person; because there were many among the Hebrew believers who were still babes in grace: immature and 'dull of hearing'. If he gave them strong meat, he knew that they would choke on it. Therefore, before moving on to weightier matters (as he does in chapter 7), the Holy Spirit inspired him to reprove those who continue in immaturity and urge them to grow up.

Unacceptable

It is a sad fact, but a fact nonetheless, that many who have been believers for a long time and ought to be mature in the things of God remain babes (v. 12). Immaturity is acceptable in children; but immature adults are an embarrassment to their families and repulsive to others. The apostle is here saying, 'Brethren, it's time for you to grow up. Stop acting like children'.

Babies require milk, 'first principles', ABC blocks, and colouring books. Mature believers need and feed upon the strong meat of the Word. Being unstable in the Word of righteousness, spiritual babies must be spoon fed, lest they be tossed to and fro with every wind of doctrine (vv. 13-14). Incapable of discerning good and evil (doctrinal good and evil), such infantile men and women must be constantly given the ABCs of the gospel, the first principles of divine truth.

Unprofitable

As long as a person is satisfied with such spiritual immaturity, he both robs himself of great joy and blessedness, and remains unprofitable in the kingdom of God. Babies have childish minds, behave in childish ways, are greatly affected by childish toys, and provide no real usefulness to others. If we would be useful to others, we must seek grace from our God to grow in the grace and knowledge of our Lord Jesus Christ (2 Peter 3:17-18).

Therefore leaving the principles of the doctrine of Christ, let us go on unto perfection; not laying again the foundation of repentance from dead works, and of faith toward God, Of the doctrine of baptisms, and of laying on of hands, and of resurrection of the dead, and of eternal judgment. And this will we do, if God permit. For *it is* impossible for those who were once enlightened, and have tasted of the heavenly gift, and were made partakers of the Holy Ghost, And have tasted the good word of God, and the powers of the world to come, If they shall fall away, to renew them again unto repentance; seeing they crucify to themselves the Son of God afresh, and put *him* to an open shame. For the earth which drinketh in the rain that cometh oft upon it, and bringeth forth herbs meet for them by whom it is dressed, receiveth blessing from God: But that which beareth thorns and briers *is* rejected, and *is* nigh unto cursing; whose end *is* to be burned. But, beloved, we are persuaded better things of you, and things that accompany salvation, though we thus speak. For God *is* not unrighteous to forget your work and labour of love, which ye have shewed toward his name, in that ye have ministered to the saints, and do minister. And we desire that every one of you do shew the same diligence to the full assurance of hope unto the end: That ye be not slothful, but followers of them who through faith and patience inherit the promises.

Hebrews 6:1-12

Chapter 18

Read: Hebrews 6:1-12

'Let Us Go On'

I am aware that Hebrews 6 is one of the most controversial chapters in the New Testament. Heretics frequently point to the opening verses of this chapter and use them to try to prove that saved men and women may be lost again, that those who are the objects of God's grace today may be the objects of his wrath tomorrow. That is both blasphemy and nonsense.

Immutable Grace

The gifts and callings of God are without repentance. His mercy, love, and grace are unchangeable. The grace of God is both immutable and indestructible (Malachi 3:6, Romans 11:29). He gives eternal life to whom he will, and declares that those to whom eternal life is given in Christ are saved forever. 'I give unto them eternal life; and they shall never perish!'

> Grace is Jehovah's sovereign will,
> In an eternal covenant sure;
> Which for His seed He will fulfil,
> Longer than sun and moon endure.
>
> Lord, help us on Thy grace to stand,
> And every trial firm endure;
> Preserved by Thy sovereign hand,
> And by Thy oath and covenant sure.

Instruction, not Debate

This is also a chapter about which faithful men, men who believe and preach the gospel of God's free and sovereign grace in Christ, are often in disagreement. It is not my intention here to explore or settle those conflicts of interpretation. I gladly leave that task to those who enjoy such things. My desire is to give the instructions set before us in this passage of inspiration, not to debate the questions men raise about it. The fact is, this is a very instructive, encouraging passage of scripture. If you will read the entire passage carefully, beginning at chapter 5 verse 11, you will see that the Spirit of God has specific reasons for giving us the instruction found in these verses. Please take a moment and read Hebrews 5:11-6:3.

Perseverance and Maturity

These things are written to encourage us to persevere in the faith of Christ, to continue looking to, trusting, following, and obeying Christ. These words were written during a time of great apostasy, much like the day in which we live (2 Thessalonians 2:11-14; Revelation 20:7-9). The Holy Spirit here encourages believers to grow in the grace and knowledge of Christ. We do not grow in acceptance with God; but we must grow in grace. We do not grow in our position of favour before God; but we must grow in the knowledge of Christ. This passage of inspiration is intended to encourage those who are still babes in Christ to 'go on unto perfection'; to maturity in the things of God. The passage is designed to encourage us to seek spiritual maturity: seeking to be strong, well-established, well-grounded, useful believers.

'Let Us Go On' Building on First Principles

Be sure you understand what the Holy Spirit is urging us to do here. He is not telling us that we are to forsake the first principles of the gospel, forget the first principles, deny the first principles, or cease to preach the first principles. Rather, we are to build upon them. We lay these first principles in our hearts as the foundation of all that we are and have in Christ. Then, we go on to build upon that foundation. What are these 'first principles of the doctrine of Christ'? The Holy Spirit here identifies six specific things as first principles. They are:

1. 'Repentance from dead works'. In Philippians 3:4-8, the apostle Paul exemplifies what this is. It is repentance from the dead works of religion. We must constantly cast off the filthy rags of self-righteousness, repenting of our sin and our righteousness, clinging to Christ alone for our entire salvation (1 Corinthians 1:30-31).

2. 'Faith toward God'. This is the faith of God's elect, the confession of every true believer. There is no faith toward God except that which is the faith of holy scripture (Romans 4:23-5:1). As we received Christ so let us walk in him, growing in our dependence upon him (Colossians 2:6).

3. 'The doctrine of baptisms'. Many suggest that the 'doctrine of baptisms' has reference to the ceremonial washings of the legal dispensation; but that does not fit the context, and seems to make the passage irrelevant to believers today. The word 'baptisms' is used here in the plural because the doctrine of baptism in the New Testament is twofold. First, at the inauguration of Christ as King over Zion, the church and kingdom of God was baptized in the Holy Spirit (Acts 2). Second, believers are buried with Christ in the waters of baptism, professing faith in him and identifying themselves with him and with his people in this world.

4. 'Laying on of hands'. This refers to that special power given to the apostles of Christ, by which they conveyed to others the apostolic gifts of the Spirit (Acts 8:17; 1 Timothy 4:14). In the early church, when deacons and preachers were ordained, the presbyters laid hands upon them (Acts 6:6; 13:3). Paul warned Timothy to exercise great caution in laying hands upon men (1 Timothy 5:21-22).

5. 'Resurrection of the dead'. The Lord Jesus Christ is coming again (1 Thessalonians 4:13-18). When he appears there will be a great, general resurrection. Following the resurrection will be ...

6. 'Eternal judgment'. God has appointed a day when he will judge the world by that man who died at Calvary and sits now upon the throne of glory (Acts 17:31; Revelation 20:11-12)

These are 'the first principles of the doctrine of Christ'. This is where we begin in Christ. We must always continue to believe, preach and rejoice in these things. But we do not need to prove these great, foundation truths over and over again. Rather, we are to build upon them. These things are the foundation upon which we build and grow in the knowledge of Christ, in brotherly love and spiritual unity, and mature in conformity to our Saviour. May God ever give us grace to build upon these first principles, for Christ's sake.

'If They Shall Fall Away ... '

Salvation is by God's free and sovereign grace alone. The sinner's only hope before God is the blood atonement and imputed righteousness of Christ. That salvation which God gives to and works in his people is eternal salvation. All true faith is permanent, persevering faith. However, there is a faith which is a satanic delusion.

Carnal Security

Here is a terribly sobering fact plainly revealed in holy scripture. We will be wise to lay it to heart. It is quite possible for men and women to have an undisturbed peace, unshaken assurance, and unquestioned security with regard to their eternal destiny, and yet have no saving interest in Christ. If that fact is not alarming to you, it should be. The Lord God sounds this fearful warning by his prophet Obadiah: 'Woe unto them that are at ease in Zion!' Satan is a crafty, subtle foe. He knows that the surest way to keep sinners from the saving knowledge of Christ is to give them some satisfying, conscience soothing substitute, some religious experience, or feelings, or gifts, or knowledge by which they may convince themselves that the grace of God is surely theirs.

Do not be deceived. Many have gifts who have no grace. Multitudes profess faith they do not possess. Countless thousands enjoy peace who do not have pardon. Hoards of men and women, orthodox to the core, are yet without life before God. There is a form of godliness possessed by men who deny the power of it (2 Timothy 3:5). Many have a name that they live who are yet dead in trespasses and in sins. Hell is bulging with damned souls who went to that place of eternal torment assured they were on the road to heaven. They went with a Bible in their hand, a song in their heart, and a profession of faith on their lips. At the time when Lot's wife felt most secure, she went to hell! When all the other apostles were anxiously saying, 'Lord, is it I?' Judas was content and confident.

Examine Yourself

There is nothing on this earth more destructive than the carnal security of religion without Christ. Let us bring our faith to the Word of God and examine it. May it please God to search our hearts and let us see if we have the faith of God's elect (2 Corinthians 13:5; 2 Peter 1:10; Psalm 139:23-24). If our faith is the faith of God's elect, if it is sound, if it is a God given faith, examination will only strengthen it, and cause us to cling more firmly to Christ. If our faith is false, examination may expose it. If we have built for ourselves a refuge of lies, in which we are trying to hide from God, may he graciously destroy our false refuge and hide us in Christ by his almighty grace.

A Form of Godliness

In these verses the Spirit of God shows us plainly that there are some people who have what appears to be heavenly gifts who have no grace in their hearts. Multitudes have religion who do not have Christ. Many there are who enjoy great experiences who have never experienced grace.

Many have a form of godliness who know nothing of the power of God by which sinners are born again. These verses speak of people who have experienced much, professed much, and demonstrated much in religion. Yet, they have no saving union with Christ. They have faith; but it is a false faith. They have repentance; but it is a repentance that needs to be repented of. They have experienced religion; but they have not experienced the grace of God. Beware of resting your soul upon experiences, gifts, and outward works of religion. To build your house upon these things is to build upon sand. It is possible to be ranked with the most spiritual, most gifted, most zealous men and women in the world, and yet go to hell in the end (Matthew 7:21-23). Is your faith the faith of God's elect; or is it a false faith?

> False faith may be greatly enlightened and knowledgeable of gospel truth. Judas talked the talk of the disciples. True faith receives the love of the Truth (2 Thessalonians 2:10).
>
> False faith excites the affections, like the stony ground hearers of the parable, and causes people to spring up like shooting stars, only to fade. True faith is the abiding, growing gift of God.
>
> False faith reforms the outward life and causes people to live better before men. True faith arises from a regenerate heart and causes people to seek the will and glory of God.
>
> False faith may speak well of Christ, as the Jews did. True faith loves Christ.
>
> False faith confesses sins, like King Saul. True faith confesses sin, like David (Psalm 51).
>
> False faith may humble itself in sackcloth and ashes, like Ahab. True faith humbles itself before God.
>
> False faith may repent in terror, like Esau and Judas. True faith repents in contrition, being convinced of God's way of salvation in Christ (John 16:8-11).
>
> False faith often performs religious works very diligently. Saul of Tarsus did. True faith is a faith which 'worketh by love'.
>
> False faith is sometimes very generous and charitable like Ananias and Sapphira. True faith causes ransomed sinners to be generous willingly, constrained only by love and gratitude.
>
> False faith may tremble at the Word of God, like Felix. True faith trembles and bows (Acts 24:25).
>
> False faith seeks and often enjoys the experiences of man-made religion. True faith trusts no experience, no matter how great. It looks to Christ alone.

False faith often receives great religious privileges, like Lot's wife. True faith places no confidence in the flesh.

False faith may preach eloquently, perform miracles, and even cast out demons, like Judas Iscariot. True faith rejoices in having one's name written in heaven.

False faith often attains high office in the church, like Diotrephes, and walks with great preachers, as Demas walked with Paul (3 John 9; 2 Timothy 4:10). True faith is honoured to serve the least in God's kingdom, keep the doors of God's house and walk with Christ (Matthew 20:25-28).

False faith may be peaceful and carnally secure, like the five foolish virgins. True faith presumes nothing, but looks constantly to Christ alone for grace.

Religious But Lost

Men and women often feel much, experience much, and do much in religion and religious circles who never experience God's saving grace. Neither emotional experience, nor orthodoxy of creed, nor reformation of life is necessarily a token of grace. Hebrews 6:4-6 speaks of such people. Look at what these people have experienced.

Enlightened

They were once enlightened to an understanding of Gospel truth. These were heretics. These are not Arminians, free-willers, papists, or Hindus. These people know the truth, at least mentally. They intellectually perceive and submit to the doctrinal truths of the gospel. To them, the doctrines of the gospel are logical and reasonable. They accept them as facts plainly revealed in the Word of God.

The fact is that natural man can see and understand any doctrine taught in holy scripture. He cannot see the glory of God in the face of Christ; but he can see and glory in doctrine. He cannot love Christ; but he can love doctrine. The unsaved man may be a better theologian than the believer. But the poor, uneducated believer knows and loves what the unregenerate doctor never can. The believer knows, loves, trusts, and rejoices in Christ.

Tasted Heavenly Gifts

Multitudes have tasted the heavenly gifts who have never tasted the Gift of heaven. During the Apostolic age, miraculous gifts were given to men. Some could heal diseases, speak in tongues, and prophesy. But miraculous gifts, which appear to be gifts of the Spirit, are by no means an evidence of grace, salvation and eternal life. Gifts of the Spirit can be, and often are, counterfeited by Satan (2 Thessalonians 2:7-10).

Tasting the heavenly gifts and powers of the world to come is not salvation. Salvation is eating the Bread of Life. Salvation is not in miraculous gifts, but in immutable grace. Salvation is not in feelings, emotions, and experiences, no matter how great and life changing they may be. Salvation is in Christ! A man can preach with power and eloquence, and yet not know Christ. Judas did. A man can perform miracles, and not know God. Pharaoh's magicians did. A man can cast out demons, and yet be the messenger of Satan (Matthew 7:21-23). A person can speak in tongues, and yet speak by the power of the devil. A man can preach, promote, and defend righteousness, and yet speak by him who transforms his ministers into angels of light and preachers of righteousness. Spiritual gifts and usefulness must not be looked upon as evidences of grace and salvation.

Partakers of the Holy Ghost

This passage even speaks of lost men and women who have been made partakers of the Holy Ghost. Many people look at that and say, 'Without question, these were once saved people'. But that is not the case at all. We read of wicked King Saul that, 'The Spirit of God came upon him, and he prophesied', but the Spirit of God was not in him. Balaam spoke by the Spirit and prophesied of Christ's coming, but never knew the Christ of whom he spoke. In fact, Balaam's ass even spoke a word from God by the power of his Spirit; but neither Balaam, nor his ass, were born of God. Caiaphas, the high priest, spoke by the Spirit of God, declaring the gospel as plainly as any man ever did. Yet, he was a lost man.

It is possible for men to say and do things which, considered by themselves, make it appear that they are partakers of the Holy Spirit, though they are not born of the Spirit. There were many in our Lord's day, as there are today, who believed; but the Master did not commit himself to them, because he knew what was in them (John 2:23-25).

Tasted the Word of God

We are told in verse 5 that these people have even tasted the good Word of God and the powers of the world to come. They love good preaching, and are moved by it. You find them at every Bible conference. Their emotions are stirred by the preaching of the Word; but it never reaches their hearts. This is what the Holy Spirit teaches us in this passage: it is possible for men and women to enjoy rare, unusual gifts and experiences without experiencing God's saving grace in Christ. Outward gifts and heartfelt emotions impress and deceive. We must have something more. We must have Christ (1 Corinthians 13:1-3).

Lost Forever

Here is a fact that must be faced and dealt with, if we would be honest with the Word of God and honest with the souls of men. Those who fall away are lost forever. What does that mean? Be sure you understand the doctrine of holy scripture on this important matter.

Never Perish

The Word of God tells us plainly and unmistakably that God's elect shall not and cannot fall away and perish. True believers never cease to be true believers. Those to whom Christ gives eternal life shall never perish. Concerning these matters, the Word of God is crystal clear. If salvation is God's work alone (and it is), then it is forever (Ecclesiastes 3:14). The gifts and callings of God are without repentance. Eternal life is eternal life. The promise of grace and the immutability of our God assure us of the infallible and everlasting security of all who are the objects of his mercy, love, and grace in Christ (Malachi 3:6).

Those Who Fall

Yet, there are many who do fall away. Many who were once numbered *among* God's elect in the house of God and were thought to be true believers, even looked upon as examples of faith and faithfulness, have forsaken Christ and the gospel (John 6:66; 1 John 2:19). 'Remember Lot's wife'! Those who do fall away are lost forever. They 'crucify the Son of God afresh and put him to an open shame'.

What is This Falling Away?

What does the Holy Spirit mean by those words 'If they shall fall away?' This is not talking about some specific act of sin. David's adultery did not separate him from the love of God in Christ. It is not even talking about the sin of denying Christ. Peter did that; but he was not lost. This is not even talking about doctrinal error, or even doctrinal error concerning vital issues. All these things may be and are forgiven. Though God's people do fall into these grievous evils, our God lifts us up and sets us upon the Rock Christ Jesus. What then is this fall that results in the eternal, unrecoverable ruin of men's souls? In the Word of God two things are described in these terms.

First, to depart from the faith of the gospel is to fall away and perish forever (Galatians 5:1-4). Those who have been enlightened to the truth of the gospel and then turn from it, for whatever reason, blaspheme the Spirit of God and fall away, and shall not be forgiven. 'There is a sin unto death. I would not that you should pray for it'. That sin which brings eternal reprobation is described in Matthew 12:31-32. There the Lord Jesus Christ declares, 'Wherefore I say unto you, All manner of sin and blasphemy shall be forgiven unto men: but the blasphemy against the Holy Ghost shall not be forgiven unto men. And whosoever speaketh a word against the Son of man, it shall be forgiven him: but whosoever speaketh against the Holy Ghost, it shall not be forgiven him, neither in this world, neither in the world to come'.

Second, to forsake the assembly of God's saints, the fellowship of the gospel; and the ministry of the Word; to abandon the worship of Christ is to fall away and be lost forever (Hebrews 10:25-31; 2 Peter 2:20-21). There are many, I fear, who tenaciously hold to and defend the doctrine of Christ who have fallen away and abandoned Christ altogether. They have no interest in the kingdom of God, no commitment to the cause of God, no fellowship with the people of God, no concern for the glory of God. They have fallen away. In forsaking the worship of God, they have fallen away.

Something I have Observed

The first step toward total apostasy is the neglect of public worship. When men and women begin to find comfortable excuses for neglecting the assembly of God's saints, I tremble for them. By their wilful neglect of public worship they declare to all who observe them that the ministry of the Word, the fellowship of God's saints, the songs of Zion, and the praises of our God are really unimportant. If that which they declare by their actions is, indeed, a declaration of their hearts, such neglecters of divine worship are apostate.

Let us never look upon the assembly of God's saints lightly, or treat it as a contemptible thing, a thing to be despised. To absent yourself from the house of God is to choose something else above the worship of God. To neglect the worship of God's church is to neglect the worship of God. To abandon the church of God is to abandon God.

Something I have Never Seen

In thirty years of pastoral experience I have seen believing men and women recovered from falls into many evils. I have seen some who, like Peter, after their fall, were stronger and more faithful than ever. But this I have never seen: I have never seen a man or woman recover after willingly walking away and abandoning the worship of God! I have seen many, perhaps trying to silence some sting of conscience, come back for a while; but I have never seen it last. I have never yet seen a man or woman willingly walk away from and abandon the worship of God recover!

'We Are Persuaded Better Things Of You'

It is a sad fact, but a fact nonetheless, that many who begin the race well soon fall by the wayside. Many, who run well for a season, in time, walk no more among us. Tares are always sown among the wheat. Goats will always be found amongst God's sheep in this world. Often, those who were once named among God's saints and honoured as brothers and sisters in Christ abandon Christ, his gospel, and his people. Thereby proving that they never were truly one of us (1 John 2:19). Such apostates are described in Hebrews 6:1-6.

A Distinction Illustrated

In verses 7 and 8, the Holy Spirit illustrates the fact that the preaching of the gospel, like rain falling from heaven, has profoundly different results upon the people who hear it. To some it is a savour of life unto life. To others it is a savour of death unto death.

When the gospel is blessed of God to the hearts of chosen, redeemed sinners, by the power of his almighty grace, it springs up unto life everlasting (v. 7). But those who hear the gospel and reject it as a thing to be despised, are themselves rejected of God, cursed forever, and shall be burned like useless weeds in hell (v. 8).

Let us lay these things to heart and soberly consider them. May these warnings and examples ever cause us to run to Christ, lay hold on him with both hands, and hold him with a death grip. However, the passage does not end with such terrifying warnings. Lest any true believer be terrified with the fear that he may, after all, perish, the Holy Spirit inspired the Apostle to speak in verses 9 and 10 of …

A Persuasion of Grace

'But, beloved, we are persuaded better things of you, and things that accompany salvation, though we thus speak. For God is not unrighteous to forget your work and labour of love, which ye have showed toward his name, in that ye have ministered to the saints, and do minister'.

How sweet! How blessed! How encouraging! Though he solemnly warned these men and women, because he cared for their souls, of the danger of apostasy and the necessity of perseverance; he saw in them evident tokens of grace, 'and things that accompany salvation'. We do not have to guess what these things are. He names them for us.

Things that Accompany Salvation

There are some things which always accompany God's salvation and are tokens of grace wrought in the hearts of men. The Holy Spirit here declares what some of those things are. 'Your work'. The work to which he refers is, first and foremost, the work of faith (1 Thessalonians 1:3; 2 Thessalonians 1:11; Hebrews 11:1-2). 'Your labour of love, which you have shown toward his name'. Believers are a people who labour together in the kingdom of God, for the glory of God, serving Christ, being constrained by the love of God in Christ. That which compels us in the service of our God is his love for us, our love for him, and our love for one another. This love for God and his people is manifest in free, voluntary service to his people, 'in that ye have ministered to the saints, and do minister'. Faith in Christ and the love that flows from it causes those who are born of God to minister to, and serve, his saints. As our Saviour washed his disciples' feet, those who follow his example wash one another's feet, willingly serving one another.

An Assurance of Hope

'And we desire that every one of you do show the same diligence to the full assurance of hope unto the end: That ye be not slothful, but followers of them who through faith and patience inherit the promises' (vv. 11-12).

In the light of the things we have seen in this chapter, you might ask, 'How can anyone have assurance that he will, indeed, endure to the end and be saved?' It seems that this is the very question anticipated by the Holy Spirit in these last verses of chapter 6. Here are seven specific things by which every sinner who looks to Christ alone for salvation may have what the Holy Spirit calls 'the full assurance of hope'.

1. The promise of God (vv. 13-15)
2. The oath of God (vv. 16-17)
3. The immutability of God (vv. 17-18)
4. The place of our Refuge (v. 18)
5. The anchor of our Souls (v. 19)
6. The finished work of Christ (v. 20)
7. The priesthood of Christ (v. 20)

In the light of these things, every saved sinner, looking to Christ alone, can and should confidently say, 'If God be for me, Who can be against me? I know whom I have believed, and am persuaded that he is able to keep that which I have committed unto him against that day!'

Assurance is not a matter of presumption on the part of a saved sinner. It is a matter of faith. Any lack of assurance is a manifest lack of faith. Our great God, who has begun his good work of grace in us, will perform it until the day of Jesus Christ. He who saved us will also keep us. He who gave us grace will also give us glory.

'He Sware By Himself'

The Apostle Paul is urging us to go on in faith, trusting Christ alone as our Saviour. He is urging us to persevere unto the end. That has been his purpose since the opening words of chapter 2. He has been urging us not to let Christ and his gospel slip from our hands. He has told us plainly that some who once professed faith in Christ have fallen away, and that if any fall away, it is impossible to renew them again unto repentance.

Having given us these warnings, he assures those who truly trust Christ that they shall indeed persevere. That is what the Holy Spirit tells us in verses 13 to 20 of chapter 6.

All who are truly born of God, all who trust Christ alone as Saviour and Lord, all who look to Christ's blood alone as the atonement for their sins, all who look to Christ's obedience alone for their righteousness before God, shall continue to trust him unto the end and shall be with him in glory.

Every believer, every sinner who looks to Christ alone for salvation and eternal life, can and should sing with A. M. Toplady …

> My name from the palms of His hands,
> Eternity will not erase:
> Impressed on His heart it remains
> In marks of indelible grace.
>
> Yes, I to the end shall endure,
> As sure as the Earnest is given:
> More happy, but not more secure,
> The glorified spirits in heaven!'

How can this be? How can any of us be sure of grace? How can anyone be assured of his salvation? Our adversary, the devil, seeks to devour us. Our temptations are many and great. Our trials are many and heavy. Our hearts are sinful and our flesh weak. Yet, in these verses the Spirit of God speaks to us of 'the full assurance of faith'. What is the basis of this assurance? The text speaks of men and women in this world having 'a strong consolation' and a 'hope as an anchor of the soul'.

Full Assurance

Paul opens this section, dealing with 'the full assurance of hope' (v. 11), by urging us to diligence. To many, that may seem strange, but not to a believer. Nothing so inspires diligence in the life of a believer as the assurance of his hope in Christ (Colossians 1:5, 23). John Trapp put it like this, 'A man may as truly say the sea burns, or fire cools, as that certainty of salvation breeds looseness'.

The Apostle urges us to continue in faith and love, and in serving one another, with the desire that we might all arrive at 'the full assurance of faith' in Christ. Yet, two things are obvious. First, some true believers do not enjoy the blessed peace of 'the full assurance of faith'. Second, it is possible for us to have assurance in this world, and we should seek it.

What could be more blessed and more inspiring to our soul in this world than a well-grounded full assurance of the election of grace with its saving interest in Christ as our Substitute and Redeemer and of the Holy Spirit's work of grace in us?

'Be Not Slothful'

Let us not be slothful concerning our souls and the things of God (v. 12), but diligent, following the examples of those who have gone before us into glory; who through faith and patience have inherited the promises of God in Christ.

Grace, salvation and eternal life in and by Christ are things bestowed upon sinners by the promise of God. This is stated here to show us that salvation is not by our works or human merit, but is entirely the work and gift of God's free grace in Christ. It is a gift that shall assuredly be obtained by God's elect. It shall be obtained by that faith and patience which God gives to his people by the power and grace of his Spirit.

This gift of grace is expressed in the plural number, 'promises', because it is the great all-inclusive promise of God. It is described as an inheritance because the whole thing is ours in Christ, as the sons of God, as 'heirs of God and joint-heirs with Christ'.

Yet, this is a promise that shall be obtained after much trouble, after faith has been tried and proved, through 'patience', as illustrated in the life of Abraham (vv. 13-15).

For when God made promise to Abraham, because he could swear by no greater, he sware by himself, Saying, Surely blessing I will bless thee, and multiplying I will multiply thee. And so, after he had patiently endured, he obtained the promise. For men verily swear by the greater: and an oath for confirmation *is* to them an end of all strife. Wherein God, willing more abundantly to shew unto the heirs of promise the immutability of his counsel, confirmed *it* by an oath: That by two immutable things, in which *it was* impossible for God to lie, we might have a strong consolation, who have fled for refuge to lay hold upon the hope set before us: Which *hope* we have as an anchor of the soul, both sure and stedfast, and which entereth into that within the veil; Whither the forerunner is for us entered, *even* Jesus, made an high priest for ever after the order of Melchisedec.

Hebrews 6:13-20

Chapter 19

Read: Hebrews 6:13-20

'Let Us Therefore Come'

Abraham is here used as a pattern, because he was the father of all believers. The promises God made to him of blessedness and of being made a blessing, are ours, for all the promises of God are in Christ, and are yea and amen in him. T. Greene wrote:

Why should my fears so far prevail,
When they my hopes accost?
My faith, though weak, can never fail,
Nor shall my hopes be lost.

A thousand promises are wrote
In characters of blood;
And those emphatic lines denote
The ever faithful God.

Through those dear promises I range;
And, blessed be His name,
Though I, a feeble mortal, change,
His love is still the same.

Promise to Abraham

The promises referred to here are found in Genesis 22:15-18. This is the place where God's promise was enforced with his oath. This promise to Abraham was made by Christ himself, the Angel of the Covenant, who swore by himself because he could swear by none greater (Isaiah 45:23). Yet, it was a promise concerning Christ, Abraham's Seed, and all God's elect in him (Galatians 3:14-16, 29).

When the scriptures speak of God swearing by himself, it is a display of his condescension. He condescends to our weakness, assuring us, by his oath, that his promise is good. All who are chosen of God, all who are called by his grace, all who believe on the Lord Jesus Christ, are hereby assured that all spiritual blessings are and shall be ours in Christ forever (Ephesians 1:3-6).

Immutable Purpose

The oath of a man is given to put an end to strife, doubts, and questions about what he has promised. How much more shall God's oath put an end to all our doubts and questions concerning his promise of grace in Christ? The counsel of God, as the term is used here, is his everlasting purpose of grace in Christ, his eternal decree concerning the salvation of his elect (Romans 8:28-31). This is, like God himself, here declared to be a matter of absolute immutability.

God's purpose of grace is immutable. It must be immutable, because it is the purpose and grace of the immutable God (Malachi 3:6; James 1:17); whose wisdom is infinite, whose power is omnipotent, whose will is unalterable, whose grace is unconditional. God's purposed and promised grace is ours immutably because it comes to us through the merits of our eternally accepted Surety. This is what the phrase, 'confirmed it by an oath', suggests. It speaks of the interposition of a Mediator, Christ our Surety.

Two Immutable Things

The two immutable things in verse 18 are the decree of God and the oath of God. By the decree of his will and the oath of his covenant, knowing that 'it is impossible for God to lie', we find in Christ our 'strong consolation'. Our assurance and consolation before God are not found in our feelings, experiences, personal holiness, or even in our faith, but in God our Saviour, the Lord Jesus Christ. Believers are men and women who have fled for refuge unto him, like the man slayer in the Old Testament who fled for refuge to one of the cities of refuge.

Even the names of the cities were typically significant and instructive (Exodus 21:13; Numbers 35:6, 11, 14; Deuteronomy 21:2, 9; Joshua 20:1-9). Kedesh means, 'holy'. Christ is holy, both as God and man, and is our holiness before God, that 'holiness without which no man shall see the Lord'. Shechem means, 'the shoulder'. Christ not only bore our sins in his own body on the tree, he bears and carries us; and the government of his church and kingdom is on his shoulders. There, on his omnipotent shoulders, we are safe and secure. Hebron means, 'fellowship'. Believers have fellowship with Christ and with the Father in him; and in him we have fellowship with one another. Bezer means, 'a fortified place'. Christ is our stronghold, our high tower, and our place of defence. To him we run; and in him we are safe and comforted. Ramoth means, 'exaltations'. Our Lord Jesus Christ is exalted at God's right hand, and in due time he will exalt those that trust in him. Golan means 'manifested'. Christ is God 'manifest in the flesh'. The Son of God was manifest to take away our sins and destroy the works of the devil; and he will be gloriously manifest and revealed at the last day.

The words 'lay hold upon' are very strong. They mean to lay hold firmly, as with a death grip. When Satan would pull us off of Christ, we hold him fast. It is our faith in Christ, our hope in him that the fiend of hell would destroy. His messengers are preachers who cunningly try to get us to take refuge somewhere else, to seek our comfort outside of Christ.

An Anchor

Our hope is fastened within the veil. It is 'a nail in a sure place'. It is a sure and steadfast hope. Our ship may be tossed to and fro, but it cannot be wrecked. Christ is the Pilot. The scriptures are the compass. God's promises are the tackling. Hope is the anchor. Faith is the cable holding it. The Holy Spirit is the Wind that drives it.

The Forerunner

As the high priest in Israel entered into the holy of holies once a year, the Lord Jesus Christ, our great High Priest, has gone into the Holy Place. There he has taken possession of Heaven as our Forerunner. By the merit of his own blood he has obtained eternal redemption for us (Hebrews 9:12). Our great Forerunner has gone to heaven to make intercession for us (Hebrews 7:25; 1 John 2:1-2) as a Priest after the order of Melchisedec. Christ is a Priest after the order of righteousness and of peace. The order of his priesthood is an everlasting and unchangeable order.

For this Melchisedec, king of Salem, priest of the most high God, who met Abraham returning from the slaughter of the kings, and blessed him; To whom also Abraham gave a tenth part of all; first being by interpretation King of righteousness, and after that also King of Salem, which is, King of peace; Without father, without mother, without descent, having neither beginning of days, nor end of life; but made like unto the Son of God; abideth a priest continually. Now consider how great this man *was*, unto whom even the patriarch Abraham gave the tenth of the spoils. And verily they that are of the sons of Levi, who receive the office of the priesthood, have a commandment to take tithes of the people according to the law, that is, of their brethren, though they come out of the loins of Abraham: But he whose descent is not counted from them received tithes of Abraham, and blessed him that had the promises. And without all contradiction the less is blessed of the better. And here men that die receive tithes; but there he *receiveth them*, of whom it is witnessed that he liveth. And as I may so say, Levi also, who receiveth tithes, payed tithes in Abraham. For he was yet in the loins of his father, when Melchisedec met him. If therefore perfection were by the Levitical priesthood, (for under it the people received the law,) what further need *was there* that another priest should rise after the order of Melchisedec, and not be called after the order of Aaron?

Hebrews 7:1-11

Chapter 20

Read: Hebrews 7:1-11

Christ: Priest After the Order of Melchisedek

In the last verse of chapter six, the Holy Spirit declares that our Lord Jesus Christ has been 'made an high priest after the order of Melchisedek'. Here he proceeds to show us the beauty and greatness of Christ as our Great High Priest, as he was typified in this man, Melchisedek.

We first meet with this great man, Melchisedek, in Genesis 14:18-20. When Abraham returned from the slaughter of the kings of the plain, after delivering Lot from his captors, Melchisedek met him with bread and wine, received tithes from the patriarch, and blessed him.

After he left Abraham, we have no mention of his name again, until we get to Psalm 110. There, David gave a prophetic psalm of praise to the Lord Jesus Christ as the exalted Mediator and King, Saviour and Great High Priest of God's elect. In verse 4, he tells us that our Lord Jesus, in his exaltation glory, is 'a priest after the order of Melchisedek'.

No other mention is made of this great man until we get to the book of Hebrews. He is mentioned frequently in this book. In fact, Psalm 110:4 is quoted twice in chapter 5 (vv. 6 and 10), and again in chapter 6 (v. 20). Then, this entire seventh chapter is taken up with this eminent type of Christ. Here, the Holy Spirit calls for us to pause and 'consider how great this man was'. The Spirit's point in calling our attention to the greatness of Melchisedek is that we might be made to see the infinitely superior greatness of our Lord Jesus Christ, as he was 'made an high priest after the order of Melchisedek'.

We are not told who Melchisedek was. Some think he was one of Shem's sons. Others suppose that he was a descendent of Ham, a Canaanite Priest and King. There are some who think that he was an angel who appeared in the form of a man. Many teach that he was Christ himself, appearing to Abraham in a preincarnate human body.

In verse 15, we are told that our Saviour is a Priest after the similitude of Melchisedek. It is evident, therefore, that he was a man, a priest, and a king; but one whose place, ancestry, life, and death have been purposefully hidden from us, so that he might be a great type and picture of Christ.

Unlike any other man, this man pictured our Saviour in that he was both a king and a priest, a priest upon a throne (Zechariah 6:13). Like Melchisedek, he was without father as a man, without mother as God, without beginning of days, without end of life, and a continual, abiding Priest.

If Abraham honoured Melchisedek with tithes, how much more we ought to honour God our Saviour with our substance, consecrating all to him who loved us and gave himself for us. As Melchisedek was greater than Abraham, greater than Levi, greater than all the great ones who came from the loins of Abraham; so the Lord Jesus Christ is infinitely greater than all. In his deity, in his humanity, in his offices, in his work, in his accomplishments, and in his intercession, Christ excels all.

All other priests died. Their priesthood ceased. Christ lives forever. His priesthood will never cease (Hebrews 5:6; 6:20). The reason why the priests, sacrifices, ceremonies, and ordinances of the law have all ceased is simple. They could not save. Christ can! Christ does! Christ has! Therefore, he continues forever (Galatians 2:21; Hebrews 7:18-19; 8:7).

'An Unchangeable Priesthood'

We cannot come to God without an altar, a priest, and a sacrifice. But those Old Testament priests, altars, and sacrifices could never bring anyone to God. Therefore, a change had to come. The picture had to be replaced with the Person. The shadow had to give way to the Substance. The law had to give way to grace. The Levitical priesthood had to die to make room for a Priest after the order of Melchisedek from the tribe of Judah (Isaiah 11:1; Matthew 1:3; Luke 3:33; Romans 1:3; Revelation 5:5)

The Lord Jesus Christ, our great High Priest, entered into and exercises his everlasting and efficacious priesthood by virtue of his resurrection glory. The law made nothing perfect. It was never intended to do so, but only to point sinners to Christ who would make everything perfect (Romans 8:3-4; Hebrews 10:1-4; Acts 13:38-39; Romans 3:20, 21, 28; 8:1-4; Galatians 2:16; Hebrews 9:9). By his perfect obedience to God in the room and stead of his people, the Lord Jesus has brought in a better hope (Hebrews 6:18; 8:6). In him believing sinners have a good hope, hope founded upon righteousness established, justice satisfied, and grace bestowed. Christ has given us such absolute perfection before God that we can now draw near to God himself with confidence, peace and assurance (Romans 5:1-2; Ephesians 2:18; 3:12; Hebrews 4:16; 10:19).

Our Great High Priest is our covenant Surety, the Surety God himself has accepted as our Representative (Psalm 110:4; Hebrews 8:6; 9:11-15; 12:24; 13:20-21). Our Saviour is an unchangeable, immutable, irrevocable, eternal, effectual Priest! The virtue of his sacrifice is everlasting and unalterable! Read verses 25-28 of Hebrews chapter 7 and rejoice! Now read Romans 8:33-34; 1 Timothy 2:5; Hebrews 9:24-26, 28; 1 John 2:1-2 and rejoice again!

'The Bringing In of a Better Hope'

There is no hope in the law, because the law provides no perfection. There is no peace in the law, because the law can only condemn. But the gospel gives us a better hope than could ever be found in the law. That hope is 'a good hope', 'a blessed hope', a hope that 'maketh not ashamed', because that hope is Christ! Blessed is that person who has learned to look to Christ alone for the whole of God's salvation, the whole of his acceptance with the holy Lord God.

Acceptance

The whole of our acceptance with God is in Christ. It is the Person and work of Christ alone, which makes us acceptable and accepted with the thrice holy Lord God.

The whole of our assurance before God is in Christ. Be sure you understand this. Our relationship with God does, in great measure, determine what we do; but what we do does not in any way, or to any degree, affect our relationship with our God.

The whole of our security in grace is in Christ. We being in Christ are accepted because Christ is accepted. We are secure, because Christ is secure. We are holy, because he is holy. We have no sin, because he has no sin. He put away our sins. Therefore, God will not charge his elect with sin, at any time, or for any reason (Romans 4:8; 8:1).

Near, so very near to God, nearer I cannot be,
For in the person of His Son I am as near as He.
Dear, so very dear to God, dearer I cannot be,
For in the person of His Son I am as dear as He!

Good Shepherd

Christ is our Good Shepherd, as such, he gave his life for his sheep. He seeks his sheep, each one of them and every one of them, until he finds them all. When he finds one of his sheep, he lays it on his shoulders and carries it all the way home. The Good Shepherd knows his sheep. He calls them by name. He leads them, feeds them, protects them, and preserves them. He gives them eternal life and declares, 'They shall never perish!' My heart rejoices in the knowledge that Christ is my Shepherd and I am his sheep (Ezekiel 34:11-16; John 10:1-30).

Substitution

The Lord Jesus Christ, the Son of God, is our Substitute. He lived in righteousness and died in shame as the Representative of his people. Substitution is the basis of hope for fallen man, the foundation and essence of the gospel; the message God's servants are sent to declare, and good news for guilty sinners. 'In due time, Christ died for the ungodly ... Who his own self bear our sins in his own body on the tree' (Romans 5:6; 1 Peter 2:24).

For my own heart there is nothing so deep and mysterious, so profound and awesome, so wonderful and inspiring, so full and joyful, so comforting and assuring as the glorious, God honouring, gospel doctrine of substitution. Indeed, substitution is the very fabric from which all biblical truth is made. How I rejoice to know and to declare, 'He hath made him to be sin for us, who knew no sin; that we might be made the righteousness of God in him'.

High Priest

Christ is our great High Priest. As the high priest had the names of the tribes of Israel engraved upon the ephod, attached to the breastplate, so Christ has our names engraved upon his heart (Ezekiel 28:28-29). 'By his own blood, he entered in once into the holy place, having obtained eternal redemption for us'. The Lord Jesus Christ deals with God on our behalf. He makes intercession with the Father for us. He represents his people continually. He who entered into heaven as our Forerunner and sat down on the right hand of the Majesty on High is Christ, our great High Priest.

This great High Priest is God; but he is also a man, a man touched with the feeling of our infirmities. He knows our trials, temptations and troubles. He knows our weaknesses and our woes and he sympathizes with us. He intercedes for us, pleading our cause with the Father. Christ is a Priest we can safely trust. His sacrifice has been accepted in heaven (Hebrews 10:1-14).

Advocate

The Son of God is our Advocate with the Father (1 John 2:1-2). What could be more blessedly consoling to sinful men and women? The Son of God is our Advocate with the Father. 'We have an Advocate with the Father'! He is a gracious, loving Advocate, a righteous Advocate, a full time Advocate, and an effectual Advocate

Do you see how careful the Holy Spirit is for believing sinners to enjoy the comfort and assurance of our souls' salvation? He not only tells us what Christ has done, is doing, and shall yet do for us, he uses metaphor after metaphor to assure God's believing people that all is well between us and our God.

For the priesthood being changed, there is made of necessity a change also of the law. For he of whom these things are spoken pertaineth to another tribe, of which no man gave attendance at the altar. For *it is* evident that our Lord sprang out of Juda; of which tribe Moses spake nothing concerning priesthood. And it is yet far more evident: for that after the similitude of Melchisedec there ariseth another priest, Who is made, not after the law of a carnal commandment, but after the power of an endless life. For he testifieth, Thou *art* a priest for ever after the order of Melchisedec. For there is verily a disannulling of the commandment going before for the weakness and unprofitableness thereof. For the law made nothing perfect, but the bringing in of a better hope *did*; by the which we draw nigh unto God. And inasmuch as not without an oath *he was made priest*: (For those priests were made without an oath; but this with an oath by him that said unto him, The Lord sware and will not repent, Thou *art* a priest for ever after the order of Melchisedec:) By so much was Jesus made a surety of a better testament. And they truly were many priests, because they were not suffered to continue by reason of death: But this *man*, because he continueth ever, hath an unchangeable priesthood. Wherefore he is able also to save them to the uttermost that come unto God by him, seeing he ever liveth to make intercession for them. For such an high priest became us, *who is* holy, harmless, undefiled, separate from sinners, and made higher than the heavens; Who needeth not daily, as those high priests, to offer up sacrifice, first for his own sins, and then for the people's: for this he did once, when he offered up himself. For the law maketh men high priests which have infirmity; but the word of the oath, which was since the law, *maketh* the Son, who is consecrated for evermore.

Hebrews 7:12-28

Chapter 21

Read: Hebrews 7:12-28

Surety

Among the many descriptions used in holy scripture to describe our Saviour's glorious person and redemptive work, none can be more instructive, consoling, and assuring than that which is spoken of in Hebrews 7:22.

Here the Holy Spirit tells us that the Lord Jesus Christ is our Surety, the Surety of the everlasting covenant. As Judah became surety for Benjamin (Genesis 43:8-9), the Lord Jesus Christ became Surety for God's elect in the covenant of grace. That is to say, the Lord Jesus Christ the Son of God, voluntarily assumed the total, complete responsibility for our souls before his Holy Father; making himself honour bound to save us!

A surety is one who approaches one person on the behalf of another person. He is a representative man who lays himself under obligation to another person for the one he represents. It is in this sense that Christ is our Surety. He drew near to his Father on our behalf, and laid himself under obligation to God for us (Psalm 40:7-8).

A Matter of Honour

Suretiship is, to a man of honour, a voluntary bondage (Proverbs 6:1-2). A surety is one who strikes hands with another in solemn agreement. He gives his word that he will fulfil his agreement. Thus he binds his honour to the fulfilment of that which he has agreed to do.

When the Lord Jesus Christ became our Surety, he voluntarily placed himself in bondage to his Father until his service was performed (Isaiah 50:5-7; John 10:16-18). The Son of God, as our Mediator, as our covenant Surety, assumed total responsibility for the everlasting salvation of God's elect, and willingly bound himself to the work of saving us.

An Eternal Surety

This is what the Lord Jesus Christ did as our Surety in the Covenant of Grace before the world began. He drew near to God on the behalf of his elect. He promised to faithfully perform all that God required for the salvation of his people. He struck hands with the Father in solemn agreement.

A Trusted Surety

God the Father trusted Christ as our Surety from eternity. He entrusted his elect people into the hands of his Son as our Surety, and the matter of our salvation was then and there settled forever. This is exactly how the Word of God describes the eternal aspect of salvation (Romans 8:28-30; Ephesians 1:3-6, 12; 2 Timothy 1:9-10).

God the Father put his chosen into the hands of his own dear Son, who volunteered to bring in everlasting righteousness for them, and to put away their sins by the sacrifice of himself. The Father, trusting the Son as our Surety, looked upon his people in him as redeemed, justified, sanctified, called, and glorified from everlasting. As such, he has, from eternity, made his elect to be 'accepted in the Beloved'. He has blessed all his chosen with all the blessings of grace and salvation in Christ the Surety.

How did the Lord Jesus Christ become our Surety? The Holy Spirit tells us: 'By so much was Jesus made a surety of a better testament'. He was made our Surety by the oath of God himself (v. 21), by the eternal decree of the Almighty God, who accepted him for us and accepted us in him (vv. 20-22).

An Absolute Surety

With men a surety is a mere guarantor, a co-signer who is jointly responsible with the principle debtor for the payment of a debt. Not so with Christ! Our Lord Jesus Christ did not merely agree to meet our obligations to God's law if we, by some circumstance or condition, became incapable of meeting our own obligations. Our blessed Saviour, as our Surety, took the whole of our obligation before the law of God upon himself.

A Voluntary Surety

With men a surety may be legally forced into suretiship. A man is legally responsible for the debts of his wife. A father is legally responsible for the debts and legal liabilities of his minor children. But Christ voluntarily, cheerfully placed himself in servitude to God's law and will, as the Surety of his own elect. From the instant he became Surety for his people, he became servant to his Father (Isaiah 42:1-4; 49:1-4; John 10:17-18). The Lord Jesus Christ is an absolute Surety by voluntary consent.

Transferred Responsibility

When he became our Surety, Christ took the whole of our debt upon himself. He became responsible for our obligations. As soon as he was accepted as our Surety, we were released from all of our debts and obligations to God's holy law. As soon as God accepted his Son as our Surety, he set us free. He ceased looking to us for satisfaction. He freed us from all bondage, all curse, all penalty, and all obligation; and looked to his Son for satisfaction of our debts (Job 33:24; Philemon 1:18). When Christ became Surety for us, our sins were imputed to him. By divine imputation, our sins were placed to his account. He became responsible for them. The Lord Jesus Christ was made to be sin for us when he hung upon the cursed tree. But he became responsible and accountable for sin when he became our Surety (2 Corinthians 5:21; Isaiah 53:6; Psalm 40:12; 69:5).

The Result

When Christ became our Surety, we were then and there redeemed, justified, pardoned, and made righteous in the sight of God (Romans 8:28-30; Ephesians 1:3-6; 2 Timothy 1:9-10). God's forbearance, patience, and long-suffering with this world are due to the suretiship engagements of Christ on behalf of his elect. God's eye has always been on the blood. It is the blood of Christ our Surety that held back the hand of God's judgment when Adam sinned.

The Old Testament saints were pardoned, justified, and forgiven upon the basis of Christ's obedience as our Surety; though he had not yet actually rendered that obedience (Isaiah 43:25; 45:24-25; Hebrews 11:13-16). Those saints of old, like believers today, had knowledge of and faith in Christ as their Surety (Job 19:25-27; Psalm 32:1-4; 119:122; Isaiah 38:14).

'Knowing therefore the terror of the Lord, we persuade men'. It is my responsibility as God's messenger to your soul to persuade you to trust Christ, our Surety. How can I do so? What words shall I use?

Lost

I cannot imagine a sadder word than the word 'lost'. If you are yet without Christ, you are a lost sinner (1 John 5:10-12). How those words ought to alarm you! If you are without faith in Christ, the wrath of God is upon you! You are guilty, depraved, helpless. You are justly condemned. The flaming sword of divine justice thirsts for your blood! Unless God is pleased to save you, you will soon be in hell. You know that this is the sad state of your soul. Your conscience bears witness to the fact that you are lost.

Righteousness

The holy Lord God demands righteousness from you, perfect righteousness. It is written, 'That except your righteousness shall exceed the righteousness of the scribes and Pharisees, ye shall in no case enter into the kingdom of heaven'. Yet, you cannot produce righteousness. The polluted fountain of your depraved heart can never bring forth the pure water of righteousness.

Satisfaction

As God demands righteousness, so he demands satisfaction. Sin must be punished. 'The soul that sinneth, it shall die'. 'Every one shall die for his own iniquity'. 'The wages of sin is death'. Again, your very conscience tells you this is so. Yet, death, even the everlasting death of men in hell, can never satisfy the infinite justice of God.

Christ

Never can a lost soul find a sweeter word than this! Christ is the Son of God. Christ is the Mediator between God and men. Christ is the Saviour of lost sinners. Christ is hope. Christ the Substitute, the Surety, is life. Christ is able to save unto the uttermost all who come to God by him! (v. 25). Christ and Christ alone can save you (1 Timothy 2:5-6; Acts 4:12).

The Lord Jesus Christ came into this world, God in human flesh, as a representative Man. He lived in perfect obedience to the law and will of God as a man, bringing in everlasting righteousness for all who look to him alone for righteousness. Once he had fully obeyed the demands of the law as the God-man Mediator, the Lord Jesus Christ took the sins of his people upon himself and died the ignominious death of the cross as the sinners' Substitute, satisfying all the law and justice of God for his people. Now, he is able to save to the uttermost all who trust him, because in him, by the merits of his blood and righteousness, God is both 'a just God and a Saviour'. May God be pleased now to grant you faith in him to the saving of your soul.

Come to God

The Bible alone tells us what salvation is and how it may be obtained. The scriptures alone are able to make us wise unto salvation. Only in the Bible do we read of God's mercy, love, and grace toward fallen man. The Word of God alone shows us how that a holy God can both be just and the Justifier of the ungodly. Salvation is revealed only in the scriptures; and salvation is the primary, essential doctrine of holy scripture.

The Bible was not written to teach us history, but to teach us grace. The Bible was not written to instruct us in philosophy, but to instruct us in divine truth. The Bible was not written to teach us morality, but to teach us the way of salvation and life in Christ. Salvation by Christ, the Substitute and Surety for his people, is the message of holy scripture.

One Way

In order to be saved we must come to God by Christ Jesus. 'He is able also to save them to the uttermost that come to God by him'. Saving faith is described by many metaphors in the Word of God. Faith is looking to Christ. Faith is leaning on Christ. Faith is embracing Christ. Faith is receiving Christ. Faith is laying hold of Christ. Here, faith is coming to Christ and coming to God by Christ. Our Lord Jesus Christ is the only way of approach to God.

Coming

What is this coming to God? Please understand that coming to God is not a physical act. In this day of high-pressure evangelism, altar-call salvation, and decisional regeneration, I cannot stress this enough. Coming to God is not a physical act. It is a spiritual act.

No one has ever been saved by a physical act. You do not get saved by coming to church; but by coming to God. You do not get saved by coming to the front, or coming to an 'altar', or coming to a confessional booth; but by coming to God. You do not get saved by saying 'the sinner's prayer'; but by coming to God. You do not get saved by coming to baptism, but by coming to God. You do not get saved by coming to the Lord's Supper; but by coming to God.

Coming to God is a spiritual act of the heart. It is not coming to him now and then, but coming to him continually, sincerely, whole-heartedly. This deliberate, wilful, whole-hearted coming to God is faith (Hebrews 11:6; 1 Peter 2:4-5).

Coming to God implies that you must leave something else. If a person comes to God, he must leave his sins and he must leave his righteousness.

He must leave his bad works and his good works. The gate is too strait to carry anything in with you; and the way is too narrow to allow you to pick up anything along the way.

Coming to God implies a sense of need. Coming to God implies a reconciliation of the heart to him, as he is pleased to reveal himself in holy scripture. Above all, coming to God is to believe him. It is exercising faith in him.

Mediator

How do we come to God? There is but one way for sinful men and women to come to God. All who come to God have to come the same way. We come to God 'by Him'. Christ is the only Way to God (John 14:6; Hebrews 10:20). Christ is the only Door of Entrance into life (John 10:9). Christ is the only Mediator between God and men. God will never accept any who come to him without a suitable Sacrifice, and that Sacrifice is Christ. God will never accept any who come to him without a spotless garment of righteousness. That garment is Christ (Matthew 22:11-13).

Five Superiorities of Christ's Priesthood

In the last three verses of Hebrews 7 we are given a marvellous display of Christ's superiority over all the priests of the Old Testament. The Holy Spirit would have us marvel at the superiority of Christ's priesthood over the Aaronic order, which he came to fulfil and replace.

A Sinless Priest

First, our Lord Jesus Christ is a sinless priest (v. 26). We have a High Priest who is 'holy, harmless, undefiled, separated from sinners, and made higher than the heavens'. No other priest could ever say that. They were all sinful, like you and me. But not Christ. He was tempted but never yielded to the point of sin.

Needed No Sacrifice

Second, because he was sinless, our Priest did not need to make atonement for himself. Therefore, he could and did offer himself as a sacrifice to God for us (v. 27). The Lord Jesus did not have to offer sacrifices for himself, but instead could offer himself as a sacrifice. He did not need, like those high priests of old, to offer up daily sacrifices, first for his own sins, and then for the sins of the people. Therefore, he was able to atone for the sins of his people, which were imputed to him, by the sacrifice of himself. This He did once for all when He offered up himself.

The Lord Jesus Christ is radically different from all those priests. They had sins of their own that had to be dealt with first. Never in a million years would it have entered their heads that they could actually be the sacrifice for the sins of others. Christ changed everything. He needed no sacrifice for himself. Rather, he became a sacrifice in himself.

'Once For All'

Third, our Lord's sacrifice of himself was 'once for all' (v. 27). 'This He did once, when He offered up Himself.' What a great declaration! One time, conclusively, with finality, the Son of God made atonement for all God's elect by the sacrifice of himself!

This great work of redemption is the centre of all history. Every work of God's grace in history before the sacrifice of Christ looked forward to the death of Christ for its foundation. And every work of God's grace since the sacrifice of Christ looks back to the death of Christ for its foundation.

Christ is the centre of world history, the centre of Bible history, and the centre of the history of grace. There is no grace without him. Grace was planned from all eternity, but it was planned with Christ at the centre and his death as the foundation (Romans 8:28-30; Ephesians 1:3-6; 2 Timothy 1:9-10; Revelation 13:8).

Divinely Appointed

The fourth superiority of Christ over all the priests of the Old Testament is this: they were appointed by the law in their weakness; but he was appointed by the very oath of God himself as the perfect Son (v. 28).

The oath of God here is the oath given in Psalm 110:4, 'The LORD has sworn and will not repent, Thou art a priest forever according to the order of Melchisedek'. The oath came after the law and pointed to the end of the law even in David's day, 'for Christ is the end of the law'. The Lord Jesus Christ is the termination of the law, because he is the complete fulfilment of it.

The oath was spoken to Christ as our Mediator. In Psalm 110:1, David says, 'The Lord (God, Jehovah) said to my Lord (Christ our Mediator, the Messiah) sit at my right hand'. Thus, David declared that the final High Priest is the Messiah, the Son of God, after the order of Melchisedek, not after the order of Levi or Aaron, One who was installed by the oath of God, not by the law of a carnal commandment, which has now passed away. Therefore, we read in Psalm 110:3, 'Thy people shall be willing in the day of thy power'.

A Priest Forever

The fifth superiority of Christ over all other priests is that He is a Priest forever (v. 28). The oath 'makes the Son, (a Priest) who is consecrated forever.' The Lord Jesus Christ, our great High Priest, shall never die. He shall never be replaced. He has an indestructible life. He will outlive all his foes. He will be there for us long after everyone we depend on is dead.

Children sometimes fear that their parents will not live to take care of them and sometimes parents fear they will not be alive to take care of their children. Here is something peculiarly precious to the believer. That One who is our great High Priest, our Advocate with the Father, that One who prays for us, with all the tenderness and sympathy of his infinite Being, has been perfected forever! Not for a decade. Not for a century. Not for a millennium. For ever!

The Point

The great point of this text is this: We have a great High Priest, the Lord Jesus Christ, the Son of God, who came into the world in human flesh, lived a perfectly righteous life as a man, offered himself as a perfect sacrifice for the sins of his people, rose to everlasting life, and sat down at the right hand of the Majesty on High. There he who loves us with a distinguishing, everlasting love, prays for us and bids us draw near to God through him. There is no priest between God and man, but Christ. Oh, but what a Priest he is! In John 17 we are given a glimpse of our great High Priest's intercessory work, as he prays for his elect, seeking for us all things necessary for our souls' everlasting good; and this prayer, his prayer, the Father always grants!

Now of the things which we have spoken *this is* the sum: We have such an high priest, who is set on the right hand of the throne of the Majesty in the heavens; A minister of the sanctuary, and of the true tabernacle, which the Lord pitched, and not man. For every high priest is ordained to offer gifts and sacrifices: wherefore *it is* of necessity that this man have somewhat also to offer. For if he were on earth, he should not be a priest, seeing that there are priests that offer gifts according to the law: Who serve unto the example and shadow of heavenly things, as Moses was admonished of God when he was about to make the tabernacle: for, See, saith he, *that* thou make all things according to the pattern shewed to thee in the mount. But now hath he obtained a more excellent ministry, by how much also he is the mediator of a better covenant, which was established upon better promises.

Hebrews 8:1-6

Chapter 22

Read: Hebrews 8:1-6

This Is Our Priest

We bow to no earthly priest. Our great High Priest, the only Mediator and Priest by which sinners may approach the holy Lord God is in heaven. The eighth chapter shows us the superiority of Christ's ministry as our High Priest over the ministry of the Aaronic priests in the Old Testament. The superiority of our Saviour's priestly ministry is here demonstrated in three ways.

A Seated Priest

Our great High Priest, the Lord Jesus Christ, is a Seated Priest. 'We have such a high priest, who is set' (v. 1; Psalm 110:1; Hebrews 1:1-3; 10:12-13). The fact that he sat down declares that his work was done. When our Lord Jesus cried, 'It is finished', he meant, 'It is finished!' What was finished? All the types, promises and prophecies concerning him were fulfilled and finished. All the commandments and ceremonies of the law were fulfilled and finished. All the work of redemption, which he came into the world to perform, was finished. No priest ever sat down in the typical holy of holies, because none of those priest could ever finish their work. Their sacrifices could never put away sin. The Lord Jesus Christ sat down, because his work was finished.

Seated Upon A Throne

Our great High Priest is seated upon the throne of God! 'On the right hand of the throne of the Majesty in the Heavens' (v. 1). The fact that he is seated upon the throne of God, the throne of universal monarchy, the throne of grace, declares that he is, indeed, able to (and most assuredly will) save all his people unto the uttermost, for he has been given power over all flesh for that purpose (John 17:1-2; Romans 14:9).

The True Sanctuary

All earthly priests served in the earth. Theirs was an earthly, carnal ministry. Our Lord Jesus Christ is 'a minister of the true sanctuary' in heaven (v. 2). The fact that he sat down declares that his work is done. The fact that he sat down on the throne of God declares that he is able to save all for whom he died: whose interests he serves as God's High Priest. And the fact that he sat down in heaven declares that his work has been accepted. Hallelujah!

Be sure you do not miss this. When he sat down in heaven, our Saviour sat down as our Forerunner, and our Covenant Head; and we sat down in him (Ephesians 2:4-7). He took possession of eternal salvation and all the glory of heaven in the name of his people, as our representative. That means that we entered into heaven and sat down with him. He entered into and took possession of heaven as our Forerunner. That means that we, for whom he entered in, shall also enter into heaven by him.

Our great High Priest, the Son of God in human flesh, ministers for us continually in the holy of holies; not on earth, but in heaven itself, in that holy place not made with hands, in the very presence of God (Hebrews 9:24). This is the superiority of our Saviour's priestly ministry. Our great High Priest is interceding for us in heaven (Romans 8:33-34). That is the work of a priest. He makes intercession; and the intercession of that Priest who has been accepted in heaven for us, is infallibly effectual.

> The Father hears Him pray,
> His dear anointed One,
> He cannot turn away
> The presence of His Son!

The Main Point

How often have you read an article or a book, or heard a sermon and said to yourself, 'I wish he would just give me the main point'? That is exactly what Paul does in Hebrews 8:1-5. In fact, the words, 'this is the sum' (v. 1), would be better translated, 'this is the main thing'. Here the Holy Spirit tells us that what is before us in this eighth chapter of Hebrews is the main, primary, most important thing for us to know and understand regarding the priesthood of our Lord Jesus Christ.

Shadows Replaced

The Lord Jesus Christ did not come to fit into the old system of priestly sacrifices; he came to fulfil them, to put an end to them, and to replace them. He is the reality; they were but shadows, types, and pictures of him. When the Reality, the real thing, came the shadows passed away. That is what we are told in verse 5.

The last words in the verse are a quotation from Exodus 25:40. They were God's words to his servant Moses. The Lord commanded his servant to make all things according to the pattern he showed him. All the furnishings and the actions of the Old Testament tabernacle were but types, shadows, and pictures of Christ; they served only to point to heavenly, spiritual things. Once the heavenly, spiritual things came, they vanished forever.

The whole point of the book of Hebrews is that Jesus Christ, God's Son, came to fulfil and forever abolish that system and to turn our hearts to himself, ministering for us in heaven. The Old Testament tabernacle and priests and sacrifices were shadows. Now the reality has come and the shadows have passed away. That is the message of Hebrews 8:1-5. The Lord Jesus Christ is precisely the kind of Priest spoken of and typified in the Old Testament scriptures.

A Priest Upon a Throne

He is a Priest in Heaven, seated upon his royal throne as God in human flesh (v. 1). 'My little children, these things write I unto you, that ye sin not. And if any man sin, we have an advocate with the Father, Jesus Christ the righteous: And he is the propitiation for our sins: and not for ours only, but also for the sins of the whole world' (1 John 2:1-2).

A Minister of the Sanctuary

His body is that true tabernacle, which the Lord pitched and not man (v. 2). 'Christ being come an high priest of good things to come, by a greater and more perfect tabernacle, not made with hands, that is to say, not of this building; Neither by the blood of goats and calves, but by his own blood he entered in once into the holy place, having obtained eternal redemption for us' (Hebrews 9:11-12).

A Priest With a Sacrifice

Our Lord Jesus, as our Priest, must have something to offer as a Sacrifice to God (vv. 3-4). 'Wherefore when he cometh into the world, he saith, Sacrifice and offering thou wouldest not, but a body hast thou prepared me' (Hebrews 10:5). That Priest who stands between us and God our Father, that One who makes us right with God, who prays for us before God is not an ordinary, weak, sinful, dying, priest like Aaron and Levi. Our Lord Jesus Christ is the Son of God, omnipotent, sinless, with an indestructible life. Not only that, he does not minister in an earthly tabernacle with all its limitations of place and size, a tabernacle that must wear out with time and use. Our Priest is ministering for us in a 'true tabernacle, which the Lord pitched, not man'. Christ is the real thing in heaven. Christ is the pattern shown to Moses in the Mount.

I've found the pearl of greatest price,
My heart doth sing for joy;
And sing I must, for Christ is mine,
Christ shall my song employ.

Christ is my Prophet, Priest, and King:
My Prophet full of light,
My great High Priest before the throne,
My King of heavenly might.

For He indeed is Lord of Lords,
And He the King of Kinds;
He is the Sun of Righteousness,
With healing in His wings.

Christ is my peace; He died for me,
For me He gave His blood;
And, as my wondrous sacrifice,
Offered Himself to God.

Christ Jesus is my All-in-all,
My comfort and my love;
My life below; and He shall be
My glory-crown above.

John Mason

Implications
What is implied by all this? What does this mean to us? 'Christ is the end of the law!' The High Priesthood of Christ fulfilled and forever brought to an end all the carnal ordinances of legal worship required under the Mosaic law (Colossians 2:11-23). The tabernacle, the temple, the priesthood, the priestly garments, the priestly service, the priestly sacrifices, holy days, sabbath keeping, the commandments, the whole thing (Romans 10:4).

The worship of God has been radically altered. Divine worship is no longer an external, material thing, but an internal spiritual matter. The external is still important, but now the spiritual is radically pervasive. We do not worship God at specified holy places, or upon specified holy days, or under the rigours of specified vestments, liturgy, etc. The believer's life of faith in Christ is a life of worship (Romans 12:1-2; 1 Corinthians 6:19-20; 10:31). Indeed, our very acts of obedience to Christ are now, in Christ, by his merits and his blood, accepted of God as a sweet smelling sacrifice (Philippians 4:18; 1 Peter 2:5).

Salvation is life in the Spirit. It is worshipping God in the totality of our beings. It is the continual consecration of our very lives to Christ. All true worshippers worship God in the Spirit and in truth (John 4:23-24; Philippians 3:3). We have nothing holy, but Christ. There is no place in the worship of God for religious symbols, crosses, images, icons, etc.. We have no altar but Christ; no priest but Christ; no sacrifice but Christ; no sabbath but Christ; no access to God but Christ; no mercy-seat but Christ; no ark but Christ; no holy thing but Christ! Salvation is doing business with God in the holy place. Worship is living for the glory of God. Evangelism is carrying Christ, to poor needy sinners by the gospel.

The covenant of free grace,
As made with Christ our Head,
Is stored with precious promises,
By which our souls are fed.

The solomn oath of God
Confirms each promise true;
And Jesus, with his precious blood,
Has sealed the covenant, too!

Hence all our comforts flow,
And balm for every fear;
May we by sweet experience know
How choice, how rich they are.

A Better Covenant and Better Promises

It is of utmost importance that we understand the teaching of holy scripture with regard to the old and new covenants. It is not possible to understand the work of Jesus Christ as our Substitute and the saving operations of our God in grace; until we understand the distinction between works and grace, between the old covenant of the law and the new covenant of grace.

This distinction is a matter of great confusion to many in the religious world today. I have no doubt that it is a matter of some confusion to some who read these lines. Can you imagine how confusing it must have been to those believers of the first century, especially to those who were Jews?

The Temple was still standing; but God was no longer worshipped there. The ordinances of the Levitical priesthood were still being performed; but God had set aside both the priesthood and the ordinances. Sabbath days were still meticulously observed; but Christ, the Lord of the Sabbath, had already finished his work and entered into his rest, fulfilling the sabbath and setting aside the carnal ordinance. The Sun of Righteousness had risen; but the moon had not yet vanished from view. It was waning and ready to vanish, but had not yet disappeared. There was still a high priest in Israel; but the High Priest of God's Israel was in Glory!

The religious, but unbelieving, Jews were (as most religious people are today) still trying to live by and worship God by the commandments and ceremonies of the Mosaic law; but Christ, who is the end of the law, had fulfilled it and had forever abolished the legal covenant by his obedience to God as our Substitute.

The new covenant had been established and the old forever abolished; but almost all the emblems of the old covenant were still standing. That time of transition, between the resurrection of Christ and the destruction of Jerusalem in 70 AD, must have been very confusing to the Jewish believers. Many of the Gentile churches were plagued by the infiltration of Judaisers who attempted to bring them under the yoke of legal bondage by mixing law and grace. Let the confusion forever end (Romans 6:14-15; 7:1-4; 8:1-4; 10:1-4; Galatians 1:6-9; 3:1-3; 5:1-4; Colossians 2:8-23).

The book of Hebrews was written specifically to correct the confusion by showing the great superiority of the gospel, the superiority of the new covenant over the old, the superiority of this present gospel age to the former legal dispensation. In the seventh chapter the Holy Spirit irrefutably displayed the superiority of Christ's priesthood over the Aaronic priesthood of the Old Testament. The eighth chapter displays the superiority of the new covenant over the old. The new covenant is altogether spiritual, a covenant of grace, pure, free grace, flowing to sinners through the mediation of Christ, established upon the unconditional promises of unconditional grace.

This is Our Priest

The one great, constantly recurring message of the book of Hebrews is this: Everything is better now! In this glorious gospel day everything is better than it was in that Old Testament legal age of carnal ordinances. Our Lord Jesus Christ's kingship is superior to the kingly types of the past, his prophetic ministry is more revealing of God's redemptive purpose, his priesthood more effective and complete. Everything is better now that the shadows and types have been swept away in the glorious manifestation of Christ himself.

Better Sacrifice

The Old Testament priests dared not come to God without a sacrifice. If our Lord Jesus is to be our Priest before God, he also must have something to offer as a Sacrifice to God (vv. 3-4; Hebrews 10:1-5). But his sacrifice is infinitely better than any of those offered in the Old Testament.

Those sacrifices were only pictures. His is real. Those priests offered animals. Christ sacrificed himself. Those sacrifices were but animals. Christ is God and man in one glorious Person. Those sacrifices had no merit. Christ's sacrifice is of infinite merit. Those sacrifices could never put away sin. Christ has forever put away the sins of his people by the sacrifice of himself!

Everlasting and Indestructible

All the law and services of the Old Testament were but pictures of true, heavenly, spiritual worship (vv. 5-6). This is a principal point of the whole book of Hebrews: We have such a high priest, who has taken his seat at the right hand of the throne of the Majesty in the heavens, a minister in the true sanctuary, 'the true tabernacle, which the Lord pitched, and not man' (v. 8)

That great High Priest who stands between us and God our Father, that One who has made us right with God, who makes intercession for us to the Father is not an ordinary, weak, sinful, dying man like Aaron or Levi. Our Lord Jesus Christ is the Son of God, omnipotent, sinless, glorious and everlasting. His precious blood avails for me! Hallelujah! God be praised! The blood of Christ avails for all for whom he died. As his life is indestructible, his priesthood is also enduring and indestructible.

The law by Moses came,
But peace, and truth, and love
Were brought by Christ (a nobler name)
Descending from above.

Amidst the house of God
Their different works were done;
Moses a faithful servant stood,
But Christ a faithful Son.

Then to his new commands
Be strict obedience paid;
O'er all his Father's house he stands
The Sovereign and the Head.

Isaac Watts

For if that first *covenant* had been faultless, then should no place have been sought for the second. For finding fault with them, he saith, Behold, the days come, saith the Lord, when I will make a new covenant with the house of Israel and with the house of Judah: Not according to the covenant that I made with their fathers in the day when I took them by the hand to lead them out of the land of Egypt; because they continued not in my covenant, and I regarded them not, saith the Lord. For this *is* the covenant that I will make with the house of Israel after those days, saith the Lord; I will put my laws into their mind, and write them in their hearts: and I will be to them a God, and they shall be to me a people: And they shall not teach every man his neighbour, and every man his brother, saying, Know the Lord: for all shall know me, from the least to the greatest. For I will be merciful to their unrighteousness, and their sins and their iniquities will I remember no more. In that he saith, A new *covenant*, he hath made the first old. Now that which decayeth and waxeth old *is* ready to vanish away.

Hebrews 8:7-13

Chapter 23

Read: Hebrews 8:7-13

'After This ... '

It is necessary for us to realize the importance of the book of Hebrews. Here the Holy Spirit shows us how all things relating to the carnal, ceremonial, outward, legal aspects of Jewish worship were forever fulfilled and forever abolished by the coming of Christ. The accomplishment of redemption by his death at Calvary, his enthronement and exaltation as God's King upon his holy hill of Zion, and the outpouring of His Holy Spirit upon the nations of the world brought the old worship to an end.

That is what this eighth chapter of Hebrews is about. In these 13 verses the Holy Spirit declares that God has abolished the old covenant by bringing in the new and by fulfilling all the types and shadows of the old. All the carnal, earthly priests of the Old Testament, all the laws given to Israel, all the ceremonies of legal worship in the Mosaic age were ordained for, and served, only one purpose. They pointed to Christ! They had no other function!

In this gospel day, the Lord Jesus Christ has 'obtained a more excellent ministry, by how much also he is the mediator of a better covenant, which was established upon better promises' (v. 6). Our all-glorious Christ is the Mediator of a better covenant, established upon better promises. That better covenant, established upon better promises, is the covenant of grace, the new covenant. Why was this new covenant necessary? That question is answered in Hebrews 8:7-13.

The Old Covenant

The old covenant had to be replaced by a new covenant because the old covenant was faulty (v. 7). That first covenant was the covenant of the Levitical priesthood. It was a covenant made with physical Israel and delivered to that nation by Moses. It was a typical covenant, only typical and altogether typical (Hebrews 7:11,18).

The people with whom the old covenant of the law was made were typical of the true Israel of God, that is, the church of God's elect. The blessings promised in it were shadows, types and pictures, of good things to come. The sacrifices of it were pictures of Christ and his one great sacrifice for sin. The priests, the mediators of that covenant, were typical of Christ, our great High Priest.

That old covenant was faulty, deficient, non-saving, non-effectual. It was weak and faulty simply because it was only typical. Its priests were all sinful men. Its sacrifices were only animals. Its offerings could never put away sin. If this covenant, its priests and sacrifices, laws and ceremonies, commandments and ordinances, could have redeemed and saved, there would have been no reason for Christ to come (Hebrews 10:1-4, 9).

The New Covenant

The new covenant (v. 8) of this Gospel age is the covenant of grace promised back in Jeremiah 31. Finding fault with the people, the priests, the sacrifices, and the ceremonies of the old covenant of the law, the Lord God said, 'Behold, the days come, when I will make a new covenant with the house of Israel and with the house of Judah'. This is a direct quotation from Jeremiah 31:31-34. This prophetic passage is referred to again in precisely the same way in Hebrews 10:15-17.

This covenant of grace is not called 'a new covenant' because it is newly made, or of a new origin. We know that because this covenant is elsewhere called 'the everlasting covenant'. It is a covenant made with Christ our covenant Surety before the foundation of the world (Hebrews 13:20; Revelation 13:8).

It is called a new covenant because it is newly revealed in this gospel age. That which is revealed second was made first. It is called a new covenant, because it is always new and fresh. It will never grow old or give place to another. It is called a new covenant, because it gives the believer a new record, a new heart, a new nature, and a new spirit. Indeed, for those who are in Christ, those who are partakers of this new covenant, all things are new (2 Corinthians 5:17).

Covenant of Grace

This new, everlasting covenant is a covenant of pure, free, immutable grace in Christ. This is the covenant which gave David hope and confidence on his death bed (2 Samuel 23:5). This new, everlasting covenant is immutable and sure, its blessings are all infallibly secured to God's elect, because this is a one-way covenant. It was made between God the Father, God the Son, and God the Holy Spirit before the worlds were made. In that sense it is a trilateral covenant. However, insofar as we are concerned it is a unilateral covenant. Its blessings are secured by the will of God alone.

The Lord God declared in eternity what he would do for all his people in this gospel day by his free, sovereign, saving grace in Christ: 'I will make with the house of Israel after those days, saith the Lord; I will put my laws into their mind, and write them in their hearts: and I will be to them a God, and they shall be to me a people … I will be merciful to their unrighteousness, and their sins and their iniquities will I remember no more.' (Hebrews 8:10-12). Praise God!

Covenant Promises

In these verses God the Holy Spirit gives us five blessed covenant promises, promises and blessings of grace which the Lord our God declared in eternity. These are promises 'steadfast and sure' to all God's elect; promises of grace flowing freely to chosen sinners, 'according as [God] hath chosen us in [Christ] before the world began' (Ephesians 1:4). This is what the Lord God declared he would do for all his people in this gospel day by his free, sovereign, saving grace in Christ. These are matters as infallibly secure to God's elect as the very throne of God himself.

1. 'I will put my laws in their minds and write them in their hearts'. God's laws here cannot possibly have reference merely to the moral law. We know that because God's moral law is inscribed upon every man's conscience by nature in creation (Romans 2:14-15; 1:18-20).

The laws of God here refer to the commandments of the gospel, all the commands of Christ with respect to repentance, faith and godliness (1 John 3:23-24). Indeed, the whole Word of God is included. Saving grace gives the believer a genuine love for the whole of God's revelation and causes us to cherish it.

These things are written not on tablets of stone, but on every believer's heart and mind. Believers think on the things of God, meditate upon them, love his Word and his way, and walk in the light of his revealed will. 'I love thy law, O Lord!' His commandments are not grievous, but precious to the renewed heart (Psalm 119:97-104; Matthew 11:28-30; 1 John 5:1-4).

2. 'I will be to them their God and they shall be my people'. He who is our God is the God of all creation. He is the God of all men, all angels, and all devils. But this is a promise of special grace, special grace, indeed!

Here God almighty promises that he is the God of his covenant people, just as he is the God and Father of our Lord Jesus (John 17:21; 1 John 1:3). Yes, we who believe on Christ are his people in the sense that all mankind are his people; but this is a promise of grace. It goes far, far beyond man's creature relationship to God. We are the sons of God, whom he loved distinctly and chose in Christ. We are the family of God (Romans 8:14-17; 1 John 3:1-3).

3. They 'all shall know me, from the least to the greatest'. Hebrews 1:1 sheds some light on this. In the Old Testament, God spoke to his people through the prophets and the priests. If a man wanted to know what the Lord had to say, he inquired of the prophet. If he wanted to offer a sacrifice, he went to the priest. That is not the case in this gospel age. Every believer has an unction from the Holy One (1 John 2:20). We all have the mind of Christ (1 Corinthians 2:14-16).

All who are born of God are taught of God; and all who are taught of God are well-taught. They are taught to come to Christ for all things (John 6:44-45). Every believer is a son of God by adoption. Every believer is a student of the Word. Every believer is taught of God. Every believer is a priest to offer sacrifices of prayer and praise. Every believer has the Spirit of God dwelling in him. Every believer has the mind of Christ and discerns all things.

The Lord Jesus today has given his church pastors and teachers that we may grow in grace through the ministry of the Word; but those pastors are not priests. All believers know the Lord, pray to the Lord, and walk with the Lord. In Christ, we are kings and priests unto God (Hebrews 4:14-16; 10:19-22; Revelation 1:4-6).

4. 'I will be merciful to their unrighteousness'. This refers to our sin. All unrighteousness is sin. The phrase tells us that God will forgive our sins (1 John 1:8-10). God will pardon freely those to whom he is reconciled in Christ. This forgiveness of sin is more than an act of mercy. It is an act of justice. Christ has paid for our sins (1 John 2:1,2). When the Lord God forgives sin he is 'faithful and just' in doing so.

5. 'Their sins and iniquities I will remember no more'. What a blessed promise of grace this is! God remembers our sins no more! All our sins of all kinds: original and actual, before conversion and after conversion, God remembers them no more! They are cast into the depths of the sea. They are cast behind his back. They cannot be found ever!

Then, in verse 13, the Holy Spirit tells us one last thing about the old covenant. Learn it and learn it well. That old, carnal, legal covenant is gone forever! 'In that he saith, A new covenant, he hath made the first old. Now that which decayeth and waxeth old is ready to vanish away'.

The establishing of the new covenant meant the abolition of the Levitical covenant. It served its day and purpose; but it is now taken away, never to be used again. As a garment rots and vanishes away, so that old garment of law and works has been put away forever (Galatians 5:1-6). 'Christ is the end of the law!'

> Children of God, O glorious calling!
> Surely His grace will keep us from falling!
> Passing from death to life at His call,
> Blessed salvation, once for all!

'He Hath Made the First Old'

It was never God's intention for sinners to be saved by the observance of the laws and ceremonies given in the Old Testament. Those laws and ceremonies were intended only to serve as types and pictures of Christ to turn us to him. Now that Christ has come, any observance of those laws and ceremonies he fulfilled as our Substitute is worse than ingratitude. It is idolatry!

Removing the First

The opening words of verse 13, 'In that he saith a new covenant', refer us back to verses 7 and 8 and to Jeremiah 31:31, the Old Testament passage being expounded in this chapter. If the first covenant (the law) had been faultless, if sin could have been put away by the observance of the legal statutes given at Sinai, there would have been no need for another. As Paul puts it in Galatians 2:21, 'If righteousness come by the law, then Christ is dead in vain!'

'He hath made the first old'. If the second is new, the first must be old. This is very much the same thing we read in Hebrews 10:9 'He taketh away the first that he may establish the second'. Finding fault with the first covenant, it had to be set aside to make room for the new covenant, the covenant of grace to which it pointed.

Establishing the Second

Once Christ came, the old covenant was out of date; and made old, made old by God's design and purpose. Therefore, it vanished away. Why it is so difficult for people to see this I cannot imagine. Why religious people insist upon trying to mix law and grace is, to me, unfathomable. Why multitudes try to mix the old covenant ceremonies with new covenant ordinances, or old legal precepts with spiritual worship, is baffling.

Perhaps you are thinking, 'How do people try to mix the old and the new?' Those who imagine that sprinkling a little water on a baby's head (a perversion of Christ's ordinance of baptism) brings their child into a covenant relationship with God, are not only guilty of perverting God's ordinance but also of trying to maintain the Jewish law of circumcision. Those who try to enforce sabbatical laws and mix them with the worship of God try to mix law and grace. Those who would make believers live by the rule of the Mosaic law try to mix law and grace.

The scriptures are crystal clear in declaring that the old Mosaic covenant is totally fulfilled and brought to its conclusive end by the gospel. In this gospel age, it is emphatically, the *old* covenant. 'We are not children of the bondwoman (the law), but of the free (the gospel). Standfast therefore in the liberty wherewith Christ hath made us free, and be not entangled again with the yoke of bondage' (Galatians 4:31-5:1).

Gradual, but Sure Dissolution

'Now that which decayeth and waxeth old is ready to vanish away'. This sentence is translated in Young's Literal Translation: 'He hath made the first old, and what doth become old is obsolete and is nigh disappearing'.

The Amplified Bible gives us the exact meaning of verse 13. 'When God speaks of a new [covenant or argument], He makes the first one obsolete (out of use). And what is obsolete (out of use and annulled because of age) is ripe for disappearance and to be dispensed with altogether.'

The dissolution or disappearance of this covenant was both gradual and climactic. It began when the Chaldeans took possession of the land of Canaan and the ark of the covenant, which was a type of Christ. When the Chaldeans stole the ark, the temple was empty, void, and meaningless. The old covenant was waxing old. Both the civil government and the worship of the Jews was, during that time, cast into terrible confusion, exactly as it had been prophesied in Genesis 49:10.

When John the Baptist came, proclaiming 'Behold, the Lamb of God, which taketh away the sin of the world', asserting that the Messiah had come, the Messenger of the covenant promised by Malachi, that his kingdom was being established in the earth; he was declaring to all Israel that the old covenant, the old, legal, ceremonial Mosaic covenant, was vanishing away.

Then, once the Lord Jesus had finished his work, made an end of sin and brought in everlasting righteousness by his obedience and death as our covenant Surety. Once he was risen from the dead, and was exalted to the throne of God as King of kings and Lord of lords, the old covenant was completely, climactically abolished. When, on the Day of Pentecost, he poured out his Spirit upon all flesh, fulfilling Joel's prophecy, God gave testimony that another order was established (John 4:21-26).

Yet, the temple was still standing in Jerusalem. The Jewish order of worship, insofar as the outward symbols of it were concerned, were not yet physically destroyed, as our Lord had prophesied (Matthew 24:1-2). However, at the time the book of Hebrews was written, the time was rapidly approaching when God would destroy even the visible symbols of the old covenant. That is what is described in Hebrews 8:13. 'In that he saith, A new covenant, he hath made the first old. Now that which decayeth and waxeth old is ready to vanish away.'

Jerusalem Destroyed

The destruction of Jerusalem in 70 AD stands as a witness to the truth of Christianity. The Lord Jesus had declared that it would take place (Matthew 24:1-2); and it did. God's people did not fight against Israel in this revolt. In fact, believers suffered in Jerusalem with the unbelieving nation of Israel. As far as Rome was concerned Christianity was just one of Judaism's many sects which they were determined to eliminate. That is why Christians and Jews suffered the horrors of Titus together in the slaughter of 70 AD.

Divine Judgment

The destruction of Jerusalem was not an act of anti-Semitism. Rather it was an act of divine judgment (Mark 12:1-11). The Son of God came in judgment upon that nation (Matthew 24:34; Luke 19:43-44). These things came to pass because the nation of Israel knew not the time of their visitation. They did not recognize the coming of the Messiah. The destruction of Jerusalem was God's testimony that the coming of Christ was, in fact, what the book of Hebrews says it was: The replacement of shadows with the Substance, Christ himself.

One of the early church fathers, Athanasius (b. 373 AD), wrote, 'It is a sign, and an important proof, of the coming of the Word of God, that Jerusalem no longer stands ... For ... when the truth was there, what need was there any more of the shadow? And this was why Jerusalem stood till then namely, that the Jews might be exercised in the types as a preparation for the reality.'

The destruction of Jerusalem and of Judaism was visibly a declaration of that which is verbally declared in the book of Hebrews. God has made the first old. He has taken away the first, that he might establish the second. But what does this mean to us? Basically, it means three things.

1. Shadows Replaced

It means that the shadows of the old covenant have been replaced with the substance, the reality, of the new. The temple and tabernacle, the sacrifices and priesthood, the feasts and laws of the Old Testament were all shadows. They were all types and pictures of the reality in heaven: the Lord Jesus Christ and his work as our High Priest and our Sacrifice. Our focus of worship is heaven. Our object of worship is Christ. The Lord Jesus Christ fulfilled and replaced all the types and shadows of the Old Testament.

2. Heart Worship

The second thing is this. God makes Christ and his work real to his elect personally by the work of the new covenant when he writes his will in our hearts (v. 10). The fact that Christ has come means that shadows are replaced with Reality. Old Testament types have given way to the Original; Christ our Saviour. It means that God almighty invades and occupies the hearts and minds of chosen, redeemed sinners by almighty, irresistible, effectual grace. He overcomes our resistance to the claims of Christ and makes us willing in the day of his power, by writing his will upon our hearts, revealing Christ to us and in us by his Spirit (2 Corinthians 4:4-6). God stamps his revelation upon our hearts and thus makes us willing and eager to trust his darling Son and follow him. He works his grace from the inside out, so that we serve Christ freely, without the constraint and rule of law (2 Corinthians 5:14).

3. God is Merciful

Here is the third meaning of this passage. God is merciful! He 'delighteth in mercy!' He declares, 'I will be merciful to their unrighteousness, and their sins and iniquities will I remember no more' (v. 12). The foundation and basis for all the promises of the new covenant (in verses 10-11) is the finished work of Christ: 'The blood of the everlasting covenant' (Hebrews 13:20). If Christ had not died for our sins, God could not be our God or write the law on our hearts or cause us to know him personally. All this covenant mercy flows freely and unconditionally to chosen sinners through the sin-atoning blood of Christ. This is why our Lord called the wine of the Lord's Supper, 'the new covenant in my blood' (Luke 22:20).

This is what the Holy Spirit means for us to understand. In Jeremiah 31, written five hundred years before Christ came into the world, the Lord God promised that he would do something new. He declared that he would replace shadows with the Substance. That he would powerfully and effectually move into the lives of chosen and redeemed sinners and write his will on our hearts. Thus, we would serve him willingly; love him sincerely; trust him completely, and follow him because we want to.

A Problem

But there was a huge obstacle: our sin. Our separation from God because of our unrighteousness. How can a holy and just God deal with sinners in mercy? How can God be just and yet forgive sin? The answer is that which was promised in the covenant, portrayed in the law, accomplished at Calvary, and explained in the book of Hebrews: Substitution (2 Corinthians 5:21; Romans 3:24-26). Christ bore our sins in his own body when he died (1 Peter 2:24). He took our judgment. He cancelled our debt. That means that our sins are gone. They do not remain in God's mind. He has forgotten them! They were consumed in the death of Christ (v. 12).

God is now free, in his justice, to lavish us with all blessings of grace in the new covenant. He gives us Christ, and all things in him and with him, for our everlasting salvation and enjoyment. He writes his own will, his own heart, on our hearts so that believers are made to love, trust, and follow Christ from the inside out, with freedom and joy.

Christ is the Goal, the Reality, the Substance. When Jerusalem fell to the Romans in 70 AD, and the temple was burned, the sacrifices ceased, the priesthood came to an end, and the law was brought to its conclusion. When the sceptre departed from Judah (Genesis 49:10), God said to the world, 'Shiloh has come!'

Christianity is woven into history. It is not a mere set of ideas. It is about a person, the Lord Jesus Christ, who came into history, died and rose again. It is about God who both rules and intervenes in history to bear witness to his Son, Jesus Christ. The destruction of the old Jewish way of life and worship tells the world that Jesus the Messiah, the Son of God, has come. That he has forever put and end to the old covenant and has brought in a new covenant.

Judaism Destroyed

'In that he saith, A new covenant, he hath made the first old. Now that which decayeth and waxeth old is ready to vanish away.' (Hebrews 8:13)

This is one of the most important, but least understood texts in the book of Hebrews. When he established the new covenant, the Lord God made the old, Levitical, legal, ceremonial covenant obsolete. It served its day and its purpose by the will of God; but that old covenant and all that pertained to it is now dissolved. It is no longer of any use to anyone for any purpose. Like an old, tattered garment, it has been laid aside, never to be used again (Galatians 5:1-6).

Spiritual Worship

All true worship is spiritual, heart worship. We are no longer under the law. We no longer live under that carnal, legal covenant (Colossians 2:6-23; Philippians 3:3). All who know God worship him in spirit and in truth, trusting Christ alone for righteousness, and place no confidence in the flesh.

The Destruction of the Old

The coming of Jesus the Messiah meant the dissolution of Judaism. Hebrews 8:13 was more than a prediction. It was an inspired prophecy of the destruction of Jerusalem, the temple at Jerusalem, and of Judaism. For those people whose entire way of life was defined by this first covenant, this prophecy must have been shocking, at the very least. The Jews understood exactly what the claims of Christ meant. I do not suggest that they believed him. Obviously, they did not. But they understood that his claims and his doctrine meant the complete dissolution of Judaism (John 8:59; 10:30-34; 11:47-54).

In the Old Testament God commanded the Jews to maintain an elaborate system of sacrifices, priestly services, feasts and rituals and required them to live under a rigid legal system; a system of law that covered every aspect of their lives (political, religious, moral, and dietary). That entire legal system pointed to and typified the Lord Jesus Christ and the work he would perform for the redemption of his people. These things typically, symbolically, and ceremonially defined the gospel and pointed to One by whose coming they must and would be fulfilled.

The gospel of Christ threatened the very core of Jewish life and religion. Jesus of Nazareth declared Judaism null and void by declaring that the Messiah had come, and that he was himself the Christ, who is God the Son. The vast majority of the people rejected his claim and despised him, his gospel and his people. That hatred of God resulted in the crucifixion of the Lord of Glory and the persecution of his disciples.

The claims of the Christ raised a huge question for the Jewish people as a whole. What would become of their way of life? This new faith was incredibly radical. For example, in Acts 6 Stephen proved, irresistibly, by scripture and history, that the claims of Christ were true, and thus, that the gospel of Christ is true. To stop him, false witnesses were brought in. And what is their charge? They claimed that Stephen spoke against Jerusalem, the temple, and the law (Acts 6:13-14).

The Threat of Christianity

There you have the meaning of Christianity, as far as the Jews were concerned. It meant the destruction of their 'church', indeed, of their entire way of life, the vanishing away of the first covenant. They sensed it keenly when Stephen, as they perceived his words, spoke against Jerusalem and the law. They believed that Christianity threatened the existence of the temple itself and of Judaism; and it did. If the temple fell, then what would become of all the customs and traditions they cherished? What would become of their religion? It had to be utterly annihilated. The old had to vanish if it were to be replaced by the new. Few today seem to understand this; but the Jews of that day understood it clearly. Therefore they stoned Stephen to death. They had reason to be afraid. Not only had the Lord Jesus actually said that the temple would be destroyed, he had predicted the entire destruction of Jerusalem (Luke 19:43-44).

The Cause of Persecution

Nothing stirs up violence like fear; and the Jews had reason to fear Christ, his followers, and the gospel they preached. They despised the Word of God, refused to submit to the righteousness of God in Christ, and clung tenaciously to their legal religion, ritualism, and personal righteousness, as do all man-centred systems of free-will, works religion today.

Though the followers of Christ are meek and peaceful people, people who would rather die than live by the sword, nevertheless at the very heart of our faith is the implicit end of the Jewish way of life, and of all other systems of works religion. Nothing enrages legalists like a threat to their refuge of lies, and the denial of their personal righteousness. It was this perceived (and very real) threat that provoked the Jews to crucify the Lord Jesus Christ and persecute his church mercilessly. It is still this threat that stirs the fears of religious people to this day, enrages them, and inspires the persecution of God's church in every community where the gospel of God's free grace in Christ is preached.

The problem is not that men and women do not understand what we preach. The problem is that they do. They understand that to embrace the gospel, they must count all their former religion dung. They understand that if they embrace the grace of God, they must repent of their dead works, turning from all their efforts to establish their own righteousness.

They understand that if they trust Christ, they must cease to trust themselves.

Just as the Jews' priesthood, animal sacrifices, carnal ordinances, legal hopes, and temple were utterly abolished by Christ; so when Christ comes in saving power into the hearts of chosen sinners, all their former way of life, all their former hope is utterly abolished; never to rise again.

Then verily the first covenant had also ordinances of divine service, and a worldly sanctuary. For there was a tabernacle made; the first, wherein was the candlestick, and the table, and the showbread; which is called the sanctuary. And after the second veil, the tabernacle which is called the Holiest of all; Which had the golden censer, and the ark of the covenant overlaid round about with gold, wherein was the golden pot that had manna, and Aaron's rod that budded, and the tables of the covenant; And over it the cherubims of glory shadowing the mercyseat; of which we cannot now speak particularly. Now when these things were thus ordained, the priests went always into the first tabernacle, accomplishing the service *of God*. But into the second *went* the high priest alone once every year, not without blood, which he offered for himself, and *for* the errors of the people: The Holy Ghost this signifying, that the way into the holiest of all was not yet made manifest, while as the first tabernacle was yet standing: Which *was* a figure for the time then present, in which were offered both gifts and sacrifices, that could not make him that did the service perfect, as pertaining to the conscience; *Which stood* only in meats and drinks, and divers washings, and carnal ordinances, imposed *on them* until the time of reformation. But Christ being come an high priest of good things to come, by a greater and more perfect tabernacle, not made with hands, that is to say, not of this building; Neither by the blood of goats and calves, but by his own blood he entered in once into the holy place, having obtained eternal redemption *for us*. For if the blood of bulls and of goats, and the ashes of an heifer sprinkling the unclean, sanctifieth to the purifying of the flesh: How much more shall the blood of Christ, who through the eternal Spirit offered himself without spot to God, purge your conscience from dead works to serve the living God?

Hebrews 9:1-14

Chapter 24

Read: Hebrews 9:1-14

The Ark of the Covenant

The purpose of the Holy Spirit in this chapter is to demonstrate three things. (1) Christ is pre-eminent over the Old Testament tabernacle, its furniture, priesthood and sacrifices. Those Old Testament types were all completely and perfectly fulfilled by our Saviour. (2) That the Old Testament sacrifices and services of the tabernacle had no redeeming, saving efficacy (Hebrews 10:1-4). The Lord Jesus Christ alone is our sin-atoning High Priest and Sacrifice (Hebrews 10:5-14). (3) All the Levitical ceremonies, sacrifices, and services of the first covenant have come to their appointed end (Hebrews 10:9; Romans 10:4).

Christ Pictured

The most sacred of all things in the Jewish worship of the Old Testament was the Ark of the Covenant. Hebrews 9:1-5 describes the tabernacle, the ark, and those things which were in the ark: the golden pot that had manna, Aaron's rod that budded, the tables of the covenant, the cherubims of glory, and the mercy seat.

We have reason to thank God that no one has ever found that ark! If anyone were to find it, foolish men and women would make an idol of it, make pagan pilgrimages to the 'holy land' to see it, and worship it. But in its day, under the ceremonial, typical religious service of the Old Testament, the Ark of the Covenant was one of those 'ordinances of divine service' which beautifully typified and pictured the Lord Jesus Christ and our redemption by him.

All the 'ordinances of divine service', all the rites and ceremonies, and the 'worldly sanctuary' itself, the tabernacle, were types of Christ. We can never understand the Old Testament scriptures until we see that everything in the Old Testament scriptures represents, points to, and pictures Christ, our Substitute (Luke 24:27, 44-45).

Christ Pre-eminent

In these opening verse of Hebrews 9 the Holy Spirit uses the tabernacle and the furniture in it to show us the excellence, pre-eminence, and glory of Christ. The tabernacle portrayed Christ in that it was glorious within, though very humble without. The brazen altar was that place where our Lord's sufferings and death were set forth. The laver spoke of Christ our Fountain, opened for cleansing. The candlestick pictured Christ as the Light of the world. The table of showbread represented Christ as the Bread of Life. The altar of incense portrayed the Lord Jesus Christ as our Intercessor. The veil was typical of Christ the Door, the Way, whereby sinners must come to God. The Ark of the Covenant spoke of Christ as our Reconciliation.

The Ark of the Covenant is a beautiful type of Christ. It was made out of shittim wood, overlaid on the inside and the outside with pure gold, representing both the incorruptible humanity and glorious deity of our Saviour. The ark was the symbol of God's holiness, power, and glory. It was carried about from place to place upon the shoulders of the priests by staves, fitted into rings attached to the ark. Even so, Christ is carried throughout the world upon the shoulders of chosen men, through the preaching of the gospel.

Redemption Obtained

How can men and women who know they are guilty sinners, having all their lives wilfully and consistently broken God's law in thought, word, and deed; who know their own hearts to be a fountain of defilement, and who are in action and attitude rebels; how can such men and women approach the Holy Lord God with confidence, peace, and assurance of acceptance? That is a huge question. But the answer to that question is given plainly and clearly in Hebrews 9:1-14.

The Tabernacle

In verses 1-7 we are given a brief description of the ordinances of divine worship in the Old Testament. That typical, ceremonial dispensation had a tabernacle (a temporary place of worship) made according to the pattern God showed Moses in the mount. It was an earthly tabernacle, and the rules and regulations for sacrifice and worship were carnal ordinances (Hebrews 9:10). The tabernacle was forty-five feet long, fifteen feet wide, and fifteen feet high. It had two sections separated by a heavy veil.

In the first section, called 'the holy place', there were three pieces of furniture. (1) The table of showbread was a wooden table overlaid with gold, picturing both the humanity and deity of Christ. The bread (twelve loaves) represented Christ, the Bread of life. (2) The golden lamp stand portrayed our Lord Jesus Christ as the Light of the world. It was made of pure gold, representing our Lord's deity. There were seven candles in the lamp stand, portraying the perfection of his being and the completeness of his revelation. (3) The altar of incense (Exodus 30:1,6-9), with its continual, sweet burning incense before the veil, typified Christ's intercession as our great Advocate and High Priest before the Father.

The second section of the tabernacle was called 'the holiest of all'. In that room there was one piece of furniture with two parts. That one piece of furniture was the ark of the covenant, the most important thing in the Jewish worship in the Old Testament. It was made of wood covered with pure gold, and contained the tables of the law, Aaron's rod that budded, and the golden pot of manna. The mercy-seat was a solid lid of pure gold. It completely covered the ark and the tables of God's broken law, which were in it. The mercy-seat, the place of atonement and propitiation, was overshadowed by the cherubims of glory (Romans 3:24-26).

The Sacrifices

In verses 6 and 7 the sacrifices, required by God's law in the Old Testament are described. The common priests went every day into the holy place, the first tabernacle, every morning and every evening, accomplishing the service of God. None of the common priests were allowed to go beyond the veil into the holiest of all. The high priest alone was allowed to enter in behind the veil. He went in once every year, on the day of atonement, with the blood of the paschal lamb, and sprinkled the blood of the lamb on the mercy-seat covering the broken law (Exodus 30:20; Leviticus 16:15-17).

The Meaning

These things may seem strange to us. Many look at these things and say, 'Well, that has no meaning for us today'. What a tragic mistake! In verses 8-10 the Holy Spirit tells us that these divinely ordained ordinances signified the necessity of Christ's accomplishments at Calvary. The Holy Spirit used those ordinances to declare that the way to God was not yet revealed (Hebrews 10:18-20). The tabernacle, its priesthood, and its services were only symbols, types, and pictures of Christ and the accomplishment of redemption by him. Those sacrifices and services could never take away sin (Hebrews 10:1-4). All the carnal ordinances and legal services of the Old Testament were imposed upon the children of Israel until the coming of Christ, who put an end to them by fulfilling them.

Redemption Accomplished

In verses 11-14 the Holy Spirit tells us that Christ, our great High Priest, our sin-atoning Substitute, by the sacrifice of himself, has actually accomplished and obtained eternal redemption for God's elect by the infinite merit and efficacy of his shed blood.

Verses 11-12 declare the efficacy of Christ's shed blood. The Lord Jesus Christ has, by the sacrifice of himself, fully satisfied the law and justice of God, and has thereby obtained eternal redemption for us. At God's appointed time Christ came, made of a woman, made under the law, to redeem and save his people (Galatians 4:4,5). He came to bring the good things of everlasting salvation and ultimate glory to God's elect (Ephesians 1:3-6). He dwelt (tabernacled) among men as a man. In him men meet God, and in him God deals with men. He is our Representative, our wisdom, righteousness, sanctification, and redemption (1 Corinthians 1:30). He died in our room and stead (2 Corinthians 5:21). By the merit of his blood, our great High Priest entered into the true holy place, having obtained eternal redemption for us. By his one offering the Lord Jesus Christ perfected forever all who were sanctified; all those set apart by God for himself in eternal election (Hebrews 10:11-14). Now, because Christ has made us priests, believing sinners can come boldly before the very throne of grace (Hebrews 4:14-16; 10:19-22; Luke 23:45).

Not only is his blood efficacious with God, Christ's blood is efficacious to purge the consciences of believing sinners, when applied to our hearts by the Holy Spirit (vv. 13-14). When the holy Lord God looks on the blood of Christ, he says, 'ENOUGH'. When the believing sinner looks on that same blood, his conscience says, 'ENOUGH!' Thus, redemption was obtained. Thus redemption is applied!

Inside the Ark

Come into 'the Holiest of all', by the 'golden censer' of our Saviour's merits, asking God to show you Christ our Ark as he was portrayed in that Old Testament type. What can be found in the ark? Let us do by faith what no mortal man could ever do in those days of types and shadows. Let us lift up the mercy-seat and look inside the ark. Remember, the ark was but a picture of the Lord Jesus Christ. What do we see in the ark? We see the two tables of the law of God, which we have broken by our sins, covered by the mercy-seat on which the blood of atonement was sprinkled; thus, our sins are under the blood (Leviticus 16:15; Hebrews 12:24; 1 Peter 1:2).

God's Purpose

Those broken tables of the law, under the blood, represent God's purpose of grace. The law was written upon tables of stone, representing both the hardness of our hearts and the inflexibility of God's law. The law represents our curse and condemnation by reason of sin. The tables of God's broken law were always kept in the ark, under the mercy-seat (Exodus 25:16, 21), representing perfect redemption by Christ. That perfect redemption of his elect is the purpose of God (Romans 8:28-31). The law of God, being perfectly satisfied by Christ, now cries as strongly for our salvation as does the grace of God. We are, in Christ, free from the law, because the law's demands have been fully met for us by Christ's obedience and blood.

God's Power

Look again, there is something else inside the ark. There is Aaron's rod that budded. That rod represents God's power. Aaron's rod that budded portrayed the gospel of Christ, the Man whom God has chosen (Numbers 17:1-5, 8). By Aaron's rod the serpents of false religion were swallowed up, representing the triumph of the gospel of Christ, which is the power of God unto salvation; before which the Dagon's of idolatry must fall (Exodus 7:8-12; 1 Samuel 5:1-4; Romans 1:16-17). It was this same rod in the hand of Moses, representing God's holy law, that smote the rock from which living water flowed; and that Rock was Christ, from whom the water of life flows out to sinners (Exodus 17:5-6; 1 Corinthians 10:1-4).

God's Provision

There is one more thing inside the ark, the golden pot that had manna. That is a picture of Christ, God's Provision (Exodus 16:33-34). It was a golden pot, portraying the richness of God's free grace in Christ. It was a big pot, holding an omer of manna; and Christ is a great Saviour, a bounteous store of mercy and grace! This golden pot had manna, the bread of heaven, portraying Christ, the Bread of Life. All God's provision for sinners is in Christ Jesus. His name is Jehovah-jireh, the Lord will provide (Ephesians 1:3). All the provisions of grace, of providence, and of eternity are in Christ! Come to the Ark Christ Jesus. The way is open.

All who come to God by Christ are forever saved. All we need, all God requires, all that heaven can bestow is in Christ, the Ark. Come to the Ark!

The Messengers of the Mercy-Seat

God's preachers are not priests. We detest idolatrous priestcraft, be it Roman, Anglican, or Mormon. God's preachers are his angels; his messengers of mercy and grace to his people in this world; they ought to be treated as such (Isaiah 52:7). Like the cherubim of glory shadowing the mercy-seat, the preacher's eyes are always towards the mercy-seat; they look to the blood of Christ's atoning sacrifice (Hebrews 9:12). Their message is the message of sins forgiven by the blood atonement, and the glory of God is revealed by the message they proclaim.

And for this cause he is the mediator of the new testament, that by means of death, for the redemption of the transgressions *that were* under the first testament, they which are called might receive the promise of eternal inheritance. For where a testament *is*, there must also of necessity be the death of the testator. For a testament *is* of force after men are dead: otherwise it is of no strength at all while the testator liveth. Whereupon neither the first *testament* was dedicated without blood. For when Moses had spoken every precept to all the people according to the law, he took the blood of calves and of goats, with water, and scarlet wool, and hyssop, and sprinkled both the book, and all the people, Saying, This *is* the blood of the testament which God hath enjoined unto you. Moreover he sprinkled with blood both the tabernacle, and all the vessels of the ministry. And almost all things are by the law purged with blood; and without shedding of blood is no remission. *It was* therefore necessary that the patterns of things in the heavens should be purified with these; but the heavenly things themselves with better sacrifices than these. For Christ is not entered into the holy places made with hands, *which are* the figures of the true; but into heaven itself, now to appear in the presence of God for us: Nor yet that he should offer himself often, as the high priest entereth into the holy place every year with blood of others; For then must he often have suffered since the foundation of the world: but now once in the end of the world hath he appeared to put away sin by the sacrifice of himself. And as it is appointed unto men once to die, but after this the judgment: So Christ was once offered to bear the sins of many; and unto them that look for him shall he appear the second time without sin unto salvation.

Hebrews 9:15-28

Chapter 25

Read: Hebrews 9:15-28

The Mercy-Seat

If we could go behind the veil with the High Priest on the day of atonement, into the holy of holies, the very first thing that would strike our eyes would be 'the cherubim of glory shadowing the mercy-seat' but we would not look long at the cherubim. Their eyes, their faces, their wings direct our attention away from themselves to the mercy-seat.

Christ Our Propitiation

The mercy-seat represented Christ, God's propitiation, the propitiation for our sins (Exodus 25:17, 21-22; 1 John 2:1-2; 4:9-10; Romans 3:24-26). In fact the word translated 'propitiation' elsewhere in the New Testament is the same word that is translated 'mercy-seat' in Hebrews 9:5.

The Day of Atonement

In the Old Testament, on the Day of Atonement, Aaron took the blood of the paschal lamb behind the veil, into the holy of holies, and sprinkled the blood on the mercy-seat; making ceremonial atonement for the sins of the people of Israel. The holy Lord God promised to meet his people there upon the blood-sprinkled mercy-seat, in peace, forgiveness, and reconciliation.

That ceremonial service was a beautiful, instructive picture of the obtaining of eternal redemption for God's elect by Christ, our great High Priest: 'By his own blood (by the merit of his blood) he entered in once into the holy place, having obtained eternal redemption for us.' The mercy-seat of the Old Testament was typically what Christ is in reality: the place of substitution, sacrifice, satisfaction, atonement, reconciliation, forgiveness, peace and worship.

The Publican

The Publican in Luke 18 cried, 'God, be merciful to me, a sinner.' He understood exactly what was portrayed in the Old Testament mercy-seat and it is reflected in his prayer. He prayed, 'God, look on the blood upon the mercy-seat, the blood covering your holy law, which I have broken, and be propitious to me, the sinner, forgiving my sin for Christ's sake.'

God's Presence

Standing in the holiest of all with Christ, our Aaron, our great High Priest, suddenly, we realize that we are standing before the mercy-seat, the symbol of God's presence. With blood upon the mercy-seat, covering the broken tables of the law, there we see the glory of God in the pardon of sin by the sacrifice of Christ (Leviticus 9:23-24; Isaiah 6:1-6; Psalm 85:9-11). The holy Lord God not only meets us upon the mercy-seat; in Christ, he abides with us. No matter where we are if we are in Christ, the Lord is there. Our lives are hid with Christ in God (Isaiah 43:1-2; Colossians 3:3).

Inside The Ark

The Word of God has a scarlet thread running through it, like the cord Rahab hung out of her window. That scarlet thread by which the 66 books of inspiration are bound together unifies everything written upon the pages of scripture. It is the precious blood of Christ.

The scriptures speak constantly about the blood. It is written in the books of the law, 'The life of the flesh is in the blood.' God told Moses, 'The blood shall be to you for a token'. He said, 'When I see the blood, I will pass over you.' When the high priest went into the holy of holies on the Day of Atonement, he went in with blood. No man can come to God without blood atonement.

When our Lord instituted the Lord's Supper, he took the cup of wine, held it before his disciples and said, 'This is the blood of the New Testament, shed for many for the remission of sins.' In Hebrews 9:22, we read, 'Without shedding of blood is no remission.' That makes the blood a matter of immense, infinite importance.

These days, it is common for preachers, churches, theologians, and hymn writers to say as little as possible about the blood. We have become so educated, refined, and sophisticated that talking about blood is considered improper, gross, and rude. But it is still true that 'without shedding of blood is no remission.' Nothing is more important and nothing more precious than the blood of Christ (Hebrews 9:12; 1 Peter 1:18-21). The shedding of his precious blood was and is absolutely essential to the saving of our souls. Let us ever cherish the blood of Christ as that which is precious above all things.

Effectual Blood

The blood of bulls and goats could never take away sin (Hebrews 10:4). That was never God's purpose. The animal sacrifices were given as types and pictures to illustrate and point to the great, sin-atoning sacrifice of our Lord Jesus Christ. However those Old Testament sacrifices did purify the people in an external, ceremonial way. How much more shall the blood of Christ, God's own dear Son, spotless, sinless blood of infinite value offered to God by the Holy Spirit, cleanse us, purify our souls, and deliver us from seeking acceptance through our dead works! The blood of Christ is effectual. It has satisfied the wrath and justice of God. By it our sins have been put away. Therefore the believer's conscience condemns him no more (Romans 8:1, 33-34; 1 John 1:7-10; 3:5).

The Cause

There was a cause, a necessity for the great sacrifice of Christ. The cause was just this: God's covenant grace could not come to sinful men without blood atonement. We could not be made righteous apart from the sacrifice of God's own Son in our room and stead at Calvary (Galatians 2:21; 3:21).

Here the Holy Spirit shows us that Old Testament believers were redeemed by the death of Christ in the same way we are, and for the same reasons. Justice must be satisfied before mercy can be given; and the only One by whom redemption could come is the God-man Mediator, Christ Jesus, of whom all the prophets spoke (Acts 10:43). The promise of eternal inheritance was made to God's elect in and by Christ, the Mediator of the covenant (testament) (1 Corinthians 10:4; Luke 24:44-47).

However, that promise could not come without the death of Christ, the Testator, the Mediator of the covenant. Wherever there is a testament, there must be the death of the testator. No claim can be made by the heirs of the testament until the testator dies (John 3:14-16; Romans 3:19-26). There was an absolute necessity for the death of God's Son as our Substitute and the Testator of the covenant. Christ must suffer and die if we are to be redeemed (1 Peter 1:18-21).

Promise Received

Those who are called receive by faith the promise of eternal salvation, our inheritance of grace in Christ (v. 15). Our faith does not in any way secure the inheritance. It simply receives what God our Father secured for us by his purpose and promise in eternity and Christ secured for us by his death. In fact, faith in Christ is itself a part of the inheritance. We believe because God the Holy Spirit, 'the Blessing' of the covenant has been sent into our hearts in saving power and grace (Galatians 3:13-14; 4:6).

The very heart of the gospel is the finished work of Christ at Calvary: unconditional, particular, and efficacious. We believe, according to holy scripture, that the sin-atoning death of our Lord Jesus Christ is of infinite merit, value and efficacy, and that the blessings and benefits of our Saviour's great sacrifice are limited by the purpose of God to his elect. I know that this glorious gospel doctrine is offensive to unbelieving men, offensive to all who wish to make man a co-Saviour with Christ; but that only demonstrates the fact that 'the offence of the cross' has not ceased.

No Blood, No Remission

God almighty will not and cannot forgive sin without blood atonement. He cannot do so because he is holy, just and true. He has sworn, 'The soul that sinneth, it shall die.' His justice must be satisfied; and the only way God's holy, infinite justice could ever be satisfied is by the righteous obedience and sin-atoning death of his own dear Son, the God-man, our Saviour, the Lord Jesus Christ.

Remission Pictured

Under the Mosaic law virtually everything relating to the worship of God was ceremonially sanctified and purged of corruption by blood. The reason for this is clearly stated in Hebrews 9:22-23. 'Almost all things are by the law purged with blood; and without shedding of blood is no remission. It was therefore necessary that the patterns of things in the heavens should be purified with these.'

When Moses gave the pattern for the tabernacle and its services, he took the blood and water[1] and sprinkled the book, the people, the tabernacle and all the vessels used in the worship of God. Almost all things were purified by means of blood (Leviticus 17:11). Other things were ceremonially purified by water and fire; but without the shedding of blood there was no forgiveness of sin! There is no example of pardon and

---

[1] The blood and water typified the blood and water which flowed from our Lord's pierced side, and our justification and sanctification by his blood.

forgiveness without blood. The Old Testament sacrifices and ceremonies as well as the very fact that Christ's blood has been shed makes it foolish to suppose that pardon might be had without it (1 Corinthians 5:7; Galatians 2:19-21).

Fulfilling the types and patterns of heavenly things given in those Old Testament symbols (Hebrews 8:5; 9:23), the Lord Jesus Christ, our great High Priest, entered into heaven. There he appears before the holy Lord God as the Representative and Mediator of God's elect, the true, spiritual Israel, 'the Israel of God'. Having fully satisfied the law; he atoned for our sins with his blood. He makes intercession for us in the holy place, in heaven itself, presenting the infinite merits of his blood and righteousness perpetually (1 John 2:1-2).

Remission Performed

Remission was only pictured in those Old Testament ceremonies. It was actually, once and forever performed and accomplished by the sacrifice of Christ at Calvary.

The Lord Jesus, our great God-man Mediator and High Priest, did not enter into an earthly, material holy place, but into heaven itself. Yonder, seated upon the throne of God is a Man, the God-man, Christ Jesus. He perpetually appears in the presence of God on our behalf, interceding for us, representing us, possessing all things as our Forerunner.

His one great, infinitely meritorious sacrifice for our sins was and is enough (Hebrews 10:11-14). Because his blood is of infinite merit, it is infinitely effectual. By his one sacrifice for all the sins of all his people, he put them away forever (Isaiah 53:4-6; Hebrews 10:17-18).

Be sure you understand the doctrine of holy scripture. The Son of God did not die merely to make it possible for sins to be put away. He did not merely provide a way for sins to be put away. He has, by the sacrifice of himself, put away all the sins of God's elect which were imputed to him. He has put our sins away fully and forever (Romans 4:8).

Blessed Hope

As men die just once and face judgment but once, so Christ was once offered to bear the sins of many, to bear the sins of God's elect. They are now fully paid for and forever put away. It is not possible for the sins he put away to be imputed to his people again. Justice will not allow it.

Let every ransomed sinner rejoice in this fact: Christ has put away our sins. We met God in judgment at Calvary in the person of our Substitute. God punished us in him for all our sins to the full satisfaction of his holy justice. Now, we have every reason to look forward to Christ's coming.

Unto all them who believe on him and look for him, he will appear without sin unto eternal glory (Romans 8:1-4, 33-39). This is blessed hope, indeed!

Either God rules, or he is ruled. Either he is in control, or he is controlled. Either he is absolutely and universally over all things at all times, or there is something, somewhere that is bigger, better and sovereign over him.

Once Only, Once Enough!

In Hebrews 9:24-28 the Spirit of God tells us of three great appearances of our Saviour. He appeared once in the world to put away sin by the sacrifice of himself. This is our atonement (v. 26). In verse 24 we are told that our great Saviour now appears 'in the presence of God for us' as our Advocate. This is our assurance (1 John 2:1-2). In verse 28 the inspired writer declares that the Lord Jesus Christ shall appear to them that look for him the second time 'without sin unto salvation'. That will be our advancement. What an advancement it will be! 'Now once in the end of the world hath he appeared to put away sin by the sacrifice of himself.'

Our great Redeemer, the Son of God, came into this world in human flesh to put away sin by the sacrifice of himself. He came but once. He died but once. He made but one great sacrifice for sin. Once was enough!

A Horribly Evil Thing

What a horribly evil thing sin must be! Sin is rebellion against God. Sin is treason against God's throne. Sin is man's attempt to defile the Holy One. Sin is the expression of fallen man's enmity against God, the display of our natural heart hatred of God. Sin is that which makes us obnoxious to the holy Lord God. Sin is the defilement of our race. Sin has brought us under the curse of God's holy law. Sin has put us under the sentence of death, eternal death. Sin shuts the door of hope upon all the human race.

No Easy Task

It is not easy for sin to be put away. No carnal sacrifice can put away sin. No work of man can put away one sin. No amount of repentance can put away sin. Not even our faith can put away sin. Toplady knew this:

> Not the labours of my hands
> Can fulfil Thy law's demands;
> Could my zeal no respite know,
> Could my tears forever flow,
> All for sin could not atone;
> Thou must save, and Thou alone!

Even God himself cannot, in his pure, absolute character as God, put away sin. If sin is to be put away, it must be put away by the sin-atoning death and substitutionary sacrifice of the incarnate God, the God-man Mediator, the Lord Jesus Christ. But his sacrifice was enough. He died but once; but once was enough! That is the meaning of these words: 'Now once in the end of the world hath he appeared to put away sin by the sacrifice of himself.'

Christ Did It

Christ's sufferings and death for sin are of infinite value, merit, and efficacy. Therefore, he suffered for sin only once. He appeared once, in the end of the world to put away sin; and he has done it!

Our Lord Jesus Christ put away the guilt of sin by his atoning sacrifice. He put away the punishment of it by his sufferings and death as our Substitute. The incarnate Son of God put away the penalty of the law by his satisfaction of divine justice. He put away the consequences of sin by his obedience unto death. He puts away the dominion of sin in his people by the power of his grace in the new birth. He puts away the filth of sin by his sanctifying grace. And he shall put away the very being of sin in resurrection glory.

This work of putting away sin was accomplished by him bearing our sin in his own body upon the cursed tree. He carried it and took it away. This is what was pictured in the Old Testament type of the scapegoat (Leviticus 16:7-10, 15, 21-22).

The Lord Jesus has removed sin from us as far as the east is from the west, by finishing and making an end of it. He disannulled and abolished it, insofar as the law and justice of God is concerned. When he paid our debt, he cancelled it in one day, by his one sacrifice. In one great day, the whole work was done (Zechariah 3:9). Our sins, being forever, put away by the sacrifice of Christ, shall never be found and can never be charged to us again (Jeremiah 50:20; Romans 4:8).

> My sin, (O the bliss of this glorious thought!)
> My sin, not in part, but the whole,
> Is nailed to His cross, and I bear it no more.
> Praise the Lord! It is well with my soul!

'After This The Judgment'

This text speaks of death. We naturally shun the subject of death. We do not like to think about it; but we should. 'It is better to go to the house of mourning, than to go to the house of feasting: for that is the end of all men; and the living will lay it to his heart. Sorrow is better than laughter: for by the sadness of the countenance the heart is made better. The heart of the wise is in the house of mourning' (Ecclesiastes 7:2-4).

'It is appointed unto men once to die'. This sentence speaks particularly of physical death, the death of the body, not spiritual and eternal death. Even this physical death of the body is the wages of sin.

Divine Appointment

The all-wise God has from eternity appointed and decreed the length of every man's life and the time, place, and means of every man's death. Our days can neither be lengthened nor shortened.

Some imagine that there is a contradiction here because we are plainly told that both Enoch and Elijah escaped death and that some will be translated into heaven at the second advent of Christ. But all undergo that change which is equivalent to death. For the believer, death is but release from this body of sin. That is what Enoch and Elijah experienced. That is what the saints living at the time of Christ's second advent will experience. And that is what our departed friends have experienced. The believer's death is not death at all, but release from this body (John 11:25-26). Blessed release!

For the believer death is to be experienced but once! On those who are born of God, those who are partakers of the first resurrection, the second death shall have no power (Revelation 20:6, 11-15).

Blessed Comfort

It is the statute law of heaven for men to die, and that but once. So our Lord Jesus died once, only once. He will die no more. This is our souls' great comfort. Though we must die the first death, we shall not be hurt of the second death, because Christ died for us, enduring all the penalty of God's holy law as our Substitute to the full satisfaction of justice.

You who are yet without Christ have no such consolation. The Lord God has appointed the day and place of your death as well. Soon, you must meet God; but for you, the death of your body will be but the beginning of everlasting torment. Oh, may God be pleased to grant you faith in Christ. If you die without Christ, you shall be forever damned!

Urgency

Since our days in this world are numbered by our God let us be diligent in the days he has given us, serving him with meekness and fear. The day of our departure is certain to God, though unknown to us. None of us know how much time we have left in this world. Yet, this is certain: No one has time to spare! The very thought of this ought to make rebels tremble. Oh, be wise! 'Seek ye the Lord while he may be found! Call ye upon him while he is near!' 'Prepare to meet thy God!'

Every believer should seek wisdom and grace to live every day as though he was certain it would be his last. Whatever it is that we have to do for the glory of Christ, the furtherance of the gospel, the increase of God's kingdom, and the good of men's souls, let us do it today! We ought to live every day with a sense of urgency. Life is urgent, for 'time is short!' We would be wise to pray with Moses, 'Teach us,' O Lord, 'to number our days, that we may apply our hearts unto wisdom.'

Death

The Lord God has appointed the day of our death; but death does not put an end to our existence. We are all men and women with living, undying, immortal souls. We will spend eternity somewhere. Either we will spend eternity with Christ, his holy angels, and all the saints of God, in the beauty, bliss, and glory of heaven; or we will spend eternity in hell, with the damned, in the everlasting torments of God's offended justice.

Judgment

There is also a day of judgment appointed by God. There shall be, in the last day, a great, general resurrection and judgment. We must all appear before the great white throne judgment. In that great day Christ will be the Judge. I do not doubt that there is a judgment which all experience immediately after death, by which, the souls of men are condemned to their proper state of bliss in glory or banishment in hell. But there is also that final, eternal judgment, at which all must stand to be either declared holy or filthy, blessed or condemned. This great day has been appointed by God from eternity. How will it be for you in that day? Will you stand before the bar of God in the linen white, blood washed robe of perfect righteousness in Christ, holy and unblameable; or will you be found in the filthy rags of your own self-righteousness? (Revelation 22:11-12). There is a day coming in which God shall judge all men. Every man will be judged according to exact truth, righteousness, and justice. 'It is appointed unto men once to die, but after this the judgment' (Hebrews 9:27).

The Standard

The standard by which we shall be judged is the holy law of God himself. We shall be judged according to the books of God, in which are recorded all our earthly thoughts, words, and deeds (2 Corinthians 5:10-11; Revelation 20:11-12; Matthew 25:31-46).

In that great and terrible day of the Lord, everyone will receive exactly what is justly due to him. None will be punished who do not deserve to be punished. None will be received into heaven's eternal glory who do not deserve to enter in. Those who are found guilty of any sin, or infraction of God's holy law, shall be cast into hell. Those who are perfectly holy, holy as God himself, shall enter into heaven (Psalm 24:3-4; Revelation 21:27; 22:11).

In that day the Judge of all the earth, who must do right, will do right. He who sits upon the great white throne will not show any leniency, partiality, or favouritism. He will not bend his law. At the bar of God there will be no mercy and no grace. The judgment seat is not a place of mercy. It is a place of strict, unbending, unwavering, immutable justice. Only the facts will be considered when we stand before God. Guilty or not guilty, righteous or unrighteous, holy or unholy, these will be the only matters of consideration in that day. 'Evil pursueth sinners: but to the righteous good shall be repayed' (Proverbs 13:21). 'The soul that sinneth, it shall die' (Ezekiel 18:20). He that 'hath done that which is lawful and right shall surely live' (Ezekiel 33:16). God will by no means clear the guilty. Neither will he punish the righteous.

Our Only Hope

In the light of these facts, most plainly set forth in the Word of God, it is obvious that the only hope any sinner has of eternal salvation and acceptance with God is that he might be saved by the infinite merits of an able, all-sufficient Substitute.

That Substitute is the Lord Jesus Christ, the Son of God! Christ, by his precious blood, has completely washed away the sins of his people, so that they are no longer recorded against us in the book of God's law and justice (Isaiah 43:25; 44:22; Jeremiah 50:20); and his righteous obedience to God is imputed to all who believe on him, making us worthy of eternal life (Romans 5:19; Colossians 1:12).

'Them That Are Sanctified'

God will by no means clear the guilty; and he will not punish the righteous. How, then, can we, who are the fallen sons and daughters of Adam, stand before the holy, just, and true God in judgment? Is there no hope? As long as we are guilty, as long as there is one remaining spot of sin upon us, unless we are made perfectly righteous, there is no hope.

No Sin

The only hope any sinner has of eternal salvation and acceptance with the holy God is that he might be saved by the infinite merits of an able, acceptable, all-sufficient Substitute. The Lord Jesus Christ, by his own precious blood, has completely washed away the sins of his people. By his blood he fully satisfied the penalty required by God's law for our sins. Christ paid our debt to God's law. Now we have nothing to pay!

Perfect Righteousness

The Lord Jesus Christ is 'the Lord our righteousness' (Jeremiah 23:6). His righteous obedience to God as the God-man, as our Mediator and Representative, has been imputed to all who believe on him; so that in the sight of God's holy law, according to the record of God's own books, we are perfectly righteous. We have been made the very righteousness of God in him (Romans 5:19; 2 Corinthians 5:21). Believer, hear these words and rejoice:

> In thy Surety thou art free,
> His dear hands were pierced for thee;
> With His spotless garments on,
> You're holy as the Holy One!

No Condemnation

If we are in Christ, united to him by faith, washed in his blood and robed in his righteousness, the day of judgment will not be for us a dreaded day of doom, or even of sorrow; but a day of victory, triumph, and glory! Let us look upon that day with sobriety, but not with fear. We must not be presumptuous. But we must not be unbelieving. We have nothing to fear. We will endure no punishment. We will suffer no loss. We will receive the full reward of eternal glory, purchased by his blood and earned by his obedience on our behalf. Our Mediator's record before God is our record. His merit is our merit. His reward is our reward!

For the law having a shadow of good things to come, *and* not the very image of the things, can never with those sacrifices which they offered year by year continually make the comers thereunto perfect. For then would they not have ceased to be offered? because that the worshippers once purged should have had no more conscience of sins. But in those *sacrifices there is* a remembrance again *made* of sins every year. For *it is* not possible that the blood of bulls and of goats should take away sins. Wherefore when he cometh into the world, he saith, Sacrifice and offering thou wouldest not, but a body hast thou prepared me: In burnt offerings and *sacrifices* for sin thou hast had no pleasure. Then said I, Lo, I come (in the volume of the book it is written of me,) to do thy will, O God. Above when he said, Sacrifice and offering and burnt offerings and *offering* for sin thou wouldest not, neither hadst pleasure *therein*; which are offered by the law;

Hebrews 10-1-8

Chapter 26

Read: Hebrews 10:1-8

Why Did Christ Come?

The most amazing thing in all the world is the fact that the Lord Jesus Christ, the Son of God, should condescend to become a man that he might live and die in the place of sinful men as our Substitute upon the cursed tree. I hope I never get over the wonder of redeeming love.

Could we with ink the oceans fill,
And were the skies of parchment made,
Were every stalk on earth a quill,
And every man a scribe by trade,
To write the love of God above
Would drain the oceans dry,
Nor could the scroll contain the whole,
Though stretched from sky to sky!

When I meditate upon this great, stupendous fact: that the Lord of glory came here to live and die for me; to be made sin for me; to bring in everlasting righteousness for me; to put away my sin by being made sin; to give me life by laying down his life; that he came here to save me; I am compelled to ask with reverent astonishment, Why? Why did Christ come?

This question is answered in many ways and in many places in holy scripture. But it is not answered more fully or more clearly in any single passage than it is in Hebrews chapter ten. Here, the Holy Spirit tells us specifically why the Lord Jesus Christ came into this world and died in our room and stead at Calvary.

No Other Way

Our Lord Jesus Christ, the Son of God, came here to put away sin because there was no other way for sin to be put away (vv. 1-4). 'For the law having a shadow of good things to come, and not the very image of the things, can never with those sacrifices which they offered year by year continually make the comers thereunto perfect. For then would they not have ceased to be offered? because that the worshippers once purged should have had no more conscience of sins. But in those sacrifices there is a remembrance again made of sins every year. For it is not possible that the blood of bulls and of goats should take away sins.'

Good Things To Come

The law of God given by Moses, with all its rituals, sacrifices, and ceremonies, was a shadow, type, or picture of the good things to come in Christ. Among those 'good things' pictured and typified in the law are: the forgiveness of sin; justification with God; peace with God; rest in Christ; fellowship with the Holy Lord God; preservation by grace; salvation and eternal life in Christ; and the blessed assurance of faith.

Pictures of Christ

The tabernacle, the priesthood and the law were not given to put away sin, but only to serve as a pattern, a blueprint, a picture of the true Tabernacle and true Sacrifice, which is Christ himself (Colossians 2:16-17; Hebrews 8:4-5). Those Old Testament sacrifices could never put away sin (v. 2). Be sure you do not miss the argument given in verse two. If those sacrifices could put away sin, they would have ceased to be offered! If I bring a sacrifice of any kind that could make atonement for my sin, then there would be no need of offering another sacrifice (Hebrews 10:12-14).

Once sin has been put away the sinner is discharged. Guilt is gone. Condemnation is impossible. This is the reason we have assurance and confidence in Christ (Romans 5:1; 8:1-4; 8:33-34). Our Lord Jesus Christ has offered one sacrifice; believing on him we have complete, total confidence and assurance that our sins are gone (Hebrews 10:17; Isaiah 53:4-6).

Remembrance Made

In verse 3 the Holy Spirit tells us that those carnal, legal sacrifices of the Old Testament only reminded the worshippers of God that someone must yet come to put sin away. Those sacrifices offered on a regular basis and by divine appointment gave a fresh remembrance of sin. The sin for which the sacrifices were made was not put away. They were still there. The sacrifices themselves only reminded the people of their sins. The sacrifices must and did continue until the Christ came, who put an end to them and to sin by his sacrifice.

Not Possible

In verse 4 we are told, 'it is not possible' for such carnal sacrifices to put away sin. It is not possible for an animal's blood to take away sin. Let me give you four reasons why sin could never be put away by such sacrifices.

(1) Sin is the transgression of God's moral law but animals are creatures of instinct, not moral prescription. These sacrifices belonged to the ceremonial law. Christ was born under and obeyed the moral and the ceremonial law (Galatians 4:4-5). (2) The blood is not the same blood. It is not from the same kind who sinned. But Christ is bone of our bone and flesh of our flesh (Hebrews 2:16-18). (3) Sin deals with the mind, the heart, the soul, and conscience, to which no animal can relate. Christ made his soul an offering for sin. He was a man of sorrows and acquainted with grief (Isaiah 53:10-11). (4) If sin could be put away by some other means, then Christ died in vain (Galatians 2:21).

'Lo, I Come To Do Thy Will, O God'

Our Lord Jesus Christ came here as a Man, as our Mediator, Substitute and Representative. He came to do and fulfil the will of God, and to bring in a better covenant. Verses 5-8 are a quotation from Psalm 40:6-8 in which David, by the Spirit of inspiration wrote of Christ who was to come.

A Body Prepared

The sacrifices and offerings of the Old Testament continued only for a set time until Christ came (1 Corinthians 5:7). God never accepted them as a term of righteousness. But, when the fulness of time came, he clothed Christ in a human body prepared by the Holy Spirit, that his own dear Son might (in the body of a man) obey the law and suffer for sin (Romans 5:19; 1 Corinthians 15:21-22). God the Holy Spirit prepared a body for him (v. 5), a real human body and soul for the infinite, eternal, incomprehensible Son of God, so that he could bear our sins in his body on the cursed tree and die as our Substitute.

A Voluntary Substitute

In verse 6 we are again told that it was impossible for animal blood to put away human sin. Burnt offerings and sacrifices could never satisfy God's justice, appease his anger, honour his law, or put away sin (Isaiah 1:11-18). Our Lord Jesus Christ came here as a voluntary Surety, as Jehovah's voluntary Servant, to die as our Substitute by the will of God (v. 7). In the book of God's decrees and in the book of God's revelation (the Bible) it is clearly written that Christ would come to work out the redemptive will of God (Luke 24:44-47).

The First and The Second

In order to fulfil and bring in the new, everlasting covenant and the blessings of it, our Saviour completely took away the old (vv. 8-9). In verse 8 the prophecy of Psalm 40 is repeated. Here, however, all the sacrifices are included. That means this: when Christ fulfilled them all he replaced them all. Those sacrifices gave no pleasure to God except as they were offered in faith toward Christ (Hebrews 11:4, 17, 28).

By completely fulfilling the redemptive will of God (John 6:38), the Lord Jesus Christ has put away all sacrifices, all offerings, the priesthood and all that was associated with that covenant. 'Christ is the END of the law!' He stands in the place of all that was represented in the law. Now, having Christ, we have all things in him (1 Corinthians 3:21-23; 1:30; Colossians 2:9-10). He who was made to be sin for us is made of God unto us Wisdom, Righteousness, Sanctification, and Redemption. Let us ever glory in him!

A God given and God sustained faith in Christ is not only sufficient to enable the most feeble believer to overcome the corruptions of the flesh, the allurements of the world, and the temptations of the devil; but also to give him an easy, triumphant passage through death into glory (Exodus 15:16-18). In a sense, faith's last work shall be its greatest. When I am leaving this world, my body may convulse with pain, physical unconsciousness may set in, and I may have many spiritual struggles. Yet, once my soul is freed from this body of flesh, I shall be blest with such a sight and sense of my blessed Redeemer as I never had and never could have in this mortal state (Acts 7:55).

'A Body Hast Thou Prepared Me'

If the Son of God would be our Redeemer and Saviour, it was necessary for him to become one with us, one of us, God in our nature, Immanuel. Therefore, in order to redeem and save his people, a body was prepared for him.

It was not necessary for the Lord of glory to redeem and save anyone. The Triune God is independent and self-sufficient. He does not need us! There is nothing man could do to cause God to save him. But, having purposed to be gracious, having purposed to save a people for the glory of his name, the only way it could be done was for God himself to take humanity into union with himself (Hebrews 2:16-17).

There was no other way of atonement whereby God could be both a just God and a Saviour. There was no other way whereby he could both forgive our sins and satisfy his own holy law and justice. So the Son of God entered into Mary's virgin womb; into 'that holy thing' prepared by the Holy Spirit. Because no sacrifice would do but the sacrifice of One who is both God and man in one glorious being, we read: 'Then said I, lo, I come (in the volume of the book it is written of me,) to do thy will, O God.' Thus, it pleased our Great Triune God to manifest his divine glory: a body was prepared for his Son by the Holy Spirit in the womb of the virgin. A body which our blessed Saviour gladly took into indissoluble union with himself (1 Timothy 3:16).

This is, indeed, the great mystery of godliness God was manifest in human flesh! As we consider this great mystery, the mystery of the incarnate God, let us do so with reverent, believing hearts. If Moses, when he stood before the burning bush, was required to take off his polluted shoes, how much more must we, as we stand before the incarnate God (of whom the burning bush was but a type), take off the polluted shoes of carnal curiosity, speculation, and reason! We must stand here, upon this holy ground, upon the bare feet of reverence and faith.

J. C. Philpot wrote, 'The sacred humanity of the blessed Lord consists of a perfect human body and a perfect human soul, taken at one and the same instant in the womb of the virgin Mary, under the overshadowing operation and influence of the Holy Ghost'. That is precisely the meaning of the angel's message to Mary. 'The Holy Ghost shall come upon thee, and the power of the Highest shall overshadow thee: therefore also that holy thing which shall be born of thee shall be called the Son of God' (Luke 1:35).

The Glorious Humanity of Our Lord Jesus Christ

A body was prepared for the Son of God in eternity, in the everlasting covenant of grace. Our Saviour was not a man before he came into this world. Neither his human body nor his human soul is eternal. Yet, his human nature was prepared by God in predestination, in the arrangements of the covenant of grace, before the world began (Psalm 139:13-16). The incarnation of our Saviour has always been the purpose of God. When the Lord God made Adam in his own image and likeness (Genesis 1:27), he had in his mind's eye that Man who, in the fulness of time would come, who would be 'the express image of his person' (Hebrews 1:3).

These words also reveal the sure salvation of God's elect. As the Lord God prepared a physical body for our Lord Jesus Christ, in which he fulfilled all righteousness and accomplished eternal redemption as the federal Head and Representative of his elect, he has also prepared a spiritual, mystical body for his Son as the Mediator of his elect and the Surety of the covenant. The church of God is the fulness of Christ as his mediatorial body (Ephesians 1:22-23). As God, Jesus Christ needs us for nothing. But as the Mediator, Christ must have all his elect, every member of the church, which is his body, that he may be complete and full in his mediatorial glory. In order that Christ may enjoy the fulness of his glory as the Mediator of the covenant, a body of elect sinners has been prepared for him from eternity.

The Lord God prepared a body for his Son in eternal election. All the elect were chosen in Christ to be his body before the world began (Ephesians 1:3-4). Christ was chosen to be our Head. And we were chosen in him. And the salvation of that elect body is as sure and certain as the exaltation and glory of Christ himself.

This body has been prepared for Christ by the satisfaction of divine justice (Romans 3:24-26). God's chosen ones, before they could be brought into union with his Son, must be both redeemed from all sin and made perfectly righteous before the law. It is true, Christ himself has made us righteous and redeemed us to God by his own obedience and death. But the scheme of redemption was devised by the Triune God, for the glory of Christ, that he might have a body of redeemed sinners for his praise (Job 33:24; Ezekiel 16:62-63).

And the church is a body prepared and made ready for Christ by God the Holy Spirit in regenerating grace (Ephesians 1:20-23). In divine regeneration the Spirit of God gives each of God's elect, those men and women redeemed by Christ, a new, holy, righteous nature. The righteousness of Christ has been imputed to us in justification. The righteousness of Christ, his righteous nature, is imparted to us in regeneration. By making us righteous, sanctified, giving us to be partakers of the divine nature, God makes us a body prepared for Jesus Christ, his dear Son.

Then said he, Lo, I come to do thy will, O God. He taketh away the first, that he may establish the second. By the which will we are sanctified through the offering of the body of Jesus Christ once *for all*. And every priest standeth daily ministering and offering oftentimes the same sacrifices, which can never take away sins: But this man, after he had offered one sacrifice for sins for ever, sat down on the right hand of God; From henceforth expecting till his enemies be made his footstool. For by one offering he hath perfected for ever them that are sanctified.

Hebrews 10:9-14

Chapter 27

Read: Hebrews 10:9-14

The Great Transaction's Done

'Tis done, the great transaction's done! I am my Lord's and He is mine! Redemption's work is done, completely finished. Nothing is to be added to it to make it complete. Nothing can be added to it. If we attempt to add anything to it, we make it of none effect to ourselves (Galatians 5:1-4). When our Lord Jesus Christ cried, 'It is finished,' he had finished the work he came here to do. He had redeemed his people. He had finished the entire will of God he came here to fulfil. That is the entire basis of our faith and confidence in him as our Saviour. It is Christ's finished work of redemption as the sinner's Substitute which the Holy Spirit declares in Hebrews 10:9-14

The Father's Will

The Lord Jesus Christ came here to die at Calvary to redeem God's elect (vv. 9-10). Carry these two verses with you as you make your pilgrimage through this world. When Satan roars against you and your heart trembles because of your own sin, remember what the Lord God here declares in his Word for your soul's comfort. Rejoice in these blessed facts. Turn them over in your heart. Worship God and give him thanks for great gospel truths.

The Son of God came into this world in human flesh to offer himself as a sin-atoning sacrifice to God at Calvary. He came here to die as our Substitute by the will of God. He came here specifically to die in the room and place of God's elect ('Them that are sanctified'!) as our great Substitute. And he has successfully, effectually redeemed all God's elect by the sacrifice of himself (vv. 11-14). There is no possibility that even one of those sanctified and made perfect by his blood shall ever be charged with sin (Romans 4:8), condemned for sin (Romans 8:1, 33-34), or separated from the love of God that is in Christ Jesus (Romans 8:35-39).

My Hope

Here is the basis of my soul's hope, comfort, and expectation before God. I have hope of eternal life, I expect to stand accepted before God forever, not because of anything I have done, experienced, and, or felt, but because of what Christ has done for me.

I have hope before God because the Son of God stood as my Surety in the covenant of grace before the world began. By his own oath, from which he will not repent, the Lord Jesus Christ was made 'a Surety of a better testament' in the eternal councils of the triune God (Hebrews 7:22; Genesis 43:8-9; Job 33:24). In that covenant, the Son of God agreed to satisfy the law and justice of God for his people and bring all the hosts of God's elect safe into glory. God the Father trusted his elect people into the hands of his Son as a Surety (Ephesians 1:12). Christ's suretiship engagements will not be finished until all that the Father gave him have come to him, and he has raised them up at the last day, presented them to the Father, and said, 'Behold, I and the children which God hath given me'. See John 6:37-40; 10:16; Hebrews 2:13.

The fact that God the Son came into this world as a man gives me hope as well. Immanuel, God with us, God in our nature, is God come to save (Matthew 1:21). The Son of God would not have become one of us were it not his purpose to show us mercy. 'For God sent not his son into the world to condemn the world; but that the world through him might be saved' (John 3:17). This is good news indeed: 'The Word was made flesh and dwelt among us' (John 1:14).

I have hope before God because the Lord Jesus Christ obeyed the law of God as my representative. Though I am a sinner, without any ability to produce righteousness, I have hope before God who cannot accept anything less than perfect righteousness. My hope is 'The Lord our Righteousness' (Jeremiah 23:6). Christ lived in this world in perfect obedience to God as my Representative and brought in an everlasting righteousness. It is this righteousness, the righteous obedience of Christ, which God has imputed to me and imputes to all who believe (Romans 5:19). But before righteousness could be lawfully imputed to me, my sins had to be both atoned for and put away.

I have hope before God because the Lord Jesus Christ died as my Substitute under the penalty of God's holy law (Romans 3:24-26; 2 Corinthians 5:21). My God, by a marvellously legal but gracious transfer, transferred my sin to Christ and punished him for my sin; then transferred Christ's righteousness to me and rewards me for his righteousness. Christ became what we were, so that we might forever be what he is. Christ stood in our place, so that we might forever stand in his place. Christ died, the just for the unjust, that he might bring us to God; so that we might live forever with God. And, now, God is faithful and just to forgive the sins of all who confess their sins, believing on the Lord Jesus Christ (1 John 1:9).

I have hope before God because this Christ, who lived and died as the sinner's Substitute, arose from the grave, ascended back into heaven, and has been exalted as King over the universe. The Lord Jesus Christ, 'when he had by himself purged our sins, sat down on the right hand of the majesty on high' (Hebrews 1:3). The fact that he arose from the grave assures us that Christ has completely satisfied the law's claim against our sins. The fact that he ascended back into heaven assures us that he is accepted of God as the Representative of his people. And the fact that he is enthroned as King over all things assures us that 'he is able to save them to the uttermost that come unto God by him' (Hebrews 7:25).

Faith

I am confident that Christ has done all of this for me, as my Surety, my Representative, my Substitute; because I honestly acknowledge my sin before God and trust him alone as my Lord and Saviour. My faith does not save me. Only Christ can save. But my faith gives me a confident hope that I have been saved by the grace of God through the righteousness and shed blood of the Lord Jesus Christ (1 John 5:10-13).

Christ Exalted

Here the Holy Spirit describes Christ's glorious exaltation. The priests of Israel stood and offered everyday the same sacrifices, which could never take away sins (as do the pretentious priests of Rome today). 'But this man (the God-man, our Saviour), after he had offered one sacrifice for sins forever, sat down on the right hand of God; from henceforth expecting till his enemies be made his footstool.'

In this chapter the Holy Spirit shows us the superiority of Christ over the Levitical priesthood of the Old Testament. Those priests under the law were many. Christ is one High Priest over the house of God forever. They offered many sacrifices. Christ made one sacrifice. They offered their sacrifices often, everyday. Christ offered one sacrifice (himself) once.

They stood ministering in the holy place. Christ sat down. Their sacrifices could never take away sins. Christ by his one great sacrifice 'hath perfected forever them that are sanctified', having put away all our sins.

Not all the blood of beasts
On Jewish altars slain,
Could give the guilty conscience peace,
Or wash away the stain.
But Christ, the heavenly Lamb,
Takes all our sins away;
A sacrifice of nobler name
And richer blood than they.

Isaac Watts

Expiation Made

Our Lord's work of redemption is done. His atonement is complete. The sins, which he bore in his body on the tree, have been fully purged away, completely atoned for, and entirely removed. All that Christ came to do he has completely done. The priests of Israel could never sit down, because their work was never done, their sacrifices could never take away sin. 'But this man, after he had offered one sacrifice for sins forever, sat down on the right hand of God.' Here is proof positive that the work of redemption is done, completely and perfectly done: Christ is sitting at the Father's right hand.

Sat Down

Sitting is a posture of rest. A man does not rest until his work is finished. Christ came to do his Father's will, 'By the which will we are sanctified', and he would not rest until he had completely and perfectly done his Father's will. Christ's sitting in heaven is our assurance that everything required for the salvation of all his people is done (Romans 8:34). Righteousness has been established. Atonement has been made. Sin has been put away. God's elect have been made perfect (Hebrews 10:10, 14).

Christ's sitting at God's right hand also implies that he enjoys great pleasure. The psalmist, when he spoke of Christ's exaltation, wrote, 'Thou wilt show me the path of life: in thy presence is fulness of joy; at thy right hand there are pleasures for evermore' (Psalm 16:11). The highest joy and pleasure of our Saviour is the salvation of his people. Our salvation was the joy set before him, for which he endured the cross, despising the shame (Hebrews 12:2).

How could he enjoy pleasure, if his people were in jeopardy? How could he have any joy, if he had not secured the salvation of every lamb of his flock? If he had not rendered the eternal salvation of every blood-bought soul as secure as his own throne, he would have no pleasure. There is a smile of pleasure upon our Redeemer's face as he sits in glory, because all his ransomed ones are perfectly safe.

Sat Down Forever

Not only is Christ seated in the posture of rest and at the place of pleasure; but our text tells us that, he 'forever sat down on the right hand of God!' Christ, as our Surety, has undertaken to save all of God's elect. He has sworn to bring all the elect to glory and present them perfect, without blemish, without fault, holy before his Father. If that is not already secured as the result of his finished work, then he would be obliged at some point to get up off his seat and go to work again. But our all-glorious Christ has so thoroughly redeemed us that he forever sat down. He will never have to leave his throne, because he finished the work he came to do.

God's Right Hand

Here is another proof that our sins are completely expiated by Christ: He is seated on the right hand of God. The very fact that Christ is in heaven, accepted by God as our Substitute, is proof that his work is done and that, as the result of his finished work, God has no quarrel with us. As long as the United States has an ambassador in Moscow, there is peace between America and Russia. As long as Christ is at the Father's right hand, we may be assured that there is peace between his people and God.

Since Christ is seated in heaven forever, it is no assumption, but a matter of infallible certainty, that our peace with God can never cease, and that the atonement for sin is both complete and effectual! God almighty made Christ to be sin for us, and as a sinner, he could not enter heaven until he had washed all our sins away in the fountain of his own precious blood. This Man, being our Substitute, could not enter heaven without two things: perfect righteousness and complete satisfaction. But, inasmuch as he is seated on the right hand of God forever, we cannot question this fact: redemption is done!

Christ Exalted

Having completely put away our sins by his one great atoning sacrifice, the Holy Spirit declares, 'This man, (Christ, the God-man, Our Divine Mediator and Substitute) after he had offered one sacrifice for sins forever, sat down on the right hand of God'.

As God the Son, our Lord Jesus Christ was always on the Father's throne. Even when he was upon earth, he was in heaven. The Son of God did not cease to be omnipotent and omnipresent, even when he was wrapped up in human flesh. Insofar as his divinity is concerned, our Lord never left his Father's throne. He who is everywhere present cannot be anywhere absent. Our Lord himself said to Nicodemus, 'No man hath ascended up to heaven, but he that came down from heaven, event the Son of man which is (at this very time) in heaven' (John 3:13).[1]

As the Man-God, our Lord Jesus has assumed the glories and honours of heavenly exaltation. This Man who died as the sinner's Substitute reigns as the sinner's God on the right hand of the glorious Trinity, Father, Son, and Holy Ghost. The Man Christ Jesus is exalted to the right hand of the Majesty on high. He is that One whom John saw as a Lamb that had been slain rising up in the midst of the throne (Revelation 5:6, 7:17).

Pre-eminent Exaltation

Our Saviour's exaltation is a pre-eminent exaltation. The triune God has ordained, 'that in all things Christ might have the pre-eminence' (Colossians 1:18). And he has given him the place of pre-eminence. God has crowned him with glory and honour above all the works of his hands. God has exalted Christ 'Far above all principality, and power, and might, and dominion, and every name that is named, not only in this world, but also in that which is to come: And hath put all things under his feet, and gave him to be the head over all things to the church, which is his body, the fulness of him that filleth all in all' (Ephesians 1:21-23).

The dignity which Christ now enjoys is a surpassing dignity. No angel rivals him. No creature can compare with him. Christ is pre-eminent in all things. He is the pre-eminent Prophet; the pre-eminent Priest; the pre-eminent King; the pre-eminent Sacrifice; the pre-eminent Saviour; the pre-eminent Brother; the pre-eminent Friend; the pre-eminent Husband.

Real Exaltation

Our Saviour's exaltation is a real exaltation (Acts 2:33-36). A good many men seek empty, meaningless titles, titles which give them a name, but no power or authority. Our Lord does not wear a meaningless title. He wears a name that is above every name, and he has power above all power (John 17:2). The sceptre of universal monarchy is in his hand (Romans 14:9).

---

[1] This verse shows the uniqueness of our Saviour God. Jesus is the only One to have ascended to heaven in such a way as to return as the One who has permanent abode in heaven. Though incarnate as man, as God he never left heaven, but was both here on earth and in heaven as only the omnipresent One can be.

He upholds all things by the word of his power. He is able to save to the uttermost all who come to God by him. He is able to work all things together for the good of his own elect. He is able to subdue all things unto himself. He is able to preserve his own and to present them faultless before the presence of his own glory.

Deserved Exaltation

Our blessed Redeemer's exaltation is a deserved exaltation (Philippians 2:5-11). If the Lord God should put it to a vote, as to whether Christ should be exalted, it would be carried by universal acclamation. All would shout,

> Crown Him with many crowns,
> The Lamb upon His throne!
> Hark how the heavenly anthems drown
> All music but its own!

All the holy angels would acknowledge Christ's right to be exalted (Isaiah 6:2-3; John 12:37-41). All the saints in heaven acknowledge Christ's right to be exalted (Revelation 4:10-11; 5:9-10). Every believer upon the earth would have Christ exalted (Colossians 3:11; 1 Peter 2:7). Every creature of God will in time acknowledge Christ's right to be exalted (Revelation 5:11-14). No other being in heaven deserves to be there but Christ. The angels of God are kept in heaven by grace. The saints of God enter heaven by grace. Only Christ is in heaven by right.

Representative Exaltation

Our great Saviour's exaltation is a representative exaltation (Hebrews 6:20; Ephesians 2:5-6). Just as you and I have our representatives in the houses of congress, or parliament, every true believer has a Representative before God in heaven. Yet, Christ is more to us than a legal Representative, he is also a real Representative, because we are really and truly one with him. He is the Vine. We are the branches. He is the Head. We are his body. We are one with Christ!

> One when He died, one when He arose,
> One when He triumphed o'er His foes.
> One when in heaven He took His seat
> And angels sang all hell's defeat.

Is Christ on a throne? He will give us to sit on the throne with him. Does Christ wear a crown? He will give us a crown that fades not away. Is Christ triumphant? He will make us triumphant too.

Child of God, set your heart's eye upon your exalted Saviour. Behold him seated upon his throne in glory, with many crowns upon his head; and remember this: You will soon be with him and like him! Let us be content now to live in obscurity or even in banishment for Christ's sake. Soon we shall wear the crown of glory!

Good News to Needy Sinners

The Holy Spirit assures us of the accomplishment of redemption by our Lord Jesus Christ. This is the gospel we declare to needy sinners: Christ has accomplished redemption by the sacrifice of himself (Hebrews 10:12). This text does not refer to the great high priest in Israel; nor to that great multitude of priests who offered daily sacrifices for the people (Leviticus 1-7). Standing before the altar, they offered the same sacrifices day after day, week after week, month after month, year after year, sacrifices that could never take away sins. Those earthly priests never sat down in the holy place, because their work was never done.

We are told three things in this 12th verse, which are absolutely essential to the saving of our souls. Apart from these three things redemption could not be accomplished. First, the Son of God became a man (Isaiah 7:14; 9:6; Matthew 1:21-23). Then, this almighty God-man offered one sacrifice for sins forever. Finally, he sat down in heaven. He sat because his work was done, his sacrifice was accepted, his people were sanctified by his blood, and our sins were pardoned. He could not have gone to the Father as our Mediator, had he not put away our sins (John 16:10). These things were written to show the excellence and superiority of Christ as our great High Priest. Those priests in Israel were numerous. Christ is one! They offered many sacrifices. He offered only one! They stood continually. He sat down! Their sacrifices were only typical of redemption's great work. His sacrifice effectually accomplished eternal redemption for us!

Blessed be God, all the enemies of Christ and his people shall be subdued to him and put under his feet! (Read Psalm 110:1; Isaiah 45:20-25; 1 Corinthians 15:24-28.) Behold the Son of God sitting in heaven, patiently anticipating the subjugation of all things beneath his feet, giving everlasting praise to him. Let us both admire and imitate our Saviour's patience. The God of Peace shall bruise Satan under our feet shortly (Romans 16:20).

This is why he sat down. This is why he expects his enemies to be destroyed. This is why he is at the right hand of the Father. Our Saviour has fully and forever, perfectly and permanently, accomplished what he came here to do. He has completely cleansed, perfected, and made holy all who were given him by the Father: his chosen and sanctified ones.

To be sanctified is to be set apart by the Father in electing love (Jude 1), to be declared holy by the Son in justification (1 Corinthians 1:2), and to be made holy by God the Holy Spirit in the new birth (2 Thessalonians 2:13). No sinner will ever be saved, no sinner has faith in Christ, until he learns this blessed fact revealed in the gospel: Redemption is done! Blessed are the eyes that see this glorious, soul comforting, Christ honouring truth of holy scripture!

> Nothing, either great or small; nothing, sinner, no;
> Jesus did it, did it all, long, long ago!
> When He, from His lofty throne, stooped to do and die,
> Everything was fully done; hearken to His cry
>
> 'It is finished!' Yes indeed, finished every jot.
> Sinner, this is all you need. Tell me, is it not?
> Weary, working, plodding one, why toil you so?
> Cease your doing. All was done, long, long ago!
>
> Till to Jesus' work you cling by a simple faith,
> Doing is a deadly thing. Doing ends in death!
> Cast your deadly 'doing' down, down at Jesus' feet.
> Stand in Him, in Him alone, gloriously complete!

Whereof the Holy Ghost also is a witness to us: for after that he had said before, This *is* the covenant that I will make with them after those days, saith the Lord, I will put my laws into their hearts, and in their minds will I write them; And their sins and iniquities will I remember no more. Now where remission of these *is, there is* no more offering for sin. Having therefore, brethren, boldness to enter into the holiest by the blood of Jesus, By a new and living way, which he hath consecrated for us, through the veil, that is to say, his flesh; And *having* an high priest over the house of God; Let us draw near with a true heart in full assurance of faith, having our hearts sprinkled from an evil conscience, and our bodies washed with pure water.

Hebrews 10:15-22

Chapter 28

Read: Hebrews 10:15-22

'A New and Living Way'

Everything relating to this gospel age, everything relating to the worship of God in this age, everything relating to the believer's life in Christ in this gospel age is described as 'new' and 'living'.

New

We are partakers of a new covenant. We come into the kingdom of God by a new birth (John 3:3-7). We are new creatures in Christ (2 Corinthians 5:17). We have been given a new name (1 John 3:1-3). We live under the rule of a new commandment (1 John 3:23). We are citizens of the New Jerusalem. We sing a new song. We look for a new heavens and a new earth.

Living

As all things in Christ are new, so, too, all things in the kingdom of God are living. Our hope in Christ is a living hope (1 Peter 1:3). We drink from the fountain of Living Water. We eat that Living Bread which came down from heaven. We are built upon Christ as living stones upon the Living Stone, the Living Foundation.

Spiritual

Everything relating to the knowledge, worship, and service of God is spiritual, not carnal. 'True worshippers shall worship the Father in spirit … God is a Spirit: and they that worship him must worship him in spirit and in truth' (John 4:23-24). 'The kingdom of God is not meat and drink; but righteousness, and peace, and joy in the Holy Ghost' (Romans 14:17). 'We are the circumcision, which worship God in the spirit, and rejoice in Christ Jesus, and have no confidence in the flesh' (Philippians 3:3).

True worship is a matter of the heart, and altogether spiritual. We worship God by faith in Christ, upon the grounds of justice satisfied. Hebrews 10:11-25 describes both the foundation and the exercise of grace.

We worship the Lord our God, trusting his Son, drawing near to him upon the basis of redemption accomplished by Christ (vv. 11-14). We come to God, confident of acceptance with him because of the complete remission of sins by his grace through the redemption Christ accomplished at Calvary (vv. 15-18). This freedom in worship, this freedom in drawing near to God arises from the blessedness and realization of our complete, perfect reconciliation to God by and in Christ (vv. 19-22). This is what Paul declares in 2 Corinthians 5:17. We are reconciled to God, perfectly, completely, and immutably!

'From Henceforth Expecting'

We have seen the expiation of our sin by our Saviour's blood atonement, and his exaltation as Lord as the reward of his obedience to the Father's will as our covenant Surety and Mediator. Here the Holy Spirit shows us that which our great Saviour yet expects to be the reward of his labour as our Mediator.

As we have seen, he who redeemed us with his blood and saved us by his grace has been exalted to the throne of sovereign dominion. He reigns upon that throne of universal monarchy, 'From henceforth expecting till his enemies be made his footstool.' His foes shall all, without exception, become his servant and his footstool (Psalm 110:1-2).

Present Subjugation

In one sense, this crushing of his enemies into subjection beneath his feet has already begun. Our Lord Jesus Christ is the sovereign ruler of the universe. All creation, all events, all animals, and all rational beings, either willingly or unwillingly, are his servants. He has power over all flesh (John 17:2).

Be sure you understand this. Satan himself is Christ's slave, beaten into subjection (John 12:31; Revelation 20:1-3). Wicked men and women are the servants of Christ, the errand boys of his providential rule. Satan cannot tempt God's servant Job without first obtaining permission from the Lord God; and having the limits of the temptation set by God. Not even demons of hell can run into a herd of hogs without the permission of

Christ their Lord. Yes, the Lord God our Saviour rules the universe totally and absolutely for the everlasting salvation of his own elect (Romans 8:28-31; Psalm 76:10).

Gracious Subjugation

Many of Christ's enemies are conquered by his grace through the preaching of the gospel (2 Corinthians 10:4-5). How I thank God for conquering grace! Nothing else could have broken this rebel's heart. Nothing less than sovereign, omnipotent, conquering grace could have stopped me in my mad rush to hell. Nothing else could have brought me to Christ and reconciled my heart to my God, making me willing in the day of his power to gladly bow to Christ as my Lord (Psalm 110:3). My heart sings with David, 'Blessed is the man whom thou choosest and causest to approach unto thee' (Psalm 65:4).

Final Subjugation

When Christ comes the second time, he will come to crush all rebellion. The second advent will not be a time of salvation for rebels; but of judgment and wrath. 'The Lord Jesus shall be revealed from heaven with his mighty angels, in flaming fire taking vengeance on them that know not God, and that obey not the gospel' (2 Thessalonians 1:7-8). In the last day, in the day of judgment, every enemy shall bow to Christ as Lord. At the name of Jesus every knee shall bow and every tongue shall confess, in heaven, earth, and hell, that Jesus Christ is Lord. And God shall be all in all (Philippians 2;10-11).

In the end, because Christ is exalted, he shall have his expectation. All his enemies shall be made his footstool. All who believe shall be saved: 'He shall see of the travail of his soul, and shall be satisfied'. All his foes shall be destroyed. All of God's elect shall be saved (Romans 11:26). Christ shall be triumphant and glorious forever in all things and over all things (Revelation 19:6).

'One Offering'

God's elect are a sanctified people. All believers are sanctified. There is no such thing as an unsanctified believer. If we are saved, we are saints. If we are not saints, we are not saved. This is exactly what Paul told the Corinthian believers (1 Corinthians 6:11).

Sanctification is altogether the work of God's free and sovereign grace in Christ. Our sanctification, like our redemption and justification, is the work of God Almighty in the trinity of his sacred Persons. We are sanctified by God the Father in election, by God the Son in redemption, and by God the Holy Spirit in regeneration. Sanctification is not something we do for ourselves. It is something God does for us and in us.

The words 'sanctify', 'sanctified', 'sanctifieth', and 'sanctification' are used more than thirty times in the New Testament. We are said to be sanctified by the purpose of God, by the blood of Christ, by the Spirit of God, by faith in Christ, and by the Word of God. But never, not even once, are we said to sanctify ourselves. Sanctification is the work of God alone.

Sanctified in Eternity

All who are God's were sanctified by God the Father in eternal election. All believers were sanctified by God the Father in eternal election, set apart by God's decree, and separated unto him (Ephesians 3:11; Jude 1).

This is the character of God's distinguishing grace. It sets some people apart from others and sanctifies them unto the Lord. Grace makes men to differ (1 Corinthians 4:7). We were secretly set apart for God in his secret, eternal decree of election before the world began. We were legally set apart from Adam's fallen race by the purchase of Christ at Calvary when he ransomed us from the curse of the law. And we were manifestly set apart and separated unto God by the effectual call of God the Holy Spirit in regeneration.

Every believer has been, in this sense, eternally sanctified, completely set apart by God and for God. The practical importance of this glorious doctrine is this: that which has been set apart for God ought never to be used for common purposes again. 'Ye are not your own. For ye are bought with a price: therefore glorify God in your body, and in your spirit, which are God's' (1 Corinthians 6:19-20). We belong to the Lord our God. Let us therefore consecrate ourselves to him and serve him in all things (Romans 12:1-2). We belong to God. Be assured, God almighty will protect all who belong to him in all their appointed ways, even as he protected the ark of the covenant in the Old Testament (Psalm 91:3-13).

Sanctified at Calvary

We were sanctified by God the Son in redemption at Calvary. All of God's elect were perfectly sanctified by the blood of Christ when he died as our Substitute (Hebrews 10:10-14). Christ is our Sanctification (1 Corinthians 1:30). We have been and are forever 'sanctified in Christ Jesus' (1 Corinthians 1:2). Believers are addressed throughout the Epistles as 'saints', that is as 'sanctified ones' in Christ.

This is what I want you to see and rejoice in: in the Lord Jesus Christ we who believe are regarded by God as perfectly holy, treated as if we were perfectly holy, and declared to be perfectly holy, because in Christ we are perfectly holy! We do no believe in imputed sanctification any more than we believe in imputed justification. We believe in imputed righteousness, by which we are both justified and sanctified. The righteousness of Christ has been imputed to us; we are by his righteousness both justified from all things and declared to be holy. Sanctified in the sight of God, 'With His spotless garments on I am as holy as God's Son!'

Sanctified by The Spirit

Every chosen, redeemed sinner is sanctified by God the Holy Spirit in the new birth. All believers are actually made holy by God the Holy Spirit in regeneration. Holiness or sanctification, like regeneration or the new birth, is complete at once. A man is either dead or alive, he is either holy or unholy, he cannot be more or less either of these. Through the instrumentality of gospel preaching, the Spirit of God effectually applies the blood of Christ to the hearts of God's elect, purifying our hearts and implanting a new, holy nature within us. This is regeneration, the new birth. This is our sanctification by the Spirit (2 Thessalonians 2:13-14; 2 Peter 1:4; 1 John 3:9; 1 John 5:18).

Someone once wrote, 'We are a people with two natures, one that is holy and seeks after righteousness, and one that is corrupt and seeks after sin. However, these two natures are not equal in power. The divine nature rules and reigns; but the evil nature will not bow nor serve'.

While we live in this world we must continue to live with this old, sinful nature. But we do have a new nature created in us, in the image of Christ, a nature that cannot sin (1 John 3:9). It is the old man that sins, not the new. It is written, 'Now if I do that I would not, it is no more I that do it, but sin that dwelleth in me' (Romans 7:20). By glorification the old man shall be totally eradicated from us, not until then. Eradication of the old man is not a gradual, progressive thing. It is the radical, climactic change experienced by God's saints in death, and ultimately in resurrection glory.

Understanding that sanctification is altogether the work of God, the work of God's grace, it is obvious that there is no such thing as 'progressive sanctification' taught in the book of God. Believers grow in grace, but not in holiness. We grow in faith, but not in righteousness. There is no sense in which our sanctification depends upon us. It is God's work.

'The Judgment'

The book of Hebrews constantly shows us that the work of Christ as our sin offering to God was a work done but once. This emphasis is made throughout the book to teach us forcibly that the sacrifice of Christ was an effectual sacrifice; that our Lord Jesus Christ has by his one great sacrifice as our Substitute accomplished everything he intended to accomplish by his death. Look what this book tells us Christ accomplished by his one offering. By his one offering, the Lord Jesus Christ has purged our sins (Hebrews 1:1-3; 7:26-27). By his one offering, the Lord Jesus Christ has obtained eternal redemption for us (Hebrews 9:12, 26-28). By his one offering, he has perfected all God's elect (Hebrews 10:12-14).

The Context

Look at this text in its context. The Son of God, by his one offering for sin, has perfected forever them that are sanctified. What does this mean? In the ninth chapter the Apostle spoke to us about the tabernacle, the candlestick, the table, the showbread, the sanctuary, the golden censor, the ark of the covenant overlaid with gold and the pot of manna. In other words, he has been talking to us about priests and priestly things.

Holy Things and Holy Men

All these things were sanctified things, holy things. However, though they were sanctified, holy things, they needed to be made perfect. They had to be sprinkled with blood to be made perfect. Granted, those things were only ceremonially sanctified and ceremonially perfected. But the ceremonies were designed of God to show us something. They were intended to teach us what sanctification is in a very practical way.

There were certain golden vessels used in the sanctuary, which were never used for anything else but the service of God. They were set apart, made holy, and kept strictly as vessels of the sanctuary for service of the Lord God. They were sanctified things.

There were also specific, chosen men who did nothing else but wait upon the Lord. They were consecrated to their offices. God chose the tribe of Levi, and out of the tribe of Levi he chose the house of Aaron. These men were chosen, and then they were prepared by divine order for their work. They underwent specific, divinely ordained ceremonies and washings, and were thereby made ceremonially holy. These priests were ceremonially sanctified. That is to say, they were set apart, dedicated and reserved to the special service of the Lord God.

Set Apart for God

That is just what you and I (if we are believers) are, and what we ought to be. If we are God's, we are sanctified men and women. We are chosen by

God to be the peculiar vessels he will use in performing his work, in pouring out his mercy to his people (Ephesians 3:8; 2 Corinthians 4:7). We are the people God has chosen and sanctified, by whom he is served, by whom he does good to chosen sinners in this world.

No man had the right to use the things of the sanctuary for himself. If he did so, he did it to his own destruction. Ask Belshazzar. He took the cups, the golden candlesticks, and so forth, and used them in his debauchery and pleasure. When he did, he was swept away in God's wrath. The handwriting on the wall foretold his doom (Daniel 5:17-31).

So it is with us. We are not to be used (or to use ourselves) for anything but for God. We are a people set-apart; we are vessels of the Lord's house. We are not for the devil's use, the world's use, or our own use. We have been made, chosen, and set apart for our Master's use!

That is what is meant in this text by 'sanctified'. We are sanctified people, set apart for God's use, consecrated to God, just as the vessels, the cups, the candlesticks, the tables, and the altars of the sanctuary were sanctified unto God and set apart for his service.

We are priests, sanctified to God, not because of any personal holiness in ourselves. Some of those priests were downright scoundrels; but they were priests nonetheless. Hebrews 10 does not deal with the matter of our character. Hebrews 10 is talking about our position in the sight of God. We are not perfect in character. We are only perfect in position.

We who are God's are sanctified, sanctified to offer spiritual sacrifices unto God through Christ (1 Peter 2:5). We have no right to do anything else but serve God. Christ has made us kings and priests unto God, a royal priesthood, a people whose whole and only purpose in life is his service!

Perfection Accomplished

The Holy Spirit declares that all who are God's are a people perfected, a people whose perfection is a done deal. What does that mean?

When the golden vessels were brought into the temple or into the sanctuary, they were sanctified the very first moment that they were dedicated to God. No one dared to employ them for anything but holy uses. But they were not perfect. What did they need then, to make them perfect? They needed to have blood sprinkled on them; and, as soon as the blood was sprinkled on them, those golden vessels were perfect vessels, officially perfect. God accepted them as being holy and perfect things. They stood in his sight as instruments of an acceptable worship.

The same was true regarding the Levites and the priests. As soon as they were set apart to their office, as soon as they were born, in fact, they were consecrated to God. They belonged to God. They were his peculiar priesthood. But they were not perfect until they had passed through divers washings, and had the blood sprinkled upon them. Then God looked upon them in their official priestly character as being perfect before him.

They were not perfect in character. They were only perfect officially; perfect in the sight of God; and they stood before him to offer sacrifice as acceptably as if they had been pure as Adam in Eden.

How does this refer to us, and what is the meaning of this text, that 'by one offering he hath perfected for ever them that are sanctified'? The answer is found in Hebrews 9:6-7. 'Now when these things were thus ordained, the priests went always into the first tabernacle, accomplishing the service of God. But into the second went the high priest alone once every year, not without blood, which he offered for himself, and for the errors of the people'.

The only way the high priest himself could come before God and be accepted was by blood atonement. In the context here, the Holy Spirit is telling us that we are made perfect—to be accepted a sacrifice had to be perfect, without blemish—by the blood of Christ: made perfect before God himself, so perfect that we may freely and boldly come to God by the blood of Christ with full assurance that we are accepted (Leviticus 22:17-22; Hebrews 10:22).

To be made perfect by Christ is to stand before God Almighty himself accepted in the Beloved, accepted by blood! The blood of the Lamb slain from the foundation of the world! The blood of the Lamb crucified at Calvary! The blood of the Lamb sprinkled upon our hearts in saving grace. This is our standing and our position in Christ. We enjoy it now by faith in him. But, blessed be God, soon, this shall be our experience.

Perfection Promised, Perfection Done

Someone said, 'The Old Testament is the New Testament concealed and the New Testament is the Old Testament revealed'. In the Old Testament believers anticipated that which the Lord would do, believing his Word of promise. In this New Testament age believers rejoice in that which the Lord has done, believing his Word of grace. We have a perfect example of this in Hebrews 10:14.

Read Psalm 138:7-8. We see a believer in the Old Testament speaking in confident faith about that which God promised he would do. 'Though I walk in the midst of trouble, thou wilt revive me: thou shalt stretch forth thine hand against the wrath of mine enemies, and thy right hand shall save me. The Lord will perfect that which concerneth me: thy mercy, O LORD, endureth for ever: forsake not the works of thine own hands'.

In Hebrews 10:14 we saw a believer in this gospel age looking back to the finished work of Christ and declaring in the joy of confident faith what the Lord has done for him and for all who are his. 'By one offering he hath perfected for ever them that are sanctified.'

In the Old Testament, the believer's faith rested on the promise of God and the work of Christ as things unseen. His heart yearned for salvation as an inheritance yet in reserve. Today, we look upon the same thing, trust the same Saviour and the same work; but we possess God's salvation as a thing accomplished. It is true, there is a very real sense in which we yet look to the future, confidently hoping for God's salvation, because we have not yet experienced the fulness of it. (Oh, what that will be!) Still, we do possess it now in Christ. Christ has obtained eternal redemption for us by his blood (Hebrews 9:12); and we have obtained an eternal inheritance in him (Ephesians 1:11). Righteousness has been brought in. Our Saviour has made an end of our transgressions. These are not things we hope for, but facts. They are things we now possess by faith in Christ. 'For by one offering he hath perfected for ever them that are sanctified.'

I have turned this text over and over in my mind I have prayed about it, looked into it, and sought illumination from the Holy Spirit for years. It is one of those verses my mind keeps going back to virtually every day, sometimes countless times in a day. I love to roll it around in my soul like a good piece of candy in my mouth. It is a text to mull over. The more I think about it, the bigger it gets. Every time I open one of its doors I see another. Here the Holy Spirit declares that our Lord Jesus Christ has, by his one offering for sin, perfected all God's elect and perfected them forever.

Where is Your Evidence?

Here the Spirit of God describes the remission of our sins by covenant grace. These verses are from Jeremiah 31:31-34, where God described the covenant of grace and promised its fulfilment in Christ. There are many things promised in the covenant and here four wonderful gifts of grace are set forth. Eternity will be spent learning the meaning of these mercies. Meditate on them in your heart until you too are amazed by the fact that God has done these things for you. If you are a believer, if you trust Christ, these four great covenant blessings are yours in Christ.

1. Regeneration

The God of all grace has put his law, his gospel, his Word into our hearts (v. 16). He has written his law in our hearts with the finger of his grace, causing us to love him, his will, his way, and his Word. His commandments are no longer grievous to us (1 John 5:3).

2. Forgiveness

The God of glory says, concerning you and me, 'Their sins and iniquities will I remember no more' (v. 17). Oh, my brother, my sister, rejoice in this. There is forgiveness with our God! His name declares it. His glory demands it. His Son came to obtain it. All the prophets and apostles proclaim it. Multitudes in heaven and earth have experienced it (Psalm 32:1-5; 103:1-5; 130:1-8). He who is our God is God who 'delighteth in mercy'.

3. Satisfaction

'Where remission of these is, there is no more offering for sin' (v. 18). Justice satisfied demands no more. The blood of Christ is enough! God requires no more offering for sin. My conscience requires no more offering for sin. There is no more offering for sin. Why? Because Christ has put away our sins! Condemnation is no longer a possibility (Romans 8:1, 33-34). Henry Mahan points out, 'Where there is absolute remission, forgiveness and cancellation of penalty, there is no longer any offering or sacrifice to be made. If we are in Christ and redeemed by Christ, it is dishonouring to our Saviour not to rest in his grace and his atonement.'

4. Reconciliation

We are all by nature enemies towards God. Our hearts, by nature, are enmity against God. But God has reconciled us to himself in Christ. In the new birth, he brings us into the blessedness of that reconciliation. Reconciliation is what gospel preachers gladly proclaim: reconciliation accomplished! (vv. 19-20).

Twofold Work

Reconciliation is a twofold work of grace. Judicially, it was accomplished at Calvary when Christ died as our Substitute. God was in Christ reconciling the world of his elect unto himself by blood atonement. When atonement was made, reconciliation was done (Romans 5:10-11; 2 Corinthians 5:17-19). Experimentally, God's elect are reconciled to him by faith in Christ. Though Christ put away our sins and justified us, we were born 'children of wrath, even as others'. Hating God, we came forth from the womb as rebels against him, and lived as such, until he conquered us by his grace, and reconciled us to himself, granting us life and faith in his dear Son.

In Christ every believing sinner has full freedom and confidence to enter the very presence of God in the name of Christ, by the power and virtue of his blood, because he and God are at peace, by the work of God himself. When our Saviour died at Calvary the veil in the temple was rent in two, and the ceremonies and sacrifices were all fulfilled and forever ended by Christ's effectual sacrifice in the flesh (Galatians 5:1). Christ is our great, eternal High Priest. He is a Priest upon a throne, the King-Priest, who rules and reigns by virtue of his atonement, who is accepted and has absolute authority! We are forever, immutably accepted in him (Ephesians 1:6).

Gospel Persuasion

In preaching the gospel, God's servants speak as his ambassadors to rebel sinners who deserve his wrath, and we seek to persuade them to be reconciled to God (2 Corinthians 5:11-21). All who come to God by Christ, finding peace with God in his dear Son, enjoy the blessedness of perfect, indestructible reconciliation. Reconciled sinners stand before the holy Lord God in Christ as new creatures. Their old record of sin has been obliterated by the blood of Christ. A new record of perfect righteousness (the righteousness of Christ) has been written in heaven in their name. God himself has no quarrel with believing sinners, because God found a way to both punish our sins to the full satisfaction of justice, and justify us by his grace. 'For he hath made him to be sin for us, who knew no sin; that we might be made the righteousness of God in him.'

'Let Us ... '

When reading holy scripture, we sometimes pass over small, familiar words and phrases, or statements of fact, without much thought. Personally, I must confess, I am far too often guilty of reading over things in the scriptures, when it appears that the context is just moving from one thing to another. We ought never do that with the Word of God. If we do, we are sure to miss precious, exquisite pearls hidden in what seem to be very common shells. Every word in this book is written by divine inspiration for a divine purpose, for our comfort, instruction, and edification in the saving knowledge of Christ.

In reading the book of Hebrews, have you ever noticed how often we are admonished to do something with the words, 'Let us'? These two, very familiar words are used powerfully in this Epistle. Twelve times in these thirteen chapters the apostle Paul calls us to action, and inspires us to do something of tremendous importance by these two words, 'Let us' (Hebrews 4:1, 11, 14, 16; 6:1; 10:22, 23, 24; 12:1, 28; 13:13, 15).

Three Responsibilities

In Hebrews 10:19-25 God the Holy Spirit uses these two words, 'Let us', to call us to three very important responsibilities and privileges as God's saints in this world. (1) We must ever draw near to our God by faith in

Christ (vv. 19-22). (2) We must hold fast the profession of our faith (v. 23). And (3) we must consider one another (vv. 24-25).

In these verses of holy scripture the apostle Paul is urging us, as believers, to persevere in the faith. In the face of trials and temptations, difficulties and dangers, heretics and hecklers, we must persevere in the faith. It is written, 'He that endureth unto the end shall be saved.' It is not the person who begins the race, but the one who finishes it that wins the prize. If we would persevere in the faith, steadfast unto the end, we must continually draw near to our God.

Draw Near

'Let us draw near' to our God (vv. 19-22). 'Let us draw near with a true heart in full assurance of faith, having our hearts sprinkled from an evil conscience, and our bodies washed with pure water' (v. 22).

This text does not stand alone. It is part of a sentence which begins in verse 19. Believing on the Lord Jesus Christ, sinners have free access to God Almighty upon his glorious throne, by Christ's precious blood. 'Having therefore, brethren, boldness to enter into the holiest by the blood of Jesus' (v. 19).

Through the merit and mediation of Christ, by faith in his sin-atoning blood, you and I can now approach that God who is 'the blessed and only Potentate, the King of kings and Lord of lords, Who only hath immortality dwelling in light which no man can approach unto; whom no man hath seen, nor can see: to whom be honour and power everlasting' (1 Timothy 6:15-16).

'Brethren'

Did you also catch that sweet word 'brethren' as you read verse 19? 'Brethren' is a term of family oneness, spiritual unity, common blessedness, and tender affection. As brethren, you and I have this common privilege. We are here called to enter into the holy presence of God with boldness by the blood of Jesus, our one Saviour, our only Saviour, our common Saviour, our accepted Saviour, our enthroned Saviour.

The Holiest

The place we may enter with boldness is heaven itself, 'the holiest', referring to the holy of holies in the tabernacle, which was the type of heavenly glory. This is the most holy place, the place of God's manifest majesty, glory, and presence, the place of mercy. This is the place where our Father is, where our Saviour is, where our brethren are, where our Sacrifice is!

Heaven was symbolically shut by the sin of man when he was driven out of the Garden of Eden. It was typically opened by the entrance of the high priest into the holy of holies on the Day of Atonement. But now, it really is open. 'Behold, a door opened in heaven'. That door is Christ. He has in person entered into it by his blood. He has opened the way for us. In him and by him we may and do now 'enter into the holiest by the blood of Jesus'! (Genesis 3:22-24; Leviticus 16:2; Hebrews 9:7-9; John 10:9; Revelation 4:1; Hebrews 9:12, 24; 10:19).

Here we come and present our prayers and praises to God by Christ. Here we pour out our hearts to the Lord. Here we find mercy, grace, and peace. Soon, we shall enter personally, like our Lord himself, and it will be all by his blood!

The Way

The way of entrance is 'by the blood of Jesus'. It is his blood, which gives both entrance and boldness. By his blood sin is removed, both from the sight of God and the conscience of the believer; peace is made with God and spoken to our hearts; pardon is procured; law and justice are satisfied and no more to be feared. By his blood the everlasting covenant is ratified and confirmed.

A High Priest

We may approach God himself with boldness, drawing near to him by faith, because we have a great High Priest sitting in his presence, sitting with him on his throne, accepted forever! We draw near to God in the holiest 'by a new and living way, which he hath consecrated for us, through the veil, that is to say, his flesh; And having an high priest over the house of God' (vv. 20-21; cf. 1 John 2:1-2)). Therefore, 'Let us draw near with a true heart in full assurance of faith, having our hearts sprinkled from an evil conscience, and our bodies washed with pure water' (v. 22).

Let us hold fast the profession of *our* faith without wavering; (for he *is* faithful that promised;) And let us consider one another to provoke unto love and to good works: Not forsaking the assembling of ourselves together, as the manner of some *is*; but exhorting *one another*: and so much the more, as ye see the day approaching. For if we sin wilfully after that we have received the knowledge of the truth, there remaineth no more sacrifice for sins, But a certain fearful looking for of judgment and fiery indignation, which shall devour the adversaries. He that despised Moses' law died without mercy under two or three witnesses: Of how much sorer punishment, suppose ye, shall he be thought worthy, who hath trodden under foot the Son of God, and hath counted the blood of the covenant, wherewith he was sanctified, an unholy thing, and hath done despite unto the Spirit of grace? For we know him that hath said, Vengeance *belongeth* unto me, I will recompense, saith the Lord. And again, The Lord shall judge his people. *It is* a fearful thing to fall into the hands of the living God. But call to remembrance the former days, in which, after ye were illuminated, ye endured a great fight of afflictions; Partly, whilst ye were made a gazingstock both by reproaches and afflictions; and partly, whilst ye became companions of them that were so used. For ye had compassion of me in my bonds, and took joyfully the spoiling of your goods, knowing in yourselves that ye have in heaven a better and an enduring substance. Cast not away therefore your confidence, which hath great recompense of reward. For ye have need of patience, that, after ye have done the will of God, ye might receive the promise. For yet a little while, and he that shall come will come, and will not tarry. Now the just shall live by faith: but if any man draw back, my soul shall have no pleasure in him. But we are not of them who draw back unto perdition; but of them that believe to the saving of the soul.

Hebrews 10:23-39

Chapter 29

Read: Hebrews 10:23-39

'A True Heart In Full Assurance'

Because we have such a great High Priest seated in heaven, because his blood has been forever accepted upon the mercy-seat, and he ever lives to make intercession for us, we have every reason to come to God by him. Christ has opened the way, Christ is the way, and every sinner who comes to God by this way is welcome in the holiest. Let us therefore draw near to God (Hebrews 10:21-22).

A True Heart

We come to God with our hearts, not with mere bodily religious exercise, but in true godliness, with a new heart. A heart that is right with God, and is single, sincere, hearty in its desires, and upright in its ends. Everything in the worship and service of our God must arise from and be done with a true heart.

Full Assurance

If we believe God, if we have faith in and toward the triune God, if we trust the Lord Jesus Christ alone for the whole of our acceptance with God, we may come to him, being fully assured of our acceptance by the blood, righteousness, and mediation of Christ. We cannot draw near to God in any other way. God is seen by faith, known by faith, honoured by faith, and worshipped by faith in Christ.

Blessed assurance! Jesus is mine!
Oh what a foretaste of glory divine!
Heir of salvation, purchase of God,
Born of His Spirit, washed in His blood!

A Clear Conscience

Our consciences are by nature evil, blind, perverse, corrupt, and pronounce us guilty before God. Once the blood of Christ is sprinkled on the conscience by the Spirit of God it is thereby purged from dead works; it is cleansed from all sin, and granted the blessed peace of full pardon and forgiveness upon the ground of justice satisfied. It is this that gives the believing sinner boldness to draw near to God.

Cleansed Life

Having our consciences and our bodies washed with pure water, is not talking about the water of baptism (v. 22). But rather about the grace of God the Holy Spirit, often compared to water in scripture (John 7:37-39). The body as well as the soul needs washing and renewing. Grace in the heart cleanses the life and sanctifies the whole man. 'The allusion', John Gill tells us, 'is to a custom of the Jews, who were obliged to wash their bodies, and make them clean, when they prayed, worshipped, and offered sacrifice to God.'

Hold Fast

Yes, we are kept in grace and kept in faith by the power of God's grace, the blood of Christ, and the seal of the Spirit. If he did not hold us by his grace, we could not and would not hold him; but true faith holds him and holds him fast. Faith holds Christ to the end. He will not let us go; and we will not let him go.

Let us ever hold fast the doctrine of our profession, the gospel of God's grace and glory in Christ, our crucified, risen, exalted Substitute, the Object of our profession. Here is our encouragement to do so: 'He is faithful that promised', God is faithful (Lamentations 3:21-26).

Our faithful God has promised us eternal life and salvation in the Lord Jesus Christ to all who seek him. Truly, his faithfulness is great! His compassions never fail! His mercy, love and grace are immutable. His gifts and callings are without repentance. He will bring us safely home to heaven at last!

Matters of Responsibility

'Let us draw near with a true heart in full assurance of faith, having our hearts sprinkled from an evil conscience, and our bodies washed with pure water. Let us hold fast the profession of our faith without wavering; (for he is faithful that promised;) And let us consider one another to provoke unto love and to good works: Not forsaking the assembling of ourselves together, as the manner of some is; but exhorting one another: and so much the more, as ye see the day approaching'. (Hebrews 10:22-25)

What great privileges of grace we enjoy in Christ! The triune God has covenanted to save us! The Son of God has redeemed us by his own precious blood! We are forgiven of all sin, sanctified by the grace of God, and given permanent access to and acceptance with the holy Lord God in Christ. Being made the recipients of such mercies by the power and grace of God the Holy Spirit, by whose saving operations we now believe, we are heirs of God and joint-heirs with Jesus Christ. With such great privileges come great responsibilities. Here the Spirit of God shows us some of our responsibilities as God's people in this world. They are responsibilities relating to ourselves, to our God, and to one another.

Draw Near

Let us draw near to God (v. 22). Let us ever come to our God in prayer and praise with honest, open and sincere hearts. He will receive us, for our hearts have been sprinkled with the blood of Christ and our bodies have been washed or purified by his Spirit through the Word and by the power of his grace.

A true heart, wrote John Trapp, is 'a heart truly and entirely given up to God, delighting to do his will, desirous rather that God's will be done than our own, that he may be glorified though we be not gratified, acknowledging the kingdom, power, and glory to be his alone'.

If our hearts are true, if we truly trust Christ alone for the whole of our everlasting acceptance with God, we can and shall come to him with 'the full assurance of faith', being confident of acceptance with him because of Christ's finished work.

This assurance is altogether a matter of faith in Christ. It is based entirely upon the work of redemption accomplished outside our experience. Yet, it arises from the experience of grace in our souls. It is the result of having our hearts sprinkled from an evil conscience. We enjoy this blessed assurance by having the witness of the blood of Christ in our hearts, having our bodies washed with pure water, that is to say, being born again by the Spirit of God (1 John 5:7-14).

'Let us hold fast the profession of our faith without wavering: (for he is faithful that promised)' (v. 23). It is our responsibility to continue steadfast in the faith of the gospel, because God is faithful. We must allow nothing to turn us aside from Christ (Philippians 3:4-14). Whatever the trial, the fear, the doubt, or the trouble, let us believe God. 'Faithful is he that calleth you, who also will do it' (1 Thessalonians 5:24).

Consider One Another

As we make our pilgrimage through this world of woe, let us ever consider one another (v. 24). Let us ever consider and be considerate of one another, both as frail, fickle, sinful men and women, and as brothers and sisters in Christ, companions in the grace of God, companions in tribulation, and companions in this hostile world. If we make it our business in life to love one another and care for one another, we will have less time to complain of being neglected. If we will each consider one another, that will help to kindle and rekindle love and grace in others.

Public Worship

Let us never forsake the assembly of God's saints in the worship of our God (v. 25). This, too, is a matter of urgent, pressing responsibility. It is the blessed duty and great privilege of believers to meet together for worship, praise and fellowship. We ought never to take this for granted.

Our great God has appointed it, approves of it, is glorified in it, and deserves to be worshipped. We need to be edified, instructed, refreshed, and comforted. Others need to be convinced, converted and brought to a knowledge of Christ. There are yet some sheep who must be called. This is the place where our Lord has promised to meet with his people (Matthew 18:20; Psalm 122:1-9; 133:1-3).

The assembly of God's saints for public worship, the gathering of God's people to hear his Word, seek his face, and sing his praise is prominently set before us in the New Testament as a matter of great privilege and great responsibility. When God's saints come together in the name of Christ, that assembly is 'the house of God' (1 Timothy 3:15). It is 'the temple of God' (1 Corinthians 3:16). It is a 'habitation of God through the Spirit' (Ephesians 2:22). This is the place, the only place, where the Lord God promises to meet with, speak to, and instruct his people. Nothing is more important for the spiritual health and well-being of our souls than the assembly of the saints for worship.

Will we ever learn that the plain statements of holy scripture alone must be the basis of our faith and practice, not the tortuous deductions of depraved minds, not the self-promoting creeds of denominationalism, and not traditions of the 'church fathers'. It is the revealed will of God in holy scripture that is and must be, our solitary rule in all things. All our doctrine, all our ordinances of divine worship, and all our judgment in all spiritual matters must arise from 'thus saith the Lord'. We dare not add or take away anything from the book.

'Let Us Consider One Another'
Brethren should always be thoughtful and considerate of one another.

As Men
We are all but men, men and women of like passions and infirmities. We should consider one another's weaknesses and make allowance for them. We should consider one another's outward state and condition in the world, and try to understand one another's needs, and help each other.

As Believers
As saints, as believers, as men and women in Christ, we are all partakers of the same grace, loved with the same love, conceived and brought forth in the womb of God's eternal electing grace. We are all interested in the same covenant, redeemed by the same blood, and have the same graces and privileges. We all have the same and an equal right to heaven and eternal glory in Christ. We all have one Spirit and the same Spirit, the same grace of faith, the same righteousness, the same fountain to wash in, the same fulness to partake of, the same throne of grace to go to, and the same inheritance to enjoy.

As Members
As church members, members of the same family and the same body, may God grant us grace always to consider one another in this light. Let us ever endeavour to provoke one another to brotherly love, to stir it up because it is always apt to wax cold. This is our Lord's new commandment, the bond of perfection, the evidence of regeneration, that which makes the saints' communion comfortable and delightful. Without this brotherly love, a profession of faith is empty, meaningless, and vain.

Let us provoke one another to good works, too. Good works are works of grace, kindness, forgiveness, patience, forbearance, and faithfulness. Good works are never set before us in the New Testament as works of self-righteousness and severity, but as works of mercy, love, kindness, forbearance, and forgiveness. They are not works by which we make ourselves righteous (or more righteous), but works arising from righteousness. How can we fulfil this admonition?

Not Forsaking

Believers are people who find great pleasure and satisfaction in daily worship: in prayer, praise, and meditation. Daily, private, personal worship is a characteristic of every believer's life. With the rising of the morning sun his heart is lifted up to God. Every morning he directs his prayer to the throne of grace and looks to his Lord with a heart of faith. Every evening he gives thanks to God and lays his head upon his pillow in the sweet rest of faith.

That is the way to begin and end every day! Blessed is the man or woman who worships God in private. Let all who know and trust the living God worship him daily. Let all who follow Christ in the path of faith and obedience follow him also to the solitary place of private prayer. I would do everything within my power to promote and encourage private worship among the saints of God. Let every priest of God offer the daily sacrifices of prayer and praise to the Lord. But there is something even more important than private worship.

Does that last statement surprise you? I know that most people who are genuinely concerned for the glory of God and the worship of God rank personal, private worship above all things in the life of faith. But I am convinced that public worship, if it is true worship, is even more important than private worship.

An Example

David, the sweet singer of Israel, gave the highest possible regard to the matter of public worship. Without neglecting private worship, he said, 'As for me, I will come into thy house in the multitude of thy mercy: and in thy fear will I worship toward thy holy temple' (Psalm 5:7).

He could not force others to worship God, and would not if he could. 'But', he says, 'as for me, I will come into thy house'. That is to say, I will come into the place of public worship in the assembly of God's saints to worship the Lord my God.

When he came into the place of worship with the saints of God, David was determined truly to worship the Lord. He says, 'In thy fear will I worship toward thy holy temple'. David was resolved in his heart, at every appointed time, to come with God's saints into the place of public worship, so that he might worship God in heaven, in the temple of his holiness.

Five Reasons Not to Abandon the Assembly of the Saints

In recent days, some have begun to call for believers to abandon the worship of God in local churches, declaring that, 'the era of the church age has come to an end.' Throughout the history of the church, men seeking to promote their own cause and their own name rather than the cause and the name of Christ have made such baseless statements.

Be assured, God has not quite yet finished using his church. He says so (Ephesians 3:20-21). Without question, those who worship God must abandon all synagogues of Satan where men and women are made drunk with the wine of Babylon (Revelation 18:4). Those who follow Christ cannot and must not give any credence to will worship (Colossians 2:16-23). But we will not abandon the worship of God in the assembly of his saints so long as the world stands. Here are five reasons why.

1. Where God Meets Sinners in Saving Mercy

It is true that God uses personal witnessing, tracts, tapes, books and other instruments of gospel instruction to call his elect to life and faith in Christ, but generally God saves his sheep in the congregations of his saints, when they are gathered for worship (Acts 2:1, 37-41). Sinners in need of mercy should seek mercy where mercy is always found in great, overflowing abundance; and mercy is always found in the house of God. God's saints know themselves to be sinners in need of mercy; so they come, with all their needs, to the house of mercy, seeking the Lord.

2. Where Our Family Gathers

Every true local church is a family of believers. When the church gathers for worship, it is the gathering of our family for sweet and blessed fellowship in the gospel. Family members need each other, comfort each other, and help each other, because they love each other.

3. Where the Lord Jesus Christ Meets With His People

Our Saviour has promised that, wherever his people gather in his name, he will be with them (Matthew 18:20). To gather in Christ's name is to gather by faith in his name, for the honour of his name and to worship in his name. If only two or three gather to worship the Son of God, he will meet with them. The old man, Simeon, found God's salvation, the Lord Jesus Christ, in the temple, the appointed place of public worship (Luke 2:25-32); and if we would see Christ we must come with his saints when they gather in the place of public worship.

4. Where God Deals With Men

Each local congregation of believers is the house and temple of the living God (1 Corinthians 3:16-17; 1 Timothy 3:15). No material building is the house and temple of God; but the gathering, the assembling of his saints in the name of Christ, to worship him is! When redeemed sinners gather in Christ's name, God the Holy Spirit makes the assembly his house. Such an assembly is 'a habitation of God through the Spirit' (Ephesians 2:22). God reveals his glory, gives out his law, makes known his will, bestows his blessings and instructs his people in his temple, his church. It is in this place that God speaks to men by his Spirit through his Word.

In all ages the people of God have been known and identified by their public gatherings for worship. Wherever God has had a people in this world, he has had a congregation to worship him. Sheep are always found in flocks. The only sheep who are alone are either lost or sick. And God's elect are sheep. No matter how few, they have always gathered together in public worship. In the public assembly they bear public, united testimony to the world of their Saviour's grace and glory. As an assembled body of believers they strengthen, cheer, comfort, encourage, edify, and help one another by prayer, praise, and the preaching of the gospel.

From the beginning of the Bible to the end, there is a clear line of succession in this matter of public worship. Cain and Abel came to worship God in a public assembly. Noah's first act after the flood was an act of public worship to celebrate God's saving grace. Wherever the patriarchs pitched their tents in days of old, they erected an altar for worship. Throughout the Mosaic economy, the Jew who did not worship God in the tabernacle or temple was cut off from the congregation. Throughout the book of Acts, wherever God's children were scattered by persecution, they soon gathered in public assemblies for the worship of God.

Public worship is one identifying mark of true believers. With David, every saved sinner is resolved to worship God, saying, 'As for me, I will come into thy house in the multitude of thy mercy: and in thy fear will I worship toward thy holy temple.' By this let everyone examine himself or herself. Those who willingly and habitually absent themselves from the worship of God do not know God. A person may be outwardly faithful to the church of God who does not know God, but no one is faithful to Christ who is not faithful in the public assembly of his church for worship.

5. Neglect of Public Worship Is the First Step Towards Apostasy

Seldom do men and women turn away from Christ and the gospel of his grace suddenly. Usually the charms of the world take men by degrees, gradually. Apostasy is usually so gradual that those who forsake Christ do not even realize they have forsaken him. How many there are who never attend, or seldom attend, the worship of God, who yet foolishly presume they are children of God! But their continued forsaking of the assembly of God's saints is proof that they never really knew the Lord

Jesus Christ in saving faith (1 John 2:19). Those who wilfully neglect the assembly of God's saints for public worship, though they know the truth of God, tread underfoot the Son of God, count the blood of the covenant a useless thing, and despise the Spirit of grace.

The House of God

David, a man after God's own heart, declared, 'As for me, I will come into thy house in the multitude of thy mercy: and in thy fear will I worship toward thy holy temple' (Psalm 5:7). 'I will come into thy house'. The house of God is the congregation of the saints, wherever they gather in public assembly to worship God. When we come into the assembly of God's saints, we come into the house and temple of the living God (1 Corinthians 3:16; 1 Timothy 3:15).

'I will come into thy house in the multitude of thy mercy'. It is not enough merely to 'go to church'. We must come into the house of God in faith, trusting the Lord's mercy. And there are a multitude of mercies with God in Christ. Sinners need mercy. We must come to the place of public worship as sinners trusting God's abundant mercy in Christ. If we do not come as sinners seeking mercy, we will not worship. But sinners looking to Christ for mercy always find a multitude of mercy in him (Luke 18:13-14). In him we find …

Everlasting, covenant mercy (Jeremiah 31:31-34)
Sin-atoning, redeeming mercy (Romans 3:24-26)
Effectual, saving mercy (Micah 7:18-20)
Immutable, preserving mercy (Malachi 3:6)
Daily, providential mercy (Romans 8:28)

Truly, 'It is of the Lord's mercies that we are not consumed, because his compassions fail not' (Lamentations 3:22), and every worshipper in God's house finds it to be so. 'And in thy fear will I worship toward thy holy temple'. We must come to the house of God with reverence and godly fear to worship him, that is, to see him, to hear him, to adore him, to praise him and to obey him. This was David's resolve. May it ever be yours and mine. May God give us grace to make public worship our delight and truly to worship him in the assembly of his saints.

Most Important

Public worship is the single most important aspect of the believer's life. When David was banished from Jerusalem, the place of public worship, he envied even the sparrows who made their nests in the house of God.

His heart longed not for the throne, the riches, or the power that had been taken from him, but for the assembly of God's saints in public worship. When the privilege of public worship is taken from him for a short time, nothing is more important or precious to God's child (Psalm 84:1-4).

The fact is, all who are born of God love the assembly of God's saints in public worship, and love the ministry of the gospel. There are no exceptions. God's people will not willingly absent themselves from the worship of God. It is true, there are many who very strictly attend, and even love, the outward service of public worship, who do not know the Lord. Their outward worship is nothing but a show of hypocrisy, for they never worship God in private. Anyone who wilfully neglects and despises the public assembly of the saints for worship, also neglects and despises private worship. Those who do not worship God do not know God.

People are busy with all kinds of things. The cares and pleasures of this world consume almost all their time and attention. When convenient they attend church, give God a little tip and sing, 'Oh, how I love Jesus!' But any time something more important comes up (a good football game, a special television show, a visiting relative, or a sick dog!), they absent themselves from the house of God with little regret. They say, 'I can always go to church next week. God knows my heart'. Of that you can be sure: the Lord does know our hearts, and he will judge us accordingly!

Those who are truly God's people love the house of God and the worship of God. They arrange their lives around the worship of God. Nothing ever comes up, over which they have control, to keep them from the house of God. They see to it that when the saints of God gather for worship, they are among them, unless their absence is genuinely unavoidable. Their faithfulness in the matter of public worship is much more than a matter of duty. It is their delightful choice. Public worship is the single most important aspect of their lives in this world. Nothing is more important to the children of God in this world than the public assembly of the saints for worship; and that public assembly of the saints for worship is the local church, the congregation of the Lord, the house of God.

Why do God's people place such importance upon the public worship of the local church? Remember what we said:

This is the place where God meets sinners in saving mercy.
This is the place where our family gathers.
This is the place where the Lord Jesus Christ meets with his people.
This is the place where God deals with men.
The neglect of public worship is the first step towards total apostasy.

Trampling Underfoot the Son of God

Those who wilfully neglect the assembly of God's saints for public worship, though they may mentally know the truth of God, tread underfoot the Son of God, count the blood of the covenant a useless thing and despise the Spirit of grace. Let us see if that is not what the Holy Spirit tells us in Hebrews 10:24-29.

This passage is pressing upon us the necessity of perseverance in the faith, and the need for each of us, by every means we can use, to encourage one another to 'hold fast the profession of our faith without wavering'. Look at the admonition and warning here given by our God to all who profess faith in his dear Son.

'Provoke Unto Love'

'And let us consider one another to provoke unto love and to good works'. May God give us grace ever to consider one another, to encourage and be encouraging to one another, for Christ's sake. As we have seen, if we devote ourselves to loving and serving others, we will have less time to feel sorry for ourselves and complain about being neglected by others. Also, as we serve each other, we provoke others to love and good works, kindling in them a desire to serve rather than be served.

Not Forsaking

'Not forsaking the assembling of ourselves together'. This is talking about our regular gathering together unto Christ (2 Thessalonians 2:1), the act of meeting together in one place for the worship of our God and Saviour, by the ministry of the Word, prayer and praise, and in observing ordinances of the gospel: Believer's Baptism and the Lord's Supper.

To 'forsake' the assembling of God's saints in public worship refers to wilful neglect in attending the gathering of God's saints. Many wander from place to place, never really committing themselves to the building of God's church and kingdom, but ever seeking personal gratification. This abandoning of God's church is an abandoning of God, the gospel of his grace and the glory of his Son. It is apostasy, departing from the faith, letting go our profession.

Privilege and Duty

It is both our highest privilege and greatest duty in this world to assemble with God's saints for public worship. Our heavenly Father has appointed it and approves of it. His glory is concerned in it. And his gospel is advanced by it. Both we and our brethren need it, that we may be revived, refreshed, comforted, instructed, edified, and enabled to grow in the grace and knowledge of Christ (2 Peter 3:17-18). The unconverted need our faithfulness in worship as well. We ought to maintain the worship of God for their sake, as well as our own, that they may be convinced of the gospel, converted by the grace of God, and brought to the knowledge and faith of Christ.

John Gill wrote: This 'assembling together ought not to be forsaken; for it is a forsaking God, and our own mercies, and such are like to be forsaken of God; nor is it known what is lost hereby; and it is the first outward visible step to apostasy, and often issues in it.'

The Manner of Some

'As the manner of some is'. As in those early days, so in our day, it is the practice of many who profess faith in Christ to absent themselves from the house of God, showing by their neglect an utter contempt for Christ, his church and the gospel of the grace of God. I know that is strong language; but that is the language of this passage.

Rather than abandoning one another, let us exhort and encourage one another to prayer, to attend the worship of God, to adhere to Christ, and the faith we have professed. Let us ever encourage one another to consider Christ and cling to him. It is in this way that we most effectually serve, comfort and edify one another. Here we share (in conversation, prayer, preaching and praise) our experiences of grace, the doctrine of Christ, and the things of God. Here, in the house of God, we put one another in remembrance of God's faithfulness, his promises, our responsibilities, and of our Lord's coming; 'And so much the more, as ye see the day approaching'. Do you see the day approaching? The day of death? The day of Christ's advent? The day of judgment?

Sinning Wilfully

'For if we sin wilfully after that we have received the knowledge of the truth, there remaineth no more sacrifice for sins.' When a person abandons Christ, when he abandons the worship of God, when he abandons the gospel, he abandons hope. Sinners have no hope but him! If we were to leave him, we have nowhere else to go! (Read John 6:66-69.) Those who abandon Christ abandon everything, except the wrath of God. There is nothing left for the apostate, 'But a certain fearful looking for of judgment and fiery indignation, which shall devour the adversaries.'

How important is the worship of God? It is just this important. The worship of God displays faith in Christ, love for Christ, devotion to Christ, and great need of Christ. The forsaking of the assembly of God's saints displays contempt for Christ (vv. 28-29).

Cling to Christ as a drowning man clings to the life rope. With every apparent slip of our hands, let us grip more firmly than ever, knowing all the while that we must be held by him if we are to hold him.

'We Are Not of Them Who Draw Back'

There are many who begin the race but never finish. Many run well for a season, but in time fall by the wayside. Like Judas, Demas, and Diotrephes, many seem to be stalwart examples of faith and faithfulness; but at last deny the faith, forsake Christ and his people, and make shipwreck of their profession. These facts, so often illustrated in holy scripture and verified by observation, cause great concern in the hearts of men and women like us who struggle with sin. True believers are often like the true apostles of our Lord. On that night when he announced that one of them would betray him, those whose hearts were true quaked with fear, saying, 'Lord, is it I?' After reading the warnings given to us in this tenth chapter of Hebrews against such apostasy, when we read verse 39, we have reason to shout with joy and thanksgiving to our God who keeps us by grace. 'But we are not of them who draw back unto perdition; but of them that believe to the saving of the soul.'

This last section of Hebrews 10 was written specifically to encourage us in perseverance; and the source of encouragement is the assurance that true believers shall persevere unto the end. The righteous shall, indeed, hold on his way. Christ's sheep shall 'never perish'. Nothing shall be able to separate us from the love of God in Christ. God's elect shall persevere unto the end, because we shall be preserved and kept unto the end by God's almighty, immutable grace.

Apostasy and Wilful Sin

Once again, we have here a word against apostasy. In verses 26 and 27, the apostle describes what apostasy is. This description must be understood in its context. Here the Holy Spirit clearly makes apostasy to be connected with the forsaking of Christ, his gospel, his church, and the worship of God in the assembly of his saints.

These verses are perverted by many in their attempts to prove that true believers can be lost; that people who commit sin after being saved by the grace of God are lost. Such heresy is so totally contrary to the scriptures that it needs no more refutation. Yet, an incorrect interpretation of this passage has caused great distress to many genuine believers. The fact is, honest hearts, burdened with a sense of inward sin, realize that all of our acts of sin are, to one degree or another, wilful acts.

This is what the text means. After a person has embraced and professed the gospel of Christ (and particularly the great truths revealed in this chapter: that the Lord Jesus Christ is the only and all-sufficient High Priest of God's elect, that his blood is our only effectual atonement, and that his sacrifice is the end and fulfilment of all the types and shadows of the law) and yet, against all evidences, light, and revelation, wilfully denies the sufficiency of Christ and the efficacy of his sacrifice, there is no other sacrifice for sin; there is no other Saviour! There is no help for him, no hope for him, but only a certain fearful judgment awaiting him eternally. There is no going back to the Mosaic law, rituals and ceremonies. So if anyone wilfully turns from Christ, there is no hope! (Acts 4:12; 1 Corinthians 3:11). The wilful sin spoken of in verse 26 is the abandonment of Christ, his gospel, his worship, and his people. It is going back to the law, going back to works religion, going back to the world.

That is exactly the way this apostasy is described in verses 28-29. God gave the law to Israel by Moses. Anyone who rejected God's law or set at naught the rules and sacrifices of the law was put to death (Deuteronomy 17:1-6). While the tabernacle, temple, and ordinances of the law stood, they were binding upon the people. If God poured his wrath upon those who made light of the types, think how severe his judgments shall be upon those who reject and make light of the precious blood of his dear Son! A return to circumcision and ceremony is turning away from Christ! It is bringing contempt upon the Son of God and the gospel of God's free grace (Galatians 5:1-4; 4:21).

We must not shy away from the very strong words the apostle was inspired to use in describing what this apostasy involves. It is treading under foot the Son of God. It is counting the blood of the covenant, wherewith a person has been outwardly sanctified (by the profession and practice of religion), an unholy, common, ordinary, meaningless thing. It is doing despite to the Spirit if grace.

Awaiting Judgment

Those who abandon Christ and the gospel of God's grace and glory in him never knew him. Nothing awaits them but wrath and judgment (vv. 30-31). 'They went out from us because they were not of us.' Such people, those who choose will-worship, circumcision, works and law in the stead of the revealed Christ, have every reason to expect the wrath and judgment of God to fall on them (Deuteronomy 32:35-39). It is a fearful thing to incur the wrath of the eternal and living God. Ask Noah's generation, the inhabitants of Sodom, or the sons of Korah. 'Be not highminded, but fear' (Romans 11:21-22; John 3:35-36).

Assurance

In verses 32-34, the Holy Spirit calls us to remembrance. Paul thus urges us to remember the early days of faith when we endured mocking, ridicule and affliction. He does this to encourage us to perseverance in keeping the faith, trusting in Christ, even in the face of great temptation and opposition. He would have us to hold to our confidence in Christ and not be disturbed and discouraged by false prophets, ceremonialists, and legalists. These would only rob us of liberty in Christ, and take us away from the simplicity that is in him.

When you left the world to walk with Christ, the world did not allow you to leave peacefully; but you knew that in heaven you had a family, an inheritance and an everlasting glory, even if you lost everything here. The people you lost for Christ's sake are nothing compared to the family you have gained. The comforts, pleasures and fame of the world are nothing but soap bubbles. The glory of heaven is eternal.

'We Have Need of Patience'

Paul concludes this chapter with a comforting, assuring, and challenging word of admonition. He urges us not to cast away our confidence, our confidence in Christ, our confident hope of everlasting salvation in him. He is telling us not to take our eyes off Christ, to let nothing and no one come between us and him. Trials will come upon us. Temptations will assail us. Satan will roar against us. The world will allure us. Those things are certain; but so is this: 'The sufferings of this present time are not worthy to be compared with the glory which shall be revealed in us' (Romans 8:18).

There is indeed, 'a great recompense of reward' at the end of our pilgrimage. We shall be with Christ! We shall be like Christ! We shall see him as he is, 'face to face'! Our God shall wipe away all tears from our eyes forever! When we have entered into and taken possession of glory with Christ, there will be no more sorrow, for there shall be no more sin! For now, let us exercise 'patience, that, after ye have done the will of God, ye might receive the promise'.

Here is the promise by which the Holy Sprit inspires our perseverance. 'For yet a little while, and he that shall come will come, and will not tarry.' When our Lord Jesus Christ comes, he will put an end to all suffering and death and sorrow (John 14:1-3; Revelation 21:4-5).

Now faith is the substance of things hoped for, the evidence of things not seen. For by it the elders obtained a good report. Through faith we understand that the worlds were framed by the word of God, so that things which are seen were not made of things which do appear.

Hebrews 11:1-3

Chapter 30

Read: Hebrews 11:1-3

In Hebrews 10 the Spirit of God gave us words of warning, encouragement, and instruction about true persevering faith: that faith by which chosen, redeemed sinners are experimentally united with Christ, faith which does not draw back unto perdition, but perseveres and continues to the salvation of their souls. In this chapter the inspired writer speaks of the nature of faith, the works of faith, and the response of faith to the Word of God. Then, the chapter concludes by giving us numerous examples of Old Testament saints who believed God.

'Things Hoped For'

In verse 1 the Holy Spirit tells us that 'faith is the substance of things hoped for'. What are the things for which we hope? Deliverance and eternal salvation, preservation in Christ, eternal glory, and everlasting fellowship with God. Faith is the ground, foundation, and support of our hope. We have a reasonable well-grounded hope of these things, of eternal salvation and all that it includes, because we believe God, because we have confidence in his Word. Faith gives us the possession of these things beforehand. Faith gives us the reality of them, the first fruits of them (Romans 8:23). These things are certain, as certain and sure as the very throne of God. It is our faith in Christ that gives us confidence concerning them (Romans 4:17-25; Acts 27:21-25). With Paul, all who trust Christ have reason to be of good cheer, because we can honestly say, 'I believe God, that it shall be even as it was told me.'

'Things Not Seen'

'Faith is ... the evidence of things not seen.' Faith looks not at the things that are seen, but at those things that are unseen (2 Corinthians 4:17-18). 'Things not seen' are things done in eternity: the counsel, covenant, and decrees of the triune God. They are things done in time: the incarnation, obedience, death, resurrection, ascension, and exaltation of Christ our Mediator. They are things being done now: the intercession of Christ in heaven, the works of God the Holy Spirit in grace, and the goodness and wisdom of God's providence. They are also things yet to be done: the resurrection of the dead, the judgment, and eternal glory.

These are all unseen things; but faith in the Lord Jesus Christ gives our hearts proof and evidence of them. His Word, his Spirit, and his work of grace in us assure us of all these things (Romans 10:17; Hebrews 11:6). Let us then consider this faith.

'Faith'

Ours is a life of faith. It is written, 'The just shall live by faith'. So let us exercise the patience of confident faith in Christ. True believers live by faith, not by law, works, merit, or ceremony. We receive spiritual life by faith in Christ. That life is sustained and kept by the power of God through faith. That life shall be perfected by faith. The whole of our salvation is by faith. 'It is of faith that it might be by grace; to the end the promise might be sure to all the seed' (Romans 4:16).

Works make no contribution to our life in Christ; and if any professor of faith draws back to ceremonialism or turns away from the simplicity of faith in Christ, God says, 'My soul shall have no pleasure in him'.

'But we are not of them who draw back unto perdition; but of them that believe to the saving of the soul.' True believers cannot, will not, and do not leave Christ, nor will they take up the weak and beggarly elements of the law and their own works in the place of Christ. 'To whom shall we go?' Christ alone has life. Christ alone gives life. Christ alone is life! He who saved us and has kept us thus far will keep us to the end and will present us, at last, faultless before the presence of his glory (John 10:27-30; Romans 8:38-39; Jude 24-25).

I want every child of God, every true believer, to know and enjoy the full assurance of a saving interest in Christ. I want all who are God's to have an assurance based upon evidence that arises from the Word of God and satisfies the enlightened conscience. Where can such evidence be found? The Holy Ghost tells us. 'Now faith is the substance of things hoped for, the evidence of things not seen.'

Faith Alone

The only evidence I have of my saving interest in Christ is faith in Christ. All other evidence, all other confidence, all other assurance, I altogether repudiate. When Satan accuses me, when my own heart condemns me, when my sin torments me, when I examine myself I find comfort, peace, and assurance only by faith in Christ. I have no evidence of a clear title to heaven but by faith, and faith is evidence enough; God says that it is enough, and my conscience says it is enough.

The Gift of God

This faith in Christ is the gift of God the Holy Spirit (Ephesians 2:8; Philippians 1:29; Colossians 2:12). It is given to us, wrought in us, and sustained in us by the gracious operations of God the Holy Spirit. Faith is not natural to man. No man can believe on Christ unless God gives him faith. We are responsible to believe, but we cannot. Unless God the Holy Spirit gives us faith, we will go to hell clinging to our own works of righteousness. If we would have faith, we must seek it from the God of all grace, crying out, as we bow before his throne, 'Lord, I believe, help thou mine unbelief'. Let us cry out to the Saviour like Peter, 'Lord, bid me come unto thee' (Matthew 14:27-33). If he bids us come, we can come and we shall come.

God's Appointed Means

The preaching of the gospel is God's appointed means of grace, by which chosen, redeemed sinners are born of God and granted faith in Christ. Faith in Christ is born in the hearts of God's elect only by the preaching of the gospel (Romans 1:16-17; 10:17; James 1:18; 1 Peter 1:23-25).

Faith without knowledge is impossible and faith based upon false knowledge is false faith. True faith is faith based upon and born of the knowledge of the gospel. Quit trying to convince yourself that you were saved before you learned the gospel. You were not. No one can or will trust Christ until he sees his need of a Substitute, sees how God can be just and yet justify the ungodly through the merits of Christ, and sees that salvation is by grace alone.

The Evidence of Grace

Faith in Christ is the sure, certain, infallible evidence, proof, and assurance of eternal salvation. 'Now faith is the substance of things hoped for, the evidence of things not seen.' Faith is not the cause of grace, salvation, and an interest in Christ; but faith is the evidence of these things.

'Faith Is The Substance of Things Hoped For'

The word 'substance' means 'the essence, the assurance, or the certainty' of things hoped for. Faith possesses beforehand what God has promised to give, 'Verily, verily, I say unto you, he that believeth on me hath (in possession) everlasting life' (John 6:47).

Did the Lord God promise to preserve and keep all who believe in his grace? Faith possesses that blessed security in grace. Did our God promise us resurrection glory? Every believer has been raised from spiritual death unto spiritual life in the new birth. This is the first resurrection (Revelation 20:6). And the first resurrection is God's own pledge of the second. The second death shall have no power over any believer. Has God promised believing sinners all the glory and bliss of heaven? In Christ, it is ours. It is the present possession of all who believe. We are already seated with the risen Christ in heaven (Ephesians 2:4-7).

'Faith Is The Evidence of Things Not Seen'

The word 'evidence' means proof. Faith is the proof or verification of things not seen. By faith in Christ I read my name in the Book of Life. Faith did not write it there. God wrote it there before the world began. But faith in Christ verifies that my name is there. Faith verifies things past, those things done by God for us in eternity. We read our names in the Book of Life, in the registry of heaven, only by faith in Christ. We know our election only by faith. We understand God's predestinating purpose by faith.

Faith Verifies Things Done in Time, But Now Unseen

We know that the worlds were framed by the word of God, only as we believe. Believing God's revelation, we understand creation. Apart from faith, no one can understand it. So, too, we understand who Christ is and what he did as the sinner's Substitute, only by believing God's revelation of his Son in the scriptures. Only when a sinner is granted faith in Christ is redemption, righteousness, justification, and forgiveness verified to his own heart and conscience. Faith does not redeem us. Faith does not make us righteous before God. Faith does not accomplish our justification. Faith does not put away our sin and guilt. These things were accomplished by Christ alone. But faith verifies that they are ours when God the Holy Spirit applies the blood to our hearts and speaks peace in our souls by giving us faith in the Son of God (Hebrews 9:11-14).

Faith Verifies Present Things Unseen

I know that I am born of God, because I trust Christ (Mark 16:16). I know that God's providence accomplishes good for me, because I have been called by his Spirit and granted faith in his Son (Psalm 57:2; Romans 8:28-32). I know that Christ makes intercession for me in heaven, because I come to God by faith in him (Hebrews 7:25; 1 John 1:9-2:2).

Faith Verifies Future Things Now Unseen

'For if we believe that Jesus died and rose again, even so them also which sleep in Jesus will God bring with him.'

Believe on the Lord Jesus Christ and eternal life, with all the blessings of grace and glory included, is yours in him, because of him, and by him (1 John 5:1, 5-13).

'The Elders'

In verse 2 we are called to remember that God's saints of old walked by faith just like we do. The only difference between their faith and ours is this: they did not have nearly as much to go on as we do. We have the whole Revelation of God in holy scripture; they did not. But they had the very same faith we have, 'For by it the elders obtained a good report'.

These elders were men of faith who lived in the earliest days of the Old Testament: Abel, Job, Enoch, Noah, and Abraham. These men were justified and accepted in Christ, through faith, just like we are, not because of their works, but by faith alone. Paul mentions this because the Jews tended to elevate the elders too highly. Here the Holy Spirit tells us that Abel, Enoch, Noah, and Abraham were all saved by grace, through faith in the Lord Jesus Christ, just like we are (John 8:39-40).

'We Understand'

In verse 3 we are told that true, saving faith is given understanding in the things of God. 'Through faith we understand that the worlds were framed by the word of God, so that things which are seen were not made of things which do appear.'

All who believe God understand how all things were created. The visible creation was formed from nothing. It all came into existence by the command of our God, who made all things out of nothing and gave it form as it pleased him (John 1:1-3; Colossians 1:16-18).

As we understand the works of God in creation and providence only by faith in his Word, only by bowing to his Word, so we understand the works of God in grace and in judgment, because we have the mind of Christ (1 Corinthians 2:12-16).

This is not something we have achieved by research and study, or even by prayer. This is the gift of God. It is that which we have received by faith in Christ. 'Now we have received, not the spirit of the world, but the spirit which is of God; that we might know the things that are freely given to us of God. Which things also we speak, not in the words which man's wisdom teacheth, but which the Holy Ghost teacheth; comparing spiritual things with spiritual. But the natural man receiveth not the things of the Spirit of God: for they are foolishness unto him: neither can he know them, because they are spiritually discerned. But he that is spiritual judgeth all things, yet he himself is judged of no man. For who hath known the mind of the Lord, that he may instruct him? But we have the mind of Christ.'

Faith is the Evidence

Faith is the evidence of God's great eternal blessings for his people. We see the plans and purposes of God unfold in the work of redemption and salvation through faith.

Chosen

The Lord God almighty, the sovereign God of grace and truth has chosen a people in eternal election, whose names were written in heaven in the Lamb's Book of Life before the world began (Ephesians 1:3-6; 2 Thessalonians 2:13-14; Philippians 4:3; Luke 10:20; Revelation 13:8). These men and women are the objects of God's eternal love, sovereign grace, and immutable purpose. They must be saved. It is not possible for an elect sinner to perish.

Redeemed

The Lord Jesus Christ, the Son of God, redeemed that elect multitude from the curse of the law by his death upon the cross as their Substitute (2 Corinthians 5:18-21; Galatians 3:13; Hebrews 9:12, 26). The blood of Christ was not shed in vain. Every sinner for whom the Lamb of God died shall be saved. If even one of those for whom Christ shed his blood to make atonement by the satisfaction of justice were to perish under the wrath of God and be forever lost, the Son of God would be a frustrated failure. That cannot be! That sin which was transferred from God's elect to Christ the Substitute, the sin for which he suffered and died under the wrath of God, can never be transferred back to those for whom Christ died. As Mr Toplady reminds us, 'Payment God cannot twice demand, first at my bleeding Surety's hand, and then again at mine!'

Called

We also know that God the Holy Spirit effectually regenerates, calls, and saves the elect by almighty, irresistible grace (Psalm 65:4; 110:3; John 3:8;

6:63; Ephesians 2:1-8). All those whose names were written in heaven in eternal election, all those who were redeemed by the blood of Christ shall be effectually called by God the Holy Spirit in time. They shall be born again and saved by the almighty power of his irresistible grace. When the Spirit of God calls, when he draws sinners to Christ, he effectually brings them to Christ. Salvation is not by the will of man, but by the will of God. Salvation is not by the power of man, but by the power of God. Salvation is not by the work of man, but by the work of God. Salvation is not by the choice of man, but by the choice of God. 'So then it is not of him that willeth, nor of him that runneth, but of God that sheweth mercy' (Romans 9:16). 'Salvation is of the Lord'! (Jonah 2:9).

Every sinner in the world who believes on the Lord Jesus Christ has everlasting life (John 3:16, 18, 36; Romans 10:9-13; 1 John 5:1). All who have faith in Christ have salvation. All who look to Christ live. Every sinner in the world who believes on Christ was chosen by God in eternal election, and redeemed by Christ at Calvary, and has been called to Christ by the Holy Spirit's irresistible grace.

All who read the Bible with any measure of spiritual understanding and discernment know these things. These are simple, elementary truths of the gospel, plainly revealed in the holy scriptures. All who were chosen by God in election were redeemed by Christ at Calvary and shall be called by the Holy Spirit in time. All who are called by the Spirit of God shall come to Christ and live forever.

A Question

How can any mortal in this world know whether he is, indeed, chosen of God, redeemed by Christ, and called by the Holy Spirit? The answer is clear and simple: 'faith'! Faith is the evidence! (v. 1). If you believe on the Lord Jesus Christ, then God the Father chose you from eternity, God the Son redeemed you at Calvary, and God the Holy Spirit has called you by his almighty grace.

Your Evidence?

Let us put ourselves on trial. We claim title to a saving interest in Christ. But what evidence do we have that our title is good? For some, nothing in all the world is of more vital concern than this. Your soul is vexed continually with the matter:

> 'Tis a point I long to know, oft it causes anxious thought.
> Do I love the Lord, or no, am I His, or am I not?

Let us examine the evidence and find out. If we can rightfully lay claim to that eternal salvation which is in Christ Jesus, with full assurance and confidence, we must be able to verify that it is ours by the evidence God has given in his Word. We must be able to point to the Word of God and given reason from holy scripture for the hope that lies within us (1 Peter 3:15). The assurance of a saving interest in Christ must be built upon evidence that is acceptable, both in the court of heaven and in the court of my own conscience. We claim to be Christians. We hope that we are the children of God. We hope that we are heirs of God and joint-heirs with Jesus Christ. Where is your evidence? Where is mine?

Not In Experiences

No experience of grace, feeling of spirituality, no work performed by me, past or present, is evidence that I am a child of God.

I know that all who are born of God experience regeneration, conversion, and faith. I know that every true believer feels remorse for sin, conviction, inner conflict, love, joy, and peace. I know that everyone born of God maintains good works in the tenor of his life. But you may experience, feel, and do all these things, and not be born again. Lot's wife, Ananias and Sapphira, Simon Magus, and Saul of Tarsus all testify plainly that neither religious experiences, nor good works, nor feelings of spirituality are evidences of faith in Christ.

Feelings come and feelings go;
And feelings are deceiving.
I trust the living Word of God.
Naught else is worth believing!

What evidence do you have that you are a child of God? When your conscience disturbs you, how do you silence it? When doubts arise, how do you settle them? When you examine yourself, if you are honest enough to do so, by what do you prove to yourself that you are in the faith? Does your heart go back to an experience, or remember a feeling, or hold forth a work you have performed and say, 'There, I know that I am saved, because I could never have experienced, felt, or done those things if I were not one of God's children'?

If your assurance of a saving interest in Christ is built upon such a foundation of sand, I must tell you this: either you are a very proud, self-righteous hypocrite, deceiving your own heart with a refuge of lies, or you have no real peace of heart, assurance of faith, and confidence before God at all! In your inmost soul, you cannot say with Paul, 'I know whom

I have believed, and am persuaded that he is able to keep that which I have committed unto him against that day' (2 Timothy 1:12). The evidence you offer to silence your conscience does not hold up in the court of conscience. Experiences of grace, feelings of spirituality, and good works are no evidence that I am born of God. These things can never give assurance to an honest man, because any grace I experience may be a counterfeit work of Satan. All feelings I have may be no more than natural emotions. Every work performed by man is marred by sin.

Not In Graces

Those graces and works which may convince other men and women that I am a child of God, can never convince my own heart and conscience. Even that which appears to be the fruit of the Spirit is no sure evidence that I am one of God's elect. There are many things by which others are convinced that we belong to God, many things which cause both the world and the church to call us the disciples of Christ (Matthew 5:13-16). But those who make the flattering opinions of others the evidence of their salvation deceive their own souls.

What about gracious influences of the Holy Spirit in a believer's life? Does not the fruit of the Spirit prove that a person is truly born of God? Without question, all who are born of God have the Spirit of God and the Holy Spirit bears fruit in them (Galatians 5:22-23). Fruit toward God: 'love, joy, and peace'. Fruit toward man: 'longsuffering, gentleness, and goodness'. Fruit within: 'faith (faithfulness), meekness, and temperance'. But these things, when held up as the evidence of life to my own conscience, can never give me assurance, if I am honest with myself.

My love, joy, and peace toward God are, at best, fluctuating, sometimes hot, sometimes cold, sometimes fervent, and sometimes languid. My longsuffering is impatient. My gentleness is awfully hard, and my goodness is terribly selfish. My faithfulness is unpredictable. My meekness is full of pride. My temperance lacks discipline. My conscience will accept none of these things as evidence that I belong to God, because conscience, like the law itself, demands perfection.

If you look to the fruit of the Spirit in you as the evidence of your election, redemption, and regeneration, I say again: either you are a proud, self-righteous, hypocrite, deceiving your own heart, or you have no real assurance, confidence of heart, and peace of conscience before God. You may sing, 'Blessed assurance, Jesus is mine!' You may protest vehemently against the possibility that you are not yet saved, a child of God, and an heir of eternal salvation. But in your inmost soul, in the quiet, still, lonely watches of the night, your conscience torments you and says, 'You have no evidence of life. You are lost. You are dead in sin. You are a hypocrite!'

Not In Brotherly Love

Even my love for you, my brethren, is no sure evidence of a saving interest in Christ. Yes, all of God's people love one another. If a man does not love his brethren, he does not love God. I do not deny that at all. Our Lord said, 'By this shall all men know that you are my disciples, if ye have love one to another' (John 13:35). But the issue is not what other men know. The issue is what I know. I want personal, full assurance that I have legitimate title to eternal life. I want evidence that will satisfy my own conscience and heart, answering to the Word of God, that I am one of God's elect, one who's sins have been put away by Jesus Christ, one who is born of God.

I do love my brethren. I can even say, with honesty, that I do love the Lord Jesus Christ. But my love for my brethren and my love for Christ are not sufficient evidences to convince my heart and conscience of my saving interest in Christ.

What about 1 John 3:14? 'We know that we have passed from death unto life, because we love the brethren.' Does not John tell us that our love for the brethren is a basis for assurance? No. John is telling us that we know one another to be the children of God by our love for one another. This is the way we judge between men in this world. The children of God love one another and do righteousness. The children of the devil are malicious and wicked. But love toward the brethren can never be a basis of personal assurance for two reasons: (1) I cannot know with certainty who my brethren are. (2) My love for my brethren does not measure up to the requirements of holy scripture, and cannot honestly be called love at all (1 Corinthians 13:4-8). Personally, I find any comfort, peace, and hope in that passage only by reading 'Christ' in every place where the word 'charity' is found.

Still, this is certain: if you make your love toward your brethren the basis of your assurance and the evidence of your salvation, either you are a proud, self-righteous hypocrite, deceiving your own heart, or you have no assuring evidence of a saving interest in Christ. Certainly, the lack of these things is evidence that a man is not saved. But their presence is not evidence that he is saved. Evidences drawn from personal experience, spiritual feelings, gracious attitudes, and good works, when fairly and honestly examined, are no evidence of a saving interest in Christ. If these things are not evidences of salvation, it is certain that legal deeds are not! The believer's only ground of assurance is faith in Christ.

By faith Abel offered unto God a more excellent sacrifice than Cain, by which he obtained witness that he was righteous, God testifying of his gifts: and by it he being dead yet speaketh. By faith Enoch was translated that he should not see death; and was not found, because God had translated him: for before his translation he had this testimony, that he pleased God. But without faith it is impossible to please him: for he that cometh to God must believe that he is, and that he is a rewarder of them that diligently seek him.

Hebrews 11:4-6

Chapter 31

Read: Hebrews 11:4-6

Abel's Faith

'By faith Abel offered unto God a more excellent sacrifice than Cain, by which he obtained witness that he was righteous, God testifying of his gifts: and by it he being dead yet speaketh.' (Hebrews 11:4).

Because he believed God Abel brought the sacrifice God required of him, trusting the Lord Jesus Christ alone for righteousness, redemption and acceptance with the holy Lord God. Paul's declaration of Abel's faith in Christ arises from that which is recorded in Genesis 4:1-10. Here the Holy Spirit tells us three things about Abel and his faith. (1) Abel offered a more excellent sacrifice than Cain. (2) He obtained witness that he was righteous. (3) Though he is dead, he yet speaks.

'A More Excellent Sacrifice'

First, we are told, 'By faith Abel offered unto God a more excellent sacrifice than Cain'. We must not presume, as many have, that since Adam and Eve are not mentioned in this chapter as examples of faith they must have been unbelievers. There are many men and women of true, saving faith who are not mentioned in this chapter. It appears to me that this inspired list of the great examples of faith begins with Abel because Abel was the first man mentioned after the fall who exemplified true faith in the worship of God and because he was the first person martyred because he believed God.

An Act of Faith

Abel's sacrifice was superior to Cain's because he offered the kind of sacrifice God required: a blood sacrifice upon the altar of God as an act of faith. Abel looked beyond his sacrifice to the sacrifice of Christ. Cain, in his sacrifice, looked only to himself and his works. Abel's sacrifice was a lamb, a type of Christ, the Lamb of God. Abel offered the Lord a firstling of the flock, a picture of Christ who is the firstborn of every creature. He also offered the fat of the lamb, or one of the fattest of his flock, which speaks of the excellence of Christ. His sacrifice was offered up, 'in the process of time' (at the end of days), as Christ came 'in due time', 'when the fulness of time was come', in the end of the world, 'to put away sin by the sacrifice of himself'. Thus the Lord God accepted Abel's sacrifice, 'had respect' to it, and rejected Cain's sacrifice.

Abel's sacrifice of faith was the response of his heart to the Word of God. Faith in Christ presupposes divine revelation. As mentioned above, we must not infer, simply because Adam is not mentioned in this chapter, that he was an unbeliever. There are many reasons for believing otherwise. One reason is this: 'Faith cometh by hearing and hearing by the Word of God' (Romans 10:17). Abel learned the gospel from someone. He did not come up with the idea of blood atonement by a whim of his mind. Abel learned how to worship God from his father. The Word of God is always operative in the conversion of sinners, in the worship of God, and in faith. That word came to Cain and Abel through their father Adam. Faith is the response of the heart to the Word of God (Romans 1:15-17; 1 Corinthians 1:21-23; Hebrews 4:12; James 1:18; 1 Peter 1:23-25).

The Lord God revealed four specific things to Adam and Eve in the garden that are clearly manifest in Abel's worship. (1) In order for a sinner to stand accepted before the thrice holy God he must have a covering. The Righteousness of Christ! (2) That which is of human manufacture (fig leaves) is worthless before the Lord. (3) God himself must provide the covering (righteousness) for us. The sinner's only righteousness before God is the righteousness God gives by imputation. (4) The covering God requires can only be obtained by death, by blood-shedding. The blood of an innocent victim! (Genesis 3:4-8, 14-21)

A. W. Pink points out, 'In Genesis 3:15 and 21 we have the first Gospel sermon which was ever preached on this earth, and that, by the Lord Himself. Life must come out of death. Cain and Abel, and the whole human race, sinned in Adam (Romans 5:12, 18, 19), and the wages of sin is death, penal death. Either I must pay those wages and suffer that death, or another an innocent one, on whom death has no claim must pay those wages in my stead. And in order to my receiving the benefit of that

Substitute's compassion, there must be a link of contact between me and him. Faith it is which unites to Christ. Saving faith, then, in its simplest form, is the placing of a Substitute between my guilty self and a sin-hating God.'

Cain's Offering

What was wrong with Cain's offering? In Genesis 4:3 we read, 'Cain brought of the fruit of the ground an offering unto the Lord.' Cain was not an open infidel. He acknowledged the existence of God. He was not irreligious. He came before God as a worshipper; but he refused to conform to the Word of God. Clearly, four things were amiss in his sacrifice. (1) It was a bloodless sacrifice; and 'without shedding of blood is no remission' (Hebrews 9:22). (2) It was but the fruit of his hands, the product of his work. (3) Cain deliberately ignored the curse of God upon the ground (Genesis 3:17). (4) He despised the grace and trampled under his feet the blood of Christ made known in Genesis 3:15-21.

Cain was a hypocrite. He refused to comply with the revealed will of God. Yet, he attempted to cover his rebellion by coming before God as a worshipper. He would not obey God's revelation. Yet, he brought an offering to the Lord. He did not believe God. Yet, sought to patronize him. This is the 'way of Cain' spoken of by Jude (Jude 11). It is the way of self-will, self-righteousness, unbelief, disobedience, and religious hypocrisy.

Cain and Abel

In Hebrews 11:4-40 Paul gives examples of faith among the Old Testament believers: before the flood (vv. 4-7), from the flood to Moses (vv. 8-29), from Moses to the prophets, kings and judges (vv. 30-40). In this fourth verse the Holy Spirit draws our attention to Cain and Abel, the first sons born to Adam and Eve after the fall.

Two Religions

In these two the world's two religions are pictured: freewill or free grace, salvation by Christ or salvation by works (Genesis 4:3-5). Cain believed, as all the fallen sons of Adam do until God saves them by his grace, that man's acceptance with God is determined by something he does. Abel believed God. He trusted Christ. He looked for acceptance by grace, by the merits of Christ. Cain was a will worshipper. Abel worshipped God. Cain believed man must do his part, or God cannot do his part. Abel believed 'Salvation is of the Lord'! Abel, being one of God's elect, rejoiced in electing love and free grace. Cain despised God's grace and God's Sacrifice, because he despised God, though he pretended to worship him.

Abel's Sacrifice and Cain's Offering

Abel brought a blood sacrifice to God because he believed God! By nature he was no better than Cain; but his sacrifice was better than Cain's, because his sacrifice typified and pointed to Christ. It was a lamb, the firstling of the flock. It was slain: its blood poured out before the Lord.

'By faith Abel offered unto God a more excellent sacrifice than Cain's, by which he obtained witness that he was righteous, God testifying of his gifts: and by it he being dead yet speaketh.' Abel was not righteous by his sacrifice, nor by his faith, but by the righteousness of Christ, to which his faith and sacrifice looked. We stand righteous before God by blood atonement! Through faith, by trusting Christ crucified represented in the sacrifice, Abel obtained a witness in his own conscience, by the Spirit of God, that he was a justified person, righteous before God. Therefore he is called 'righteous Abel' in the book of God (Matthew 23:35).

Though Abel is dead, 'he being dead yet speaketh'. His faith, and the example of it testifies loudly that believers today receive witness of righteousness before God in exactly the same way Abel did. As we believe God, we have the witness of God the Holy Spirit, by his Word, that we are righteous: totally, completely righteous before God by the blood of Christ (John 16:8-11; Romans 8:16; Hebrews 9:12-14; 1 John 5:7-13).

Cain's offering was 'of the fruit of the ground' by his own works and effort. It was as a bushel of turnips, and you cannot get blood out of a turnip! It had no reference to Christ at all.

'He Being Dead Yet Speaketh'

The first and most obvious significance of these words is that, by his obedient faith as recorded in Genesis 4 and Hebrews 11, Abel preaches a very important and necessary sermon to us.

Substitution

There comes to us a voice from the far distant past, from the other side of the flood, saying, 'Fallen man can only approach unto God through the death of an innocent Substitute. No sinner will ever, if left to himself, know and acknowledge his need of such a Substitute. None will set aside their own righteousness and their own inclinations, bow to God's revealed will, and submit to the righteousness of God in Christ. Only those chosen sinners called by his grace, and made willing in the day of his power will trust Christ for acceptance with God, finding all their righteousness in him alone. Still, all who do so trust the Lord Jesus Christ obtain witness that they are 'righteous', and receive divine assurance that they are accepted by God and heirs of eternal life in Christ (Matthew 13:43).

Offence of The Cross

Abel declares that 'the offence of the cross' shall never cease as long as the world stands. Abel died by the murderous hand of a religious hypocrite who hated him. His own brother! The seed of the serpent murdered the seed of the woman. 'He that was born after the flesh persecuted him that was born after the Spirit' (Galatians 4:29). In fact, Abel's death foreshadowed and represented the death of Christ himself. Like his Redeemer, Abel was murdered by the religious world. Those who are approved of God must ever expect to be disapproved of men, particularly by self-righteous religionists. But the time is coming when the present situation shall be reversed.

Judgment

In Genesis 4:10 God said to Cain, 'The voice of thy brother's blood crieth unto me from the ground.' Abel's own blood spoke, crying to God for vengeance, 'And by it he being dead yet speaketh'. He is among that multitude John saw under the altar, 'the souls of them that were slain for the Word of God, and for the testimony which they held, and they cried with a loud voice, saying, How long, O Lord, holy and true, dost thou not judge and avenge our blood on them that dwell on the earth?' (Revelation 6:9-10).

Thus, Abel is not only a type of the persecution and suffering of the godly, but also a pledge of the certain vengeance God will take in due time upon all who despise and persecute his people in this world. God shall yet avenge his own elect (those in heaven as well as those on earth) who cry unto him day and night for him to avenge them (Luke 18:7-8). For now, let us seek grace to possess our souls in patience. Soon God almighty will publicly own and honour his own with everlasting glory and punish the wicked with everlasting fire and confusion in hell.

Lessons From Cain and Abel

There are some very important lessons for us in the things recorded in the book of God about Cain and his brother Abel. They are important and practical.

1. Public worship is now and always has been the ordinance of God. Let self-serving men say what they dare against it. God has always ordained the assembling of sinners in the name of his Son for worship. Adam and Eve set a time and place for public worship, and taught their children to do the same (Genesis 3:8-9).

2. The only way sinners can approach and find righteousness with God is by the shed blood of the Lord Jesus Christ, by faith in him. Cain was rejected of God because he trampled under his feet the blood of Christ and sought to climb into heaven by the merit of his own works. Abel was accepted because he trusted Christ alone (Genesis 4:6-7).

3. There are only two religions in the world. The religion of Cain and the religion of Abel; works and grace; carnal and spiritual.

4. Our acceptance with God precedes our faith in Christ. Abel did not earn divine approval by bringing his sacrifice of faith. His sacrifice of faith was the witness of his righteousness, not the cause of it (Genesis 4:4-5).

5. Salvation is by grace alone. Grace does not flow in bloodlines. Grace does not depend upon works. Grace is the sovereign prerogative of God and the work of God (Romans 9:15-18).

6. 'Whatsoever is not of faith is sin'. Cain's worship, his sacrifice, that very thing by which he hoped to be accepted of God, was as much an act of sin as rape and murder, a sin of much greater portion than rape and murder. His worship was and act of defiant unbelief and rebellion.

7. That which distinguishes one man from another is the grace of God and the grace of God alone (1 Corinthians 4:7) It is the grace that elects redeems, regenerates, and keeps. It has no equal and all believers gladly acknowledge, 'By the grace of God I am what I am'!

> Naught have I gotten, but what I received,
> Grace hath bestowed it since I believed.
> Boasting excluded, pride I abase,
> I'm only a sinner saved by grace!

The Witness Abel Obtained

By faith in Christ Abel 'obtained witness that he was righteous'. He was not made righteous by his sacrifice (Hebrews 10:1-4). Neither was he made righteous by his faith. He was made righteous in exactly the same way we are, by the righteousness of Christ, which was imputed to him. By faith he looked to Christ and his sacrifice, as he offered up his lamb before God. John Owen points out concerning Abel:

> He was not made righteous, he was not justified by his sacrifice, but therein showed his faith by his works; and God, by acceptance of his works of obedience, justified him, as Abraham

was justified by works, namely, declaratively. He declared him so to be. Our persons must be first justified, before our works of obedience can be accepted with God; for by that acceptance He testifies that we are righteous.

Abel's Witness

However, it was by his faith that he obtained, or received witness in his own conscience, from God the Holy Spirit, that he was righteous. The Holy Spirit sprinkled the blood of Christ on Abel's heart, testifying that he was a justified person (Romans 4:25-5:2, 11).

The Lord Jesus Christ, 'was delivered for (because of) our offences (imputed to him), and was raised again for (because of) our justification (accomplished by his sacrifice). Therefore being justified (by his one great sacrifice), by faith we have peace with God through our Lord Jesus Christ. Remember, faith does not justify us. Christ justified us. Faith gives us the blessed peace of assured justification by Christ. By whom also we have access by faith into this grace wherein we stand, and rejoice in hope of the glory of God ... And not only so, but we also joy in God through our Lord Jesus Christ, by whom we have now received the atonement.' Faith does not make atonement, but simply receives it and enjoys it.

Because he believed God, Abel had an outward testimony given to him in the scriptures, that he was a righteous person. Therefore he is called righteous Abel (Matthew 23:35).

God's Testimony

'God testifying of his gifts' (v. 11). God gave testimony of Abel's gifts, the sacrifices he offered. He testified of them by accepting them. We are not told exactly how the Lord God showed his acceptance of Abel and his sacrifice, only that he did. Perhaps he spoke audibly of his acceptance. Perhaps fire fell from heaven and consumed the sacrifice. But this is certain, by one means or another God publicly proclaimed Abel's acceptance and Cain knew of the proclamation.

Enoch's Faith

In verse 5 we read, 'By faith Enoch was translated that he should not see death; and was not found, because God had translated him: for before his translation he had this testimony, that he pleased God.' True saving faith gives believing sinners the witness and testimony of God the Holy Spirit that in Christ, because of Christ, we please God. Enoch was caught up to heaven, not temporarily as Paul, but like Elijah, forever! He was changed from mortality to immortality without dying. Let us learn these lessons:

There is an intimate relationship between this life and glory. Enoch walked with God on earth, and one day he did not return from his walk. God took him to glory. Old Testament believers knew, expected, and enjoyed eternal life through faith, just as we do (Philippians 1:21-23; 2 Corinthians 5:1-8; Romans 4:3).

Enoch went to heaven, as some shall at the coming of Christ, without dying. 'We which are alive and remain shall be caught up together' with those who have gone before us into heaven. The resurrection of all believers is here exemplified. Enoch went to glory as a whole man, body and soul (1 Corinthians 15:51-52; 1 Thessalonians 4:13-18; 1 Corinthians 15:42-44).

But the primary thing to be learned here is the fact that Enoch walked with God by faith. It is faith in Christ that pleases God (John 6:28-29). And it is faith in Christ that receives testimony from God that like Christ himself, because we are in him, the Father says of us 'I am well pleased'!

Like Enoch, God's people in this world please him, satisfy him, and are accepted by him, only by faith in Christ. Enoch did not please God by his own works of obedience, but by faith in Christ, for 'without faith it is impossible to please him'. In other words every true believer pleases God, just like Enoch did.

Like Enoch, all who trust Christ, being partakers of the first resurrection, the new birth (Revelation 20:6), shall 'not see death'. Then, on that great day of judgment, it shall be declared that we please God, perfectly, completely, without flaw, because we have fully obeyed him and satisfied him in the obedience and death of Christ, our Substitute (Revelation 21:27; Ephesians 5:25-27).

Three Practical Questions Concerning Faith

1. How Can I Obtain Faith?

There are many who vainly imagine that faith is a hereditary gift, that if one's parents were believers, or if he was raised in a believing home, then he is automatically a believer. Others imagine that faith comes to the children of believing parents by means of the parents' faith, the ceremony of sprinkling (or pouring) water on the baby, catechizing the child, and raising it to be a believer. Many who reject both these false teachings imagine that faith can be communicated to children by the will of others, suggesting that if we pray earnestly enough for someone to be saved they will be saved. Still others have the idea that faith can be secured by religious education.

John 1:11-13 specifically repudiates all such teaching about faith in Christ and God's great gift of grace in salvation. 'He came unto his own, and his own received him not. But as many as received him, to them gave he power to become the sons of God, even to them that believe on his name: Which were born, not of blood, nor of the will of the flesh, nor of the will of man, but of God.'

Faith in Christ cannot be obtained or communicated to anyone by inheritance, education, human reason, or religious ceremony. Faith in Christ is the free gift of God's sovereign grace. Any sinner who obtains faith in Christ gets it by God's appointed means, through the preaching of the gospel (Romans 10:13-17). Faith comes by divine revelation, by Christ being revealed in us (Matthew 16:16-17; Galatians 1:15-16). Faith is the gift of God the Holy Spirit, the result of the operation of his grace in regeneration (John 6:63; Ephesians 1:15-20).

2. Do I Have True, Saving Faith In Christ?

Is it possible for men and women to know whether or not they have faith in Christ? Indeed, it is. 'These things have I written unto you that believe on the name of the Son of God; that ye may know that ye have eternal life, and that ye may believe on the name of the Son of God' (1 John 5:13).

If a person is born of God, if God has given the gift of faith in the Lord Jesus Christ to a person, he renounces all personal righteousness, acknowledging that Christ alone is his righteousness before God (Jeremiah 23:6; 1 Corinthians 1:30; Philippians 3:3-11). It is impossible to look to Christ alone for righteousness while going about to establish your own righteousness (Romans 9:31-10:4). The believer looks to Christ alone for his acceptance with God. We trust his blood alone for atonement and satisfaction. We look to his obedience alone for righteousness (Romans 5:18-19).

Trusting Christ alone as our only Redeemer and Saviour, all who are born of God, all to whom God the Holy Spirit has given the gift of faith, bow to Christ as their Lord. Faith, in its essence, involves surrender to Christ as Lord (Luke 14:25-33). Christ's lordship is not a theological point about which believers argue. All who are taught of God know that he is Lord over all. The believer wants him to be Lord over all. He rejoices in the fact that he is. And he voluntarily surrenders the rule of his life to his Lord. Faith is the giving up of my life to Christ, willingly.

This surrender to Christ is not a once for all thing. It is not something done at the time of conversion, never to be experienced again. As we must daily say no to all confidence in the flesh, daily look to Christ for grace, so we must daily take up our cross and follow him, daily surrendering our will to his will, our way to his way, and our lives to his dominion.

All who have faith in Christ love him and love one another. 'Whosoever believeth that Jesus is the Christ is born of God: and every one that loveth him that begat loveth him also that is begotten of him' (1 John 5:1). We do not and cannot love Christ or one another as we ought, any more than we can trust our Saviour as we ought; but all who are granted faith in Christ love him and his people.

3. Where Is Assurance of Faith Found?

Without question, faith is accompanied by the fruit of the Spirit (Galatians 5:22-23). All believers renounce all personal righteousness before God, bow to Christ as their Lord, and walk in love. Yet, our assurance is not found in the degree to which we renounce our own righteousness, the degree of our surrender, or the degree of our love for him and one another. The assurance of faith is found in the Word of God alone.

It is written, 'He that believeth and is baptized shall be saved; but he that believeth not shall be damned' (Mark 16:16). 'He that believeth on the Son of God hath the witness in himself: he that believeth not God hath made him a liar; because he believeth not the record that God gave of his Son. And this is the record, that God hath given to us eternal life, and this life is in his Son. He that hath the Son hath life; and he that hath not the Son of God hath not life. These things have I written unto you that believe on the name of the Son of God; that ye may know that ye have eternal life, and that ye may believe on the name of the Son of God' (1 John 5:10-13).

Faith

There is nothing in the world more important, and nothing about which there is more confusion than faith. I dare say men and women in our society are more ignorant and confused about faith than about any other subject they presume to understand.

It is written, 'the just shall live by faith', and those who have this faith in Christ 'believe to the saving of the soul'. Faith is not our Saviour; but there is no salvation without faith (Hebrews 10:38-39).

The substance, the ground, the foundation of our confident hope of eternal salvation is our faith in Christ. That faith is the evidence of our eternal justification and everlasting salvation. Faith looks not to evidences for evidence of salvation, but to Christ alone!

Faith understands what the most learned scientists cannot fathom. Faith understands that 'the worlds were framed by the Word of God', for faith simply believes God. Faith does not come by understanding. Understanding comes by faith!

Abel understood that the only way a guilty man can approach the holy Lord God is by blood atonement. His brother, Cain, did not. Cain thought that a man can please God and win his favour by works. Abel believed God. Cain believed not.

Enoch understood that the only way a man can please God and be accepted of him is by faith. So Enoch walked with God by faith. And when he left this world, he had this testimony, that he pleased God.

The only way fallen, guilty sinners can ever be saved, the only way we can find acceptance with God, the only way to walk with God, the only way to please God is by faith, faith in the Lord Jesus Christ. If we would be saved, we must personally believe God, we must personally trust the Lord Jesus Christ.

> O gift of gifts! O grace of faith!
> My God, this grace give me.
> Give me the gift of faith in Christ.
> That I may live with Thee!

Believing God

Faith is more than merely believing in God. Faith, true saving faith, is believing God. To be sure, faith is believing what the Bible says about God, but even more, faith is believing God. Without such faith it is impossible to please God. He both 'is' and 'is a rewarder' of them that seek him (v. 6). Those who are without faith are without God, without life, and without hope, because they are without Christ (Romans 8:8; Ephesians 2:12-14). Christ is our peace! Christ is our Wisdom! Christ is our Righteousness! Christ is our Sanctification! Christ is our Redemption! Christ is our All! Here are the four vital, essential, basic, fundamental aspects of all true faith.

1. Coming to God

Faith is coming to God (Hebrews 7:25). Many physical acts are used to describe spiritual things. Faith in Christ is no exception. Faith in Christ has nothing to do with physical motion, posture, or location. You cannot come to God by a physical act (going to a confessional booth, going to an altar, walking an aisle, or saying a scripted prayer). Faith is a work of the heart. It is coming to God through Christ our Mediator. It is looking to Christ our Substitute. It is leaning on Christ our Beloved. It is bowing to Christ our King.

2. Believing God

He that comes to God in Christ must believe that he is. He must believe that God is, not only that there is a God, but that God is who he says he is, Father, Son and Holy Spirit, as revealed in the holy scripture. God is holy, eternal, and immutable. God is mercy, grace, and love. God is righteousness, justice, and truth. God is omnipotent, omniscient, and omnipresent. God is good. God is sovereign. He is the God of creation, providence, and grace. He does as he will in all, with all, at all times.

3. God's Promises

He that comes to God must believe that he is and believe that he is the Rewarder of them that diligently seek him. Faith is not believing that God can do anything. Faith is believing that God will do everything he says in his Word he will do. Faith is always connected with the Word of God. We must believe that God will fulfil every promise and purpose toward believers in Christ Jesus. True faith actually believes and is confident that God will give us all that Christ purchased (Romans 8:31-34; 1 Corinthians 1:30).

4. What Is Faith?

There are many forms of false faith by which the souls of men are deluded. James tells us that even the devils have faith. What is that true, saving faith, that faith by which a man pleases God? That is the question that must be answered. And it is answered, answered with emphatic clarity, in the book of God. There is but one true faith. We must examine ourselves and prove ourselves on this point, whether we be in 'the faith' (2 Corinthians 13:5).

The Three Elements of Saving Faith

Saving faith consists of three things: knowledge, assent, and trust. If we would be pleasing to God, if we would come to him and be saved by him, we must know the revelation of God in the gospel, we must give assent that God's revelation is truth, and we must trust him whom God reveals.

1. Knowledge

The first aspect of faith is knowledge. Knowledge is not faith. Yet, there is no faith without knowledge. Paul says, 'He that cometh to God must believe that he is, and that he is the rewarder of them that diligently seek him.' Knowledge is essential to faith. We cannot trust an unknown Christ. Faith in Christ is a heart work. But it is not a leap in the dark. It is based upon knowledge. In order for us to trust, there must be someone, or something known for us to trust (Isaiah 53:11; John 17:3).

Knowing That 'God Is'

In order for anyone to have faith, he must know the Lord God, as he is revealed in the Person and work of Christ (John 1:18; 14:6-9; Hebrews 1:1-3). We must know that God is, that he is who he says he is, and that he is what he says he is: Sovereign and Good (Exodus 33:18-19), Just and Gracious (Isaiah 45:20-22), Holy and Merciful (Isaiah 6:3, 7). The only way any man can attain this knowledge is by the revelation of God in Christ, the God-man (2 Corinthians 4:5-6).

Knowing God 'The Rewarder'

We must also know that God is the rewarder of them that diligently seek him (Isaiah 55:3, 6, 7; Jeremiah 29:13-14). All who seek the Lord, all who come to God by faith in the Lord Jesus Christ, shall be rewarded with eternal life and everlasting salvation. This, too, must be known. But how can we know that God will reward every believer with eternal salvation? By the Gospel (1 Corinthians 15:3; Romans 3:24-26)! The Lord Jesus earned righteousness for his people (Romans 5:19). The Son of God purchased salvation for his elect (Galatians 3:13; Hebrews 9:12). God has promised that salvation to all who trust his Son (John 3:14-16, 36; Romans 10:9-13).

Gospel knowledge is essential to saving faith. And the matter of paramount importance in the knowledge of the gospel is the redemptive work of Christ. Because he is the God-man, we are assured that he is an able Redeemer, a willing Redeemer and an effectual Redeemer (Isaiah 53:5-7, 10-11). Unless a person knows these things, he cannot have faith, he cannot please God, he cannot be saved; but merely knowing these things is not faith. Knowledge is necessary, but knowledge alone is not faith. John Owen says,

> Of all the poison which at this day is diffused in the minds of men, corrupting them from the mystery of the gospel, there is no part that is more pernicious than this one perverse imagination, that to 'believe in Christ' is nothing at all but to 'believe the doctrine of the gospel!' which yet we grant is included therein.

2. Assent

The second element of saving faith is that along with that knowledge, our hearts must give assent that these things are true. Many people know the truth. They have heard it for years. They have been catechized and trained in gospel truth from their infancy. But saving faith involves a willing, voluntary, deliberate, considered assent to the truth of God. Faith simply embraces the revelation of God as the revelation of God.

Hearing the gospel, sinners are being confronted with the truth of God. The Word of God is open on their laps. The truth stares them in the face. God speaks directly to their hearts. As that happens, each one makes a decision, wilfully and deliberately. Each one either embraces the testimony of God as the Truth, or he rejects it and declares that God is a liar (1 John 5:10).

Have you embraced this gospel of God's free grace as the truth? If you have, you are not far from the kingdom of God. Still, something else is necessary. Faith knows the gospel and gives assent to the gospel of the truth. But there is more

3. Trust

The third element of saving faith is trust. True faith trusts the Lord Jesus Christ. A person acts upon what he believes, and the act of faith is trusting Christ. The woman with an issue of blood did not simply say, 'I believe Christ can heal me'. She touched him. The publican did not merely believe there is propitiation at the Mercy Seat; he sued for mercy upon the grounds of propitiation made. The leper did not simply think within himself, 'Christ can make me whole if he will'. He came to the Master.

Faith is more than knowledge and assent. Faith is acting upon that revealed knowledge of which we are convinced. Faith is trusting the Son of God! Thomas Brooks puts it like this:

> He that believeth on the Lord Jesus Christ shall be saved, be his sins never so many; but he that believeth not in the Lord Jesus must be damned, be his sins never so few.

The Necessity

Why is faith in Christ necessary? Why is it necessary for sinners to trust the Lord Jesus Christ alone in order to be saved? It is necessary, because no sinner can be accepted of God upon any other ground. Hebrews 11 records the names of 17 men and women, whose histories are well known, who pleased God. How did they do it? By faith alone! Many others, mentioned in the Bible perished under the wrath and curse of God, though they did some good and commendable things.

Repentance will not save you. Esau, King Saul, and Judas all repented, but still went to hell. The confession of sin will not save you. Both Saul and Ahab confessed their sins, but perished still. Self-denial and sacrifice will not save you. Ananias and Sapphira made great, costly sacrifice; but their very sacrifice was a lie, for which they fell dead in the house of God. Only faith pleases God, because only faith gives all praise, honour, and glory to the Son of God.

Faith is necessary because without faith there is no vital union with Christ. Faith is necessary because God plainly declares that works have nothing to do with salvation (Ephesians 2:8-9). Faith is necessary because salvation is by grace alone (Romans 4:16; Galatians 5:2-4; 2 Timothy 1:9). Faith brings nothing! Faith promises nothing! Faith does nothing!

Because faith looks to Christ alone for everything, the cry of faith is, 'By the grace of God I am what I am. Not unto us, O Lord, not unto us, but unto thy name give glory, for thy mercy and for thy truth's sake!' Faith understands that all who are in Christ are in him by God's work alone. Faith understands and rejoices in the fact that Christ is made of God unto us wisdom and righteousness, sanctification and redemption. Faith hears God say, 'He that glorieth, let him glory in the Lord'. And faith says 'AMEN!'

By faith Noah, being warned of God of things not seen as yet, moved with fear, prepared an ark to the saving of his house; by the which he condemned the world, and became heir of the righteousness which is by faith.

Hebrews 11:7

Chapter 32

Read: Hebrews 11:7

'By Faith Noah ... '

Noah is held before us here as an example of faith in Christ. His name means 'rest, or resting place'. Here the Holy Spirit tells us that Noah found rest for his soul by faith.

In Genesis 6 we are told that all the world was lost, cursed of God, and sentenced to suffer the wrath of God, because of man's sin and apostasy from God. God was justly angry with all men and determined to rid the world of fallen men by the flood of his wrath; but in wrath, he remembered mercy. We are told 'But Noah found grace in the eyes of the Lord.' The scriptures do not tell us that the Lord God found grace in the eyes of Noah, 'But Noah found grace in the eyes of the Lord.'

All men deserved God's wrath; but one man was chosen. All men were condemned, justly condemned; but one man was justified. All men went astray from God; but one man was called. All men were lost; but one man was saved. All men were unbelievers; but to one man faith was given. Noah found grace (not merit, but grace!) in the eyes of the Lord. There is always a remnant according to the election of grace.

A Divine Gift

Faith is a divine gift. Noah's faith, like ours, was the gift and operation of God's grace upon him (Ephesians 2:8). True saving faith is something that is bestowed upon and wrought in chosen, redeemed sinners by God's saving grace. Faith in Christ is not the cause of God's salvation, but part of it.

A Divine Revelation

Noah's faith was the result of God's revelation of his purpose of grace toward him (Genesis 6:13-14, 18, 22). Faith arises from, is built upon, and believes God's revelation. Faith is no more and no less than believing God's word. God told Noah what he would do; and Noah believed him.

Noah's Ark: An Example

Noah's faith is held before us by God the Holy Spirit as an example of how sinners are saved by faith. We are told that, 'a picture is worth a thousand words.' Here is a picture of faith. God help us to see it and obey the example he has set before us. As Noah fled into the ark, which he had prepared, we must flee into the Ark, Christ Jesus, if we would be saved. The only way sinners can obtain that salvation, which is in Jesus Christ, is by faith. 'Believe on the Lord Jesus Christ, and thou shalt be saved.'

Long ago Martin Luther wrote, 'If you want to interpret (the Word of God) well and confidently, set Christ before you, for he is the man to whom it all applies, every bit of it.' Edmund Clowney said much the same thing in recent times: 'We do not find Christ in the Old Testament by spotting accidental references or similarities here and there. He is the centre, the structure of the whole history of the Old Testament.'

God the Holy Spirit is showing us how that 'faith is the substance of things hoped for, the evidence of things not seen.' He is showing us how that without faith it is impossible to please God (v. 6). The example he selects and holds before us in this seventh verse is Noah.

The Basis of Faith

The basis of Noah's faith was the Word of God: 'By faith Noah, being warned of God of things not seen as yet'. Faith must have a foundation, and the foundation of all true, saving faith is the Word of God (Romans 10:17). Noah believed, because God spoke. He believed what God spoke, though it was contrary to all reason, experience, and science. God warned him of things not seen as yet: the universal flood though it had never rained; the building of an ark though no ship had ever been built; the saving of himself and all creatures in the ark and the destruction of all who were not in the ark.

The Evidence of Faith

The evidence of Noah's faith was his reverence for and obedience to the Lord God. 'Moved with fear, (He) prepared an ark to the saving of his house'. Noah feared God, because he believed God. He had an awesome sense of God's holiness, justice, and truth. He was overwhelmed with the sense of God's goodness. His reverence for the Lord God caused him to obey his Word. Immediately, without delay, before the first raindrop fell, Noah began preparing an ark exactly according to the pattern God had given him. His object in doing so was that he and his family might be saved from wrath, according to the promise of God. Noah showed his faith by his works. Faith believes the Word of God and acts upon it. Show me a man who believes God, and I will show you a man who reveres God and obeys God. James instructs us in this very thing, using Abraham and Rahab as examples (James 2:18-26).

The Fruit of Faith

The fruit of Noah's faith was justification. By his faith in and obedience to the Word of God, 'he condemned the world'. As a preacher of righteousness, he declared the certain condemnation of all who would not believe. By his actions he both reproved the unbelieving and aggravated their guilt. At the same time, Noah himself 'became heir of the righteousness which is by faith'. Neither his faith nor his obedience made him righteous. But by faith he received the righteousness of God in Christ, which is justification and eternal life.

Will you, or will you not, believe God? There is a storm of wrath approaching. God will punish sin. But he has made a way for sinners to escape his wrath (John 3:14-16). By his obedience to God, Jesus Christ, the Son of God, the sinner's Substitute, has become the Ark of deliverance for God's elect. I hold before you the Ark of God, Christ Jesus. Will you enter in? Will you trust the Son of God and discover, as a personal reality, the salvation that is found in him?

Warned of God and Moved With Fear

Noah was 'warned of God of things not seen as yet' (Genesis 6:1-3, 7). Noah's faith was the response of his heart to God's Word. God told Noah that his Holy Spirit would not always strive with man, that his longsuffering is for an appointed time, and that after the appointed days of mercy were ended, he would destroy man from off the face of the earth.

God's Warning

The Lord God has warned you of these things. Has he not? Your days on this earth are numbered, 'now is the day of salvation' (2 Corinthians 6:2). Salvation belongs to all who trust Christ. But if you will not trust Christ, you must be forever damned!

You have a Bible. What mercy! God has given you his Word in book form to warn you of wrath, impending wrath, eternal wrath, inexpressibly horrible, infinite wrath (Romans 3:23; 6:23; 1:18). Read the book. In it is written, 'The soul that sinneth, it shall die' (Ezekiel 18:20). Noah's generation, the men of Sodom, Korah and his followers, all stand as beacons to warn sinners of divine judgment. 'Except ye repent, ye shall all likewise perish' (Luke 13:5).

You have been warned, some of you, hundreds of times by the faithful preaching of the gospel. It is the responsibility of God's servant to receive the word at God's mouth and faithfully warn you of wrath to come: the certainty of it, the justice of it, the imminence of it, the eternality of it, the horror of it, and the singular means of escape from it. Hell is the portion of every rebel, eternal hell! The only way of escape from the wrath of God, the only refuge for your soul is Christ. Escape for your life! Flee to Christ! There is no other Saviour.

How often God has warned you of his wrath upon you, by his acts of providence. You have seen immortal souls cut down, without warning, and swept away into eternity to meet an angry God, without Christ, without hope. They are forever damned; but you are left! For now, you are spared! Be warned.

God speaks to you by your conscience, too, warning you of impending hell. You know that you are lost. You know that you are a guilty sinner. You know that the wrath of God is upon you. Do not stop your ears and run madly into hell!

Moved With Fear

Noah, being warned of God, was 'moved with fear'. He was not moved by fear for himself. He believed God. He was moved by fear for his family, his neighbours, those who were yet rebels to God. He feared for the souls of men.

Had Noah been like most, he would have said, 'God is merciful, he will not really send men to hell', or 'There will be time enough to repent later', or 'I am not bad enough for God to send me to hell.' But Noah was not so foolish and senseless. He was 'moved with fear'.

Perhaps you are thinking, 'Why do you frighten us? You know that fear will not save a sinner.' That is true. It is the goodness of God that leads you to repentance. Only the love of God in Christ can melt the sinner's heart, draw us to Christ, and constrain us to believe; but you will never be drawn to Christ by the cords of love until you are driven from your carnal security by the fear of God's impending wrath. You must be driven from your carnal security by fear, so that you may be drawn to Christ by his grace. You have only two options: repent or perish. Which will it be?

Historic Facts

The ark of Noah and the flood are facts of history, plainly revealed in the Word of God. The ark is not a myth. It is a fact. The flood is not a piece of fiction. It is a fact. Let the critics, the infidels, and the scoffers say what they will. We look upon them with disdain, as ignorant fools and liars. The Word of God is true. We rest our souls upon the validity and veracity of holy scripture.

The Cause of Divine Judgment

The cause of God's judgment upon the earth was the sin and depravity of the human race. Only 1,000 years after the fall, man had become so degenerate that 'the thoughts of his heart were only evil continually' (Genesis 6:5). Generation after generation, man became more and more vile until at last 'it repented the Lord that he had made man upon the earth, and it grieved him at his heart.' God did not change but he was so grieved by man's sin that he turned against the human race in wrath and justice. Having rejected the counsel of God and despised the longsuffering of God man was about to feel the holy indignation of God.

Grace Granted

'But Noah found grace in the eyes of the Lord' (Genesis 6:8). The cause of Noah's salvation was God's sovereign grace. The scripture does not say, 'The Lord found grace in the eyes of Noah.' The scripture clearly says, 'Noah found grace in the eyes of the Lord.' Because God from eternity set the eye of his grace upon Noah, the Lord God found a way to be gracious to Noah. God found a way to save Noah. The ark was devised by God, not Noah. Noah alone was chosen as the object of God's grace. Because he was chosen of God, Noah was effectually delivered from the wrath of God. The Lord God established his covenant, preserved his seed, and accomplished his purpose with Noah.

The Means of Salvation

The means of salvation was an ark. Noah and his family were saved in the flood by a ship, an ark, which God commanded him to build. It saved those who were in it from the violent wrath and vengeance of an angry God. As there was but one ark in the days of Noah, there is but one way of salvation. The whole world was drowned under the flood of God's wrath, except for those eight happy souls in the ark. Christ alone is the Saviour of men. 'There is none other name under heaven given among men, whereby we must be saved.' If you would be saved you must be robed in Christ's righteousness and washed in his blood. You must come to the Ark, Christ Jesus.

Because Noah found grace in the eyes of the Lord, he was given the blessed gift of faith in Christ. He believed God. Believing God, he acted upon God's revelation, 'being warned of God'. Every act of faith is the response of the believing heart to God's Word (Romans 10:17).

'Prepared An Ark'

Noah prepared an ark according to God's command (Genesis 6:14, 16, 21, 22). The ark was built by God's design and purpose and was a strong, mighty ship. The ark was a beautiful picture of our Lord Jesus Christ and the salvation of our souls by him (Romans 8:28-39; Ephesians 1:3-14). There was plenty of room for all who entered into that ark, but room only for those for whom it was prepared (Hebrews 7:25).

The ark had a door made in the side of it, but only one door (Acts 4:12). It had a window in the top of it to let in light, but only one window. Thank God, there is a Door of access to God, but only one Door. That Door is Christ. There is Light for sinners lost in darkness; but there is only one Light to show us our way. That Light is Christ, the Light of the world.

The ark had no steps leading up to it. There are no steps by which sinners ascend up to God. We must come to God as sinners, trusting Christ alone. If we try to ascend to God upon steps of experience, repentance, knowledge, progressive holiness, or anything else we will only expose our shameful nakedness (Exodus 20:24-26).

The ark had everything needed by Noah and his family (1 Corinthians 1:30-31; Ephesians 1:3-6). The ark bore all the storm of God's wrath (Isaiah 53:10; Galatians 3:13; 1 Peter 1:18-20; 2 Peter 3:18). The ark was covered with pitch which speaks of blood atonement! All for whom the ark was designed entered into it (Isaiah 53:10-11). All who entered in were saved.

'To the Saving of His House'

God the Holy Spirit tells us that Noah saved his house. He 'prepared an ark to the saving of his house'. How can that be? We know that, 'Salvation is of the Lord'. We know that no man can save himself, much less save his family; but God says that Noah saved his house. The meaning is this:

Noah was the instrument God used to save his household physically, symbolically, and spiritually. This is the responsibility of all parents, especially fathers! How did Noah save his family? He entered into the ark himself and led his sons, his daughters-in-law, and his wife into the ark.

He was called into the ark (Genesis 7:1). He went into the ark (Genesis 7:7). Noah left everything and everyone else behind, and went into the ark at God's command. 'And the Lord shut him in' (Genesis 7:16).

That is exactly what we must do. We must enter into the Ark, Christ Jesus, by faith. We must forsake all other arks. We must not stop at the threshold and look into the ark. We must enter in. It is not enough to hear about the Ark. We must enter in! It is not enough to know about the Ark. We must enter in! It is not enough to admire the Ark. We must enter in! It is not enough to defend the Ark. We must enter in!

'Condemned the World'

When Noah entered into the ark, he condemned the world. That is to say, he declared the world to be condemned. When Noah entered into the ark, he declared that everyone outside the ark was condemned. Those who mocked the ark. Those who chose other arks. Those who helped to build the ark, but never entered it. Those who saw no need of the ark. All were condemned by Noah as he walked into the ark (Matthew 24:37-39).

'Became the Heir of Righteousness'

Noah 'became the heir of righteousness'. He became the heir of that righteousness represented in the ark, the righteousness of God in Christ, that everlasting righteousness imputed to all who trust the Lord Jesus Christ.

All Noah did and all he obtained, he did and obtained by faith. Noah believed God. He believed God's Word concerning sin and judgment, salvation by the ark, and his promise of grace to all who entered it.

By faith Abraham, when he was called to go out into a place which he should after receive for an inheritance, obeyed; and he went out, not knowing whither he went. By faith he sojourned in the land of promise, as in a strange country, dwelling in tabernacles with Isaac and Jacob, the heirs with him of the same promise: For he looked for a city which hath foundations, whose builder and maker is God. Through faith also Sara herself received strength to conceive seed, and was delivered of a child when she was past age, because she judged him faithful who had promised.

Hebrews 11:8-9

Chapter 33

Read: Hebrews 11:8-9

The Obedience Of Faith

The life of faith begins with the call of God; and it is a life which is characterized by obedience to God. Though true faith is characterized by obedience, neither our faith in Christ nor our obedience to him is perfect. Far from it! Our faith is ever mingled with unbelief and our best obedience with disobedience. This, too, is evident in Abraham.

Incomplete Obedience

There is no indication that Abraham hesitated in his obedience to God. Yet, it is evident that Abraham, the father of all who believe, did not comply with God's command completely. When the Lord God called Abraham, he specifically told him to leave his country, his people, and his father's household. Indeed, he left his country and his people, but he did not leave his father's household immediately.

Terah was Abraham's father. But God came to Abraham, not Terah. God told Abraham to leave all ties in Ur. God gave Abraham the promises, not Terah. But we read in Genesis 11:31-32 that it was Terah who led the way. It was Terah who bound himself to Abraham's promise. And it was Terah who settled his family in Haran. A. W. Pink comments on this:

> [Abraham] left Chaldea, but instead of separating from his kindred, he suffered his nephew Lot to accompany him; instead of forsaking his father's house, Terah was permitted to take the lead; and instead of entering Canaan, Abraham stopped short

> and settled in Haran. He yielded to the affections of the flesh ... Though Abraham had settled down in Haran, God would not allow him to continue there indefinitely. The Lord had purposed that he should enter Canaan, and no purpose of His can fail. God therefore tumbled him out of the nest which he had made for himself (Deuteronomy 32:11), and very solemn is it to observe the means which He used: 'And Terah died in Haran' (Genesis11:32; Acts 7:4). Death had to come in before Abraham left Halfway House. He never started across the wilderness until death severed that tie of the flesh which held him back.

Complete Grace

I point out the weakness of Abraham's faith, because I want us ever to understand that God's goodness, grace and mercy, his faithfulness, does not at all depend upon ours; 'If we believe not, he abideth faithful'. It is not our imperfect faith that is imputed to us for righteousness, but the Lord Jesus Christ, the perfect Object of our faith.

Understand this, too, 'The gifts and callings of God are without repentance.' God did not forsake Abraham. Indeed, our God will never forsake one of his own (Mark 16:7).

Let us ever remember that our Heavenly Father will see that all his children obey him, even if it means he must take from us those who are dearest to us (Hebrews 12:5-11). The Lord God says, 'My son, give me thine heart'. And he means to have it. 'Faithful is he that calleth you, who also will do it.' 'God is faithful, by whom ye were called unto the fellowship of his Son Jesus Christ our Lord.'

Abraham Went Out

Because God is faithful even when we are not, because he will not forsake his own even when we forsake him, because he is true even when we are not, because he who gave Abraham faith kept him in faith, we are told that Abraham went out of Ur. He sojourned in the land of promise as a pilgrim in a strange land.

All the days of his pilgrimage, he lived among men and women who had no regard for God; but he made his dwelling with those who were heirs with him of the same promise. Abraham, Isaac, and Jacob lived like they did, believing God, because they had his Word of promise for the basis of their faith. The promise was and is a promise of grace. Isaac and Jacob were heirs with him of the same promise because they, too, believed God.

They dwelled in tents because they were pilgrims. Pilgrims do not built their homes in the land of their pilgrimage. Let us never forget that we are pilgrims here. This world is not our home. May God give us grace never to loose sight of this fact.

Abraham

God's grace was set upon Abraham from eternity (Romans 8:28-30). He was the object of God's everlasting love, chosen to salvation before the world began. Therefore, at the appointed time of love 'the grace of God that bringeth salvation' came to Abraham while he was in Ur of the Chaldees, a land of idolatry (Genesis 12:1-4; Joshua 24:2-3). While Abraham was yet in the darkness, death, and degradation of sin and unbelief, the Lord God called him to life and faith in Christ.

Called to Believe

Because the Lord chose Abraham, he called him. Because the Lord called him, Abraham believed God and journeyed to a land he had not seen. It was not Abram's faith that caused the Lord to choose him and call him. It was God's election and God's call that caused Abram to believe. Faith is the gift of God's grace, not the cause of it (Ephesians 2:8-9). The Lord changed his name from Abram (a father) to Abraham (a great father, or a father of great multitudes) fifteen years after he left Ur (Genesis 17:1-5).

Called to Go Out

Abraham was called of God to go out to a place unknown to him and to be a sojourner, a pilgrim, in that land. The Lord God leads his people in the way he has determined, in ways known only to him. We know neither the way we should take nor the way we shall take; both are determined by our God. Faith follows his direction when it knows not where it shall go, how, or why (Acts 27:21-25).

Abraham lived in Canaan, the land of promise, by faith. He lived in that land for a little more than seventy-five years. He fully believed that God would give this land to his seed. Yet, he never had an inheritance in it (Acts 7:4-5).

He died when Isaac was seventy-five years old. Jacob was fifteen. All that time they dwelled in tents. Israel later possessed the land (Joshua 23:14). But God's promise and Abraham's faith looked far beyond the physical land of Canaan. Abraham looked for a permanent home with Christ in heaven. His hopes and expectations were upon the world to come. He lived in this world with the eyes of his heart fixed upon another world.

It was this faith, faith in the Lord God who revealed himself to him in Mesopotamia, which moved Abraham to obey the Word of God and enabled him to do and suffer all that God required (Romans 8:17-18).

God's Purpose

These things are not written in the scriptures merely to give us a biographical account of a great man, or merely to inspire us with admiration for Abraham. They are recorded by Divine Inspiration to teach us what faith is and how we must live by faith while we live in this world.

Abraham is not merely the physical father of the Jewish race; he is the spiritual and exemplary father of all God's elect, the father of all true believers, the true Israel of God.

Abraham Our Father

The word 'father' conveys much more than the physical head of a family. It is often used to speak of the first of a specific class. George Washington is called 'The father of our nation' because he was the first President of the U.S.A. Thomas Jefferson is called 'the father of democracy' because he was a very dominant influence in the development of our democratic government. Abraham is called 'the father' of all who believe not because we get our faith from him or by connection with him, but because he is the first man mentioned in the Bible as one who believed God (Genesis 15:6); because he so greatly exemplified what it is to believe God, and because the Lord Jesus Christ in and by whom we are saved is Abraham's Seed (Romans 4:11, 16; Galatians 3:6-9, 13-14, 16, 29).

The Call of God

Whenever we discuss the life of faith, we must begin with the call of God by which Abraham was brought to faith in Christ. Genesis 12:1 (compare Acts 7:2-3) gives us the historical account of that to which the Holy Spirit here alludes.

A Divine Gift

Faith is the gift of God. The life of faith begins with the call of God. Salvation does not begin with man, but with God. It is not in any sense of the word caused by man. It is not to any degree or at any point dependent upon man. Salvation is God's work, and God's work alone. 'Salvation is of the Lord.' Abraham was not seeking the Lord. The Lord sought him. Abraham was not looking for God. God was looking for him. Abraham did not come to God. God came to him. Abraham's faith was not the cause of

God's grace to him, but the result. Faith in Christ is the gift of God bestowed upon, wrought in, and given to sinners who otherwise could not and would not believe God.

Faith in Christ is given to lost men and women according to God's eternal purpose of grace in election (Ephesians 1:3-4). It is the result of Christ's atonement (Hebrews 9:12). It is wrought in chosen, redeemed sinners by the power and grace of the Holy Spirit's omnipotent, irresistible, effectual call (Ephesians 2:1-10). They and they alone are 'the called' according to the purpose of God for whom all things work together for good (Romans 8:28).

Two Calls

There are two distinct calls from God set forth in holy scripture: a general, outward call and a particular, inward call; a call that men resist and reject, and an effectual, irresistible, almighty, saving call of omnipotent grace. The general, external call is given to all who hear the Gospel, or come under the sound of the Word of God (Proverbs 8:4; Matthew 20:16; Luke 14:17-18; Proverbs 1:24-28). All men and women, without exception, stoutly resist this general call.

The special, inward, and efficacious call of God comes only to his elect. This call is always effectual. It is always saving. It always results in faith. It always brings the chosen, redeemed sinner into the arms of his omnipotent Saviour. Examples of this omnipotent, irresistible call are scattered throughout the scriptures. Abraham is here held before us as one of the examples in the Old Testament. In the New Testament era God still works irresistibly in the salvation of his elect (Luke 5:27-28; 19:5-6; Acts 9:4-5; John 5:25; 10:3, 4, 16; Romans 8:30; 1 Corinthians 1:26-31).

This invincible call of God is an act of God's sovereign grace, accompanied by all-mighty, irresistible power, giving life to men and women who are dead in trespasses and sins. It brings life, eternal, spiritual life. It brings us 'out of darkness into God's marvellous light' (1 Peter 2:9). No wonder David sang about it as he did 'Blessed is the man whom thou choosest and causest to approach unto thee' (Psalm 65:4).

A Call From Death To Life

Like all others, Abraham was a lost man, dead in trespasses and in sins, when the Lord God called him by his grace (Joshua 24:2). He belonged to a heathen family He lived as an idolater in the midst of idolaters until he was seventy years old. Then God called him! Until God stepped into his life, Abraham lived just like everyone else in that massive, pagan land. He was content with the husks of this world upon which the swine feed. He was without God, without Christ, without hope, without life! Abraham's experience is repeated and attested by every one of God's elect people (Ephesians 2:1-4).

A Divine Revelation

This effectual call of God comes with the revelation of Christ (Acts 7:2; Zechariah 12:10; 2 Corinthians 4:6; Galatians 1:15-16). What marvellous grace! The God of glory condescends to draw near to and reveal himself to lost sinners, immersed in idolatry, having no concern for his honour and glory! There was nothing in Abraham to deserve God's notice, nothing to merit his esteem. Yet, God called him!

This call is a work of God's sovereign, distinguishing grace. Grace singled out one man from the midst of many. God says, 'I called him alone, and blessed him' (Isaiah 51:2). Why did God call Abraham but not his father and kinsmen? No answer can be given but this: God has mercy on whom he will have mercy (Romans 9:18). He called Isaac and refused Ishmael. He loved Jacob and hated Esau. He accepted Abel and rejected Cain. Why? Because he would. No other explanation is or can be given (Romans 9:16).

'The God of glory appeared unto our father Abraham' (Acts 7:2). I do not know all that is included in those words, but of two things we may be certain: (1) For the first time in his life God was real to Abraham and (2) Abraham beheld God in his glory as God his Saviour. Sooner or later, this is what God does for every chosen, redeemed sinner. In the midst of their worldliness, self-serving, self-seeking and self-pleasing rebellion and death, God steps in and makes himself known! Then, they can say with Job, 'I have heard of thee by the hearing of the ear: but now mine eye seeth thee.'

This is how God saves sinners. He 'who commanded the light to shine out of darkness, hath shined in our hearts, to give the light of the knowledge of the glory of God in the face of Jesus Christ' (2 Corinthians 4:6). The chosen, redeemed sinner in whom this miracle of grace is wrought is brought by the power and grace of God out of darkness, bondage and death into the light and life and glorious liberty of the sons of God!

For he looked for a city which hath foundations, whose builder and maker is God. Through faith also Sara herself received strength to conceive seed, and was delivered of a child when she was past age, because she judged him faithful who had promised. Therefore sprang there even of one, and him as good as dead, so many as the stars of the sky in multitude, and as the sand which is by the sea shore innumerable. These all died in faith, not having received the promises, but having seen them afar off, and were persuaded of them, and embraced them, and confessed that they were strangers and pilgrims on the earth.

Hebrews 11:10-13

Chapter 34

Read: Hebrews 11:10-13

'A City Which Hath Foundations'

Faith lives in expectation of eternity, looking for that which God has promised. The life of faith is a life of hope, the hope of glory. Abraham sojourned here; but he lived for eternity. 'For he looked for a city which hath foundations, whose builder and maker is God.' That keeps things in perspective!

'Heaven hath foundations', wrote John Trapp, 'earth hath none, but is hanged upon nothing, as Job speaketh. Hence things are said to be on earth, but in heaven.'

The spies who went in to spy out the land with Joshua and Caleb saw nothing but giants in the land. They were terrified by what they saw. Abraham looked not at the giants but at the promise of God and fully expected God to fulfil his promise in spite of the giants. He believed God. He saw the same thing John saw, the New Jerusalem. He walked with it ever before him, seeing it as a city that hath foundations, whose Builder and Maker is God!

Faith's Expectation

When God the Holy Spirit tells us that Abraham 'looked for a city', he does not mean for us to understand that Abraham was searching for that city, but that he expected it. He fully expected to enter into and take possession of the heavenly Jerusalem as a rightful heir to it. This was not a matter of presumption, but of faith. You see Abraham really did believe God. Do we?

Has not God promised eternal life and heavenly glory to every sinner who trusts the Lord Jesus Christ? Indeed, he has (John 3:14-16). Does the Lord God not declare that every sinner washed in Christ's blood and robed in his righteousness is worthy to enter into and take possession of the inheritance of the saints in heaven? He clearly does (Colossians 1:12). It is, therefore, most reasonable that we should expect all the fulness of heavenly glory if we trust the Son of God, just as Abraham did.

The City's Foundations

What are the foundations of that city? We are told that the foundations of the city have inscribed upon them the names of 'the twelve apostles of the Lamb' (Revelation 21:14). That is to say, the city of God, the Heavenly Jerusalem, is a city built upon that which the twelve apostles of Christ taught, the gospel of God's free and sovereign grace in him.

Heaven is a city built upon the foundation of God's everlasting purpose of grace in Christ (Romans 8:28-31; Ephesians 1:3-14; 2 Timothy 1:9). The foundation of the city is God's everlasting love for his elect, his eternal covenant of grace, his sovereign election, his absolute predestination, his unalterable Word, the precious blood of Christ, and his almighty, free grace. In a word, the foundations of the city are those foundations of grace and truth in Jesus Christ crucified (Ephesians 2:20). Let us ever keep the city in sight! Do not look at the giants in this dark land, but set your heart on things above (Colossians 3:1-5, 15-17).

'She Judged Him Faithful'

Isaac was pre-eminently a child of faith. His birth was a supernatural work of God, a work of grace, for his birth was typical and prophetic of our Saviour's incarnation. But his birth was no less miraculous, no less supernatural, no less the work of God's grace than the fact that Sarah believed God would do it!

Abraham was 100 years old when Isaac was born. Sarah was 90! Not only was she well past the age of bearing children, she had never given birth to a child. Her womb was dry and barren. It was, as they say, 'biologically impossible' for her to give birth to a son; but she did. It was totally contrary to 'common sense' for her to bare a child; but she did. It was totally contrary to reason for her to believe that God would do this thing; but she did!

Believed God

Sarah believed God. 'Through faith Sarah also herself received strength'. Here is a happy, blessed family. Both Abraham and Sarah believed God!

What a blessing it is when both husband and wife are believers, when both in the same yoke pull together. They were heirs together of the same promises. They lived by the same principles, sought the same things, loved the same things, and sought to avoid the same things, because both believed God. Blessed is that house where a husband and wife love someone else more than they love each other, their children, or themselves. Where Christ is loved supremely! Like Zechariah and Elizabeth, Abraham and Sarah 'were both righteous before God, walking in all the commandments and ordinances of the Lord blameless' (Luke 1:6).

Example of Faith

Here is an exemplary woman of faith. Abraham did not and could not believe God for Sarah. Sarah herself believed God. Her faith is specifically mentioned so that all might understand that in Christ all social distinctions are insignificant (Colossians 3:10-11). Sarah is held before us as an example for all to follow, particularly for all women to follow (1 Peter 3:6).

Display of Grace

Here is a marvellous display of grace. In the Genesis record no mention is made of Sarah's faith, only of her unbelief. Here no mention is made of her unbelief, only of her faith. Her unbelief is forgiven and hidden by the inspired writer. Her faith is recorded and honoured. How gracious our God is. Let us ever seek to be like him (Ephesians 4:32-5:2).

Received Strength

Because she believed God, Sarah received strength to conceive. 'Through faith Sarah also herself received strength to conceive seed'. The word 'herself' is emphatic; Sarah did not receive the strength she needed from Abraham, or from Abraham's faith. She received it from God by the gift of his grace through her own faith.

By believing God, Sarah obtained that which she did not have before and could not get any other way. Her dead womb was given life to conceive. The Lord did the same thing for Sarah that he did for Abraham (Romans 4:17-21). Sarah discovered the answer to the angel's question for herself. 'Is anything too hard for the Lord?' (Genesis 18:13-15; Matthew 19:26; Mark 9:23).

Patience

Sarah waited for God to fulfil his promise for twenty-five long, long years. In that time, she erred greatly, failed miserably, and brought upon herself and her house great pain and sorrow. Yet, all that time, she believed God and waited. At last, she received the strength she required (Psalm 27:13-14; Isaiah 40:31; Lamentations 3:25-26).

Like Sarah, you and I obtain strength by faith in Christ by believing God. Our God has promised to honour those who honour him (1 Samuel 2:30). Nothing honours God like faith. God always honours faith. His word to us is, 'Lay hold of my strength' (Isaiah 27:5; Job 8:7; Ephesians 6:10; Philippians 4:12-13; 2 Timothy 2:1).

Delivered

Because she believed God, Sarah 'was delivered of a child when she was past age'. Her faith was persevering. This ninety year old woman went into labour with confidence and nursed a son like a twenty year old! There was no abortion and no miscarriage! Why? Because Sarah believed God (1 Timothy 2:15).

Rachel died in giving birth. Phineas' wife did too, as have many, many others. The pain and travail of giving birth is but a part of the curse. God has arranged that the birth of a child, perhaps the happiest of all human experiences, has with it a reminder of the curse and the threat of death.

Most women are delivered from death in child bearing, believers and unbelievers. The one who delivers them is God, whether they know it or not. But believers worship God in all things. We live by faith! Sarah believed God, worshipped him, gave birth to Isaac by faith (worshipping God), and gave thanks to God for the child he gave (Proverbs 3:5-6).

'When She Was Past Age'

The Holy Spirit emphasizes the fact that Sarah received strength to conceive and bear a son 'when she was past age'. He hereby heightens the sense of the miraculous and the supernatural because he would have us understand that no difficulty, no obstacle, no hindrance, should cause us to not believe our God.

The omnipotent God is not limited by nature. He rules nature and alters it as he sees fit! He who brought water out of the Rock, poured bread down from heaven, and caused an axe to swim has no difficulty with anything. The greater the apparent difficulties, the greater reason we have to believe God.

When all the streams of nature are dry, then we should most reasonably expect the waters of God's grace and goodness to pour out in a flood of mercy! Whatever the difficulties are before us, whatever the obstacles may be that are in our way, let us 'be strong in faith' being fully persuaded that 'what he has promised he is able to perform'.

Sarah believed God, 'because she judged him faithful who had promised'. Faith looks to God, not to self. Faith looks to God, not to circumstances. Martin Luther said, 'If we would trust God we must crucify the question, "How?"'

Let it never be forgotten that Sarah had the Word of God for what she believed. It was not a whim, a figment of her imagination, or simply something she desired which gave her faith. God made a promise, and she believed the Word God gave. Let us take heed that it is God's Word and God's testimony that we believe. Let us take heed that we really believe God's revelation. Let us take care that we cherish no hope but that which the Word of God promises. If we have the Word of God for the foundation of our faith, then it is impossible for our faith to be too confident or our hope to be too firm. He that promised is faithful!

He who is our God is a God of promised goodness. His promises of goodness to his people extend to all things temporal, spiritual and eternal. His promises are free, unconditional and sure. God who is faithful, all-wise, immutable, omnipotent and true cannot fail (Lamentations 3:22-26).

Faith's Fruit

'Therefore sprang there even of one, and him as good as dead, so many as the stars of the sky in multitude, and as the sand which is by the sea shore innumerable.' Because Sarah believed God, God's promise to Abraham was fulfilled.

Sarah's faith was as essential to the fulfilment of the promise as Abraham's. Yes, it is God who fulfils the promise. Yes, it is God who gives us faith. But, still, faith, personal faith exercised toward God is essential to receiving the blessing he has promised (Luke 7:50).

Because she believed God, Sarah became the mother of a great nation: the Church of God. You and I, like Isaac, are the children of our mother in faith, Sarah! Because Sarah believed God, the Lord Jesus Christ came into this world in the fulness of time to redeem us. A. W. Pink wrote:

> The opening 'Therefore' of verse 12 points the blessed consequence of her relying upon the faithfulness of God in the face of the utmost natural discouragements. From her faith there issued Isaac, and from him, ultimately, Christ Himself. And this is recorded for our instruction. Who can estimate the fruits of faith? Who can tell how many lives may be affected for good, even in generations yet to come, through your faith and my faith today! Oh how the thought of this should stir us up to cry more earnestly 'Lord, increase our faith' to the praise of the glory of Thy grace.

Oh, gift of gifts! Oh grace of faith!
My God, how can it be
That You, in free and sov'reign love,
Should give that gift to me?

Sweet grace! Into the vilest heart,
It is God's boast to come,
The glory of His grace to set,
In darkest souls His throne!

Your choice, Father, (Great God of grace!),
I lovingly adore.
Thank You for this great gift of faith,
And grace to long for more!

'Through Faith ... '

Sarah believed God. She believed his promise, trusted his Word, without anything to back it up, without any evidence, without any basis in human science, history, or reason. She just believed God, because God gave her the blessed gift of faith.

All things spiritual are utterly beyond the scope of human reason. The gospel of Christ and all that is revealed in the gospel is irreconcilable to human reason. The things of God are totally contrary to what the depraved mind and heart of man considers common sense. The Divine Trinity, the Fall of our race in Adam, Eternal Election, the Incarnation, Substitutionary Redemption, and Free Salvation are all matters utterly beyond the reach of human reason.

These are things which every heaven born soul sees, believes and rejoices in; but things which no unregenerate man can reconcile in his own mind with 'common sense'. Why? The Holy Spirit gives us the answer in 1 Corinthians 2. That which is the wisdom of God is hidden from the wise and prudent of this world. It can be known only by divine revelation (1 Corinthians 2:7-16).

Not only is it true that the gospel itself is beyond the reach of human wisdom, contrary to the depraved mind's idea of 'common sense', but faith, true faith, faith in the Lord Jesus Christ, in and by whom alone the triune God reveals himself, is totally contrary to human reason, contrary to it because it is so far above it that reason cannot grasp it.

True saving faith, faith in Christ and faith in the living God, is a supernatural thing. Faith does the impossible, sees the invisible, hears the inaudible, and touches the intangible. I fear that the vast majority of those who profess to have faith in Christ have nothing more than faith in their faith. Their faith is all talk, theory and emotion. Not so with true faith! Most religious people have a faith that has been, in one way or another, produced by men. There is nothing at all supernatural about it. True saving faith, this supernatural faith that believes God without evidence, without proof, without any foundation except God himself, is the gift and operation of God. In other words, no one can or will believe God until and unless God the Holy Spirit gives him faith.

If you and I believe God, if we truly believe God, it is because God has wrought his work of grace in us by the omnipotent power and goodness of his Spirit; as Paul puts it, 'according to the working of his mighty power, which he wrought in Christ, when he raised him from the dead' (Ephesians 1:19-20). This faith is the gift and operation of God (Ephesians 2:8; Colossians 2:12; Philippians 1:29). It cannot be had or explained in any other way.

'Not Having Received The Promises'

These saints of old 'died in faith, not having received the promises'. They had not yet received the promised blessings of their inheritance in Canaan. They had received and believed God's word of promise; but they had not yet received the fulfilment of the promises God made to Abraham. In a word, they had not yet seen Christ and the accomplishment of redemption by him. They lived by faith, as you and I do. They had the Word of God and promise of God as we do. They had it in part. We have it in its fulness. They had the same word we have; and they believed it just like God's people believe it today. They received it by faith.

Faith is the gift of God; but we must never look upon faith as a speculative thing. Faith is not an inactive fact, or a mere intellectual acquirement. True faith is always a living principle. It is an active grace, doing and experiencing the very things here declared.

'They Saw'

They saw God's promises afar off. They saw by divine revelation, that the Lord God would send Abraham's Seed, the Lord Jesus Christ, and all the blessings of grace and glory by him. The Lord God gave them a seeing eye, a hearing ear, and an understanding heart. The eyes of their understanding had been enlightened (Ephesians 1:18). Like Abraham, these all saw Christ's day and rejoiced.

They Were Persuaded

They were persuaded of the promises. They set to their seal that God is true (John 3:33). These chosen, redeemed sinners, believed God, and had that confidence in their souls that only God-given faith can give. The believer is persuaded, confident, assured of some things, the believer knows some things others can never know in this world, because we know that God is true.

We know that Jesus is the Christ. We know the Shepherd's voice. We know that we know him. We know that we have passed from death unto life. We know whom we have believed. We know that all things work together for good to them that love God, to them that are the called, according to his purpose. We know that when our earthly house of this tabernacle is dissolved we have a building of God, a house not made with hands, eternal in the heavens. We know that when we see him we shall be like him.

They Embraced

Seeing God's promises afar off, being persuaded of them, they embraced them. Faith received. The understanding was persuaded. And the heart loved the revelation of God in the Gospel (Psalm 119:14). John Trapp said, 'They kissed Christ in the promises and were kissed by him in them, being drawn together by mutual dear affection.'

They Confessed

The blessings promised were the objects of their confident hope, joyful expectation, and invigorating affection. Therefore, they confessed that they were strangers and pilgrims on earth. Abraham sought no inheritance here, but only a place to bury his wife and himself. Jacob made the same confession to Pharaoh (Genesis 47:9). But the confession went far beyond the earthly inheritance in Canaan.

We know this because David made the same confession long after that earthly inheritance had been obtained (Psalm 39:12; 119:19; 1 Chronicles 29:15). God's people in this world are all strangers here, because our home is in another country. We are pilgrims because we are simply passing through this strange land on our journey home (Philippians 3:20-21; Colossians 3:1-3).

They Lived By Faith

Four times in holy scripture, we read, 'The just shall live by faith' (Habakkuk 2:4; Romans 1:17; Galatians 3:11; Hebrews 10:38). Our faith in Christ is as essential to our salvation as his death for us. Our faith in God is as necessary to the salvation of our souls as God's election of us unto salvation. Our believing by the Spirit is just as necessary to our everlasting salvation in Christ as our being born of the Spirit. Faith is not our Saviour. Christ alone is our Saviour; but we can no more be saved without faith in Christ than we could live without breathing. 'The just shall live by faith'.

Bible Doctrine

Be sure you understand the doctrine of holy scripture. Faith in Christ is not the cause of our justification or of our regeneration. We are justified by the grace of God through the redemption accomplished by the shedding of Christ's precious blood at Calvary (Romans 3:24). It was the blood of Christ that satisfied the justice of God, not our faith. It was the blood of Christ that put away our sins, not our faith. It was the blood of Christ that redeemed us, not our faith. In the matter of regeneration, too, the work is altogether the work of God's free, sovereign, omnipotent, irresistible grace. Faith is not the cause of the new birth, but the result. We believe by the working of God's almighty power; by the operation of God. Yet, we must believe on the Lord Jesus Christ. 'He that believeth on the Son of God hath everlasting life. He that believeth not the Son of God shall not see life; but the wrath of God abideth on him.' But faith in Christ is much more than most people imagine. Most vainly imagine that since they decided to believe in Jesus, since they believed in him (yesterday, this morning, or 30 years ago) they are saved forever. The scriptures never use such language. The testimony of holy scripture is, 'The just shall live by faith'. Faith in Christ is not an act of life, but a way of life.

Dying in Faith

All who live by faith shall die in faith (Job 17:9; Psalm 138:8; Isaiah 46:4; Jeremiah 32:40). The house built on the Rock shall not fall. Those to whom Christ gives eternal life shall never perish. The gifts and callings of God are without repentance. The sons of Jacob shall never die, because our God cannot and does not change. The seal of God's Spirit cannot be broken. The merit of Christ's blood can never be made of none effect. The power of God's grace can never be resisted. The purpose of God's love can never be overturned.

Who are these of whom the Apostle says, 'These all died in faith'? Perhaps he is speaking only of those believers who lived after the flood and before the giving of the law, of those who lived in the patriarchal age (Abraham, Sarah, and their immediate descendants). But I think that places a limitation on the text that is unnecessary. The words 'these all' refer to all who have been mentioned as examples of faith.

The faith in which all these believers died is that faith defined in verses 1-3. It is that faith which is the substance of our hope. The revelation of the Gospel! It is that faith which is the evidence of our salvation. Faith in Christ, the evidence of election, redemption, and calling. It is that faith which gives us an understanding of all things spiritual (Proverbs 28:5; 1 Corinthians 2:12, 14-15).

Abel

Abel died in faith. Though he was murdered by his own brother, he died believing God (v. 4). It does not matter how we die, when we die, or where we die, so long as we die in Christ, so long as we die believing God. It is written, 'Precious in the sight of the Lord is the death of his saints.' This faith in which Abel died is that faith by which he received witness that he was righteous. His faith did not make him righteous. Christ alone has made us righteous. By faith we receive the witness of God the Holy Spirit that we are righteous (Romans 4:25-5:2; 5:10-11; 8:15-16).

Enoch

Can Enoch be included among these all who died in faith? I am sure he can. Enoch died in the same sense that all believers do (v. 5). It is true, he did not see death; but none of God's elect ever die (John 5:24). We simply depart from this life into glory (John 11:25-26). Like Enoch, we walk with God by faith. Like Enoch, we have testimony that we please God by faith (v. 6). Like Enoch, if we believe God, we shall soon be translated into heaven. Being absent from the body, we shall be present with the Lord. Yes, our bodies shall die, unless the Lord Jesus comes again beforehand; but we shall not die.

The Patriarchs

Abraham and Sarah, and Isaac and Jacob, also died in faith. They died as believers, expecting the fulfilment of God's promises. 'These all died in faith'. Because they were born of God, they believed God. Because they believed God, they died as they lived, 'in faith'. That which is true of these is true of all who live by faith in the Lord Jesus Christ. All of God's elect die in faith.

For they that say such things declare plainly that they seek a country. And truly, if they had been mindful of that country from whence they came out, they might have had opportunity to have returned.But now they desire a better country, that is, an heavenly: wherefore God is not ashamed to be called their God: for he hath prepared for them a city. By faith Abraham, when he was tried, offered up Isaac: and he that had received the promises offered up his only begotten son, Of whom it was said, That in Isaac shall thy seed be called: Accounting that God was able to raise him up, even from the dead; from whence also he received him in a figure. By faith Isaac blessed Jacob and Esau concerning things to come.

Hebrews 11:14-20

Chapter 35

Read: Hebrews 11:14-20

'Strangers And Pilgrims On The Earth'

A. W. Pink wrote,

> The figure of the 'stranger' applied to the child of God here on earth, is very pertinent and full. The analogies between one who is in a foreign country and the Christian in this world, are marked and numerous. In a strange land one is not appreciated for his birth, but is avoided (John 15:19). The habits, ways, language are strange to him (1 Peter 4:4). He has to be content with a stranger's fare (1 Timothy 6:8). – He needs to be careful not to give offence to the government (Colossians 4:5). He has to continually enquire his way (Psalm 5:8). Unless he conforms to the ways of that foreign country, he is easily identified (Matthew 26:73). He is often assailed with homesickness, for his heart is not where his body is (Philippians 1:23).

Seeking A Country

The Holy Spirit draws his own conclusion to this confession. 'For they that say such things declare plainly that they seek a country' (v. 14). The word translated 'country' would be better translated 'fatherland'. Heaven is our fatherland, the land where our Father dwells, the land he possesses as his own and for his children. The fatherland is the land where the children want to live, have a right to live, and seek to live.

A Choice Made

Because they were strangers and pilgrims in the earth, they chose not to go back to Chaldea. 'And truly, if they had been mindful of that country from whence they came out, they might have had opportunity to have returned' (v. 15).

Chaldea, the land from which they had come, was never very far away. There were no obstacles to prevent them from returning. But they were never inclined to return. Abraham made his servant take an oath, swearing that he would do nothing to induce Isaac to return to that pagan land. Though Jacob did once sojourn there, he did not and could not stay. His God would not allow it. Why? Because they looked for their happiness and satisfaction somewhere else.

Application

What do these things tell us about God's people in this world? How do they apply to us? Spiritually, believers today are precisely like those people. Many who profess faith in Christ do depart from him. But when the Lord Jesus asked his disciples if they would also go away, Peter answered for all when he said, 'Lord, to whom shall we go? thou hast the words of eternal life' (John 6:65-69). We 'desire a better country'.

All who know God, all who live by faith desire, yearn for, and pant after a better country, a heavenly country. We long for a country where everything is better! A heavenly country! Therefore, God is not ashamed to be called our God: for he has prepared for us a city.

Here is the inconceivable greatness and glory of our Fatherland. It is a land prepared specifically for us, the people of God's peculiar love. In preparing this land for us and bringing us home to it, the Lord God fully answers all the hopes, expectations and desires that are aroused in our hearts and minds by him calling himself our God and us his people. When we are at last brought home to glory, we shall say (of that which till then we have only seen afar off), 'Now I understand what he meant when he said, "I will be their God, and they shall be my people!"'

Travelling to Another Country

Almost every year I travel to a foreign country preaching the gospel of Christ. I have crossed the borders of our nation north, south, east, and west many times. Whenever you leave this country and cross into another, three things are required. (1) You must have a birth certificate to prove your citizenship. (2) You must have a visa from the country receiving you. (3) You must have no criminal record.

Soon I will leave this land of sorrow and sin. I hope to enter into the bliss and glory of heaven. I hope to stand forever accepted as a citizen of the New Jerusalem. What is the basis for this hope?

I have a birth certificate. The Lord God has given me a new nature (2 Corinthians 5:17). There is in me a new man, created of God in righteousness and true holiness.

I have a visa. I have a right to enter into heaven itself by the blood of Christ, because I am washed in his blood and robed in his righteousness (Colossians 1:14). God says, 'It must be perfect to be accepted,' and in Christ I am perfect! He has made me perfectly righteous before God! (1 Corinthians 1:30).

And I have a clear record. The Lord Jesus Christ has purged away all my sins with his own precious blood. Therefore God will never charge me with any sin (Romans 4:8). When I stand before God and he searches the books for iniquity and sin under my name, he will find none (Jeremiah 50:20).

Abraham's Great Trial

In Hebrews 5:8 we read that our Saviour, the Lord Jesus Christ, 'Though he were a Son, yet learned he obedience by the things which he suffered'. And that which was true of our Redeemer, when he walked upon this earth as a man, is true of us. If we are the children of God, as long as we live in this body of flesh, we will be required to learn obedience. And we learn obedience by the things which we suffer by the hand of God's wise and good providence.

The life of the believer is a series of trials, by which his faith is tested, proved, and strengthened. Character is developed by discipline. And God will develop the character of his saints. It appears that frequently there is one great trial of faith, for which all other trials seem to be preparatory. Certainly, that was the case with Abraham and the great trial of his faith described in these verses.

'By faith Abraham, when he was tried, offered up Isaac' (v. 17). God's will is the rule of justice and goodness, and whatever he requires is just and good. We dare not attempt to call the Almighty to our bar. He gives no account to us of his matters. His command to Abraham to offer up his son Isaac may be confusing to men. Men may use it to blaspheme his name; but the Lord our God is the Lord of life. He gives it, he preserves it, and he takes it as he will, by whatever means he pleases.

Abraham showed no reluctance. As soon as he had God's command, he travelled three days' journey to the place of sacrifice. He took the wood for the burnt offering, laid it on his son; took fire, and carried a knife in his hand to slay his son. He built an altar, laid the wood in order on it; and bound his son, laid him on the altar before the Lord, took the knife, and stretched forth his hand to slay his darling son. He fully intended to kill his only son upon the mount of sacrifice. In fact, God declares that he that received the promises actually 'offered up his only begotten son', because in his heart the deed was already done.

For this, he is held before us as a great example of faith. Had God not stopped him, Abraham would have killed his son by faith. He believed God. He trusted the equity, justice, and wisdom of his God and his God's command. Believing God, he was fully assured of the truth and faithfulness of the Lord's promises, no matter how his providence and commands might seem to contradict them. Moreover, Abraham was fully persuaded that God would, one way or another, fulfil his promises, raise Isaac from the dead, and save his people through that Saviour who was to come through Isaac's loins! This was great faith indeed! Being great faith, it was greatly tried.

God's Sure Promises

The Lord God promised Abraham that he would have a son, that a great multitude would be born of him, a people who would inherit the land of Canaan, a people who would inherit the earth. The promise of God to Abraham was that the Messiah himself, (the Woman's Seed, the Christ, the Redeemer) would come into the world through Isaac! The Holy Spirit calls our attention to this fact specifically in verses 18-19.

'And he that had received the promises offered up his only begotten son. Of whom it is said, That in Isaac shall thy seed be called.' Accounting that God was able to raise him up, even from the dead'! Commenting on these words, John Gill wrote,

> Abraham did not go to the place of sacrifice without thought. Yet, he did not consult with flesh and blood. His reasoning was the reasoning of faith; and the conclusion of it was, that God was able to raise him from the dead. He knew that he had received him at first, as it were, from the dead; he sprung from his own dead body, and out of Sarah's dead womb; and though his faith did not prescribe to God, yet he believed that God would raise his son from the dead, rather than that his promise should fail; and this conclusion proceeded upon the power and faithfulness of God.

Abraham received Isaac as one raised from the dead, 'from whence also he received him in a figure', for the purpose of teaching us about faith.

Blessings?

We almost always judge God's providential acts wrongly. We almost always mistake evil for good and good for evil. We almost always mistake God's curse for his blessing and God's blessing for his curse.

Without question, the countless evils that befall our nation and the other nations of the world in these dark, dark days are displays of the providential judgments of God upon a generation that has persistently turned its back upon God and despised him. Let us be warned. These things are but a foretaste of things to come. Indeed, they are but a foretaste of that great and terrible day when God shall bring us all to stand before his bar.

Yet, we must never imagine that God's providential acts of judgment upon this nation or any other are acts of judgment against his own elect. Those things that appear to the natural mind to be God's judgments are, in reality, God's blessings upon his own; and, more often than not, those things that appear to the natural mind to be God's blessings upon unbelieving people are acts of divine judgment against them (Psalm 73). It is written, 'There shall no evil happen to the just: but the wicked shall be filled with mischief' (Proverbs 12:21). God always does good for his own (Jeremiah 32:38-42; Isaiah 3:10), giving them grace they do not deserve, and always brings judgment upon the wicked, giving them their just reward (Isaiah 3:11). Even when it appears that he is blessing them, 'it is that they shall be destroyed forever' (Psalm 92:7).

When David thought on these things, he wrote, 'Surely thou didst set them in slippery places: thou castedst them down into destruction. How are they brought into desolation as in a moment! They are utterly consumed with terrors!' (Psalm 73:18-19).

Esau's Blessing

The Holy Spirit tells us that Isaac blessed both his sons, Jacob and Esau, concerning things to come by faith. The blessing of Isaac upon Esau was, in reality, the curse of God upon him. God gave him all that his heart desired of this world. He was 'blessed' as the world would say, in health, prosperity, power, influence, and family; but God had set the world in his heart, and that reprobate man whom God hated was and is forever cursed by his blessings (Ecclesiastes 3:9-11).

Isaac knew that was what he was doing by the blessing he pronounced upon Esau. He knew God had justly rejected his beloved son. When the old patriarch was dying, he acted in faith, bowing to the will of God. Esau was cursed, though he appeared to be blessed. It looked like God loved Esau, though he hated him.

Jacob's Blessing

Jacob was blessed, though he appeared to be cursed. It looked like God hated Jacob though he loved him. Jacob's life, to all outward appearance, seems to have justified his cry, 'all these things are against me' (Genesis 42:36). In reality, though all the things he experienced, bitter and painful as they must have been, were working together for his everlasting good.

When Isaac was about to die he called Esau and told him to go out, kill a deer, and make a batch of his favourite stew, and promised when he returned that he would pass along to him the patriarchal blessing, the blessing of God's covenant. But Esau had already sold his birthright and the blessing of it to Jacob (Genesis 25:29-34).

Rebekah overheard the conversation between Isaac and Esau. Therefore, she called Jacob and urged him to pretend to be Esau that he might deceive Isaac into blessing him instead of Esau. Because Isaac was an old man and nearly blind, their scheme worked. By the time Esau returned to Isaac, Jacob had already obtained the blessing (Genesis 27:1).

Esau was so angry that he swore he would kill Jacob as soon as Isaac died. So Jacob fled from his brother and took refuge under the roof of Rebekah's brother, Laban. Laban may have been the only man living more conniving than Jacob; but that is another story. Jacob spent fourteen years serving his uncle Laban, married his daughters Leah and Rachel, and was greatly blessed of God in everything he touched. The Lord gave him a huge family, tremendous herds of sheep and cattle, and great wealth.

Enough

After serving Laban for twenty years, Jacob said, 'I've had enough of this' and resolved to return to the land of his fathers. Always the schemer, on his way home, he began to make plans to appease Esau. He sent huge presents, one on the heels of another. Yet, when he heard that Esau was coming with four hundred men to meet him, he was scared to death. When the two brothers finally met (Genesis 33:1-11), Esau said to Jacob, 'I have enough'.

Both Esau and Jacob declared themselves content with that which they possessed. What a rare sight this is. Seldom do we meet any who are content, who have enough to satisfy them. But here are two men who were content. More than that, these two men were brothers. Yet, the only thing in the characters of these two men, which they had in common, was the fact that they were content with what they possessed. In every other way, these two brothers were as unalike as two brothers could be.

But the words that Jacob used when he said, 'I have enough', and the words Esau used were completely different. When Jacob said, 'I have enough', he was referring to much more than his earthly, material riches. In fact, those things really had nothing at all to do with what he was talking about. Jacob said what Esau could never say. He said what every true believer can and should say; but it was something the unbeliever can never say. Jacob said, 'I have all things' (Genesis 33:11). Truly, that person who has all things has enough! Esau had the world, and was content with it. Jacob had Christ and, having Christ, had all things; and he was content (Genesis 32:24-30). Let us return to Isaac's blessing.

Isaac: An Example of Faith

Were I searching for an example of faith, a single act of faith, by which I wanted to instruct, comfort and encourage God's elect in the matter of believing God, I am certain I would never have thought about the example given here. In fact, that which is here held before us, as a great example of remarkable faith, I have always thought of as an example of great weakness. But 'the Lord seeth not as man seeth … the Lord looketh on the heart' (1 Samuel 16:7).

Isaac and His Family

Hebrews 11:20 refers us to chapter twenty-seven of Genesis. Isaac and Rebekah had twin sons, Jacob and Esau. Esau, the firstborn, was exactly the kind of son every man wants. Judging by the description we are given of him, he probably was not much to look at; but he was all boy. He was strong, manly, an outdoorsman, a sportsman, a great hunter. He and Isaac were very close. Esau appears to have endeavoured to honour his father.

Jacob, on the other hand, was apparently quite the opposite. He was soft, delicate, and always hanging around his mother's apron. Jacob was as conniving and scheming, as Esau was plain and forthright. He was as weak as Esau was strong.

The Birthright

When it came time for him to die, Isaac was anxious to give the blessing of God to his beloved son Esau. This patriarchal blessing was very, much more than a father's wishes for his son. It was the blessing of God in the firstborn, passed on from generation to generation in the patriarchal ages.

It represented Christ and all the blessings of God's boundless grace in Christ.

This birthright should have been Esau's, being the firstborn and Jacob wanted Esau to have it. Who better to represent him and carry on his family than Esau? So he sent Esau out to kill a deer and prepare him a pot of stew so that they could have their favourite meal together, reminisce about the things they had enjoyed together, and then Isaac would bless his favourite son.

But there was a problem with Isaac's plans. Isaac's plans, desires, will and purpose were directly contrary to God's purpose. God loved Jacob and hated Esau. God chose Jacob. God had ordained that Jacob be the one through whom the covenant would be established; through whom Christ should come into the world; through whom he would accomplish his purpose of grace; by whom he would bring salvation to all his elect.

The Birthright Despised

Esau had long before sold his birthright to Jacob in a moment of trial (Genesis 25:27-34). It wasn't much of a trial. He had been out in the fields, as usual; and as usual, Jacob had been in the kitchen with his mother. When Esau came in from the fields he was hungry and desperately wanted something to eat. Devious Jacob saw his opportunity, and made a deal with his elder brother: Jacob would give him a bowl of the lentil stew he was cooking, if Esau would give him his birthright in exchange. To gratify the lust of his flesh for a moment, Esau agreed, and swapped eternal redemption for the sake of his appetite. He traded the Son of God for bread and a bowl of stew!

Rebekah's Plan

When Isaac was dying and wanted to bless Esau, Rebekah overheard the conversation between them and came up with a plan of her own, by which to deceive her husband and secure God's blessing for her favourite son, Jacob. She had Jacob to kill a kid of the goats and bring it to her. She made a stew for him to take to Isaac, and put the skin of the goat on Jacob, so that Isaac would think he was Esau and bless him. Jacob was scared to death; but the plan worked, because Isaac was blind.

A Picture of The Gospel

What a blessed picture this is of the gospel! This is exactly how sinners receive the blessing of God. I make no excuse for Rebekah's actions, or Jacob's; but this much is clear: Rebekah knew what God's purpose was; and she was determined that the promise of God be Jacob's. Jacob knew what that birthright represented; and he was determined to have it. They both hazarded everything to get it. If we would have that same blessing, the blessing of God's grace, we must do exactly what Jacob did. A Lamb must be killed. No blessing can be had from God without a sacrifice being made. We must bring the holy Lord God that savoury meat he loves: Christ himself (Ephesians 5:2). We must come to the holy Lord God in the skins of his darling Son. As Jacob came to Isaac wearing Esau's clothes and in the skins of the slain goat, so we must come to him robed in the righteousness of Christ, wearing his garments of salvation. Coming to God in Christ, he cannot see us. All he sees is Christ and us in him.

Isaac's Great Faith

Faith bows to the will of God. The flesh resists it, but faith bows to it. Isaac proved himself to be a man of faith. When he, at last, saw that his will was in direct opposition to God's will, he humbly bowed to the will of God, saying, 'I have blessed him? Yea, and he shall be blessed' (Genesis 27:33). He lifted his heart to heaven, and said, 'Not my will, thy will be done'. That is great, remarkable, exemplary faith.

Isaac's Blessing Upon Jacob and Esau

The purpose of God stands fast. It is unalterable. It cannot be hindered. The Lord our God always does all his pleasure. How clearly this fact is demonstrated in Isaac's two sons, Jacob and Esau! Jacob, the younger, was to be served by Esau, the elder. Does this purpose come to pass? All parties involved sinned against God: Esau by godless unbelief, Jacob and Rebekah by deceit, and Isaac by giving way to human passions. Thus, everything known was contrary to God's purpose. Yet, we see God overruling everything by his providence to accomplish his purpose.

Rebekah's Presumption

Isaac's wife, Rebekah, acted in terrible unbelief and presumption, attempting to secure by the arm of the flesh what God had promised to do by his free grace (Genesis 25:23). Both Rebekah and Jacob knew and believed the promise of God. They knew God's purpose in the matter. Though his father may have refused to recognize it and honour it, Jacob had purchased the birthright lawfully. Rebekah's faith failed when she decided to scheme and through deceit get the blessing for Jacob; and Jacob's when he agreed to it. They should have left it to the providence of God, and waited for him to perform the work. They were working in the energy of the flesh to prevent the thwarting of God's purpose (compare 2 Samuel 6:6-16).

Isaac's Perversity

Isaac's affections were perverted. Isaac loved Esau more than Jacob, but it was a selfish, human love. How often displaced affections lead to sin! Esau was his elder son. He was likely the more masculine of Isaac's two boys. And Isaac loved the 'savoury meat' Esau provided for him. Isaac was determined to bless Esau, contrary to the revelation of God. Truely, 'his eyes were dim'!

Prophetic Blessings

Isaac's blessings upon his sons were prophetic (Genesis 27:28-40). The significance of the blessings was clear. Jacob was promised both spiritual and temporal blessings. The coming Seed, the Lord Jesus Christ, the Saviour of the world, was confirmed to him. Esau was blessed, but only temporally. Both Jacob and Esau were descendants of Abraham, but only Jacob was 'a prince with God'. The people of God, in any age, are those who believe him. They are the Israel of God, God's true covenant people.

The sovereignty of God was manifestly displayed in the blessings of Isaac's two sons. Isaac believed that the one he blessed would have the promise of God. When he perceived that the providential hand of God had crossed his own affections, he did not murmur and rebel, but he yielded and submitted to the Lord. (Believers always, in the end, yield to the will of God, no matter how God's will may cross their plans and schemes!) The object of his faith was God. The ground of his faith was God's revelation. He did not try to recall the blessing, but he accepted God's providence. Esau found no repentance in him (Hebrews 12:17). He could not get back the blessing he despised in his youth. He had sold Christ for a bowl of beans, and thereby 'fitted' himself to destruction.

God Prevailed

Once more, we see that 'the heavens do rule'! The Lord God prevailed; he always does; his will was accomplished; it always is. His purpose was performed; as always. Our God prevails and ever shall. He works his will even through the weaknesses and sins of others, yet he is in no way affected by their sin or weakness.

Though it will never thwart the purpose of God, unbelief does reek havoc in our lives and in the lives of those who are under our influence, as it did in Jacob's household for many years. If we are taken up with satisfying the flesh, we are terribly dim sighted spiritually, and are sure to act in unbelief. Let us, rather, believe God, trusting our Heavenly Father to accomplish his will and wait for him to perform his purpose (Proverbs 3:5-6; Romans 8:28-31; Isaiah 40:27-31).

Isaac's Remarkable Faith

Read Genesis 27, the passage to which Paul refers, and you will see why Isaac is held before us here as a man of remarkable faith. The Holy Spirit specifically declares that Isaac, in an act of faith, blessed both his sons, both Jacob and Esau. Here are eight things to be gleaned from the record God has given us of this event.

1. God Almighty Saves Whom He Will

Let men rant and rave all they may, gnashing their teeth upon the Word of God, the fact remains 'Salvation is of the Lord'! God has mercy on whom he will. He chooses some and passes by others. The purpose of God according to election stands firm. 'The foundation of God standeth sure: the Lord knoweth them that are his'! Read Romans 9:11-16.

2. God's Elect Are Almost Always Those We Least Suspect

God's ways are not our ways. God's thoughts are not our thoughts. And God's choices are not our choices. Isaac chose Esau; but God chose Jacob (1 Corinthians 1:26-29). Let us never imagine that we know the purpose of God concerning another person. No one is beyond the reach of omnipotent grace. No one, no matter how excellent he may appear to our eyes, has anything to commend him to God's favour.

3. Faith Cherishes and Prizes Christ Above All Things

Faith chooses Christ. Faith seeks Christ. Faith counts Christ precious and all things but dung in comparison to him (1 Peter 2:6-8).

4. Unbelief Despises Christ and Cherishes the Lusts of the Flesh

Esau despised Christ but Jacob chose him. Esau counted Christ but dung for the momentary gratification of his appetite. Jacob counted that dung which Esau cherished, that he might win Christ and be found in him (Philippians 3:3-14). Multitudes are like Esau. The sons of Korah, Elimelech, Judas and Demas stand before us as glaring examples of men in whose heart the world was so set that they could not behold the works of God (Ecclesiastes 3:11). Jacob preferred Christ to anything and everything. Few there are like him. The birthright Jacob chose represented Christ and God's salvation in him. For that, Jacob was willing to incur his father's wrath, a life of separation from family and friend, and anything else.

5. God Gives Every One of Us Exactly What We Want

This fact deserves consideration. If you desire Christ, I am fully aware that God himself has made you want him; but if Christ is what you want,

Christ is what you shall have (Jeremiah 29:11-14). If you want the world, if you want self-gratification, if you want what all men naturally want and choose, if you despise Christ and choose your own lusts, God will give you that. Oh, how I pray that God will cause you to seek Christ. But if you despise him and choose to serve your own lusts, God will give you what you want. Esau found enough to gratify his heart in the portion with which he was blessed ('I have enough' Genesis 33:9). His blessing proved to be his everlasting curse (Proverbs 1:23-32, Hebrews 12:16-17). Jacob, when he had given everything away, found that which satisfied his heart and soul ('I have enough' Genesis 33:11). His blessing is Christ!

6. When God Shuts a Sinner Up in Reprobation, He Is Doomed Forever

If God gives a person up, if God turns a sinner over to himself and lets him have his own way, he is as good as in hell. When God shuts the door, the door is shut! He shut the door going into the ark before the first raindrop fell from heaven! Esau set his heart upon the world; and God set the world in his heart (Ecclesiastes 3:11).

7. Nothing Stands in the Way or Hinders the Purpose of God

Yes, God always has his way, overruling our wills, our desires, our purposes, and even our most reprehensible behaviour, to accomplish his everlasting purpose of grace! The purpose of God shall stand.

8. Faith Ultimately Bows to the Will of God

Faith says, 'Thy will be done!' This is what we see in Genesis 27:33-41 and Hebrews 11:20. Though the purpose of God was in direct opposition to all that Isaac wanted, purposed, planned and worked to secure, in the end, he bowed to God's will.

Jacob and Esau

Predestination is God's sovereign eternal decree, his foreordination and purpose of all things that come to pass in time. It is his everlasting purpose by which he has ordered all things from eternity for the salvation of his elect. Providence is the accomplishment of all things in time according to the purpose of God in predestination (Romans 8:28-30).

Predestination

Divine predestination is clearly seen in Jacob and Esau. The book of God teaches the doctrine of absolute, universal, and particular predestination. In providence, God fulfils his will of predestination, unerringly and absolutely (Acts 2:23; Romans 8:28-30; Ephesians 1:3-6, 11).

Nowhere is the purpose of God in eternal predestination more fully set forth than in the birth, lives, and ultimate end of those twin boys born to Isaac and Rebekah. The purpose of God regarding Jacob and Esau was made known to Rebekah when the children strove in her womb, when he said to her, 'The elder shall serve the younger' (Genesis 25:23).

God's eternal purpose for Jacob and Esau was made known before they were born (Romans 9:13). Jacob was loved before he was born, before he was capable of doing good. Esau was hated before he was born, before he was capable of doing evil. What was said to Rebekah concerning them was intended by God to be an illustration of his eternal purpose of grace in predestination concerning all his elect. These things are plainly revealed in Romans 9:11-18.

Esau

Esau proved himself to be a man in every way worthy of divine hatred. He was worthy of God's hatred before his birth, because he was a son of Adam. As such, he was a child of wrath and a fit object for hatred.

I do not read in the scriptures of anyone going to hell because of God's predestination. Predestination includes all things, even man's rebellion, sin, and everlasting ruin. But the cause of eternal damnation is always set forth in the Word of God as being man's wilful rebellion and unbelief (Proverbs 1; Romans 1). Neither do I read in the book of God of any being punished eternally for Adam's transgression. Sinners go to hell because of their own rebellion and their own chosen course of iniquity; but all are born children of wrath, under the sentence of condemnation, and go astray as soon as they are born speaking lies.

Esau proved himself a rebel who lived and died under the wrath of God. He was conceived in sin. He manifested the depravity of his heart in the actions of his life and lusts of his flesh. He profanely despised God's blessing by selling his birthright for a moment's satisfaction. He took wives of the women of Canaan, contrary to the holy example of Abraham, and was determined to murder his brother (Genesis 26:34-35; 27:41). He turned his back on the habitation of his fathers, and departed forever from the land of promise (Genesis 36:6-8). The apostle Paul, writing by divine inspiration, refers to him as a 'profane person' (Hebrews 12:16).

Jacob

As Esau was justly the object of God's hatred before he was born, because he was viewed in Adam as a sinner, Jacob was justly the object of God's love before he was born, because he was viewed in Christ as righteous. He was numbered among those chosen in Christ from eternity, redeemed by the blood of the Lamb slain from the foundation of the world, and 'accepted in the Beloved' before the worlds were made (Romans 8:29-30; Revelation 3:5; 20:12, 15; Ephesians 1:6).

Loved and Hated

The words 'loved' and 'hatred' must be viewed in the full force of their meaning. The Holy Spirit gives no qualifying sense in his usage of these terms as they relate to God's love of Jacob and his hatred of Esau (Romans 9:11-17). God loved Jacob in the sense that he was fully devoted to him from eternity. He hated Esau in the sense that he passed by him, giving him no consideration, but left him entirely alone.

Two Seeds

That which is said of Jacob and Esau must be said of all men before they are born. All are either loved of God or hated of God from eternity. Genesis 3:15 marks the announcement of the coming Redeemer, but it also divides all mankind into two 'seed' the seed of the woman and the seed of the serpent. There are some in this world—God's elect—who are of the Seed of the woman, that is, Christ's. It is written, 'A seed shall serve him' (Psalm 22:30). 'He shall see his seed' (Isaiah 53:10). All the sons and daughters of Adam are either sheep or goats by the decree and purpose of God. Sheep will never become goats, and goats will never become sheep. This fact is illustrated throughout the scriptures (Cain and Abel, Ishmael and Isaac, Jacob and Esau). It is God alone who makes the distinction between men (1 Corinthians 4:7). He has mercy on whom he will have mercy. He has compassion on whom he will have compassion. Whom he will he hardens. Robert Haldane wrote that: Jacob and Esau ...

> ... illustrate by their particular examples both sides of the important doctrine of God's sovereignty in the election, and of his justice in the reprobation of fallen man. For, by acting in this manner, God has clearly shown that he is the sovereign Master in their calling and election, and of their rejection, that he chooses and rejects as seems good to him any of the sinful race of Adam, all of whom are justly objects of his displeasure, without regarding natural qualities which distinguish them from one another.

The Purpose of God Shall Stand

God's promise is, 'It shall be well with the righteous'. His Word declares, 'There shall no evil happen to the just'. The Lord God promises his own,

'I will not depart from them to do them good'. 'And we know that all thing work together for good to them that love God, to them who are the called according to his purpose.'

Vexing Providence

Yet, our lives are frequently vexed with trials and circumstances that make it appear that God's promises have failed, and his purpose has been nullified. It sometimes seems as though evil and not good is our lot.

We are often like the weeping prophet in Lamentations 3, crying, 'He hath led me and brought me into darkness, but not into light … against me is he turned; he turneth his hand against me all the day … and compassed me with gall and travail. He hath set me in dark places … when I cry and shout, he shutteth out my prayer. He hath enclosed my ways with hewn stone, he hath made my paths crooked. He was unto me as a bear lying in wait, and as a lion in secret places. He hath turned aside my ways, and pulled me in pieces: he hath made me desolate … He hath filled me with bitterness'.

Remembering our affliction and misery, the wormwood and the gall, how often, like Jeremiah, our circumstances cause us to think, even if we do not express it in words, 'Thou hast removed my soul far off from peace … My strength and my hope is perished from the Lord' (Lamentations 3:17-18). How foolishly and ignorantly we behave when we judge the goodness of God by the things we see, feel, and experience!

Judge not the Lord by feeble sense,
But trust Him for His grace.
Behind the frowning providence,
He hides a smiling face!

His purposes will ripen fast,
Unfolding every hour;
The bud may have a bitter taste,
But sweet will be the flower!

May God give us grace, in the teeth of adversity, to trust him! What he has promised, he will perform. What he has purposed, he will do. God's providence is sure. His decree is firm and unalterable. His will must and shall prevail. If everything around us crumbles to the ground, though heaven and earth pass away, the purpose of God must stand! Nothing hinders his purpose, alters his will, or stands in his way!

Isaac's Faith

This great truth is nowhere more clearly demonstrated than in the life of God's servant, Isaac. Though Isaac lived longer than any of the other patriarchs, less is recorded about him than any of the others. In fact, the entire history of this man, Isaac, is recorded in two short chapters of Inspiration (Genesis 26 and 27).

In Hebrews 11:20 the Holy Spirit uses that which, at least to me, appears to be very incidental to display the greatness of Isaac's faith. However, when the event here described is closely examined, it proves to be a truly remarkable example of faith. Here the Spirit of God calls our attention to Isaac's act of faith in blessing his sons, Jacob and Esau, in his old age. 'By faith Isaac blessed Jacob and Esau concerning things to come.'

Faith Bows

Faith bows to the will of God. It may not do so initially. I do not suggest that faith never struggles; it does. But, ultimately, faith bows to God's will. Isaac wanted the blessing of the birthright to go to Esau. He wanted God's bounty and goodness for Esau; but when the Lord God made it clear to him that Jacob would be blessed and Esau cursed, Isaac bowed to the will of God. By faith, that is to say, trusting God, Isaac blessed both his sons, Jacob and Esau.

God's Purpose Unalterable

This event shows us the wisdom, faithfulness, goodness, and sovereignty of God, overruling and using the frailties, infirmities, and even the sins of men to accomplish his purpose (Psalm 76:10). The fact is God's purpose is unalterable. It cannot be thwarted, hindered, or changed in any way. No matter how our circumstances may appear to oppose it, no matter how disobedient men and women are, no matter how cunningly Satan works, the purpose of God must and shall stand. 'The foundation of God standeth sure, having this seal, The Lord knoweth them that are his' (2 Timothy 2:19).

By faith Jacob, when he was a dying, blessed both the sons of Joseph; and worshipped, leaning upon the top of his staff. By faith Joseph, when he died, made mention of the departing of the children of Israel; and gave commandment concerning his bones.

Hebrews 11:21-22

Chapter 36

Read: Hebrews 11:21-22

Brother Jacob

Jacob was a believer, a man of true faith. He is held before us by the Spirit of God as an example of faith. He had great weaknesses, great faults, and great failures, as all believers do. Yet, Jacob was a man who believed God. He was a prince with God, a man chosen in eternal love, washed in the blood of Christ, robed in his perfect righteousness, born of the Spirit. Jacob was one of us.

Jacob's Life

Above all the other patriarchs, Jacob's life was marked with trials and temptations; and he therefore furnishes us with many illustrious testimonies of faith.

The life of faith is not like the shining of the sun on a calm and clear day, meeting with no resistance from the atmosphere. Rather it is like the sun rising on a foggy morning, its rays struggling to pierce through and dispel the opposing mists.

Jacob lived by faith, but in the exercise of faith he encountered many struggles. His was an uphill struggle from beginning to end. In spite of all his faults and failings, Jacob dearly prized his interest in the everlasting covenant. He trusted God and highly esteemed his promises. He believed and cherished his Redeemer.

We all are as full of error as Jacob. We are all like Jacob, if we are born of God, a people with two warring natures. But that which is most prominent about this man Jacob is this fact He believed God. He valued the birthright Esau despised. Jacob esteemed Christ and his salvation of greater value than anything else. He coveted the promises of God's free, covenant grace in Christ. He chose the Lord to be his God (Genesis 28:21). Though he was terrified at Esau, nevertheless, he sought the Lord, pleaded his promises, and obtained the answer of peace (Genesis 32:12). Though he cringed at the feet of his brother, he prevailed as a prince with God (Genesis 32:28). Like his fathers Abraham and Isaac, 'by faith he sojourned in the land of promise, as in a strange country, dwelling in tents' (Hebrews 11:9).

Jacob's Maturity

Like all believers, Jacob grew in grace. During the closing days of his life, His faith was brightest. When he gave permission for Benjamin to accompany his brothers on their second trip to Egypt, he said, 'God almighty (or God the Sufficient One) give you mercy before the man' (Genesis 43:14). He rested his soul on his God. It is delightful to see the conduct of this man, this believing sinner, when he was brought before Pharaoh, ruler of the greatest empire of the world. Instead of grovelling before him, we are told, 'Jacob blessed Pharaoh' (Genesis 47:7). He acted as a child of the King of kings (Hebrews 7:7). He carried himself with dignity as the ambassador of the Most High God.

Jacob's Deathbed

When he was dying, this old believer blessed his sons, leaving them a rich, rich heritage by faith. Jacob's benediction upon his sons was a great act of faith (Genesis 48:8-20). We can learn much from its circumstances.

Jacob exercised faith in his old age and in the immediate prospect of death (Genesis 47:29; 48:21). In spite of all his trials and conflicts, the weaknesses and discomfort of old age he was vigorous and firm in faith, believing God with his dying breath. His natural decay did not cause any abatement in his spiritual strength.

In his blessing upon Joseph and his sons Jacob solemnly recognized, pleaded, and asserted the covenant made with Abraham (Genesis 48:15). 'And he blessed Joseph, and said, God, before whom my fathers Abraham and Isaac did walk'. This is the very core and essence of faith. Faith lays hold of God's covenant, and draws strength from it (Romans 8:28; 1 Corinthians 3:21, 23; 2 Corinthians 4:15). Faith walks in the light of God's everlasting covenant of grace as the foundation of all blessedness

(Ephesians 1:3). It is the charter of our heavenly inheritance. It is the guarantee and security of our eternal glory.

A clear, firm view of Christ and the covenant of God's grace in him secures the hearts of dying saints and gives them a peaceful end, and a God-honouring exit from this world of suffering and sin (2 Samuel 23:1-5). Jacob declared that all temporal, as well as spiritual mercies were his by virtue of the covenant. 'The God which fed me all my life long unto this day' (Genesis 48:15). John Owen, wrote, 'It was a work of faith to retain a precious thankful remembrance of divine providence in a constant provision of all needful temporal supplies, from first to last, during the whole course of his life'.

Jacob never forgot God's mercy to him in redemption, calling Christ, 'The Angel which redeemed me from all evil' (Genesis 48:16). His faith was in Christ, the Son of God, the Angel of the Covenant (Genesis 32:24-30), who redeemed him. In his old age Jacob's hands were guided wittingly, understandingly, so that he blessed the sons of Joseph and pronounced their future according to the purpose of God (Genesis 48:14, 16-18). He desired the blessings of God's grace in Christ for his sons rather than the wealth of Egypt. Even in his dying hour, when the will of his most favoured relative crossed the will of God, the old man wisely taught Joseph to yet submit to the will of God (Genesis 48:18-19). Jacob understood, at this stage of life, that obedience to God was the great thing. He had heard from God (Romans 10:17). He believed God. And he submitted to God.

Comfort and Encouragement

Had I been given the task of choosing an example of faith to hold before us, by which to comfort and encourage God's saints in this world, I would never have chosen Jacob; but God did; and I am thankful. The fact that Jacob's faith is held before us by the Spirit of God as an example of faith in Christ is a very great source of comfort and encouragement to me.

Jacob was a man very much like me. He was a believer, but often very unbelieving. He was a righteous man, but often did things totally contrary to his true character. He was a man who loved God, but often appeared to love himself more than anything. Jacob was a faithful, faithful man, but often appeared unfaithful. He was a strong pillar of God's church, but often seemed to be fickle as the wind. He was a saint, robed in the righteousness of Christ, but often did what was horribly sinful.

Perhaps you are thinking, 'How do those facts comfort and encourage you?' Jacob is with Christ in glory! As he left this world, the Holy Spirit tells us he left here worshipping God.

Jacob is with Christ in glory because God chose him. He is seated with Christ in heaven because Christ redeemed him. He is with Christ because God the Holy Spirit called him. Jacob entered heavenly glory by grace alone. The Lord God kept him by his grace, giving him faith to the end, enabling that poor sinner to trust Christ until he drew his last breath and obtained that salvation which his brother Esau despised.

This is my prayer: O Lord my God, let me die like Jacob. Give me grace to die like this, looking to Christ. Nothing will give us peace in the hour of death like a clear, firm view of Christ, the Angel of the Covenant, and God's covenant grace in him. If we would leave a rich heritage for those who follow us, let us leave with them the gospel of God's free grace in Christ. When we come to death let us rejoice in God our Saviour and leave here worshipping God, leaning upon our Staff, Christ crucified.

Why do we mourn departing friends, or shake at death's alarms?
'Tis but the voice that Jesus sends, to call them to His arms.
Are not we tending upward too, as fast as time can move?
Nor should we wish our hours more slow, to keep us from our love.

The graves of all the saints He blest, and softened every bed;
Where should the dying members rest, but with their dying Head?
Thence He arose, ascending high, and showed our feet the way;
Up to the Lord our flesh shall fly, at the great rising day.

Let Me Die Like This!

There is no gift in all the world to be compared with God's gift of faith. Rich indeed is that immortal soul to whom God has graciously granted faith in Christ!

Oh, gift of gifts! Oh, grace of faith! My God, how can it be
That Thou, Who hast discerning love, should'st give that gift to me!

Ah, Grace! Into unlikeliest hearts it is thy boast to come,
The glory of thy light to find in darkest spots a home.

Thy choice, O God of goodness, then I lovingly adore;
O, give me grace to keep Thy grace, and grace to long for more!

Faith is a precious gift! We find it precious in life. In trials and temptations, in heartaches and sorrows, in troubles and tribulations, in the fiery furnace and in the raging sea, faith proves itself blessed. But never is faith so precious as it shall be when the cold sweat of death is on our brow and we are about to leave this world. Matthew Henry wrote,

> Though the grace of faith is of universal use throughout our whole lives, yet it is especially so when we come to die. Faith has its greatest work to do at last, to help believers to finish well, to die to the Lord, so as to honour him, by patience, hope, and joy so as to leave a witness behind them of the truth of God's Word and the excellency of his ways, for the conviction and establishment of all who attend them in their dying moments.

How greatly God is glorified when His people leave this world with their flag flying at full mast. His worthy name is marvellously honoured when the Spirit triumphs over the flesh, when world is consciously and gladly left behind for heaven.

Three Examples of Faith

In Hebrews 11:20-22 the Holy Spirit furnishes us with three examples of faith in the final crisis and conflict of life (Isaac, Jacob, and Joseph). God hereby assures his trembling and doubting children, that he who has begun a good work in us will perform it unto our last day. He who has sovereignly and graciously given us this precious grace of faith will not allow it to languish when its support is most needed. God, who enables us to exercise faith in the vigour of life, will not withdraw his quickening power and grace when we are about to leave this world (Isaiah 46:4).

I do not suggest that all true believers leave the world in triumphant jubilant confidence. I do not suggest that God's saints have no struggles in their dying hour. But I am saying what the scriptures clearly teach: God will sustain our souls in faith unto the end (Philippians 1:6).

Preparation for Death

Though we naturally shy away from thoughts about death and try to avoid talking about it, we must all prepare to meet God. As believers, we need instruction from the book of God in preparation for death and the comforts that can be ours in those last hours. Satan is ever seeking to strike terror in the hearts of God's children. I want you to know the groundlessness and hollowness of his lies.

A God-given and a God-sustained faith is not only sufficient to enable the feeblest saints to overcome the weakness of the flesh, the attractions of the world, and the temptations of Satan, but it is also able to give us a triumphant passage through death. I love that passage in Moses' song of triumph that speaks of God silencing our enemies and giving his people easy passage through death unto heavenly glory.

'Fear and dread shall fall upon them; by the greatness of thine arm they shall be as still as a stone; till thy people pass over, O Lord, till the people pass over, which thou hast purchased. Thou shalt bring them in, and plant them in the mountain of thine inheritance, in the place, O Lord, which thou hast made for thee to dwell in, in the Sanctuary, O Lord, which thy hands have established. The Lord shall reign for ever and ever.' (Exodus 15:16-18)

Precious Deaths

It is written, 'Precious in the sight of the Lord is the death of his saints.' Balaam said, 'Let me die the death of the righteous, and let my last end be like his!' (Numbers 23:10). Well might he wish to do so! The believer's last experience in this world shall be his best. 'The path of the just is as the shining light, that shineth more and more unto the perfect day' (Proverbs 4:18).

This body may convulse with pain, and physical unconsciousness set-in, yet my soul, once it is freed from this body of flesh, shall be blest with a sight and sense of my precious Redeemer such as I have never yet enjoyed! We see this verified in Acts 7, where we read about Stephen's very last experience in this world. 'He being full of the Holy Ghost, looked up steadfastly into heaven, and saw the glory of God, and Jesus standing on the right hand of God' (Acts 7:55).

'Mark the perfect man, and behold the upright; for the end of that man is peace' (Psalm 37:37). A peaceful death has concluded the troublesome life of many. C. H. Spurgeon wrote, 'With believers it may rain in the morning, thunder at midday, and pour torrents in the afternoon, but it must clear up ere the sun go down.'

Jacob's pilgrimage through this world was stormy; but the waters were smooth as he entered his desired haven. Much of his life was cloudy and dark; but it was radiant in the end. Blessed is that man or woman who dies like Jacob. Jacob died worshipping God. Let me die like that; worshipping God. Truly, faith's last act is its most blessed and delightful act, bringing us into heaven's glory land with Christ!

Joseph's Bones

At the early age of seventeen Joseph was carried away into a foreign, heathen country. There he remained for many years surrounded by idolaters. It is unlikely that during all that time he came into contact with another believer, not even one, who knew and worshipped God. He was a lone believer in a land of unbelievers, a land of idolatory.

Kept Faithful

In those days there was no Bible to read, for none of God's Word had been committed to writing. Yet, amid strong temptations and various trials, Joseph was steadfast in his faith. He was a faithful man, though he was utterly without the aid of another. His solitary aide was the one aide he needed: Jehovah was his strength. The grace of God was sufficient for him. Grace gave him faith in Christ and grace kept him faithful to Christ. Thirteen years of imprisonment did not make him bitter. Being made lord over Egypt did not ruin him. Evil examples all around did not corrupt him.

The Lord God, who has promised, 'My grace is sufficient for thee', has proved the sufficiency of his grace many times. Here he gives us one more example, by which he would encourage our faith.

Joseph's Early Training

We recognize that Joseph was the object of God's free grace. We know that salvation is God's work alone. Grace chose him. Grace redeemed him. Grace called him. Grace kept him.

Yet, we also recognize that the Lord God graciously and wisely uses specific means in the exercise of his grace. This, too, is obvious in the life of Joseph. In his earliest years Joseph was taught to worship God, instructed in the gospel of Christ, and encouraged to believe God. How this ought to encourage believing parents. May God give us grace and wisdom to faithfully instruct and train our children by word and by example, committing them to his hands, his grace, and his care. If he is pleased to call them and grant them life and faith in Christ, he will keep them even in our pagan, heathen society.

The Example Chosen

Why did the Holy Spirit choose this particular example of Joseph's faith to use as an encouragement to us? Had we been making the choice there are many things we might have selected as being far more significant.

The Holy Spirit is demonstrating great examples of faith. He is encouraging us to believe God and to be faithful to him in all things. Yet, he makes no mention here of Joseph's faithfulness in declaring the revelation of God, in benevolence, in the exercise of wisdom and prudence, or in enduring great adversity, slander, and unjust imprisonment. He makes no mention of Joseph's great compassion, overcoming evil with good, or his reverence and obedience to his father. Joseph was a remarkable man with a remarkable life. But his entire life is passed over, all his mighty deeds and his examples of devotion, and we are introduced to the final scene of his pilgrimage.

The Purpose

The purpose of Hebrews 11 is to encourage us to believe God, to remain faithful to the end, and to help us to overcome the fears with which God's saints are vexed in every age. The Lord here very graciously shows us that he who gave us faith will keep us in faith unto the end, and will carry us safely through every trial into heavenly glory. Nothing inspires faith and faithfulness like the assurance God gives us of his faithfulness (1 Corinthians 10:13; Philippians 1:6; 1 Thessalonians 5:18-24; 2 Timothy 2:19, Revelation 3:12).

The Time

Joseph's faith in Christ kept his soul in peace, composed, and expectant, 'when he died'. Nothing but the faith of Christ can enable rational, thinking men and women to enter with composure and delight into the unseen world of eternity.

It is the faith which is wrought in men and women by Christ, and that alone, which can enable dying sinners to rejoice in the dissolution of 'our earthly house of this tabernacle', and to sing in their souls, 'O death, where is thy sting? O grave, where is thy victory?'

Joseph's Faith

Because he believed God, Joseph refused to become or even be regarded as an Egyptian. His faith in Christ compelled him to identify himself with Christ, his people, and his worship.

Joseph was not asked merely to be an Egyptian, or even one of the nobles of the land. He was made the prime minister of the land, but refused even the place afforded him by Pharaoh. He was a loyal citizen in the land where God placed him. He served the land of Egypt better than any man in the history of that nation. But, because he was an Israelite indeed, a true believer, he would not be identified with the Egyptians. C. H. Spurgeon made the following, interesting observation.

> In Sakhara, hard by the pyramid of Pharaoh Apahis, stands at this day the tomb of a prince, whose name and titles are in hieroglyphic writing. The name is 'Eitsuph', and from among his

> many titles we choose two 'Director of the king's granaries', and the other an Egyptian title, 'Abrech'. Now this last word is found in the scriptures, and is that which is translated, 'Bow the knee'. It is more than probable that this monument was prepared for Joseph, but he declined the honour. Though his resting-place would have been side by side with the pyramid of one of Mizraim's greatest monarchs, yet he would not accept the dignity, he would not be an Egyptian.

Following Christ

If we would follow Christ, we must always refuse to align ourselves with this world. We must choose rather to identify ourselves with the people of God and the worship of God (1 John 2:15-17; 2 Corinthians 6:14-7:1).

Faith in Christ is seen by love for God's people (1 John 3:14). Joseph demonstrated, both in his actions and in the most public manner possible, his love for his brethren. At the very time of his death Joseph's heart was engaged with the future happiness of Israel (Psalm 137:5-6). This same unselfish faith and love was later demonstrated by Eli's daughter-in-law as she was leaving this world (1 Samuel 4:22). It is that same love which was perfectly and infinitely demonstrated by our Saviour (John 13:1).

Believing God

As Joseph believed God, though everything seemed to contradict his Word, let us believe God, though everything seems to contradict his Word (Isaiah 59:19; Matthew 16:18). Faith in Christ caused him to see the unseen, and to look to the spiritual blessings of grace pictured in the carnal things that represented them. Faith gave him an eye to the spirituality of the covenant. His hope was not in the earthly Canaan, but in the spiritual.

'And Joseph said unto his brethren, I die: and God will surely visit you, and bring you out of this land unto the land which he sware to Abraham, to Isaac, and to Jacob. And Joseph took an oath of the children of Israel, saying, God will surely visit you, and ye shall carry up my bones from hence. So Joseph died, being an hundred and ten years old: and they embalmed him, and he was put in a coffin in Egypt' (Genesis 50:24-26).

Joseph believed that God would graciously visit his people in deliverance, bringing them out of bondage. That salvation which Moses would accomplish was typical and prophetic of our salvation by Christ. He believed not only that God would bring them out of Egypt; but that he would bring his chosen, redeemed people into Canaan, which portrayed the believer's heavenly inheritance of grace in Christ, in resurrection glory.

Assurance

Joseph so thoroughly believed God that he was assured that he would, himself, enter into the land of promise. He made his brothers swear that they would not bury him in Egypt, but embalm him and carry him into Canaan. Embalming, though an Egyptian custom, was adopted by Joseph, by an act of faith, to be an emblem of the hope of the resurrection. Joseph's bones were buried in Canaan with Joshua's, after the Lord God fulfilled every promise he had made to Abraham and the nation of Israel concerning that land (Joshua 24:29-32).

Submission

Faith in Christ involves the resignation of my life to his dominion, the resignation of my will to his will (Luke 14:26-33). Joseph's faith in Christ made him submissive to the will, purpose, and glory of God. Because he believed God, Joseph was willing to await God's time for the promised blessing. He waited for God to exalt him. He bowed to God's providence. He waited for God to deliver Israel.

His bones were not buried until Joshua had conquered and divided the land. But Joseph believed that God would do as he had promised. And he waited for his God in patient faith unto the end. May God the Holy Spirit give us such confident, submissive faith.

Joseph's Last Days

The reference to which our text points is Genesis 50:22-26. Joseph believed God amidst severe and persistent trials. Because this text passes over the other events in Joseph's extraordinary life, I will too. Joseph's life was remarkable. His trials were remarkable. His faith was remarkable. Like the Lord Jesus Christ, of whom he was an eminent type, Joseph shows us by example how that we ought ever to bow to the will of God, believing him (Genesis 50:18-21). But the Holy Spirit here points us to Joseph's display of faith and faithfulness in his last days when he was at the very height of his glory in Egypt. Here was a man who believed God in circumstances that cause most men to forget him.

Faith and Prosperity

Joseph was a man tempted by the possession of great prosperity. The Lord God does call some men to high positions. Some of his servants are found in Caesar's court, some in Uzziah's, some in Pilate's, and some in Pharaoh's. That in itself is a great trial of faith. Joseph was the highest ranking official in a land of idolaters, serving a mighty king who was a base idolater. He was wealthy beyond imagination. Riches, of themselves, do not injure a person. Whether we are rich or poor, we simply must not set our hearts upon material things. That is the danger (Philippians 4:12; Psalm 62:10; Proverbs 30:7-9; Matthew 6:31-34; Colossians 3:1-3).

Faith and Death

When he knew he was dying, Joseph believed God. Death is a great tester of man's sincerity. It shakes down bowing walls and tottering fences. The brightest instance of faith in this grand old man was at his death. In his death he remembered God's covenant. His heart was totally baptized with the thoughts of heaven. He did not dwell upon the past, but hoped for the future (Hebrews 11:1). He rested his soul upon his God, believing his Word, trusting his promise.

Faith and Reason

Joseph believed God, though that which God had promised was totally contrary to reason, to the things which he saw, and to all outward appearance. Israel was in Goshen. Why should they leave? But God had promised that after 400 years, he would bring them out of that land; and Joseph believing God, 'made mention of the departing of the children of Israel' (Genesis 50:24). He knew that his brethren would be slaves to the Egyptians. How could they escape? Faith does not reason, but believes.

By faith Moses, when he was born, was hid three months of his parents, because they saw he was a proper child; and they were not afraid of the king's commandment.

Hebrews 11:23

Chapter 37

Read: Hebrews 11:23

Hidden In The Ark

There are three arks mentioned in the Word of God. Each was a place of refuge, shelter, and safety. Each is typical of the Lord Jesus Christ, and God's salvation in and by him.

Noah's Ark

The ark that Noah built secured those who were in it from the vengeance and violent wrath of an angry God. That is Christ our Substitute. All the terror of God's wrath fell on Noah and his family in the ark; but no wrath touched them. The ark absorbed all. So, too, all the fury of God's wrath fell on his elect in Christ; but no wrath can ever touch us. Christ absorbed it all. Noah and his family were saved when all the world was drowned in the wrath of God. In Christ all God's elect shall be eternally saved when all the world is destroyed forever.

The Ark of The Covenant

This ark sheltered the two tables of God's holy law, and, being covered with blood, was the place of atonement, mercy, and acceptance with God for sinners. Where the ark went God went. That ark is Christ our Mercy-Seat. In him we have perfect righteousness and complete atonement. He kept the law for us as our Substitute, in his life of obedience to God, and satisfied its justice by his death in our place at Calvary. If we are in the Ark, Christ Jesus, God is reconciled to us and we to him. The holy Lord God bids needy sinners to come to him at the Mercy-Seat, Christ Jesus. He promises to meet with mercy all who come to him there.

Moses' Ark

Moses' parents hid him for three months in an ark (a basket) made of bulrushes. That ark protected one of God's chosen ones, Moses, from the murderous designs of a wicked ruler, Pharaoh. That ark, too, was a picture of Christ, into whom from eternity chosen sinners were placed by our loving, heavenly Father. As that ark of bulrushes was the means by which Moses was saved from drowning in the Egyptians' river, God's elect are saved from drowning in that infernal lake of his wrath, which burns forever with fire and brimstone (Revelation 19:20; 20:10).

From the beginning there has been but one place of refuge for sinners, only one way of salvation. That refuge, that way, that salvation is Christ! If we would be saved, we must be robed in Christ's righteousness and washed in his blood. We must be in Christ by faith. Only Christ can bear our souls above the flood of God's wrath. Only the Lord Jesus Christ can save us.

When Change Comes

A considerable length of time elapsed between the death of Joseph and the birth of Moses. That interval is bridged by what is recorded in Exodus 1. There we see a marked change in the lot of the Hebrews. In the days of Joseph the Egyptians had been very kind to the descendants of Abraham, giving them the land of Goshen to dwell in.

Another Pharaoh

But there arose another Pharaoh in Egypt who did not know Joseph. The policy of this new monarch was one of tyranny (Exodus 1:9-10). But his policy of tyranny and persecution could not alter the purpose of God. 'There are many devices in a man's heart, nevertheless, the counsel of the Lord shall stand' (Proverbs 19:21). We read in Exodus 1:12 that 'the more they afflicted them, the more they multiplied and grew'. Indeed, 'The Lord bringeth the counsel of the heathen to nought: He maketh the devices of the people of none effect. The counsel of the Lord standeth forever, the thoughts of this heart to all generations' (Psalm 33:10-11).

Moses' Birth

Moses' birth came in the very height and fury of persecution. After Pharaoh failed in his design to destroy the male children of Israel by the midwives who served them, he ordered the execution of all the male Hebrew babies. His soldiers, complicit in the barbarism, dutifully carried out their orders. Their object was the utter annihilation of God's people. It was but one more attempt by Satan to destroy the woman's Seed and topple the throne of God. But it was as vain as it was inhumane.

When the rage of the Egyptian was most fierce, in the wise disposal of divine providence, Moses was born and miraculously preserved. Indeed, the Lord God overturned Pharaoh's wicked designs and made him to be the very one by whom the deliverer of his people would be preserved and brought to power! Never were the words of Psalm 76:10 more powerfully illustrated in the Old Testament. 'Surely the wrath of man shall praise thee: the remainder of wrath shalt thou restrain'. John Owen wrote:

> How blind are poor sinful mortals, in all their contrivances against the church of God! When they think all things secure, that they shall not fail of their end; that their counsels are laid so deep as not to be blown up; their power so uncontrollable, and the way wherein they are engaged so effectual, as that God himself can hardly deliver it out of their hands; He that sits on high laughs them to scorn, and with an almighty facility lays in provision for the deliverance of his church, and their utter ruin.

The Faith of Moses' Parents

Faith is a gift of God's grace that enables the believer to look away from human terrors, and gives courage and boldness by enabling us to trust God our Father, though we see him not.

In other words, faith prevails over fear. I do not mean that believers know nothing of fear. It is a sad fact, but a fact nonetheless, that we are all, at times, fearful. But faith prevails over fear and says with David, 'What time I am afraid, I will trust in thee. In God I will praise his word, in God I have put my trust; I will not fear what flesh can do unto me' (Psalm 56:3-4). Here in Hebrews 11:23, the Holy Spirit holds before us the faith of Moses' parents as an instructive, encouraging example for us to follow.

Moses Hid

'By faith Moses, when he was born, was hid three months of his parents'. The Apostle mentions the faith of both of Moses' parents. Moses, in his account mentioned only his mother; Stephen, speaking to the Sanhedrin mentioned only his father (Exodus 2:3; Acts 7:20). In this verse Paul combines two inspired narratives.

Happy is that home in which husband and wife, mother and father walk together in faith, in the fear of God. Blessed, blessed beyond what words can express, are those children born into such a home! 'It is a happy thing,' wrote Matthew Henry, 'when yoke-fellows draw together in the yoke of faith, as heirs of the grace of God; and when they do this in a religious concern for the good of their children, to preserve them not only from those who would destroy their lives, but corrupt their minds.' Moses' parents show us three things about faith.

1. Faith Fears God

Pharaoh had given orders that every male child born among the Jews be thrown immediately into the Nile. Instead of complying with this atrocious command, Moses' mother and father concealed their infant son for three months. Without question, we are to be in subjection to the higher powers. We are to be obedient to our divinely appointed civil rulers, no matter who they are (Romans 13:1-7). But we have a higher authority than any earthly monarch. Our God is our King. 'We ought to obey God rather than men' (Acts 5:29). As those noble brethren in Daniel 3, we cannot do that which God has forbidden, no matter who demands it. And, like Peter and John in Acts 4, we must obey God's will, no matter who opposes it.

2. Faith Removes the Fear of Man

The fear of God dispels the fear of man. 'The Lord is my light and my salvation; whom shall I fear? The Lord is the strength of my life; of whom shall I be afraid?' (Psalm 27:1).

3. Faith Obtains God's Salvation.

Deliverance came to Israel because Moses' parents, believing God, hazarded their lives to do what they knew to be his will. Fearing God, they obeyed his Word, though obedience might cost them their lives.

'Three Months'

'Moses was hid three months'. Faith proves itself by works. Moses' parents, like Abraham before them and Rahab after them, showed their faith by their works. They concealed the birth of their son, not fearing the wrath of the king. From the beginning they showed greater concern for Moses' soul than for their own lives. They hid him for three months. Theirs was a persevering faith. No doubt they made many cries unto God. Can you imagine the faith it required to put that baby in a basket and leave him alone to God's care in the Nile River?

Such faith is both well founded and most reasonable. God preserves his own. Nothing can harm them, much less destroy them! In the preservation of Moses we have an illustration of how God preserves his elect from infancy to the day of their calling (Jude 1).

'A Proper Child'

Their faith was not so much a parental act of love as it was the act of two people who believed God. That which motivated the faith of these godly parents was that which the Lord God had made known to them. 'They saw he was a proper child'. The Holy Spirit is not talking about Moses' being a physically beautiful child, too good looking to murder! This was an act of faith. They saw that Moses' was beautiful to God, chosen of God to be Israel's deliverer (Acts 7:20). It is obvious from the book of Exodus that they taught him this from his youth. Had this not been a matter of divine revelation, something specifically made known to them by God, it would not have been an act of faith, but of desperation. They believed God's word, the promise he had given to Abraham and Joseph, and had confirmed to them.

'By Faith'

We know this because the Holy Spirit tells us specifically that the hiding of Moses was 'by faith'. It was an act of faith, God given, God wrought, God sustained faith. The principle of their actions in the preservation of Moses was faith. Paul's purpose in this chapter was not to honour men, but to honour faith. Particularly, their faith was in Christ, the Deliverer of his people, of whom Moses was both a type and one by whom the Seed of the woman must be preserved. They had a particular revelation from God. They had a firm faith in the deliverance of the children of Israel in the appointed season. And they had faith in him whom Abraham believed. They trusted Christ.

'Not Afraid'

'And they were not afraid of the king's commandment.' Their faith was eminent in this: In the discharge of their duty they did not fear the kings command. No doubt they had fear, but not such as would prevent the performance of their duty; 'What time I am afraid, I will trust in thee'.

Because they believed God, Moses' parents secured for themselves and for the nation of Israel the promised blessing of God's salvation. Israel was delivered by the faith of a godly mother and father. Let us train our children for God, heaven, and eternity. Train them, first and foremost, by believing God ourselves, by making the will and glory of God the rule of all things in our lives.

By faith Moses, when he was come to years, refused to be called the son of Pharaoh's daughter; Choosing rather to suffer affliction with the people of God, than to enjoy the pleasures of sin for a season; Esteeming the reproach of Christ greater riches than the treasures in Egypt: for he had respect unto the recompense of the reward. By faith he forsook Egypt, not fearing the wrath of the king: for he endured, as seeing him who is invisible.

Hebrews 11:24-27

Chapter 38

Read: Hebrews 11:24-27

Moses' Faith

Perhaps, above all other Old Testament believers, Moses is the example of faith best suited to us. Those men of God who are mentioned in the first part of this chapter are all examples to be followed. But we cannot literally do what most of them did. We follow them in spirit, but not in deed. God has not called us to offer up a literal sacrifice, like Abel. God has not called us to build a literal ark, like Noah. God has not called us to literally leave our homeland and families, to dwell in tents, or to offer up our Isaac, like Abraham. But the faith of Moses exactly tallies with the experience of all God's saints. Moses' faith made him walk in the same path, make the same sacrifices, and endure the same trials as true faith requires of us today. As it was with Moses, so it is with all believers. True faith in the heart manifests itself by certain characteristics of life.

Moses' Sacrifices

Moses gave up some things he would have preferred not to give up. Here we are told that Moses gave up three things for the sake of his soul. He could not have followed Christ; he could not have been saved, had he kept them, so he gave them up. He sat down, counted the cost of following Christ, and willingly paid the price of doing so. Moses made three of the greatest sacrifices a man could ever make.

First, Moses gave up rank, position, and greatness. 'When he was come to years, [he] refused to be called the son of Pharaoh's daughter'. We are told, by tradition, that Pharaoh had but one daughter, his only child; and that Moses was her only child. She had adopted him as her son. He was next in line for the throne of Egypt, the greatest nation in the world. He could have been a great man, the most powerful, influential man in the world. But Moses refused it. This was a very great sacrifice. He refused the throne of Egypt. He forsook his family, a mother whom he loved. He made this decision when he was a man of forty years of age.

Second, Moses gave up earthly ease and pleasure. The pleasures he gave up would have been for other men matters of indifference, involving no sin in themselves. They were simply the pleasures of wealth, security, comfort, luxury, and ease of life. But for Moses, they would have been 'the pleasures of sin', because they were contrary to the will of God. This, too, was a great sacrifice. Moses gave up that which all men and women of all ages and social conditions most naturally seek. Pleasure!

Third, Moses gave up great riches. 'The treasures of Egypt' would have been his. This, I dare say, was his greatest sacrifice. Most men are far more willing to give up both position and pleasure than give up prosperity. Yet, Moses did not give away only a portion of his wealth; he gave up all his wealth. Consider how great these sacrifices were. He gave up all of these things: position, pleasure, and prosperity, all at one time. He gave them up deliberately, as a wise, well-educated, mature man, a full forty years old (Acts 7:22). His was not a hasty, rash decision, made in an emotional moment, but a deliberate, wilful, calculated choice.

He was in no way obliged to give these things up. Pharaoh did not disown him. The children of Israel did not beg him to become their leader. He was not a dying man who was about to leave the world, and therefore willing to give it up. He was not a beggar who had no rightful claim to or hope for these things. He was not an old man who could no longer enjoy these things. Moses willingly made these sacrifices for the honour of God and the good of his people, expecting nothing in return.

Moses' Choices

Moses chose some things he would have preferred not to choose. His choices were as great as his sacrifices. He chose to walk in a path that was completely contrary to the flesh, contrary to worldly wisdom, and contrary to personal desire. The Holy Spirit tells us that Moses chose three things. They were hard, costly choices. But they were necessary to the salvation of his soul. The things Moses chose did not in any way earn, or cause his salvation. But had he not done these things, he could not have been saved (James 2:17; Matthew 6:14-15). Obedience to Christ is necessary.

First, Moses chose a path of affliction. He chose conflict instead of comfort; adversity instead of prosperity; sorrow instead of satisfaction; pain instead of peace; suffering instead of solace.

Second, he chose the company of God's despised people. He left his family and friends and became one with the people of God. Their troubles became his troubles. Their sorrows his sorrows. Moses not only preferred God's people to the people of this world, he preferred them to himself.

Third, Moses chose a path of reproach and scorn. He was mocked, belittled, ridiculed, and laughed at. He was the joke of Egypt. He saw reproach and scorn before him, and deliberately chose them. For most, little is as difficult to face as scorn and ridicule.

Never was there a man, but the God-man, who made such sacrifices and choices as Moses. He gave up a king's throne and chose slave's rags. He gave up a palace for a place among God's people. He gave up riches for poverty, respectability for reproach. Why would a man do this?

Moses: A Man who Believed God

What is the principle that compelled Moses to act as he did? The Holy Spirit tells us 'By faith Moses'. Moses believed God. Faith motivated him, directed and controlled him. Moses acted because he believed.

Moses believed on the Lord Jesus Christ. He believed God's promise that he would send a deliverer, a Redeemer, a Saviour, a King of the seed of Abraham in whom all the nations of the earth would be blessed. He believed God would fulfil his covenant. He would deliver his people. He would never forsake his own.

Believing God, Moses knew that with God nothing is impossible. The deliverance of Israel and the overthrow of Pharaoh seemed impossible. But Moses believed God! Moses trusted the wisdom and goodness of God's providence. He trusted God's faithfulness (Lamentations 3:21-26). He trusted God to be faithful to his purpose, his promise, and his people.

Faith in Christ caused Moses to see things that had not yet come to pass. Faith caused him to see temporal things as temporal and eternal things as eternal (2 Corinthians 4:18). As a man of faith, he interpreted divine providence by faith. The Lord showed Moses what he would have him do; and faith gave him strength to do it.

Marvellous as Moses' sacrifices and choices seem to be, they are really not very marvellous at all. He believed God and acted accordingly. His God given faith in Christ made Moses such a meek man that he feared neither Pharaoh's wrath nor Egypt's armies; nor the depths and breadth of the Red Sea[1]. Faith made him so utterly humble before God that he dared not cower before anything or anyone else!

---

[1] Located north of the Gulf of Suez and adjacent to the Land of Goshen where Israel was settled (Genesis 45:10; Exodus 8:22; 9:26).

Lessons from Moses' Faith

What lessons are we to learn from this man who believed God? We have seen what Moses did. He denied himself, took up his cross, and followed Christ. We have seen why he did it. He believed God. What does this show us? What does the Lord intend us to learn from Moses' example?

First, if I would be an heir of eternal life, I must deny myself, take up my cross, and follow Christ. This is clearly the doctrine of Christ (Luke 14:25-33). There is no such thing as salvation separated from discipleship. There is no such thing as faith without consecration. Where there is no cross, there is no crown. Where there is no sowing, there is no reaping. Where there is no battle, there is no victory. Where there is no struggle, there is no triumph. Faith in Christ requires a denial of self. Faith in Christ willingly, deliberately takes up the cross, the way of offence for the glory of Christ. Faith in Christ follows Christ. Nothing will cause a man in his heart to truly deny himself and forsake this world, except faith in Christ. If I believe Christ I can and will follow him, regardless of cost or consequence.

Second, if I live for myself and refuse to forsake this world, I cannot have faith, I cannot have Christ, I cannot have eternal life (Mark 8:34-38). The issue between God and man, since the fall of our father Adam, has always been God's right to be God, God's right to exercise dominion everywhere and rule all things as he will. Faith voluntarily surrenders to Christ's dominion as Lord and King. Faith bows to God's throne. This is the very first act of faith. Wherever Christ comes in saving grace he comes with a royal crown upon his head. If I prefer my will to God's will and seek my way rather than my Lord's way; if I prefer the world to Christ, and place the things of time before the things of eternity; if I live for the comfort of my body, rather than for the welfare of my soul; then in my heart I prefer myself to Christ, I do not know Christ and I have no faith. No man can serve two masters. You will either serve self, or serve Christ. You will either deny self, or deny Christ. You will either live for the world, or live for Christ. Choose you this day whom you will serve.

Third, if I believe Christ, follow Christ, and seek the will of and glory of Christ, my God will take care of all my earthly and eternal interests (Matthew 6:33; 10:28-33). The righteous shall never be forsaken. His seed will never go begging for bread. God provides for his own. His children ought never give the slightest concern to such matters. Our only concern ought to be the will and glory of our God and the good of his people.

Moses: Three Views

Moses was pre-eminently a type of our Lord Jesus Christ. In fact, he seems to have known that he was specifically raised up by God as a type of his coming Saviour. This is not commonly the case. I do not know of another example. Adam, Enoch, Noah, Abraham, Joshua, Boaz, David, Solomon, Hosea, and Jeremiah were all typical of the Lord Jesus; but there is no indication that they knew it. Moses, on the other hand, seems to have known his typical significance (Deuteronomy 18:15-18).

Moses as a Type of Christ

Not only was he typical of Christ as our great Prophet, by whom God makes himself known to, teaches, and directs his people in this world, Moses was typical of our great Saviour in many ways. He was the meekest man in the earth. Yet, never was there a man more courageous and bold. For the sake of his people and the glory of his God, Moses hazarded everything. He delivered Israel from Pharaoh and from Egypt at the time appointed by God. Moses was a mediator between God and his people as Christ is ours. He was, while he walked on the earth, the only man by whom God spoke to men. He led the chosen nation through the wilderness to Canaan as Christ leads us through the wilderness of this world.

Moses as a Type of The Law

Yet, he could not bring Israel into Canaan, the land of promised rest and inheritance (typical of heaven), because he also represented the law. As a type of the law and justice of God, there are three specific things to be seen in Moses' actions and in his death. He smote the rock out of which flowed the water of life in the wilderness of death; 'and that Rock was Christ'. He smote the rock a second time and died because of it. The law, having once smitten Christ, is dead! He could not enter into the land of Canaan with Israel, because salvation cannot come by law (Romans 8:4).

Moses as a Man of Great Faith

Still, this man, Moses, was a man of great faith. As such he is held before us as an example to follow in Hebrews 11:24-27. In verse 23, we read of the faith of Moses' parents in hiding him. In these four verses the Holy Spirit describes Moses' own faith in Christ.

It was seeing the invisible God, seeing him by the revelation of the glory of God in the face of Christ, that gave Moses' faith and sustained him in faith. And it is only as we see him by divine revelation that we can have faith and walk in faith (2 Corinthians 4:6).

'Seeing Him Who Is Invisible'

Here are seven specific things the Holy Spirit tells us about Moses and his faith, by which he instructs us in this matter of faith. 'By faith

Moses, when he was come to years, refused to be called the son of Pharaoh's daughter'. He chose 'rather to suffer affliction with the people of God, than to enjoy the pleasures of sin for a season'. Moses held 'the reproach of Christ greater riches than the treasures in Egypt'. He did so because 'he had respect unto the recompense of the reward'. 'By faith he forsook Egypt'. He forsook it, 'not fearing the wrath of the king'. He did not fear Pharaoh's wrath 'for he endured, as seeing him who is invisible'.

First, because he believed God, Moses refused to be called the son of Pharaoh's daughter (v. 24). When he openly took the part of the Israelite against the Egyptian, Moses publicly identified himself with the people of God. The Holy Spirit tells us that when Moses' slew the Egyptian, he did so as an act of faith. He preferred Israel to Egypt. He preferred being an Israelite to being the most prestigious, powerful man in the world. He preferred the care of God's church and people to his own honour and well-being. This is what God's elect do in believer's baptism. We publicly identify ourselves with Christ, his gospel, and his people.

Second, believing God, Moses' chose the afflictions of God's people (v. 25). It is true, he was chosen of God to be one of his own; but Moses' chose to be numbered among God's people. At first glance, this might not seem to be a very difficult choice for anyone to make. After all these were the chosen, redeemed, peculiar people of God. These were the people to whom alone God gave his Word and ordinances of divine worship. God himself was with them. Canaan was promised to them.

But Moses counted the cost and chose rather to suffer the afflictions of God's elect than to enjoy the pleasures that were his in Egypt. He knew that the afflictions they endured were hard afflictions indeed; but he also knew that they were afflictions endured as the people of God. They were divinely appointed chastisements of their heavenly Father. They were ordained of God for the spiritual, eternal benefit of his people and the glory of Christ's own great name (1 Peter 1:3-9).

Third, because he believed God, Moses esteemed the reproach of Christ to be far greater riches than the treasures of Egypt (v. 26). He considered it his greatest wealth and honour to be allowed to personally bear the reproach of Christ: reproach for his word: reproach for his worship; reproach for being numbered as one of his people (1 Peter 2:19-24).

Fourth, believing God, Moses had respect unto the promises of God (v. 26). That is, he believed, looked for, and anticipated the fulfilment of all the Lord God had promised: the deliverance of Israel from bondage in Egypt, the blessings of Canaan, and eternal glory. These promises are ours too: freedom from the bondage of sin and death, the blessings of heaven, and the glory of Christ our redeemer (2 Timothy 1:7-12).

Fifth, 'by faith he forsook Egypt, not fearing the wrath of the king' (v. 27). Though this may have reference to Moses leading Israel out of Egypt and across the Red Sea, I do not think that is the primary thing referred to here. Rather, this sentence speaks of Moses' flying away to Midian. The deliverance of Israel as a nation is described in verse 29.

After he had slain the Egyptian and taken up the cause of Israel, Moses made no effort to appease Pharaoh's wrath. His fleeing was not an act of cowardice, but of obedience to the will of God. There he must wait for God to send him for the work to which he was ordained. He must be trained in the prophecy school of hardship, isolation, and trouble in the Midian desert.

Pharaoh was a roaring lion, but Moses did not fear him. Those who are called by the grace of God out of a state of darkness and bondage, and out of a strange land forsake this world and everything that is near and dear when it is in competition with Christ; not fearing the wrath of any temporal king or prince; nor of Satan, the prince of this world.

Sixth, because Moses believed God, 'he endured'! That is what faith does. Faith endures to the end. It endures the trials of providence. It endures the afflictions of the gospel. It endures the rod of chastisement. It endures the relentless warfare in the soul between the flesh and the spirit. Faith never quits!

Seventh, the cause of Moses' great faith, the thing that sustained him to the end, was simply this: Moses had seen him who is invisible; and lived (v. 27). This was not a one time sight, but an ever-increasing sight, a sight which guided, sustained and refreshed this man Moses unto the end. He saw the Lord God in Christ. He saw him in the Word he was taught; in the burning bush, in the paschal lamb and sprinkled blood; in salvation experienced at the Red Sea; in the tree at Marah, in the manna, in the rock, and in the cleft of the rock (Exodus 33:13-19).

This sight of the invisible God was a spiritual sight. It was 'by faith' that Moses saw the Lord. It was a glorious and a humbling sight, a transforming and a separating sight, and an inspiring and a sustaining sight. It was a costly, but a satisfying sight. Oh, may God give us grace ever to see him!

Through faith he kept the passover, and the sprinkling of blood, lest he that destroyed the firstborn should touch them. By faith they passed through the Red sea as by dry land: which the Egyptians assaying to do were drowned.

Hebrews 11:28-29

Chapter 39

Read: Hebrews 11:28-29

Blessed Salvation

The event here stated in two verses is described fully in Exodus chapter 14. That which Israel experienced in deliverance from Egyptian bondage and the crossing of the Red Sea was a picture of our salvation by Christ. When the children of Israel were hemmed in on every side, when they were brought into a position of utter helplessness, hopelessness, and despair, they murmured in unbelief against God and against his servant Moses.

Moses was undeterred by the murmuring of the people. He did not respond to their gripes. Instead, he turned their minds away from their outward danger and directed their hearts to their God. They had 'lifted up their eyes and beheld the Egyptians' (v. 10), and were sore afraid. They should have been looking to Christ, to the throne of God and the promise of God. If they had been steadfastly occupied with God's salvation, they would never have known fear.

Instead of responding to Israel's accusations, Moses continued doing what God had sent him to do; he proclaimed God's salvation. 'Moses said unto the people, Fear ye not, stand still, and see the salvation of the Lord, which He will show you today: for the Egyptians whom ye have seen today, ye shall see them again no more forever' (Exodus 14:13).

God's Work

Salvation is altogether God's work. It is not something we do. It is something done for us by our God which we see, receive, and experience when the Lord God graciously forces us to stop doing, stand still, and look to Christ.

Yes, the children of Israel fled across the Red Sea from the armies of Pharaoh, but how? The Lord God brought them to the place that they had to look to him. There was no human strength to which they could turn. Pharaoh and the armies of Egypt terrified them. They were as helpless as they were afraid.

Is that not the experience of every chosen sinner? Legal fear and terror of itself never saved anyone. The fear of eternal damnation and a sense of utter helplessness and despair is not necessarily Holy Spirit conviction (John 16:8-11). But I never knew anyone to fall into the arms of mercy who was not driven there by the terror of the law. I never knew anyone to flee away to Christ who was not driven to him by Moses. When Israel stood trembling, as it were upon the very brink of hell, Moses commanded them to 'stand still, and see the salvation of the Lord'.

Our Trials

That which is true of our salvation, our deliverance from the terror of the law and the guilt of sin is also our experience in times of great trial. Believers are sometimes called upon to face great trials. A Red Sea of difficulty and trouble confronts us. It was not Pharaoh who put the sea in Israel's way, but God. It is the Lord our God, our heavenly Father, who tries the faith of his children. He uses Satan to do it; but the trial is his work. The deliverance is his as well!

How often a new born believer emerges from Egypt, thinking that now it will be easy to surrender everything to God, but after a while there is a Red Sea of testing before him, which seems impossible to cross. We are often terrified by powerful enemies. How often the Egyptians (our sins) come upon us and we discover another law warring in our members, bringing us into captivity of the law of sin and death. Our sins are more bitter than ever. In Egypt Israel's task masters only had whips. Now they are mounted on chariots! Satan hurls all the power of hell at us.

We are often troubled with fainting hearts, too. A faint, unbelieving heart is the worst foe a believer has in this world. While faith is anchored upon Christ, the Rock of our salvation, all is well. But when the eye of faith is dim and we look at the storms without and our weakness within, we are tossed upon the sea.

Divine Revelation

Faith comes by and acts upon the Word of God (Romans 10:17). Moses had a revelation from God, which he communicated to the people. It was a revelation to the heart, of what God would do (Romans 8:26). If he had not had the revelation of God's salvation, he would have drowned as he presumed to cross the sea.

Faith acted upon God's revelation. By faith Moses stretched out his rod and stepped into the sea. The Red Sea was parted by the rod of Moses. Similarly, the way of salvation, our way of access to God, was opened for us by the law of God, by the satisfaction of justice by the blood of Christ (Hebrews 10:19-22). As the waters parted before them the hosts of Israel walked through the sea with confident, full assurance; and their enemies were 'as still as a stone' (Exodus 14:22; 15:16).

Believer's Baptism

The scriptures (1 Corinthians 10:1-2) tell us plainly that the passage of Israel through the Red Sea was a baptism unto Moses. It signified the same thing as believer's baptism does today. It exposed the distinction God put between Israel and Egypt, as does believer's baptism. It was an act of obedience to God's command, as is believer's baptism. Both Israel's baptism unto Moses and the believer's baptism with reference to the finished work of Christ are acts of obedience performed to the command of God (Exodus 14:13-16, Matthew 28:19, Mark 16:16). As Israel followed Moses through the Red Sea, so believers follow Christ through the waters of baptism, symbolically declaring salvation to be the work of God alone by Christ's fulfilling all righteousness as our Representative and Substitute.

Lessons from The Red Sea

Hebrews 11 shows us, by numerous examples, what true, saving faith is. By contrast, it also shows us what faith is not. In this chapter, we see faith doing things that are impossible with men, doing that which only God almighty, with whom nothing is impossible, can do. You see, the power of faith, the strength of faith, lies not in us but in the Lord Jesus Christ, who is the Object of all true faith. So when men and women do things believing God, it is not them, but Christ who is doing the work; doing it through them, yes, but he is the One doing the work. This blessed gift of faith, the work and operation of God in his people, performs great works indeed. Faith in Christ enables weak, helpless sinners, sinners who believe God, to perform supernatural acts, overcome impossible difficulties, and endure trials that are impossible for flesh and blood to endure.

We are told that Israel passed through the Red Sea as by dry land, because they believed God. The Egyptians, attempting to do the same thing in the strength and energy of the flesh, were destroyed. It was faith that enabled Israel to enter a miraculously formed valley between two mountainous walls of water, crossing over safely to the other side of the Red Sea. In much the same way, true, saving faith, faith in Christ, is that which enables believers to pass through and overcome trials and troubles that utterly destroy others. As it was faith in Christ that enabled those men of old ultimately to enter into and take possession of Canaan, so it is faith in Christ that will soon land us safe on Canaan's happy shore and enable us to take possession of heaven's eternal bliss.

There is no greater example of the contrast between faith and presumption in the whole book of God than that which is before us in Hebrews 11:29. Here we see the ultimate end and result of the long controversy between the Egyptians and the Israelites. This is clearly a type and picture of what will be the last end of the conflict between the world and the church. It has been a long and bitter conflict. It began with Cain and Abel and continues to this day. But it shall soon end in the sudden appearance of Christ for the complete salvation of his church and the utter destruction of his enemies. The example of faith before us in Hebrews 11:29 is truly remarkable. It was night when the children of Israel undertook their flight out of Egypt. Through the darkness they fled, moved by faith. Through the darkness Pharaoh and the huge Egyptian army presumptuously and blindly pursued them, moved by envy, hatred and lust. At last, the hour arrived when the long-insulted forbearance of the Almighty was to be avenged (Exodus 14:24-25).

The Egyptians cried, 'Let us flee from the face of Israel; for the Lord fighteth for them against the Egyptians'. But it was too late. The Lord had begun to fight against them. Once the Lord God unsheathes his sword of justice, he does not put it away until he has dipped it into the blood of his enemy! The proud monarch of Egypt and those who followed him learned suddenly and everlastingly that it is a vain thing to be found fighting against God! That which was the path of deliverance for the believing Israelites (the Red Sea) was made the very gate of hell for the Egyptians. You see, every attempt of men to obtain in unbelief that which is obtained only by faith is doomed to everlasting disappointment.

Oh, may God the Holy Spirit teach and convince you who believe not how vain it is to fight against God. Turn to him now. Sue for mercy, pleading the merits of Christ for your soul, lest he begins to fight against you this very hour!

'They Passed Through The Red Sea'

Faith in Christ enabled Moses, Joshua, Caleb, Aaron, Miriam and the believing Israelites to obtain what they could never have otherwise obtained. Faith gave them strength to obey the command of God and pass safely through the roaring Red Sea with complete safety.

Great Danger

Hebrews 11:29 takes us back to what is recorded in Exodus 14. There we are informed that shortly after Pharaoh had consented to let Israel go, he hardened his heart again. His spies informed him that the Israelites were trapped. So he went after them in fury, determined to destroy them. As the armies of Egypt drew near, the children of Israel began to murmur in unbelief (Exodus 14:10-12). They were hemmed in. They were shut in with the wall of Egypt on one side, the wilderness on the other, the Red Sea before them, and Pharaoh behind them. What did they do? They murmured against God. They ate the Passover and God protected them from the destroying angel. They walked out of Egypt with a high hand. Now, they trembled in unbelief. They looked to their own strength rather than the power of God, and their hearts failed them.

Forced Faith

Thanks be unto God, he will not forsake his own! He will never leave his chosen to themselves. Rather than leave us in our unbelief, by the inner workings of his Spirit and his sovereign arrangement of providence, the Lord our God graciously forces us to believe him. (Sweet grace! Immaculate mercy!) The Lord brought Israel to such a helpless and hopeless condition that they were constrained to trust him. What could they do? Fight they dare not. Flee they could not. If the Lord had not shown himself strong on their behalf they would surely have perished. God brought them to this place! He had promised to be for them. Now he was teaching them to rest confidently in his Covenant. Let us be wise, and learn from their mistake. Has he not promised us, 'When thou passest through the waters I will be with thee; and through the rivers, they shall not overflow thee' (Isaiah 43:2)? No matter how deep the waters, no matter how dark the storm, no matter how strong the oppressor may be, God who cannot lie has said, 'They shall not overflow thee'!

Remember The Red Sea

Israel was constantly reminded by the Lord to ever recall and learn from their experience at the Red Sea. The psalmist taught them to sing, 'Come and see the works of God: he is terrible in his doing toward the children of men. He turned the sea into dry land: they went through the flood on foot: there did we rejoice in him' (Psalm 66:5-6). Let all the Israel of God learn the lessons of the Red Sea.

Faith

Here we are taught how we ought to behave in times of great trial (Exodus 14:13-15). Moses said to the people, 'Fear not'. They were terrified by their foes because they did not trust their Father. How we need to learn to trust our God and cease from fear! Nothing so dishonours our God as our unbelief. Nothing causes us more trouble. Then God's prophet called for his people to 'Stand still'. Stand still, with foes pursuing? Stand still, with no visible means of deliverance? Stand still, in utter helplessness? Yes, if ever there is a time to stand still, it is when there is absolutely nothing else you can do! It is only when we cease from all reliance upon ourselves that we will stand still. And it is only when we stand still that we will 'see the salvation of the Lord'.

That is what faith does. It sees God's salvation. It contributes nothing to it and does nothing to get it. Faith simply beholds what God has done and is doing. It matters not whether we apply the word 'salvation' to the everlasting salvation of our souls, which is what the Red Sea experience typifies, or to deliverance from any temporal trouble, the instruction is the same. We will see God's salvation only as we stand still before him in faith, trusting our heavenly Father with all the affairs of our lives. Be assured, my brother, be assured, my sister, 'The Lord shall fight for you'. When we are confident of this, we shall hold our peace.

Then, the Lord commanded Moses to tell the people to 'Go forward'. They were commanded to 'go forward' before the sea was parted. Faith sees deliverance, faith apprehends the promise of God in his Word and acts upon it before it is actually performed. The believer is ready to go forward when by faith he has seen the deliverance of the Lord, before it is actually accomplished. Who would ever have imagined that Israel's way of escape and victory over her foes was to be the Red Sea? That was the very last thing any form of human reason would have expected. But God commanded them to go forward; and as soon as they stepped into the sea, obeying the revealed will of God, he turned the sea into dry ground, made its waters a wall of protection, and caused his people to go through the waters rejoicing (Exodus 14:22; Psalm 66:6).

Security

There may have been some trembling Israelites who passed through the sea, as terrified by the walls of water as they were by the pursuing armies of Pharaoh. They walked through the sea by faith, but not in the 'full assurance of faith' (Hebrews 10:22). They passed through the sea just as safely as the others, but with much less enjoyment. What a pity! Those who walked through the Red Sea 'in full assurance of faith' walked through it in the 'joy of faith' (Philippians 1:25).

They looked neither at the waters of the sea, nor at the might of their foes, nor at the reasonableness of their behaviour, but at the Word of God. Believing God, they walked through the Red Sea confident that God would deliver them. God who made the sea for them could certainly guide them through it (Romans 8:1). May the Lord be pleased to constantly teach us thus to trust him. He who makes our trials will also guide us through them and keep us safe and secure until he brings us home at last (Romans 8:28-30; 11:36, 1 Corinthians 10:13, John 10:28-30).

More on Judgment

Without question, the decrees and purposes of God are eternal, absolute, and immutable. Pharaoh was raised up by God, according to his eternal purpose, as a vessel of wrath (Romans 9:15-18; Proverbs 16:4). But the judgment of God upon Pharaoh and his armies was not an arbitrary thing. He was judged of God upon the basis of his own, wilful rebellion and sin (Exodus 14:17-25). I will leave it to others (who think they can do so) to work out the theological details, but these two facts are revealed in the book of God: (1) Reprobation, like election, is an eternal act of God. And (2) divine judgment is always the result of man's disobedience. God fought against Pharaoh because Pharaoh fought against God.

The Egyptians resolved to pursue Israel into the sea. But they entered the sea not in faith, but in rash presumption. What multitudes follow their example, rushing into eternity, presuming that all is well, when all is ill! There God will fight against them. The Egyptians drowned the firstborn of Israel, now they are drowned. There is always an element of retribution in God's judgment. In hell the damned shall but 'eat of the fruit of their own way' (Proverbs 1:31).

Recognition

When the Lord was done with his wonders at the Red Sea, exactly as he had purposed, both Israel and the Egyptians knew and acknowledged that Jehovah is God alone and God indeed. When the Lord our God has finished all his works all creation shall know and glorify him as God alone, either to the everlasting torment of their souls in hell or to the everlasting bliss and satisfaction of their souls in heaven (Exodus 15:1-6).

By faith the walls of Jericho fell down, after they were compassed about seven days.

Hebrews 11:30

Chapter 40

Read: Hebrews 11:30

'By Faith the Walls of Jericho Fell'

No man's ministry lasts forever. The best of prophets, pastors, and leaders will soon die and their ministries will come to an end. When the prophet dies, he needs to be buried, preferably buried in obscurity, lest his garnished sepulchre hinders his successor.

God's cause is not wrapped up in a man; and we must not wrap it up in a man. God's church and kingdom does not depend upon a man; and we must not make it, or act as if we make it, dependent upon a man.

Moses

Under the leadership of Moses, God accomplished great things for his people, Israel. He had revealed to Moses what he was going to do for his people, and Moses acted upon the divine revelation by faith. He brought the children of Israel out of Egypt by a mighty hand. They crossed the Red Sea as upon dry ground; and God slew the armies of Pharaoh in that same body of water. Because of Moses' intercession the children of Israel were fed with manna from heaven. Because of his earnest prayer in their behalf God preserved the nation. Still, throughout his ministry, he had the heartache of a grumbling, discontent, and rebellious congregation.

Joshua

God raises up specific men for specific purposes. When the servant has accomplished the purpose for which the Lord raised him up, God takes him. When Moses' work was done God took him. Then God raised up another man, a new leader for the people of Israel. A man like Moses, yet altogether different from Moses; a man trained by Moses, but a man trained by God through Moses; a man to take the place of Moses, but a man standing in his own place to do his own work for the glory of God. Joshua was God's chosen servant to lead the Israelites into the Promised Land.

Faith Displayed

Hebrews 11:30 displays the triumph of faith under the leadership of Joshua. In verse 29 we saw what faith accomplished during the exodus from Egypt. Now we see what it achieved as Israel entered the land of promise. The yoke of cruel bondage was broken asunder by faith, and by the same faith the people of God obtained the blessings of the Promised Land. 'By faith they passed through the Red Sea as by dry land: which the Egyptians assaying to do were drowned. By faith the walls of Jericho fell down, after they were compassed about seven days.'

The Life of Faith

By these two things, we see again that the believer's life is from beginning to end a life of faith. Without faith no progress can be made, no victories can be obtained, and no fruit can be brought forth for God's glory. It is written, 'The just shall live by faith'. 'As ye have received Christ Jesus the Lord, so walk ye in him'. 'Looking unto Jesus, the author and finisher of our faith' (Romans 1:17; Colossians 2:6; Hebrews 12:2; cf. John 1:29; 1 John 3:2; Revelation 22:4; Isaiah 45:25).

40 Years

It is solemn to note that an interval of forty years duration comes in between Hebrews 11:29 and 30. Those years were spent in the wilderness. They were years of judgment from God because of the unbelief and disobedience of the people. The Lord gave them a sentence of forty years of wandering in the wilderness, one year for every day the spies were in the land. They roamed about in the wilderness until every unbelieving rebel had died. That generation could not enter into and take possession of Canaan because of unbelief. They are forever a reminder of the importance of believing God and obedience to his revealed will. Nothing is more dishonouring to our God than unbelief; and nothing brings greater trouble and sorrow into our lives than that disobedience that arises from it.

Joshua 6

Hebrews 11:30 is an inspired commentary on the sixth chapter of Joshua, which begins by telling us, 'Now Jericho was straitly shut up, because of the children of Israel: none went out, and none came in.' Israel had reached the borders of Canaan. They had safely crossed the Jordan River; but they could not enter the land because of Jericho, which was a powerful fortress barring their way. This was one of the cities which had frightened the spies, causing them to say, 'The people is greater and taller than we: the cities are great and walled up to heaven' (Deuteronomy 1:28). To their eyes of unbelief the cities appeared impregnable, and far too secure for them to take.

Jericho was a frontier town. It was the gateway to Canaan. Its capture was absolutely necessary before any progress could be made by Israel in conquering and possessing their promised inheritance. Failure to capture Jericho would not only discourage the Israelites, it would give strength to the Canaanites. It was the enemies' leading stronghold, their most invulnerable fortress.

Yet, it fell to a people who possessed no artillery, and without them fighting a single battle. All they did, in obedience to God's Word, was to march by faith around the city once each day for six days and seven times on the seventh day. On that seventh day (in scripture seven is the number of completion), the trumpets of rams' horns were blown and when the people shouted the walls collapsed before them. By faith they destroyed Jericho and obtained their promised inheritance.

Jericho Taken

John Brown wrote, 'Faith, persevering faith, enabled Joshua and the Israelites to do what otherwise they could not have done, and by doing so, to obtain what otherwise they could not have obtained.'

Their Captain

Israel's Captain was her God (Joshua 5:13-15). The man Joshua saw with 'his sword drawn in his hand ... the Captain of the host of the Lord', was none other than the Lord Jesus Christ, the Prince of Israel, the Captain of our salvation (Hebrews 2:10). Christ is the great 'I Am'. Jehovah himself, who had commissioned Moses, stood before Joshua, assuring him of success in the work he was sent to perform. This is God our Saviour, the covenant keeping God who promised to Abraham the land of Canaan.

God's ways are not our ways. His ways are never our ways. God never does things the way we would do them; and we would never do things the way God would have them done if he did not compel us to walk in his way and follow him (Isaiah 58:5).

Moses was preserved in the ark of bulrushes. No mere man would ever have thought of such a method of saving a helpless boy from the king's slaughter. David was chosen above his brothers and all the men of Israel as Israel's king, though his own father considered him an impossible choice. The giant, Goliath, was slain by a shepherd boy's sling. Elijah was fed by a raven. Joseph was put in prison and Daniel cast into the den of lions, only for God to raise them up to their respective positions of usefulness for his people. The Lord Jesus, the King of Israel, was born in a stable and laid in a feeding trough. God's ways always involve staining the pride of man. In all things, our God teaches us to trust him and not ourselves, to lean upon his omnipotent arm and never upon the arm of flesh. Our God is totally independent of all natural means, and superior to all 'laws of nature'.

Their Commission

The children of Israel had a distinct and specific commission from the Lord. It was clear and unmistakable. The Lord told them to take Jericho (Joshua 6:1-5). These herdsmen were required and responsible to conquer a city with nothing but the word of God for their weapon. But they had the power of God and the promise of God to accompany his word.

We, too, are engaged in a warfare. The believer's life is a constant warfare, a warfare waged in hostile enemy territory (Romans 7:14-23; Galatians 5:17-26). Formidable enemies, great difficulties, and powerful oppositions are encountered in the warfare of faith. We are constantly at war in this life with the world, the flesh, and the devil. The warfare is real, the struggle difficult. But Christ our God, the Captain of our salvation goes 'conquering and to conquer', assuring us of triumph at last.

We cannot take possession of our promised inheritance except we conquer the enemy. But conquer we have, conquer we do, and conquer we shall. Christ conquered the enemy for us (John 12:32; Romans 8:39; Colossians 2:13-15). And the Lord God gives us grace, day by day, to prevail over our enemies (2 Corinthians 12:9). 'We are more than conquerors through him that loved us' (Romans 8:37).

God's elect shall prevail at last over all our foes (Romans 16:20; Galatians 2:20-21; Philippians 4:13; 2 Timothy 1:12; 1 Peter 2:5; Revelation 3:5; 20:6). We each have our swelling rivers to cross, impregnable walls to overcome, and mighty enemies to conquer in this warfare. But whatever our difficulties are, our God has put them before us. They are placed in our path on purpose by the hand of our unerring, all-wise, ever good and faithful God. Our God will cause us to trample them beneath our feet. Satan's strongholds cannot stand before a people who believe God. The very gates of hell shall fall before us (Matthew 16:18). So let us ever follow our Saviour, obeying his voice, doing his will, fearing no evil.

Another Question

With such promises of grace and glory, with such assurances of victory, one question must be faced and answered honestly. Why does it appear in this day that the church of God is so impotent? Why is it that we do not see God's mighty arm stretched out and his glory revealed? Is his arm shortened that it cannot save? No! The problem is not with our God, but with us. The problem is altogether with us. We do not see Jericho's walls fall before us and the enemies of our God conquered for two reasons. The first is our shameful, sinful failure to believe God (John 11:40; Matthew 13:58; Isaiah 48:17-19). The second is disobedience.

David could not bring the ark of God up to Jerusalem because he sought not the Lord after the due order (1 Chronicles 15:13). God will be served in the way he prescribes. His work will be done in his way. 'Not by might nor by power, but by my Spirit'! God's work will be performed in a way that honours him. I cannot help wondering what the Lord might do today, if we simply believed him and obeyed him. Let us go forth doing God's work in his way, and dependent upon his power.

The Walls Must Come Down

Jericho's walls fell because Israel believed God. Yet their faith had to be tried and proved. They prevailed against their foes by persevering in the trial God put before them. When Israel crossed Jordan, they burned their bridges behind them. They were cut off from flight; they had no houses to which they could flee, no fortresses to which they could retreat. They were in hostile enemy territory. They would either conquer their enemies and take Jericho, or they would perish. There was no way back. They must move forward. Jericho must fall.

Degrees of Faith

Faith is much more than a matter of speculation or theory. It is a living principle; and every living thing grows. There are degrees of faith. We do not grow in justification, holiness, and acceptance with our God. But believers do grow in faith as we grow in grace. We grow in grace as we grow in the knowledge of our Lord Jesus Christ. We grow in faith by the blessed discipline of grace (Hebrews 12:5-11).

Faith receives Christ (John 1:12). Receiving Christ, we are taught to reckon as our God does. We are taught to reckon that we are justified before him by Christ's obedience and death as our Substitute (Romans 6:11). As the Lord God graciously causes believing men and women to grow in grace and grow in faith, they become more and more confident of him, being confident and persuaded that he will perform his Word, fulfil his promises, and accomplish all that he has undertaken on behalf of his people (Philippians 1:6; 2 Timothy 1:12).

It is confident faith that enables insignificant nobodies to accomplish impossible things, because the strength by which faith operates belongs to the God upon whom faith relies. Believing God, Moses dared defy Pharaoh and the armies of Egypt. Believing God, and for the cause of his honour, David took on Goliath, fully confident that he would slay the giant and save Israel. Believing God, Elijah delivered Israel from the idolatry of Baal worship and the influence of his vile prophets. Believing God, Paul was comfortable in the face of sure and certain death.

God Honoured

God always honours those who honour him (1 Samuel 2:30), and nothing so honours our God as believing him. God honours faith because faith honours him. It is said that the missionary, William Carey, once challenged an assembly of preachers to, 'Ask great things of God; expect great things from God, undertake great things for God.' He accepted his own challenge and was honoured of God with success beyond human measure. Joshua and the children of Israel were obedient to God because they believed God (Joshua 6:3-4, 6-8). They honoured God by their faith; and God honoured them with victory. 'Lord, I believe. Help thou mine unbelief'.

Faith in Four Forms

The Lord told Joshua and the children of Israel exactly what they were to do to take Jericho (Joshua 6:3-4), and promised them that Jericho's wall would fall down flat before them (Joshua 6:5); and it came to pass (Joshua 6:6-25). 'By faith the walls of Jericho fell down,' but not until 'after they were compassed about seven days'.

True saving faith is much more than an idea or an ideal. It is much more than the acceptance of facts, believing specific doctrines, believing that God is, or believing that Jesus Christ died, was buried, and rose again the third day. Faith in Christ involves confidence in him and submission to him, as well as relying upon the merits of his blood and righteousness. There is much to be learned about faith in the fall of Jericho. What is recorded in Joshua 6 shows us four aspects of faith.

Obedience

Here is faith obeying God. That is what faith does. I do not suggest that believers are perfectly obedient. We are not. But believers do bow to and obey the Lord their God. These people were required to march around Jericho in utter silence. They were required to do this for six days, and then a seventh. Thus the Lord taught them patience (Psalm 37:4-7).

God's ways often seem strange to us. I am sure every man in Israel, when he heard Joshua's declaration of God's word, must have thought, 'That sure seems like a strange way to conquer a place.' Who would ever dream of conquering a city with nothing but the blowing of a ram's horn and carrying an ark? No matter how contrary it may appear to be to human reason, no matter how unpopular it may be for us to do so, it is our responsibility and blessedness to obey implicitly our God's will, revealed in holy scripture. We cannot do his work any other way.

The ark that Israel carried was typical of redemption accomplished by Christ. The blowing of the rams' horns was symbolic of the preaching of the gospel. These and these alone are the weapons of our warfare, by which the church and kingdom of God assaults the gates of hell.

Patience

The children of Israel obeyed God and waited for Jericho's wall to fall. Nothing is more contrary to our proud flesh than waiting on God. We want action, and we want it right now. But faith must and will wait on the Lord. 'Wait on the Lord: be of good courage, and he shall strengthen thine heart: wait, I say, on the Lord' (Psalm 27:14). 'Wait on the Lord, and keep his way, and he shall exalt thee to inherit the land: when the wicked are cut off, thou shalt see it' (Psalm 37:34). 'Say not thou, I will recompense evil; but wait on the Lord, and he shall save thee' (Proverbs 20:22). 'But they that wait upon the Lord shall renew their strength; they shall mount up with wings as eagles; they shall run, and not be weary; and they shall walk, and not faint' (Isaiah 40:31). 'The Lord is good unto them that wait for him, to the soul that seeketh him. It is good that a man should both hope and quietly wait for the salvation of the Lord' (Lamentations 3:25-26).

Anticipation

Waiting in faith is not lazy idleness, excused by claiming to believe in divine sovereignty and absolute predestination. Faith in God's sovereignty and confidence in his eternal purpose inspires obedience to his Word and confidence in his Word. The waiting of faith involves anticipation. We wait on God to work when we expect him to do so.

The faith by which Jericho fell was an expectant faith (Joshua 6:20). The people shouted before the walls fell down. Because they believed God, they expected those mighty, huge walls to fall. We who believe God ought to expect him to do all that he has promised. What could be more reasonable? If in the middle of a severe drought we pray for rain, we ought to walk around with an umbrella in our hands. We ought to expect the preaching of the gospel to bring forth fruit (Isaiah 55:11). We ought to expect the triumph of the gospel. We ought to expect our God to do us good, and nothing but good, all the days of our lives (Romans 8:28). We ought to expect goodness and mercy to pursue us everywhere we go (Psalm 23:6). We ought to live every day in the expectation of Christ's coming (Titus 2:11-14).

Perseverence

Israel persevered in their task and took Jericho (Joshua 6:20). The walls fell down flat before them. God made a promise; they believed it, and faith prevailed. They conquered their enemies. Let us likewise believe our God (Matthew 17:20; 1 John 5:4). 'Believe in the Lord your God, so shall ye be established; believe his prophets, so shall ye prosper' (2 Chronicles 20:20). 'If ye have faith as a grain of mustard seed, ye shall say unto this mountain, Remove hence to yonder place; and it shall remove; and nothing shall be impossible unto you' (Matthew 17:20). Yes, faith in Christ always prevails. We shall prevail over every obstacle, over every foe, inward and outward, over death, over hell, and over the grave (Revelation 19:1-6; 20:6).

By faith the harlot Rahab perished not with them that believed not, when she had received the spies with peace'.

Hebrews 11:31

Chapter 41

Read: Hebrews 11:31

A Chosen Harlot

God our Saviour saves sinners, real sinners. The Lord Jesus Christ takes the gutter-most and saves them to the uttermost by his omnipotent mercy, through the merits of his blood and righteousness. Here we read of a woman who was once a harlot who is now seated among the redeemed, made to be a chaste, pure, undefiled, perfectly holy virgin before God (Revelation 14:4). How can that be?

Rahab was the object of God's sovereign, electing love. What a picture this woman is of God's sovereign mercy and grace in Christ to sinners like us! Rahab was a sinner by birth, and a notorious sinner by choice and practice. Religious moralists and legalists try their best to make us believe that the word 'harlot' simply means that Rahab was an innkeeper. But the kind of inn Rahab kept was a brothel. The only women in those times and countries who kept public houses and inns were prostitutes.

I do not understand why people have so much trouble with that. The Lord Jesus Christ came into this world to save sinners; real sinners (1 Timothy 1:15; Matthew 9:10-13; Romans 5:6-8).

Mercy is for the miserable. Grace is for the guilty. Redemption is for the ruined. Righteousness is for the rotten. Rahab was a cursed woman, in a cursed profession, dwelling in a cursed city, from a cursed race (an Amorite); yet she obtained mercy.

A Cursed Woman

Why did this cursed woman obtain mercy? It was not because of anything in her, or anything done by her, but because the Lord loved her and chose her as the object of his grace. It is true that she and her house were saved because she received the spies, hid them, and sent them out another way. But that was an act of faith, faith which God gave her; not to get mercy, but because she had obtained mercy.

Faith is not the product of natural religion, logic, or human reason. Faith is the gift of God (Ephesians 2:8-9). Faith is the fruit of the Spirit (Galatians 5:22-23). Faith is the operation of God in the souls of chosen, redeemed, called sinners (Colossians 2:12).

No Accident

It was not by accident that the spies stumbled into Rahab's house when they came in to spy out the land. They came to Rahab's house because God had purposed it from eternity. If you will read her conversation with the spies, you will see how this harlot's experience of grace is described (Joshua 2:8-19). By some means or another, this woman heard the gospel of God's salvation (v. 10). Rahab's heart withered before the august, sovereign majesty of the true and living God (v. 11).

The other inhabitants of the land withered in the dread and fear of God's wrath and power; but Rahab's heart withered in repentance and faith, as is evident from verse 9. When she heard the report of God's wondrous works, Rahab believed God. 'And she said unto the men, I know that the LORD hath given you the land, and that your terror is fallen upon us, and that all the inhabitants of the land faint because of you.'

Under The Blood

Not only was Rahab an object of God's amazing, free, and sovereign grace in Christ; her house could not fall under the wrath of God because it was under the refuge and protection of the precious blood of Christ. That is what was symbolized by the scarlet cord hanging from her window (Joshua 2:18-21). This scarlet cord that Rahab dropped from her window was, like the blood of Abel's lamb, the blood of the passover lamb upon the houses of the Israelites, and the blood of sin-offering in the tabernacle, a picture and type of the precious blood of Christ.

Let others mock and deride us as being outdated in our religion, if they must, but among the saints of God the precious, sin-atoning, redeeming blood of the Lord Jesus Christ is not only prominent, it is everything! We glory only in the cross of our Lord Jesus Christ (Galatians 6:14). How we thank God for the blood!

It is by the blood that we are redeemed (1 Peter 1:18-20; Revelation 5:9-10). It is by the blood that we have forgiveness (Ephesians 1:7). It is the precious blood of Christ that gives us access to and acceptance with the Lord our God (Hebrews 10:19-22). It is the blood of Christ, sprinkled upon our hearts, that gives us the blessed peace and full assurance of faith that under it we are safe and secure from the avenging wrath and justice of God (Romans 8:1-4, 33-34).

The Lord our God declares, 'When I see the blood, I will pass over you'! Rahab believed him. Do you? When Joshua saw the scarlet cord hanging in her window, when he saw the blood upon her house, 'Joshua saved Rahab the harlot alive'. This one house on the wall could not fall because it was protected by grace. It could not fall because it was protected by blood.

Faith and God's Promise

I recall seeing a scene from a movie in which a gambler is shown looking intently at a deck of cards, obviously concentrating as completely as possible. When he drew the card he needed and won the hand, he said, 'My pappy always told me that if I just believed strongly enough that I could do it, I could draw any card I wanted from the top of the deck.'

Sadly, multitudes think of faith in just that way, as though it is a magical power by which we get what we want from God. Nothing could be further from the truth. Such ideas about faith are nothing more than superstition. Faith is not believing God for selfish gain. Faith is believing God's Word, trusting God's revelation. Faith is our response to God's revelation. As it is written, 'Faith cometh by hearing, and hearing by the Word of God.'

Rahab's Faith

Rahab believed God. She is held up before us in faith's hall of fame, in Hebrews chapter eleven, along side Abraham, Moses, and Joshua, as an example of faith (v. 31). James uses her, side by side with Abraham, as an example of what it means to prove our faith by our works (James 2:25).

Rahab's faith was not an empty, unfruitful, meaningless profession of faith. She believed God and proved that she believed him by her works of obedience. She believed the report she heard of God's salvation (Joshua 2:9-10). Rahab received, cared for, and protected God's messengers in her home, at the risk of her own life. Believing God, she also sought mercy for her household (vv. 12-13). Rahab hung everything upon the blood of the covenant represented in that cord hanging from her window. Rahab the harlot so thoroughly believed God that she brought all her family into her house and thus into the pale of grace!

This old harlot, who had been the shame of her family, was made, in the hands of God, the primary instrument and means of eternal salvation to her family. Rahab the harlot, believing God, obtained a place in the family tree of the incarnate Son of God, the Lord Jesus Christ (Matthew 1:1-5). Matthew identifies her as the wife of Salmon (a prince of the tribe of Judah), mother of Boaz, and great-great grandmother of King David.

In the genealogy of our Saviour only four women are mentioned. All four of them have a specific taint upon them. Tamar was guilty of incest. Rahab was a harlot. Ruth was a cursed, unclean Moabitess. Bathsheba was an adulteress. Thus, even in his genealogy and birth, our Saviour associated himself with sinners. The Son of God came to save sinners.

God's Promise

Rahab's faith was based upon God's promise. She had the promise of God for her security and the security of her house. If you read Joshua chapter two again (vv. 12-21), you will see that the messengers of God made a solemn promise to Rahab. They said, 'You go get your family, bring them into your house, bind this scarlet cord to the window, and stay in the house. When the Lord gives us this city, "We will deal kindly and truly with thee."' This is our security, too. We have the promise of God: 'I give unto them eternal life; and they shall never perish, neither shall any man pluck them out of my hand' (John 10:28; Romans 8:32-39; 16:20; Philippians 1:6; 1 Thessalonians 5:24; Hebrews 13:5; 1 John 5:11-13).

Rahab's Perseverance

Rahab was saved because she persevered in faith. She stayed in the house. God's faithful messengers told her that if she went out of the house, she would perish with all the rest of Jericho. There was no safety in any house in the city except in that house protected by the ever-abiding scarlet cord, the house under the ever-abiding protection of the blood. Just as the Israelites were to stay in their houses while God judged Egypt, so Rahab and her family had to stay in her house while God judged Jericho. Even so, you and I must cling to Christ alone. Abiding in him, we are safe from the wrath of God. But if you go out of this house, you will perish without mercy.

Five Characteristics of Faith Displayed in Rahab

Saving faith, that faith by which chosen redeemed sinners receive God's free salvation in Christ, is a faith that is displayed in the radical change it works in the lives of regenerate sinners. Without question, God's saints in this world are sinners still, and humbly acknowledge and confess their sin before him (1 John 1:7-10). There is no aspect of our lives and no act performed by us that is not constantly marred by sin. Yet, faith in Christ radically changes the lives of saved men and women. This is clearly demonstrated in Rahab's faith.

Singular Faith

Rahab's faith was a singular faith. The city of Jericho was about to be attacked. Within its walls there were hosts of people of all classes and characters. They knew that if Joshua and the children of Israel came against them, they would all be put to death. They had heard clearly what God had done and would do.

Yet, strange as it may seem, there was not another person in the entire city, young or old, male or female, who believed God and sought his mercy; except this woman who had been a harlot. Rahab and Rahab alone believed God!

If we would believe God, there is a sense in which we, too, must be singular in believing him. Faith is always an individual matter. Each of us must believe God for ourselves. Faith always stands alone. It is not dependent upon and does not seek reinforcement from others. Faith always swims upstream, against the tide. It is never the way approved by the majority. Faith always stands by itself before God. It is never the result of group therapy!

Steadfast Faith

Rahab's faith was also a steadfast faith. Her faith stood firm in the midst of trouble. She believed God when everything she hoped for seemed most unlikely; and she believed God to the end. When Jericho was gone, when the storm was over, she was right where she was when the walls began to fall. She was in the house marked by blood, kept by a covenant, and secured by the very Word of God!

Self-denying Faith

This woman's faith was a self-denying faith. She dared to risk her life for the sake of the spies. She knew that if they were found in her house she would be put to death. Yet she ran the risk of being put to death to save these two men. True faith is always self-denying faith.

I read this statement years ago and wrote it down. I do not know who the person was, yet I have seen his like many times. He said, 'I have got a good religion; it's the right sort of religion; I do not know that it costs me a cent a year; and yet I believe I am as truly a religious man as anybody.' That is the kind of religion you get from Babylon, not from God. Faith which is the gift and operation of God is faith that sacrifices all to Christ, and never looks upon it as a sacrifice (Luke 14:25-33).

Sympathizing Faith

Rahab's faith was a sympathizing faith. She was not content to go to heaven alone. She desired the mercy and grace of God for her family, and got it for them (Acts 16:31-34; Romans 9:1-3; 10:1).

George Whitefield put into words what Rahab displayed in her concern for her family. He wrote, 'As soon as I was converted, I wanted to be the means of the conversion of all that I had ever known'. Religion that has no concern for spreading itself and makes no effort to do so is religion that is not worth having. All God's people are his witnesses, evangelists sent forth by him to make disciples (Isaiah 43:10-11).

Sanctifying Faith

Let me show you one more thing about Rahab's faith. It was sanctifying faith. Rahab was no longer a harlot. Faith in Christ brings with it both justification and sanctification. The grace of God that brings salvation teaches all who experience it to live graciously, to live as unto the Lord (Titus 2:1-14). When God saves a person even his dog benefits from it, because the man becomes a better master.

God's Gift To Rahab

People everywhere honour the great triumphs of their heroes with monuments. Most of the monuments are raised in honour of great soldiers. Sometimes they are raised in honour to those who have performed great works of philanthropy, self-sacrifice, or individual heroism.

It seems most reasonable to me that there should be a monument to faith in Christ, which is the greatest, most noble, most honourable of all things on this earth. It is the most honourable of all things because faith in Christ is that which is both most honouring to our great God and that which makes men and women honourable.

Faith's Monument

The apostle Paul undertook, by Divine Inspiration, to raise a monument to faith in this eleventh chapter of Hebrews. What an extraordinary monument it is! In this chapter God the Holy Spirit, by whom faith is created in the hearts of men, by whom it is sustained, and by whom it works, shows us many of the great triumphs of faith.

Like most monuments, the names recorded here are the names of common, ordinary men and women. There is nothing really striking about any of them, except that for which their names are inscribed in this chapter. They were people like us, ordinary Bobs and Sallys, nothing but sinners who believed God.

Faith's Triumphs

The chapter begins with one triumph of faith, and then proceeds to others. If I have counted them correctly, there are 48 distinct acts of faith set before us in this chapter. All are extraordinary in that they are all acts beyond the realm of human ability. Yet, there is a sense in which they are very ordinary in that these acts of faith and the triumphs of them are common to all who believe God.

Like Abel, all who believe God obtain witness that they are righteous before God. Like Enoch, all who trust Christ are delivered from death because they please God. Like Noah, all who are born of God are heirs of righteousness. Like Abraham, all believers are strangers and pilgrims in this world, receiving life from the dead. Faith always (ultimately) triumphs over natural affection, as displayed in Abraham's sacrifice of Isaac. Faith stands firm against the allurements of the world, as in the case of Moses. Faith keeps the passover and the sprinkling of blood, trusting Christ, who is our Passover. Faith worships God. Faith is patient in trial. Faith endures to the end, seeing him who is invisible.

Here, in verse 31, as though the greatest victory of faith should be recorded last, Paul shows us a picture of faith waging war with sin, battling with iniquity, and coming away more than a conqueror. 'Rahab perished not with them that believed not, when she had received the spies with peace.'

There is no doubt at all Rahab was indeed a harlot. She was not a mere hostess in a local Jericho hotel. If the Lord had meant to tell us that she was an innkeeper, he would have used the word 'innkeeper'. He did not do so. He used the word 'harlot', because Rahab was a harlot. Nothing but contempt for the free grace of God would ever have led any to deny this fact.

The harlot Rahab believed God! What grace is displayed here! What a great, encouraging picture we have before us of …

> The change that's wrought in a sinner's heart,
> By the touch of the Master's hand!

The most hideous lusts are conquered by the revelation of Christ. The most bestial debauchery is defeated by the grace of God. The most useless, most worthless dregs of fallen humanity are made the instruments of the greatest possible usefulness by faith in Christ.

God's Gift

Let us see, and see clearly, that faith in Christ is the greatest gift God almighty can or will ever give to any sinner upon the earth. Seek it for yourself. Seek it for others. Thank God if you have it. Faith is the gift of God's grace (Ephesians 2:8-9) and the operation of God's Spirit (Colossians 2:12). It comes to redeemed sinners as the fruit of Christ's atonement (Galatians 3:13-14). Rahab believed God because God gave her faith. He chose her in eternal love and caused her to believe him (Psalm 65:4).

Oh, gift of gifts! Oh, grace of faith!
My God, how can it be
That Thou, Who hast discerning love,
Should'st give that gift to me!

How many hearts Thou might'st have had
More worthy, Lord, than mine!
How many souls more worthy far,
Of that pure touch of Thine!

Ah, Grace! Into the most unlikely hearts
It is thy boast to come,
The glory of thy light to find
In darkest spots a home!

Thy choice, O God of goodness, then
I lovingly adore!
Oh, give me grace to keep Thy grace,
And grace to long for more!

Saving Faith

Rahab's faith was saving faith, 'By faith the harlot Rahab perished not'! She was delivered from destruction and death, though all around her perished under the wrath of God, because she believed God. Her salvation, however, was not merely of a temporal nature, not merely the deliverance of her body from the sword, but redemption of her soul from hell. Oh, what a great gift faith is. It is that which saves the soul from hell! C. H. Spurgeon said,

> So mighty is the ever-rushing torrent of sin, that no arm but that which is as strong as Deity can ever stop the sinner from being hurried down to the gulf of black despair, and, when nearing that gulf, so impetuous is the torrent of divine wrath, that nothing can snatch the soul from perdition but an atonement which is as divine as God himself. Yet faith is the instrument of accomplishing the whole work.

Great Salvation

What a great thing the salvation of a soul is! You can never know how great it is until you experience it. There are only two people who know what salvation is: the saved and the Saviour! No one knows what liberty is except a freed captive, and the Deliverer. No one knows what redemption is but a ransomed soul, and the Redeemer. No one knows what forgiveness is but a forgiven sinner, and the Forgiver. No one knows what salvation is but a saved soul, and the Saviour.

Great Faith

'By faith, the harlot Rahab perished not'. God sent his Word, and she believed it. God showed her the blood and she hung everything on it. The same faith that saved Rahab saves us. Believe on the Lord Jesus Christ, and you shall perish not, even if your name is Rahab! Christ's gospel is a declaration of free salvation for sinners. Thieves, murderers, and harlots find in his blood full absolution from all sin (Romans 8:1-4, 33-34).

Great Hope

The fountain filled with Immanuel's blood was opened for the cleansing of souls as black as hell. The robe of Christ was woven for naked sinners, guilty before God. The balm of Calvary is for sin-sick souls. He who is Life came into the world to raise the dead. Oh, perishing and guilty soul, may God give you Rahab's faith! If he does, you shall have Rahab's salvation, and shall with her stand in heaven, where the white-robed spotless hosts sing unending hallelujah to God and the Lamb.

'The Harlot Rahab'

When the Lord God sent Joshua and the children of Israel across the Jordan River and into the land of Canaan to take possession of the land, the first order of business was to destroy the city of Jericho. Jericho was one of the largest, most prosperous, and best fortified cities in the land. But the city was cursed of God and marked for destruction. The sentence of death had been passed upon it forty years earlier (Exodus 23:27-28).

Though the inhabitants of Jericho prospered in the world; though they worked and played, laboured by day and partied by night; though they filled their lives with every amusement, comfort, and pleasure they could find; though they were utterly ignorant of it, they were a people cursed of God, a people whose numbered days were up, and a people about to be forever damned!

They were as sure for hell as if they were already there when Joshua and the children of Israel crossed over the river Jordan; but they were oblivious to the fact of it! The scriptures tell us that the children of Israel marched around Jericho, carrying the ark of the covenant everyday for seven days. On the seventh day, they marched around the city seven times, blew their trumpets and shouted. When they did, the walls of Jericho came tumbling down and fell flat to the ground. The whole city was completely destroyed at once, except for one house. There was one small section of the wall that did not fall because there was a house on that section of the wall that could not fall.

Why? Why was that house preserved? The answer is found in Hebrews 11:31. There was a woman in that house who believed God. There was a woman in that house who was sheltered by a scarlet cord, which represented the precious blood of Christ. The story is recorded in Joshua six. Though all of Jericho was destroyed under the wrath of God, Rahab and her father's house were saved; the house of the town's most notorious harlot could not fall.

When I read that, being the kind of curious, inquisitive person I am, I want to know why? Why was this one house left standing, while all the other houses were destroyed? Why, when the entire wall surrounding the city collapsed under the weight of God's wrath, was this harlot's house left standing? The book of God shows us clearly that there are five reasons why Rahab's house did not and could not fall when the judgment of God fell on Jericho:

1. Rahab was the object of God's sovereign, electing love.
2. Rahab's house was under the blood.
3. Rahab believed God.
4. Rahab had the promise of God for her security and the security of her house.
5. Rahab stayed in the house.

And what shall I more say? for the time would fail me to tell of Gedeon, and of Barak, and of Samson, and of Jephthae; of David also, and Samuel, and of the prophets:

Hebrews 11:32

Chapter 42

Read: Hebrews 11:32

Examples of Diversity

Believers are not all the same. We all have the same faith. We all have the same hope. We all have the same redemption, the same righteousness, the same heaven, and the same promises of grace to sustain us along the way. Still we are not the same. Paul could not have given us six names that more clearly reflect the great diversity there is among God's people than those given in this verse. Gideon, Barak, Samson, Jephthae, David, and Samuel were all men who believed and served God; but they were unique individuals.

A Question

Verse 32 begins with a question: 'And what more shall I more say?' Need he add more examples of faith? Need he say anything more to prove the necessity and effectiveness of faith in Christ? He admits that he does not have the space or time to do it, 'for the time would fail me to tell of Gideon, and of Barak, and of Samson, and of Jephthah; of David also, and of Samuel, and of the prophets'.

We might wish he had written several more chapters on faith. But he has made his point without being redundant. Faith in Christ satisfies believers through the ages, cultures, circumstances, and personalities represented in human history.

Great Diversity

Yet, the six examples here used by the Spirit of God to exemplify faith in Christ show us that true believers are people of great diversity with varying personalities. God does not stamp us out with a cookie cutter, making us all alike. Each of us is dealt with personally by the Lord, and individually shaped in the image of Christ. Each one experiences the providential working of God in his life, tailored to affect every detail to bring the whole of his existence into conformity with Christ and to the glory of God.

Four of these men are identified in the book of Judges during a period when 'every man did what was right in his own eyes', and faith appeared to be almost non-existent. David and Samuel appear in the book of 1 Samuel, with David following in many other portions of scripture. As we have seen, Paul picked these names somewhat randomly rather than chronologically. They are paired out of order. His purpose was not to chronicle their acts of faith but to give us a broad display of those who believe God. In doing this, he assures us of the legitimacy of our own faith, though it is housed in the weakness of our personalities.

Weakness and Sin

All believers face the fact that they are weak and sinful, always weak and sinful. This we acknowledge before God (1 John 1:7-10). Yet, nothing causes us more pain and difficulty. Our faith is never perfect. Far from it; it is always marred by our unbelief. The men here set before us as examples of faith were no different. They all had defects in their faith.

Gideon was slow to take up arms against God's enemies, slow to obey the revealed will of God. He did conquer the massive Midianite army with his 300 men, but was slow to take action. Barak hesitated and went forward only when Deborah encouraged him. He did lead the charge against the army of Sisera, the Canaanite commander, but he refused to lead without Deborah the prophetess at his side. He was a man of faith, but a man with such shameful weakness that he had to be led by a woman into battle.

Samson was enticed by Delilah. He was a remarkable man and did great things. Yet Samson was a man of great weakness, whose life is shrouded under a cloud of great sin. Jephthah made a rash vow. He is to be commended for much. He was a man of remarkable character; but his rash vow was terribly costly to him, his daughter, and his family.

Samuel was a great prophet and a mighty judge in Israel. He was a man who seemed to know no fear, because he believed God. Yet, he was fearful and hesitant in anointing David as king, because Saul might kill him.

David was a man after God's own heart. What a remarkable man of faith he was! Yet, his name is always linked with great shame because of the matter of Bathsheba and Uriah. In shameful pride, he numbered Israel, ignoring God's law. He even got mad at God for killing Uzza, when he put his hand to the ark of God.

Not Faith But Christ

John Calvin stated, 'In every saint there is always to be found something reprehensible. Nevertheless, although faith may be imperfect and incomplete, it does not cease to be approved by God'.

It is not the perfection of our faith that God honours, but the perfection of its Object. God approves faith even when it is displayed through the weakness of flawed personalities, because faith looks to Christ. It is not our faith that gives us acceptance with God, but Christ, the Object of our faith.

Lights Shining In Darkness

It is written, 'The path of the just is a shining light' (Proverbs 4:18). Certainly, that fact is manifest in the lives of these faithful men. One thing was common to them. Each one lived and served the cause of Christ in a day of great spiritual darkness and evil. The times in which they lived are described at length in the book of Judges. Following the deaths of Moses and Joshua, Israel forsook her God. She cast off his law, worshipped the idols of the heathen, and 'every man did that which was right in his own eyes'! Darkness covered the earth, and gross darkness the people.

God's Provision

Yet, even in those days God did not leave himself without a witness. In the midst of great darkness, these six men stood in their day as bright, shining lights. In the midst of terrible idolatry, they stood as beacons of truth. In the midst of utter apostasy, they stood as walls and pillars of steadfast faith in and love for the God of all grace, whose grace they had proved. They were just the men needed for the day in which they lived. And the day in which they lived was just the day for them.

In this text six specific men are named. Then, these six are linked to the 'prophets', who also served God in times of great apostasy. So the number of those mentioned here is seven, the number used in the scriptures for completion, grace, fulness, and perfection. In other words, we are told that God's provision is always exactly what is needed, always complete, and always full.

This inspired description of faith could not have been complete if Paul had not given us these examples from Israel's darkest days. A. W. Pink writes, 'It was during seasons of great spiritual darkness and gloom that faith wrought many of its mightiest works and achieved some of its most notable victories.' It was during these days of terrible darkness, idolatry, and unbelief that grace shone brilliantly.

Encouragement

Our God is not constrained by our circumstances! Grace is not limited by our limitations. The Word of God is not bound by our bondage. Faith is not weakened by unfavourable circumstances, but thrives in such. These things are written for our encouragement (Romans 15:4). We, too, live in days of darkness, utter darkness and apostasy. But the arm of the Lord is not short that it cannot save. His ear is not heavy, that it cannot hear. Let us cry to him. He will hear us. Let us lean heavily upon his omnipotent arm. He will help us. Who knows what wonders he may do in our day. Never was a day riper for the showing forth of his greatness, his glory, and his grace. In this apostate generation, we have reason, as much and more, as Gideon, Barak, Samson, Jephthah, David, and Samuel, to believe God, rejoice in his goodness, and give thanks to his holy name.

'Of Barak'

Barak was raised up by God after Jabin the king of Canaan had 'mightily oppressed the children of Israel' (Judges 4:1-3) for twenty years. Deborah acted as judge in that day. Israel had fallen into such a low condition that God gave them a woman to rule over them (Isaiah 3:12).

Deborah the Prophetess

Deborah was not a 'judge' in the strict sense of the word (cf. Judges 4:4 Judges 2:18). She was a 'prophetess' (a worshipper of God), one by whom God spoke his word to his people, a mouthpiece of the Almighty. The word 'prophetess' in the Old Testament does not refer to female preachers, but simply to women who were singularly known for their worship of God. Sometimes the word is used simply to speak of a woman who was the wife of a prophet (Isaiah 8:3). Yet, even if those Old Testament women spoken of as prophetesses actually stepped into a pulpit and preached, that does not nullify the specific prohibition of the New Testament concerning female preachers (1 Corinthians 14:34; 1 Timothy 2:11-12). It was through Deborah that God spoke to Barak, saying, 'Hath not the Lord God of Israel commanded, Go and draw toward mount Tabor, and take with thee ten thousand men of the children of Naphtali and of the children of Zebulun? And I will draw unto thee to the river Kishon Sisera, the captain of Jabin's army, with his chariots and his multitude; and I will deliver him into thine hand' (Judges 4:6, 7).

Barak's Faith

Faith is not an unguided impulse. Faith is a believer's response to God's revelation. 'Faith comes by hearing, and hearing by the Word of God.'

The word from God that Deborah delivered to him was the basis of Barak's faith. He was given the sure promise of divine revelation that the thing to be 'hoped for', Israel's salvation, would be accomplished.

Barak is here held before us as an example of faith. How thankful we should be that the Spirit of God gives us such an example. His faith was exemplary; but it was not perfect. Like all God's saints in this world, Barak's faith acted through the infirmity of a sinful man. That infirmity is seen in Judges 4:8. 'Barak said unto her, If thou wilt go with me, then I will go: but if thou wilt not go with me, then I will not go'. Yet, he was obedient to the Lord God, walking before him in faith (Judges 4:10). The Lord went before him and delivered Sisera into his hand (Judges 8:14). Barak heard God's Word, believed it, and obeyed it. It was by faith in God's promise that Barak went forth against the enormous army of Sisera and vanquished it. His obedience of faith brought Israel deliverance by the hand of God.

'Of David'

It was not Paul's purpose here to direct our attention to all the wonders of David's remarkable life, but to the remarkable conquests of his faith in Christ. David alone is that man who is described by the Lord God as a man after his own heart (1 Samuel 13:14; Acts 13:22). That which made David a man after God's own heart was not his personal righteousness, but his faith in Christ, who 'is the Lord our Righteousness'.

There is no need, here, for me to mention David's great sin. That matter is recorded plainly in the scriptures and is well known by almost all men the world over. Even the man after God's own heart, while he lived in this world, was a sinner. He was, like all God's elect, a man blessed of God, to whom the Lord would not impute sin; redeemed and forgiven by the blood of Christ (Romans 4:8). Like you and me, David's only righteousness was the righteousness of God imputed to him. As with us, the Lord God wisely and graciously overruled David's sin for his good, the glory of his own great name, the accomplishment of his purpose, and the salvation of his elect. It must never be forgotten that Solomon, through whom Christ came into the world, was the son of David and Bathsheba (2 Samuel 12:24). David's experience of God's grace in forgiving his sin made his sin bitter to him and made his Saviour precious (Psalm 32 and 51).

Perhaps the Holy Spirit has particular reference to David's victory over Goliath (1 Samuel 17). When David was just a teenage boy, totally inexperienced in combat of any kind, he engaged Goliath in the name of God. Armed with nothing but a sling and a few small rocks, David went to war with the mighty giant of the Philistines, and cut off Goliath's head with his own sword

How did he accomplish this? How do we explain his courage, his boldness, and his victory? David had the revelation of God's own Word of promise (1 Samuel 17:46-47). He believed God's Word, resting upon it with implicit confidence, and acted accordingly. By faith he ventured; by faith he overcame.

David was, in this, an eminent type of Christ. David stood on the field of battle representing the whole nation of Israel. He conquered Goliath, and delivered Israel out of the hand of the Philistines single-handedly. Our Lord Jesus Christ, representing the whole of God's spiritual Israel, conquered Satan as our Representative and saved all the hosts of God's elect from all their souls' enemies single-handedly. As David used Goliath's own sword to cut off his head, so our omnipotent Redeemer, by his death upon the cross, defeated Satan. As David said of Goliath's sword, 'Give me it, there is none like it' (1 Samuel 21:9-10), we ought to say concerning the message of the cross, 'Give me it, there is none like it'. By the preaching of Christ crucified, our God still defeats his foes and saves his people.

'Of Jephthae'

Gideon was a farmer. Barak was a soldier. Samson was a Nazarite. David was the youngest of Jesse's sons and was despised by his brothers. Samuel was the first used by God while he was still a child. Our great God delights to use weak, insignificant, despised instruments to accomplish his greatest works in this world (1 Corinthians 1:26-29).

This fact is never more demonstrably illustrated than in the case of Jephthah. Jephthah was born in shame, the bastard son of a harlot (Judges 11:1, 2). He bore all his life the pain and shame of his mother's immorality. He was by law excluded from the congregation of Israel (Deuteronomy 23:2). But Jephthah was beloved of God, chosen in Christ, and ordained as an instrument by whose hand he would save his people.

The Lord God poured out his Spirit upon Jephthah and exalted him to the highest dignity and usefulness among his people. Jephthah was one of God's elect. As such, he was prospered in all that he did. No outward condition, be it ever so base, can hinder God's purpose, or thwart his grace. Jephthah feared God (Judges 11:9-10) and believed his Word (Judges 11:14-28). His faith was evident in ascribing Israel's conquests to the Lord (Judges 11: 21, 23). He called on the God of all truth to judge between Israel and Ammon (Judges 11:27).

The Lord God honoured the faith that honoured him by delivering the Ammonites into Jephthah's hand. Jephthah's fidelity and perseverance in the faith is seen in the keeping of his vow (Judges 11:30-32). He had no idea that the one who would come out of his house and be the first to meet him would be his only child. But when he saw her, though his vow caused him great pain, he kept it. He said, 'I have opened my mouth unto the Lord, and I cannot go back' (Judges 11:35). In accordance with his oath, he offered his only child as a burnt-offering to God, banning her to continual virginity.

Let us follow noble Jephthah's example of faith. In our baptism we publicly avowed ourselves God's forever. We are, as it were, willing burnt-offerings to our God (Romans 6:4-6). We present our bodies a living sacrifice, holy, acceptable unto God, that we might prove what is that good, and acceptable, and perfect, will of God. Let us live as those who are God's (Romans 12:1,2). When we united with God's people in church membership, we publicly wed ourselves to God's saints in that local assembly. Let us live for the good of and serve the interests and needs of that local assembly into which God has placed us. Brothers and sisters in the household of faith serve one another in love. They do not seek to be served, but to serve.

'Of Samson'

Samson's many mighty deeds are recorded by divine inspiration in the book of Judges, beginning at chapter thirteen. He was, in many ways, typical of Christ.

Like our Saviour, his birth was foretold by the angel of the Lord (Judges 13:7). As our Lord Jesus chose his bride from a cursed race, Samson went down to Timnath and found a wife there among a cursed people, among the Philistines who were his most implacable enemies (Judges 14:1-4). His wife was taken from among those who most deserved his just wrath. She was taken from Timnath, which means, 'portion allotted, given, assigned portion'. So God's elect are Christ's assigned portion. As that Philistine woman 'pleased him well', so the Lord Jesus is well-pleased with his bride, the church of God's elect. As we are the bride of Christ by the will of God, she was taken to be Samson's wife by the will of God, because he sought an occasion against the Philistines.

As our Saviour conquered Satan, the lion that roars against us, Samson tore a lion to pieces, as though it had been a kid (Judges 14:5-6). One day he killed a thousand Philistines, single-handedly, with the jawbone of an ass! So the Son of God slew all our enemies, using the most despised of all instruments, the death of the cross (Galatians 3:13). As Samson carried off the gates of Gaza with their posts on his shoulders up a steep hill, our almighty Saviour carried the gates of death away as he broke the iron bars and ascended up into heaven. As he tore asunder the strongest cords when bound by his enemies, our great Redeemer foiled every temptation of the devil, conquered death in his death, and broke the cords of death in his resurrection. As Samson overturned the pillars on which the great temple of Dagon stood, our great Samson, the Lord Jesus Christ, has overturned the kingdom of darkness. As Samson was divinely anointed for his work, the Lord Jesus is the Christ, the Anointed One of God.

How did Samson perform these great and mighty deeds? By faith. In the book of Judges we read, 'The Spirit of the Lord came upon him'. But that does not mean he was forced involuntarily by divine power, like a tornado carries things through the air blindly and unwittingly. God the Holy Spirit does not use men passively like we use wood, rocks, steel, and mortar. God uses people by making them his willing servants, enlightening their minds, controlling their hearts, inclining their wills, and supplying grace and strength to do what he has for them to do.

'Faith cometh by hearing'. In Samson's case he heard through his parents the promise which God had made concerning him (Judges 13:5). He was raised in a home where God was believed and honoured. His parents taught him the Word and worship of God in an age when few knew him, believed him, and worshipped him. But their faith was not his faith. He believed the Word he 'heard' from God through his parents; but Samson also believed God for himself. He grew up in the confidence of that faith and conducted himself accordingly. His last act was his greatest and best (Judges 16:28-30). As he had lived in faith, he died in faith.

Ordinary Men Trusting an Omnipotent God

It is commonly thought that Paul's purpose in writing Hebrews 11 is to extol the greatness of those men and women whose names are mentioned in these verses, or at least to extol the greatness of their faith. Neither is true. Paul's purpose here is to extol the greatness of their God, the Giver and Sustainer of faith. In this chapter the Holy Spirit is encouraging believers, in the midst of great trials, facing great dangers, enduring great opposition, to continue trusting Christ. Let me remind you of some things clearly revealed in the book of God about faith.

The singular Object of all true faith is the triune God, revealed and known in the Lord Jesus Christ, our Substitute. Faith looks to Christ alone for righteousness and atonement. But there is more to faith than trusting Christ as our sin-atoning Saviour. Faith trusts Christ as Lord, as the God of all providence and grace, ruling and disposing of all things for the salvation of his people. True, saving faith is the gift and operation of God (Ephesians 2:8-9; Colossians 2:12). Faith is not a work of man's free will; something we have a natural ability to perform. Faith is the gift of God. Faith is the fruit of the Holy Spirit (Galatians 5:22).

Faith is given by, arises from, and acts in obedience to the revelation of God in the scriptures. Every act of faith described in this chapter, every act of faith described in the entire Word of God, was in direct response to God's revelation (Romans 10:17; 1 Peter 1:23-25).

Faith is the gift of God; the operation of his grace in us. We cannot and will not believe apart from the gift and operation of God's grace. Yet faith is not passive, it is an active thing. Faith acts in response to God's revelation. The power, strength, and efficacy of faith is not in us, or the strength of our faith, but in our God, the Object of our faith.

These were ordinary men, sinners saved by the grace of God, washed in the blood of Christ, robed in his righteousness, born of his Spirit; just like us. Saved sinners, but sinners still! Ordinary men, just like us, who trusted an omnipotent God. Faith is not dependent on favourable outward conditions. Faith rises above circumstances. Faith is sustained and energized by One who is infinitely superior to all circumstances. Trusting God our Saviour, we shall be delivered from all our enemies, and sustained and enabled to do his will in this age for the glory of his name. Yes, we can do all that he would have us do, by his all-sufficient grace in Christ (Philippians 4:12-13).

Samuel and The Prophets

We have a brief summary of Samuel's life in 1 Samuel 1:24-28. This remarkable man was typical of our Lord Jesus Christ in many ways. He grew in wisdom and stature, finding favour with God and with men. He was bold and courageous. He was a man of prayer, ever interceding for a rebellious, sinful people. He was a prophet. And he was faithful all his life. That last thing is, I am sure, what the Holy Spirit intends for us to grasp. Samuel was faithful from his youth, faithful to God's glory, faithful to his will, faithful to his Word, and faithful to his people. Samuel is one of very few men mentioned in the scriptures against whom no evil, no weakness, no flaw of character is recorded. That is the remarkable thing! God took an ordinary man, used him all his life, used him in the most ordinary way, and used him for the establishing of his kingdom. Indeed, it is God's habit (if I may use such a word in reference to our God) to do so (1 Corinthians 1:26-29).

The Prophets

Those men who were God's prophets were ordinary men like us, sinners who were saved by the grace of God. They were men who believed God. Believing God, they served him and his people well. They preached nothing but what God told them to preach. Their watch-word was, 'Thus saith the Lord'. They concealed nothing they received: though it was a 'burden' to them (Malachi 1:1). They were undaunted by opposition. Setting their faces as a flint, they delivered God's message (Ezekiel 3:8, 9). Samuel's first task as God's spokesman was to expose Eli's failure. Nathan had to confront the king of Israel (David) with his sin. Elijah had to stand against Ahab, Jezebel, and all the prophets of Baal in a day when all Israel readily worshipped at the altars of Baal. Jeremiah had to warn Israel, the people he loved and served faithfully, of God's impending judgment and the righteousness of it. These faithful men, God's prophets, defied the entire religious world and the gods of men.

Prophets Today?

Someone wrote the following many years ago. I do not know who the author was, or when he wrote it. But what he wrote concerning prophets is too important for me not to insert it here.

'Along with the evangelist, pastor and teacher, the New Testament lists, the ministry of the prophet. It is difficult to find anything said or written about the prophet's ministry. Like the prophet himself, his work is difficult to define. We know the old definition, "A forth teller rather than a foreteller." We apply the term generally to preachers as spokesmen for God. Yet, there appears to be a distinct calling somewhat different from that of evangelist, pastor, or teacher. There never have been many prophets; and certainly there are few today. Never was the need greater and the supply smaller than today.

The prophet is a voice in the wilderness. It is his business to sound the trumpet, proclaim the ideal, not work on details or set up programs. He does not devise ways and means. He does not fit on boards and committees. The prophet is a solitary soul and does his best work alone. He is no parrot, puppet or promoter. He is nothing but a prophet, and if he tries to be anything else he is an embarrassment to himself and to everybody else. He is never popular with politicians in state or church. He is not cowed by dignitaries. He calls Herod a fox to his face if occasion demands. He is an unreconstructed rebel, an oddity in a day of regimentation. He has no more patience with mere religion than had Isaiah when he thundered, or Amos when he called on Israel to come to Bethel.

It is the prophet's business to say what others cannot, will not, or at least do not say. The politician has his eye on the next election, not the nation's welfare. It is possible for a preacher to get his mind on promotion, the next rung of the ladder, a high seat in the synagogue, and being called a rabbi. The prophet has no axe to grind. For him the grass is no greener in the next pasture. He does not want, nor does he seek any man's office.

The church today looks for scholars, specialists, socialisers, and showmen. We need some prophets who, like Isaiah, have seen God in His holiness, themselves in their sinfulness, and the land in its uncleanness. The prophet does not pack the house, nor produce impressive statistics. He may get but poor response. Yet, whether they hear or refuse to hear, those who hear him know that a prophet has been among them. People do not crowd churches to hear prophets. People with itching ears look for smooth talking men-pleasers who will scratch their ears with what they want to hear. They do not want a prophet.

The prophet is never popular with the Pharisees. 'Which of the prophets have not your fathers persecuted?' 'Ye are the children of them that killed the prophets.' So declared the Son of God to the Pharisees of his day. Religious people have always stoned living prophets and enshrined dead ones. The monuments of this generation are designed to cover the crimes of our fathers. Prophets are never popular at home. Our Lord told us that plainly. Even his family accused him of being a mad man, saying, 'he is beside himself'.

The prophet's path is not easy. John the Baptist's head is not served up on a charger these days; but such a prophet is not less despised today than John was in his. Like John the Baptist, the prophet is out to pull down the high places, build up low places and make a way for the Lord. His business is not intellectual explanation but pointed declaration! He does not lecture about mustard, he makes a mustard poultice and lays it next to the wound. Others comfort the afflicted, but he afflicts the comfortable. Today the whole religious world is trying to accomplish by pep, publicity, propaganda, and promotion what once was done by preaching. The woods are full of trained pulpit puppets. Oh, may God give us some prophets!

Any young Elisha in line for Elijah's mantle will need the mind of a scholar, the heart of a child, and the hide of a rhinoceros. He is sure to irk those who want to preserve the status quo. He is sure to be a disturber of Israel. But no one else can take his place. We must have a prophet; a man who will dare to scorn the hatred of Ahab, Jezebel, and the prophets of Baal; a man who will dare to mock the mock gods of the Baal worshipers of our day; seeking nothing but the glory of God, preaching nothing but the gospel of God, serving nothing but the cause of God!

The Faith of The Judges

This chapter begins with a definition of faith. It is, without question, both the shortest and the best definition of faith ever written. 'Faith is the substance of things hoped for, the evidence of things not seen.' The entire chapter, following verse 1, is devoted to giving us examples and illustrations that prove the truthfulness of that definition. Therefore, when Paul gets to the last section of the chapter, the last group of examples, he begins verse 32 by telling us that nothing more is needed to prove his inspired definition. By all that we have seen, it is evident that 'Faith is the substance of things hoped for, the evidence of things not seen.' That is why he opens verse 32 with a question, implying that the answer is obvious. 'What shall I say more?' Then, he says, 'Time would fail me', if I were to give you all the examples that might be given from holy scripture that illustrate my point. 'Faith is the substance of things hoped for, the evidence of things not seen.' It would be redundant to continue. Further examples are not needed. Then, he rattles off more examples in verse 32, as if to put an exclamation point to what he had just written. These examples of faith are all taken from the period of the Judges. Seven things stand out as obvious lessons we ought to lay to heart.

1. God does not see things the way we see them. We judge only by outward appearance; and judging by outward appearance we always judge wrong. Had any of us been writing this chapter, we would probably have omitted Gideon, Barak, Samson, and Jephthah. We would have included, instead, Deborah, Caleb, Hannah, and Asaph. That is because we can only look upon and judge things by outward appearance. 'The Lord looketh on the heart'!

2. It is not our faith that gives us acceptance with God and wins his approval, but Christ, the Object of our faith. My faith did not save me. Christ did! Faith did not redeem me, justify me, put away my sin, or forgive me. Christ did! It is the weakness of these men, the weakness of their faith, particularly of Gideon, Barak, Samson, and Jephthah that gets our attention when we read about them in the scriptures. Yet, they are honoured of God just as fully as Abraham, Moses, and David, because they all stood before God 'accepted in the Beloved'!

3. God's choice of any, God's election, has nothing to do with what he sees in us. It is altogether a matter of grace; pure, free, sovereign grace. Gideon was a poor man, from a poor family; but God chose Gideon to lead his people. Barak was a weak, timid man, who would not act except by the counsel of a woman. Yet, the Lord used him to deliver his people. Jephthah was a bastard, cursed, unfit, legally banned, a man who had to bear the shame of his mother's debauchery all his life; who spent his days in utter vanity, until God called him by his grace. Samson was a spoiled brat, and acted like a spoiled brat right through his adulthood; but the Lord God used him mightily. David was the weakest and most insignificant of Jesse's sons; but he was God's chosen man. Of the six named in this verse, only

Samuel seems to have been a man of obvious usefulness and of commendable character from his youth. David was as well; but he did not appear to be outwardly. Read 1 Corinthians 1:26-31 and rejoice.

4. Faith in Christ does not prohibit anyone from honest employment in any field of service to God and men. A.W. Pink wrote, 'Five of the six men named in our text were judges who ruled over Israel, though they came from very humble callings. From this we may learn that faith is a spiritual grace suited not only unto the temple, but also to the judicial bench and throne; that it is needed not only by those who occupy positions in the private walks of life, but also by those who fill public office. Governors equally with the governed require to have a true faith in the living God: instead of disqualifying them for the discharge of their important duties, it would be of inestimable value to them.'

5. That which distinguishes God's elect from other people is God's grace alone. We cannot view these men and their deeds properly until we view them in the light of what is revealed in this chapter. The book of Judges gives us the historical narrative of their lives and deeds. Hebrews 11 gives us the light to see that which set them apart from others. Others have vanquished lions, put armies to flight, and subdued kingdoms. But yet their deeds were motivated and performed by base, sensual things. The exploits of Gideon and Barak, Samson and David, were things performed by faith, for the glory of God, and for the benefit of his people. That which is honoured here is not the mere names of men, but the work of God in and through men. Their faith was God's gift, their righteousness the righteousness of another. Their strength was the strength of Christ, made perfect in their weakness (1 Corinthians 4:7; 2 Corinthians 12:9). It is our God and our God alone who makes one to differ from another.

6. God's people in this world are still sinners in constant need of mercy, grace, and forgiveness. These men believed God; but their faith was far from perfect. They believed God; but they had much instability. They trusted Christ; but they were terribly unbelieving at times. They were godly men; but they had much sin in their lives. Their faith, like ours, was mixed with fear, at war with unbelief, weakened by lust and carnal reasonings. They were men of like passions with us. The best of men are only men at best. There is much for us to learn from these examples of faith. Our only hope of salvation is God's free and sovereign grace in Christ. Our only acceptance with God is the blood and righteousness of Christ. Our perseverance in faith is the result of God's perseverance in grace. Because he changes not, we are not consumed. Though there is much about us which breaks our hearts and humbles us with shame, that constantly makes us aware of our utter insufficiency for any good, and

our total unworthiness even to call upon the name of God in prayer; we have no cause for despair, if we trust Christ (Psalm 32:1-2; Romans 4:8; 8:1, 33-39; 11:29; 1 John 1:9-2:2).

7. Grace shines brightest when things appear darkest. God never leaves himself without a witness. In every age and circumstance, in every place and situation, when the Lord God intends to perform his works of grace he has just the right person, prepared by his own grace, to perform his work. These men all lived in dark, dark times; but grace shined brightly through them in the dark age in which they lived and served God.

The Right Men for The Right Time

In this chapter Paul clearly demonstrated his assertion that 'faith is the substance of things hoped for, the evidence of things not seen' (v. 1). He has shown us that 'by it the elders obtained a good report' (v. 2). The Holy Spirit has set before us numerous and remarkable examples of that faith that he works in the hearts of chosen sinners.

Many others might have been cited; but it was not needful for him to describe each example of God given faith in Old Testament history. Therefore, as he closes this great chapter, encouraging us to go on believing God, he simply names these six prominent believers (and all the prophets of God) who lived and died by faith in Christ, and gives us a brief, general description of their great acts of faith.

Men Raised Up

These men were raised up by God for the day in which they lived, each one raised up at precisely the right time for the work to which he had been appointed from eternity. The time was right for them and they were right for the time. They were, like the apostles, like Luther, Bullinger, Calvin, Gill, Toplady, Whitefield, Edwards, and Spurgeon, ordinary men. But men raised up by God in times of extraordinary crisis, for the good of his church and kingdom; for the preservation and furtherance of his gospel; for the glory of his own great name. Bear this in mind, their calling was extraordinary, their deeds were extraordinary, but they were ordinary men, men with the same faith God has given us, raised up by God for the day in which they lived; raised up to do the work they did for God's glory.

Who Can Tell?

As Mordecai said to Esther, so I say to you, 'Who knoweth whether thou art come to the kingdom for such a time as this?' (Esther 4:14). Some time ago, a friend of mine who was a bit disheartened by the things that had transpired in his life, began to find some encouragement in God's wise and good providence, and said to me, 'Maybe the Lord has something for me to do.' As I read the stories of these men, my heart dances with this thought 'Maybe the Lord has something for me to do.' 'Who knoweth whether thou art come to the kingdom for such a time as this?'

Gideon

Israel could not have been in much worse condition than they were when God raised up Gideon to deliver his people. Three judges preceded him (Othniel, Ehud, and Barak), who delivered them from the hand of their enemies. Yet, a fourth time they departed from their God and were made to groan under the yoke of an oppressor.

Oppression

Though the oppressors did not know it, and Israel seemed to be ignorant of it, God used the oppressors (Psalm 76:10) to make his people cry out to him! By the oppression of the wicked, the Lord God separated the precious from the vile and proved his people (Judges 2:16-19). It is in the darkest days of apostasy that Gideons shine bright. Trials and persecutions only strengthen faith. They never destroy it. They only destroy that which is false. Everything that can be shaken will be shaken. But those who are God's are made manifest by the very things that destroy the hypocrite (1 Corinthians 11:19).

The Midianites held Israel in bondage. So great was the number of those who had invaded their land, that they 'left no sustenance for Israel' and 'Israel was greatly impoverished because of the Midianites' (Judges 6:4, 6). But that was by no means the worst of it. Israel was so far and so completely turned away from God to the worship of Baal, that to oppose Baal was considered a criminal act, deserving of death (Judges 6:28-30). Yet God had promised 'the Lord shall judge his people, and repent himself for his servants, when he seeth that their power is gone' (Deuteronomy 32:36), and now, once again, he would prove his word good.

A Man Prepared

God found a man named Gideon, whom he had made to be a 'mighty man of valour' (Judges 6:12). God has no trouble finding the right man for the right job at the right time. He always has the right man ready, readied by his grace. As a mighty man of valour, Gideon was clearly a picture of Christ, of whom it is written, 'I have laid help upon One that is mighty. I have exalted One chosen out of the people'. Still, Gideon had to be prepared (Judges 6:12-14). No man will ever be fit to serve God until he finds all his strength in Christ. No man will ever look to Christ for strength until he knows his utter weakness. Thus it was with Gideon; thus it is still.

Only a man purged of all self-sufficiency will look to Christ for all sufficiency. Only a man purged of all strength is made strong in the Lord and 'a vessel fit for the Master's use'. 'For when I am weak, then am I strong.' God never uses an unprepared instrument; and the first part of the preparation process is to empty the chosen instrument of all self-sufficiency that he may thoroughly trust Christ, looking to Christ alone for grace and strength. Gideon's 'might' was to be his conscious weakness. As soon as that was realized, he would be forced to believe the Lord's declaration, 'Thou shalt save Israel'. Now, look at Judges 6:15. Gideon now asks, 'Oh my Lord, wherewith shall I save Israel? behold, my family is poor in Manasseh, and I am the least in my father's house.' Now the servant is ready! The Lord God responded to Gideon's acknowledged helplessness: 'Surely I will be with thee, and thou shalt smite the Midianites as one man' (verse 16). How blessed! When the believing heart realizes this, it exclaims confidently, 'I can do all things through Christ which strengtheneth me' (Philippians 4:13).

Who through faith subdued kingdoms, wrought righteousness, obtained promises, stopped the mouths of lions, Quenched the violence of fire, escaped the edge of the sword, out of weakness were made strong, waxed valiant in fight, turned to flight the armies of the aliens.

Hebrews 11:33-34

Chapter 43

Read: Hebrews 11:33-34

Nine Feats of Faith

Reading the things here declared, one might think, 'Faith appears to be omnipotent'. How else can these things be explained? How else can we believe this record? Our Lord declares that if we have faith in him, even as a grain of mustard seed, 'Nothing shall be impossible unto you' (Matthew 17:20). How can that be? The answer is just this: the strength of faith is the omnipotent arm of our God!

Let us look at these feats of faith. As we do, I will say little about the historical events to which they refer because it is obviously the intent of the Holy Spirit to move our minds and hearts above the carnal to the spiritual, to move our thoughts about the historical events themselves to those things represented by them.

How can we be certain of that? Look at the passage. The Holy Spirit does not specify whether Joshua or David subdued kingdoms, Samuel or David worked righteousness, Abraham or Joshua obtained the promises, Samson or Daniel stopped the mouths of lions. He does not specify the historical event because he wants us to apply each of these feats of faith to ourselves, because he would have us apply them to our own lives, because he would have us accomplish the same things by faith.

In Galatians 5:22-23 the Holy Spirit speaks of the fruit of the Spirit (the fruit of faith) as being nine fold. In these two verses, he speaks of the feats of faith as being nine fold. I cannot avoid thinking there must be a deliberate correlation.

1. 'Who Through Faith Subdued Kingdoms'

The word here translated 'subdued' has the idea of fighting to subdue, or contending like warriors on the battlefield to take a place. We are not told whether this refers to Joshua subduing Canaan or David subduing the kingdoms around Israel. The important point is this: the kingdoms subdued were those kingdoms that sought to keep Israel from obtaining that which God had promised them. Neither Joshua nor David subdued any kingdom that did not stand in the way of and oppose Israel's taking possession of the land God had given them.

The lesson is obvious. The Lord God has promised us an inheritance of everlasting salvation and glory in Christ. There are two great warring kingdoms, standing in the way of us obtaining the inheritance God has promised us in Christ: the flesh, the kingdom within (Romans 8:13; 1 Corinthians 9:27,) and the world, the kingdom without (James 4:4; 1 John 2:15-17; 5:4).

2. 'Wrought Righteousness'

These words, in their strict sense, refer to the exercise of judicial righteousness; the enforcement of law. Joshua wrought righteousness in executing the king and inhabitants of Hazor (Joshua 11). David wrought righteousness in his rule over Israel (2 Samuel 8:15). And Elijah wrought righteousness in slaying the prophets of Baal (1 Kings 18).

But in the context of Hebrews 11, these words are primarily intended to tell us that faith is that by which the believer is experimentally justified before God. Just as God gave the land of Canaan to Israel before any who entered it were born, so the Lord God justified us in Christ long before we came into this world. Still, Israel had to take possession of the land by the execution of justice. So, too, the believer must be justified by faith experimentally, justified before God by the execution of law and justice. Trusting the crucified Substitute, by whose blood justice is satisfied (Psalm 15:1-2).

Certainly, this working of righteousness also refers to the believer's behaviour; his way of life in this world. Men and women who believe God, endeavour to live by his standard; our lives being regulated by the Word of God.

3. 'Obtained Promises'

Abraham got Isaac. Jacob got the birthright. Moses delivered Israel. Joshua conquered Canaan. Gideon defeated the Midianites. David got the throne. They all obtained, by faith, what God had promised; despite the forces ranged against them.

So, too, you and I shall obtain every covenant promise of our God (redemption, pardon, justification, eternal life, and everlasting glory), all those promises of God in Christ Jesus, by faith in him. All the promises of God are in Christ and in him they are yea and amen, sure and certain!

4. 'Stopped The Mouths of Lions'
Just as both Samson and Daniel stopped the mouths of lions by faith, believers still stop the mouth of the lion that roars against them, by faith in Christ. Satan roars against us. Oh, how the lion of hell roars! But faith stops the lion's mouth (1 Peter 5:8; Romans 8:31-39).

5. 'Quenched The Violence of Fire'
Paul probably had in mind those three Hebrews who were cast into the fiery furnace. But the promise of God is to us 'When thou walkest through the fire, thou shalt not be burned; Neither shall the flame kindle upon thee' (Isaiah 43:2). The fiery darts of the wicked shall do us no harm, being quenched by the shield of faith (Ephesians 6:16). The fiery trials by which God proves us in the furnace of affliction shall only refine the gold of his grace. Nothing, child of God, shall harm you (1 Peter 3:12-13).

6. 'Escaped The Edge of The Sword'
Certainly David, Elijah, and Jeremiah escaped the persecutor's sword by faith (1 Samuel 18; 1 Kings 18; Jeremiah 39:15-18). There is no question that persecuted believers escape the edge of the persecutor's sword, by the grace of God. Believing God, even when beheaded, they escape the edge of the sword. That which is intended to be the instrument of death is the instrument of life for God's elect. But this line, like all those things written in the book of God, was written for us and about us.

The Sword of the Spirit, by which we are brought under the sentence of death, that Sword whose edge slays us in Holy Spirit conviction, that Sword proceeding out of the mouth of the King of kings and Lord of lords, is itself the source of faith, by which we escape the edge of the Sword, for it brings us to our knees before the throne of grace, suing for mercy in faith (Hebrews 4:12-16).

7. 'Out of Weakness Were Made Strong'
Samson, in his weakest hour, was out of weakness made strong. Hezekiah was, upon his deathbed, out of weakness made strong and became the father of Josiah, the progenitor of the Christ.

Can this apply to us? Of course it does! Notice, the text does not simply say that these were made strong when they were weak. It says, they 'out of weakness were made strong'! Here is the great source of strength for faith. When we are weak, then we are strong, for only when we are weak is Christ made to be our Strength and trusted as our Strength (2 Corinthians 12:1-10).

8. 'Waxed Valiant in Fight'

This phrase could refer to any of the Judges, or to David, or any of those kings in Israel who were valiant in war, or to any of those mighty prophets of old. But, again, the purpose of the Holy Spirit in this place is to teach us about faith and to encourage us in faith.

This is what he is teaching us. Poor, weak, helpless, insignificant, insufficient creatures like us, when walking in faith, are made strong in the Lord Jesus Christ and are made to wax valiant in the fight of faith by his omnipotent grace. Faith refuses to be intimidated by the fiercest opposition. Faith is undaunted by reason. Faith stubbornly refuses to give in to cowardice.

The kingdoms of the flesh and of the world will not stop faith in her path. Roaring lions may make us tremble; but they will be subdued. The violence of fire will not prevent faith from pursuing Christ. The persecutor's sword will not cause faith to give up Christ. Weakness will not cause faith to give up the fight. Faith waxes most valiant when she most depends upon her omnipotent Saviour.

9. 'Turned to Flight The Armies of The Aliens'

Did not Joshua put Ai and the five kings of the Amorites to flight (Joshua 10:1-10)? Did not David put to flight the armies of the Philistines at Baal-perazim, smiting them hip and thigh, from Geba to Gazer (2 Samuel 5:17-25)? So it shall be with all who believe, with all who trust the Lord Jesus Christ. We, too, shall put to flight the armies of the aliens: our sins, Satan, and the world (Exodus 15:11-18).

Who shall condemn to endless flames
The chosen people of our God,
Since in the book of Life their names
Are clearly writ in Jesus' blood?

He, for the sins of His elect,
Hath a complete atonement made:
And justice never can expect
That the same debt should twice be paid!

Not tribulation, nakedness,
The famine, peril, or sword,
Not persecutions, or distress,
Can separate from Christ the Lord!

Nor life, nor death, nor depth, nor height,
Nor powers below, nor powers above,
Nor present things, nor things to come,
Can change His purposes of love!

His sovereign mercy knows no end,
His faithfulness shall still endure:
And those who on His Word depend
Shall find His Word for ever sure!

A Sign Sought

Many pointed to the fact that Gideon asked for a sign from the Lord (Judges 6:17-23) as an indication of the weakness of his faith. But there is no indication that Gideon's request was a sign of weakness. Having found grace in the eyes of the Lord, he asked for a sign, not because he doubted, but because he believed! Not to prove the truth of God's word, but because he would prove the truth of his grace in the acceptance of his offerings he would bring to God (vs. 17, 18). The proof of this is in the fact that God did what he asked, accepted the sacrifice he offered, and blessed him.

Idols Destroyed

Gideon showed his devotion to and faith in the Lord God by tearing down the altar of Baal his father had built (Judges 6:25-26). Like his father Abraham, Gideon believed God and obeyed his command. This act of devotion and faith may not appear so great in the eyes of those unfamiliar with the culture in which he lived, but his deed was a display of tremendous valour for God. What Gideon did that night he did at the hazard of his life (Judges 6:30-33).

Enraged at the overthrow of the altar of their god, the Midianites gathered their forces together and with their allies came up against Israel for war. When we dare invade Satan's territory, when the church of Christ marches over the gates of hell, we must expect his fury. Gideon tore down his father's altar and destroyed his father's gods with the full awareness that he would incur the wrath of both his father and the Midianites. He did it for the glory of God and the good of his people.

Then, 'the Spirit of the Lord came upon Gideon' (Judges 6:34). That supplies the key to all that follows. That which Gideon accomplished, he accomplished not by his own might and power, but by the Spirit and power of God. So it is with us. We cannot overcome Satan, or even resist his temptations in our own strength. We cannot grow in grace and faith and love, or even continue in the grace of God by will. We can do all things through Christ who strengthens us. But we can do nothing of ourselves. It is only as we are strengthened with might by his Spirit in the inner man that we are prepared for the battles that lie before us.

Gideon's Infirmity

Gideon's infirmity was that he imagined he needed a large army to defeat the Midianites and deliver Israel (Judges 6:33-35). Little by little he was taught of God and learned that God is not dependent upon numbers. His work is never accomplished by the arm of the flesh. Gideon repeatedly spread the fleece, seeking signs to confirm God's word to him (Judges 6:36-40). And the very strongest believer is very much like him. We learn to walk by faith and not by sight only gradually, by degrees. Yet the Lord our God is patient and long-suffering toward his own. He bears with our infirmities and puts up with our weaknesses, ever remembering that we are dust (Psalm 103:8-14).

The Lord graciously granted Gideon the signs requested. He corrected his notion that a large army was needed. He took only a small fragment; and they were the ones who were scared to death! The Lord God declared, 'by the three hundred men that lapped will I save you' (Judges 7:7).

Then, when Gideon believed the Lord and obeyed his Word, God said, 'Arise get thee down unto the host, for I have delivered it into thine hand' (Judges 7:9). And he did! Thus the Lord used and worked mightily by one who was poor and little in his own eyes (Judges 6:15), a man who 'did as the Lord had said unto him' (Judges 6:27). Who knows, maybe he will do the same with you. Maybe he will do the same with me. May God be pleased to show us his will, make us know our own utter weakness and inability before him, and make us find our strength in his all-sufficient grace in Christ.

Our Faith God's Gift

Though faith in Christ is the gift of God, the operation of his grace in us by the power of the Holy Spirit, it is not a passive thing. Faith is not merely something God does for us. It is a grace given by which we live. It is an active, living principle of grace. It is something we exercise, not passively but actively, purposefully, intentionally.

Our lungs are God's creation and God's gift. They function by God's power. The air we breathe is God's creation and gift. It sustains us in life by the operation of God. Yet, the lungs are ours. We exercise them. They take in the air by which we live through activity on our part.

So it is with faith. It is God's gift. God's operation, and operates by God's power. Yet it is our faith. It is that which we must exercise. In other words, we live in this world by faith, ever looking to God our Saviour: resting in him, following him, serving him, and seeking to honour him.

The exercise of faith is as prominent and essential in spiritual life as the beating of your heart is in natural life. Where faith is absent, grace is absent and life is absent. I do not suggest, and the scriptures do not teach, that faith must be perfect or even strong. But where there is no faith toward God there is no life from God.

Without question, all who are born of God err greatly in many things and in many directions. This we know by painful experience, as well as by Divine Revelation. Still, if you have faith in Christ, even faith that is no more than 'a grain of mustard seed,' the mountain of your sin has been cast into the ocean of God's forgetfulness by the blood of Christ; 'and nothing shall be impossible unto you' (Matthew 17:20). If you have faith in Christ you are born of God. You have passed from death into life by God's almighty grace.

Divinely Given

Your faith in Christ is the gift of God. Faith is the heart's persuasion that God is true, the hearts persuasion of God's Truth (Christ). It is produced in us by the omnipotent power and grace of God the Holy Spirit by the preaching of the gospel (James 1:17-18; 1 Peter 1:23-25).

Divinely Sustained

Not only do we believe by the gift of God, we continue to believe by the constant supply of God's grace. Grace gave us faith; and grace keeps us in faith. Faith depends entirely upon God. Faith lives upon Christ by the unfailing supply of grace from the throne of God.

Divinely Activated

This faith, given and sustained by God is activated and energized by him, too. Our Saviour said, 'Without me ye can do nothing' (John 15:5); and we know it. If we turn to him, he must turn us. If we run after him, he must draw us. If we open to him, he must put his hand in our hearts and open the door himself. 'Faith worketh'. 'Faith worketh by love'. But all the work of faith is God working in us both to will and to do of his good pleasure.

Divinely Increased

It is God alone who causes our faith to grow and increase. Therefore, we pray, 'Lord, increase our faith' (Luke 17:5). 'Help, thou, mine unbelief' (Mark 9:24). Our heavenly Father causes all his children to grow in faith, to grow in the grace and knowledge of Christ by the instruction of his Word, the discipline of his grace, and the experience of his providence.

Divinely Focused

As it is God who gives us faith, keeps us in faith, activates our faith, and causes our faith to grow, so it is God alone who focuses our faith on Christ and keeps it focused on Christ. In all things, the Lord God commands, 'Look unto me'! And, blessed be his name, if we are his, he graciously forces us to look to him for grace. Faith looks to Christ alone for grace; saving grace, sustaining grace, and sanctifying grace.

Here, in Hebrews 11:33-34, the Holy Spirit directs our attention to nine specific feats of faith. In these nine examples of faith meeting great obstacles and overcoming them, we are taught that faith, leaning upon the arm of Omnipotence, accomplishes that which would otherwise be impossible. We understand that these great feats of faith were God's works accomplished through the instrumentality of men. Yet, this text speaks of them as works of faith performed by individual believers. Why? It is because that faith which God gives us and works in us is our faith.

'What Shall I Say More?'

As we come to the end of this chapter Paul, (rather than focusing on specific acts of faith as he has done in the first thirty-one verses of the chapter), lumps together numerous people who believed God from the time of the Judges on. He appears to list them randomly, ignoring any chronological connection. This is on purpose, by divine inspiration, to keep us from missing his purpose to teach us that faith is enough.

When I say that faith is enough, I am not talking about faith in the idea of having faith in something or someone. I am talking about true faith in the Lord Jesus Christ, as it is set forth in holy scripture. That faith is gospel faith in the Lord Jesus Christ, the Son of God; faith that bows and surrenders to Christ as Lord. This faith is the gift of God. This is the faith held before us in Hebrews 11.

Health, Wealth, Prosperity Preaching

Faith in Christ is not what most people in this age of spiritual darkness think it is, and does not bring the results in life that most expect it to bring. These days, people tend to think that faith in Christ is manifest by tangible things. 'If we have great faith, we have great success, great wealth, great health', and so on. 'Health, wealth, prosperity' preachers have built religious empires by teaching their heresy.

The God of heaven has been reduced by these religious con men to nothing more than a dispenser of gifts that gratify the basest lusts of men, and a god that can be manipulated by positive thinking. People are led to believe that faith in Christ is synonymous with prosperity, and that our failures in business, sicknesses, and earthly troubles are outside the purpose of God and beneath the dignity of true faith. Faith is made to be the elusive secret for elitist Christians to further a Hollywood lifestyle.

Contrary to Scripture

Such teaching is totally contrary to that which is revealed in Hebrews 11, totally contrary to the experience of all believers (past and present), and totally contrary to the entire revelation of God in holy scripture. In fact, the scriptures teach and our experience confirms just the opposite.

Faith in Christ is just as active, just as real, and just as powerful when all our earthly circumstances and experiences are distasteful; when we face deep personal loss, when our enemies appear to conquer us, and when all hope of comfort and external peace are gone. Faith takes us through the rivers of woe, through the fiery furnace of adversity, over the hills of difficulty, and through many stormy seas.

Faith is a conscious dependence upon the infinite character, power, grace, wisdom, and goodness of God. Faith understands that we are depraved men and women, plagued still with sin; full of personal weaknesses, vulnerabilities, and inadequacies, and horrid unbelief.

Carries Us Through

Faith in Christ carries God's elect through every possible situation, because Christ himself is the Anchor of our souls, because we are more than conquerors (not in ourselves, but) through him that loved us, redeemed us, intercedes for us, holds us, and rules the universe for us! The world may look upon us as pathetic, hopeless people, whose lives are total losses and utter failures marked by tragedy. But faith mounts us up on eagles' wings, carrying us through great loss with peace, joy, and hope in Christ (Isaiah 40:31).

Short-sightedness

We tend to measure far too much by the level of creature comfort we attain in life. If we can achieve a certain level, (Always measured by the level others achieve or fail to achieve!), we deem ourselves successful.

What short-sighted goals we set! Man, who was made to glorify God and enjoy him forever, thinks himself something if he has a bigger hut than his neighbour and enjoys the transient smiles of fallen mortals! Worms of the earth always feel best when they are buried in a pile of manure!

Faith in Christ has absolutely no connection with those things commonly associated with it. I do not mean to suggest that God's people do not enjoy earthly comforts. Some do, and some do not. Many of those described in Hebrews 11 were people of great earthly wealth and comfort. But none of them lived for such things. Their lives were not consumed with such base things.

Above Time and Circumstances

Faith in Christ enabled these men and women to do great things because faith in Christ caused them to live above the world, above time, above circumstances, and above their own mundane interests in this world. True faith teaches us, causes us, and enables us to set our affection on things above while living in the world (Matthew 6:31-33; Colossians 3:1-4; Titus 2:11-14).

Faith in Christ will see us through. Faith will carry us through every stage and demand of life, and ultimately deliver us into the presence of Christ in heavenly glory.

Women received their dead raised to life again: and others were tortured, not accepting deliverance; that they might obtain a better resurrection: And others had trial of cruel mockings and scourgings, yea, moreover of bonds and imprisonment: They were stoned, they were sawn asunder, were tempted, were slain with the sword: they wandered about in sheepskins and goatskins; being destitute, afflicted, tormented; (Of whom the world was not worthy:) they wandered in deserts, and in mountains, and in dens and caves of the earth. And these all, having obtained a good report through faith, received not the promise: God having provided some better thing for us, that they without us should not be made perfect.

Hebrews 11:35-40

Chapter 44

Read: Hebrews 11:35-40

Three Things Observed Among Believers

If you read the lives of God's saints in any age, you will observe three things about them, three things that make it impossible for unbelievers to understand them or their faith in Christ: 1. Diversity, 2. Unity, 3. Trials. We certainly see these three things in this last section of Hebrews 11.

Diversity

First, we see a great diversity in faith, not in the Object of faith, or in the doctrine of faith, but in the people of faith. Believers are not like cookies cut out by the same cutter. We do not all look alike, talk alike, or act alike. Without question, all believers are alike in many things. All seek to obey God. All seek to honour Christ. All seek to do good in this world.

Still, we are individuals, and the Lord deals with us personally and individually. He shapes each into the image of Christ. Each experiences the workings of God's providence in his life differently. Furthermore, the workings of God's providence are tailored to affect every detail of our lives, to bring us into conformity with Christ and to the glory of God. All this is accomplished by God's free grace (Romans 8:28-31).

Unity

Second, there is a great unity in faith. All God's people are one. All these men and women named (and unnamed) in these 40 verses are (not were) one in Christ. God's church and God's kingdom is one. In verse 40 Paul says, 'that they without us should not be made perfect'. That is to say, the body of Christ was not complete and could not be complete until each of his chosen, redeemed brethren has been brought into living, vital union with him by faith (Ephesians 1:22-23).

We are all loved, chosen, and adopted as the sons of God. We are all redeemed by the blood of Christ. We are all born of one Spirit. We all have the same Father and Elder Brother. We all have the same faith. We all have the same inheritance awaiting us. We are all going to the same home. We all have the same hope. May God give us grace to live in that blessed unity, for the glory of his name (Ephesians 4:1-7).

Trials

Third, verses 33-38 show us something that almost every believer learns very quickly and continues learning all the days of his pilgrimage through this world. Wherever faith is found, trials follow (Philippians 1:29). Wherever you find a man or woman who believes God, you are sure to find a person whose faith is tried, tried by God, tried for the purpose of doing him good (James 1:1-2, 12).

Triumphant Faith

Faith in Christ does not secure a life of ease in this world, but just the opposite. Faith in and obedience to Christ meant that Abel had to be hated by his own brother. Noah had to be the object of constant scorn and ridicule for 120 years. Abraham had to leave the splendour of Ur to live as a nomad his whole life. He was required to cast one son out of his house and sacrifice the other. Isaac had to bless Jacob and curse Esau. Jacob had to be brought down to Egypt. Moses had to be hid in a basket. He had to flee the wealth and the throne of Egypt. Jericho (the cursed city inhabited by God's enemies) had to be destroyed. God's spies had to be saved by a harlot. Gideon had to fight the Midianites with a rag-tag army of cowards. Barak had to go out against a king and army that terrified him. Jephthah had to sacrifice his only daughter to the Lord. Samson had to die with the Philistines. Samuel had to anoint a king to replace his beloved Saul. David had to be hunted like a rabbit, running from one cave to another. God's prophets had to be made a gazing stock, laughed at, scorned, and abused by men from generation to generation.

Dependence

Faith is dependence upon God, not upon self. It is just as real, just as active, and just as true when all circumstances are unfavourable; when we face great personal loss, when our enemies appear to conquer us, and when all hope of comfort and external peace are gone. Faith takes us through deep waters and stormy seas, through fiery trials and the wilderness of temptation; because faith is conscious dependence upon the infinite, omnipotent, eternal, immutable God. Faith is dependence upon the Lord Jesus Christ, our almighty Saviour. It is not the strength of our faith that sustains us and carries us through these things, but the strength of Christ, the Object of our faith. He is our Strength.

Faith in Christ realizes and acknowledges personal weaknesses, vulnerabilities, and inadequacies. When we are strong, we are terribly weak. But when we are weak, then we are strong. Faith carries us through every possible situation depending on the Lord our God

To the world, to our families, to our friends, our case may be pathetic, hopeless, a total loss and failure. But inwardly, faith mounts us up on eagles' wings, carrying us through great loss with the triumph of peace, joy, and hope in Christ (Isaiah 40:27-31).

I do not suggest that the believer never receives any of those things the world craves. We have examples in this chapter of some who did. But these things are not the end of life or the great goal of our existence. Faith enables us to set our hearts on things above while living here below, even in the most distressing circumstances imaginable (Colossians 3:1-4).

Triumphant

Faith carries the believer through every stage and demand of life, and ultimately delivers him into the presence of Christ. That is the message these first century believers needed; and that is the message we need. Yes, as we believe God, you and I too can do all things through Christ, who strengthens us.

'Through Faith'

In Hebrews 11:35-38 the Holy Spirit shows us how that faith both performs the most remarkable deeds and suffers the most astonishing hardships, looking to Christ, believing Christ, seeking to honour Christ. There is no task too great for our God, no task too great for one who believes God (vv. 33-34). There is no trial too great for any of us to endure, as we believe God (1 Corinthians 10:13; Philippians 4:12-13).

Faith's Pinnacle

As the Holy Spirit directed Paul in giving us this great chapter on faith, all through these forty verses, he seems to be moving in an upward direction, showing us one great act of faith after another, each succeeding event a little greater than the one before it. When chapter 12 begins, we are immediately confronted with a great cloud of witnesses in heaven. But here, right at the end of chapter 11, the Apostle is describing faith's pinnacle, faith's highest point, faith's greatest deeds; though the faithful be destitute, afflicted, tormented.

These men and women 'of whom the world was not worthy', by enduring their great trials even unto death, displayed a faith that is completely subject to Christ and bows submissively to whatever God is pleased to send; a faith so completely welded to Christ and one with him that imprisonment, torture, and death are deliberately chosen and preferred to apostasy from him.

A 'meek and quiet spirit' is of 'great price' in the sight of God (1 Peter 3:4). The meekness of faith is true meekness. It is that meekness that comes from the realization that God is God indeed, and we are his servants. Such meekness of faith bows to the will of God. It is faithful unto death, because it arises from an unshakable confidence in God's wisdom, goodness, and power.

Faith's Strength

The strength of faith is not in us, but in God our Saviour, the Object of our faith. Faith draws strength from him, believing his Word. Faith recognizes that 'the Lord God omnipotent reigneth' (Revelation 19:6). Our God sits on his throne, Sovereign over all the universe. 'He doeth according to his will in the army of Heaven, and among the inhabitants of the earth: and none can stay his hand, or say unto him, What doest thou?' (Daniel 4:35).

The believer understands that all the affairs of the universe are ordered by his heavenly Father, and ordered by God for his good. We know that our enemies can do nothing whatever against us without his direct permission. Satan could not touch Job nor sift Peter, until he got permission from their Redeemer to do so. What a blessed, sure resting-place this is for the troubled and trembling heart! This is 'a nail in a sure place'!

Believing God, we know all things work together for our good and his glory (Romans 8:28). Satan roars fiercely; but our God reigns supremely. His malicious designs are always overruled to accomplish God's good designs (Psalm 76:10). Faith in Christ causes and enables us to look beyond time to eternity. It anticipates the heavenly glory with confident assurance that 'the sufferings of this present time are not worthy to be compared with the glory which shall be revealed in us' (Romans 8:18).

Oh, gift of gifts! Oh, grace of faith!
My God, how can it be,
That Thou, who hast discerning love,
Should'st give that gift to me!

How many hearts Thou might'st have had,
More worthy, Lord, than mine!
How many souls more worthy far,
Of that pure touch of Thine!

Ah, Grace! Into the most unlikely hearts
It is Thy boast to come,
The glory of thy light to find,
In darkest spots a home!

Thy choice, O God of goodness, then,
I lovingly adore!
Oh, give me grace to keep Thy grace,
And grace to long for more!

What Does Faith Do?

Faith receives, embraces, and bows to Christ. Faith unites us to Christ. Faith believes Christ, trusting him alone for acceptance with God. But faith in Christ is not just a dream of 'pie in the sky in the sweet bye and bye'. Faith in Christ is the believer's way of life in this world. It is written, 'The just shall live by faith.'

That does not mean that we are made alive by our faith in Christ. It is not our faith that gives us spiritual life, but God's gift of life that gives us faith. So, when the scriptures declare that, 'The just shall live by faith', the meaning is that we live in this world by faith in Christ. That is what is set before us in Hebrews 11. What does this faith, by which all justified sinners live, do?

Faith Trusts God

We trust a God who is without limitation, the Infinite Lord God with whom nothing is impossible. That enables faith (faith in this great God) to look at impossibilities and smile in light of God's wisdom, power, and goodness (vv. 33-38).

Faith still subdues kingdoms. Christ has made us kings. Faith works righteousness (Romans 5:19), obtains God's promises (2 Corinthians 1:20), stops the mouths of lions (Romans 8:33-34), escapes the edge of the sword (Romans 8:35-39), out of weakness is made strong (2 Corinthians 12:9-10), waxes valiant in conflict (1 Corinthians 15:58), turns to flight the enemies (Romans 16:20), quenches the violence of fire (Isaiah 43:1-5) receives life from death (John 11:40-44), endures great trials (Romans 5:1-5), and obtains a better resurrection (Revelation 20:6).

Faith Turns Loss To Gain

Faith turns great loss into great gain and great failure into great triumph. We sing, 'Faith is the victory'; but we tend to think of mere temporal, earthly, creature comfort as victories achieved by faith. We aim too low! That is why the rest of the chapter is needful. Read verses 35-40 carefully.

The Holy Spirit does not identify the men and women he refers to in these verses, but they have been numbered in Heaven. Read *Foxe's Book of Martyrs* or *Men of the Covenant* or *The Reformation in England* or *The Scots Worthies* or *By Their Blood: Christian Martyrs of the Twentieth Century* or biographies of William Tyndale, Hugh Latimer, Jim Elliot, and Bill Wallace, and you will discover that throughout history countless brethren have faced great suffering and inhumane, barbaric executions. There were no thoughts of 'health, wealth, and prosperity' among them, they pressed on through their trials by faith. Faith did not deliver them from the experience of suffering and death, but faith carried them through triumphantly. If need be, faith will do so for you.

'They went about in sheepskins, in goatskins, being destitute, afflicted, ill-treated (of whom the world was not worthy), wandering in deserts and mountain, and in dens and in caves of the earth.' The allurements of this world had nothing for these faithful and often penniless brethren. They lacked all the creature comforts of life but what people of faith they were! What knowledge of God they experienced in their temporal deprivations! The world was not worthy of them, though the world considered them unworthy. God judges by different standards than the world; loss, deprivation, and poverty are no failures in God's sight. The only real failure is a failure to believe God!

What do all of these believers through the centuries tell us? 'When you can have it all, faith says Christ is better; and when you lose it all, faith says Christ is better.'

Faith Unites

It is this common faith that unites all God's elect in Christ. We have different cultures, come from different races, face different experiences, but faith in the Lord Jesus Christ sustains us throughout our days. Faith carries us through good times and bad, through abundant times and lean ones, through prosperity and poverty, through health and sickness, through births and bereavements, through peace and war. Faith unites us in hope, in life, in heart, in eternity, for faith unites us in Christ (vv. 39-40).

'And these all, having obtained a good report through faith, received not the promise: God having provided some better thing for us, that they without us should not be made perfect.'

Here the Spirit of God links believers from Old and New Testaments together, showing that there is a continuity and unity in our faith. There are not 'two faiths', one old and the other new, but one common faith among all God's people in all places and in every age. Believers in the Old Testament looked to Christ in the shadows of the law, through a Levitical priesthood and animal sacrifices. We see Christ in all the fulness and sufficiency of his substitutionary death on the cross and resurrection glory on the throne. They lived under the old covenant, while looking for the fulfilment of the new covenant in Christ. Their faith looked forward. Our faith looks back. Both those of old and believers today look in faith to the Lord Jesus Christ, trusting him alone as Saviour and Lord.

In trusting Christ, faith obtains a good report, a good report before God and a good report from God. Faith waits for the promise (1 John 3:1-2; Titus 2:11-14). Faith brings all God's elect into one inheritance of perfection, called 'the glorious liberty of the children of God'. All God's elect are one in Christ now. Soon, we shall be made perfect in one.

'And Others Were Tortured'

Paul, who wrote these words, was once a persecutor and tormenter of God's saints (Acts 8:3, 9:1). After God saved him, he endured the cruelties he once inflicted upon others (2 Corinthians 11:24-27). And he chose to do so, taking up his cross, following Christ (Acts 20:22-24).

'Tortured'

'And others were tortured, not accepting deliverance'. The word 'tortured' here means 'racked'. Those Old Testament believers were put on the persecutor's rack. Their bodies were stretched until their joints were ripped apart. That horrid method of torture was a favourite of the papists during the times of Rome's open persecution of God's saints. By such means the representatives of the pope tried to force believers to recant and deny their faith in Christ. By this fearful form of suffering the graces of God's people was tested and tried. But with believers the rack was impotent!

'Not Accepting Deliverance'

Deliverance was offered, but only at the price of apostasy. Two alternatives were set before them: deny Christ, or endure the rack; surrender the gospel, or be tortured by devils in human form. History tells us that believers were not only offered freedom from torture and death, but often were promised great rewards and promotions, if they would but recant. They steadfastly refused.

The Test

Thus, the real test was this. Which did these believers esteem more highly, the present comfort of their bodies or the eternal interests of their souls? Remember they were people of like passion with us. Their bodies were just as tender and sensitive to pain as ours. But their faith in Christ and hope of a better resurrection made them faithful unto death.

We face the same trial today, only without the rack. Multitudes lose their souls eternally for the temporary gratification of their bodies. Which do you esteem the more highly your body or your soul? Which do I esteem more highly? Our actions supply the answer. Which receives the more thought, care, and attention? Which is denied? Which is pampered?

'Not accepting deliverance'. They had bought the Truth at the price of turning their backs on the world, the world's religion, families and friends, bringing down upon themselves the scorn and hatred of all. They refused to sell the Truth (Proverbs 23:23) for earthly ease or even life itself.

'A Better Resurrection'

'Not accepting deliverance, that they might obtain a better resurrection'. Here is the basis of their resolve. These tortured saints were offered a 'resurrection' if they would deny Christ. They were offered a 'resurrection' from reproach to honour, from poverty to riches, from pain to ease and pleasure, from death to life. It was a 'resurrection' from the physical torture which threatened them (Hebrews 11:19). But their hearts were occupied with something far, far better than being raised up to earthly comfort, earthly honour, and a temporary reprieve from death. They anticipated that morning without clouds, when their bodies would be raised in glory, made like Christ's, and taken to be with Him forever. It was this blessed hope that supported their souls in the face of extreme peril and sustained them in torment.

'Mockings and Scourgings'

'And others had trial of mockings, and scourgings, yea, moreover of bonds and imprisonments'. No stone was left unturned in the persecutor's merciless efforts to destroy the faith of God's saints. Let us, when we are reproached for Christ's sake and ridiculed because of the gospel of the grace of God, remember these steadfast believers of old. We have not yet 'resisted unto blood' (Hebrews 12:4).

The sneers of men, the unkind words of puny mortals are nothing, compared to what others have endured. Even the bonds of breaking hearts and the imprisonments of souls crushed in adversity and bodies decaying with age are far less than our brethren before us have endured. More than that, the things we are here called upon by our God to endure for Christ's sake are nothing compared to what the Lord of Glory has suffered for us; or to the glory that awaits us! Read Matthew 5:10-12; 1 Peter 2:21-24, and 1 Peter 1:2-9.

Faith Enduring

In this 11th chapter of Hebrews the Holy Spirit is encouraging us to perseverance. In doing so, he has shown us numerous examples of faith in Christ. He has given us examples of devotion, sacrifice, consecration, and triumph. Here he gives us examples of faith enduring great trials and hardships for the glory of Christ.

The Holy Spirit's object here is to teach us that true faith must and shall be tried and proved by divine providence, tried and proved by enduring hardship, by suffering with Christ and for Christ. All the evils here enumerated were brought upon these saints of old solely and entirely because of their faith in Christ.

Faith's Portion

It has ever been the portion of faith, the portion of God's people in this world to be derided, reproached, insulted, and abused for their faith in Christ (1 Peter 4:12; 1 Corinthians 10:13; Philippians 1:29; Galatians 4:29). Our Lord declared, 'He that endureth to the end, the same shall be saved'. Faith, true, God given faith, must endure and will endure the trials and sorrows that inevitably accompany it. To all who believe, our Saviour's promise is: 'If we suffer, we shall also reign with him: if we deny him, he also will deny us' (2 Timothy 2:12; Revelation 3:5, 12, 21).

Count the Cost

It is criminal for any preacher to call men and women to faith in Christ without warning them in advance of the cost involved in following Christ. The fact is, 'we must through much tribulation enter into the kingdom of God' (Acts 14:22). The Lord Jesus tells us plainly that we should, before we make any profession of faith in him, sit down first and count the cost (Luke 14:28).

Our Saviour dealt with this matter openly and plainly. He expressly told all who came after him that following him, being his disciples, living by faith in him, meant daily taking up their cross and following him. Things have not changed. If we would follow Christ, if we would be his disciples, if we live by faith in him, we must daily take up our cross and follow him. The path of faith is sure to take us through waters of adversity, rivers of woe, and the fiery furnace of great sorrow. The Son of God himself endured these things. All the saints of ages past have endured them, so must we.

People Who Believed God

How did these saints of God meet such tribulation with patience, such hardness with meekness, and such persecution with unwavering loyalty? Where can we find such strength of faith?

The strength of faith is not in us. The strength of faith is not in faith. The strength of faith is Christ, the Giver. Faith is a gift of grace that draws strength from its Source. Drawing strength from God, faith in Christ draws down from heaven grace to help in time of need. Faith in Christ gives believing sinners steadfastness of purpose, noble courage, and tranquillity of mind in the midst of great adversity. As A. W. Pink put it, 'Faith makes the righteous as bold as a lion, refusing to recant though horrible tortures and a martyr's death be the only alternative.'

Yes, we are weak, weaker than water. Yes, faith often falters. Yes, believers fail oft and fall oft. But though the righteous man falls seven times a day, the Lord raises him up. And faith (divinely given and divinely sustained) will rise to the occasion, saying with Christ, 'the cup which my Father hath given me, shall I not drink it?' (John 18:11). Faith, God given faith, endures all things and endures to the end. Let's look at the examples before us in this passage.

The Dead Raised

'Women received their dead raised to life again' (verse 35). The historical reference to this is probably found in 1 Kings 17:22-24 and 2 Kings 4:35-37. Our Lord tells us plainly 'with God all things are possible'. As the Lord our God raised those two boys from the dead, and restored them to their mothers by the word of his prophets Elijah and Elisha; so he is able to raise our sons and daughters from the dead by the word of his grace today. Bring your children to the Saviour like Jarius brought his daughter, like the Canaanite woman brought her daughter, like the man brought his demon possessed son. Tell him, 'My child is grievously vexed with a devil!' Bring your children to God's prophet to hear God's Word. Pray for God's blessing upon the Word preached.

Turn Us

There is another application of this to us. You and I, as we look to Christ, have our languishing graces renewed to life through faith. Thereby we 'Strengthen the things that remain, that are ready to die' (Revelation 3:2). This is God's Word to his languishing people, 'Awake thou that sleepest, and arise from the dead, and Christ shall give thee light' (Ephesians 5:14). Still, we know all too well, that our languishing souls will never take the initiative (Song of Solomon 5:2). Faith responds to grace. It does not cause it! Let us cry, with languishing saints of old, 'Draw us, and we will run after thee ... Turn us, and we shall be turned!' John Owen writes:

> It may also be observed that the apostle takes most of these instances, if not all of them, from the time of the persecution of the church under Antiochus, the king of Syria, in the days of the Maccabees. And we may consider concerning this reason: 1. That it was after the closing of the canon of the scripture, or putting of the last hand unto writings by Divine inspiration under the Old Testament. Wherefore, as the apostle represented these things from the notoriety of fact then fresh in memory, and it may be, some books then written of those things, like the books of the Maccabees, yet remaining: yet as they are delivered out unto the church by him, they proceeded from Divine inspiration. 2. That in those days wherein these things fell out, there was no extraordinary prophet in the church. Prophecy, as the Jews confess, ceased under the second temple. And this makes it evident that the rule of the Word, and the ordinary ministry of the church, is sufficient to maintain believers in their duty against all oppositions whatever. 3. That this last persecution of the church under the Old Testament by Antiochus, was typical of the last persecution of the Christian church under antichrist; as is evident to all that compare Daniel 8:10-14, 23-25; 11:36-39 with that of the Revelation in sundry places. And indeed the martyrologies of those who have suffered under the Roman antichrist, are a better exposition of this context than any that can be given in words.

A Better Resurrection

The 'better resurrection' for which the saints of old hoped, the hope of which sustained them in times of great trial and severe persecution, was exactly the same as that for which God's saints today live in confident hope. They did not hope for a superior place in heavenly glory, but for something better than mere deliverance from temporal trouble. They lived and died in the confident hope of resurrection glory with Christ. That is the 'blessed hope' of faith.

Our assurance of the resurrection is much more than belief in a point of orthodoxy. It is faith in and hope in a Person. Christ is Himself our Resurrection. This is not some fool's philosophy. It is not a mere religious tranquilizer by which we are able to cope with the trials of life. This is the calm, confident assurance of believing hearts. It is the necessary, inevitable result of faith in Christ (John 11:25-26). The Lord Jesus Christ is the resurrection and the life of all who trust him; and all who trust him shall in the last day be resurrected with him. All who trust Christ shall, indeed, 'obtain a better resurrection!' Let me show you why I hope to obtain this 'better resurrection'. I live in hope of the resurrection for three reasons:

A Representative Resurrection

First, I have been resurrected with Christ representatively (Ephesians 2:5-6; Romans 8:29-30). When the Lord Jesus Christ arose from the grave, he arose as my Representative. All that he did and all that he experienced, all of God's elect did and experienced in him, by virtue of our representative union with him. His obedience to the law was our obedience (Romans 5:12, 18-21). His death as a penal sacrifice for sin was our death (Romans 6:6-7, 9-11; 7:4). This is our atonement! His resurrection was our resurrection. This is our life!

The resurrection of Christ is an indisputable fact of revelation and history upon which we rest our souls (1 Corinthians 15:1-8). Disprove the resurrection and you disprove the gospel. 'If Christ be not raised, your faith is vain; ye are yet in your sins' (1 Corinthians 15:17).

The bodily, physical resurrection of the Lord Jesus Christ necessitates the resurrection of all who are in Christ. That which has been done for us representatively must be experienced by us personally. We are members of Christ's mystical body, the church. If one member of the body were lost, the body would be maimed (1 Corinthians 12:12, 27). If one member of the body were lost, the Head would not be complete (Ephesians 1:22-23). These bodies of ours must be fashioned like unto his glorious body (Philippians 3:21; John 17:22).

Christ was raised as the firstfruits of them that sleep (1 Corinthians 15:20). The full harvest must follow. Christ is the second Adam. We have borne the image of our first covenant head and must bear the image of the second (1 Corinthians 15:21-23, 47-49). Christ has obtained victory over all that could hinder the glorious resurrection of his people: sin, death, hell, the grave, and the Devil (Colossians 2:13-15; Hebrews 2:14-15).

The covenant engagements of Christ as the Surety of God's elect are not complete until the hour of our resurrection (John 6:37-40). He shall soon present his bride before his throne, 'holy and unblameable and unreproveable' (Colossians 1:22). In that great day he will present all his elect to the Father, saying, 'Behold, I and the children whom the Lord hath given me.' For, 'there shall be one fold and one Shepherd' (Isaiah 8:18; Hebrews 2:13; John 10:16).

A Spiritual Resurrection

Second, I have experienced the resurrection of Christ in regeneration. The new birth is nothing less than a resurrection from the dead. To be born again by the Spirit of God is the first resurrection (Revelation 20:6; John 5:25; 11:25-26; Ephesians 2:1-4). This is beautifully illustrated in Ezekiel's infant (Ezekiel 16), the dry bones that were made to live by the Spirit of God (Ezekiel 37), and by the resurrection of Lazarus (John 11).

A Better Resurrection

Third, I believe the revelation of God concerning the resurrection (John 5:28-29). Our Saviour declared, 'Whosoever liveth and believeth on me shall never die.' God's elect never die! There shall be a resurrection of life at the return of Christ (1 Corinthians 15:35-44, 51-58; 1 Thessalonians 4:13-18). This will not be a secret rapture, but a glorious resurrection. The dead in Christ shall be raised. After their resurrection, all the saints living upon the earth shall be raised into glory. Then, there shall also be a resurrection of damnation (John 5:29).

The wicked and unbelieving shall be raised by the power of Christ in order to be judged and condemned. The believer shall be raised by virtue of his union with Christ in order to be judged and rewarded with everlasting glory. The wicked shall be raised in wrath. The believing shall be raised in love. The wicked shall be raised for execution. The righteous shall be raised for a wedding. Soon you and I will stand before the living God in judgment (2 Corinthians 5:10-11). Comfort one another with these words: 'Be steadfast, unmovable, always abounding in the work of the Lord, for as much as ye know that your labour is not in vain in the Lord' (1 Corinthians 15:59). Do you desire a part in the first resurrection and in that glorious resurrection to come? Awake (Ephesians 5:14), believe on the Lord Jesus Christ, and you shall never die.

'That They Might Obtain a Better Resurrection'

We must not forget that these Old Testament believers were men and women of like passion with us. They were made of the same stuff as we are. Their bodies were the same tender and sensitive flesh as yours and mine. They felt pain just like we do. Yet, the care they had for their souls was so great that they chose to endure the tortures of their persecutors, rather than deny their God and Saviour. Their faith in Christ was so dominant in their lives, and their hope of a better resurrection was so confident and sure that they refused to accept deliverance from the persecutor's torments at the cost of denying the gospel, 'not accepting deliverance that they might obtain a better resurrection'. May the Lord grant me, too, such confident faith and such a sure hope.

Choices

You see the issue is really the same today. Those believers described in Hebrews 11:32-35 preferred the loss of all things temporal, the loss even of life in this world, to the loss of Christ, the loss of their souls, and the loss of eternity. I cannot help thinking, 'What countless multitudes, like Esau, lose their souls eternally for the temporary gratification of the flesh!'

The issue was crystal clear. They had choices to make; and we do too. Which did these saints of God esteem more highly: the present comfort of their bodies or the eternal interests of their souls? The issue is just as clear today. Which do you esteem the more highly, your body or your soul? Which do I esteem more highly? The question is not hard to answer. Which receives the more thought, care and attention; which is 'denied', and which is chosen?

These men and women refused to accept a temporal 'deliverance', (when it could have been obtained so easily) because to have obtained deliverance would have meant the renunciation of their faith and apostasy from God.

Faith

It was 'through faith' that they made their costly, but noble choice. It was love for Christ, love for the truth, love for the gospel, that caused them to hold fast that which was infinitely dearer to them than an escape from bodily suffering. A. W. Pink wrote, 'They had "bought the Truth," at the price of turning their backs on the world and their former religious friends, and bringing down upon themselves the scorn and hatred of them. And now they refused to "sell the Truth" (Proverbs 23:23) out of a mere regard to bodily ease.'

Resurrection

Here is the thing that sustained them. 'Not accepting deliverance, that they might obtain a better resurrection'! The language here is figurative.

They were offered a 'resurrection' on the condition of denying Christ. They were offered a 'resurrection' from reproach to honour, from poverty to riches, from pain to ease and pleasure. It was a 'resurrection' from the physical torture and presumed death to life and ease (cf. Hebrews 11:19). But they refused that for 'a better resurrection'.

Their hearts were occupied with something far greater than earthly comfort and honour, or even earthly life. Their faith anticipated that morning without clouds, when Christ shall appear without sin unto salvation, when their bodies would be raised up in glory and made like Christ's. They endured their great trials with patience, because they hoped for that great day when they would be taken up to glory to be with Christ forever. It was this hope that sustained their souls in the face of extreme peril and horrible sufferings.

'That they might obtain a better resurrection'. Never imagine that the saints of God in the Old Testament were ignorant of these things. Nothing could be further from the truth. The resurrection has always been the top-stone in the building of faith (Job 19:25-26; Acts 24:14-16). The faith of the 'fathers' embraced 'a resurrection of the dead, both of the just and of the unjust'. This glorious resurrection will more than compensate for any pain, persecution, or loss we must endure here for Christ's sake.

Our Hope

We live in hope of the resurrection. With Paul, we say, 'If in this life only we have hope in Christ, we are of all men most miserable' (1 Corinthians 15:19). In making that statement Paul does not mean that the believer's life in this world is a sad, morbid life; or that it is really more delightful and pleasurable to live in this world without faith; or that were it not for the hope of eternal glory, the people of God would prefer not to live as they do in obedience and submission to our heavenly Father.

When Paul says, 'If in this life only we have hope in Christ, we are of all men most miserable', he means simply that if there were no eternal life in Christ, no eternal bliss of life with Christ in glory, and no resurrection, then the believer would be the most miserably frustrated person in the world. We would never have that which we most earnestly desire. We would never see the end of our hope. We would never embrace Christ, or be embraced by him. We would never see our Redeemer. Such a thought is the most distressing thought I have ever entertained. Nothing could be more cruel and miserable than to live in hope of seeing Christ, being with Christ, and spending eternity in the presence of Christ, only to die like a dog! 'If in this life only we have hope in Christ, we are of all men most miserable.' What a horrible thought! What a tormenting supposition!

But it is not the case. We live in hope of the resurrection; and our hope is both sure and steadfast, 'For I know that my Redeemer liveth, and that he shall stand at the latter day upon the earth: and though after my skin worms destroy this body, yet in my flesh shall I see God: whom I shall see for myself, and mine eyes shall behold, and not another; though my reins be consumed within me' (Job 19:25-27). In sickness I am calm, because I live in hope of the resurrection. In sorrow I am peaceful, because I live in hope of the resurrection. In trial and affliction I am at ease, because I live in hope of the resurrection. In bereavement I am confident, because I live in hope of the resurrection. And I hope to die in confidence and joy, because I live in hope of the resurrection.

'Persecuted for Righteousness' Sake'

It has always been the lot of God's people in this world to suffer persecution at the hands of men, to suffer persecution at the hands of those who profess to be God's people. The cause of this relentless persecution is the gospel of Christ, the offence of the cross. 'Persecuted for righteousness' sake'! As Cain persecuted Abel and Ishmael, Isaac, so it has been throughout the ages, and so it shall be until time shall be no more.

The words of Jeremiah describe the condition of God's church in all ages and in all places in this world. 'Our necks are under persecution … We get our bread with the peril of our lives because of the sword of the wilderness … For this our heart is faint; for these things our eyes are dim' (Lamentations 5:5, 10, 17). Persecution is the lot of God's saints in this world (Matthew 5:10-12; Romans 8:34-39; Galatians 5:11; 6:12; Philippians 3:18-19; 2 Timothy 3:12). Sometimes the persecution is open and violent. Sometimes it is very subtle. But persecution is ever the lot of God's saints in this world.

The Persecutors

The persecutors of God's people are not usually ignorant barbarians, but men and women who are highly educated, of great respectability in society, high rank, political power and religious influence. Magistrates, governors, princes, kings, queens, popes, prelates, priests and preachers have all dipped their hands in the blood of God's saints. Such facts are so shocking that our historians and educators try as much as possible to explain them away, to find excuses for them; and invent horror stories about God's people that make such persecutions seem justifiable when they must be mentioned.

Those who have thirsted for the blood of God's saints have never been content merely to hurt, or punish, or even kill them. They have invented the most cruel, barbaric forms of torture imaginable to inflict as much pain as possible before the objects of their hellish hatred died.

God's Purpose

Why has God allowed such persecutions? What is his purpose? Unlike their persecutors, God's saints know and understand that the Lord God is in absolute control of all things and all men. 'Our God is in the heavens. He hath done whatsoever he hath pleased.' If he permits wicked men to violently abuse his people, he has good reasons for doing so. I cannot pry into the mind of the infinite Lord God. I know nothing about God's secret will. But those things that are revealed are revealed for our learning. And these things he has revealed.

All our trials come from God our heavenly Father, even when they come by the hands of wicked men. 'All things are of God'. Our trials are intended by God to strengthen our faith in Christ and make us grow in the grace and knowledge of our Saviour. 'Tribulation worketh patience, and patience experience, and experience hope' (Romans 5:1-5). By our trials our heavenly Father teaches us sympathy with and compassion for one another. By temptations, trials and persecutions, we are taught to lean on our Saviour, finding grace all-sufficient in him. Trials are designed of God to wean us from the world, set our hearts on heaven, and make Christ more precious. These trials, especially those offences that come because of the gospel, separate the precious from the vile (Matthew 13:21; Luke 8:13; 1 Peter 1:7).

That faith which is 'the gift of God' endures to the end. Only that faith which comes from God endures the testing of God. In the furnace gold and silver are made brighter. Dross is consumed. So it is in the furnace of affliction. True faith is made better. False faith is consumed.

Compare Daniel 3

We are given a strikingly solemn example of this in Daniel 3:13-30. The fires in that furnace in Babylon did not hurt Shadrach, Meshach, and Abednego. Those three men did not even have the smell of smoke on them when they came out of the furnace. The fires by which they were proved only destroyed their bonds! But they consumed the Babylonians who threw them into the furnace! Then, when Shadrach, Meshach, and Abednego came out of the burning and fiery furnace, the king promoted them. And far more importantly, God was honoured as the result of their trial in the fiery furnace (v. 29).

More Precious Than Gold

True faith is more precious than gold; and our faith itself is only made better by the fire that tries it. But the Holy Spirit would have us understand that 'the trial of your faith' (the trial itself) is more precious than perishing gold (1 Peter 1:7). The trial of faith is precious to us because it makes God's promise sweet. Our trials are precious to our brethren because one believer's endurance of hardship strengthens another in faith. Our trials are precious to our God because he is honoured by that faith that endures the trial. And the trial of our faith will be found 'precious' when the Lord Jesus comes again in his glory (2 Thessalonians 1:10). Our bitterest trials here will only serve, in the end, to make our heavenly inheritance sweeter and more glorious. 'For our light affliction, which is but for a moment, worketh for us a far more exceeding and eternal weight of glory' (2 Corinthians 4:17).

'And Others'

These few verses describe some of the heavy trials and afflictions to which many of God's saints in the Old Testament were subjected.

'They were stoned'. Because God's saints were counted as a people who were harmful, corrupting, destructive to society, they were stoned to death. Stoning was a form of capital punishment appointed by God to protect society as a whole from those who would destroy it by murder, rape, moral decadence, and idolatry (Leviticus 20:2, Joshua 7:24, 25). But that which God ordained for good, Satan perverted for evil. 'The devil is never more a devil nor more outrageous, than when he gets a pretence of God's weapons into his own hands' (John Owen).

'They were sawn asunder', as wild beasts who were feared by men. There is no record in scripture of anyone being put to death this way, though tradition tells us that God's prophet Isaiah was slaughtered by this barbaric method of execution.

'Were tempted'. They were tempted by their persecutors to repudiate their faith in Christ by the bait of having their lives spared, of being delivered from death. No doubt they were tempted of Satan to doubt the goodness and grace, power and faithfulness, mercy and love, promises and tender mercies of God; but they were steadfast.

'Were slain with the sword'. Those words would be more accurately translated, 'they died in the slaughter of the sword'. They were slain, as was Abel, because they believed God, trusting Christ alone for acceptance with him, denying salvation by any other means.

Saul slaughtered those priests of God who were faithful to the Lord (1 Samuel 22:18-21). Israel slaughtered God's prophets under the reign of

Ahab and Jezebel (1 Kings 19:10). Papists have exceeded countless multitudes in their insatiable thirst for the blood of God's saints. The Holy Spirit tells us that the whore, Babylon, is 'drunk with the blood of the saints' (Revelation 17:6). History verifies that fact repeatedly.

'They wandered about in sheepskins and goatskins' as people unfit for society. They were driven out of their homes and forced to live like animals, reduced to wearing the skins of wild beasts, instead of clothes woven by man. Any day, any one of these wanderers could have rejoined their families and former friends, enjoyed their society, and shared their comforts. But they preferred to live as wandering beasts than to deny Christ. They loved not the world. They loved not themselves. They loved their Saviour.

'Being destitute, afflicted, tormented'. 'Destitute' means they were deprived of the ordinary necessities of life. Neither relative nor friend would intervene for these banished ones. 'Afflicted' has reference to their state of mind. They were not stoics without emotion. They felt the pain of these hardships as acutely as anyone else would. There may be a reference here to Satan's harassing torments because of their inward struggles with horrid unbelief. They were 'tormented' by the taunting jeers of men, the assaults of Satan, and the lusts of the flesh with which they had to contend.

'Of whom the world was not worthy'. See the difference between God's estimate of his people and the world's. God regards his people as 'the excellent' of the earth in whom is his 'delight' (Psalm 16:3). The people of this world are altogether ignorant of it, but the fact is, all the benefits of providence they enjoy they enjoy because God's saints yet dwell among them in this world. God's people really are 'the salt of the earth'. Their presence stays the hand of divine judgment (Genesis 19:22), and brings down God's blessings upon the earth (Genesis 30:27). Their prayers secure divine healing (Genesis 20:17). Their presence brings both sunshine and rain upon their neighbours. Child of God, if your neighbours knew how much they benefit from you, rather than trying to run you out of town, they would be making your house payments for you!

'They wandered in deserts, and in mountains, in dens and caves of the earth.' The word 'wandered' suggests a wandering about as a stranger in an unknown place. It is the term used in reference Abraham in verse 8, and Hagar in Genesis 21:14. It is used in reference to wandering sheep in Matthew 18:12.

So long as we are in this world we are wanderers and strangers. The world makes us wanderers and strangers. Let us make ourselves wanderers and strangers. This world can never provide a home, a resting place, or an inheritance for our souls. It provides nothing for us but empty deserts, mountainous obstacles of trouble, and cold, damp, dark dens. But that is okay. That is just fine 'For I reckon that the sufferings of this present time are not worthy to be compared with the glory which shall be revealed in us' (Romans 8:18). Oh, may God give us grace ever to live with eternity before our eyes, with eternity in our hearts, for Christ's sake.

The Family of God

Here God the Holy Spirit tells us much about the family of God. The family of God, the church of God, and the kingdom of God are synonymous. All who are chosen by God the Father, redeemed by God the Son, and born again by God the Holy Spirit are members of his church, his family, and his kingdom.

Family Members

Who is in this family? You will notice that Paul first speaks of 'these all', referring to all those he has described in this 11th chapter of Hebrews. But he is not limiting himself to those who are specifically named. He is talking about all those men and women who believed God in the Old Testament era. Then he speaks of 'us', referring to all who believe on the Lord Jesus Christ in this gospel age. Then he speaks of them and us being 'made perfect' together.

In other words, he is telling us that the whole family in heaven and in earth, the family of God (Ephesians 3:15), the church of God, the kingdom of God is one great family, a family more numerous than the sands upon the seashore and the stars of the sky. The family of God is made up of all God's elect, all true believers, all the redeemed. The church of God really is one body, one indivisible family, one holy kingdom. All who are in Christ of every age, nationality, and language, throughout all the ages of time, and throughout all the earth are one family. It includes all the blessed company of the redeemed. The family of God is known and spoken of by many names in the book of God. This family is the body of Christ and his bride, the temple of God and the household of faith, God's royal priesthood and holy nation, the church of the Firstborn and the Israel of God.

Membership in 'the family of God', does not depend upon anything earthly. It does not come by natural birth, but by new birth. No preacher can bring you into this family. The waters of baptism cannot immerse you into this family. Parents cannot bring their children into the family of God. You may have been born to the most faithful parents in the world; but you were not born an heir of heaven. To belong to the family of God you must be born again. No one but God the Holy Spirit can make you a living member of this family. It is his special function and prerogative to bring chosen, redeemed sinners into this family by the washing of regeneration and the gifts of life and faith in Christ.

The mere exercise of your will cannot put you in the family of grace. A beggar may sooner become a king's son by his own choice than you and I could become the sons of God by our will. Entrance into the family of God is God's work alone (John 1:11-13; Romans 9:15-16; Galatians 4:4-7; Ephesians 1:3-6; 1 John 3:1-3).

One Family

The scriptures describe all God's people as one family (Ephesians 3:15). Why is it important for us to realize that God's church is one family? Why does God the Holy Spirit refer to all who are in Christ as the family of God?

All true believers are called a 'family' because we all have one Heavenly Father. We are all children of God by faith in Christ Jesus. We are all born of one Spirit. We are all sons and daughters of the Lord Almighty. We have all received the Spirit of adoption, whereby we cry, 'Abba Father' (Galatians 3:26; John 3:8; 2 Corinthians 6:18; Romans 8:15). We no longer look upon the holy Lord God with a cringing dread and fear. We no longer think of him as One always ready to punish us. Rather, we lift our eyes heavenward and look up to our God with tender confidence, as our reconciled and loving Father, as One who has forgiven all our sins, put away all our iniquities, and received us graciously for Christ's sake. We see him now as One who is full of compassion and pity. We came to him like the prodigal and he ran, fell on our necks, and kissed us. Those words, 'Our Father which art in heaven', are no longer merely the words of a prayer we learned as children in Sunday School. They are the sweetest words imaginable to our hearts.

All true believers are called the 'family' of God because we all rejoice in, have confidence in, trust in, and are named after one great and glorious name (Ephesians 3:14, 15). That name is the name of our great Head and Elder Brother, Jesus Christ the Lord. Just as a common family name is the uniting link to all the members of an earthly clan, so the name of Christ unites all believers together in one vast family in heaven and earth. As living members of Christ, we all, with one heart and mind, rejoice in one Saviour. Every heart in this family is built upon Christ as the only object of hope. Every tongue in this family will tell you that 'Christ is all'.

God's people are all called the 'family' of God, because as the sons and daughters of God and brothers and sisters of Christ, all true believers are heirs of God and joint heirs with Christ (Romans 8:14-19; John 17:1-5,

22). And we are called the 'family' of God because there is such a strong family resemblance among all who are born of God (Philippians 3:3, 9).

The Father's Promise

What has God our Father promised to do for his family? We are told in Hebrews 11:39-40 that our brethren in the Old Testament could not be made perfect, the family could not be completed and finished, without us, because God has provided some better thing for us. The Lord God has promised to make his family perfect! What does that mean? How are we to understand this?

The Lord God shall complete his family. Every adopted son shall be brought into the fulness and joy of sonship by God's sovereign grace. Every elect, redeemed sinner shall be brought into the blessed union of life and faith with Christ. Before God gets done with this world, all Israel shall be saved (Romans 11:25-27).

All the family shall be made perfect in Christ, perfectly one before God; perfect in heart and soul, mind and body! Yes, when God gets done, his whole family shall honour him forever (Ephesians 2:1-7).

Wherefore seeing we also are compassed about with so great a cloud of witnesses, let us lay aside every weight, and the sin which doth so easily beset us, and let us run with patience the race that is set before us. Looking unto Jesus the author and finisher of our faith; who for the joy that was set before him endured the cross, despising the shame, and is set down at the right hand of the throne of God. For consider him that endured such contradiction of sinners against himself, lest ye be wearied and faint in your minds. Ye have not yet resisted unto blood, striving against sin.

Hebrews 12:1-4

Chapter 45

Read: Hebrews 12:1-4

'Looking Unto Jesus'

The Holy Spirit is urging us to go on in faith, to persevere to the end, running with patience the race that is set before us, enduring hardship, overcoming difficulties, resisting temptation, laying aside every weight of care that would hinder us and the sin that so easily besets us. In a word, the Lord God here calls for every believing sinner to make whatever sacrifice is necessary, and do whatever it takes, no matter what the cost may be, and follow Christ.

The claims of grace are universal. The Lord God claims dominion over our whole life. If we would follow Christ, nothing can be held in reserve. Either he is Lord of all, or he is not Lord at all.

Upon what grounds can such sacrifice, such commitment, such consecration and devotion be expected? How can reasonable, responsible men and women be expected to live such a life? What will inspire such devotion? What will effectually motivate a person to such wholehearted consecration? We find the answer in Hebrews 12:2.

The only way we can run the race set before us, the only way we can live in this world by faith, the only way we can enter into the glory and bliss of eternal life with Christ is by 'looking unto Jesus, the Author and Finisher of our faith'. Oh, may the Lord give us grace to be found looking unto Jesus! Salvation is 'looking unto Jesus'. If we would persevere in faith, if we would continue in the grace of God, if we would keep our hearts in the love of God, we must ever be found 'looking unto Jesus'.

The Object of Our Faith

The Lord Jesus Christ is the solitary object of our faith. These three words, 'looking unto Jesus', are much, much fuller than our English translation suggests. They are immense. The words would actually be more accurately translated, 'Looking away unto and into Jesus'.

Salvation is 'looking unto Jesus'. Salvation begins, in the experience of it, looking to Christ (Isaiah 45:22). Salvation continues 'looking unto Jesus'. Salvation ends similarly, 'looking unto Jesus' (1 John 3:2). It is written, 'And they shall see his face' (Revelation 22:4).

The Holy Spirit calls for us to turn our eyes away from everything else and fix them upon the Lord Jesus Christ alone. If we would be saved, we must look to Christ alone. If we would continue in the grace of God, we must look to Christ alone. Let him have no rival. Look away from that great cloud of witnesses. They will be a hindrance to faith if they keep you in anyway from looking to Christ. Look away from yourself. Looking to yourself will keep you from looking to Christ. Look away to Christ for eternal life; for redemption, justification, faith, repentance, mortification, sanctification, and preservation. Look away from the course you must run. If you spend your soul's energy looking at the course, you will soon be overwhelmed. Look away from other runners in the race. Anything, anyone to whom you look, to any degree, takes your eyes off Christ. Look to him alone and look to him always.

These words, 'looking unto Jesus', suggest that as we run our race looking to Christ alone, we must ever be looking into him. We must look away to Christ, with the eye of faith, ever gazing into his infinitely glorious Person. Faith begins with but a glimmering revelation of the light of the glory of God in the face of Jesus Christ. The more we look unto Christ the more fully we see him; and the more fully we see him the more we see into him and perceive who and what he is.

The Author of Our Faith

Let us always be found 'looking unto Jesus the Author' of our faith. The word translated 'author' is another word that is full of meaning. It is one of those Greek words that has no exact equivalent in English. This is the word that is used in Hebrews 2:10 when Paul calls the Lord Jesus Christ, 'the Captain of our Salvation'. It comes from a root word that means 'commence'. Here, Paul holds the Lord Jesus Christ before us as that One who is the Author of faith. He is the One who commences faith. We would have no faith, if he did not give it to us and work it in us by the omnipotent power of his grace (Ephesians 1:19; 2:8; Philippians 1:29; Colossians 2:12).

But there is more here than that. Notice that the word 'our' is in italics, indicating that it was added by our translators. The scriptures universally teach that Christ is the One by whom we have that faith that looks to him alone as its Object. But the intent of the Holy Spirit here is to teach us that Christ is the One who is the great pioneer and example of faith.

That is to say, if we would know what it is to live and walk in this world by faith, we must look to Christ as the Pioneer who struck out the path and blazed the trail before us. Multitudes lived by faith in the Old Testament. Multitudes have lived by faith since. Multitudes live by faith today. But, if we would find a man who truly and perfectly lived by faith, if we would find an example to follow, we must look away from all others to Jesus, the Author, Captain, Pioneer, the One in whom our faith is perfected.

Yes, our blessed Saviour lived in this world as a man by faith, ever trusting God. Let us follow his perfect example. He said, concerning the Lord our God and his God, 'I will put my trust in him' (Hebrews 2:13). God the Father put his trust in his Son as our Surety in the covenant of grace (Ephesians 1:13). And God the Son put his trust in the Father as a Man while he lived in this world. What an example he is! What a pioneer trail he blazed for us to follow! He walked with God, looking always unto the Father, speaking and acting in childlike dependence upon the Father.

By faith he looked away from all discouragements, difficulties, and oppositions, committing his life and his cause to the Lord his God; who had sent him, to the Father whose will he had come to fulfil. By faith he resisted and overcame all Satan's temptations. By faith he endured all the trials brought upon him by his Father's wise and good providence. By faith he performed all those signs and wonders in which the power and love and salvation of God were symbolized.

Before he raised Lazarus from the grave, he thanked God who heard his prayer. By our Saviour's example we are taught what it is to believe God, what it is to live by faith. Let us ever be looking unto Jesus the Pioneer of our faith. He trusted in God. He gave us the command, 'Have faith in God', out of the fulness of his own experience (Proverbs 3:5-6).

The Connection

'Wherefore', be sure you get the connection between Hebrews 12 and what has gone before. This word 'wherefore' looks all the way back to Hebrews 10:35-39, where Paul urges us to patiently, doggedly continue in the faith, assuring us that we will need much grace to give us the patience and fortitude with which to endure unto the end. Then, in chapter 11, he gives us those great examples of faith, patience, and perseverance drawn from Old Testament history. In Hebrews 12 he picks up the admonition.

The Cloud of Witnesses

'Wherefore seeing we also are compassed about with so great a cloud of witnesses'. There is an allusion here to spectators at the ancient Olympic games. But witnesses are our brothers and sisters who have gone before us into glory. Specifically, these witnesses refer to those Old Testament saints mentioned in chapter 11. But it certainly includes all who have gone before us into heaven, because the body of Christ, the people of God, are one. Nor are these merely spectators at a games. They are men and women who have run the race before us, finished their course, and won the prize. Now, they are a cloud of witnesses urging us on in the race.

The word translated 'witnesses' is really the word from which we get our word 'martyr'. It is a word full of meaning and instruction. These witnesses are people who all voluntarily laid down their lives for Christ. They are people who bore on earth, and continue to bear in heaven, witness to Christ; to the blessed sufficiency of his grace, to his unfailing faithfulness, and to the glorious majesty of his person. Such a witness is a martyr by definition.

They are presently witnesses of those of us who are still running the race. We must not make more or less of this than the scriptures assert. This much is certain, God's saints in heaven have a keen and constant interest in his kingdom on earth.

The Charge Given

'Wherefore seeing we also are compassed about with so great a cloud of witnesses, let us lay aside every weight, and the sin which doth so easily beset us, and let us run with patience the race that is set before us'.

First, Paul calls for us to join him in laying aside every weight that hinders us in our race. Ancient Greek athletes stripped themselves of all encumbrances. The Apostle says, 'Let us, like those who have gone before us into heaven, lay aside every weight.' Obviously, he is talking about those things that weigh heavily upon us, those things that press us down and hinder us from running the race. Lay aside the terrible burden of the law that you cannot bear. The Lord God has laid it aside. Let us lay it aside. Take the weight and burden of your sin and lay it down, lay it on Christ, and quit carrying it. Our God has laid it aside. Let us lay it aside (Romans 6:11). Literally, Paul says, 'Having laid aside every weight and the sin which doth so easily best us, let us run with patience the race that is set before us'. Take all the weight and burden of your heart's care and lay it upon his broad shoulders, 'casting all your care upon him; for he careth for you'! It is both foolish and wrong for us to spend our energy and time dwelling upon and carrying burdens that we can do nothing about. Let us also, with deliberate purpose, lay aside every earthly care that would keep us from running the race set before us (Matthew 6:25-34).

Second, he says, 'Let us lay aside the sin which doth so easily beset us'. No doubt, these words may be applied to many, many things, many besetting sins. Indeed, we must not let sin have dominion over us. We must say no to the flesh and to all worldly lusts. But, if you read the words carefully, you will see that Paul uses a definite article, 'the', and refers to 'the sin' that so easily besets us all as one sin. He uses the singular form of the word 'sin', not the plural. He is talking about one, single sin that besets us all, one sin that constantly wraps around us, entangles, and trips us up. It is the same thing Jeremiah said about himself (Lamentations 1:14). The sin that so easily besets us, that is so easily and constantly committed, that so much hinders us and dishonours our God, is unbelief. Unbelief, more than anything else, hinders us in our race. Unbelief caused the disciples to cry, 'Master, carest thou not that we perish?' Unbelief caused Martha and Mary to question the Lord's goodness. Unbelief caused Peter to sink as he walked across the stormy sea. Unbelief keeps us from seeing the glory of God in the work of his grace and in the works of his providence (John 11:40). Unbelief causes our hands to hang down, makes our knees weak, and turns our feet off course!

Third, the Apostle calls for us, laying aside every weight of care and the sin that so easily trips us up, to 'run with patience the race that is set before us'. The Amplified Version paraphrases this admonition well.

> Therefore, then, since we are surrounded by so great a cloud of witnesses [who have born testimony to the Truth], let us strip off and throw aside every encumbrance (unnecessary weight) and that sin which so readily (deftly and cleverly) clings to and entangles us, and let us run with patient endurance and steady and active persistence the appointed course of the race that is set before us.

The race that is set before us is the course of our individual lives. Each course has its own obstacles, hills, valleys, and difficulties. But it is the course set before us by God our Father and Christ our Redeemer. The arena is this present evil world. The course is set before us in the Word of God and by divine providence. The race is a race that must be run. It requires effort, constant strain, relentless endurance, perseverance, patience, and determination. The Prize is Christ (Philippians 3:7-14). Read verse 2 and learn how to run this race.

'Looking Away'

The word 'looking' would be better translated 'looking away!' The only way to run this race is to look away from ourselves, our weaknesses, our troubles, the world, the cares of the world everything! Look away unto 'Jesus', Our Saviour, Our Redeemer, Our Covenant, Surety, Our Lord! Look unto him by faith. Look into him. Dive into the mystery of his person, his offices, his works, and his grace! For he is 'the Author of our faith'. He is the sole Object of our faith (2 Timothy 1:8-12).

'The Race'

The book of Hebrews, from start to finish, is an inspired admonition to perseverance. It is an inspired motivation to faith, constantly holding before us both the example of Christ as our guide and the accomplishments of Christ as our motive. In the face of trials and temptations on every hand, we are called upon to endure unto the end and persevere in the faith, to go on following Christ. We must not quit. We must not give up. We must not go back, though heresies abound on every side, though temptations of every kind allure us away from our Saviour, though troubles come hard on the heels of each other.

Many Pictures

The believer's life is compared to many things that picture the absolute necessity of perseverance in faith. We are in a warfare that will not end until we have left this world and entered into heavenly glory with Christ. We are engaged in a work, a labour, a cause from which there is no rest until our work is done. In Hebrews 12 it is compared to a race.

Our life in this world is a race, a race with a starting point, a finish line, and a prize (1 Corinthians 9:24; Philippians 3:14). Contrary to what most seem to think, the prize is obtained not when the race is begun, but when it is done (Philippians 3:3-14). It is not he who begins the race and runs well for a season that wins the prize, but he who finishes the race. It is not he who runs fast, or even he who runs well, but he who runs to the end who wins the prize. 'The race is not to the swift, nor the battle to the strong' (Ecclesiastes 9:11).

Perseverance and Preservation

The book of God teaches both the preservation of God's elect by grace and the perseverance of all believers in grace, eternal security in Christ and the endurance of faith.

Yes, it is true, the Lord Jesus Christ gives his sheep eternal life, and they shall never perish. All who are born of God are kept by God. All who are saved by the grace of God are kept saved by the grace of God. Not one of God's elect shall fail to obtain eternal glory with Christ (Ecclesiastes 3:14). There is no possibility of failure with our God.

We have been chosen and predestined to obtain God's salvation (Ephesians 1:3-6). The Lord Jesus Christ purchased and obtained eternal redemption for us (Hebrews 9:12). Our Surety has taken possession of heaven for us (Hebrews 6:20). And we are sealed by God the Holy Spirit unto the day of redemption (Ephesians 1:13-14). Yet, the Word of God is crystal clear, we must persevere unto the end. It is written, 'The righteous also shall hold on his way, and he that hath clean hands shall be stronger and stronger' (Job 17:9). 'He that endureth to the end shall be saved' (Matthew 10:22). 'We are made partakers of Christ, if we hold the beginning of our confidence steadfast unto the end' (Hebrews 3:14).

We are to persevere in faith, looking to and seeking Christ unto the end of our days on earth. 'Cast not away therefore your confidence, which hath great recompense of reward. For ye have need of patience, that, after ye have done the will of God, ye might receive the promise. For yet a little while, and he that shall come will come, and will not tarry. Now the just shall live by faith: but if any man draw back, my soul shall have no pleasure in him. But we are not of them who draw back unto perdition; but of them that believe to the saving of the soul' (Hebrews 10:35-39).

The Finisher of Our Faith

Let us ever look away to the Lord Jesus Christ as the Finisher of our faith. The word here translated 'finisher' seems to have been coined by Paul himself. It is found nowhere else. Christ is the Object of faith. Christ gives faith. Christ sustains faith, and Christ consummates, completes, and finishes faith. Paul explains what he means by the word 'finisher', or consummator, in the rest of the verse.

The Joy Before Him

The Lord Jesus has finished faith, that is to say he has finished that whole work that makes him the Object of faith, has finished that for which faith looks to him, and has finished his own life and example of faith, because he is that One 'who for the joy that was set before him endured the cross, despising the shame, and is set down at the right hand of the throne of God.'

With those words, the Holy Spirit here tells us how Christ finished faith. The word 'for' could be properly translated in two ways. Both translations are accurate. The word could be translated 'instead of', and it could be translated 'because of'. An accurate explanation of this text allows that we interpret the word both ways. This is how the Lord Jesus Christ finished that great work of redemption by which he has become both the Object of our faith and the Example of it.

Instead of the joy set before him, our blessed Saviour endured the cross. 'For ye know the grace of our Lord Jesus Christ, that, though he was rich, yet for your sakes he became poor, that ye through his poverty might be rich' (2 Corinthians 8:9).

Because of the joy set before him, the Lord Jesus Christ endured the cross. 'The joy set before him', the joy that sustained him in all his soul's trouble, sorrow, and agony was the joy of saving his people (Isaiah 53:10-11), magnifying the law of God and making it honourable (Isaiah 42:21), glorifying his Father (John 12:28), and the joy of attaining the glory he had with the Father as our Mediator and Surety from eternity (Psalm 2:8; John 17:5; Hebrews 10:10-14; Psalm 21:1-6).

The Cross Endured

In order to save us the Son of God, the Lord of Glory, the Darling of Heaven, voluntarily 'endured the cross, despising the shame'.

> O what shall I do my Saviour to praise,
> So faithful and true, so plenteous in grace;
> So strong to deliver, so good to redeem,
> The weakest believer that hangs upon Him?

With what words can such a Saviour be praised? He who endured the ignominy of the cross, despising the shame, because of his heart's love for and his soul's determination to ransom our souls, deserves infinitely greater praise than we can give him to all eternity! Because of his great love for us, the Lord Jesus Christ endured the cross. He would not go back. He would not give up. He would not quit until he had poured out his life's blood unto death for us! Yes, he endured all the wrath and justice of God and endured to the end.

The Shame Despised

Because he loved us, the Lord Jesus despised the shame of the cross. What can be more difficult for a man to bear than shame? Yet, as Moses despised the riches of Egypt, counting them nothing, so the Lord Jesus despised the shame of the cross, that he might have us freed from sin and forever glorified with him. He counted all the shame of the cross to be nothing: all the shame heaped upon him by men; all the shame of all of our sin being made to be his; all the shame of our guilt imputed to him; all the shame of being made a curse for us; all the shame of One abandoned by God. Our Saviour despised it all, counted it all as nothing, for the joy of having his elect with him in glory forever! Now the shame is all gone! He who endured the cross, despising the shame for us, even unto the end, 'is set down at the right hand of the throne of God.' His work is finished! He has entered into his rest. His glory is full! His soul is satisfied!

The Goal of Our Faith

Let us therefore encourage our hearts, ever looking away to Christ as the Goal of our faith. As he overcame and has been seated in his Father's throne, so too, as we follow him, persevering to the end, enduring whatever trial he sends us, despising whatever shame he has ordained, we shall soon be seated with Christ in his throne. Soon our work will be finished. Our rest will begin. Our glory will be full. Our souls will be satisfied!

'Consider Him'

In all things, in all circumstances, it is both our wisdom and strength, and our consolation and inspiration to look away from ourselves and our circumstances to Christ; to 'consider him'. Ever consider him as he is set forth in holy scripture (John 5:39). Open the book of God and behold him of whom the book speaks. Consider your Saviour, child of God, in humble prayer and meditation, seeking grace from God to know him and, knowing him, to be conformed to him in all things (Philippians 3:8-10).

In Trial

But these two verses specifically call upon us to focus our hearts and minds upon our Saviour when we are enduring trials and hardships. Clearly, it is the intention of God the Holy Spirit that, as we consider him, we should constantly bear in mind the infinite contrast between his sufferings and ours. As long as we are in this world, we must suffer (John 15:20; Hebrews 5:8). We must through much tribulation enter the Kingdom of God (Acts 14:22; 1 Peter 4:13). But our sufferings fade into insignificance when we consider him.

Consider Christ, always consider Christ. Before you make any decision, before you do anything, before you go anywhere, consider Christ. Throughout your race, thoughtfully consider him. Ever bear in mind who he is: your God, your Saviour, your merciful and faithful High Priest. Ever remember what he has done for you. Constantly calculate the debt you owe to him. Seek his will. Weigh everything, make every decision considering what is best for his glory, the interests of his kingdom, the service of the gospel, and the welfare of his people.

'Consider him ... lest ye be wearied and faint in your minds.' If we would but consider Christ that would, in great measure, keep us from being wearied and fainting. In the world we have tribulation, but faint not, Christ has overcome the world (John 16:33). Consider him in faith. Trust him. Believe his Word. Rest upon his promises. That will help to keep you from weariness in your race, in your warfare, and in your trials (Romans 8:18; 2 Corinthians 4:16-18).

If we faint not, Christ must be the singular Object of our faith, the Food of our souls, the Strength of our hearts, and the pattern of our lives (Philippians 2:5-16; 1 Peter 2:21-24).

Contrast

Look at v. 4 and you will see that it is the contrast between our Lord's suffering and ours that the Holy Spirit intends for us to bear in mind. Our trials, temptations, and troubles, our conflicts with sin, our opposition from those who despise the grace of God, and the many trials of life have really cost us very little. We have not yet resisted to the shedding of our blood. Our Redeemer did! Let us calculate and count the cost of following Christ (Luke 14:28). And, counting the cost, as we 'consider him', we will run with patience the race that is set before us. Soon we will win the prize (Galatians 6:9; Romans 8:18). We are in a state of warfare with the world, the flesh, and the devil (Galatians 5:17; Romans 7:14-23). Count the cost, considering Christ, and like our Master and his faithful servants of days gone by we will not faint (Acts 20:24; 21:13). If we cannot stand now what will we do in the swelling of Jordan? (Jeremiah 12:5).

Awake our souls, away our fears,
Let every trembling thought be gone;
Awake and run the heavenly race,
And put a cheerful courage on.

True 'tis a strait and thorny road,
And mortal spirits tire and faint;
But they forget the Mighty God,
Who is the Strength of every saint.

Swift as an eagle cuts the air,
We'll mount aloft to Thine abode;
On wings of love our souls shall fly,
Then we shall be at home with God!

When the Spirit of God tells us to consider Christ, he is telling us to ever remember and bear in mind who he is. Nothing more inspires faith, confidence, and a sense of security in this world like the blessed knowledge of Christ. He is the mighty God (Isaiah 9:6). He is the infinitely Holy God-man, our Mediator (1 Timothy 3:16). Our Lord Jesus Christ is both our omnipotent Saviour and our sympathizing Saviour, able and willing to save us (Hebrews 7:25).

The Spirit of God would have us constantly consider our Saviour's mediatorial offices. He ever speaks of Christ and teaches all who are taught of him ever to consider Christ. He is our everlasting Surety. He is our Prophet, Priest, and King. The Lord Jesus Christ is our mighty Advocate in heaven.

We should constantly consider our Saviour's mission, that for which he came into this world in human flesh. He came into this world for the singular purpose of saving his people from their sins for the glory of God (Matthew 1:21; John 12:28). He had no other aim, no other purpose, no other motive, no other goal.

When we are called of God to endure trials and afflictions for his name's sake, then we should especially remember and consider the patience with which our blessed Saviour endured all that he suffered for us. What relentless contradiction, what never-ceasing opposition he suffered from sinners and for sinners! He was opposed by his own kinsmen after the flesh (John 7:5). He was opposed by those very sinners for whom he suffered.

When he was born at Bethlehem, there was no room for him in the inn. He was not wanted. When he was just a small baby, Herod tried to kill him. His parents were forced to flee with him into Egypt that the scriptures might be fulfilled. Our Saviour declares in Psalm 88:15, 'I was afflicted and ready to die from my youth up: while I suffer thy terrors I am distracted'.

From the commencement of his ministry until its end he endured the unbroken, relentless, 'contradiction of sinners against himself'. He endured Satan's temptations, the slanders of men, the unbelief of his own disciples, the betrayal of his friend, mockery and shame, and all the horror of Calvary in our room and stead. And in his hour of greatest sorrow he was abandoned by the very sinners he came to save, and abandoned by his Father, because he was made to be sin for us!

Our Lord Jesus Christ felt keenly that contradiction. Let us never imagine otherwise. He was the man of sorrows and acquainted with grief. He cried, 'Reproach hath broken my heart; and I am full of heaviness: and I looked for some to take pity, but there was none; and for comforters, but I found none' (Psalm 69:20). James Montgomery wrote,

Go to dark Gethsemane, ye that feel the tempter's power;
There your Saviour's conflict see, watch Him there (O bitter hour!)
Turn not from His griefs away, learn of Jesus Christ to pray.

Follow to the judgment hall, view the Lord of Life arraigned;
O the wormwood and the gall! Oh, the pangs His soul sustained!
Shun not suffering, shame, or loss, learn of Him to bear the cross.

Calvary's mournful mountain climb, there, adoring at His feet,
Mark that miracle of time, God's own sacrifice complete;
'It is finished', hear Him cry, learn of Jesus Christ to die.

Early hasten to the tomb, where they laid His breathless clay;
All is solitude and gloom, who hath taken Him away?
Christ arisen meets our eyes, see Him seated in the skies!

In the midst of all that our blessed Saviour suffered any man might be expected to collapse, but the God-man set his face as a flint, until the work was finished (Luke 9:51; Isaiah 50:7). He would not turn back. He came here to redeem us, knowing full well the price by which we must be redeemed; and he voluntarily determined to pay it because of his great love for us. When we are tempted to murmur against his providence, give up the race, or find ourselves becoming weary and faint, 'consider him'.

The Holy Spirit tells us in verse 1 that we must lay aside every weight and the sin that easily besets us. We must lay aside every weight of carnal care and the horrid sin of unbelief if we would run with patience the race that is set before us. In verse 2 he tells us how to run this race with patience and how to run to the end. 'Looking unto Jesus the author and finisher of our faith; who for the joy that was set before him endured the cross, despising the shame, and is set down at the right hand of the throne of God.' Looking unto Jesus is not merely an occasional glance in his direction, or an occasional thought about heavenly things. What the Spirit of God is telling us to do is this: fix your eyes on Christ exclusively, looking away from everything else, ever focusing your heart and mind upon him.

That is not too difficult as we begin to run the race. But after a while we tend to get distracted, obstacles arise; the cross-country race gets difficult, and we get weary of the race. You see, the race we are running is not a sporting event, but a warfare. It is not merely a race for a crown, but for life; and the course of the race set before us carries us through hostile, enemy territory.

In addition to all the other things that might hinder us in our pursuit of Christ, we meet with opposition on every hand, from within and from without. So Paul was inspired by the Holy Spirit to use yet another motive to inspire our steadfastness in faith. He has told us that the Lord Jesus Christ is the Author and Finisher of our faith. Our all-glorious Christ looked upon the saving of our souls as the joy of his own soul. In order to obtain that great joy (our everlasting salvation) he endured the cross, despising the shame. And, having finished the work of our redemption, he sat down at the right hand of the throne of God.

Failure to 'Consider Him'

Now, may God give us grace ever to 'consider him'. How many mistakes I have made because I did not 'consider him'. How often I have behaved recklessly because I did not 'consider him'. How often I have needlessly hurt others because I did not 'consider him'. How often I have hesitated when I should have run because I did not 'consider him'. How often I have run when I should have waited because I did not 'consider him'. The little word 'for', connects what Paul says here with the race described in verses 1-2. It connects this matter of considering Christ to looking to Christ. Paul has urged us to consider Christ throughout this Epistle, ever holding him before us as the example we must follow, after whom we must pattern our lives; by whom we are constantly inspired to faith, obedience, and perseverance. But he uses a different word on all three occasions.

Observe

In chapter 3, verse 1, Paul writes, 'Wherefore, holy brethren, partakers of the heavenly calling, consider the Apostle and High Priest of our profession, Christ Jesus.' The word translated 'consider' here means to observe fully, to behold, observe and perceive. In v. 4 of chapter 7, we read, 'Now consider how great this man was, unto whom even the patriarch Abraham gave the tenth of the spoils.' The word translated 'consider' here means to look closely, like a spectator in court who has an intense, personal, experimental interest in the affairs of the court. You and I are only spectators in the affair of redemption. But we are spectators with an intense personal interest.

Analyse

But the word translated 'consider' in Hebrews 12:3 is altogether different from the words used in chapters 3 and 7. Here the word is really a mathematical term. It is the word from which we get our word 'analyse'. It means to weigh proportionately, to compare, to consider again intensely.

When you begin to think that faith in Christ costs too much, that the opposition is too great, that obedience is too costly, that the cross is too heavy, the Holy Spirit here says, 'Think again! Consider him!' And he does not leave us to guess about what he means. 'Consider him that endured such contradiction of sinners against himself'. Whenever we begin to imagine that our path is too rough, too costly, too demanding, let us look away from ourselves and consider him who endured being made sin for us, who endured suffering all the wrath of God for us, and blush with shame. Is any cost too great, any burden too heavy, any duty too demanding for Christ?

And ye have forgotten the exhortation which speaketh unto you as unto children, My son, despise not thou the chastening of the Lord, nor faint when thou art rebuked of him: For whom the Lord loveth he chasteneth, and scourgeth every son whom he receiveth. If ye endure chastening, God dealeth with you as with sons; for what son is he whom the father chasteneth not? But if ye be without chastisement, whereof all are partakers, then are ye bastards, and not sons. Furthermore we have had fathers of our flesh which corrected us, and we gave them reverence: shall we not much rather be in subjection unto the Father of spirits, and live? For they verily for a few days chastened us after their own pleasure; but he for our profit, that we might be partakers of his holiness. Now no chastening for the present seemeth to be joyous, but grievous: nevertheless afterward it yieldeth the peaceable fruit of righteousness unto them which are exercised thereby. Wherefore lift up the hands which hang down, and the feeble knees; And make straight paths for your feet, lest that which is lame be turned out of the way; but let it rather be healed.

Hebrews 12:5-13

Chapter 46

Read: Hebrews 12:5-13

Our Father's Rod

Every wise and good father has a rod by which he corrects his sons and daughters, by which he disciplines his children and focuses their attention. Our heavenly Father is a wise and good Father. Hebrews 12:5-11 tells us much about our Father's rod.

One great evidence of our Father's love for us is his rod of chastisement. When we are in trouble, when our hearts are heavy, I cannot think of anything that would be more helpful to our souls than the realisation of that fact.

Sorrow

In this world of sin, sorrow is everywhere. All who live in this world suffer many bitter things, sorrows that are deeply felt, leaving scars that never quite heal. The fact of human suffering is something that baffles philosophers and sociologists, politicians and religious leaders, moralists and educators. Try as they may to eradicate pain and poverty, it only gets worse.

The glaring fact that men and women in this world refuse to acknowledge is that all sorrow, all pain, all adversity is the result of sin. Because we live in a sin-cursed world under the judgment of God, because our human race is a race under the wrath of the Almighty, our world is a world of hurt and woe.

The Unbeliever

When the unbeliever, the man of the world, has to face pain and sorrow, he looks upon his hardships either as a matters of 'luck', or 'fate', or as things which must be blamed on someone. If his child is born with a severe handicap, or one of his family is permanently injured by an automobile accident, it is 'bad luck'. In the face of such things he either becomes bitter and cynical, or he shrugs his shoulders and tries to cope with fate with as much cheerfulness as he can muster.

The Believer

For the believer things are different. We trust God who is almighty, our heavenly Father who 'worketh all things after the counsel of his own will' (Ephesians 1:11). We know that God is love, that he loves us with a peculiar, distinguishing love. He has adopted us as his sons and daughters. He is our Father; and we are his children.

We do not feel pain any less than others. In some ways we feel it more acutely. When a child of God looks into the face of a deformed baby, or sees his teenage boy or girl maimed by some accident, as he holds the weak hand of a dying wife, as he thinks about the whole of human suffering and misery, he cries from the depth of his tortured soul, 'Why, O Lord, Why?' 'Why do the righteous suffer?'

Often our sorrows are aggravated by the apparent indifference of our God, our heavenly Father. How often the heavens seem silent and empty. We cry out in despair with the psalmist, 'Why standest thou afar off, O Lord? why hidest thou thyself in times of trouble?' (Psalm 10:1) These are questions that need to be answered. But they can only be answered by God himself. And he has answered them for us in Hebrews 12:5-11.

Consolation

As he instructs us in this matter of suffering, urging us to endure the Father's chastening rod, the Holy Spirit reminds us of a consoling fact in verses 5 and 6. 'And ye have forgotten the exhortation which speaketh unto you as unto children, My son, despise not thou the chastening of the Lord, nor faint when thou art rebuked of him: For whom the Lord loveth he chasteneth, and scourgeth every son whom he receiveth.'

The opening words of verse 5 are not incorrect, but they could be (and I think should be) translated as a question. Paul is not saying, 'You have forgotten', but 'Have you forgotten?' The word 'exhortation' would be better translated, 'consolation'. In my opinion, the opening line of verse 5 would be more accurately translated 'And have ye forgotten the consolation which speaketh unto you as unto children?' This is not intended to be an accusation, but a challenge.

The passage Paul is quoting here is Proverbs 3:11-12. 'My son, despise not the chastening of the Lord; neither be weary of his correction: For whom the Lord loveth he correcteth; even as a father the son in whom he delighteth.' This is a blessed word of consolation that we often need. Therefore it is often given in the book of God (Deuteronomy 8:5; Job 5:17; Psalm 94:12; James 1:2-3, 12; Revelation 3:19).

Love Not Wrath

We must never look upon our Father's chastisements as acts of anger, vengeance, or wrath. He is not punishing us for our sins as a judge executing the sentence of law upon us. That could never be! The Lord God punished our sins to the full satisfaction of his law's infinite justice and wrath in our Substitute, the Lord Jesus Christ, at Calvary.

Because our God's rod is the rod of our heavenly Father's love, not the rod of divine justice, we must take care that we 'despise not the chastening of the Lord'. The Lord God corrects his children in love as our Father. The very word 'chastening' implies instruction. The Lord by chastening us instructs us. The shepherd's rod was not for beating his sheep, but for guiding and protecting them (Psalm 23:1-4).

This is called 'the chastening of the Lord' because every chastening, every afflictive providence, is appointed by God, and is to be seen by us as his work. It is ordained by him, governed by him, limited by him, and overruled by him for our good and his glory! When we understand this, we will cease to look upon our trials and hardships as nauseous, loathsome things, and begin to esteem them as wonders of mercy. Mysterious? Yes! But still, wonders of mercy. Whatever my pain is, my Heavenly Father sent it. If he sent it, he will do me good by it. William Cowper understood this. That is why he could write, though he was constantly bombarded with afflictive circumstances …

God moves in a mysterious way His wonders to perform;
He plants His footsteps in the sea and rides upon the storm.

'Whom the Lord Loveth He Chasteneth'

When we understand that the afflictions, trials, and heartaches we endure in this world are not accidents or the result of blind fate, but rather the works of our heavenly Father; when we understand that they are brought to pass for the specific purpose of making us grow in faith, in grace, and in the knowledge of Christ, our hearts are comforted and our souls strengthened. Those things that might cause us to faint in the way become the very things that inspire faithfulness, devotion, and perseverance. Thus, we read, 'My son, despise not thou the chastening of the Lord, nor faint when thou art rebuked of him: For whom the Lord loveth he chasteneth, and scourgeth every son whom he receiveth' (vv. 5, 6).

Divine Rebuke

These chastisements are divine rebukes, and should be received as such. Let us not faint when we are 'rebuked of him'. Our heavenly Father has many ways of rebuking, reproving, and convincing us. He does this by his Word, his Spirit, the preaching of the gospel, and by his wise, unerring, good providence. He rebukes us for our sins, convinces us of them, and graciously forces us to acknowledge them and confess them; not because he is angry with us, but because he loves us. Afflictions are the black dogs by which God chases the evil he hates from the people he loves.

Tokens of Love

Paul tells us not to faint under the stroke of our Father's rod and tells us why we shouldn't. 'For whom the Lord loveth he chasteneth, and scourgeth every son whom he receiveth' (v. 6). Our Father's chastisements are tokens of his love for us. This statement is both a declaration of distinguishing love and an assurance of divine care. And it is a promise of divine acceptance. The fact that he will not leave us to ourselves, the fact that he disciplines us is an indication that he has received us in Christ as his own children.

Humble Submission

In verses 7-8 the Holy Spirit tells us that the difference between believers and those who merely profess to be believers is this: while religious hypocrites rebel against God's providence, believers humbly submit themselves to the will of God. I do not mean that there is no rebellion in the believer. Every child of God knows better than that. But the scriptures do clearly teach that the man or woman who trusts Christ will, by the grace of God, bow to Christ. 'If ye endure chastening, God dealeth with you as with sons; for what son is he whom the father chasteneth not? But if ye be without chastisement, whereof all are partakers, then are ye bastards, and not sons' (vv. 7-8). When our Father lays his rod upon our backs our only and our wisest course is to bow to him. Snuggle up as close as you can. The closer you snuggle up to him the lighter will be the strokes of his rod. One of Luther's friends who was terribly sick, covered with sores, and bed-ridden, was asked how he felt. Pointing to the ulcers that covered his body, he said, 'These are God's gems and jewels wherewith he decks his best friends. To me they are more precious than all the silver and gold in the world.' God's corrections are pledges of our adoption. We should always look upon them as distinct tokens of his distinct love and favour. God deals with us as with sons, when he refuses to leave us alone (1 Corinthians 11:32). Those who are without chastisement are not sons. The word 'bastard' refers to one born of an unfaithful, adulterous wife; a child of fornication. Here it refers to one who wears God's name by profession, but without right. Not all who suffer are sons; but all sons do suffer. The wicked suffer because of their impenitence, the righteous for God's glory and their good.

God's Purpose

In verses 9-10 the Lord shows us his wise and gracious purpose in chastening us with his rod. Thank God, he is not like us! He never chastens his children when there is no need, or without a purpose, or because he is angry! His rod is a rod of love, not of anger and wrath. Did he not say, 'Fury is not in me' (Isaiah 27:4)? Our Father's object in our afflictions is that we might grow in faith and in love, that we might grow in grace. He never strikes without purpose. His rod is the rod of instruction. The fact is, we read God's Word most clearly when our eyes are wet (Psalm 94:12; 119:65-72). God's purpose in all things, and distinctly in the exercise of his rod, is 'that we might live, that we might be partakers of his holiness' (v. 10). But how do our trials make us partakers of God's holiness? Our holiness before God is altogether his work of grace. We have no holiness except that which he has given us and made us in Christ. Our only righteousness before God is Christ (1 Corinthians 1:30). God's holiness spoken of here does not refer to his moral character or to that holiness which he gives, which we have in Christ by grace. Here the word simply and only means 'separation'. By the loving exercise of his rod, our Heavenly Father separates our hearts from the world, the wheat from chaff, the precious from the vile (Proverbs 6:23; 15:31).

The End

Read verse 11 and learn what our Father's ultimate end is in all our temporary adversities, trials, heartaches, and afflictions. 'Now no chastening for the present seemeth to be joyous, but grievous: nevertheless afterward it yieldeth the peaceable fruit of righteousness unto them which are exercised thereby.' The more you beat a walnut tree, the more fruit it gives. The more God chastens his children, the more fruitful they are. His vine is most productive when it bleeds. He prunes it to make it fruitful (Galatians 5:22-23). If chastisements did not hurt, they would not be chastisements (1 Peter 1:3-9). Yet, with the blessed assurance of our Father's immutable faithfulness and love, we can, even with broken hearts and weeping eyes, live in peace (2 Corinthians 4:17-5:1; Philippians 4:4-7). Soon, very soon, our Father will use his rod no more, because it will never be needed again (Romans 8:16-18; Revelation 7:14-17). When we are tempted to despair, and complain, let us remember God's faithfulness (Lamentations 3:21-23; Isaiah 63:9; 1 Corinthians 10:13). Let us ever remember, look to, and trust him who was afflicted as no man ever was. May God give us grace to both trust him and emulate him (Lamentations 1:12; Philippians 1:29; 1 Peter 2:22-24).

'Lift Up The Hands Which Hang Down'

The opening word of verse 12 connects this passage with all that has preceded it concerning our heavenly Father's chastisements. 'Wherefore'. With that word, the Holy Spirit tells us why our heavenly Father deals with us in such goodness, grace, and love when he chastens us. The Lord our God chastens us that he might keep us in his grace, that he might keep us looking to Christ, that he might keep us from the apostasy by which multitudes have perished.

Our Weakness

We all like to think we are spiritually strong, in good health, and fully capable of doing what we ought to do. But that is not the case. The fact is the Lord's sheep are sheep. Weakness is common to sheep. They are easily exhausted. Often, they are lame, lame because the Good Shepherd graciously breaks their feet. When he breaks their feet, it is that he might carry them in his arms and teach them to follow him.

Verse 12 speaks of sluggishness, weariness, and weakness. 'Lift up the hands which hang down, and the feeble knees'. Remember, the passage before us speaks of believers as a people running a race. When a runner's hands dangle at his side, when his knees begin to wobble, it is not likely that he will proceed much further. This is precisely the condition in which David found himself in Psalm 73. He wrote, 'My feet were almost gone; my steps had well nigh slipped' (v. 2).

How weak our hands are! How feeble our knees! How sluggish and inactive we are in prayer! In hearing the Word of God! In Worship! In holding fast our profession! In the performance of those things by which the gospel of Christ is to be adorned!

We are easily wearied and fatigued with weights and burdens of sins and afflictions. We are faint, fearful, and timorous, because of unbelief; because we do not trust God's goodness, grace, love, and the promises of his unfailing goodness, compassion, grace, and care.

This is the Lord's word of exhortation to you and me. 'Lift up the hands which hang down, and the feeble knees'! He here calls for us to be active in every duty, courageous before every foe, and of good cheer in every woe. He is calling for us to patiently bear every burden he puts upon us, looking to him for help, and strength, and protection.

Helping The Weak

Particularly, this is a call for us to help one another in such times of need. Eliphaz commended Job because God's servant Job had been such a helper of his weak brethren. 'Behold, thou hast instructed many, and thou hast strengthened the weak hands. Thy words have upholden him that was falling, and thou hast strengthened the feeble knees' (Job 4:3-4).

We know that Paul is primarily referring to and urging us to help one another because Hebrews 12:12 is a quotation from Isaiah 35:3-4, where the admonition cannot be mistaken. 'Strengthen ye the weak hands, and confirm the feeble knees. Say to them that are of a fearful heart, Be strong, fear not: behold, your God will come with vengeance, even God with a recompense; he will come and save you.'

When our brethren are weak, when it appears that they are ready to quit the race, let us refresh and strengthen them with love, sympathizing with them, speaking comfortably to them, and bearing their burdens. That is what brothers and sisters do for one another. It is called 'love' (Galatians 6:1-3).

'Make Straight Paths'

When one of God's children appears to be lame, perhaps lame by their own foolishness, we are to make straight paths for their feet, that they may be healed. 'And make straight paths for your feet, lest that which is lame be turned out of the way; but let it rather be healed' (v. 13). The word 'feet' refers to our walk, our manner of life, both in the church, and in the world. 'How beautiful are thy feet with shoes, O Prince's daughter'(Song of Solomon 7:1). There are straight paths made ready for our feet to walk in.

These 'straight paths' are the 'old paths' of Gospel truth (Jeremiah 6:16), the paths of holy scripture (Psalm 119:41-48). The straight path we walk is the path to the house and throne of our God (Psalm 122:1-4). We make the paths straight for ourselves and for one another by steadfastly refusing to add anything to the Word, ordinances, and worship of our God and by taking care not to neglect that which God has ordained for our souls' good. Make the paths straight for yourself. Make the paths straight by deliberate example for one another.

'The Lame'

How tenderly the Lord urges us to this business of caring for one another. 'Lest that which is lame be turned out of the way.' The word 'lame' is a very strong word. It means that which is twisted and broken. Who would not pity a man fallen in the streets, whose legs had been twisted and broken? How much more we ought to pity a lame member of Christ's body. How much more we ought to pity a lame member of our family. It matters not whether the lameness is the lameness of his corrupt nature, or lameness caused by his own foolish and sinful behaviour, or lameness caused by the neglect of his soul.

Ours is not to judge and blame, or even diagnose, but to heal: 'But let it rather be healed.' As Gill explains, 'Let the fallen believer be restored, the weak brother be confirmed, the halting professor be strengthened, and everyone be built up and established upon the most holy faith, and in the pure ways of the Gospel.' Shall we not do for one another what our God does for us? Read Micah 4:6-8 and Zephaniah 3:19-20.

How can we heed this admonition? How can we strengthen our own hands and one another's? How can we strengthen our own feeble knees and each other's? How can we make straight paths for our own broken legs and one another's? Read verse 14, and you will see. 'Follow peace with all men, and holiness, without which no man shall see the Lord.'

Follow peace with all men, and holiness, without which no man shall see the Lord: Looking diligently lest any man fail of the grace of God; lest any root of bitterness springing up trouble you, and thereby many be defiled; Lest there be any fornicator, or profane person, as Esau, who for one morsel of meat sold his birthright. For ye know how that afterward, when he would have inherited the blessing, he was rejected: for he found no place of repentance, though he sought it carefully with tears. For ye are not come unto the mount that might be touched, and that burned with fire, nor unto blackness, and darkness, and tempest, And the sound of a trumpet, and the voice of words; which voice they that heard intreated that the word should not be spoken to them any more: (For they could not endure that which was commanded, And if so much as a beast touch the mountain, it shall be stoned, or thrust through with a dart: And so terrible was the sight, that Moses said, I exceedingly fear and quake:) But ye are come unto mount Sion, and unto the city of the living God, the heavenly Jerusalem, and to an innumerable company of angels, To the general assembly and church of the firstborn, which are written in heaven, and to God the Judge of all, and to the spirits of just men made perfect,

Hebrews 12:14-23

Chapter 47

Read: Hebrews 12:14-23

Peace and Holiness

If we would serve the souls of men, if we would do one another good and serve the interests of our own souls, we must set our hearts continually upon Christ. We must earnestly and continually pursue peace and holiness.

Peace with All

The Spirit of God here tells us ever to follow the path of peace with all men. We cannot make all men peaceable, or make all men peaceable toward us. Yet, we must seek, as much as possible, to live peaceably with all. In society, in our homes, and especially in the church of God, we should always endeavour to maintain and promote peace (Romans 12:18).

'Follow peace' be in eager pursuit of peace. Use every means God gives you to live in peace. Spare no energy, no sacrifice, no cost to promote peace. Our God is the God of peace. Our Saviour is the Prince of peace. The Holy Spirit is the Spirit of peace. The Gospel we profess to believe is the gospel of peace. Let us, therefore, 'follow peace with all men', believers and unbelievers.

Promoting Peace

'Let us therefore follow after the things which promote peace, and things wherewith one may edify another' (Romans 14:19). Henry Mahan once gave nine very helpful comments on this text. They are ...

1. Be careful to love one another with a true heart. Love covers a multitude of failures.
2. Avoid a spirit of argument and debate. One may win an argument and lose a friend.
3. Beware of jealousy. Jealousy destroys happiness and builds suspicion.
4. Beware of envy. Let us learn to rejoice in another's gifts, blessings, and happiness. God gives as he will!
5. Do not meddle in the private lives and domestic affairs of others.
6. Guard against a touchy temper. For every trifling thing to take offence shows either great pride or little sense.
7. Learn to keep a confidence. 'He that repeateth a matter separateth very friends'.
8. Strive to heal differences. 'Blessed are the peacemakers'.
9. Be always ready to forgive anything. 'Forgive us our sins as we forgive those who sin against us'.

Pursue Holiness

If we would serve the souls of men and serve our own souls, if we would help the fallen and heal the broken, we must incessantly pursue that holiness without which no man shall see the Lord.

Let us ever seek to live in all holiness and godliness; but that is not the holiness here spoken of. Let us constantly observe and faithfully keep the holy ordinances of divine worship; but that is not the holiness here spoken of. That holiness without which no man shall ever see God is the holiness that is found only in Christ. The only way we shall ever see God and live, and the only way we can help one another along the way, is to set our hearts upon the pursuit of Christ and constantly urge one another to do the same (Philippians 3:1-21).

'Lest Any Man Fail'

There can be no doubt that the holiness spoken of in Hebrews 12:14, that holiness we must constantly pursue, is Christ. Not only is that the only interpretation consistent with the message of holy scripture, the illustration used in verses 15-17 is given to verify it.

Here we are warned that the turning of our hearts away from Christ and the gospel of the grace of God is sure to end in our everlasting ruin. 'Looking diligently lest any man fail of the grace of God; lest any root of bitterness springing up trouble you, and thereby many be defiled' (v. 15).

The grace of God cannot and shall not fail; but multitudes fail of the grace of God, multitudes are turned from the gospel of the grace of God (Galatians 5:1-4). 'Lest there be any fornicator, or profane person, as Esau, who for one morsel of meat sold his birthright' (v.16). Those who fail of the grace of God are those who, like Esau, sell Christ for the world. 'For ye know how that afterward, when he would have inherited the blessing, he was rejected: for he found no place of repentance, though he sought it carefully with tears' (v. 17). Esau is in hell because he sold Christ for the world.

We have entered a race that must be run to the end (1 Corinthians 9:24). The prize goes to those who finish the race (Hebrews 10:35-39). Those who, like Esau, give up Christ for something else will some day, like Esau, weep with bitter tears, when it is beyond their power to recover what they have lost.

Our Inheritance

Heaven is our eternal inheritance, purchased and obtained for us by the blood of Christ, 'In whom we have obtained an inheritance,' and he has given the earnest (i.e. pledge) of that inheritance by the Spirit of grace in the new birth (Ephesians 1:11, 13-14). But we cannot enter the kingdom of heaven, except we do so through the path of much affliction. There is no way home for God's pilgrims, but the way of the cross.

Every heir of endless bliss,
Passing through this wilderness,
Finds his journey, to the end,
Vexed with trouble and with sin.

This is God's all-wise decree.
May He give us grace to see
Thus He weans us from the earth's
Vanity and empty mirth.

Pains and sorrows, sin and woes,
Satan's roars and countless foes,
Every day our way oppose.
Still, God's grace sufficient proves!

He is strong, faithful, and true.
He will guide us safely through!
All that now our souls distress,
Will increase our endless bliss!

Life in this world is not easy. It is not easy to live by faith while we still carry in our nature an evil heart of unbelief. It is not easy to persevere in the faith when the world, the flesh, and the devil oppose us. It is not easy to live for and seek the glory of God when so many earthly cares and inward corruptions vex and torment our souls.

Heaven on Earth

Heaven is our eternal inheritance. We who believe live in hope of eternal life, which God, who cannot lie, promised before the world began. We hope to go to heaven when we die. We hope to spend eternity with Christ in heaven. Sometimes that seems like a far distant hope: far removed from the here and now. Like Israel in the wilderness, we often fail to see the glory, beauty, and fulness of the promised land for two reasons: enemies without and unbelief within. Until enemies are subdued and the unbelief is removed, we cannot enter into our rest. Hebrews 11:18-24 is a passage that ought to subdue those enemies and remove that unbelief, allowing us to know and enjoy heaven on earth.

Jewish Legend

The Jews have a legend. They say that during the days of famine in Canaan, Joseph ordered his officers to throw cartloads of wheat and chaff into the Nile River so that the people who lived below the Nile might see there was great abundance in the land of Egypt. I place no stock in Jewish legends, but I know this: Christ, our great Joseph, throws the grace of heaven into the river of life that his people on earth might taste it and, tasting it, desire more and seek those things which are above.

'For'

The opening word of verse 18, 'For', is very significant. It connects what Paul is about to say with what he has just said from verse 12, 'Lift up those hands, strengthen those feeble knees, go on, go on my brother, *for* the prize is near, and it is sure!' Read verses 18-24 in that light.

'For ye are not come unto the mount that might be touched, and that burned with fire, nor unto blackness, and darkness, and tempest, And the sound of a trumpet, and the voice of words; which voice they that heard intreated that the word should not be spoken to them any more: (For they could not endure that which was commanded, And if so much as a beast touch the mountain, it shall be stoned, or thrust through with a dart: And so terrible was the sight, that Moses said, I exceedingly fear and quake:) But ye are come unto mount Sion, and unto the city of the living God, the heavenly Jerusalem, and to an innumerable company of angels, To the general assembly and church of the firstborn, which are written in heaven, and to God the Judge of all, and to the spirits of just men made perfect, And to Jesus the mediator of the new covenant, and to the blood of sprinkling, that speaketh better things than that of Abel.'

If we belong to God, if we are numbered among those who come to God by faith in the Lord Jesus Christ, here are nine heavenly blessings that belong to us now. We will never enter into the fulness of them until we have dropped this robe of flesh, but they are ours to enjoy right now as much as they shall be when we are seated before the throne of God and of the Lamb.

Complete freedom from the curse and terror of the law (vv. 18-21).
The enjoyment of free access to God (v. 22).
The privilege of heavenly citizenship (v. 22).
The companionship of the angels of God (v. 22).
The spiritual wealth of adoption into the family of God (v. 23).
The defence and protection of God's holy throne (v. 23).
The company and fellowship of glorified saints (v. 23).
The personal care and mediation of the Lord Jesus Christ (v. 24).
Full, irrevocable salvation through Christ's precious blood (v. 24).

Not Mount Sinai, but Mount Zion

Having come to the Lord Jesus Christ by faith, we now enjoy the blessed privilege of complete freedom from the curse and terror of God's holy law. 'For ye are not come unto the mount that might be touched, and that burned with fire, nor unto blackness, and darkness, and tempest'.

Not Mount Sinai

Paul states it emphatically, 'Ye are not come to Mount Sinai.' We now have nothing to do with the law. That horrible, black, fiery mountain might be touched; but to touch it meant certain death! Sinai issued demands we could not fulfil, threatened wrath we could not endure, and exposed sin we could not remove. But Christ fulfilled the law for us. And now, in Christ, we are free from the law (Romans 7:4; 10:4). The Lord Jesus Christ (as our representative) fulfilled the righteousness of the law for us, by his obedience to God (Romans 5:19). He satisfied the penalty of the law by his death as our Substitute, redeeming us from its curse (Galatians 3:13-14). The righteousness of the law is now fulfilled in us by faith in Christ (Romans 8:4; 3:28). We are, right now, as completely free from the law of God as Abraham, Isaac, and Jacob.

But Mount Zion

In Christ Jesus, we now have the enjoyment of free access to God. 'But ye are come unto mount Sion, and unto the city of the living God, the heavenly Jerusalem, and to an innumerable company of angels' (v. 22). Mount Zion was the hill on which the temple was built. There alone, God was seen, heard, revealed, and known. There alone could men approach God on the mercy-seat, through a priest, by the blood of an animal sacrifice. But now, we are the temple of God (1 Corinthians 3:16; Matthew 18:20).

Christ is our Priest, our Mercy-seat, and our Sacrifice. And we are as free to approach God in Christ as the saints in heaven (Hebrews 10:19-22). Right now we have free access to God (Hebrews 4:16). We enjoy the perpetual presence of God (John 14:23), and are perfectly accepted by him (Ephesians 1:6).

Heavenly Citizenship

You and I, believing on the Lord Jesus Christ, possess the privilege of heavenly citizenship. 'Ye are come unto ... the city of the living God, the heavenly Jerusalem'. Our citizenship is in heaven, from whence we look for the Saviour.

I am like an American travelling through Europe. I stop along the way, enjoy the sights, eat the food, smell the flowers, and learn from the history. But my purpose is to return home soon. I want to behave so that I bring no reproach upon my homeland. But I do not, must not, set my heart upon anything along the way. And I do not, must not, let the affairs of the strange land disturb me greatly.

Angelic Companions

Are you a child of God? Do you trust Christ? If so, you have come into the companionship of the angels of God. 'Ye are come unto ... an innumerable company of angels'. I do not pretend to know much about the angels of God, but I do know some things about them. They are an 'innumerable company'. They are all ministering spirits, sent forth to minister to them who shall be the heirs of salvation (Hebrews 1:14).

The Lord has given his angels charge over his elect to protect them. 'The angel of the Lord encampeth round about them that fear him'. The angels of God meet with God's saints in our assemblies of public worship (Ephesians 3:10; 1 Corinthians 11:10).

The angels of God attend the saints in death and carry them home to glory. The angels of God will gather his elect from the four corners of the earth in the last day (Luke 16:20-22; Mark 13:27).

'Firstborn'
In Christ every believer possesses all the spiritual wealth of adoption into the family of God (v. 23). In God's family all the sons are firstborn sons. Our names were written in heaven before the world began (1 John 3:1-2). That makes us all 'heirs of God and joint-heirs with Christ'.

Perfectly Safe
Every believer is safe and secure, because we have come under the defence and protection of God's holy throne. We live in the immediate presence of 'God the Judge of all' all the time. God has judged our sins in Christ, and declares now that we are not subject to condemnation (Romans 8:1, 33-34). He who judges us righteous is our Judge in all things. He will 'plead my cause'. He will 'undertake for me'.

General Assembly
Being united to Christ by faith, we are brought into the company of glorified saints. We have (not shall, but have) come 'to the general assembly and church of the firstborn, which are written in heaven, and to God the Judge of all, and to the spirits of just men made perfect'. God's church on earth and God's church in heaven is one church. Our glorified brethren are our brethren in the body of Christ. They worship before the throne just like we do, only perfectly. They rejoice before God every time one of God's elect are saved (Luke 15:6, 7, 10). And they are very interested in those of us who are not yet made perfect (Hebrews 12:1).

Our Mediator
You and I who believe are the objects of the personal care and mediation of the Lord Jesus Christ. We have come 'to Jesus the mediator of the new covenant and to the blood of sprinkling, that speaketh better things than that of Abel' (v. 24). Our all-glorious Saviour, Jesus, is the Mediator of that everlasting and ever new covenant of grace, ordered in all things and sure from eternity; that covenant that has been ratified and put into force by his sin-atoning blood. And, believing on the Lord Jesus Christ, we have right now, as surely as the saints in heaven, full, irrevocable salvation through Christ's precious blood. Abel's blood demanded the wrath of God upon his brother who killed him. Christ's blood demands the mercy of God upon us, his brethren, who killed him. For what does the blood of Christ speak? Does it speak for forgiveness? Then we are forgiven. For justification? Then we are justified. For sanctification? Then we are sanctified. For glorification? Then we have promise of that, too. For life?

Then we have life! Let these things comfort, strengthen, and sustain you in the midst of your heartache and toil in this world.

The Covenant, The Mediator, The Blood

As Paul comes to the close of the Epistle, he seems to write as one who is running out of paper, or running out of time, as a man so excited about his subject that he cannot speak of it adequately. In Hebrews 12:22, he tells us that we have come to Mount Zion, a better place than Sinai! To the Heavenly Jerusalem, a better city than Jerusalem! To the general assembly and church of the firstborn, whose names are written in heaven, a better assembly than those who gathered at the tabernacle or temple of old, whose names were merely written on paper. To God, who is infinitely better than all the types and pictures given of him in the Mosaic age! The Judge of all, who is better than all the best judges Israel ever had. To the spirits of just men made perfect, a better company than Israel ever enjoyed.

When we come to verses 24 and 25 we shall see more of those better things that are ours in this gospel age. Let us have a quick preview.

The New Covenant

We have come by faith 'to Jesus the Mediator of the New Covenant'. The Lord Jesus Christ, to whom we look, to whom we come, is the Mediator of the New Covenant. This new covenant is called new, only because it is always new, and because it is newly revealed in Christ. The new covenant is an everlasting, eternal covenant. We read about it in Jeremiah 31:3, 31-34, 32:37-42, and in Ephesians 1:3-7.

The covenant of grace, we are told in Hebrews 8:6, is 'a better covenant'. The covenant of works was conditional. The covenant of grace is unconditional. The old covenant was based on law and works. The covenant of grace is all grace. The Mosaic covenant was broken and made void. The covenant of grace is established in Christ, and cannot be broken or nullified. That covenant revealed at Sinai was dark, shadowy, and fearful. The covenant of grace is light, clear, and delightful.

This new covenant of righteousness and grace was and is established upon better promises than that old covenant of works and law. All the promises of that covenant were made to fickle men and conditioned upon their obedience. All the promises of this covenant were made to the God-man, our Mediator, upon condition of his obedience for us! And in him, all the promises of God are 'yea, and amen'. This new covenant of grace, and all the blessings and benefits of it, comes to us through the merits of Christ's better sacrifice (Hebrews 10:1-10).

The Mediator of this covenant of grace is 'Jesus', our Saviour, the Son of God, the Christ. A mediator is a go-between, a daysman, a representative for two parties, an advocate, and a reconciler. There is only one Mediator between God and men, and that Mediator is Jesus, who came to save his people from their sins as God's appointed and accepted covenant Surety! No wonder David sang as he did about this covenant on his dying bed (2 Samuel 23:1-5).

The Blood

We have come by faith 'to Jesus the Mediator of the new covenant, and to the blood of sprinkling'. The blood of Christ is called 'the blood of sprinkling'. I am sure there is more in this than I have yet grasped; but what I do know about it is as thrilling as it is precious. His blood is the blood of the true Paschal Lamb. He is Christ our Passover, the Lamb of God, who is sacrificed for us! His blood has been sprinkled on the mercy-seat (1 Corinthians 5:7). Like the blood of that first paschal lamb, his blood has been sprinkled upon the door of our hearts and consciences, declaring that judgment is passed, convincing us of sin, of righteousness, and of judgment. With reference to the blood of his dear Son, God says to us, 'When I see the blood, I will pass over you'! In this way the 'blood of sprinkling speaketh better things than that of Abel'.

The blood of Christ speaks, ever speaks, and speaks better things than the blood of Abel. Abel's blood cried for justice and vengeance: Christ's blood cries for justice and mercy! Abel's blood spoke for punishment: Christ's blood speaks for pardon. Abel's blood spoke against his brother: Christ's blood speaks for his brethren. Abel's blood demanded death: Christ's blood demands life! Abel's blood cried from the ground to God: Christ's blood speaks in heaven before God. Abel's blood cried out against Cain in his conscience: Christ's blood speaks for us in our consciences. Abel's blood continues to speak: and Christ's blood continues to speak (1 John 1:7-2:2).

Refuse Not

'See that ye refuse not him that speaketh.' What a tender word of mercy, grace, compassion and hope this is! 'See that ye refuse not him that speaketh.' What an awful word of warning! 'For if they escaped not who refused him that spake on earth, much more shall not we escape, if we turn away from him that speaketh from heaven.' Read Proverbs 1:23-33.

And to Jesus the mediator of the new covenant, and to the blood of sprinkling, that speaketh better things than that of Abel. See that ye refuse not him that speaketh. For if they escaped not who refused him that spake on earth, much more shall not we escape, if we turn away from him that speaketh from heaven: Whose voice then shook the earth: but now he hath promised, saying, Yet once more I shake not the earth only, but also heaven. And this word, Yet once more, signifieth the removing of those things that are shaken, as of things that are made, that those things which cannot be shaken may remain. Wherefore we receiving a kingdom which cannot be moved, let us have grace, whereby we may serve God acceptably with reverence and godly fear: For our God is a consuming fire.

Hebrews 12:24-29

Chapter 48

Read: Hebrews 12:24-29

Christ Is Better

Throughout the book of Hebrews the Holy Spirit's purpose is to show us the superiority of this gospel age to that of the Old Testament. A key word in these 13 chapters is the word 'better'. It is used repeatedly.

Christ is better than the angels. 'Being made so much better than the angels, as he hath by inheritance obtained a more excellent name than they' (1:4). Christ has given us better things, things that accompany salvation. 'But, beloved, we are persuaded better things of you, and things that accompany salvation, though we thus speak' (6:9). Christ, our Melchisedek, is better than Abraham. 'And without all contradiction the less is blessed of the better' (7:7). Christ gives us a better hope ('a good hope through grace'), than the law could ever give. 'For the law made nothing perfect, but the bringing in of a better hope did; by the which we draw nigh unto God' (7:19). Christ is the Surety of a better covenant. 'By so much was Jesus made a surety of a better testament' (7:22). Christ is the Mediator of a better covenant. 'But now hath he obtained a more excellent ministry, by how much also he is the mediator of a better covenant, which was established upon better promises' (8:6). Christ is a better sacrifice. 'It was therefore necessary that the patterns of things in the heavens should be purified with these; but the heavenly things themselves with better sacrifices than these' (9:23). Christ gives us a better, enduring, heavenly inheritance. 'For ye had compassion of me in my bonds, and took joyfully the spoiling of your goods, knowing in yourselves that ye have in heaven a better and an enduring substance'

(10:34). In Christ we are made citizens of a better country. 'But now they desire a better country, that is, an heavenly: wherefore God is not ashamed to be called their God: for he hath prepared for them a city' (11:16). Christ gives us hope of a better resurrection. 'Women received their dead raised to life again: and others were tortured, not accepting deliverance; that they might obtain a better resurrection' (11:35). God has provided for us better things in Christ. 'God having provided some better thing for us, that they without us should not be made perfect' (11:40). Christ's sacrifice and blood speaks better things than the blood of Abel and his sacrifice. 'And to Jesus the mediator of the new covenant, and to the blood of sprinkling, that speaketh better things than that of Abel' (12:24).

Coming to Christ

'And (ye are come) to Jesus the mediator of the new covenant.' Faith is coming to Christ. All who are born of God and taught of him come to Christ. But coming to Christ is not at all what people imagine it to be. Coming to Christ is an act of faith. It is altogether something that is done in the heart. It is altogether a spiritual thing. Many came to Christ physically, touching him, and being touched by him, who never came to him. 'It is the spirit that quickeneth. The flesh profiteth nothing.' Multitudes come to Christ outwardly, by profession, in the place of public worship, who never come to him (Ananias and Sapphira, Simon Magus). Faith is a heart work. It is coming to Christ with a sense of need. It is coming to him as the One, the only One, who has infinite fulness to meet our souls' need. This faith is the gift and operation of God's almighty, omnipotent, irresistible, efficacious grace. Faith is coming to Christ and no one else. It is coming to him alone for everything (1 Corinthians 1:30-31). It is coming to Christ as a poor, helpless, bankrupt, naked, needy sinner. It is coming to Christ with no aide, no assistant, no mediator, no priest, and no sacrifice. It is coming to Christ bringing nothing of your own to ingratiate you. It is coming to Christ bringing nothing but your filth for him to cleanse, your sin for him to forgive, your nakedness for him to cover, and your need for him to meet. To all who come, our Saviour promises, 'Him that cometh unto me, I will in no wise cast out'!

A Divine Gift

This gift of faith is the great privilege of God's elect. It is the blessing of blessings. All who are given this great boon of grace are saved, safe, settled, secure, and at peace. They can want no good thing, for all things are theirs. We have free access to God through Christ, and a right to all privileges of the sons of God in him!

Things Shaken and Things That Cannot Be Shaken

The Old Testament passage to which the apostle refers is Haggai 2:6. 'For thus saith the LORD of hosts; Yet once, it is a little while, and I will shake the heavens, and the earth, and the sea, and the dry land.' Here, as in Hebrews 12, the Lord is reminding the people of the time when He shook the world when He descended upon Mount Sinai and gave the law to Moses (Exodus 19:16-20; Hebrews 12:26).

Things Shaken

But the Lord here speaks of a time when the shaking of the world would be far more violent and would affect the heavens and the earth. All nations would be affected and even the islands of the sea by this shaking. This is a prophecy of Christ's coming into the world. Yet, it reaches beyond his incarnation, and spans all time, from the time of his first advent to the time of his glorious second advent. This 'shaking' is a herald, a prophecy of the coming of the Lord to judge the nations of the earth. It is talking about the whole gospel age (Isaiah 13:13; 24:18-23; Ezekiel 33:19-33; Joel 3:15-21). Haggai seems to see the whole universe in convulsions that affect every nation. Peter speaks of the same thing in 2 Peter 3:10-13.

When God shakes the heavens and the earth, nothing in the universe will ever be the same again. He will break the power of the nations. The ultimate fulfilment of this passage will be, as I have said, at the second Coming of Christ (Haggai 2:21-23).

But, it is terribly erroneous to look upon this as only a prophecy of our Lord's second advent. This is a promise and prophecy of God's work today by the gospel. Our great God establishes, uses, and overthrows all the powers and kingdoms of the universe, at his will, for the building of his house, for the salvation of his people. He is sovereign over the nations. Wars and revolutions are nothing but his shaking of the Gentiles. The Lord God reigns. He uses these cosmic events to accomplish his eternal purpose of grace, which is the salvation of his elect (Romans 8:28-30). He says, 'and I will shake all nations, and the desire of all nations shall come: and I will fill this house with glory, saith the LORD of hosts' (Haggai 2:7).

The Desire of Nations

Our Lord Jesus Christ is that One of Whom the prophet here speaks. He is 'the Desire of all nations' (Genesis 49:10; Malachi 3:1). Coming to Christ, God's elect from the four corners of the earth, the whole Israel of God, come together as one. Thus, as Calvin suggested, 'The nations will come, bringing with them all their riches, that they might offer themselves and all their possessions as a sacrifice to God.'

The word 'desire' might be translated 'consolation'. The Gentile nations will come to Christ, the Desire of all nations, the Messiah. He is the object of desire in the renewed heart, that in which a man finds pleasure, joy, consolation, and value. Both Isaiah and Micah speak of all nations flowing to the mountain of God to worship him and hear His Word. Christ is the one in whom the nations find their treasure and riches. He is the 'Pearl of Great Price'.

That shaking spoken of in Haggai 2 and Hebrews 12 is followed by this result, or produces this effect, God's elect are gathered from all nations, tongues, and peoples to fill his house and make it glorious, far more glorious than the Temple of old (Isaiah 40:9-11; Micah 4:1-2).

Things Unshaken

There are, however, some 'things which cannot be shaken'. The purpose of God, and all that is involved in that purpose are things unshakable. The Lord God speaks of the great glory of his house (Haggai 2:8-9). The result of all this shaking of the universe will be the filling of the Temple with the glory of the Lord. 'The silver is mine, and the gold is mine, saith the LORD of hosts. The glory of this latter house shall be greater than of the former, saith the LORD of hosts: and in this place will I give peace, saith the LORD of hosts'.

Our God is the Possessor of all things. God's Church and Kingdom shall never lack anything. His cause, his Church, his Gospel is never in lack of supply and is never dependent upon anything outside himself. When God saves his people, they sell all they have for the Pearl of Great Price. They bring all they possess into his house (Acts 5). And, when all things have been accomplished, all the glory and honour of the universe shall be brought into the New Jerusalem (Revelation 21:22-27).

The glory of God's house, since the coming of Christ, far exceeds, and forever shall exceed, by infinite measure, the glory of the former house. That house was shaken and destroyed. This house cannot be shaken. Haggai's prophecy began to be fulfilled when Christ was brought into the temple after his birth (Luke 2:21-38). It was more fully fulfilled when he came into the temple and cleansed it. The glory of the Lord filled the tabernacle and Solomon's temple when they were dedicated. The type began to be fulfilled when the Lord God came to his temple in the person of his Son, the Lord Jesus Christ. This is what Malachi spoke of in Malachi 3:1. Christ himself, as the incarnate Word in whom the 'glory of the Lord' was and is beheld, in whom the glory of the Lord is, fulfilled Haggai's prophecy when he came into the temple. He brought a greater glory to the temple with his own presence, not in symbolic form, but true divine glory.

The glorification of the house of God commenced with the incarnate Son of God and will reach its consummation when he returns (Hebrews 12:26-27; Revelation 21:10-11, 22-24).

Place of Peace

In the last sentence of Haggai 2:9 the Lord God declares, 'In this place I will give peace'. Christ is the glory of God. He is the Prince of Peace. In him alone sinners find peace. The Prince of Peace is one who brings peace to Jerusalem. When he comes again in his glory, the world will know everlasting, perfect peace, and not until then (Micah 5:4; Joel 4:17; Psalm 72:17; Isaiah 9:7; 60:18; 66:12; Luke 2:14).

'The glory of this latter house shall be greater than of the former' (Haggai 2:9). At the second coming of Christ Haggai's prophecy will be fully accomplished and fully realized. Jesus Christ, the Desire of all the nations, will rule without rival in the hearts of all who dwell in the new creation. His is a kingdom that cannot and will not be shaken (Hebrews 12:26-28). The glory and honour of the Gentile nations will be brought into it (Revelation 21:24, 26). The promise will be fulfilled in the New Jerusalem, where 'the dwelling of God is with men' (Revelation 21:3; 22). And this shall be God's work alone (Zechariah 4:6-7).

Still, there is more. Between the first and second advents of Christ, throughout this gospel age, the Lord God continually shakes the nations. Christ, 'the Desire of all nations', comes. He fills his house with glory; and he has promised, 'In this place will I give peace' (Psalm 80:1, 3-4, 7, 14, 17-19; Isaiah 64:1-2). Once more, O Lord, once more, shake heaven and earth! Once more, O Lord, once more, come and fill your house with glory!

'Yet Once More'

In v. 26 Paul is referring us to the prophecy of Haggai. He means for us to understand that there is only one more shaking after the time of Haggai. The shaking he speaks of is not a physical, material thing (though it certainly includes all things physical (2 Peter 3), but a moral and spiritual shaking. It is a shaking that began with our Lord's first advent, continues throughout this gospel age, and will be consummated in his glorious second coming. It is a work both of God's wrath upon those who refuse to hear his Word, upon those who despise his Gospel; and of his great mercy, love, and grace upon his elect, whom he causes to hear his Word, whom he makes willing to receive, believe, and delight in his gospel.

The Lord our God will shake and remove everything that is natural, transitory, temporal, and perishable; not merely of the old Mosaic dispensation, but also every human thought and power that is opposed to Christ, his Gospel, his Church, his Kingdom, and his dominion. This shaking is the thrice repeated overturning of all things in his creation that are opposed to God our Saviour and his people (Ezekiel 21:27; Isaiah 13:13; Joel 3:16; Matthew 24:29). But that which cannot be shaken, the church and kingdom of God, the faith of God's elect, the blessed hope of the Gospel, shall remain.

Haggai

Haggai's prophecy was written more than 500 years before Christ came into the world (about 520 BC). Yet, he tells us what we should expect our God and Saviour to do in our day. Haggai was, from all accounts, born in Babylon during the time of the Babylonian Captivity. He came to Jerusalem as an old man. The Temple at Jerusalem, the House of God, lay in utter ruin, and the people were in despair. Though the Lord had brought them out of Babylon, they were reluctant to go to work rebuilding the Temple. Cyrus, their deliverer (a type of Christ) had told them to do it. But they did not believe God. They were content just to be out of Babylon. They had lost all hope of God visiting them again. Oh, they looked for him to visit the earth again and make his house glorious again, just not in their day. (Sound like anyone you know?) We see this in the opening words of Haggai's prophecy (Haggai 1:2). So the Lord God sent his prophet Haggai to his people. Haggai's name comes from a word that means 'Merry', or 'Feasting'. It might even be translated 'Time of Feasting', or 'The Feasts of the Lord'. God sent Haggai to his people to encourage them to believe him and build his house, assuring them that he would make it glorious.

He rebukes them by telling them twice in chapter 1, 'Consider your ways! Consider your ways!' Then, we read in verse 8 of Haggai 1, 'Go up to the mountain, and bring wood, and build the house; and I will take pleasure in it, and I will be glorified, saith the LORD.' In other words, he says, 'Put your shoulder to the work!'

Zerubbabel

Then (vv. 12-14) God raised up Zerubbabel (another type of Christ), who inspired 'the remnant of the people to obey the voice of the Lord their God, and the words of Haggai the prophet, as the Lord their God had sent him, and the people did fear before the Lord.' Before, while looking at themselves, they feared to believe God. Now, looking away from themselves to him, they feared not to believe him! And, we read in verse 14, 'They came and did work in the house of the Lord of hosts, their God.' They put their shoulders to the work.

Still, there were some old, old people in their midst, who had seen the Temple in its former glory. In their eyes, this new Temple was 'nothing in comparison' (2:3). Lest they should give up, God sent Haggai to them again with words of gracious encouragement (Haggai 2:4-5). Against this backdrop, the Lord God gave the promise to his ancient people, which he has repeated to us in Hebrews 12:26-27.

'For thus saith the LORD of hosts; Yet once, it is a little while, and I will shake the heavens, and the earth, and the sea, and the dry land; And I will shake all nations, and the desire of all nations shall come: and I will fill this house with glory, saith the LORD of hosts. The silver is mine, and the gold is mine, saith the LORD of hosts. The glory of this latter house shall be greater than of the former, saith the LORD of hosts: and in this place will I give peace, saith the LORD of hosts'. (Haggai 2:6-9)

Let us not despise the days of small things. God's hand is not short. His ear is not heavy. So long as the Lord our King is on his holy, sovereign throne, he will both sustain us in our work for him and make our work effectual and fruitful for the building of his true Temple, his true House, and the glory of it!

So long as Christ is King and Shepherd upon his throne we will lack nothing in the service of his Kingdom. He will provide the means of building his house and filling His temple with the splendour and glory of his grace.

Something Better

In our society a man's worth is commonly judged by his position, his power, and his possessions. We are conditioned to presume that anyone who lacks what we commonly consider obvious signs of success must be uneducated, or lazy, or both. Those who are poor are commonly considered more likely to be immoral, if not criminal. Parents are always a little concerned if their daughter shows interest in a boy who comes from 'the wrong side of the tracks'. They are always delighted to see her marry into the right kind of family: the kind with money!

Young people (and older ones, too) put themselves deeply into debt to keep up the appearance of success. Husbands and wives work every minute they can, so that they can impress themselves and their neighbours with what they have! What a sad commentary those facts are upon our society!

This perverse, proud, corrupt mentality is just as prevalent in the religious world as it is in the secular world. We have been conditioned by the 'health, wealth, prosperity' preachers of the day to think that if a person is not physically healthy and wealthy and prospering materially, there must be some fault in his character, some flaw in his faith, or something otherwise evil that is the cause of his failure. Anything less than tangible success that leads to great comfort and prosperity in life is shamed as being a defective faith.

What is the result? In the minds of most, God has been reduced to nothing more than a great dispenser of creature comforts who is manipulated by positive thinking and positive believing! The Christian is, in the minds of most, synonymous with prosperity. Failure of any kind, sickness, and tragedy are thought to be beyond God's control, contrary to his goodness, outside his will, and altogether beneath the dignity of a Christian. Faith today is made to be the elusive secret of elitist Christians by which they attain all the dreams of materialism and all the flamboyance of a Hollywood lifestyle.

Such thinking is totally contrary to the teaching of holy scripture. When we come to Hebrews 11, and read here of the great men and women of faith, men and women held before us by God the Holy Spirit as examples to follow, we see that faith in Christ, obedience to the revealed will of God, and the goodness of God to the people of his love very often bring us into the very condition and circumstances the world disdains. Faith in and obedience to Christ, God's infinite wisdom, and sovereign goodness very frequently, indeed, most commonly, prevent the souls he loves from ever attaining that which the world calls good and great. Our God has something better for us than the riches and comforts of this world. Christ is better. Eternity is better. Our hearts must be set upon these better things, if we would attain them.

Let brotherly love continue. Be not forgetful to entertain strangers: for thereby some have entertained angels unawares. Remember them that are in bonds, as bound with them; and them which suffer adversity, as being yourselves also in the body. Marriage is honourable in all, and the bed undefiled: but whoremongers and adulterers God will judge. Let your conversation be without covetousness; and be content with such things as ye have: for he hath said, I will never leave thee, nor forsake thee. So that we may boldly say, The Lord is my helper, and I will not fear what man shall do unto me.

Hebrews 13:1-6

Chapter 49

Read: Hebrews 13:1-6

'Let Brotherly Love Continue'

How often our Lord encourages us to love one another! Nothing is more like our Saviour than love. Nothing is more unlike him than the absence of love. As he brings his Epistle to its inspired conclusion, the Apostle Paul makes his final word of instruction an encouragement to brotherly love. The last chapter of the book of Hebrews begins with these words 'Let brotherly love continue.'

Paul has been encouraging us to persevere in the faith, to continue in the grace of God, to run with patience the race that is set before us. Then, he says, 'Let brotherly love continue'. It is as though he is saying, 'The way to run this race, the way to persevere in grace, the way to walk in faith is to keep on loving one another.'

Multitudes live in religious bondage, trying to obey rules and regulations imposed upon them by their leaders. These rules of bondage people everywhere call 'practical godliness'. Our Lord calls them 'vain traditions', 'works of the flesh', 'a vain show in the flesh', and 'a form of godliness'. Here, in these seven verses of Inspiration, the Holy Spirit shows us that godliness is to be measured by love. This is very much the same thing that James says in James 1:26-27.

Love Expressed by Deeds

First, we see that love is expressed by deeds (vv.1-4). As was his custom, having finished his doctrinal instruction, Paul here applies his doctrine to our everyday lives. He begins the application of his doctrine with these words, 'Let brotherly love continue.' He is saying, 'Children of God, never cease loving one another. Let nothing divide your hearts. Make it your life's business to love one another and to show your love to one another. Let brotherly love continue in you and among you.'

We are to love all men, even our enemies; but the love Paul is talking about here is that special family love that God plants in the hearts of his people for one another. It is the love of hearts united to Christ. 'The fruit of the Spirit is love' (Galatians 5:22; John 13:35; 1 John 3:7-11; 4:20; 5:1).

I am not talking about lip love. Anyone can say, 'I love you', or 'I love my brethren'. Lip love is no love. Love is manifest by deeds. And the deeds, by which the love of Christ in us is manifest, are not matters about which we have to guess. If we love one another, we pray for one another. That is how Christ loves us. Is it not? If we love one another, we bear one another's burdens. That is how Christ loves us. Is it not? If we love one another, we are forbearing, patient, longsuffering, and forgiving with one another. That is how Christ loves us. Is it not? If we love one another, we meet together to encourage and exhort one another. That is how Christ loves us. Is it not?

If we do not love one another, any profession of faith we have is but a meaningless, vain delusion (1 Peter 2:17; 1 John 3:14-18; 1 Corinthians 13:1-7). Paul says, 'Brethren, see that you make this the fixed principle by which you live, the unbroken habit of your lives. Love one another. As you grow in love for Christ, grow in love for one another.'

Hospitality

'Be not forgetful to entertain strangers: for thereby some have entertained angels unawares' (v. 2). Here the Holy Spirit tells us something about how this love for the brethren is to be expressed. Love is hospitable, given to hospitality. We know that a pastor must be a man given to hospitality; but the reason that is a requirement for one who preaches the gospel is simply the fact that faith in Christ makes people loving, gracious, hospitable.

The Amplified Version gives us an excellent paraphrase of this verse. 'Do not forget or neglect or refuse to extend hospitality to strangers [in the brotherhood—being friendly, cordial, and gracious, sharing the comforts of your home and doing your part generously], for through it some have entertained angels without knowing it.'

We must never neglect or fail to care for and meet the needs of God's people in this world. When the Apostle tells us to 'entertain strangers' he is not suggesting that we open our homes and invite people into them who are strangers to us, though that may certainly be included. We have a responsibility to protect our families. The strangers he speaks of here are the 'strangers' spoken of in verse 13 of chapter 11. They are our brethren who are 'strangers and pilgrims on the earth'. We must never fail to use that which God has trusted to our hands, as stewards in his house, to benefit, minister to, and comfort his people in this world. We are to make it a matter of conscious effort to be friendly, cordial, and gracious toward God's people (especially those who cannot return the kindness), sharing the comforts and provisions of our homes generously.

When you invite one of God's people into your home and into your life, you may just be inviting an angel of God, a special messenger of God into your home and life 'for thereby some have entertained angels unawares' (Genesis 18:1-8; 19:1-3; Luke 24:28-31). Our Lord tells us that entertaining one of his people is entertaining him (Matthew 25:38-40).

Matters Relating to Brotherly Love

In Hebrews 13:1-7 the Apostle Paul is urging us to make it our habit of life to walk in the exercise of brotherly love. We read in verses 1-2 'Let brotherly love continue. Be not forgetful to entertain strangers: for thereby some have entertained angels unawares.' In verses 3-7 he continues with the same subject, reminding us of specific matters relating to the exercise of brotherly love.

Brethren in Need

Brotherly love expresses itself by tenderly caring for brethren in need. 'Remember them that are in bonds, as bound with them; and them which suffer adversity, as being yourselves also in the body' (v. 3). This is not talking about prison ministries and caring for legally incarcerated criminals. It is talking about those who are in bonds for the gospel's sake and those who suffer adversity (particularly God's suffering people in their adversities), because we are in the same body with them. We are in the same body of this flesh, the same body of Christ, and the same spiritual body, the church of God, with them. As members one of another, as brethren in the same family, we ought to, 'weep with those that weep and rejoice with those that rejoice' (Romans 12:15).

If we love as brothers and sisters in Christ, we will see that missionaries, old people, needy people, sick people, and people out of work have their needs supplied, as we are able to supply them.

Marriage Honourable

In verse 4, Paul seems to throw in something that is unrelated to this matter of brotherly love. He speaks of the honour of marriage. But what he has to say is very much related to brotherly love. He says, 'Marriage is honourable in all, and the bed undefiled: but whoremongers and adulterers God will judge.'

Brotherly love flourishes when home love flourishes. If I do not love my wife and care for her, if I do not devote myself to her, I do not love you or Christ and will not care for you and the things of Christ. So Paul says, 'Take your marriage vows seriously.' Let marriage be held honourably and highly esteemed in all things. Your marriage bed is honourable. And there is never an excuse (religious or otherwise) for a husband neglecting his wife, or a wife her husband. Love means you keep yourself from sexual promiscuity! 'Whoremongers and adulterers God will judge.'

Contentment and Assurance

Verses 5 and 6 speak of contentment rising from assurance. 'Let your conversation be without covetousness; and be content with such things as ye have: for he hath said, I will never leave thee, nor forsake thee. So that we may boldly say, The Lord is my helper, and I will not fear what man shall do unto me.'

Here again, Paul is still taking about brotherly love. Covetousness destroys it. Contentment promotes it. Let us live free from love of money, free from craving wealth and worldly possessions, free from greed and lust for material things. Be content with what God has given you. Be content with your present position and circumstance.

Such contentment arises from the assurance spoken of in verse 6. God has said, 'I will not in any way fail you, nor give you up, nor leave you without support.' 'The Lord is my shepherd, I shall not want' (Matthew 6:25-34; Philippians 4:6,11,12; 1 Timothy 6:6-8). Because we are so slow to believe him, our God has given this promise to us five times in his Word (Genesis 28:15; Deuteronomy 31:6-8; Joshua 1:5; 1 Chronicles 28:20; Hebrews 13:5).

This is God's promise to every believing sinner in this world, 'I will never leave thee, nor forsake thee'. It is given to us that we may, as Isaiah puts it, 'Suck, and be satisfied with the breasts of her consolations; that ye may milk out, and be delighted with the abundance of her glory.' (Isaiah 66:11; Psalms 37:25; Philippians 4:6, 11-12; 1 Timothy 6:6-8).

Pastors

In verse 7 the Holy Spirit calls for us to remember God's servants as rulers worthy of allegiance. 'Remember them which have the rule over you, who have spoken unto you the word of God: whose faith follow, considering the end of their conversation.'

This is not talking about political rulers, but spiritual rulers, those men who are given the responsibility for ruling God's house. The word would be better translated 'guides' or 'governors'. Gospel preachers are men who rule the house of God by the Word of God and the example of faith, by which they guide God's people to glory (Jeremiah 3:15; Ephesians 4:11-13).

Remember them, respect them, follow them, pray for them, provide for them, and honour them for Christ's sake, as his servants by which he serves you (1 Thessalonians 5:12-13; Ephesians 4:1-13). 'Obey them that have the rule over you, and submit yourselves: for they watch for your souls, as they that must give account, that they may do it with joy, and not with grief: for that is unprofitable for you' (Hebrews 13:7).

A Motive For Contentment

This is what Paul says, 'Let your conversation be without covetousness; and be content with such things as ye have.' He gives this for the motive: 'For he hath said, I will never leave thee, nor forsake thee.' If the Lord my God is with me, and promises never to forsake me, want should never be an emotion felt in my heart (Philippians 4:12-13).

This is my earnest prayer to my God: Lord give me a contented heart. Teach me contentment! I want to be content with your providence, content with your provision, and content with your presence. He who possesses him, to whom all things belong, possesses all things (Romans 8:32; 1 Corinthians 3:21-23).

Child of God, let your riches consist not in the largeness of your possessions, but in the fewness of your wants. Contentment makes poor men rich; and a lack of it makes rich men poor. Our wants ought to be always limited to our present possessions and present circumstances.

This I know: it is my responsibility, if I follow Christ, to make all material things immaterial, and simply trust my heavenly Father for all things. If I believe him, I will (Matthew 6:20-34; 10:39). Because God has said, 'I will never leave thee, nor forsake thee,' we may boldly say, 'The Lord is my helper, and I will not fear what man shall do unto me.' The Lord, my Helper, is greater than all my foes. All my foes are entirely in the hands of my Lord, and under his control. It matters not what men do to me, the Lord will sustain me.

Child of God believe him. Trust his promise. Trust his grace. He will not leave you in the time of your greatest guilt and sin (1 John 2:1-2). He will not leave you in the time of great temptation, trial, and danger (1 Corinthians 10:13). Though others forsake you, and they surely will, the Lord will not forsake you (Lamentations 3:21-26).

For six thousand years, the Lord has confirmed his promise. It never was broken yet and it never shall be. 'He hath said, I will never leave thee, nor forsake thee' How far does that word 'never' reach? It reaches deeper than the deepest agonies of your soul! It reaches lower than the lowest pit into which you may fall! It reaches beyond the grave! It reaches as high as the judgment seat of God himself! It reaches to eternity!

Robert Murray M'Cheyne wrote,

> Eternity alone will unfold the riches of this promise. He who died for us will be our eternal Friend; and he who sanctifies us will forever dwell in us; and then God, who loved us, will be ever with us. Then will we get into the meaning of his promise 'I will never leave thee, nor forsake thee'.

'Never'!

Here is a promise from the Triune God to every sinner who trusts his darling Son. 'He hath said'. I like that! God has said, 'I will never leave thee, nor forsake thee'. This is a remarkable, unconditional promise. Literally, 'God has said, I will never, no never, no never leave you or forsake you'. The Amplified Version gives this paraphrase of Hebrews 13:5-6:

> Let your character or moral disposition be free from love of money [including greed, avarice, lust, and craving for earthly possessions] and be satisfied with your present [circumstances and with what you have]; for He [God] Himself has said, I will not in any way fail you nor give you up nor leave you without support. [I will] not, [I will] not, [I will] not in any degree leave you helpless nor forsake nor let [you] down (relax My hold on you)! [Assuredly not!]'
>
> 'So we take comfort and are encouraged and confidently and boldly say, The Lord is my Helper; I will not be siezed with alarm [I will not fear or dread or be terrified]. What can man do to me?

This promise assures us of God's constant help. It guarantees the greatest possible good. It secures all our needs. It gives comfort for every trouble. It is substantiated by God's immutability, faithfulness, and love. And it is confirmed by the observation of faith. These are not the words of an angel, a mere man, or any creature. These are the words of God himself. 'I will never leave thee, nor forsake thee.'

God the Father will never leave his children, nor forsake them (Isaiah 49:13-15; 54:7-10, 14-17). God the Son will never leave nor forsake the people for whom he suffered and died (Matthew 28:18-20). Once the Lord Jesus comes to a sinner to be his all, he will never forsake that sinner and be nothing at all. His immutable love will not allow it. His precious blood will not allow it. His covenant engagements will not allow it. His faithfulness will not allow it. And God the Holy Spirit will never leave nor forsake those in whom he dwells (John 14:16; Philippians 4:4).

God forsook the tabernacle in the wilderness, and the temple at Jerusalem, but he will never forsake his living temple. We are the habitation of his delight. God once forsook his darling Son, when he was made to be sin for us. But, since Christ has put away our sins, God will never forsake any sinner for whom Christ died, because he can never have any reason to do so! This is the sweet promise of God to every believer. 'I will never leave thee, nor forsake thee.' Read it as it is given repeatedly in his Word and rejoice (Psalm 27:10; 73:25-26). 'I will never leave thee, nor forsake thee.'

God's Word to You

Paul is rapidly bringing his epistle to the Hebrews to its conclusion. This epistle was written specifically to Jewish believers in the first century. But we must never imagine that it was not also specifically written for us. Paul's personal intent was to minister to those earliest men and women among Abraham's physical descendants who were born of God. But the Holy Spirit's intent in all the scriptures is to minister to the needs of all God's people in this world, throughout this gospel age (Romans 15:4). Throughout these thirteen chapters, the Spirit of God is speaking directly to us (as he does in all the Word of God). He is encouraging those who have been saved by the grace of God to persevere in the faith of Christ. Though we are required to constantly engage in spiritual warfare, though the religious world we have left despises us and ridicules us, though family and friends forsake us, we cannot go back. We must run with patience the race that is set before us. We must follow Christ, who 'endured such contradiction of sinners against himself'.

Be Faithful

The message to us is this: 'Let us go forth therefore unto him without the camp, bearing his reproach. For here have we no continuing city, but we seek one to come' (vv. 13, 14). Here Paul admonishes us to faithfulness in all things. He urges us to be faithful in love to one another (v. 1) and faithful in hospitality, charity, and kindness (v. 2). We ought always to use what God has given us to minister to the needs of others. With open heart, open hand, and open doors, let us serve the needs of others. God never gave us anything, except that which he intends for us to share with others.

Be faithful in intercessory prayer for your suffering, tried, afflicted brethren (v. 3), and be faithful in your homes (v. 4). Let every man have his own wife and every woman her husband. And let them love, serve, and care for one another with tenderness and faithfulness in every aspect of life. Marriage is honourable among all and the marriage bed is undefiled.

Be faithful to Christ in all things (vv. 5-6). The word 'conversation' means 'manner of life'. Paul says, 'Let your life be without covetousness; and be content with such things as you have; for he hath said, I will never leave thee, nor forsake thee. So that we may boldly say, The Lord is my helper, and I will not fear what man shall do unto me.'

God's Promise for Today

Here is a word of promise from our great God. 'I will never leave thee, nor forsake thee.' Here is a word from God that is full of spiritual meaning and instruction. This is bread for the Father's children. This is a staff upon which weary pilgrims may lean. It will give us strength for our journey, comfort for our souls, and vigour for our hearts. This sentence is a chest full of rich treasure. May God the Holy Spirit graciously open it and cause our souls to be enriched by it. 'I will never leave thee, nor forsake thee.' The Lord our God promises his perpetual presence and care to every believer forever.

This is a quotation from the Old Testament scriptures. How many times have you heard someone deny the application of a promise, a warning, or a doctrine by saying, 'That is in the Old Bible', or 'That is in the Old Testament'? Many are of the opinion that only a very small portion of the Bible was really intended for us in this day. They say, 'The Old Testament was for the Jews. The four Gospels are for the "tribulation saints". The book of Revelation is for the "Millennial saints". The epistles of Peter, James, and John were for Jewish believers in the first century. And Paul's epistles alone are really intended for the Gentile believers of this age'. Rubbish!

In this text the Holy Spirit led Paul to quote a promise from the Old Testament. In doing so, he is teaches us to honour the Old Testament scriptures as the Word of God, just as we do the New Testament. He tells us that the promises of God made to his ancient people are the promises of God made to his people today (2 Corinthians 1:20).

Five Times

We find this promise given five times in the Old Testament. (1) It was given to Jacob at Bethel when he was on his way to Laban's house and fourteen years of great trial (Genesis 28:15). (2) It was given to Moses just before the Lord took him up into the mountain where he died (Deuteronomy 31:16; 34:4-7), a promise by which God assured Moses that everything would be well with Israel after he was gone (Deuteronomy 31:6-8). (3) It was given to Joshua when he was commissioned to lead the people of God in Moses' place and again just as he began the work to which God had called him (Deuteronomy 31:7-8; Joshua 1:5). (4) It was given to Solomon when he was about to assume the throne of Israel and was commissioned to build the house of the Lord (1 Chronicles 28:20). And (5) it was given to God's afflicted people when they had to face their mighty enemies (Isaiah 41:10-14; Isaiah 43:1-5).

Lessons

What are we to learn from the fact that Paul, by inspiration, gives us the same promise that God gave to Moses, Jacob, Joshua, Solomon and Israel? You will notice that Paul gives us the sense of the promise, not the very words of the promise, teaching us that the sense of scripture, the spiritual message of scripture, is the meaning of scripture. Many know the scriptures 'by heart' who do not know the heart of the scriptures!

I know there is a danger here. We believe in the verbal, plenary inspiration of holy scripture. But we do not interpret the scriptures in a strictly literal way. The Spirit of God gives us spiritual understanding to discern the message of scripture. And the message is always a spiritual, Christ centred, Christ honouring message (Luke 24:27, 44-47).

It is also evident that every word from God to any believer is the Word of God to every believer. God who made the promise never changes (Malachi 3:6; Hebrews 13:8). All the promises of God in Christ Jesus are yea and amen (2 Corinthians 1:20) conditioned on Christ alone! The promises made to one are made to all, for all believers in Christ are one body (Ephesians 4:4).

This makes the Bible a book written for me. It is a word from the Lord directed to me. 'Every word of divine love and tenderness that he has written in this book belongs to me' (M'Cheyne). So this promise from the Lord is God's promise to me particularly. 'I will never leave thee, nor forsake thee.' This, my brother, my sister, is God's promise to you.

Remember them which have the rule over you, who have spoken unto you the word of God: whose faith follow, considering the end of their conversation. Jesus Christ the same yesterday, and to day, and for ever. Be not carried about with divers and strange doctrines. For it is a good thing that the heart be established with grace; not with meats, which have not profited them that have been occupied therein. We have an altar, whereof they have no right to eat which serve the tabernacle. For the bodies of those beasts, whose blood is brought into the sanctuary by the high priest for sin, are burned without the camp. Wherefore Jesus also, that he might sanctify the people with his own blood, suffered without the gate. Let us go forth therefore unto him without the camp, bearing his reproach. For here have we no continuing city, but we seek one to come.

Hebrews 13:7-14

Chapter 50

Read: Hebrews 13:7-14

'Established With Grace'
The Holy Spirit focuses our attention on our immutable Saviour in verse 8. 'Jesus Christ the same yesterday, and to day, and for ever.' In verse 7 Paul exhorted us to remember, respect, acknowledge, and follow those faithful pastors the Lord has been pleased to give to us. Here he says, 'Consider the subject and object of their ministry Jesus Christ, who is the same yesterday, today and for ever.' All God's servants say with Paul (and tell the truth when they say it), 'We preach not ourselves, but Christ Jesus the Lord, and ourselves your servants for Jesus' sake.' (2 Corinthians 4:5).

Our Saviour
A faithful pastor preaches Christ. The goal of his life and ministry is to know Christ. The glory of Christ is the object of his conversation and conduct. Christ is the same yesterday, today, and forever. What does that mean?

Christ is the same in his glory, his offices, his purposes, and his work 'yesterday', in all times past. In the beginning of the world he was the everlasting 'I AM', the Lamb slain, the Surety of his people. In Old Testament times he was the substance of the sacrifices, the types and the promises.

'Today', in this gospel age, he is still the same. In his person he is the God-Man; in his offices he is Prophet, Priest and King. He is 'forever' the same, because he is our unchanging, unchangeable, immutable God and Saviour. See him now on his throne. He is the same Lamb of God who died for us at Calvary! His kingdom is an everlasting kingdom and his priesthood an unchanging priesthood. His love and care for his people can never change (Malachi 3:6; Romans 11:29; Philippians 1:6).

Our Hearts

Next, the Holy Spirit calls for us to remember and consider our own hearts. 'Be not carried about with divers and strange doctrines. For it is a good thing that the heart be established with grace; not with meats, which have not profited them that have been occupied therein' (v. 9). Let your hearts 'be established with grace'. Conviction, repentance, faith, and the knowledge of Christ are heart works, not just mental acceptance of facts and doctrines (Romans 10:9-10). Let your hearts be convinced, persuaded, settled and established regarding the righteousness of God and the way to God. By 'Grace' we understand that salvation, justification, and eternal life are the result of God's grace to us in Christ Jesus, not by deeds of the law nor works of the flesh (Titus 3:5-7; 2 Timothy 1:8-11).

Let us not be unsettled, tossed about and carried way from the gospel of the grace of God by the many winds of strange doctrine which come our way from the lips of men. They are called 'strange doctrines' because they are not taught in the Word of God, because they are doctrines inconsistent with the person and work of Christ, and because they are contrary to the doctrine of grace. Those who are occupied with the ceremonial law, eating certain meats, keeping sabbath days or engaging in religious ceremonialism have not profited in their souls by such conduct. These things cannot sanctify, justify, establish the heart, or give peace to the soul (Romans 14:17; Colossians 2:16-23).

Our Altar

Next, we are urged to set our hearts upon Christ our Altar, so that our hearts may be established with grace. 'We have an altar, whereof they have no right to eat which serve the tabernacle' (v. 10). The reference here is to the eating of the sacrifices of the Old Testament by God's priests (Leviticus 6:14-16). The sacrifice was offered, burned upon the altar, and eaten by the priests. We, too, have an Altar. Not the cross, or the Lord's Table, or a bench at the front of the church, but Christ himself. He is our Altar, our Sacrifice, and our Priest. We have the right to come to Christ and, therefore, to eat of his flesh and drink of his blood (John 6:53-57).

That is what it is to live by faith. Those who seek salvation and acceptance with God by the works and duties of the law have no right to this Altar. They have fallen from grace. They have forsaken the Altar, Christ Jesus himself(Galatians 5:1-4).

Our Sacrifice

The Altar at which we feed, upon which we must set our hearts, is Christ, our Sacrifice. 'For the bodies of those beasts, whose blood is brought into the sanctuary by the high priest for sin, are burned without the camp. Wherefore Jesus also, that he might sanctify the people with his own blood, suffered without the gate' (vv. 11-12).

On the Day of Atonement the bullock and goat were slain and the blood was brought into the holy of holies and sprinkled on the mercy-seat to make an atonement. The bullock and goat were then taken outside the camp and burned (Leviticus 16:15-17, 27, 28). In order to sanctify us with his blood and to fulfil this typical picture, the Lord Jesus was crucified outside the walls of the city of Jerusalem, represented by the camp of Israel in the wilderness. The flesh, skin, and dung of the sin-offering were unclean before God and had to be carried and disposed of outside the camp. Even the men who handled it were unclean. We see in this not only the suffering of our Lord for sin but the shame and reproach he endured as our sin-offering. Bearing our sins in his own body, he was unclean and must die outside the camp.

Our Place

'Let us go forth therefore unto him without the camp, bearing his reproach. For here have we no continuing city, but we seek one to come' (vv. 13-14). Christ is our sin-offering, our hope of redemption, and our Redeemer. Where he is, there we must be (John 14:3). In his shame and reproach he suffered without the camp. So, being one with him, we must quit the camp of ceremony, legalism, human works, worldliness, and all that is opposed to him, to be identified with our Lord. Whatever reproach we incur from the natural or religious world is welcome, because we find in him all we need (1 Corinthians 1:30; Colossians 2:9-10). The world and everything in it are unstable and temporary. The riches, honours, and pleasures of the world, the people in it, and the fashion of it pass away. Though we are in the world, we are not of it, and when the will of God is done, we will be taken out of it to heaven, where all is peace, perfect love, and eternal (John 17:16; 1 John 2:15-17). In the light of these things, it is indeed a good thing 'that the heart be established with grace'.

'Them Which Have The Rule Over You'

The preaching of the Gospel is ordained of God for many good purposes. As I prepare to preach, and when I stand to preach the gospel of God's grace and glory in Christ, I try to keep these things constantly in mind: the glory of God, the salvation of God's elect, and the comfort and edification of your souls.

God has promised to give his church pastor/teachers, after his own heart to feed you with knowledge and understanding (Ephesians 4:11; Jeremiah 3:15), to guide you in the old paths of gospel truth, that you may constantly find rest for your souls in Christ that your hearts may be 'established with grace'.

If we would have our hearts established with grace, we must constantly set our hearts upon Christ, living in the pursuit of him (Philippians 3:7-14). In Hebrews 13:7-14 we are given six important, pressing admonitions; admonitions we need to constantly heed. They are admonitions concerning faithful pastors (v. 7), our immutable Saviour (v. 8), our hearts (v. 9), our Altar (v. 10), our Sacrifice (vv. 11-12), and our place (vv. 13-14). The admonition in verse 7 concerns the believer's attitude and responsibility toward his pastor. 'Remember them which have the rule over you, who have spoken unto you the word of God: whose faith follow, considering the end of their conversation.'

Rulers

Christ's church is a kingdom. He is King. Faithful pastors of local churches are his subordinates, his appointed governors over his churches. They are here called 'them which have the rule over you,' because they are men appointed and gifted by God to rule his house, just as a husband is to rule his house for the glory of God (1 Timothy 3:4).

God's servants do not rule his churches arbitrarily, according to their own wills, but according to the Word and Spirit of Christ. They rule his house faithfully, with prudence, exercising great diligence, seeking the will and glory of God, the good of his people, and the furtherance of the gospel.

God's servants are not, and do not wish to be demigods. They are not little tyrants and dictators over the souls of men. But neither are they puppets on a string, controlled by men. They are God's servants, men who watch over you, and serve the eternal interests of your immortal souls, for the glory of God.

The word 'rule' could be rendered 'guidance' or 'leadership' and means that the gospel preacher is one who points out the way of peace, life, and salvation to men, directing sinners to Christ. He is one who guides men and women into the understanding of the scriptures, and the truths of the gospel, and leads them in the paths of faith, faithfulness, and true godliness, by word and by example. The admonition here is threefold.

Remember

First, God admonishes his people to 'remember' those men who serve their souls by the gospel. Own and acknowledge them, respect and obey them, submitting to the Word of God they deliver to you. To remember them involves knowing them, making yourself acquainted with them and their labour for your souls (1 Thessalonians 5:12-13). To remember them is to treasure up, remember and heed the gospel they preach to you (2 Timothy 1:13-14). To remember them is to remember their needs and supply them with their needs. To remember is to remember those who preach the gospel to you before the throne of grace (2 Thessalonians 3:1-2).

The reason given for this admonition, the encouragement to heed it is the fact that faithful pastors are men 'who have spoken unto you the Word of God'. Without question, this refers to the faithful exposition of holy scripture. God's servants are faithful to God's book. But the word used here for 'Word' is commonly used in holy scripture to refer to the Lord Jesus Christ, who is the living, eternal Word, of whom the written Word speaks. The singular subject of holy scripture is the love, mercy and grace of God in Christ, the sinners' Substitute.

Follow

Second, the apostle says, 'whose faith follow'. Here God's people are urged to follow the faith of their pastors, as the pastors guide them in the way of life, and faith, and godliness. Faithful pastors are faithful men, responsible to set before men an example of faith and faithfulness, so that they can say to those who hear them what Paul said to the Corinthians and the Thessalonians, 'be ye followers of us' (1 Corinthians 4:16; 11:1; 1 Thessalonians 1:6). In verse 17 he speaks of obeying their doctrine. Certainly, to follow a faithful pastor is to follow his instruction; but here (v. 7) Paul is urging God's people to imitate those men who lead them by example. Be wise, my friends, and follow the example of faithful men. Follow them in their doctrine, in the faithful discharge of their responsibilities, in the worship and service of Christ, in faith and patience, in love and good works, and in steadfastness and perseverance.

Consider

Third, Paul urges believers to remember and follow their pastors, 'considering the end of their conversation'. This third part of Paul's admonition includes a reason for following such men. Paul urges believers to consider the end of their conversation; to consider the consummation, and glory awaiting such faithful men. The end, the drift, the scope of such conduct is the glory of Christ, the good of men, and everlasting salvation. What a motive this is!

Four Responsibilities of a Gospel Pastor

In these verses we are told that gospel pastors are specifically responsible for four things. (1) It is the responsibility of every gospel pastor to rule the house of God. A gospel church is a kingdom under the rule of Christ her King. Pastors called by God are the overseers, governors, and rulers of his churches. Christ is the Shepherd. Faithful pastors are his under-shepherds. The pastor's rule of God's house is like a husband's rule of his own house. It involves direction, provision, and protection. (2) The way God's servants rule his church is by the declaration of God's Word, by the preaching of the gospel. 'Who have spoken to you the Word of God'. (3) To preach the Word of God is to instruct eternity bound men and women in the way of faith. When Paul says, 'whose faith follow', he is both telling us that the gospel preacher must be a man of faith and faithfulness, and that the faith he preaches and the faithfulness he exemplifies are to be followed by those over whom the Lord has placed him. (4) These things God's servants are responsible to do as watchmen, as men who 'watch for your souls, as they that must give account'. But Paul's primary object in these verses is to show God's people what they ought to do, how they ought to behave, in relation to 'them which have the rule over you'. The scriptures give clear instructions about these things. Here are five things every church and every believer within the church ought to do for the man who preaches the gospel of Christ to them, labouring for their souls' eternal good.

1. Remember him (Hebrews 13:7) – Ever keep your pastor close to your heart in fond remembrance. Remember him at the throne of grace when you pray, but particularly, the admonition here is to remember his messages and the doctrine he preaches. Listen carefully to what he preaches. Take notes to aid your memory. Discuss his sermons at home and among your brethren, and store up his doctrine in your mind, so that you can apply it to yourself as you seek to live in this world for the glory of God. As you read the Word of God in your private worship, if you remember what has been preached to you, the Word will open before you and be blessed of God to your heart. Here are two reasons for remembering your pastor, particularly, for remembering his messages. First, he has the rule of the church. His word is to be remembered, because God has made him your

spiritual guide in this world. Second, he speaks to you the Word of God. He does not come in his own name, teaching his own opinions, or the philosophies of men. If he is God's man, your pastor comes to you with God's message, armed with God's authority: and what he says you are responsible to hear, remember, and obey. He preaches to you the Word of God.

2. Follow him (Hebrews 13:7) – Believers and churches are to follow their pastors. Your pastor is your leader and guide in the kingdom of God. You are to follow his example of faith and faithfulness. Follow the pure gospel doctrine that he preaches to you. It leads to life everlasting. Follow his example of devotion to Christ. Your pastor, if he is truly the servant of God, is a man of resolute heart devotion to Christ, his church, his gospel and his glory. He guides God's people by his own example of consecration to Christ. Follow his example of faithfulness. The one thing God requires of his servants is faithfulness, and if you would be serviceable to the cause of Christ in your own sphere of responsibility, you will learn how by following your pastor's example. This is not blind allegiance to a man. This is obedience to Christ. If you would follow Christ, you must follow the man he has made your guide, 'considering the end of his conversation, Jesus Christ the same yesterday, and today, and for ever' (Hebrews 13:8). Christ is the object of our faith, the pattern of our faith, and the end of our faith. Follow your pastor in the life of faith, as he presses towards the mark, Christ Jesus (Philippians 3:14).

3. Obey him (Hebrews 13:17) – Obedience is not servitude, but it does mean submission. God's people are expected and required to obey their pastors. In spiritual, doctrinal matters, in all things regarding the affairs and work of the church, the pastor is to be obeyed. If he is not worthy of obedience, he should not be the pastor. Elders are to serve the church in obedience to the pastor. Deacons are to serve the church in obedience to the pastor. Teachers are to serve the church in obedience to the pastor. Every member of the congregation is to serve the church in obedience to the pastor. The pastor is the captain of the ship. All the crew must serve in obedience to him. Obey his message, the gospel of the grace of God. Hear it. Receive it. Love it, and order your life by it. Obey his direction in the worship of Christ. Every aspect of the worship and work of the church should be carried out in accordance with the pastor's instruction. The order of the services, the selection of music, the administration of the ordinances and the activities of the church are to be performed in the way required by the pastor, as he is guided by the Word of God. There is no need for committees and societies within the church body. The pastor's voice, as he seeks the will and glory of God, is to be obeyed in all things.

Obey his admonitions and reproofs. No pastor is infallible. He will often err. But if he is a faithful man, his errors will be errors of judgment, not errors of principle. You can safely follow such a man and obey him. His admonitions and reproofs, if he is God's servant, are not personal attacks or fits of passion. They are thoughtful, needed, God-given warnings and directions for your soul's eternal good.

4. Submit to him (Hebrews 13:17) – The admonition here is to submit yourself to the Spirit led, faithful care of your pastor. Do what he tells you to do, even if you do not really understand why. That may seem a little too much to expect, but a little consideration will show that it is not. A few years ago, I was dying with cancer. The doctors wanted to treat my disease by injecting me with a series of drugs and cobalt treatments. The drugs and the treatments could prove deadly themselves, if they were not properly administered. I do not understand how they work, but, being confident of my physicians' abilities, I submitted myself to them and did what they told me to do, because I knew that they knew better than I did what was needed. You are to submit to your pastor in just that way. If he is a faithful man, he probably knows better than you what is best for your soul, the cause of Christ, the welfare of the church and the furtherance of the gospel. He will not wilfully mislead you, and he will not abuse you, or take advantage of you. Your pastor's concern is for the welfare of your soul. He watches for your soul as one who must give account, both to his own conscience and at the judgment bar of God. Every faithful pastor exercises great care and diligence as he watches over God's people, for he desires to give account of his hearers with joy and not with grief.

5. Pray for him (Hebrews 13:18) – Let every child of God pray continually for all who faithfully preach the gospel of Christ; but every believer should especially pray for his own pastor. Pray for your pastor as he seeks a message for your soul in his private study and preparation for the pulpit, as he preaches the gospel to you, and with regard to his life and conduct in this world. He is a man like yourself, weak, frail, sinful and tempted. Pray that God will ever give him grace to seek neither to avoid the disfavour of men, nor to crave the favour of men. Call upon God to preserve him in grace, in usefulness, in health and strength. Pray for your pastor's constant and increasing usefulness in the cause of Christ.

Blessed Immutability!

Everything changes, nothing remains the same. Sometimes the changes are delightful. Sometimes they are almost unbearable. But change is inevitable. Winter turns to spring, spring to summer, summer to autumn, and autumn to winter again. Everything changes, nothing stays the same.

In this world there is nothing solid, stable, and substantial. Everything we grasp is air. Everything we seek is vanity. Everything we build upon is sand. Everything in this world that gives us joy will, in time, cause our hearts to break with grief! 'Vanity of vanities; all is vanity!' That is not the cry of hopelessness and despair. That is just a statement of fact. 'Vanity of vanities; all is vanity'.

Is there no solid rock upon which to stand? Is there no immovable anchor by which we can find stability? Is there no sure foundation upon which to build? Blessed be God there is one! 'Jesus Christ the same yesterday, and today, and forever.' The Lord Jesus Christ never changes! He upon whom we have set our hearts, he who is the Object of our faith, he who sits upon the throne of the universe, never changes. Our Lord Jesus Christ is immutable. He cannot change or be changed. He is always the same. What does this mean?

Yesterday and Today

All that our Lord Jesus Christ was yesterday, he is today. All that he was in the yesterday of eternity past, he is today. Was he the object of his Father's delight before ever the world was made (Proverbs 8:30)? Then he is the Father's delight today. Was he the Bearer and Dispenser of all the blessings of life and grace before the world began (Ephesians 1:3-6; 2 Timothy 1:9)? Then he has all life and grace in himself today.

All that he was yesterday, in his life upon the earth, he is today. He was tender, kind, sympathetic and approachable then. And he is exactly the same now. He was the one in whom God was well pleased then. And he is the one, the only one, in whom God is well pleased now. He was made of God unto us wisdom, righteousness, sanctification, and redemption then. And he is made the same to us now (1 Corinthians 1:30).

All that he was in the yesterday of more than 2000 years since he ascended to the throne of glory, he is today. Did he take dominion over the universe as King? He is still reigning today. Did he send down his Spirit upon his church? He is still sending down the Spirit today. Did he do mighty works yesterday? He is still doing mighty things today.

All that Christ ever has been to his people yesterday he is to his people today. All that Christ ever did for his people yesterday he does for his people today. And the only reason you and I ever look back to a yesterday that appears to be better than today is that we fail to trust Jesus Christ who is the same yesterday, and today, and forever. If we did not fail to trust him, today would be but a new revelation and a larger experience of the grace revealed and experienced yesterday. All that Christ was yesterday he is today.

And Forever

Our all-glorious Christ is the same yesterday, and today, and forever! All that he is and has been he will forever be; and all that he will be forever, he is at this moment. All that he is to your soul and mine, he will be forever. And all that he will forever be, he is right now!

Try to grasp this. All that Christ will be in the fullest revelation of his glory and grace in heaven, all the inconceivable closeness of love and communion, all the indescribable excellence of our union with him in heaven, all that he can in eternity be to me, he is to me, and to all God's elect, right now! Amid all the changes that take place in this world and in our hearts, here is a message from God containing joy and strength which nothing can take away, 'Jesus Christ the same yesterday, and today, and forever'.

Today

'Today'. I love that word. Jesus Christ is immutable! 'Today if ye will hear his voice, harden not your hearts'. I want you to know, trust, and love Christ today. Look not to yourself, your fickle feelings, or your unstable works. Trust him who changes not. Build upon this sure foundation, and you shall live forever. 'Jesus Christ the same yesterday, and today, and forever'.

Read verse 7. 'Remember them which have the rule over you, who have spoken unto you the word of God: whose faith follow, considering the end of their conversation.' The apostle admonishes us to remember those men who have preached the gospel to us and to follow their examples of faith and faithfulness, keeping our hearts and minds fixed upon 'Jesus Christ the same yesterday, and today, and forever.' If we would believe God, obey the gospel, and be faithful, we must ever look to Christ (Hebrews 12:1-3).

Look at verse 9. 'Be not carried about with divers and strange doctrines. For it is a good thing that the heart be established with grace; not with meats, which have not profited them which have been occupied therein.' The admonition here is to doctrinal steadfastness. If our hearts are established with grace, firmly fixed upon the doctrine of the grace of God, our hearts must be fixed upon the immutable Christ.

Do you see how everything is built upon, flows from, and points to Christ? Christ is the source of all, the foundation of all, the centre of all, the object of all, and the end of all. In the life of a believer, in all true doctrine, in all true faith, in all the church of God, Christ is all. And he is immutable. He never changes!

Our Immutable Saviour

Our all-glorious Saviour, Jesus Christ, is immutable in his person. He is himself God. He never has changed and never can change in the essence of his Person, because he is perfect. Perfection cannot change. It is true, when he came into this world, the Son of God assumed our nature; but he did not change at all. He took our human nature into union with his divine nature; but nothing about his Person changed (Malachi 3:6). Though he died as our Substitute upon the cursed tree, his Person never changed. Our Master is forever the same. Nothing changes him. His attributes never change. His purpose of grace never changes. His great love never changes. The objects of his purpose, grace, and love never change. Christ's person never changes. What he was before the world began he is now. What he is now, he shall forever be. What he shall forever be he now is and always was (Lamentations 3:22; Romans 11:29, James 1:17). As our Saviour is immutable in his person, he is immutable in all his works.

His Covenant Offices

Our dear Saviour is immutable in all his covenant offices and relationships. Our God is very accommodating to our weakness. In order to communicate to us, he condescends to use human language. He describes himself to us in human terms in his Word. But whenever you read anything that implies change or limitation about God, it must not be taken literally. This must especially be understood of the covenant offices and relationships of Christ toward his elect. What Christ is to us and for us, he always was and forever shall be.

He is a Prophet who shall be heard, a Priest who makes satisfaction, and a King who rules from everlasting to everlasting. Jesus Christ is the eternal Husband of his church, a Husband who 'hateth putting away' (Malachi 2:16). The Lord Jesus is an eternal Brother, born in time for adversity, but set up from everlasting. He is an eternal 'Friend that sticketh closer than a brother' (Proverbs 17:17). He was from everlasting the Friend of sinners, and still is! He is just as ready today to pardon sinners, as he was when he forgave the woman taken in adultery. He is just as anxious to comfort his afflicted ones, as he was when he came to Bethany to comfort Martha and Mary. He is just as ready to meet the needs of his people today as when he washed his disciples' feet. All that Christ ever was, he always was, and is now. He is the eternal Surety of an eternal covenant (Hebrews 7:22). He is the eternal Lamb who obtained eternal redemption (Revelation 5:6, 9, 12; Hebrews 9:12; Romans 8:28-34). He is an eternal Advocate who makes eternal intercession (1 John 2:1-2). He is an eternal Saviour who gives eternal salvation (2 Timothy 1:9-10; Hebrews 5:9). We rejoice to know that all these things were revealed in time, accomplished in time, and applied in time. Our joy is in the experience of grace. But the pillar of our faith does not rest upon anything in time. We rest our souls upon the sure foundation of an eternal, immutable Saviour.

His Doctrine

The doctrine of Christ is immutable. Certainly Paul had this in mind when he wrote, 'Jesus Christ the same yesterday, and today, and for ever.' I know that he meant for us to understand that our Saviour's immutability includes the immutability of his doctrine, because in the next verse he tells us that it is the message of Christ that establishes our hearts with grace and prevents us from being 'carried about with divers and strange doctrines.' Truth never changes. In the matter of doctrine anything that is reported to be 'new and improved' is false and damning. We walk right only when we walk in the old paths (Jeremiah 6:16). Divine truth does not change. The gospel, the doctrine of Christ, does not change.

His Grace

The Son of God is immutable in the operations of his grace. His doctrine never changes. His method of operation never changes. He is 'the same yesterday, and today, and forever.' Whenever God has a work to do among men; whenever God is pleased to pour out his grace upon sinners; in the Bible and in history he always does four things. (1) He raises up men to use, like Moses. (2) He sends men with a message, the Gospel. (3) He sends a spirit of prayer upon his people (2 Samuel 7:27, Daniel 9:3-4; Acts 8:14-15; 13:2-3; 14:23). (4) He grants the power and grace of his Spirit to accomplish his purpose. This is our Lord's method of grace. 'It pleased God by the foolishness of preaching to save them that believe'. The church of God needs three things, only three, to accomplish her work in this world: God's man, God's message, and God's power. Everything else is a hindrance and liability.

His Power

Our great Saviour is immutable in his position, possessions, and power (John 17:2; Philippians 2:9-11). He is on his throne. He possesses all things. He has all power. He is 'the blessed and only Potentate', the only possessor of power! We live in dark times, perhaps the darkest this world has ever seen. I cannot exaggerate the gravity of this hour. Never has error been more widespread and popularly received. In the 'dark ages' the papacy reigned by the sword over the bodies of men. In these darker ages free-willism reigns over the hearts of men. But there is no cause for despair.

Jesus Christ is the same yesterday, and today, and forever. He has not abdicated his throne. He has not relinquished his power! He still holds all the resources of the universe, all the resources of God, in his hand. Does the church need messengers? Christ has plenty! Do we need grace? Christ has plenty! Do we need power? Christ has plenty! We have changed. The world has changed. But Christ has not changed. He is eternally the same.

For Me

Allow me to interject a personal word. The Lord Jesus Christ is immutable to me. For thirty-seven years now, I have found him immutable. I have never known him to change. He abideth faithful. All that he was to me when I first came to him, he is now (2 Samuel 23:5). Christ is all my Wisdom. Christ is all my Righteousness. Christ is all my Sanctification. Christ is all my Redemption. Christ is all my Hope. Christ is all my Desire (Psalm 73:25). I trust nothing but Christ. I have nothing but Christ. I want nothing but Christ (1 Corinthians 1:30, 2 Thessalonians 2:16).

Immutable Forever

This immutable Christ shall be the eternal glory, reward, and joy of our inheritance in heaven. Soon we shall depart from this changing world and enter that world where change is unknown. And if we are in Christ, we shall forever be with Christ and find him to be 'Jesus Christ the same yesterday, and today, and forever.' All that he has been, all that he is he shall forever be. When everything around you seems to crumble like dried flowers in your hand, when it seems to you that the very foundations of all things temporal crumble beneath your feet, look away to our great, immutable Saviour, and be at peace.

> Swift to its close ebbs out life's little day.
> Earth's joys grow dim; its glories pass away;
> Change and decay in all around I see.
> O Thou who changest not, abide with me.

Established Hearts

Multitudes are 'carried about with divers and strange doctrines' (v. 9). Many and strange are the different doctrines of men; doctrines that are foreign to the scriptures and contrary to the gospel of Christ, the character of God, and the person, work, and offices of Christ as our Mediator. (1 Timothy 4:1-3; 2:5). The doctrine of Christ is one. Truly, it is a good thing to have our hearts established with grace.

'Hearts'

It is written, 'With the heart man believeth unto righteousness' (Romans 10:10). The Lord God requires, 'Apply thine heart to understanding' (Proverbs 2:2). 'Let thine heart keep my commandments' (Proverbs 3:1). 'Write mercy and truth upon the table of thine heart' (Proverbs 3:3). 'Let thine heart retain my words' (Proverbs 4:4). 'Keep thy heart with all diligence'(Proverbs 4:23). 'My son, Give me thine heart' (Proverbs 23:26). All true religion is a matter of the heart. Faith is a heart work. Repentance is a heart work. The confession of sin is a heart work. Prayer is a heart work. Worship is a heart work. Our Lord declares in Matthew 5:8 that the pure in heart shall see God, and no one else. In all things spiritual the heart is the principle thing.

'Established'

The grace of God establishes the hearts of men. It does not leave us floundering in religious mysticism, religious intellectualism, and philosophical speculation. Believing hearts are convinced, persuaded, and settled regarding the righteousness of God and the way to God. Being built upon that foundation God himself has laid, Christ Jesus, we are established in the love of God, convinced of acceptance with God, the complete expiation of our sins, and our righteousness before God in and by Christ. Trusting Christ, we are no longer looking for the way to God and eternal life, but are established in the way. We no longer grope about in the blindness and darkness of religious confusion, but walk in the light of revealed truth, firmly looking for and expecting eternal happiness by, with, and in Christ, rejoicing in hope of the glory of God.

'Grace'

Our hearts are established with the gospel of the grace of God, the doctrine of the grace of God, the truth of the grace of God, and by the work of the grace of God. We understand that salvation, justification, and eternal life are the result of God's grace to us in Christ Jesus, not by deeds of the law or works of the flesh (Titus 3:5-7; 2 Timothy 1:8-11). Let us never be unsettled, tossed about and carried away from the gospel of God's free and sovereign grace in Christ, by the many winds of strange doctrine, which come our way from the lips of men.

'Not With Meats'

Work-mongers and religious legalists are occupied with outward, carnal things: eating and not eating certain meats, the keeping of sabbath days, and the observance of religious ceremonies. Such carnal practices gratify the flesh, but do not profit their souls. These things cannot justify, sanctify, establish the heart, or give peace to the soul (Colossians 2:16-23; Romans 14:17). It is Christ alone who is all our acceptance with God (1 Corinthians 1:30).

Christ Our Altar

Moses describes the altar of sacrifice for us in Exodus 27:1-8. All that the altar of the tabernacle and the temple signified typically is fulfilled for us really and truly in the Lord Jesus Christ. Christ is our Altar.

The Altar's Use

The altar of sacrifice typified Christ in the use for which it was made. The altar sanctified the gift, the sacrifice, which was placed upon it, and made it acceptable to God (Matthew 23:19). Christ sanctifies us. He makes the believing soul and our sacrifices acceptable to God (1 Peter 2:5). There was one altar for all the people, one altar for all their sins, one altar for all their sacrifices. There is one Altar for sinners; and that Altar is Christ.

The altar bore the violent heat of divine wrath, so that the sinner might go free. While the fire consumed the sacrifice on the altar, the altar itself was not destroyed. Even so, Christ our Altar bore the violent heat of God's wrath. He poured out his soul unto death for our sins as a sacrifice to God of a sweet-smelling savour. Yet, he is not destroyed. This sacrifice, rather than being consumed by the wrath of God, has consumed the wrath of God (Romans 8:1).

The altar was a place of refuge for guilty men (1 Kings 1:50; 2:28-30). What else can a guilty man do but take hold of the horns of the altar? Christ alone is the Refuge for guilty sinners.

There were four horns on the altar. These four horns represented the universality of Christ's redemption, reaching to the four corners of the earth. It is written, 'Whosoever shall call upon the name of the Lord shall be saved.' You will be wise to lay hold of the horns of the Altar, and plead for God's mercy. What encouragement the Holy Lord God gives to sinners to do just that in the invitations and commands of the gospel (Isaiah 43:25-26).

The Altar's Position

The altar of Sacrifice was typical of Christ in its position. The moment the sinner entered the door of the tabernacle to approach God, the first, the most important, most prominent thing he saw was that huge brazen altar. As he left the tabernacle and went out to live in the world, the last thing he saw was the altar.

In all things spiritual Christ is pre-eminent (Colossians 1:18). All the fulness of grace dwells in him (Colossians 1:19). Indeed, all the fulness of the eternal Godhead dwells in him (Colossians 2:9). In order to approach God, we must come by the Altar, Christ Jesus (Hebrews 7:25, 13:10). As we attempt to live in the world, we must live with the Altar of Sacrifice, the Lord Jesus Christ, ever before our heart's eyes. Every relationship in life is affected by this Altar.

The Altar's Form

The altar of sacrifice was typical of Christ in its form. It was four square, like Christ our Altar: full, complete, perfect. All the fulness of God's love is revealed in him and resides in him (Ephesians 3:19). All the fulness of God's covenant grace and promises is in Christ (Isaiah 49:8; 2 Samuel 23:5). All the fulness of God's salvation and grace is in Christ (1 Corinthians 1:30; Ephesians 3:8). He is the Creator of all things, the Upholder of all things, the Ruler of all things, and the Heir of all things.

There were no steps going up to the altar, because there is no possibility of sinners approaching God by the steps of their own works. There are no steps of preparation before we come to the Altar. When the priest approached the altar, no nakedness could be seen, because there were no steps to the altar. So it is with sinners coming to God by faith in Christ. Because we come to him by faith alone, the shameful nakedness of our souls is altogether unseen. We are washed in his blood and robed in his righteousness. The altar was completely covered with blood, because sin can only be put away by blood (Hebrews 9:22). Justice must be satisfied; and nothing but the blood of Christ could ever satisfy God's holy, inflexible, infinite justice.

The Altar's Materials

The altar of sacrifice was typical of Christ in its materials. The shittim wood represented the incorruptible humanity of Christ. The brass represented the eternal Godhead of Christ. The shittim wood overlaid with brass represents the eternal duration of the sufficiency of Christ's sacrifice.

Shittem wood, also called 'incorruptible wood' from the Shittah or Acacia tree, is a hard wood, resistant to corruption by insects, and able to flourish in barren places where other trees fail. The Lord Jesus, the incorruptible man, 'that holy thing', succeeded where all other men failed.

Brass is metal able to withstand great heat and speaks of the strength and power of the Lord Jesus to endure the fiery trials of his suffering, and to endure the cross, because he is God.

The Altar's Fire

And the fire, which continually burned upon the altar of sacrifice, was also typical of Christ. That perpetual flame represented the eternal love of Christ for his people, the zeal of Christ for the glory of God, the purifying of God's elect by the blood of Christ, and the unfailing intercession of Christ for us.

Come to Christ our Altar. He is the only Altar, the appointed Altar, a living Altar, a lasting Altar, an accessible Altar, and a saving, sin-atoning Altar. Sinners have no hope but to lay hold of the horns of this Altar. Horns suggests strength. Christ is able to save. Horns imply sufficiency. Christ is the Horn of salvation (Psalm 18:2; Luke 1:69). He is a Horn of plenty (Psalm 86:5). Child of God, come to Christ your Altar. Come continually (1 John 2:1-2). Eat of the Altar. Come and offer yourself to God upon this Altar (Romans 12:1-2). We cannot come to God any other way (John 14:6). And we cannot be rejected if we come to God by means of the Altar he has established (Hebrews 10:19-22).

One Altar

There is but one Altar by which sinful men may approach the Holy God. In the Old Testament there was but one altar of sacrifice by which men could ceremonially approach God; and that one altar finds its fulfilment in the Person of the Lord Jesus Christ. The only altar, which can sanctify us and make us acceptable to God, is Christ.

Today all physical, carnal, ceremonial altars are instruments of idolatry. Use anything as an altar for acceptance with God other than Christ and you have no right to the merits of Christ. If you have another altar, your altar will drag your soul down to hell.

Not the Cross

There are many who think of the cross upon which our Lord died as an altar. I have heard it said that the cross was the altar upon which our Lord offered himself as a sacrifice for sin. But it is not so. That cross upon which our Lord was crucified was nothing more than the instrument of his torture. It is no more to be reverenced as an altar than the whips of Pilate's soldiers, or the spit of those Jews, which defiled his holy face. I would no more wear a cross around my neck than I would take the dagger a murderer used to kill my wife and wear it on my belt.

Not Your Heart

Sometimes men talk of the heart as an altar to God. I know what they mean. They mean that sincerity makes our service to God acceptable. It is true that there must be sincerity in our service to God, or it will never be acceptable. But sincerity itself will never make our most solemn devotion acceptable to God. Nothing but blood will ever make a man acceptable to God. Only the blood of Christ, shed for the atonement of our sin, can make us accepted with God.

Not a Family Altar

It is common for men to talk of having a family altar. It is good to worship God in your home, with your family. But your family devotions will never make you acceptable to God. The church of God is a family, and we have a family altar. His name is Jesus Christ our Substitute.

Not a Church Altar

In many churches the table used for serving the Lord's Supper is looked upon as an altar. But the scriptures never speak in such a way. The table spread before you is a table of communion; not a table of sacrifice. It is a place of remembrance, not a place of atonement. It is a solemn feast, not a sanctifying feast.

Today many churches are removing their pulpit from the front of the congregatrion and placing it on a side wall. In its place is a table reminiscent of an altar. This might appear to be a mere re-arrangement of furniture or simply an architectural preference. But it is more subtle than that. It is a symbolic supplanting of the pre-eminent place of preaching in the church, and its replacment with an altar in the old Romish tradition. Our reforming forefathers purposefully placed the pulpit front and centre in their churches. We need not change their priorities.

Not an Altar Call

Perhaps the most deceptive of all idolatrous notions is the idea that there is an altar of salvation at the front of the church. You can no more obtain salvation by walking down the aisle of a Baptist church to an altar, than the papists can by going to a confessional booth, making a pilgrimage to Rome, and climbing the stairs to the pope's seat of infamy.

Christ Our Altar

There is but one Altar. There is but one place of salvation. That Altar is Christ. He is God's salvation. God only meets with men in his Son. We read in Exodus 20:23-26:

'Ye shall not make with me gods of silver, neither shall ye make unto you gods of gold. An altar of earth thou shalt make unto me, and shalt sacrifice thereon thy burnt offerings, and thy peace offerings, thy sheep, and thine oxen: in all places where I record my name I will come unto thee, and I will bless thee. And if thou wilt make me an altar of stone, thou shalt not build it of hewn stone: for if thou lift up thy tool upon it, thou hast polluted it. Neither shalt thou go up by steps unto mine altar, that thy nakedness be not discovered thereon.'

Christ is our Altar of earth. He is our Altar of stone. He is the Altar of God's making. 'If thou lift up thy tool upon it, thou hast polluted it'. That is to say, if you add anything to his work for acceptance with God, you pollute the Altar and the Sacrifice. Christ is the Altar with no stairs for men to climb. We do not come to God by degrees of holiness and sanctification, but by faith in Christ alone.

All forms of carnal worship, all forms of physical things that men call 'holy', all attempts to place any merit of any kind or any reverence of any kind in material things is base idolatry (Exodus 20:23; John 4:23-24; Philippians 3:3). Let us once and for all put away every form of idolatry from our midst (2 Kings 18:4), and worship God in spirit and in truth. We must worship God spiritually, from within, by the power and grace of the Holy Spirit. We must worship God truthfully, in truth and sincerity and according to the revealed truth of holy scripture. We must worship God in Christ who is the Truth.

'We Have An Altar'

Since the fall of our father Adam, God has never allowed man to approach him without an altar and a sacrifice of blood. In the old days of the patriarchs, from Adam to Moses, God's saints built altars of unhewn stone, upon which they offered sacrifices to God (Exodus 20:25; Genesis 22:9; Joshua 8:31). Whenever men drew near to God, whether to offer praise or to seek mercy, they built an altar and offered a sacrifice of blood. Even in those days, men of faith knew that God's justice could only be satisfied for sin by blood, even the blood of God's own Son, the Redeemer who must come into the world to put away sin.

Typical Altars

Then, when God called Moses up into the mount and spoke to him face to face he appointed one altar of sacrifice to be built, and appointed a place for that one altar in Israel alone. One spot was selected, and only one. All the rest of the world was left without an altar and without a sacrifice.

At first the altar was placed in the tabernacle. Later it was placed in the temple at Jerusalem. This was the only altar of sacrifice by which men might approach the holy Lord God. From time to time, the prophets of God, by God's special command, raised up other altars. But for all others the rule was unbending. One altar! All other altars erected by men were erected in defiance of God's command; and their pretended sacrifices to God were an abomination to him.

The True Altar

As in the typical, legal dispensation, so it is now. There is but one altar upon which the holy Lord God meets sinners in mercy, only one altar upon which God can and will be worshipped; and that Altar is Christ. The altar of sacrifice, in the tabernacle and in the temple, was typical of our Lord Jesus Christ (his Person, his work, and his merit) as our Substitute before God. This is what Paul teaches us in Hebrews 13:10. 'We have an altar, whereof they have no right to eat which serve the tabernacle.' The only access which sinners have to God, and the only acceptance we have with God is Christ our Altar.

A Heavenly Altar

Our Altar is in heaven. We recognize no altar upon the earth. He who has an Altar in heaven needs no altar upon the earth. He who has an altar upon the earth has no altar in heaven. The Holy Spirit tells us plainly; 'We have an altar, whereof they have no right to eat which serve the tabernacle.'

We cannot approach God without a Mediator, without an Altar, and without a Sacrifice. We are all guilty men and women, our best and holiest acts are but the sinful deeds of sinful men, and our purest worship is but the worship of depraved hearts. Who can bring a clean thing out of an unclean? No one. Before we can ever be accepted with God, before we can ever bring an acceptable offering or service to God, there must be a shedding of blood for the removal of our sin and guilt. We must come to God by way of the Altar and Sacrifice he has appointed, the Lord Jesus.

There is no door of acceptance for us except through the merit of our great Surety, who laid down his life for us. There is but one way by which we who are washed in the blood of Christ can offer unto God our prayers, our gifts, our praises, or our service, and that is by the Lord Jesus Christ, who alone is our Altar. We must give ourselves to him as living sacrifices, only in Christ will God accept our reasonable service (Romans 12:1).

Without The Camp With Christ

There are many who take great pride in being 'without the camp', after a fashion. But that is all that can be said of them. They are 'without the camp' in exactly the same sense that one might say a Mormon, a Russellite, or a Hindu is without the camp. They seem to think that godliness and gossip, holiness and haughtiness, separation and isolation are all synonyms. They think that meanness and meekness is the same thing. Merely being 'without the camp', is meaningless; we must be 'without the camp' with Christ. That is the instruction of Hebrews 13:11-13.

As the Lord Jesus Christ voluntarily identified himself with us, bearing our reproach for the salvation of our souls, let us ever go forth unto him, bearing his reproach for the glory of God.

The Day of Atonement

First, the apostle Paul points us once more to typical sacrifices of the Old Testament offered unto God on the day of atonement. The opening word of verse 11, 'For', refers us back to verse 10. There, Paul spoke of Christ our Altar, that Altar which we have in heaven, by whom we come to God. Here he speaks of the sacrifices offered on that old, carnal altar. As that altar was typical of the true Altar, all those sacrifices were typical of Christ, our one, great, sin-atoning Sacrifice.

The bodies of those animals, which were sacrificed year after year as sin-offerings for the priests and the people of Israel, were completely burnt without the camp of Israel. 'Without the camp' was the place of uncleanness, the place of God's curse, and the dwelling-place of lepers.

The sacrifice was carefully chosen, precisely according to the rigid requirements of the law. The sins of the people were imputed to the innocent victim. The blood was carried by the priest into the holy of holies and sprinkled upon the mercy-seat. And the body of the slain sacrifice was burned without the camp, symbolizing the wrath of God against the cursed thing.

The Sufferings of Christ

'Wherefore Jesus also, that he might sanctify the people with his own blood, suffered without the gate' (v. 12). Here, the Holy Spirit shows us the parallel between the burning of those sacrifices on the day of atonement in the Old Testament and the sufferings of the Lord Jesus Christ, our sin-atoning sacrifice, for us. In order to fulfil the type, the Lord Jesus who came to save his people from their sins, that he might sanctify and save us with his own blood, suffered all the horrid wrath of God for us, as our Substitute; as our sin-atoning Sacrifice to God 'without the gate', out in the place of uncleanness, the place of God's curse, where lepers dwelt.

In order to redeem and save his people from their sins, it was necessary for the Lord Jesus Christ, the Son of God, to suffer all the horrid terror of God's holy law, inflexible justice, and infinite wrath against us. In order to redeem and save his chosen people, the Son of God had to suffer all the consequences of our sins to the full satisfaction of divine justice as our Substitute.

Much we talk of Jesus' blood,
But how little's understood!
Of His sufferings so intense
Angels have no perfect sense.
Who can rightly comprehend
Their beginning or their end?

'Tis to God and God alone
That their weight is fully known.
See the suffering Son of God
Panting, groaning, sweating blood!
Boundless depths of love divine!
Jesus, what a love was Thine!

Our sins were imputed to the Son of God! That fact in itself is overwhelming. But I am certain that there is more to the sufferings of our Lord for us than the mere legal, or forensic term 'imputation' implies. His heart was not broken simply because he was made to be legally responsible for the debt of our sins. Our sins were not pasted on him, or merely placed to his account. The Lord Jesus Christ, God's Darling, our all-glorious Saviour, was made to be sin for us! (2 Corinthians 5:21).

Our Reasonable Response

Since the Lord Jesus Christ so willingly bore our reproach and suffered the wrath of God for us, let us go forth unto him without the camp bearing his reproach. Let us ever 'glory in the cross of our Lord Jesus Christ' (Galatians 6:14). Though the offence of the cross is ever increasing, let us never flinch to bear the offence of Christ and his gospel, and do it with patience, counting it our great honour to bear his reproach (1 Peter 2:21 4:12-19). Is anything too much for us to suffer for Christ? Is any sacrifice too great for us to make for him? Is any devotion to the Son of God extreme?

By him therefore let us offer the sacrifice of praise to God continually, that is, the fruit of our lips giving thanks to his name. But to do good and to communicate forget not: for with such sacrifices God is well pleased. Obey them that have the rule over you, and submit yourselves: for they watch for your souls, as they that must give account, that they may do it with joy, and not with grief: for that is unprofitable for you. Pray for us: for we trust we have a good conscience, in all things willing to live honestly. But I beseech you the rather to do this, that I may be restored to you the sooner.

Hebrews 13:15-19

Chapter 51

Read: Hebrews 13:15-19

'With Such Sacrifices God Is Well Pleased'
May God the Holy Spirit cause us to hear and heed the admonition here given and give us grace to 'offer the sacrifice of praise to God continually, that is, the fruit of our lips giving thanks to his name.'

'By Him'
'By him'. Everything begins with Christ. We cannot worship God without Christ. We cannot come to God without Christ. We cannot be saved without Christ. In all our approaches to God, we must have Christ. When Paul says, 'by him', he means by faith in him, through his mediation, by the merit of his blood, and upon the ground of his righteousness.

My first word is to you who have not yet come to God 'by him'. I bid you now, right where you are, to come to God by him (Hebrews 7:25). The Lord Jesus himself calls you to come to him (Matthew 11:28-30). This is the day for you to come to Christ (2 Corinthians 6:1-2). The Lord God, in his Word, promises salvation and eternal life to all who come to him by faith in Christ (John 3:16-18, 36; 1 John 1:9; 5:10-14).

Let us who have come to Christ ever come to him. Let us ever have our hearts and minds fixed upon Christ, consciously coming to God by him (1 Peter 2:4). At the very threshold of all worship and of all sacrifice to God, we begin with Christ. We cannot go a step without Christ. Without a Mediator we can make no approach to God. Apart from Christ there is no acceptable prayer, no pleasing sacrifice of any kind. 'By him therefore' we cannot move our lips acceptably without him who suffered without the gate. The great High Priest of our profession meets us at the temple door, and we place all our sacrifices into his hands, that he may present them to our God for us. That is just the way we want it. If we could do anything without him, we would be afraid to do it. We are safe only when Christ is with us. We are 'accepted in the beloved', only 'in the beloved'. And our sacrifices are acceptable to God only because of his great sacrifice (1 Peter 2:5).

Behold our great Melchisedek meets us! Let us give all to him and receive his blessing, which will repay us a thousand-fold. Let us never venture upon a sacrifice apart from him, lest it be the sacrifice of Cain, or the sacrifice of fools (Ecclesiastes 5:1). Christ is that altar which sanctifies both gift and giver. 'By him' therefore let us offer our sacrifices unto God.

'Therefore'

'By him therefore'. The word 'therefore', as you know, points us back to the context. First, 'We have an Altar' (13:10). Christ is the Altar upon which we offer sacrifice to our God. Second, Christ has sanctified us 'with his own blood' (13:12). Therefore we are worthy to come to God. Third, we must go forth unto Christ 'without the camp'. We must go forth unto him, bearing his reproach, serving the interests of his kingdom, his glory, and his people.

'The Sacrifice of Praise to God'

'By him therefore let us offer the sacrifice of praise to God'. We have no carnal, material altar; and we offer no carnal, material sacrifices. The sacrifices God requires are sacrifices of the heart (Psalm 51:15-17, 19). The first sacrifice we present to God is Christ, our sin-atoning Substitute. The second sacrifice is ourselves (2 Corinthians 8:5; Romans 12:1-2). As Christ gave himself for us, we now give ourselves back again to him.

Here, we are called to offer the sacrifice of praise to God, the God of all grace (Psalm 100:1-5). The sacrifice of praise involves the adoration of his person, ascribing to him all the honour, and glory, and majesty that belongs to him as God alone. Adoration and praise implies a delight in him. This praise, adoration, and delight in God imply a confident trust in him as God our Father. We believe that he is; and we believe that he is the Rewarder of them that diligently seek him. We trust him, delight in him, and find satisfaction with him.

When we understand who God is and delight in him, we understand that he always does right and always does us good. As we trust him and delight in him, giving praise to him, we praise him for all his works, both in providence and in grace (Psalm 92:1-15). This praise, adoration, delight, and confident trust of God our Father arises from a heart of true, intense love for him as God (1 John 4:19; Psalm 116:5, 8, 12-13, 16-18).

'Continually'

'By him therefore let us offer the sacrifice of praise to God continually'. Oh for grace to do so! Worship is not something we are to do at specific, appointed times only. It ought to be the habit, the dress, the adornment of our lives. Let us worship our God 'continually': in prosperity and in adversity; in wealth and in poverty; in sickness and in health; in good times and in bad times. Our circumstances do not reflect any change in our God. He is good, always good, only good, and righteous altogether.

'The Fruit of Our Lips'

'By him therefore let us offer the sacrifice of praise to God continually, that is, the fruit of our lips'. There is a reference here to Hosea 14:2. 'Take with you words, and turn to the LORD: say unto him, Take away all iniquity, and receive us graciously: so will we render the calves of our lips.' Let us praise our God and Saviour continually (1 Chronicles 16:9; Psalm 105:2; Romans 11:33-36; Ephesians 1:3).

'Giving Thanks To His Name'

'By him therefore let us offer the sacrifice of praise to God continually, that is, the fruit of our lips giving thanks to his name.' Thanksgiving is the essence of worship and praise. Let us engage in it continually, privately and publicly. Continually give thanks to God for all that he is, for his darling Son our Saviour, his blessed Spirit our Comforter, his purpose, his grace, his providence, and his presence.

'Do Good'

'But to do good and to communicate forget not'. Here Paul puts his admonition into shoe leather. He is telling us that thanksgiving and gratitude, praise and worship, make people gracious, kind, and generous. When he speaks of us doing good, notice that he is not talking about what men look at, approve of, and applaud as good, but doing good to one another.

That is exactly how our Lord describes good works in Matthew 25:31-46. To do good is to love one another, help one another, and communicate with (provide for) one another.

'God Is Well Pleased'

'For with such sacrifices God is well pleased'. Our sacrifices of praise, thanksgiving, and love are not meritorious before God. What we give is but what God has given us, and cannot be profitable to him. Yet doing good in this way, when it is done in faith, springs from love, and is directed to the glory of God, is well pleasing to him (Hosea 6:6). God is pleased with our feeble efforts at pleasing him when, as our sacrifice of praise, we do good to one another because we are in his Son, in whom he delights, and our sacrifices are bathed in his blood and robed in his righteousness (1 Peter 2:5).

What Is A Good Conscience?

In Bible terms, a good conscience is a conscience purified from the guilt of sin by the grace of God and purged from reliance upon dead works by the blood of Christ. It is a conscience purged and purified by the blood of Christ (Hebrews 9:9-14; 10:22). A pure conscience may still be a weak conscience, not always free from the taboos of religion and society (1 Corinthians 8:7-12). But a good conscience is a conscience freed from both the guilt of sin and the dead works of legal religion, relying upon Christ alone for all things. The good conscience sees and understands that 'Christ is All!'

A good conscience is a conscience that seeks to be void of offence (Acts 24:16). A good conscience is pure, honest, and sincere. 'Now the end of the commandment is charity out of a pure heart, and of a good conscience, and of faith unfeigned' (1 Timothy 1:5). Faith unfeigned is true faith, not the pretended faith of the hypocrite. A man with a pure conscience really believes what he says he believes. It is holding the mystery of the faith in a good conscience.

A good conscience is a believer's source of peace and joy (2 Corinthians 1:2; 4:1-2). It is a conscience that is submissive to the will of God (1 Peter 2:19) and obedient to Christ (1 Peter 3:21). A good conscience causes people to live right (1 Peter 3:16). Do you have a good conscience? May God be pleased to give you a good conscience by the sprinkling of the blood of Christ.

Your Conscience

Is it right to follow your conscience? Should we let our consciences be our guide, as we make our way through this world? What is the conscience? What does it do? Should I trust my conscience? We all have a conscience. Someone said, 'The conscience is the voice of God in a man's soul.' I do not know whether that is true or not; but I do know that

God has put a conscience in every person, which either accuses or excuses him in all his actions.

Conscience is that voice inside you that you simply cannot silence. You can muzzle it. You can sear the conscience, but you cannot silence it. It is that faculty of the mind, which God has put in us all, by which we judge the moral character of human conduct, our own and others. It is an inborn sense of right and wrong. As Charles Buck put it, the conscience is 'the secret testimony of the soul, whereby it approves things that are good, and condemns those that are evil'.

Your conscience is the law of God written on your heart (Romans 2:14-15). All men have a sense of right and wrong which, to a greater or lesser degree, reflects the law of God written upon the heart in creation. The conscience of a man often produces a sense of guilt, legal fear, which many mistake for conviction (John 8:9).

Conviction

But the conviction of sin is more than a sense of guilt and just condemnation. The conviction of sin arises from the revelation of Christ in the heart and is accompanied by a conviction of righteousness and of judgment. Holy Spirit conviction is that gracious work of God the Holy Spirit by which he effectually applies the gospel to the hearts of chosen, redeemed sinners, causing them to see that Christ alone is and must be the object of faith; that righteousness has been established by the obedience of the God-man, and that divine justice has been satisfied by the sin-atoning blood of Christ (John 16:8-11).

It was conscience which caused Adam and Eve to hide from God after the fall. It was conscience that made them know their nakedness and filled them with shame. The fact that they could appease their consciences with fig leaf garments, made by their own hands, shows that the conscience of man is, like every faculty of human nature, perverted and depraved.

Do Not Trust

We must not trust our consciences. The conscience cannot be trusted any more than the thoughts of the depraved mind or the emotions of the depraved heart can be trusted, because our depravity has made us perverse in all our faculties.

The scriptures tell us plainly that the conscience of fallen man is 'an evil conscience', from which we must be cleansed by the blood of Christ (Hebrews 10:22). The consciences of lost religious men are 'defiled' (Titus 1:15), so defiled that they may, in a sense, have 'a good conscience' while performing abominable things (John 16:2; Acts 23:1; 26:9).

The Apostle Paul, writing by divine inspiration, tells us that when he was persecuting the church, he was fully convinced that he was doing the right thing (Philippians 3:6; Acts 22:3-4; 26:9-10). But now his conscience bearing witness, he who once persecuted the church preaches the gospel, and seeks the salvation of those he once persecuted to prison and death (Galatians 1:13, 23; Romans 9:1-3).

Some, however, are so hardened by free will, works religion or by ungodly behaviour, often by both, that they live with a 'seared' conscience (1 Timothy 4:1-2). Such men and women, even children (as we have seen in our newspapers in recent years) have consciences which are so cauterized and hardened that they are past feeling. They have no regard for the rightness or wrongness of what they say or do. They have no conscience of anything. John Gill wrote, 'Under a cloak of sanctity they commit the most shocking impieties'.

If you work at it, if you hold down the truth of God long enough and persistently enough, you can cauterize your conscience. You can so sear your conscience, so harden yourself, that your conscience will excuse your wickedness and even justify your self-righteousness. We must never trust our consciences.

Let us ever be careful not to violate our consciences, not for anyone. But do not trust your conscience. He who trusts his own conscience, like he who trusts his own heart, trusts both a fool and a devil. Our guide in all things must be the Word of God alone! Not our feelings! Not our desires! Not the opinions of others! The Word of God alone!

'A Good Conscience'

A good conscience is something everyone wants, but few possess. Do you have a good conscience? Do I? Does the Word of God have anything to say about the conscience? Indeed, it does. There are numerous references to the conscience in holy scripture. The Word of God talks about a good conscience, a conscience void of offence, an accusing conscience, an excusing conscience, a weak conscience, a pure conscience, a defiled conscience, a seared conscience, an evil conscience, a purged conscience.

What kind of conscience do you have? What kind of conscience do I have? What do our consciences tell us about ourselves? We all want a good conscience, a quiet, peaceful conscience. What would you not give to have a good conscience? A conscience that will let you sleep at night? A conscience that would let you draw near to God with full assurance? A conscience that gives you ease, real ease and peace of heart and mind in the prospect of death, judgment, and eternity?

All the religion and religious practices, ceremonies, and sacrifices in the world cannot obtain a good conscience. All the gifts, works of charity and philanthropy imaginable cannot buy a good conscience. Good works of moral reformation and religious devotion, no matter how earnest and sincere, can never earn you a good conscience.

Demands

Our consciences demand what we cannot give. Your conscience and mine demands and can only be satisfied with perfection. As I said before, the conscience echoes God's holy law. Echoing the law, the conscience demands the same thing God's law demands. Our consciences demand perfection. Our consciences demand and will only accept perfect atonement for sin. Our consciences demand and will only accept perfect righteousness. That perfect atonement and perfect righteousness is found only in Christ's obedience and death as our Substitute (Hebrews 10:1-22). Horatius Bonar wrote, 'In another's righteousness we stand, and by another's righteousness we are justified.' All accusations against us, founded upon our unrighteousness, we answer by pointing to the perfection of the righteousness which covers us from head to foot, in virtue of which we are unassailable by law as well as shielded from wrath.

> Thy work alone, O Christ, can ease this weight of sin;
> Thy blood alone, O Lamb of God, can give me peace within.
> Thy love to me, O God, not mine, O Lord, to Thee,
> Can rid me of this dark unrest, and set my spirit free.

Blood Sprinkling

The only way we can ever obtain a good conscience is by the sprinkling of the blood of Christ upon our hearts by the Spirit of God (Hebrews 10:22). In the Old Testament, the law required that if anyone so much as touched a dead body, he was ceremonially unclean. If one person died in the tent, all the family and the tent itself were ceremonially defiled and unclean. That is a picture of our sin and uncleanness in our father Adam.

When Adam sinned against God, we all sinned. When he died, we all died in him (Romans 5:12). From the moment of Adam's fall, the conscience of man (the ability to know God in truth) has been defiled. By Adam's disobedience, all human kind was plunged into darkness. Men are totally incapable of knowing God, truth, or good, unless and until God himself purifies the conscience (Ephesians 4:18-19).

The sprinkling of blood in the Old Testament was ordained of God to make defiled things ceremonially clean. This was a type of the true cleansing of the hearts and souls of sinners by the blood of the Lord Jesus. 'The blood of Christ' is a phrase that refers to his atoning sacrifice for the sins of God's elect (Hebrews 10:10). It is his perfect obedience to God's holy law, his suffering and death that cleanses condemned sinners whom God the Father chose by his eternal grace in Christ (2 Timothy 1:9). The blood of Christ alone answers all the demands of God's holy law. And the blood of Christ alone answers all the demands of the conscience. 'Without shedding of blood is no remission'.

Peace

God the Father ordained peace by the blood. God the Son, our Lord Jesus Christ obtained peace, by the shedding of his blood. God the Holy Spirit gives the sinner peace, speaking peace to the conscience, by sprinkling our hearts with the blood of Christ. Faith receives peace by believing on the Lord Jesus Christ. I have peace with God because my heart, my conscience, looking on the shed blood of Christ echoes what the holy law of God says about the blood: 'Enough!'

Why An Everlasting Covenant?

A covenant has specific stipulations which each of the contracting parties is honour bound to fulfil. If ever one stipulation is not met, then the entire covenant is nullified and made void. As we saw previously, God's covenant had stipulations. But they are stipulations made, accepted, and sworn to by the Triune God. Therefore, the covenant never was and never can be in jeopardy. The covenant of grace was made in anticipation of the fall of our father Adam and the ruin of his race. The object and goal of the covenant is the restoration of God's elect from the ruins of the fall for the glory of the Triune God. When all the stipulations of the covenant had been agreed upon all the blessings of grace were fully and infallibly bestowed on God's elect in Christ, our covenant Head (Ephesians 1:3-6).

The Beneficiaries

The beneficiaries of this everlasting covenant were named from eternity and their names written in the book of life of the Lamb slain from the foundation of the world (Revelation 13:8; 17:8). The covenant is not for all men. If that offends some, I am sorry. But man's offence does not nullify God's work. This covenant is a work of God's unconditional grace and absolute sovereignty, performed for his elect from eternity (Romans 9:13-18), for the praise of his glory (Ephesians 1:6, 12, 14).

Do you ask, 'Who are God's elect?' They are those sinners for whom Christ died (John 10:11, 15, 26) and for whom he makes intercession (John 17:9, 20). God's elect are those who are called to life and faith in Christ by God the Holy Spirit (Psalm 65:4). God's elect are all who trust the Lord Jesus Christ as their Saviour (1 Thessalonians 1:4-10).

Why Everlasting?

In other places it is called, the 'covenant of peace', 'covenant of life', 'better covenant', and 'new covenant'. Why does the Holy Spirit here and elsewhere describe the covenant of grace as the 'everlasting covenant'? It is described in just these words seven times in the Word of God (2 Samuel 23:5; Isaiah 55:3; 61:8; Jeremiah 32:40; Ezekiel 16:60; 37:26; Hebrews 13:20). Why?

First, it is called 'the everlasting covenant' to identify its antiquity. The covenant of grace is the oldest of all God's works. It is from everlasting. The covenant of works had a beginning and an end. The covenant of grace has neither. Believer, think about that fact and let it thrill your soul.

Before anything that is existed God loved you and made a covenant of grace for you. Before the mountains, the stars, or the seas were brought forth, God thought of you. Before Adam fell, God covenanted with God for you. Before you sinned, help was laid upon One who is mighty for you. Before you went astray from your mother's womb speaking lies, the Triune God found a way to bring you home to glory. Before he made the angels to minister to you, God's heart was devoted to you in covenant grace. The Triune God, who has had his heart upon you from eternity, will never forget you, or forget to be gracious to you (Isaiah 54:7-10).

Second, the covenant of grace is called 'the everlasting covenant' to assure us of its sureness (2 Samuel 23:5). Here is something that stands sure and stands forever! Its mercies are sure mercies. Its blessings are sure blessings. Its promises are sure promises.

On our part, it is an unconditional covenant. Nothing was left to chance. Nothing was left to be determined by our wills. Nothing about it depends upon our works. There are no 'ifs', 'maybes', 'buts', or 'perhaps' in this everlasting covenant. Every line is punctuated by God's 'shall' and God's 'will'. It is a covenant ordered in all things and sure from everlasting: ordered by God's decree and made sure by his power.

Third, the covenant of grace is called 'the everlasting covenant' to show us its immutability. Anything everlasting must be immutable. Not one line of the covenant can be erased, not one word blotted out. God is immutable in all things. His love is immutable love (Romans 9:13). His grace is immutable grace (Malachi 3:6). His forgiveness is immutable forgiveness (Romans 4:8). His favour is immutable favour (Ephesians 1:6). His blessings are immutable blessings (Romans 11:29; Ephesians 1:3). His covenant is an immutable covenant (Ecclesiastes 3:14).

Fourth, this covenant is called 'the everlasting covenant' to teach us that it will never cease to be enforced, no, not even in eternity. It shall one day be consummated, but never terminated. All the heirs of grace shall be the heirs of grace forever: for the same reason (because God chose us), upon the same basis (the blood of Christ), and, therefore, to the same degree! Well may we sing with Phillip Doddridge ...

My God, the covenant of Thy love abides forever sure;
And in its matchless grace I feel my happiness secure!
Thy covenant the last accent claims of this poor, faltering tongue;
And that shall the first notes employ of my celestial song.

Now the God of peace, that brought again from the dead our Lord Jesus, that great shepherd of the sheep, through the blood of the everlasting covenant, Make you perfect in every good work to do his will, working in you that which is wellpleasing in his sight, through Jesus Christ; to whom be glory for ever and ever. Amen. And I beseech you, brethren, suffer the word of exhortation: for I have written a letter unto you in few words. Know ye that our brother Timothy is set at liberty; with whom, if he come shortly, I will see you. Salute all them that have the rule over you, and all the saints. They of Italy salute you. Grace be with you all. Amen

Hebrews 13:20-25

Chapter 52

Read: Hebrews 13:20-25

'Our Lord Jesus'

We have seen our Lord Jesus throughout this great Epistle. Our all-glorious Christ is the theme and message of these thirteen chapters. We have been told repeatedly of his supremacy, his greatness, and his glory as our God, Mediator, High Priest, Surety, and Substitute. We have come near to him, heard from him, enjoyed him, and worshipped him as …

God's final Word by whom he has spoken and revealed himself to men (1:2). The Creator of all things, whom the angels worship (1:6,10). The Captain of our salvation who was made perfect through suffering (2:10). Our divine Mediator who was made flesh that he might die in our place and free us from the fear of death (2:14). Our sovereign Saviour who took hold on the seed of Abraham to save us (2:16). That Prophet who is better than Moses and that Son who is better than a servant (3:5-6). Our Sabbath in whom we find rest for our souls (4:1-11). Our sympathizing High Priest who bids us come by him to the throne of grace to obtain mercy and grace in every time of need (4:14-16). The Anchor of our souls, both sure and steadfast (6:18-20). Our ever living High Priest and omnipotent Saviour, one who saves to the uttermost all who come to God by him (7:25). The Surety and Mediator of a better covenant (7:22; 8:10-12). The Redeemer who obtained eternal redemption for us (9:12). The Sacrifice who, by his blood, purifies our consciences from dead works to serve the living God (9:14). The Sacrifice who put an end to all sacrifices by putting away sin once for all through the sacrifice of himself (9:26). The Servant whose obedience has perfected forever all God's elect (10:1-14). The new and living Way by whom we have access to God (10:18-22). The Author and Finisher of our faith who for the joy set before him endured the cross, despising the shame and sat down at the right hand of God until all his enemies are made a stool for his feet (12:2; 1:13). He whose blood speaks in heaven and speaks better things than the blood of Abel (12:24). The God and Saviour who will never leave us nor forsake us (13:5-6; 7:16). Our immutable God and Saviour (13:8). Our Altar (13:10). The One who suffered outside the camp that he might sanctify us by his own blood (13:12).

Again and again the Lord Jesus reveals himself to encourage our perseverance, strengthen our faith, inspire our hope, and assure our hearts. Now, we come to the last verses of this great, instructive, comforting epistle.

How do you end an epistle like Hebrews? Paul must have contemplated this for some time, praying and mulling over the contents of his letter to these struggling brethren. He had spoken rapturously of God's revelation of himself and his Son, and of his eternal work. He has brought them face to face with our doubts, fears, and unbelief.

Though it is commonly called one of the 'General Epistles', the book of Hebrews is truly a 'pastoral' Epistle. It deals with the most sublime depths of sacred theology and makes piercing, personal applications of divine truth to our hearts. Paul was inspired by God the Holy Spirit to bring his Epistle to its conclusion by reminding us again of the greatness, glory, and supremacy of God our Saviour, ascribing all praise to him, and by declaring his heart's desire and prayer to God for his elect (13:20-25).

'Now the God of peace, that brought again from the dead our Lord Jesus, that great shepherd of the sheep, through the blood of the everlasting covenant, Make you perfect in every good work to do his will, working in you that which is wellpleasing in his sight, through Jesus Christ; to whom be glory for ever and ever. Amen. And I beseech you, brethren, suffer the word of exhortation: for I have written a letter unto you in few words. Know ye that our brother Timothy is set at liberty; with whom, if he come shortly, I will see you. Salute all them that have the rule over you, and all the saints. They of Italy salute you. Grace be with you all. Amen'.

What a picture this is of a faithful pastor's tender heart. Knowing that his words were, at times biting, and stinging, and hard to bear, knowing the terrible reluctance of proud flesh to take rebuke, but knowing that what he had written was indeed God's Word to his people, he urged these believers and urges us, to receive, bear, and heed the word of exhortation.

The Everlasting Covenant

With these words the Apostle Paul gives his benediction, the Holy Spirit's benediction to all who are in Christ, to every sinner in this world saved by the grace of God. This is God's benediction of grace to us.

He who is our God is here called 'The God of peace'. He is 'the God of peace, that brought again from the dead our Lord Jesus'. Our Lord Jesus Christ was raised up from the dead as 'that (one and only) great Shepherd of the sheep' who came here to save his sheep, and in order to do so laid down his life for the sheep. The Lord Jesus has been raised up from the grave and is now seated in heaven as our great Shepherd of the sheep, 'through the blood of the everlasting covenant'.

Now, look at the first three words of verse 21. See the object and purpose of the Triune God in this everlasting covenant of grace, and the blood by which that covenant was ratified at Calvary, to 'make you perfect'.

In this everlasting covenant, the covenant of grace and peace, the covenant of salvation made between the three Persons of the Triune God before the world began, through the blood of the everlasting covenant, the salvation of God's elect was fixed and settled from eternity. This everlasting covenant of grace is a compact of love, an agreement of mercy, a contract of goodness, a sovereign disposition of grace made between God the Father, God the Son, and God the Holy Spirit in eternity. And in that covenant our salvation was immutably secured.

Every saved sinner traces the origin of his salvation back to eternity, for the origin of all saving grace is the firm and everlasting covenant spoken of in our text. God always deals with men and women upon the basis of a covenant. Though he brings the blessings or the curses of the covenant upon individuals, God always deals with people collectively, in covenant terms, through a representative. According to his own sovereign purpose, he has arranged that he will not deal with man except in covenant terms. And he will not allow us to deal with him in any other way.

'The Blood of the Everlasting Covenant'

What is the connection between the shed blood of Christ and the everlasting covenant? The precious blood of Christ has a fivefold connection to the covenant of grace.

God the Son

With regard to God the Son, our Saviour, his blood is the fulfilment of every stipulation agreed to in the covenant. When he had finished his work of establishing righteousness for us by his life of perfect manhood, a life of total obedience to the will of God, he said to the Father, 'I have finished the work which thou gavest me to do' (John 17:4). Then, when he had fully satisfied the holy wrath and justice of God, when he had paid our debt to God's offended justice, when he had put away our sins, our Saviour cried, 'It is finished', and triumphantly breathed out his life.

God the Father

With regard to God the Father, the precious blood of Christ puts the Almighty under inescapable obligation. Having fully met all the requirements of God in the covenant, God must now (justice demands it) save every redeemed sinner, pardon every ransomed soul, and give grace and glory to all for whom atonement has been made!

God the Spirit

With regard to God the Holy Spirit, the blood of Christ is what he sprinkles (effectually applies) to the hearts of sinners, by which he proclaims peace and reconciliation upon the ground of sin put away, righteousness brought in, and justice satisfied (judgment finished) (John 16:8-11).

The Believer

With regard to the believing sinner, the precious blood of Christ is the solitary ground of his peace and assurance. Christ's blood is God's token to us for good. Do you rely entirely upon the blood of Christ for all your salvation? If you do, be at peace. Let nothing disturb you. This covenant was made for you. All its blessings are yours forever. You are one of God's elect.

The Guilty Soul

With regard to guilty sinners, the precious blood of Christ is your only way of access to God; but this way of access is the way by which you may come to God with full assurance of faith, being confident that you are accepted at the throne of grace (Hebrews 10:22).

There is no remission of sins without the blood (Hebrews 9:22); and there can be no condemnation with the blood (Romans 8:1). He who died to ratify this covenant lives and reigns to enforce it (2 Samuel 23:5). He and he alone is able to save to the uttermost all who come to God by him (Hebrews 7:25).

The Everlasting Covenant

God made a covenant of works with the first man, Adam, soon after he was created (Genesis 2:15-17). When Adam broke that covenant, everything God did with him and everything he has done with his sons in the punishment of sin has been according to the terms of that covenant (Romans 5:12-14). The covenant of works, because of Adam's sin and our sin in him, has always been a covenant of death. Later, when God gave the law at Sinai by the hand of Moses, it was a covenant of death from the beginning, because righteousness and life could never come to sinners by their works of righteousness (Galatians 3:10, 21). No sinner can ever perform righteous works. The giving of the law at Mount Sinai was nothing more or less than the revelation of God's justice in punishing every transgression under the covenant of works. It was never intended by God to be a way of life for men, a rule of life for his children, or a code of moral ethics. The law was given by God to be a messenger of death, a messenger of justice, wrath, and condemnation to fallen men; that sinners might be driven to Christ and to the covenant of grace established with him.

Another Covenant

However, long before God made the covenant of works with Adam in the garden, he had made a covenant of grace with Christ, his Son. It was made for us. But it was made with Christ our covenant Surety and Mediator in eternity before the world was made. In fact, Adam, as the federal head and representative of all men in the covenant of works, was a type and picture of the Lord Jesus Christ (Romans 5:14), who is called 'the last Adam' (1 Corinthians 15:45) and is the federal Head and Representative of God's elect in the covenant of grace (Romans 5:12-19).

The covenant of works was broken by the first Adam. The covenant of grace was fulfilled by the last Adam. Death and sin came by the first Adam's disobedience. Life and righteousness came by the last Adam's obedience. Wrath came upon all men by the fall of the first Adam. Grace comes to all God's elect by the success of the last Adam (1 Corinthians 15:21-22).

This everlasting covenant of grace was also typified in the covenants God made with Noah (Genesis 6:8, 18; 8:1, 20-22; 9:11-15), Abraham (Genesis 15), and David (2 Samuel 7:8-17). It was often spoken of in the Old Testament (Psalm 89:19-31; Isaiah 49:1-12; 54:9-10; Jeremiah 31:31-34; 32:37-40; Ezekiel 36:21-38; 2 Samuel 23:5). God's saints in those days prior to the coming of Christ found in this everlasting covenant a solid foundation upon which to stand and a soft pillow upon which to rest their weary souls. Believing God, they said to the comfort of their souls, 'The Lord hath made with me an everlasting covenant, ordered in all things and sure. This is all my salvation and all my desire'!

This everlasting covenant of grace is 'the foundation of God that standeth sure'. It cannot be shaken by the changing tides of time and trouble. That which inspired David in life and comforted him in death, the everlasting covenant, is the inspiration of our lives and the comfort of our souls today.

The New Covenant

What is the covenant spoken of in this text? This is not the first time the word 'covenant' is mentioned in the book of Hebrews. It is first mentioned in chapter 7, verse 22, where Christ is called, 'the Surety of a better testament (covenant)'.

This is the 'better covenant' described in chapter 8, verses 6-12. It is the 'new covenant' of Hebrews 8:13, and the 'new testament' (covenant) of chapter 9, verse 15, by which we 'receive the promise of eternal inheritance'. When we read Hebrews 10:15-17, we discover that this is the very same covenant that was spoken of in Jeremiah 31:31-34, which the Lord Jesus came to fulfil by his obedience to God as our Representative.

The covenant spoken of in Hebrews 13:20-21 is the new covenant of the gospel, the covenant of grace made in eternity for the salvation of God's elect. Yet, it is ever fresh and new. It is the covenant by which God makes all things new in the new creation of grace. This everlasting covenant is the whole will of God, the whole purpose of his grace concerning the salvation of his elect.

God's Purpose of Grace

The will and purpose of God regarding the salvation of his people is revealed in the Bible as a covenant. I do not pretend to understand all that I know about this subject. But I do know that a covenant was made. It might be called 'God's sovereign purpose of grace', or 'God's sovereign decree of grace'. But the Bible calls it, 'the everlasting covenant'. It does so because God's purpose and decree of grace, as it is revealed to us, bears all the marks of a covenant.

Contracting Parties

A covenant is a contract, or an agreement made between two or more contracting parties. The high contracting parties between whom the covenant of grace was made before time began were the three Persons of the Eternal Godhead. The Triune God asked, 'Who will go for us?' Christ, the Son, volunteering to be our Surety, arose and said, 'Here am I, send me'. When he came to fulfil his covenant engagements he said, 'Lo, I come to do thy will, O God'. When he ascended back into heaven, the

Father said to his victorious Son, 'Ask of me, and I will give thee the heathen for thine inheritance, and the uttermost parts of the earth for thy possession.' And again he says, 'Sit thou upon my right hand, until I make thine enemies thy footstool.' And the exalted Son of God, our Saviour, poured out his Spirit upon all flesh to gather his elect from the four corners of the earth (Isaiah 6:8; Psalm 2:8; 110:1; Joel 2:28-32; Acts 2:16-27).

Christ stood as our Representative, Mediator, Substitute, and Surety from everlasting. In that blessed, everlasting covenant the salvation of God's elect was decreed, purposed, predestinated, and made sure. God the Father pledged himself to God the Son, saying, 'I will save these whom I have loved and chosen.' God the Son pledged himself to God the Father, saying, 'I will satisfy all the demands of your law and justice, so that God can be both "a just God and a Saviour".' And God the Spirit pledged himself to God the Father and God the Son, saying, 'I will sanctify every chosen, redeemed soul.'

Done from Eternity

When the three persons of the adorable Trinity struck hands together, the deal was done. The salvation of an elect multitude, which no man can number, was made sure and looked upon by the Triune God as a thing already done (Romans 8:29-30; 2 Timothy 1:9).

'The God of Peace'

Some time ago, the husband of a friend was diagnosed with a terminal disease, a form of cancer the doctors expected would lead to a prolonged death. She asked me with tears in her eyes, 'Brother Don, how do I prepare for what I am going to have to face?' I paused for a moment and said, 'There is no way you can prepare yourself; but our heavenly Father, the God of peace, will prepare you.'

As Paul closes the book of Hebrews, he directs our hearts to the God of peace. What could be more fitting? We have no idea what trials, temptations, and troubles we may yet have to face before our time on this earth is done. We do not know how Satan may assail us. We do not know what heaviness and heartache lie before us in this world. We do not know what work the Lord has for us to do by which we are to glorify him. But I do know what we need. I do know what it will take for you and me to persevere unto the end. We need 'the God of peace'.

The God of peace bids you cast all your care upon him, assuring you that he cares for you.'The Lord will not forsake his people for his great name's sake: because it hath pleased the LORD to make you his people ...

Only fear the LORD, and serve him in truth with all your heart; for consider how great things he hath done for you' (1 Samuel 12:22-24).

Try to get the sweet milk that is here set before us. Our heavenly Father, the God of glory, is here called 'the God of peace' because his thoughts toward you are thoughts of peace (Jeremiah 29:11). He has made for you a covenant of peace (Numbers 25:12-13; Ezekiel 34:25; 37:26). The Lord God has laid on his Son the chastisement of our peace and thereby made peace for us (Isaiah 53:5; Colossians 1:18-21). His gospel is the gospel of peace, the good news of peace accomplished (Isaiah 40:1-2). Our heavenly Father has given us his Spirit, who dwells in us as the Spirit of Peace. He assures us that he will keep us in peace in this world and will bring us into a world of peace at last.

The Resurrection of Christ

Here is the basis of and assurance of that peace revealed and proclaimed in the gospel. Our heavenly Father, the God of peace, has raised Christ from the dead. He 'brought again from the dead our Lord Jesus, that great shepherd of the sheep, through the blood of the everlasting covenant.'

Assured Grace

After giving us those words of assurance, Paul tells these saints what he desired for them. That God might 'Make you perfect in every good work to do his will, working in you that which is wellpleasing in his sight, through Jesus Christ; to whom be glory for ever and ever' (v. 21). Let us remember that, though this is Paul's prayer for these believers, people he knew and loved, it is more than that. This is what he was inspired of God to write. With these words, the Holy Spirit assures every believer that the God of peace, who brought Christ forth from the dead, shall complete his work in us and for us. He who has 'begun a good work in you' will make you everything you ought to be and want to be (Philippians 1:6). He will work in you that which is well-pleasing in his sight (Hebrews 13:21; Jude 24-25). He will do it through Christ Jesus your Mediator and Saviour, and do it in such a way that Christ shall have glory forever and ever. Then, he says, 'Amen', so shall it be.

The Word of Exhortation

We are sometimes hesitant to believe and to obey the Word of God. So Paul here urges us to receive and heed the word of exhortation he has given us in this epistle, and persevere in faith.

It appears that Timothy had been imprisoned for preaching the gospel and was now at liberty again. Paul hoped to visit these friends, his beloved brethren, his truest family, again soon, and says so; sending greetings to the people and their pastors, conveying with his own the greetings of the saints in Italy.

Grace Be With You

Here is the source from which all that I want for you must come. 'Grace be with you all' (v. 25). This was Paul's usual salutation (2 Thessalonians 3:17-18) expressing his desire that God's elect might enjoy renewed discoveries of his mercy, love, and favour, and fresh manifestations of grace in Christ. Grace is what we need! It is what we must have: covenant grace, saving grace, sustaining grace, forgiving grace, reviving grace, daily grace, sufficient grace, everlasting grace, and nothing but grace! This grace, as one older writer put it, 'is a stream of living water flowing through the desert, a power which enables us to withstand every adversity and to reach the promised land, the place of our rest, the heavenly Jerusalem.' This grace is for all and assured to all who trust the Lord Jesus Christ.

Amen

Index of Bible Verses

Old Testament

New Testament

www.ingramcontent.com/pod-product-compliance
Lightning Source LLC
Chambersburg PA
CBHW030942150426
42812CB00062B/2690

9780954862442